THE HISTORY OF THE LONDON RIFLE BRIGADE 1859–1919

THE HISTORY OF THE LONDON RIFLE BRIGADE

1859—1919

WITH INTRODUCTION

BY

MAJ.-GEN. SIR FREDERICK MAURICE

K.C.M.G., C.B.

LONDON

CONSTABLE & COMPANY LTD

10 & 12 ORANGE STREET LEICESTER SQUARE WC 2

1921

Field Marshall H.R.H George William Frederick Charles Duke of Cambridge, K.G., K.T., K.P., G.C.B., G.C.S.I., G.C.M.G., G.C.I.E., G.C.V.O. Honorary Colonel of the London Rifle Brigade, 1860—1904

INTRODUCTION

By Major-General Sir Frederick Maurice,
K.C.M.G., C.B.

EVERY soldier knows that *esprit de corps* is a part, and a great part, of the foundation of efficiency. It is one of the prime elements which go to make up that potent but indefinite force, *moral*, a force more powerful than the heaviest bombardment, than the most deadly poison gas, than thousands of tanks and squadrons of aeroplanes, than all the destructive forces of science. It is the force which keeps weary and hungry men together amidst confusion and apparent defeat, which refuses to recognise the possibility of failure, decides the fortune of the doubtful struggle, and turns initial success into complete triumph; the force, in short, which enables the spirit to triumph over the body. How often in our games have we seen a weak team, which had played together and represents some ancient school or college with a long and proud tradition, defeat a scratch side of which the individual members are incontestably the better players. The saying that Waterloo was won on the playing fields of Eton may or may not have come from the Iron Duke. Whether he or another was its author it is a true saying, though its meaning and application are not those popularly ascribed to the phrase. It does not mean that the battle of Waterloo was won because the British officers were better athletes or physically stronger than the French officers, that a Briton could knock down a Frenchman when he met him, but that the British of the Army of Waterloo had learned to play for the side, to work together as a team, to put love of country and love of corps above love of self, whereas the French officers of those days were distracted by political jealousies and intrigues, by suspicion and distrust, and too many of them were playing not for the side but for their own hand. Now the foundation of team work is pride in the team and in what the team stands for, in other words *esprit de corps*.

George Eliot has said, " Our lives make to themselves a moral tradition, and to have acted nobly once seems a reason why we should act nobly always."

If this is true of the individual it is still more true of the corporate body. If *esprit de corps* is part of the foundation of efficiency, tradition, the record of past achievement, is the foundation of *esprit de corps*. Therefore the compilers of this history of the London Rifle Brigade have not merely fulfilled a pious duty to the memory of those who fought and suffered and fell in the Great War, they have done much to promote the future efficiency and well-being of a great regiment.

I will not refer here to the proud record of achievement of the London Rifle Brigade in the greatest test to which soldiers have ever been submitted. It is set forth in these pages, but I would ask those who are now joining the ranks of the regiment and those who will join the ranks in after years, to think, when they read, what that record means and how the achievements here described became possible. The London Rifle Brigade is not the creation of a day; it represents the history of the Volunteer movement in this country. As the opening pages of this history tell, the regiment came into existence at a time when the Crimean War had exposed the weakness of our regular army, at a time when we appeared to be threatened with invasion by our late ally France. From that date, 1859, the Volunteers became a definite part of our military organisation. Volunteers had been created before to meet a special danger and they had disappeared once the danger was passed, but in 1859 they came to stay. The history of the Volunteer movement is an index to our national attitude towards our military forces. In times of danger the Volunteers have been greeted with enthusiasm, which has not infrequently degenerated into flattery. They were so received in the early days of the French Revolution, they were so received when Napoleon's Grand Army was encamped around Boulogne waiting to cross the Channel, they were so received during the South African War. Few who saw them will forget the scenes in the City of London when the C.I.V.'s left for South Africa and were welcomed home. But times of danger are fortunately rare, and in the intervals the Volunteers have had to fight their way forward against indifference, against patronage which has been almost contemptuous, and against ridicule. The London Rifle Brigade may be said to be, if not historically, at least spiritually, the descendants of the Trained Bands of London Town, and I dare say that the clearest recollection which the average citizen has to-day of the Trained Bands is that a certain famous mercer of Cheapside, by name John Gilpin, was a captain in that Force. The fun which Cowper poked at the Trained Bands and Leech, during the period in which the London Rifle Brigade was born, at the "Brook Green Volunteers," is an indication of the difficulties which the Volunteers had for long years to contend against.

These difficulties were in great measure surmounted when Lord Haldane created the Territorial Force. It is of interest now to recall the fact that one of the chief assistants of Lord Haldane in his scheme of Army Reform was Sir Douglas Haig, then the head of a directorate of the General Staff at the War Office. Under the Haldane scheme the Volunteers were given a definite organisation analagous to that of the Regular Army, they were provided with adequate staffs and some approximation to modern equipment. Even so the battle was not won. There remained the doubts of the professionals to overcome. With certain notable exceptions the regulars openly expressed their opinion that citizen soldiers could not be made fit to take their place in the line of battle against an European enemy. This is the national attitude of the professional in all trades towards the amateur, and it was an attitude which was not peculiar to British soldiers. I well remember talking to a French officer, who has since risen to great fame, shortly after the creation of the Territorial Force and hearing him say: "Territorial infantry? That may be, but Territorial artillery—Pouff!"

Well, even these doubts have now vanished. They vanished more than six years ago when in November, 1914, the first Territorial battalions, the London Rifle Brigade amongst them, came out to France. Our little regular army, exhausted by the retreat from Mons, the battles of the Marne, the Aisne and of Ypres, was holding on in the mud and slime of that first winter in Flanders by the skin of its teeth. It is difficult for those who saw only the trenches of the later years of the war to envisage the conditions of those days, when our parapets were dissolving under the steady rain, when communication trenches were nothing but water channels, when we had few sand bags, few guns, few shells, no trench mortars and few hand grenades; when "trench feet" thinned our ranks more than the enemy's fire. It was in these conditions that the first Territorial battalions reached the front. Their arrival meant for the least thinking regular a day or two less in the trenches, a night or two more in a warm billet. That was enough. No more questions were asked as to whether the Territorials were fit to fight the Germans. From that beginning the Territorials went on winning the confidence of the Army and of the Nation, till at the end their divisions were ranked by friend and foe alike as peers of the best.

The men who achieved these results have left to their successors a great tradition and a great responsibility. In one way the task of these successors has been made easy, they have no longer to contend against the indifference and the ridicule which their military forebears had to live down. In another way it has been made more difficult, for it is no light task to maintain a great record. That task can only be accomplished by work, and by earnest endeavour after joining a great regiment to act in all ways worthily of its great history.

F. MAURICE.

February, 1921.

CONTENTS

LIST OF ILLUSTRATIONS

LIST OF MAPS AND PLANS

The maps illustrating this history are of two kinds :—

1. Copies of the Official War Office maps, as used in France, on the scale of 1/40000, which have been specially printed by the Ordnance Survey.
   (A) Sheet 28, covering the area Poperinghe—Passchendaele on the North to Bailleul—Ploegsteert on the South and including Ypres as its central feature.
   (B) Sheet 51 B., Arras, which covers all the fighting in which the Regiment took part to the East of that town.
   (C) Albert combined sheet, which covers all the Somme fighting, from September, 1916.
2. Sketch maps based in all cases on official maps and therefore "squared," with the one exception of the sketch illustrating the final advance in November, 1918. These have been reproduced to no particular scale, but solely with the idea of making the resulting map as large and clear as possible. The scale is, however, easy to read when it is remembered that in every case the smallest square shown on any map is 500 yards. This is invariable.

In addition to the above, two diagrams are given illustrating the journeyings of the two Battalions. These are not drawn to scale.

The attention of those who are not accustomed to reading squared maps is drawn to the instructions which appear in the margin of the W.O. map C referred to above.

The map references to A, B, and C are in Roman type ; *the references to the sketch maps are in italics.*

For A, B, and C see above. These maps and the two itinerary plans are in the pocket of the cover.

First Battalion.

·REFERENCE·

ENEMY TRENCHES
BRITISH TRENCHES
ROADS
HEDGE, FENCE OR DITCH

SUNKEN ROADS
BUILDINGS
VILLAGES
RAILWAYS

CHURCHES
SHRINES
RIVERS

FOREWORD

MANY perhaps who joined the regiment during the war may have realised that the lot had fallen to them in a fair ground, without quite fully grasping that it was no natural soil, but rather a goodly heritage, that had been prepared for them by the faithful toil and loving service of those who had preceded them.

The story of the early days of the Volunteers tells how through difficulties, disappointments and ridicule, the regiment was most devotedly served by those who put personal advantage and leisure on one side, and gave it their help and allegiance, while others stood aside and mocked. Had the way not been an uphill one and the going anything but smooth, it is not likely that the spirit called forth which placed the cause and the regiment before personal considerations would have been of the same unswerving and steadfast type.

Things relating to the spirit can at best be only felt and not described, and even then the mere fact of feeling does not always carry with it the comprehension of the underlying reality, but the results form an indisputable witness. The efficiency of the London Rifle Brigade in 1914 and the whole of its subsequent war record are indications of what it implied. Throughout can be traced the determination of all ranks that their Regiment should have the first claim at all times, and that the tradition should be upheld of a service united by friendship and fellowship, that would bring out all that was best in each individual member.

The pre-war History revives a picture of an almost forgotten past and narrates the many vicissitudes of varying importance through which the regiment went, with the culminating change from Volunteers to Territorials. All through can be traced the spirit that built up the L.R.B. and led to its being found on the outbreak of war a unit worthy of the labour of love that had been bestowed upon it.

The story of the first battalion from the earliest days of mobilisation, through the succeeding three months of rumours and strenuous preparation up to the day on which it crossed to France, is underlined with the same spirit—if possible emphasised by the return of so many old members. From November 4th, 1914, its history is not merely regimental but, along with those of other Territorial battalions selected for early service at the Front, tells a tale of the Citizen Army, which has made history in the truest sense for all time. Properly understood, it cannot but stand for ever as a witness that service as a soldier offered by citizens in the right spirit, so far from being the last hope of a decadent militarism, is the crowning glory of a nation.

The early history of the second battalion is one of a different sort. The persistent bad luck and perpetual rumours, the changes and indecision with which the Higher Authorities saw fit to afflict it, and the loss of men who were drafted to the first battalion, only served to call out a keenness and strenuous application to securing efficiency that were worthy of tradition. That the battalion kept together so well and, when at length opportunity offered, gave such an excellent account of itself speaks volumes for the spirit which Lieut.-Col. Tod and the other old members of the regiment put into their work.

The third battalion was wholly engaged in spadework without being put to the supreme test, so that its merits are more difficult to gauge, but its labours from the highest motives for the welfare of the battalions in France were unceasing. Those at the Front could always rely upon drafts from the reserve unit, however short their training, being not only efficient soldiers but also true members of the regiment. Interference in recruiting and interference with the training staff made anything but plain sailing for those responsible; the drafting of men to other regiments might well have taxed the patience of the most loyal; but to the third battalion was entrusted the proud honour of instilling the regimental spirit into all who joined it and of ensuring that, whatever mistakes were made, no one could leave without having realised what it meant to be in the true sense members of the regiment.

This work has been planned with the object of giving, as far as possible, a representative picture of the L.R.B. in its various phases, and not as a war history in the technical sense. Forced by its nature to fall into very definite sections, many writers have contributed to the several parts and no attempt has been made to assimilate their styles. This is no reason for looking upon the whole as disconnected, and those who read between the lines and have known the regiment should have no difficulty in supplying any links that may be missing. In order to keep within reasonable limits, only typical examples of the various operations in which the battalions took part have been described in detail, and these have been selected according to the amount of material available, not necessarily on account of their importance.

No account of the splendid work carried out by the L.R.B. from the date of its foundation, culminating in a war record that cannot be easily surpassed, can do full justice to its subject. If, however, those members, who have long retired, find that these pages bring back to them some of the events in which they took part; if those who served in the critical years from 1914 to 1918 are led to recall some of the scenes that they witnessed and the comrades who were by their side; and if above all those whose loved ones fell are helped to realise how they upheld the honour and glory of the regiment, this book will have achieved its purpose.

EDITORIAL NOTE

A PUBLICATION of this sort brings to mind the old deaf scholar, who went each day to the Cathedral to say his prayers. Owing to his deafness he was not aware when his words were audible, and one day was overheard giving thanks to God for the labours of compilers of dictionaries, statistics and books of reference! That the labour put into these chronicles has been one of love cannot in any way prevent the reader from having the same feeling of gratitude to all those who have helped to make the record complete.

The early history of the regiment has been obtained from the old Orders, from the Minutes of the Finance Committee, and from scrapbooks containing newspaper extracts carefully preserved by old members as reflecting credit on the regiment. In addition a great debt is due to Capt. F. R. Gale, who founded and for some years produced the *L.R.B. Record*, containing many details about the early history which have been freely used. Major Guppy and the Rev. A. Dawson Clarke have also helped by recalling their impressions.

The history of the 1st Battalion is based upon the war diary, supplemented by a mass of invaluable material diligently collected by Lieut.-Col. A. S. Bates. Major F. H. Wallis allowed free use to be made of his private diary; Col. N. C. King, Lieut.-Col. C. D. Burnell, Capt. J. H. Stransom, Capt. F. H. Crews, Capt. W. C. von Berg and Lieut. J. S. Lindsay helped with their recollections, and Capt. E. H. Slade is responsible for preparing the itinerary plans.

The first part of the history of the second battalion was written by Lieut. C. Harrison Jones, and the latter part, dealing with events after embarkation, by Major H. G. Wilkinson. The account of the third or reserve battalion was drafted by Col. N. C. King.

When the circumstances of the war have been forgotten, the frequent changes up and down in the rank of officers may be puzzling. They were due to temporary or acting rank being given to those who carried out certain duties, e.g. commanding officers, company commanders, and adjutants, which was relinquished when the duty had ceased to be performed.

Every effort has been made to ensure accuracy, and care has been taken to verify statements and data upon which there might be doubt, but even with such pains some errors may have crept in, and (if any are discovered) it is felt that they should be condoned and overlooked in view of the necessity that there is for early publication.

HISTORY OF THE LONDON RIFLE BRIGADE

OLD HISTORY

1859–1914

> "Come the three corners of the world in arms,
> And we shall shock them: nought shall make us rue
> If England to itself do rest but true."
>
> *King John*, Act V, Scene 7.

IT has been well said of the English that they are a warlike, but not a military people. Ever since the days of Cromwell there has been a prejudice against a large standing army; yet the approach of danger has always been the signal for an outburst of voluntary patriotism that turns the whole nation into a martial one.

In 1789, when the French had overrun Europe, and their fleet combined with that of the Spaniards was increasing in strength, a Bill was introduced into Parliament for the first time to provide for the raising of Volunteer Corps in every part of the kingdom. Such was the spirit of the people that in a few weeks 150,000 volunteers were under arms in Great Britain.

In 1803, when Napoleon was rising to the height of his power and planning the invasion of England, the Government contemplated raising 50,000 men by conscription for home service. In addition to this the King was to call on a *levée en masse* to repel the invasion of the enemy, and the Lord-Lieutenants were to enrol all the men in the kingdom between seventeen and fifty-five years of age. But—and this was a most important but—any man was to be exempt who was a member of a Volunteer Corps. The result was that in a few weeks 300,000 men were enrolled, and training, in all parts of the kingdom, and the compulsory conscription fell to the ground.

After Waterloo "the land had rest forty years" and this martial spirit disappeared. The Volunteers were disbanded, and England, weary of war, dismissed all thought of it from her mind. "Business as usual" was the cry, and the great Exhibition of 1851 was supposed to usher in a reign of everlasting and universal peace.

It seems impossible for the nation to realise that, so long as human nature remains what it is, wars can never cease, and that it costs far less in blood and gold to insure steadily by being prepared for war than it does to improvise at the last minute.

The Crimean War proved a rude awakening; the blunders and mismanagement of the authorities and the sufferings of our men roused the nation to uneasy consciousness that all was not well. The Indian Mutiny came as a second shock, and by 1859 all thinking men were of opinion that the time had come to act. The dismissal by the United States of the British Ambassador, the war in China, and, above all, renewed fears of a French invasion under a Napoleon, revived the idea of a Volunteer Force to defend the country. Some sort of formation had been continued by Volunteers in Devonshire, and the Victoria Rifle Club still maintained the tradition of their old corps. A book entitled *The Rifle and How to Use it*, by Mr. Hans Busk, which appeared about this time, seems to have done a good deal towards transforming the ideas afloat into concrete shape, and Tennyson's poem, "Form, Form, Riflemen, Form," had its due share in stimulating the movement towards establishing Rifle Volunteers.

1859

In May the Secretary of State for War issued a circular to the Lord-Lieutenants of Counties authorising the formation of Volunteer Corps, but, by some inadvertence, no copy was sent to the Lord Mayor of London, with the result that the City was late in setting to work, and its Regiment appears some way down the list in order of seniority. On Thursday,

21st July, 1859, a public meeting was held in the Guildhall. The Lord Mayor, the Rt. Hon. David Williams Wire, was in the Chair, and he stated that he had called the meeting of Citizens in obedience to the following requisition which he had received :—

"My Lord,

"We, the undersigned, sharing in the unanimous determination of the Government and people of this country to maintain a strict neutrality during the present Continental complications, desire to testify our high appreciation of a measure calculated greatly to secure that object by providing for possible contingencies.

"Mindful of the advice contained in the circular letter of the Rt. Hon. the Secretary of State for War issued on 12th ulto., and having reference to the formation of Volunteer Corps, we are of opinion that the establishment of a comprehensive and efficient Volunteer Rifle Brigade in the Metropolis would be a judicious measure, and, in order to its immediate formation, beg respectfully to request your Lordship will convene a public meeting to consider the subject forthwith.

"We feel assured that your Lordship's desire on all occasions to recognise efforts to promote the public weal will induce your immediate and hearty concurrence with our wish."

Then follow the names of 152 of the leading firms of merchants in the City of London. It was moved by Alderman John Carter, seconded by the Rt. Hon. Lord Elcho, and unanimously resolved, "That this meeting is of opinion that it is expedient to form a Volunteer Rifle Corps to be called 'The London Rifle Brigade,'" etc. It was further resolved, on the motion of Admiral Sir Charles Napier, K.C.B., M.P., seconded by Sir F. H. C. Doyle, "That the Brigade should be governed in everything not appertaining to military affairs by a Council of Twelve, three being Field Officers and nine being members not on the effective strength of the Regiment, with the Lord Mayor for the time being as President." This constitution was embodied in a regimental rule which stated that, "For the promotion of the interests of the Brigade, there shall be a Board of Patrons, consisting of the Court of Aldermen of the

City of London, with the Rt. Hon. the Lord Mayor (for the time being) as President of the Board," but it had long been a dead letter when it was annulled on the formation of the Territorial Force in 1908. Amongst the names of the Members of the Council in the early days are those of Alderman Rose (Vice-President), Lord Denman, Sir F. C. H. Doyle, Aldermen Carter, Allen and Mechi, Mr. W. Gardner, Mr. W. Cubitt, M.P., Capt. G. M. Hicks, Earl Grosvenor, Lord Elcho, Admiral Sir C. Napier, Sir P. Laurie, Sir Joseph Paxton, Baron Lionel Rothschild and Mr. R. W. Kennard, M.P. A fund was opened to meet preliminary expenses, and an advertisement was inserted in the leading newspapers asking for funds to equip the corps. An office was opened at 8 Great Winchester Street, in a building which has since been demolished, and by August 9th £1022 had been subscribed.

Alderman John Carter was elected Colonel, and Capt. Hicks (late of 41st Welsh Regt.), Governor of Whitecross Street Prison, Lieut.-Colonel. An advertisement was inserted in the papers for an adjutant, who was to be an ex-regular and to be paid £50 a year with 2s. 6d. capitation fee for each recruit, and, out of twelve candidates, Capt. C. F. Mackenzie was selected, while Robert Southgate, a Yeoman Warder of the Tower, was appointed sergt.-major. The following officers were elected: Captains: Aldermen W. A. Rose and W. F. Allen, W. Gardner, H. R. Poole, W. Gardner, junr., and H. W. Masterson. Lieutenants: T. D. Sewell, J. W. Carter and G. Simm. Ensigns: F. G. Finch, G. Dolland, W. Hopkinson, W. McLachlan. Surgeons: W. C. May and John Propert. The establishment of officers allowed by the War Office for a regiment of ten companies, in a letter dated 28th October, was 1 Lieut.-Colonel, 2 Majors, 8 Captains, 8 Lieutenants, 2 Adjutants, 1 Surgeon and 1 Assistant-Surgeon. The letter continued: "If the Corps now numbers 480 men the title 'London Rifle Volunteer Brigade' will be allowed at once. But the designation of a Brigade is only allowed to a Corps of more than one Battalion, and it is given in this instance on the distinct understanding that every endeavour will be made to enrol a thousand members. As soon as this number has been attained the establishment of officers will be 1 Colonel Commandant, 2 Lieut.-Colonels, 2 Majors, 16

Captains, 16 Lieutenants, 18 Ensigns, 2 Adjutants, 1 Surgeon, 2 Assistant-Surgeons. . . . The City of London holds forty-ninth place in the Rifle Volunteer Force of Great Britain, and this Brigade will rank as the first Division of the Force in the City of London."[1]

The Honourable Artillery Company was asked to give facilities for drill in its grounds, the first of several applications all of which were refused, and in the reply the suggestion was made, but not followed, that, instead of forming a new corps, rifle companies should be attached to that body. The Corporation granted the regiment leave to drill in the Guildhall, and, although this privilege was not exercised for some years after the building of the present head-quarters in Bunhill Row in 1893–4, drills were held there during the great rush of recruits in the South African War of 1900, while up to 1914 the thanks of the regiment were conveyed to the Corporation every year for the concession which had never been withdrawn. The War Office empowered the Commissioners of Lieutenancy of the City to grant the aid of two sergeants of the Royal London Militia to teach drill for a period of three months, remuneration to be paid by the corps at the rate of one shilling a day and fourpence lodging money.

Accommodation for shooting secured the early attention of the Council, and Battersea Park was suggested, but considered too difficult of access. An alternative site was proposed near the City Prison, Holloway, then in occupation of Mrs. Blyth, a cow-keeper, but it was eventually decided to build a range at the Crystal Palace, of which more will be heard later on. Capt. Hicks suggested that a central committee should be formed for the establishment of an annual rifle gathering, and, after the question had been discussed on more than one occasion by the Council, Lord Elcho took the matter in hand. This was the origin of the National Rifle Association, and the L.R.B., which has done such good work for shooting during its existence, may take credit for having initiated a

[1] When the Territorial Force was established in 1908 the Volunteer Battalions of the Royal Fusiliers were granted the precedence, and the L.R.B. with its proud motto, "Primus in Urbe," was relegated to the fifth place and became the 5th (City of London) Battalion The London Regiment. This change created a sore which has never healed.

project that has proved to be of far-reaching importance in the development of the power of the rifle, as was well exemplified during the Great War.

A meeting of those interested in rifle shooting was held, at which it was said, "It was feared that the nation, which had suddenly been awakened to a sense of insecurity, might, in the course of time, gradually relapse into a state of supineness should the state of continental affairs assume a less unsettled aspect; and it was felt that something more than temporary excitement, something more even than a sense of duty, might be required permanently to maintain a Volunteer Force. This, it appeared to the originators of the N.R.A., could, in a great measure, be effected by bringing to bear upon the Volunteer Force that healthy, manly spirit of rivalry and competition which is so characteristic of Englishmen, and which is the life and soul of all our sports." A meeting was held at which the promoters declared that, in view of the action taken by the London Rifle Brigade, national action could not be taken without "complete union among those interested." The National Rifle Association was then formed, and the resolution to hold a general meeting contains the following important passage: "In order that the Association should be established on a satisfactory footing, Lord Elcho undertakes to communicate with the Lord Mayor, and request his Lordship's attendance and co-operation on behalf of the London Rifle Brigade." At the first rifle meeting of the N.R.A. at Wimbledon, in 1860, the second prize in the "Prince Consort's" competition was a fifty-guinea cup presented by the L.R.B. The regiment had its separate camp at the meetings during the whole time that these were held at Wimbledon.

The Government undertook to provide rifles for 25 per cent of the strength, and it was decided to purchase rifles out of the corps funds for those who were unable to buy them for themselves. The original intention was to use the short Enfield rifle, but eventually the War Office decided to issue the Long Enfield (pattern of 1853), and in addition promised to supply a further 25 per cent, making 50 per cent in all. Authority was also given for the issue of ammunition on repayment at the rate per man of 200 rounds of ball, 120 rounds of blank, 352 percussion caps and 40 extra caps for snapping practice.

By August 30th matters had so far progressed that it was decided to apply for leave to enrol men, as already 87 had applied to enlist. The Early Closing Association asked for the co-operation of the Council in trying to induce bankers to close at two o'clock on Saturdays, but this was refused.

The question of uniform received much attention, and a contract was made with Messrs. Silver and Co. to provide tunic, trousers, shoulder and waistbelts, pouches, shako, plume and badge, forage cap and cover and badge, for £5 5s. There is, however, a bill in existence which shows a charge of £4 4s. for a full-dress tunic, £1 12s. for trousers, £1 for shako and plume, 8s. 6d. for a shoulder belt, and £2 11s. for a cloak, so that the prices were soon altered. The plume was of black cock's feathers: those of the men were short and only reached the top of the shako, while those of the officers reached the peak in front and the bottom of the shako behind. The Standing Orders prescribed the following:—

Review Order. Full dress tunic and trousers (gaiters if ordered), shako and plume, shoulder and waist-belts, black gloves.

Heavy Marching Order. Same as Review Order. Shako without plume, but with oilskin cover: undress kit and great-coat carried in pack, gaiters.

Light Marching Order. Undress tunic and trousers, gaiters, forage cap and oilskin cover, waist and shoulder belts, pack and great-coat.

Drill Order. Same as Light Marching Order, but without pack or great-coat.

These Orders are not very clear, but it may be noticed that shoulder belts were worn by privates, and that they had pouches. Honorary members wore the same uniform as privates, excepting all belts, with a red sash round the waist and silver shako plate and chain. The Council were entitled to wear officers' uniform with red sash, but without belts or swords. The Court of Lieutenancy approved the uniform proposed "except that they would suggest that the buttons upon the tunic project so much as to form an impediment to the free use of the rifle, and might, as well as the braid, be reduced with advantage: and that Section 19 of the War Office Memorandum for the formation of Volunteer Corps requires a 20-round pouch only." The undress cap followed the pattern of the French *képi*. The frequent references to alterations in dress and accoutrements are more interesting to those immediately concerned than to the general reader. The entrance fee at this time was a guinea, and the subscription was also a guinea. In addition subscriptions ranging from £10 10s. for field officers to £1 1s. for corporals were required for the band, the cost of which in the earlier years, even after instruments had been provided, amounted to £600 per annum.

On the 5th November the regiment marched from Zion College in London Wall to the Mansion House, where the Oath of Allegiance was administered, and by the 15th of the month the subscriptions amounted to £3550 and the enrolled members to 407.

The first Order issued by Lieut.-Col. Hicks is dated from head-quarters, 8 Great Winchester Street, 30th December, 1859, and is as follows:—

"VOLUNTEERS,

"The Court of Lieutenancy have this day conferred on me the honour of commanding you.

"In the organisation of a freshly formed Corps many difficulties exist, and I therefore trust that you will, by attention to your military duties and cheerful submission to necessary discipline, assist me in my earnest desire to render this Brigade second to none in the Kingdom. In unity is strength. We must all work willingly and together, remembering that we are not only Englishmen, ready to bear arms in our country's cause, but comrades bound by the additional tie of serving Her Majesty in the ranks of the London Rifle Volunteer Brigade."

1860

By the 10th January over 1100 men had been enrolled, and by the end of February nearly 1400. Lieut. A. T. Ewens (60th Rifles) was appointed adjutant in the place of Capt. Mackenzie, and it is no exaggeration to say that he *made* the regiment in these early days. His devotion to its best interests, his military instinct, and his universal popularity at once made their mark and left the stamp "Thorough" (Lord Kitchener's motto) on everything that made for efficiency. The subscriptions by this time amounted to over £4400, but unfortunately the Secretary proved dishonest and had to be prosecuted though, as the net amount of his defalcations amounted to only some £186 while the cost of the prosecution was £457, good money was thrown after bad. Arrangements were made for a range and armoury at the Crystal Palace at a cost of £157, for which purpose butts were erected and all members were given season tickets. Drill took place on the cricket ground. In the Standing Orders forty-five minutes were allowed for parade. The first bugle was for Staff Parade : the "Assembly" went ten minutes later for falling in. "Coverers" (or "Markers") was sounded five minutes before forming up, and the "Advance" for marching on markers. Companies at this time were called "Divisions." N.C.O.'s were appointed for the first time, and forty-seven corporals were made who were permitted to attach to their shoulder belt a bronze chain and whistle as a distinguishing badge. The regiment was formed into two battalions of eight companies each, and one man was sent to Hythe for instruction in musketry. Sergeants were ordered to carry rifles on parade, but were allowed to wear swords off parade. Privates, however, were forbidden to wear swords at all. Members were reported to have been seen in public places in uniform, an irregularity which "the Commanding Officer trusts will not occur again." Attention was drawn in Orders to the necessity "of exercising the utmost courtesy towards each other, and the C.O. trusts that on every occasion all orders will be given and corrections at drill made firmly and patiently without irritation."

The Duke of Cambridge was appointed Colonel in the place of Col. Carter, about whose appointment there had apparently been no little difference of opinion, and this led to a strange scene at the Mansion House in January of this year, for Col. Carter, who had become Lord Mayor in the previous November, called a meeting there of the members of the regiment and addressed them as follows :—

". . . You are no doubt aware that on 21st July last, in this hall and in the presence of a much larger number of my fellow-citizens than I now have the pleasure of addressing, Lord Elcho proposed, and that gallant old sailor, Sir C. Napier, seconded, a motion that I should be nominated to the colonelcy of the intended Brigade." (Strong symptoms of mutiny, manifested by groans, hisses and cries of "Oh, oh.") "At that time the Brigade numbered nearly 500, but so steady has been its progress since that it now nearly numbers 1200 efficient men. When the Brigade took a flourishing position a rumour gradually spread abroad that H.R.H. the Duke of Cambridge would not object to accepting the colonelcy. Deeming it my duty to make myself acquainted with the real sentiments of His Royal Highness on the subject, I sought an interview with the illustrious Duke, who frankly and fairly stated that if I, as Lord Mayor of London, requested him to take command of the London Rifle Brigade, he should not be unwilling to comply with the request, though his time was already occupied by many other important duties. Feeling that such an appointment—that of His Royal Highness the Commander-in-Chief—would confer no small distinction upon you, I considered it to be my duty at once and without hesitation to resign my appointment into the hands of the Duke who, on the 9th inst., kindly consented to accept the title of Colonel of the London Rifle Brigade." (Tremendous and long continued applause.)

The Duke of Cambridge inspected the regiment, in the welfare of which he always took the keenest interest, for the first time on 5th May, and, with scarcely an exception, was present at every succeeding inspection until his death. The regiment seems to have acquitted itself creditably, for Lieut.-Col. Hicks received a letter from Col. Raines, late Commanding 95th Regiment, whom he describes as "an old and distinguished officer," in which he writes: "I congratulate you with all my heart on the splendid show your regiment made yesterday, and at the steadiness and correctness with which they performed the manœuvres you put them through. I could scarcely have believed it possible with the materials you possess—men of independent means—you could have done so much in so short a time and got on so gloriously," etc. The regiment with other London units was reviewed by Queen Victoria in Hyde Park during the following month, when 1300 men were present. The Duke said that "There was no corps on the ground superior in any respect to the L.R.B."

Col. McMurdo had by this time been appointed Inspector of Volunteers, and wrote early in the year to the Commanding Officer: "Col. McMurdo, Inspector of Volunteers, presents his compliments to the Officer Commanding the London Rifle Brigade, and, having observed that corps in a march on Saturday evening last at half-past six as it passed along London Bridge, he thinks it due to the members who compose it to express the high opinion he entertains of their efficient and soldier-like appearance. A tolerably accurate estimate of the state of discipline existing in a regiment can generally be made by observing it on an ordinary march (perhaps more so than on parade), and the example of perfect steadiness and formation on this occasion, when the evening was dark and the thoroughfare on the Bridge sufficient to distract and confuse older soldiers, was very creditable and promises to confirm the most favourable expectations which have been formed of the present important movement." As the gallant colonel seems to have gone out of his way to make this communication it may be accepted as an honest statement, and is therefore the more gratifying.

At this time shooting was a difficulty, as the Crystal Palace range had to be abandoned in consequence of an injunction threatened by the neighbours, who regarded it as a dangerous nuisance. As £2300 had been spent and only £600 was recovered from the Crystal Palace Company the loss was a heavy one. Sites which were inspected at Forest Gate and Bromley were found to be unsatisfactory, but the London Scottish very kindly came to the rescue and granted the use of their range at Wimbledon on certain days. A Whitworth rifle was presented to them for competition as a small token of gratitude. Company silver medals were shot for, which became the property of the winners and were worn when in uniform as long as the wearer was the best shot in his company.

In the early part of the year a Church Parade was held at St. Paul's, and the bandmaster was instructed to play sacred music on the march. A proposal was made about the same time that, in order to distinguish bandsmen from privates, the former should have red piping on their uniform and red horsehair plumes. This was negatived by the Commanding Officer, who said, "Should it be deemed advisable to make any alteration or addition, I would advise some change being made consistent with good taste." The City of London Engineers proposed amalgamating with the L.R.B. and forming a third battalion, but the idea was rejected. A suggestion was also made to have an artillery company and a mounted company, but nothing came of it. On drill nights a guard was mounted at the Guildhall, whose duties were to fulfil the ordinary functions of sentries, and to enforce compliance with orders as to dress, smoking, etc. When marching out from the Guildhall the guard had to fall in under the sergeant and follow "next after the advance guard," doubling out to the front when ordered to take post in order to take up and keep the ground.

The regiment was inspected by Col. McMurdo in September, and he said, "I have had many opportunities of seeing Volunteers in different parts of the country, and for rapidity and steadiness of movement, I say it again, gentlemen, for steadiness of movement, you have surpassed anything I have seen in any corps, and it is my opinion that your movements are admirable."

For the first time the regiment found the Guard of Honour at the Guildhall on Lord Mayor's Day, a duty which was performed without break for many years. The cadet corps was started in this year.

1861

A serious difference of opinion seems to have arisen between Lieut.-Col. Hicks and the Court of Lieutenancy on the subject of the promotion of officers. The Court appears to have had some jurisdiction in the matter, and to have decided to promote by seniority, while the Commanding Officer had instituted an arrangement under which a Board made recommendations to him based on an examination and on the number of drills put in. Although the relations between the Court and the Commanding Officer were evidently strained, the feeling of the regiment was naturally with its chief, and, when he resigned in the following year, at a special general meeting resolutions were passed regretting the resignation of Lieut.-Col. Hicks and thanking him for his valuable services to the regiment. At the meeting the opinion was also expressed that it was absolutely necessary for the beneficial existence of the regiment that its two Lieut.-Colonels should now and always be officers of professional military experience and ability; and a further resolution was passed to the effect that the Court of Lieutenancy was dilatory in regard to promotions, over which it had a measure of control, and that it had ignored some of Lieut.-Col. Hicks' recommendations. The meeting also hinted that it would be glad if the Court would mend its ways.

The following extract from the *Daily Telegraph* of October 21st is not without interest :—

"The presentation of colours, silver bugles, and prizes won at the annual competition in July last took place on Saturday at the Crystal Palace with all the éclat that the presence of the Lord Mayor and Lady Mayoress and a most distinguished company could add to the occasion. . . . In front of the platform were displayed the complete set of regimental colours which the Corporation had honoured themselves and the Brigade by presenting. The Queen's Colour and regimental flag bearing the initials 'L.R.B.', the City arms and motto, occupied the posts of honour to the right and left of the steps leading from the dais to the transept. Eight marching-past points, white flags with red St. George's Cross, were draped at intervals around the edge of the platform with the battalion aides beneath them. The regiment mustered at three o'clock on the upper terrace, in front of the central transept, under the command of Major and Alderman Rose, and Capts. and Adjts. Ewens and Smith. Sixteen companies were formed, bringing the numbers up to nearly 900 men. Both bands and the Cadet Corps attached to the brigade were present. After proving the companies, they were marched in succession to the open space preserved in front of the Handel Orchestra, and formed in triple lines round three sides of a square, the cadets in front of a raised dais forming a fourth. Every point from which a view of the ceremony could be obtained was completely filled, the dark uniforms and waving plumes of the brigade forming a barrier beyond which the spectators extended in a solid mass in every direction. . . . The Lord Mayor and Lady Mayoress having taken their seats, a representation was made to Major Rose that the troops in front of the reserved seats facing the orchestra entirely obstructed the view of the occupants of those seats. An order was therefore given, and as promptly obeyed, for that side of the square to lie down. This manœuvre was rewarded by hearty plaudits from all quarters, but, not being exactly the position in which troops usually receive colours, it evidently excited the surprise of Lord Clyde, whose stern features relaxed to a grim smile on the motive for this novel procedure being explained."

The colours were then presented by the Lady Mayoress, who "stepped forward and in a low silvery voice, rendered slightly tremulous perhaps by the consciousness of the important part she was performing in the imposing spectacle, addressed the brigade." The Lady Mayoress then presented the silver bugles, the funds for which had been collected from the ladies of the City. After this followed the presentation of prizes, about which the account says: "Hitherto the motionless, statuelike attitude and the deathlike silence in the ranks had borne testimony to the high state of discipline in the ranks. Now, however, the *esprit de corps*, which sends every man of soldierlike spirit to rejoice over the success of a comrade as an honour to the regiment and to mourn over every disgrace as something affecting his own person, triumphed, and each prize winner was greeted, as he descended the dais, in the cheers of his comrades." The colours were never carried on parade because rifle regiments have no colours, but they were always used for marching past; the aides were small flags inserted in the muzzles of the rifles of the "coverers" or "markers" to facilitate dressing.

During this summer arrangements were made for a fortnight's camp at Aldershot in August, probably the first of its kind, but at the last minute His Majesty's Secretary of State for War having positively refused the issue of tents, camp equipment, etc., for the use of the London Rifle Brigade, the Lieut.-Colonel Commanding "regrets that he is obliged to cancel all orders published in reference to the proposed encampment." At this time shooting took place at Plumstead and near the Royal Pavilion Hotel, North Woolwich, and drills took place at Zion College, the Guildhall, London Fields, and also at Blackheath, to which the troops proceeded by boat. The regiment seems to have offered itself for active service, but the offer was declined as "if the country was at war, it would only be employed under Act 44, Geo. III., Cap. 54."

The School of Arms began its activities this year, and the first practices were at Cowper Street Schools, but subsequently for many years use was made of the London Coal Exchange. A ball also was given at the Guildhall, a contemporary account of which states in journalese style: "There was room for dancing. When a polka, galop, a waltz, a quadrille, a schottische, a Lancers or a Caledonian was announced, people were not compelled to confine their saltatory exertions within a circle of a few square inches. On the contrary, they had full scope to move uninterruptedly, if they pleased, along the whole length of the spacious hall, nay, to cross audaciously from side to side if they could elude the active vigilance of the masters of the ceremonies. Thus it was quite possible, nay exceedingly easy, for any person present not of misanthropical tendencies, and possessing a knowledge of the mysteries of dancing, to partake of a very pleasant evening's amusement, and enjoy himself as a man should who puts on patent boots with the special intention of availing himself of their elastic capabilities to the greatest extent. . . . A large proportion of the gentlemen wore uniform, and martial enough they looked in costumes to which all had now evidently grown accustomed."

1862

There was considerable difficulty in finding a successor to Lieut.-Col. Hicks, so the Duke of Cambridge was approached for help, and eventually, in March, Capt. George Warde, late of 35th and 51st Light Infantry, was appointed. At a general meeting of the regiment a resolution was passed that the

Commanding Officer should in future always be an officer of professional military experience and ability. This rule, which has been strictly adhered to, except that Lieut.-Col. Haywood had command for about a year and Col. Edward Matthey for a short time during the South African War, is undoubtedly largely responsible for the efficiency which the regiment has maintained, and is a thoroughly sound one because the second in command may, or may not, be suitable for Commanding Officer, and, if he is not, the regiment is bound to suffer; whereas, through looking for someone outside it, so far the right man for the post has always been found.

The first of the long series of Easter Reviews at Brighton took place in this year. A notice appeared in Orders that, "The Brigade has the honour of covering the front of the division, and the C.O. trusts that all officers will be alert for any bugle sound or word of command which may be given." The work was confined to Easter Monday, and it was not till later that the training was extended so as to cover the four days from Good Friday. In May a sham fight took place at Epsom, and a quotation from an article in the *Daily Telegraph* about it may be interesting :—

"A very successful Volunteer Brigade Field Day took place at Epsom under command of Col. McMurdo, Inspector General of Volunteers. The following paraded : Inns of Court, 6 companies, 300 men; L.R.B., 9 companies, 450 men; West Middlesex, 3 companies, 150 men; Queen's Westminsters, 12 companies, 600 men; London Scottish, 6 companies, 300 men; 38th Middlesex (Artists), 1 company, 60 men. The troops drew up 'in line of contiguous columns,' the Inns of Court on the right and the London Rifle Brigade next. The Inns of Court advanced, changed front to the right, and threw out skirmishers who lined the S.W. side of the race-course, they and their supports sheltering themselves behind the furze bushes and hillocks by assuming a recumbent position. As soon as the skirmishers had occupied the ground, the remainder of the Brigade advanced by mass of columns on the right battalion along the hollow, hidden from the view of the enemy by the intervening ridge. Before this movement had commenced, however, the skirmishers opened fire across the race-course at their recondite foe, the sharp crack of rifles

A Sergeant, Corporal, and Private, 1862

from the right of sections soon becoming general along the line. The great advantage which a breech-loading rifle would be for skirmishers was here strikingly shown. Though the cover was amply sufficient for most of the men whilst lying down, the impossibility of loading in this position obliged them to expose themselves more or less for a time which would have given fatal opportunity for the exercise of an enemy's skill in sharp-shooting. . . . This and the subsequent deployments and movements of the day were performed with admirable precision by the L.R.B. at the double, the movements of the remaining Battalions in quick time appearing inordinately slow by comparison." From this it appears that the custom in old days of men firing standing was indicated not so much by courage as by necessity. An old volunteer wrote on the subject of muzzle loaders as follows: "They were often the source of much fun, and sometimes of danger. In those days loading was a long operation—none of your slipping in a cartridge and closing the breech. It entailed taking out a cartridge, tearing off the paper end, then pouring in the powder, then reversing the cartridge case and putting the bullet in the muzzle, drawing the ramrod, ramming down, returning the rod, and finally capping—all distinct movements. Again, if a rifle was not very carefully washed out after using, the fouling in the breech prevented the cap from firing the charge—thus it often happened in the excitement of a sham fight, when sometimes the whole battalion in line would fire a volley, that several men would get quite a number of blank cartridges rammed down before the rifle went off. The effect then was somewhat astonishing. Sergeants carried a kind of small corkscrew that screwed on to the end of the ramrod, so as to be prepared to draw overcharged rifles, or those that would not fire from dirt in the breech. Another awkward feature about muzzle loading was that a careless man, in the hurry of loading, often did not withdraw his ramrod after ramming down, but capped and fired, when away went the ramrod like an arrow from the bow." On one occasion a spectator was shot through the body and killed on the spot. The conditions of one of the competitions at the annual prize meeting at 200 yards were that the competitors should load at the word of command, and on the bugle sounding "commence firing," blaze away as rapidly as they liked for six minutes. Each man had 20 rounds and any position was allowed. The average results per man were 12·13 rounds fired; and 7·13 hits. The largest number of rounds fired by any man in this particular competition was 16: one man shot "from the shoulder" (i.e. standing), and the remainder "in the Hythe position from the knee, rising to load after delivering their fire."

In this year a commission appointed by the War Office to go into the matter recommended that a capitation fee of 20s. should be paid for every man who made himself efficient. Up to this time all expenses had been paid by the men themselves, so that all corps consisted solely of the well-to-do, and the working man was not in a position to join however anxious to do so, as it was contended by many that men who could not afford to pay their own expenses ought to go to the militia. If this view had been followed there can be little doubt that the movement must have died out, because the number of those who were prepared to give their money as well as their time, when the prospect of war was slight, was limited. Moreover, about this time, the playing of games became increasingly popular, and the difficulty of securing recruits became greater each year. At the close of the year the regiment had a march out in the neighbourhood of Norwood, and the *City Press* wrote: "About 200 took advantage of this method of spending a very pleasant afternoon, and of gaining practice in moving about after dark in agricultural districts."

1863

In March the regiment assisted in keeping the streets on the occasion of the arrival of Princess Alexandra prior to her marriage to the Prince of Wales, but there appears to have been some mismanagement, and it was almost impossible to control the crowd. An article appeared in *The Times* complaining that the L.R.B. had obstructed the City Police by falling in in Guildhall Yard, by marching by a circuitous route to their position in front of the Mansion House, and by arriving there an hour late. In a trenchant letter Lieut.-Col. Warde disproved all the statements of the Police, maintaining on the contrary that their arrangements were inadequate and the primary cause of all the trouble. He subsequently received from the War Office a letter signed by Col. McMurdo completely exonerating the regiment, and adding " great praise is due to the Volunteers for the moderation and good temper evinced by them under trying circumstances." History repeats itself, and similar scenes took place when the C.I.V. returned from South Africa in 1900, as the streets were allowed to be occupied so completely by the crowd that the troops on their arrival were helpless.

In June the annual inspection by the Duke of Cambridge took place. The C.O. in his preliminary order drew special attention to the importance of having the bayonets, scabbards, rifle slings and knee-caps well cleaned. The knee-caps were of stout leather, precisely similar to those worn by men when laying carpets, and were strapped on below the knee, because most of the firing was done in the kneeling position, so that the protection for the trousers was necessary, especially when drilling in plain clothes. Knee-caps were certainly worn at plain clothes drill up to 1893, when drills were carried on in the Guildhall, probably because the floor was of stone, but they seem to have disappeared when the regiment drilled in its own hall, the floor of which was of wood. It will be of interest to students of military history to record the movements carried out at this inspection : From quarter distance column, right in front, facing south, the battalion deployed on the leading company. The line advanced, halted, retired by fours from the right of companies, front turned, advanced, and left wheeled into line without halting. The line halted and file-fired. The line then retired in open column from the right in rear of the left. The column then front turned and right wheeled into line, advanced, halted and fired a volley. It formed square on No. 5 : the square retired, advanced, and then took ground to the left. The square then wheeled to the right. After preparing to receive cavalry, column was reformed, but, the cavalry again threatening, square was formed at the double on the leading division. The square advanced, took ground to the right, and prepared for cavalry. Column was then reformed, and the front changed by wheel of subdivisions. The column, then facing south, deployed on its rear division. The line then fired, and advanced by wings : line was reformed on the leading (right) wing. The line then retired, advanced, companies wheeled into open column right in front. Square was formed on No. 5, column reformed, and front changed by wheel of sub-divisions at the double so as to face east. The column deployed on a central company: the line retired, halted and fronted. Line advanced in direct echelon of companies from the right at company distance: echelon wheeled to the left, and formed company squares to receive cavalry. The standing ranks fixed swords as well as the kneeling ranks: this though not usual with rifles always seems to us preferable to the custom of the standing ranks firing with swords unfixed. Echelon reformed, companies formed line on No. 7, line formed quarter distance column, right in front, on No. 6. Column retired and wheeled to the right, front turned (facing east) and formed square on the leading company at the double. Reformed column and retired at the double: front turned and formed square on the leading company. Reformed column: took ground to the right at the double: front turned: took ground to the left: retired: took ground to the proper right: retired and deployed on No. 6, line retired and halted: then advanced in Review Order and gave the Royal Salute." This sounds a fairly formidable programme, but H.R.H. spoke very highly of the way in which the drill was done and the men were commanded.

It will be easier to reconstruct this drill if it be remembered that companies were then called divisions, and half companies sub-divisions. The counter march of sub-divisions (half companies) is an interesting example of the drill of the period, when a battalion always had a grenadier company on each flank when in line, and in front and rear when in column, while in all formations companies stood in proper order and "re-numbering" was not allowed. Consequently a retirement could not be carried out by merely "turning about," but the whole battalion had first to be inverted, which was effected as follows: All the right half companies turned about, and on the command "quick march" the battalion stepped off. The left half company of No. 1 wheeled to the right at once and followed behind its right half company, each left half company wheeling in turn when it arrived on the spot from which the left half of No. 1 started. At the proper moment when the two halves of a company came into line again the battalion was halted : the right half companies turned about and the movement was complete.

During July, just prior to the Wimbledon Meeting, a field-day took place on Wimbledon Common in conjunction with the H.A.C., the St. George's and the Queen's Westminsters. A contemporary report states : "The line then fired volleys by battalions from the right, that of the L.R.B. sounding, in its unity, like the report of a field-piece, and contrasting favourably with the straggling discharge of the battalions on the left of the line."

In those days targets were of iron, and of the Wimbledon meeting it was said in the newspapers : "At present the system of marking in general use is for a man, protected by a mantlet, to watch each shot as it strikes the target, roughly signalling its position by means of appropriate flags, and washing off the marks when they become too numerous. . . . The new system consists of having discs to show bulls'-eyes, centres, and outers, each of which has at the back a small brush. On a bullet striking the target, the marker at once erases the mark, and, in doing so, indicates to those at the firing point the exact position of the shot." In consequence of the markers being often injured by splashes, owing to their own carelessness, the Guardsmen, who usually acted as markers, were forbidden this year to perform that duty, and, in order that the meeting might not end prematurely, Lord Elcho set an example by himself marking, assisted by volunteers for the work.

At this time a rifle range in Plaistow Marshes, near the Victoria Docks, was rented from the 2nd Tower Hamlets at a cost of £130 a year, and before long a correspondence took place in regard to a cow which came to an untimely end. Eventually the regiment agreed to pay half the cost of the animal, £7 1s., but entered a protest against such payment forming a precedent.

1864

The regiment now for the first time carried off the much-coveted palm at the Wimbledon meeting, the Queen's prize being won by Pte. J. Wyatt, who served in the L.R.B. for many years and was a consistently good shot. The annual Inspection by the Duke of Cambridge seems to have gone off well. "The movements, which differed considerably from the usual routine of displays of this description and gave the whole affair more the appearance of regular troops than an official inspection of volunteers, were without a single exception executed with remarkable precision and regularity, most of them eliciting expressions of satisfaction and praise from the gallant Duke, and repeated bursts of applause from the spectators." All ranks wore a laurel leaf in the shako in honour of the Wimbledon victory. The number of members seems by this time to have shown signs of falling off, as the first enthusiasm waned, and the companies were reduced from sixteen by two, "D" and "I" being broken up. The officers were permitted for the first time to wear badges of rank on the patrol jacket, and men were allowed to put up a badge to show that they were "effective" in the previous year. At first a strip of braid was worn, but later the badge was a diamond worn on the right cuff. These badges were not worn from 1893 by the L.R.B., though they were put up by other regiments, so it can only be supposed that all the L.R.B. were effective, and that the distinction was unnecessary.

1865

The Cripplegate Trophy, a very handsome piece of plate consisting of a representation in silver of the old Cripple Gate, with figures at the base, was presented at this time.

1866

The finances of the regiment were now in a poor way, and Capt. Ewens, the Adjutant, voluntarily gave up £100, half the salary paid him by the regiment. He was not a rich man, and this act was only one of many by which he showed his deep interest in all that concerned the welfare of the L.R.B., but the full salary was paid again in a year or two. The regiment sent a detachment to Brussels as part of a composite battalion under command of Col. Sir Loyd Lindsay, V.C.

(afterwards Lord Wantage), to take part in the "Tir National," during the Belgian Fêtes of Independence, which took place from the 15th to 18th October, and drew competitors also from France and Holland. The distances mainly were 100 yards, about 240 yards, and 500 yards, the last of which was a longer range than the Belgians were accustomed to. Some 100 volunteers were present and the Lord Mayor of London attended as a guest of King Leopold II. The firing took place from a long shed in which there was a compartment for each shooter, and the noise seems to have been rather trying. The roof of the shed was made of double thickness, so that if anyone fired away his ramrod no great harm should be done. The British representatives seem to have held their own, and to have been well up in the prize lists. They were the first British troops which had been seen in the town since the days of Waterloo, and they received a great ovation. There was a constant round of festivities of all kinds, and hospitality without limit.

Head-quarters seems to have been at 17 Finsbury Place South at this time.

1867

The assembly of Volunteers took place this year at Dover, and one man, who distinguished himself by crossing to Calais in uniform, was brought back in custody, and seems to have disappeared from that time forth. One of the captains died, and crape was ordered to be worn on all silver ornaments and on the left arm.

1868

At this time each company was affiliated to one of the Wards of the City, and for many years received generous donations from the Ward Funds towards its prizes. Later on some Ward clerk started a scare that these payments were *ultra vires*, and might possibly be surcharged, which caused them to fall off, but many members of the Ward Clubs and other friends of the regiment subscribed privately and contributed materially to the funds until the Volunteers as such ceased to exist. In the winter of 1867–8 there was much Fenian activity all over England, and the regiment found a guard at its head quarters from 9 p.m. till daylight, with fixed swords and ball cartridge, for about two months. This was the first occasion that the L.R.B. were on duty with ball ammunition. The regiment for the second time suffered through a dishonest secretary, whose accounts showed a deficit of £745 in addition to defalcations which were not traceable.

1869

A committee was appointed to go into the finances, and reported that the accounts, as presented by them, they " believe for the first time are not only clear and intelligible but accurately represent the financial position of the regiment." Considering that all the members were business men, this state of affairs does not do them much credit. The duties of the secretary were for a time taken over by the adjutants and sergt.-major.

The following is an account of the Easter Monday Review :—

" We paraded at an early hour in town and detrained about 8 a.m. at Dover. A heavy gale was blowing with squalls of rain : the fleet that was to co-operate in the attack on Dover was pitching and straining at its anchors a short distance out at sea, and things generally looked nasty. The L.R.B. formed up near the Admiralty pier and quietly absorbed their share of the moisture. The storm increased in fury, and shortly the order came for all regiments to dismiss, and fall in at 4 p.m. for the return journey. About an hour later the storm ceased, and thousands of Volunteers came out from their various shelters. The Admiralty Pier was the chief centre of attraction for, opposite to it, H.M.S. *Ferret* was dragging her anchors, and coming slowly but surely on to the pier. At last she drifted right in and smashed up on the pier. The crew mainly escaped by the chain of a crane that was hanging down just at the point at which she struck : in a very short time she went to pieces. While we were watching this exciting scene, bugles were heard sounding the 'Assembly' all over the town. We hurried back to our various rendezvous, to hear that the Duke of Cambridge had ridden over from Walmer with his staff, expecting to find the troops on the heights above the town. Surprised at not finding them, he came on post haste down into the town, only to find the street filled with a mixed mass of men wandering about. The Duke soon hunted up the various Brigade Staffs, and ordered that the troops should at once fall in and march up to the hills. In an hour some 20,000 men had been got together again, and the various brigades began their march to the hills. Snow had been lying for a day or two, and the 'going' over the land was heavy in the extreme. It was the hardest bit of marching I remember. The Duke insisted on our going through the Field Day as originally laid down, although late in the day. I think few were sorry when the order came for the tired regiments to march back."

1870

The Volunteer movement had by this time felt the inevitable reaction from the enthusiasm with which it started, so that some battalions found it impossible to carry on, and two companies of the 12th Tower Hamlets (Stoke Newington) were transferred to the L.R.B. A new drill came into force.

It was somewhere about this year that the "masked lady," who became so notorious that her picture came out in one of the illustrated papers (not so numerous then as now), made her appearance. The story, as told by an old member, is as follows: "One day a lady appeared at the orderly room with a photograph of a young man whom she wanted to find, but no one could identify it. She obtained some regimental belts and, at most big reviews, she turned out, dressed in black, with an officer's belt over her riding habit and a small sword. She rode a white horse and was a fine horsewoman. Many's the time I have seen her riding after the Staff over the Sussex downs, but she always kept near the L.R.B. No one could see what she was like as she wore a half mask of black crêpe. It used to be the custom for the City Corps to have a combined march once a year to Hyde Park. On one occasion the masked lady had ridden with us. Our chief, Col. George Warde, was much annoyed and sent his adjutant, Capt. Ewens, to her with a request that she would discontinue attaching herself to the L.R.B. When we reached Hyde Park and had fallen out, I was having a look at the guns of the H.A.C. when to me rode the lady and asked why the Colonel would not let her ride with the L.R.B., and why was he angry with her. 'It would break her heart,' she said, 'if she could not go about with us as before.' She was last seen at the Wimbledon Review in 1872. Of course some said there was a love affair at the bottom of it ; but whatever it was, it has remained a mystery from that day to this."

1871

Breech-loading Snider rifles were now issued. The Finance Committee reported at the General Meeting that the Government had deducted £94 from the capitation grant for deficiencies and repairs to arms after 11 years' wear, a sum exceeding the cost of new weapons.

1872

After many years of difficulty a range was secured for some of the City corps at Rainham, which continued to be used until the Territorial Force was well established.

New Efficiency Regulations were issued which enacted, amongst other things, that a man might only belong to one corps, while a number of other points were laid down with regard to drills and musketry, from which it may be inferred that slackness had crept in, and that attendances had been allowed to count as drills which did not carry out the purposes for which they were intended. Autumn manœuvres on a large scale, the first of their kind, took place at Dartmoor, and the Regiment was represented by a company.

1873

Efficiency stars were granted for each five years' service. Men served for long periods in those days and later, and it was not uncommon to see them with five, six and even seven stars, as no age limit was enforced. Martini-Henry rifles were made available for practice. For the Dartmoor manœuvres this year, in addition to sending a company, the regiment furnished the staff for the 2nd Provisional Battalion. The men wore Army serge fatigue jackets and glengarries. They were equipped for the first time with water-bottles, consisting of covered soda-water bottles with straps, and also with half-pint horn mugs.

1874

The establishment was further reduced to twelve companies, and another offer was made to rent the ground of the H.A.C. for drill, but this was, as usual, refused. Up to this time a volunteer band had been kept up in addition to the professional one, but it seems always to have been a source of discord in more senses than one, and was now finally dropped. In the place of the autumn manœuvres, a company was sent to Aldershot in August for fifteen days with a provisional battalion.

1876

In this year, to the great regret of all ranks, Col. George Warde gave up the command of the battalion, which he had held since 1862. During this time he had seen a great decline from the original spirit, but despite the apathy, and sometimes almost opposition, of the authorities, he "carried on" and rendered great services to the regiment during a most difficult period. He died in 1877, and a monumental brass was erected to his memory by the regiment in Westerham Church. His successor was Sir Arthur Hayter, late Grenadier Guards, who had joined the regiment in 1872. Sir Arthur was in the Eton XI for three years, and at Oxford, and had served for ten years in the Guards. He commanded until 1881, and subsequently became Lord Haversham. He always took an interest in the regiment, and frequently after his retirement attended the Past and Present Officers' Dinner. The first of the Whitsun camps, which were a regular feature in the annual programme for some years, took place at Mitcham, the men sleeping in camp and doing their drills in the morning and evening, but coming up to town daily for their ordinary work.

1877

No events of note occurred during this year, but some changes in uniform may be noted. Shoulder belts, hitherto worn by all ranks, were ordered to be worn by officers only ;

but sergeants continued to wear chains and whistles which were attached to the tunics. Glengarry caps, of the Scotch pattern with two ribbon tails, were taken into use in undress by all ranks except officers, who continued to wear the round "pill-box."

1878

For the second time the Easter training was spread over the four days, and a marching party started off on Good Friday. Corporals were given permission to wear bronze chains and whistles, but these disappeared later on.

1879–80

The year 1879 seems to have been quite uneventful, but Easter 1880 was spent in the neighbourhood of Brighton, and, concerning the operations on Easter Monday for which the regiment marched over from Lewes where it had been quartered, the *Daily News* wrote: "Nothing could be finer than the push and resolution with which the L.R.B., nowise fagged by the steep slopes up which lay its road to the fray, pressed up to the edge of the wood, and finally, after a struggle which lasted quite a quarter of an hour and was by far the best episode of the fighting, carried it with a resistless rush." Of the march past the account goes on to say that the L.R.B. were "conspicuous not only by their good marching and stalwart appearance, but also by their rather old-fashioned plumes."

The Easter manœuvres at Brighton were of very little use from a military point of view. Those corps which marched down no doubt learnt something of value, but the Easter Monday field-day itself was a farce. The march past was the only item to which any importance was attached by the troops and the public, and to it everything was subordinated. The sham fight, which sometimes took place before and sometimes afterwards, generally ended in two lines of men lying down about a hundred yards apart, firing off all their blank ammunition, with a thick bank of spectators behind them. If a hare got up it was not unusual for everyone to chase it, including many of the troops, and throw anything handy at it. After Lord Edward Pelham Clinton took command this was altered so far as the L.R.B. was concerned, as the four days were spent in barracks or forts, and useful work carried out all the time. A list of the various places at which Easter was spent will be found on p. 407.

1881

The officers were all ordered to wear shoulder straps, and, those entitled to them, badges of rank on their patrol jackets. As officers had worn badges on their collars up to then, the last clause probably related to the fact that ensigns, or 2nd lieutenants, did not then wear badges of rank, and it was not till many years later that they were allowed to do so. A Royal Review was held at Windsor during the year, on 9th July. The *Standard* said that the L.R.B. went by in a style "almost faultless." In this year the regiment suffered a great loss by the retirement of Robert Southgate, who had been sergt.-major from the earliest days, and was a man of mark, with many quaint sayings. He was awarded a gratuity of £105, and made assistant secretary, the first of several similar appointments; he died a few years later, much regretted by all ranks, after having been a truly faithful servant of the regiment. Sir Arthur Hayter resigned during the year, and was succeeded by Lieut.-Col. Haywood, who had served for twenty-one years and had passed through all grades. This is one of the two instances of the L.R.B., whilst Volunteers, being commanded by an officer who had not been a regular soldier.

1882

This year saw the retirement of Lieut.-Col. Ewens, who had been adjutant of the regiment from the beginning of 1860. He had also been acting as secretary for some time, and was asked to continue to act in this capacity on his retirement, as well as being appointed one of the majors. He was succeeded by Capt. Wortham, late of the 60th Rifles, and Lieut.-Col. Haywood was succeeded in the command by Lord Edward Pelham Clinton. This was the beginning of a new era, for Lord Edward, as he was always called, was one of the first to abandon the idea that volunteering was an amusement and Easter trainings a picnic. He immediately began to deal with the regiment as a fighting unit, and great progress was made from the day on which he took over the command. Two small alterations are recorded as having been made in the uniform, the officers wearing an undress cap of a different pattern, and N.C.O.'s being ordered to wear chevrons on the right arm only. The reason for the latter change is not apparent; the H.A.C. always continued to wear chevrons on both arms, and on the introduction of service dress in 1908 the old order was restored.

1883

Lieut.-Col. Ewens died on 13th March, and the following appeared in Regimental Orders: "The loss of Lieut.-Col. Ewens as adjutant, after a service of twenty-two years, was much felt by all, but his valuable services as major and secretary still identified him with the active management of the corps. The C.O. knows well that Lieut.-Col. Ewens was beloved by all ranks, and he feels that the news of his death will occasion the greatest grief, and that in the regiment which he loved so well he will never be forgotten." Col. Ewens' devotion to the regiment was unbounded, and, as has already been said, there can be no doubt that he was very largely, if not almost entirely, responsible for the efficiency which the regiment acquired and maintained from its earliest days. He was buried in Brompton Cemetery on 20th March with full military honours, and the whole regiment attended. A monument was erected over his grave by the members as a token of their respect and esteem. Lieut.-Col. Harvey, late paymaster in the Rifle Brigade, was appointed secretary in his stead.

1884–7

These years were for the most part uneventful. In 1884 the Martini-Henry rifle was adopted at the Wimbledon Meeting, as the weapon for fine shooting in place of the Snider rifle, with which the Volunteers were still armed. In 1887 the L.R.B. took part in the Jubilee Review at Aldershot, when they paraded outside the Houses of Parliament at 3.30 a.m., trained to Farnborough, and were dismissed at Waterloo at

10 p.m. It also took part in the Jubilee Review of the London Volunteers, and "marched past" in front of Buckingham Palace.

1888

Capt. J. A. Skene Thomson (Duke of Wellington's Regt.) became adjutant in the place of Capt. Wortham. In the early days adjutants held office for practically as long as they liked, but in the early eighties regular officers were selected and were appointed, at first for five years, and, from 1903, for three years only. The object was to have young, keen men, fully up to date in their work, and this change was most successful, although many adjutants, especially in the Volunteer days, took office for reasons other than those of wishing to do the best for the forces, as some wanted to get married, and others to be settled down for a time. They also had very hazy ideas as to how any force except the Regulars could be maintained, and were quite unable at first to understand how any regiment could be run without the administration of military law. The result was that they had as much to learn as they had to teach, and it was some time before they were able to be of full use to their units.

Canon Liddon, who was one of the chaplains of the regiment from 1888 to 1890, at the request of the Rev. A. Dawson Clarke, who was his senior, wrote the following prayer, which has always been used from that time at regimental services :—

L.R.B. Regimental Prayer

"O Lord God of Hosts, who, by thy Blessed Son Jesus Christ, hast put high honour upon a soldier's calling, we pray Thee to enable by thy Holy Spirit all the officers and men of this Regiment to glorify Thee by sober, pure, upright and Christian lives, and so to serve our Queen and Country as never to forget Thee and that Blessed Land to which we beseech Thee to bring us, through the merits and mediation of the same Thy Son, Jesus Christ our Lord."

Canon Liddon died in 1890, and the regiment lined the nave at St. Paul's for his funeral. The men wore their shakos, and uncovered as the coffin passed down the nave. Liddon had the soul of a great Christian soldier, and the regiment was honoured by his chaplaincy.

1889

A curious incident occurred during the Easter training while the regiment was at Eastney Barracks. Col. Lord Edward Pelham Clinton decided to practise an attack against Fort Cumberland and sent a party up there to mark the defence, but the commander of a Volunteer Artillery Corps, which was quartered in it at the time, took exception to this invasion of his precincts without his having been notified, and opened fire with his guns. Finally, when the last stage of the attack had been reached and the men were "standing easy," the strains of the "Dead March" were heard and the gates opened to let a band come out, followed by half a company moving as mourners. The L.R.B. were at once called to "attention" and then to the "shoulder," while the procession marched slowly round them and then retired laughing. The incident roused some feeling for a while, but the matter was amicably settled in time over the mess-table.

Martini-Henry rifles were issued in this year, and were a great improvement on the Sniders; they were single breech-loaders, the breech being depressed by a lever underneath the stock. Neat and handy weapons, they had undoubtedly the best breech action for a purely single loading rifle that has ever been invented. A very unpleasant amount of recoil with the black powder then in use was the chief drawback.

Capt. Skene Thomson was keen on developing tactical ideas, and amongst other operations arranged by him was night work in Hainault forest, and it is amusing to read that the men engaged in them wore shakos. As long as the regiment wore black it was always customary to parade in London in shakos and plumes, even for field days, and those who went down to Epping Forest and similar places can easily remember that their plumes were not improved by skirmishing through the undergrowth.

1890

The L.R.B. had the misfortune this year to lose its Commanding Officer, Lord Edward Pelham Clinton, who published the following farewell Order: "The Colonel Commandant cannot take leave of the Regiment without a few words of farewell. During the nine years he has been in command, his duties have been rendered easy and pleasant by the cordial support he has received from all ranks : the slightest wish, or even suggestion, expressed by him has always been carried out without hesitation. To the Adjutant, Secretary and permanent staff he is much indebted for their energy and zeal. Such is the *esprit de corps* existing in the L.R.B. that the Colonel feels it will ever remain, as it always has been, one of the smartest in the Volunteer Force : and he will always look back with pride and pleasure to the time he was in command."

Lord Edward had a wonderful personality which endeared him to all with whom he came into contact. He was modest and unassuming, and at the same time firm and resolute, and, as he said in his "farewell," his slightest wish was law. In short, he loved the regiment and the regiment loved him. He was presented on his retirement with a silver statuette of a Private in Review Order, which on his death was returned to the regiment by his sister, and is now one of the most treasured pieces of plate. The announcement of his retirement was made on parade at Easter, which was spent in the barracks at Winchester. The city gave the regiment a great reception, and also liberally entertained it at a smoking concert on the Saturday night, with the Mayor in the chair, to which all the members were invited.

Lieut.-Col. H. C. Cholmondeley, late of the Rifle Brigade, succeeded to the command.

1891

Companies were ordered to fall in for manœuvres by sections under the command of their own N.C.O.'s. This innovation was the beginning of the system, used so greatly later on and of such vital importance in military training, of accustoming men to work together instead of being a haphazard conglomeration of individuals.

Hitherto the men had carried their great-coats *en banderole*, but this year an equipment invented by a member of the regiment, Sergt. H. Lintott, was adopted. The idea was to do away with the difficulty which had been found with all equipments up to that time, namely that, in the absence of ball ammunition from the pouches, the weight of the great-coat, etc., dragged the belt up from its proper position in front. In this equipment there were two hooks of soft metal which went over the shoulders, and could be moulded to suit the individual; these put the weight on the shoulders and relieved the belt. Up to about this time it had been customary to wear one pouch only, which was carried in the middle of the back on the belt, because it looked better and did not get in the way when handling the rifle. The position was, however, singularly inconvenient from a practical point of view, and the pouch had to be worn in front when firing was in progress. In this position the ammunition was apt to fall out; so Sergt. Lintott adopted the simple device of having the pouch made so that it opened in the usual way for inserting the cartridges, but, for extracting them, the back was separated horizontally in such a way that the part coming down slightly overlapped the part coming up, and went inside it. The hand could therefore be slipped in from above and rounds removed, but the opening closed automatically when not in use. The equipment was only a moderate success, as so many complained that the hooks cut into their shoulders, though the inventor said that this was because they were not properly fitted, but the pouch satisfied all requirements. This equipment was worn until 1908, when the web equipment came into use with the service dress. Whistles and chains were ordered to be worn by full sergeants only, and the chains were ordered to be triple instead of double as worn by most other regiments; no cross belt was worn, and the lion's head and whistle were affixed to the tunic, so that the whistle had to be taken out of its sheath before the tunic could be doffed.

In July a Volunteer Review was held on Wimbledon Common by the German Emperor, Wilhelm II. The L.R.B. formed part of the East London Volunteer Brigade, which was the 2nd Brigade of the 1st Division under H.R.H. the Duke of Connaught.

In this year the regiment, which had always been noted for its individual shooting, began its long list of successes in team-competitions, whose complete record is as follows:—

The Belgian Cup 1895, 1910; The China Cup 1892, 1901 (the City of London team for which was entirely composed of members of the L.R.B.); the Commander-in-Chief's Prize 1902, 1903 ; the Duke of Westminster's Cup 1892, 1893, 1899 ; the Mappin Cup 1891, 1894, 1895, 1896, 1897, 1900 ; the Mullens 1895 ; the Ranelagh Cup 1907, 1910 ; the *Daily Telegraph* Cup 1897, 1898 ; and the Dewar Trophy 1900, 1901. Major Earl Waldegrave, Capt. A. S. Bates, Lieut. E. Collier, Capt. E. D. Johnson, Lieut. E. Milliken, Lieut. P. W. Richardson, Sergt. W. G. Ashby, Sergt. H. G. Burr, Pte. A. Cocks, Pte. C. J. Cruse, Pte. A. Denny, Pte. F. Elkington, Pte. R. Griggs, Pte. J. P. Hope, Pte. H. Lattey, Pte. W. C. Luff, Pte. H. Mardell, Pte. H. J. Rothon, Pte. E. Skilton, Sergt. W. Barry, Pte. W. J. M. Burton and Clr.-Sergt. R. H. Tayton are names which will always be associated with these results, but there were many others who helped. These distinctions were not, however, obtained at the expense of general efficiency in musketry, as the class-firing returns, which could be relied on, always showed a high percentage of marksmen together with a small number of 3rd class shots.

1892

Easter was spent at Winchester for the second time, and the opportunity was taken to give an Assault at Arms of a unique kind, in return for the hospitality received in 1890. Capt. Alfred Hutton, late of the King's Dragoon Guards, had for a long time taken a great interest in the fencing of the L.R.B. and had taught many of the old exercises, such as sword and dagger, sword and cloak, battle-axe work, etc., on which he was a well-known authority. He arranged a display for the occasion, which was a great success, and in 1894, by invitation, took a party of the regiment over to Brussels, where a grand entertainment was given in the Opera House, at which all the performers wore the correct costume of the period to which the weapons which they were using belonged.

For many years the regiment had been endeavouring to obtain more suitable head-quarters. Application had been made to the City Fathers by a deputation headed by the Duke of Cambridge for assistance in securing ground in the City, and a vacant site was suggested on the embankment where the Metropolitan Asylums Board Office now stands, but this was considered too valuable, and no help could be obtained. However, a committee under the energetic leadership of Col. Edward Matthey was appointed to face the difficulty, and eventually a site was found in Bunhill Row. This was suitable in extent and position, but, as it was outside the City boundary, there were fears that the connection with the City might be severed. In order to obviate this, and to keep up the polite fiction that the regiment had its head-quarters in the City, a board with " L.R.B. Adjutant's Office " on it was placed at the office of a certain colour-sergeant at No. 2 Gt. Winchester Street, where it remained for many years.

In March, night operations arranged by the adjutant took place in the neighbourhood of Elstree with the aid of search-lights, a useful and novel experiment.

1893

The new Drill Hall in Bunhill Row was opened by the Honorary Colonel, H.R.H. the Duke of Cambridge. The hall was the first part of the building to be completed, and the remainder was not occupied until the next year. It was much the finest of its kind in London, and the main hall alone, without the annexe, measured 180 by 60 feet.

The annual prize distribution, which had taken place at the Crystal Palace every year since the formation of the regiment, was held this year for the first time in the regiment's own hall. From 1860 until the passing of the Volunteers in 1908, the prizes were always presented by the Lady Mayoress, and the Lord Mayor and Sheriffs attended in state.

Capt. Skene Thomson's term of office came to an end, and he was succeeded by Capt. T. G. P. Glynn (8th, King's Liverpool, Regiment). A new undress cap of fore and aft pattern replaced the old glengarry, but officers still retained the pill-box cap. Mr. Gowling, who had served the regiment well as sergt.-major, was appointed assistant secretary, and Lieut. Milliken took over the position of honorary secretary in the place of Col. Harvey.

During the year a Guard of Honour was mounted on the occasion of the wedding of the Duke of York, now King George V.

1894–5

These years were in the main uneventful. Lord Methuen, who then commanded the London District, and whose Christian name was Paul, instituted some time marches by night for the Guards and Volunteers. They were certainly useful and fairly well attended, but they were not very popular, especially with the Guards, who lost their free Saturday night, and a wag named them "Methuen's Mixtures" or "Paul, Paul, why persecutest thou me?" Up to this time it had been customary for N.C.O.'s and men to wear shoulder cords in place of the usual strap with the name of the regiment thereon, a relic no doubt of the days, when everyone, including privates, wore cross belts. These were now abolished, and a shoulder strap marked "1st Ld." was substituted. This was not popular, as everyone would have preferred the title of "L.R.B."

1896

Further small changes of uniform took place. Officers wore serge jackets in undress in the place of patrol jackets, the object being to save expense, and to enable them to wear the Lintott equipment like the men. The mounted officers still retained the round cap, but the remainder wore the "service cap" as it was called, similar to those worn by the men.

1897

In this year the regiment, which up to this time had been armed with short rifles and had carried the sword-bayonets, adopted the flat bayonet owing to the issue of long rifles —Lee-Metfords—to all Volunteer Corps. During the same year the custom that all ranks should wear black gloves was discontinued except for special parades.

In May the cup given by the proprietors of the *Daily Telegraph*, for marching from Weybridge to Bisley and then volley-firing, was won for the first time. The victory was gained not only over all the other Volunteer Battalions in the London district but also over representatives of the several Battalions of Guards. The team had been trained by Lieut. C. R. Bland

and Clr.-Sergt. Tayton, but at the last minute the former was taken ill and his place was taken by Lieut. N. C. King. This cup was again won in the following year, when Lieut. Bland, being in command, was able to glean the fruits of his exertions. The names of the members of the teams will be found on the cups in the list of regimental plate in Appendix H.

Clr.-Sergt. R. H. Tayton served in the L.R.B. from 1863 to 1906, and many of the regimental successes were due to his careful training. Not only was he a fine shot himself, for he was in the Queen's Hundred in 1890, 1891 and 1896, and in the St. George's Sixty in 1898, 1899 and 1901, but he helped to train nearly every regimental team, and won a large number of prizes for the L.R.B. He was a good all-round sportsman, and a pattern to all soldiers. He was also an active member of the School of Arms for upwards of twenty years, being secretary of it for twelve, and on the Finance Committee from 1882 to 1894, and 1901 to 1903.

The regiment found a Guard of Honour, on the occasion of the Diamond Jubilee of Queen Victoria, which was mounted at the north end of London Bridge, opposite the Fishmongers' Hall. The *Army News* reported as follows: "There was no finer turn out than the Guard of Honour and Band of the L.R.B. who took post opposite the Fishmongers' Hall. In every detail they were well-nigh perfect. Their appearance and turn out were a credit to the Corps, and they moved as one man. Officers of the Line, and there were many at the Fishmongers' Hall, all agreed it was as smart a Guard of Honour as they had ever seen." After the procession had gone past, and before the troops lining the street had broken up, the Guard was allowed to march back by way of King William Street and the Mansion House, and received an ovation from the crowds assembled there.

At the annual inspection the whole battalion went through the bayonet exercise under the adjutant, a very creditable performance, and one seldom witnessed at the inspection of other London battalions. At the Royal Military Tournament in June the L.R.B. team carried off the prize for this and made a break in the long sequence of victories which the Artists had to their credit.

1898

Capt. G. R. Tod, (72nd, Seaforths) took over the adjutancy from Capt. Glynn, of whom the C.O. wrote in Orders: "In taking leave of Capt. Glynn, the C.O. begs him to accept his own cordial thanks for the support received at all times from him, and to assure him of the hearty appreciation of all ranks for his services on behalf of the regiment." Capt. Glynn had certainly done much to improve the drill, and had smartened up the L.R.B. considerably.

For many years past the authorities had been pressing the regiment to go to camp for a week in August instead of training for four days at Easter. The August camp was without doubt preferable from the training point of view, but to attend it meant the surrender of part of the short annual holiday, whereas the men were able to go away at Easter without much sacrifice. Further, the majority of men in the ranks were juniors in their offices, and could not get away at such a favourite time of the year. In those days very few facilities were given by employers, but in later times, when the Territorials came into being, things were different. This year the regiment went into camp in August, in accordance with orders, with the result that, as had been anticipated, the attendance did not come up to the mimimum requirements, and no Government grant was received, so that all the expenses had to be paid out of regimental funds. This was bad enough, but was put into the shade by what happened the following year. The L.R.B. pointed to what had occurred in 1898, and, with some difficulty, permission was obtained to go out at Easter 1899. At the last minute, as the Commanding Officer was getting into the train to convey the troops to Brighton, a letter from the War Office was put into his hand saying that no grant would be given for the Easter outing, so regimental funds had once more to bear the whole of the expenses, a serious drain.

The regiment was quartered in a school, and for fear of fire, the men were asked not to smoke in the building. They were also told that it was not customary for the L.R.B. to smoke in the streets during daylight. Both regulations were loyally adhered to, but they meant no small sacrifice to men away on a holiday.

1899

In July, to celebrate the fortieth anniversary of the founding of the force, the Prince of Wales held a review of all the Volunteers in London, and a march past took place on the Horse Guards' Parade, with the Duke of Cambridge leading the L.R.B.

The following account of the annual inspection taken from the *Pall Mall Gazette* is worth reading :—

"The parade of the Rifles was roughly about 800 strong. The first thing that struck the onlooker as the Rifle Brigade came up was that the mounted officers were well horsed, and rode with a 'Canterbury leg.' As a rule the mounted Volunteer shows a lack of exercise in military equitation, and sits at ease shaped like a letter 'C,' which is always displeasing to the trained eye. But the officers under notice kept a correct seat, had their stirrup leathers adjusted to a nicety, and obeyed the cavalry regulations, which provide for a proper 'leg,' a bent small of the back, and correctly squared shoulders and held head. To some the point may appear a small one, but it makes all the difference between a smart and lazy, slovenly show. The corps did splendidly and was well up to regulation mark. In the marches past the lines were admirably dressed and the intervals and distances well preserved. It was impossible not to admire the black mass as it swung along, topped by the sea of cock's feather plumes that rustled and fluttered in the breeze. The manual and firing exercises were performed steadily and in good time, and when the line opened out for the bayonet exercise the battalion showed that it can be useful as well as ornamental. Unlike some corps that might be mentioned, the Brigade threw the whole weight of the body behind the lunge, and was not content with putting the power that rests in the arm from the shoulder to the wrist. There is no reason why every battalion should not do the same thing, yet the essential is too often markedly absent. The men went through an unusual number of evolutions, and all their movements, whether from the halt or on the march, were admirable."

In October the South African War broke out, and on December 26th the names were asked for of men (1) willing to serve in South Africa or anywhere abroad ; (2) willing to serve on garrison duty in the United Kingdom, this being after men had been asked to join the City Imperial Volunteers. In the event, the L.R.B. sent five officers, and, as nearly as can be ascertained, 145 N.C.O.'s and men to the war. The following officers served: Col. H. C. Cholmondeley, commanding C.I.V. M.I.; Capt. C. G. R. Matthey, and Lieut. Hon. Schomberg K. McDonnell, C.I.V. Infantry ; Lieut. E. D. Johnson, Rough Riders Imperial Yeomanry ; Lieut. Hon. Rupert E. C. Guinness, Irish Hospital. In the C.I.V. 78, and in other regiments 67, N.C.O.'s and men took part in the war. Four were killed, Sergt. D. H. Kingsford, Ptes. M. W. Holland, E. J. Campbell, and F. J. Andrew; and three died on service, Ptes. B.P. Rowley, H. E. Neal, and C. H. Clippingdale. Four received commissions in the Imperial Yeomanry, viz. Ptes. A. L. Lintott, D. W. Pollock, J. A. W. Charge, and G. C. Barton. Col. Cholmondeley was mentioned in despatches, and was granted a C.B. Lieut. Guinness was made C.M.G. Lieut. E. D. Johnson and Clr.-Sergt. T. G. Beeton were also mentioned. Some men after serving in the C.I.V. went out again in the I.Y., amongst them Corpls. A. Evans and W. Houghton. The names of those who served will be found in Appendix G, p. 409.

It was in this year that Corpl. Newton Dunn presented his cup, for an inter-company competition in marching and shooting on the lines of the *Daily Telegraph* cup. The Donor, one of the most prominent men in the City, was a fine old sportsman, and served in the ranks for many years. He was a very highly valued member.

1900

The C.I.V. M.I. under Col. Cholmondeley left London on 13th of January, having slept at Bunhill Row on the previous night. There were huge crowds to see them off, in spite of the early hour, and it took them three hours and twenty minutes to reach Nine Elms Station, the column being entirely broken up and arriving piecemeal. They embarked 250 on s.s. *Briton* and 250 on s.s. *Garth Castle*. Lieut.-Col. The Earl of Albemarle was in command of the infantry, Col. W. H. Mackinnon being in command of the whole regiment. The infantry embarked on 20th of January on s.s. *Gaul*, *Ariosto* and *Kinfauns Castle*, arrived at Cape Town on 15th of February, and moved to Witteputs, the L.R.B. detachment being in "C" Company under Capt. C. G. R. Matthey and Lieut. the Hon. S. K. McDonnell. On April 16th the infantry, which was in Brig.-Gen. Bruce Hamilton's 21st brigade in Lieut.-Gen. Ian Hamilton's division, left Naawpoort, to which they had moved, and joined the rest of the brigade, which consisted of the Camerons, the Sussex, and the Notts and Derbys. They marched continuously and, on 29th May, took part in the battle of Doorn Kop, during which the battalion fired 9500 rounds, all in volleys. On 5th June they reached Pretoria, having been on the march for 51 days (actually on the move on forty of them), during which they covered 523 miles, averaging 13 miles per marching day, with only one two days' consecutive halt, in addition to taking part in twenty-six engagements during the time. On 12th June they fought in the battle of Diamond Hill, and after spending some time in garrison duty in various parts of the theatre of war, left for home on 7th October by s.s. *Aurania*. The total casualties due to fighting were, killed 1 officer, 60 other ranks; wounded 1 officer, 60 other ranks. They reached London in November and marched from Paddington to the Guildhall, but the whole affair was so badly managed, that the column was broken up and overwhelmed by the immense crowds on the route. The L.R.B. contingent was entertained at a regimental dinner at Head-quarters, and a souvenir was presented to every man. The Duke of Cambridge was present and the affair was a great success.

Col. Cholmondeley had intended to retire at the end of 1899, but, owing to the war, continued his service, Col. Edward Matthey taking over the command in his absence, and, as there was a great rush of recruits, the regiment was in a flourishing condition. One of Col. Matthey's first actions was to take steps to provide transport and entrenching tools for the battalion. The former was arranged for by means of a contract with a firm of carriers, which continued until the Volunteers came to an end; the latter were presented to the regiment by Mrs. Matthey. A camp kitchen was also obtained, and the C.O. was in a position to report that the battalion, having been selected for mobilisation in case of necessity, was ready to move at very short notice. In May names were asked for of those willing to join the Volunteer Reserve in case of invasion, the conditions being that men must have been returned as efficient six times, and that the maximum age for officers was 62, and for other ranks 55. During this month the Dewar Trophy was won at the London District Rifle Meeting. The competition was akin to that for the *Daily Telegraph* Cup only with less marching and more shooting. In June the regiment went to camp at Perham Down on Salisbury Plain for a fortnight, which was a great innovation, and was only rendered possible by the co-operation of employers, due to the war. The marching-in strength was 627, while 335 stayed for the whole period, but some men attended for the first week only, and others for the second, because offices which had encouraged recruiting were only able to spare part of their staff at a time.

The bulk of the East London Volunteer Brigade, to which the L.R.B. belonged, trained during August at Minster, near Sheerness, and for the Whitsuntide training the regiment was attached to the Cheshire brigade. The annual Inspection took place in July as usual, and the parade state showed that 997 were present; in addition to these there were of course the men serving in South Africa on the rolls, and the strength of the L.R.B. now reached its maximum since the very early days. The Machine Gun detachment was first formed during this winter under Lieut. C. D. Burnell, and proved a very efficient addition to the regiment for many years. It was armed with one Maxim Gun mounted on a large carriage, drawn by a horse or by a team of men.

This year it is sad to have to record the loss of two old and valued members, through the death of Major and Hon. Lieut.-Col. H. C. Boyes, and the retirement of Major and Hon. Lieut.-Col. Earl Waldegrave.

Col. Boyes served in the regiment for 36 years and was latterly honorary surveyor and architect of the new headquarters. His stalwart figure was familiar to all the prominent Volunteers in the London District, and his opinion on military matters was held in high esteem. He was an able tactician and took an active part in the war games organised by the London District War Game Society. At his death he left property to the L.R.B. valued at £3000.

NOTE.—In Volunteer days honorary rank could be claimed after a certain length of commissioned service: e.g. if an officer had served for 15 years and was still a captain, he could claim the rank of Hon. Major.

Lord Waldegrave's record covered 28 years ; he commanded "D" Company for 27 years, and for 25 years was a member of the Finance Committee. Several offers of promotion were made to him, but, as they involved the severance of his connection with the L.R.B., were declined. He was a noted shot, and was for some years Chairman of the National Rifle Association. In addition to his military duties he was Chief Conservative Whip in the House of Lords, Captain of the Yeomen of the Guard, and also a Privy Councillor. Long periods of service (30 to 40 years) were by no means unusual at this time.

1901

In January the L.R.B. was represented at Queen Victoria's funeral by 3 officers and 100 men. After the death of Dr. Mandell Creighton, Bishop of London, early in the year Dr. Winnington Ingram was appointed in his place and one of his first acts was to follow the example of the late bishop by becoming one of the regimental chaplains. From the time that he joined he took the keenest interest in the regiment, almost always managed to attend the annual training for a day or two, and identified himself more closely with it than any of his predecessors with one exception. His work in peace time largely helped the growth of that L.R.B. spirit which proved itself so gloriously when tested in war, and many had reason to thank him for what he did for them. His work during the war is recorded in its proper place. The exception was the Rev. A. Dawson Clarke, who invariably was present at all the trainings, and whose good company always made him most welcome and popular.

In March Col. Cholmondeley carried out the retirement which he had contemplated in 1899, and wrote in his farewell Order :

"Colonel Cholmondeley being now obliged to relinquish the command of the L.R.B.—a command which for the past ten years has been the pride and absorbing interest of his life—he takes the opportunity to bid good-bye to the regiment, and to thank those good comrades of all ranks, past and present, whose friendship, loyalty and help have continued to make his command a period of prosperity to the regiment and of constant pleasure to himself. Col. Cholmondeley can wish the L.R.B. no better than that the same fine spirit of loyalty be transferred from himself to his successor—one so worthy of it —for therein lies the prosperity of the regiment."

Most of the period of his command was uneventful, but the progress made under Lord Edward Pelham Clinton was continued, and there is no doubt that the L.R.B. benefited greatly from the tact and professional ability of both.

In April a new scheme of organisation was brought in for Volunteers, and certain battalions, of which the L.R.B. was one, were selected for inclusion in what was called the Field Army, but the conditions of service as to camp and numbers were found to be impossible, so the distinction was declined. The Dewar Trophy was again won this year. The annual training took place in August henceforward except in 1906.

The Inspection took place in July, when there were present on parade 939 officers and men, and 323 cadets. This was the last occasion on which the Duke of Cambridge attended. For some years he used to act as Inspecting Officer, but, when it was pointed out that he could not report to himself as Commander-in-Chief of the British Army, the Brigadier inspected and the Duke attended merely as a compliment to his battalion. At the conclusion he addressed the regiment, according to his wont as "Officers and gentlemen of the London Rifle Brigade," and concluded "Good-bye, my friends." He died in 1904, and the L.R.B. was represented at his funeral by one officer as pall-bearer, by a detachment in the procession, and by a party stationed on the route. He had been a staunch friend to the regiment in every way, and his loss was a real one. The vacancy caused by his death has not yet been filled. The party stationed on the route was commanded by Capt. C. D. Burnell, who was ordered by a Line Officer to "slope" before the "present." The Line Officer failed to appreciate the importance which Riflemen attach to their special privileges, and there was a severe difference of opinion between the two officers. Fortunately, perhaps, when matters were becoming somewhat strained, the Linesman was severely taken to task by one of the Staff for ordering his men to "present" too soon, and while this was taking place the L.R.B. presented from the "order" as usual.

On Col. Cholmondeley's retirement, he was succeeded for a short time by Col. Edward Matthey. This officer, who was born in 1836, joined the Victoria Rifles in 1859, becoming a sergeant in 1872. In 1873 he joined the L.R.B. as a private, and was made an ensign in 1874, captain in 1878, major in 1884, lieut.-colonel in 1890, and hon. colonel in 1891. He was fully entitled to have kept the command, and qualified in every respect for the post, but, in accordance with tradition, he gave way in order that a regular officer might take the command. His devotion to the L.R.B. was unbounded, and he set a fine example to all who served under him. From the day on which he retired up to that of his death, which occurred in 1918, he was always in close touch with the regiment, and during the Great War he manifested his interest by making presents to all the battalions at Christmas-time. He was made a C.B. for his services to the Force. His successor was Lieut.-Col. Lord Bingham (now Earl of Lucan), who after serving in the Rifle Brigade for some years and being adjutant of his battalion, had joined the L.R.B. as major in 1900 with a view to taking the command.

1902

The very existence of the Volunteer Force was now threatened through new regulations which were issued enjoining an increased number of drills and compulsory attendances in camp for six days, as compliance with the latter was practically impossible at that time for men of the class from which the L.R.B. and other kindred regiments were recruited, while the attitude of employers was generally half-hearted and often positively hostile. The War Office, which had from the start given little and demanded much in return, now spoke in plain and almost insulting language. "For some years past the Volunteer Force has claimed to be seriously accepted as a reliable and organised section of the Army for Home Defence. It is now determined that the responsibility claimed shall be realised." In spite of would-be recruits being frightened and the numbers falling off considerably, Lord Bingham never wavered and cheerily hoped for better days, so that it is no exaggeration to say that the regiment largely owes its existence to-day to his high courage and inspiring words during a period of unexampled difficulty.

One of the changes introduced this year was the breaking up of the East London Volunteer Brigade, to which the L.R.B. had hitherto belonged, and its transformation into the 4th London Volunteer Brigade, composed of 24th Middlesex (Post Office Rifles), 1st (L.R.B.), 2nd, 3rd, and 4th London, and 1st and 2nd Tower Hamlets, but subsequently the two latter were withdrawn, and the 15th Middlesex (Customs and Docks) included.

At the camp this year all dismounted officers were ordered to carry carbines (Martini-Henry) in place of swords on service and on manœuvres. This was the result of the experience of the South African War, when it was found useful for officers to be armed with a long range weapon, but the order only continued in force for about two years. At ordinary parades officers carried sticks in place of swords, another innovation, and a convenient one. Up to this time the rank badges on officers' tunics had been of gilt thread, the reason for which is not very clear because it was not in accordance with the custom of the Rifle Brigade, but they were now ordered to be of bronze. Until this date captains wore two stars, 1st lieutenants wore one, and 2nd lieutenants were without any, but orders now laid down that three, two and one stars respectively should be worn.

In July the King's Prize at the N.R.A. meeting at Bisley was won by Lieut. E. D. Johnson, this being the second time the honour had fallen to the regiment. The victory was thoroughly well deserved, for the weather at the last stage was bad, owing to a hurricane of wind, and only a really skilled shot could have scored well under such conditions. On his return to London, Lieut. Johnson was met at Waterloo by a Guard of Honour, and escorted to head-quarters past the Mansion House by members of the regiment in uniform, with the band, being chaired for the latter part of the way.

For camp the question of the provision of khaki-drill uniform was considered, but nothing was done at the time, except to order the wearing of slouch hats with the regimental ribbon. The weather that year, with its usual perversity, turned out very wet, so that the need for protection from the sun was not great. The officers adopted a black cap with peak, over which a khaki cover could be worn.

The coronation of King Edward was to have taken place in June, but was postponed in consequence of his illness until August, and the camp was broken up one day earlier in consequence. In October he made a procession round London, when the L.R.B. found a Guard of Honour at London Bridge, as at Queen Victoria's Diamond Jubilee. In any similar event it is to be hoped that care will be taken that this privilege of the regiment, of finding a Guard of Honour and marching back down the route before the troops lining it are withdrawn, is maintained.

1903

The regiment went to Bisley at Easter for a musketry camp, those attending paying their own expenses. A new musketry course came into force, but its adoption was optional, and the only battalions in London which took it up in this year were the L.R.B. and the Post Office Rifles. It was certainly a more severe test, and the number of marksmen fell appreciably, but matters improved with experience, and the L.R.B. came again to the front as a good shooting regiment.

In May Major Tod's term of office as adjutant closed, when the following appeared in regimental Orders :—

" On termination of his period of service as adjutant, the C.O. desires to place on record his high sense of the valuable services of Major Tod in that position. In so doing he is confident that he is expressing the unanimous opinion of the members of the L.R.B. During the five years of his tenure of the adjutancy his tact, energy, and ability have contributed to maintain the maximum degree of efficiency with the minimum amount of friction : and, while the high standard of efficiency of the regiment has been fully kept up, the C.O. is sure that all have felt that in Major Tod they had a friend who thoroughly identified himself with them and with the interests of the L.R.B. All ranks sincerely regret the severance of Major Tod's official connection with the L.R.B., and wish him all prosperity in the future."

Major Tod was an ideal adjutant and was immensely popular

with all ranks. He was succeeded by Capt. B. H. Cooke, of the Rifle Brigade, the first adjutant to wear the uniform of his own regiment in the place of the uniform of the L.R.B.

At camp men provided themselves with a khaki-drill jacket, which was cooler and less absorbent of dust than the black serges worn hitherto.

1904

The regiment when it did its own training at Easter had been accustomed to send a strong company with the Post Office Rifles to their Aldershot camp in August, so that a close friendship always existed between the two battalions, and this year a joint officers' mess was arranged, which proved a success.

1905

A small but intelligent anticipation of orders which were received subsequently was made. Up to this time it had been customary for drill to take place twice a week in plain clothes, when the men fell in in two ranks to be broken up into squads or companies according to the work to be done without any special reference to their own officers and N.C.O.'s, and the men in each company were only kept together on uniform parades.

With a view to making men and officers of a company better acquainted with one another, a drill competition was instituted in which companies, in addition to marks for turn out and drill, were given points for the percentage of attendance at each parade. This proved successful in many ways and was continued for some years.

The L.R.B. was allowed to put up " South Africa 1900–02 " as a battle honour in recognition of its services in that war.

For some years prior to 1900 the battalion had consisted of ten companies, but in that year the establishment was raised to twelve, in consequence of the influx of recruits owing to the South African War. Numbers were now falling, so the establishment was reduced to ten companies again. In 1900 a new regiment, called the 4th London, had been raised from old boys of the Grocers' Company School, but its numbers fell off after the war like those of other Corps, and the remainder were absorbed by the L.R.B., to which it had always been attached and with which it had always done its training, as part of "E" Company.

For some time past an annual match had taken place at tip-and-run, rounders and tug-of-war between the two officers' messes of the L.R.B. and P.O.R., the prize being a tiny silver cup, and on this occasion the P.O.R. issued a challenge in the following form :—

"De la part de Monsieur le Président du Sporting Vingt-Quatrième Mousquetaires (Postes et Télégraphies) à Messieurs les Officiers de la Brigade Chasse-Pots de Londres :

"Nous, les avant-dits, présentons nos compliments les plus sincères, et ayant regard de l'entente cordiale et l'ardent souhaite de regagner 'Les Cindres' ;

"Nous challengons les avant-dits Chasse-Pots trés honourables au combat à l'outrance aux Jeux de 'pourboire et courrez,' et 'Plus rondes,' et, si le resultat de ces luttes n'est pas comme il faut ou décisive, alors, pour determiner le domicile annuaire de la tasse, ou pot, ou coupe, un 'Rémorque de Guerre.' Huit concurrents à chaque course.

"Agréez, Messieurs, l'expression de nos sentiments les plus distingués."

To this the following reply was sent :—

"'Primus in urbe' quae vocatur Legio Cohorti Mediorum Saxonum Vicesimae Quartae et omnibus ad quos hae praesentes litterae pervenerint—Salutem.

"Sciatis quod nos de speciali gratia et certa scientia nostra et mero motu, etc., etc., etc.

"Guadebimus suscipere (Anglice 'take on') ludibria ista quae vester magister ludorum proposuit—videlicet :

"Apicem et cursionem ; Teretiores ; et (si necesse fuerit) Tractionem de bello.

"Octeni octenis certentur. Spolia (scilicet poculum) victores suferant. Sciatis etiam quod de nostro exercitu nondum actum est.

"In cujus rei testimonium huic praesenti cartae nomina et sigilla affiximus apud castra Marivadiana (Seaford) nono die Augusti anno regis Eduardi septimi quinto, etc."

1906

In May a torchlight Tattoo given by the regiment at the Royal Military Tournament received high praise from the Press. The uniform was altered so as to allow the men to have two breast pockets in their serges, which gave great satisfaction. Capt. Cooke was succeeded in the adjutancy by Capt. A. C. H. Kennard, also of the Rifle Brigade, an old L.R.B.

As the year wore on and the number of members continued to decrease, the financial question became an acute one. The head-quarters in Bunhill Row, which had been estimated to cost about £8000, originally consisted of the drill hall, with offices facing the street, but, as a piece of ground at the side was available, this was eventually made use of, and the annexe enlarging the hall, with extra rooms for the men and officers' quarters, was added in 1895. The final cost amounted to £16,480, of which members and their friends subscribed £9530, and the City Wards and Liveries £1960, leaving a balance of about £5000 unpaid. As the ground rent, the interest on the sum unpaid, and a sinking fund to extinguish the debt which had been insisted upon by the Charity Commissioners, absorbed a large sum of money annually which was difficult to find, a suggestion was made that the premises facing the street should be let off, and that the offices, etc., should be moved to the annexe, but the cost of the alterations was found to be so great that the project was abandoned.

1907

In June the last Inspection of the regiment as Volunteers took place, and during the summer a torchlight Tattoo was given at the Royal Military Tournament for the second time.

The financial difficulties became accentuated by the publication of the regulations for the Territorial Force, which was to come into existence during the next year. These prescribed that the term of enlistment was to be for four years, and that the maximum limit of age for enlistment was to be 35 instead of 49. A medical test was laid down ; men were to be under military law whilst under arms ; they could not be ordered to serve abroad without their consent, but the force could be embodied whenever the Army Reserve was called out. Those who neglected their training were liable to fine, but those who attended the annual camp were paid. The conditions of fines and embodiment compelled many old members to resign, and the attitude of employers, who at that time were unsympathetic, prevented many from joining. Subscriptions fell off in consequence and the financial problem was a serious one.

1908

On 31st March the old Volunteer Force died and the Territorial Force reigned in its stead. It is easy to find fault with the old state of affairs, but there is no doubt that the Volunteers filled a gap in the national defences, and carried out important duties in spite of much veiled ridicule, and official neglect and discouragement, and they were responsible for many improvements in drill and musketry which were adopted by the Regular Army. Their value to the country was discussed *ad nauseam*, but those who formed a good opinion of them would not appear to have been unjustified judging by what is recorded later on in these pages.

The Easter outings were undoubtedly of great use, and especially so in later years, as the men derived very much good from being brought into contact with so many regular battalions, when quartered in or near barracks. In addition to learning the actual routine of barrack life and the practical work of a guard, men were able to see how duties were carried out by professional soldiers, which in itself was a great gain. But, especially in the early days, the Regulars as a body never seemed able to understand the constitution of a regiment like the L.R.B. The fact that the men gave up four days' holiday without pay struck them as peculiar. That the men bought their own uniforms seemed to them rather foolish, but that, in addition, they should pay an annual subscription seemed madness, and the regiment was generally viewed as rather a smart lot of cranks. Really the most wonderful part of the whole business was to find that five or six hundred young men, used to most of the ordinary comforts of life, should be able to come away from their offices and homes on a Thursday afternoon, and for four days be soldiers, live as soldiers, and work as soldiers, pay a substantial portion of the expenses, and then return to their normal conditions, not only with no regrets for what they had given up and gone through, but looking forward to the next training with pleasant anticipation.

The new scheme caused great heart-burning by converting the L.R.B., the oldest and most truly representative of the City of London Volunteer Corps, from the 1st into the 5th of the 1st London Division, and, although there were undoubtedly difficulties in the way of refusing Royal Fusiliers any of the privileges going with the name, those who were fully acquainted with all the circumstances felt very resentful. This did not encourage members to remain and the embodiment clause was a great deterrent to transferring, so that by 31st March the numbers had fallen to 465, in spite of a regimental Order which said: "The C.O. ventures to hope that a large number of the present regiment may find themselves able to follow him into the Territorial Force, thus continuing that loyal service in their Country's defence which the regiment has so well maintained in the past." By 9th May, 233 had transferred, making with 8 recruits a total strength of 241, and, as no battalion could be "recognised" or earn any grant until its numbers were 30% of its establishment, the following appeared in Orders: "The C.O. is confident that, when the regiment is once installed in the Territorial Force, its future is assured, as he is certain that it will fill up its numbers largely during the next recruiting season. He therefore most strongly urges all members to join at once, and assist in bringing about this result." The conditional permission given for men to be absent from camp eased matters, and by 6th July the regiment numbered 18 officers and 305 other ranks, while by the time it went into camp in August it had reached 332 and had been "recognised" as a unit of the 2nd London Brigade, which was composed of the 5th (L.R.B.), 6th (formerly 2nd), 7th (formerly 3rd) and 8th (Post Office Rifles, formerly 24th Middlesex).

As the khaki uniforms and all accoutrements were now issued free, the members of the L.R.B. had no longer to provide their own, as they had done from the beginning, although almost every other Volunteer Corps had long ago given this up and adopted the system of finding everything for the men in return for their signing an agreement to serve and make themselves "efficient" for 4 years. The annual subscription of 25s. was paid by all the members of the regiment until the middle of 1916, when the War Office ordered that it should be discontinued, as regiments could not be allowed to be under strength through having to refuse men because they were not in a position to meet this expense. The black uniform was also retained, but only for ceremonial parades, and the sergeants' chevrons were altered so as to be the same as those of the Rifle Brigade, edged with gold braid. After a final issue of the Volunteer Long Service Medal, but for 16 years' service instead of the original 20, a Territorial Force Efficiency Medal for 12 years' service was instituted. Unfortunately the ribbon for the new medal, green with a yellow stripe, was almost identical with that for the Territorial Decoration, which was given for 20 years' commissioned service, but this was put right in 1919 and the ribbon of the efficiency medal is now green with yellow edges.

Major C. W. Cornish, the honorary secretary since 1897, gave up his position. There can be no question that the regiment would never have survived the financial difficulties of the years immediately preceding the formation of the Territorial Force without the advice which his experience as an accountant enabled him to give. He was succeeded by Capt. E. D. Johnson, who, though compelled to resign his commission for business reasons, desired to continue his long association with the L.R.B., and gave up much of his spare time to carry on this arduous duty. Under the new Territorial scheme the regiment was compelled to hand over the premises at Bunhill Row, together with the mortgage, to the Government, who undertook to pay the ground rent, and so relieve the regimental finances of a heavy burden. It was not without great regret that the property which had been built up with so much care and labour, aided by liberal contributions from members, was given up, but there was practically no alternative. The buildings were so large that the authorities felt that they could not be utilised by one regiment only, and consequently arranged that the Post Office Rifles, who had hitherto had no proper head-quarters, should share them. This was the most satisfactory solution of the difficulty, for not only was this regiment one with which the L.R.B. had had very close and pleasant relations for many years, but most of its work was done during the day, so that the hall was generally at the disposal of the L.R.B. in the evening, when it was most needed.

1909

Early in this year journalistic efforts were made to stimulate recruiting, with the result that the numbers, which were 371 on 1st February, had risen by 1st March to 744, and were continuing to rise. The sympathies of employers were enlisted, and arrangements were made by them so that men who were willing to give up part of their holiday should be able to attend the annual camp. Early in the spring the City Territorials marched past the Lord Mayor at the Mansion House, and made an imposing show. A new spirit was infused into the force, which was smiled upon by the authorities, and many fresh arrangements were made for improving the knowledge and training of all ranks. All drills took place under the company officers instead of under the adjutant, and many staff rides and courses of instruction were provided.

The title of " London Rifle Brigade " was again officially given to the regiment, with the consent of H.R.H. the Duke of Connaught, Colonel-in-Chief of the Rifle Brigade. For some unknown reason this title had lapsed from the Army List for many years, although it had been retained unofficially. The men were provided with the web equipment, which was a great improvement on anything previously issued, because it rode equally well whether there was ammunition in the pouches or not, and was therefore much more comfortable for them, but valises were not issued, and great-coats and mess tins only were carried. At this time also the bugles were plated, in conformity with the custom of the Rifle Brigade.

The annual training took place at Lark Hill, on Salisbury Plain, then virgin turf, but since the Great War, a ghastly wilderness of huts. Most of the men were recruits, and one night when the F.O. of the day had with some difficulty induced the sentry on the Guard Tent to challenge him, and had given the reply " Grand Rounds," he was surprised to see the sentry deposit his rifle on the ground. The sergeant of the guard was told to instruct his men better, and it subsequently transpired that the sentry thought he had received the command "Ground Arms," which he proceeded to obey. Two hangars were in the vicinity of the camp, and great was the excitement when one day an aeroplane was wheeled out from its shelter. Scarcely anyone had ever seen such a thing, and all hoped that it would fly, but, after taking a brief airing on the ground, it retired modestly to its shed and never showed its paces.

The King's Prize at Bisley was won by Corpl. H. G. Burr, and thus for the third time came to the L.R.B. For the first time the prizes were not given away by the Lord Mayor, and his place was taken by the Rt. Hon. R. B. Haldane (afterwards Lord Haldane), Secretary of State for War. He was interrupted during his speech by suffragettes, who were forcibly removed. Capt. Kennard's appointment as adjutant came to an end, and he was followed by Capt. J. A. W. Spencer, Rifle Brigade, one of the most successful and popular adjutants the regiment ever had.

1910–11

These years were not very eventful, but the regiment made continued progress in efficiency. In 1910 charger loading rifles were issued. Easter in both years was spent at Shorncliffe, the regiment going over to Hythe each day for musketry, which was the object of the training. In 1911 a party of the regiment under Lieut. F. W. Bewsher and Clr.-Sergt. F. H. Wallis made a forced march to Brighton in about 18 hours, but the time was beaten shortly afterwards by the London Scottish who were old rivals in sport. The L.R.B. put up a fresh record in 1914 as will duly appear.

1912

Towards the end of this year Lord Bingham severed his connection with the L.R.B. His farewell Order was as follows :

"These are the last words that Lord Bingham issues to the London Rifle Brigade as on 1st December he is appointed to command the 1st London Brigade. He has had the honour and pleasure of commanding the L.R.B. for nearly twelve years, and he wishes to take this opportunity of expressing his gratitude to all ranks for the unfailing support he has always received. He is perfectly confident that his successor, Lord Cairns (also late Rifle Brigade) will receive the same hearty support, and that under him the L.R.B. will maintain the same high standard of efficiency which it has enjoyed in the past. In severing his long connection with them, Lord Bingham wishes all good luck and prosperity to the L.R.B. and all its members."

There can be little doubt that, but for the cheery optimism and good leadership of Lord Bingham, the L.R.B. would have failed to survive the difficult years from 1905 to 1909. He took over the command when the prosperity brought forth by the South African War was at its height, but through no fault of his own saw the regiment gradually dwindle, and get deeper and deeper into financial difficulties. During all this time his courage never failed, as he always maintained that things would come right if men would hold on, and he stayed to see his words fulfilled. When he left, the L.R.B. was far more prosperous and efficient than it had ever been, and the debt of gratitude owed to him can never be repaid in full. He was presented with a silver statuette of a private in Review Order as a mark of the great esteem and affection felt for him. Lieut.-Col. and Hon. Col. Cyril Matthey was the senior officer but he waived his claim and the new commandant was Earl Cairns, an old rifleman.

1913

The year was quite uneventful except for one tiny detail. From the earliest days the weekly orders had always been inserted in one of the daily papers, latterly the *Standard*, but they were from this time sent out each month by post. Capt. Spencer left on the termination of his appointment, his successor being Capt. A. C. Oppenheim of the K.R.R.C.

1914

It was determined this year to put up a time for a march to Brighton that would really want some beating, so a team consisting of 2 officers, 5 sergeants, and 53 other ranks, was trained under Capt. R. H. Husey, Lieut. E. L. Large, and Clr.-Sergt. F. H. Wallis, and the march took place on 18th April. The 52½ miles were covered in 14 hours 23 minutes : halts occupied 1 hour 39 minutes. The nett time therefore was 12 hours 44 minutes, which shows that the rate of marching was 4·12 miles per hour.

The march was reported in many papers, not only throughout the country, but in several circulating abroad, one of which was *The China Critic.*

It might be said that a feat of this kind has no practical value, but there is no doubt that the valuable experience gained by those who took part enabled them with advice born of practical experience to help others in the more serious field of war, and the fact that a reputation had to be sustained was responsible for some of the good work done. For instance, in 1917 the 1st Battalion L.R.B. made a long " trek " from Laventie to Arras. The winter had been spent in the trenches, and the men were by no means fit for long marches on bad roads. On the second day 19 miles had to be covered, and the battalion was marching in rear of the Brigade. After the first hour's march the roadside was scattered with men who had fallen out from units in front. This began to have a bad effect on the men of the L.R.B., many of whom had only recently been posted to the battalion from other regiments, and the second-in-command and the M.O., who were marching in rear, had a busy time persuading men to keep going. At the end of the march only eighteen men, about a quarter of the number dropped by other battalions, had fallen out, but this was not the L.R.B. standard. That night Lieut.-Col. Husey interviewed the defaulters, and next morning addressed " a few words " on marching to the battalion before it moved off for another long march. He said he had heard the remark, " It's all very well for senior officers to talk about marching ; they always ride a horse and don't know how heavy a pack feels after the first five or six miles." For the information of those who were unaware of the fact, he told them he had marched 52½ miles on his own feet, carrying a pack most of the way, in 14 hours and 23 minutes, and therefore from his own experience knew what a stiff and trying march felt like. With a few other remarks, which were characteristic of him, he conveyed to the men that he knew all there was to know about marching. The next day only three men fell out, their feet being so bad that they had to go into hospital.

For some years a race in marching order had taken place during the Territorial Sports over a course of about 12 miles, a competition of no real military value, as the men were trained to run for a large part of the distance, which would be an impossibility in ordinary circumstances. The L.R.B. had entered more than once without success, but this year, a team led by Capt. Husey beat the London Scottish, who had won on several previous occasions, handsomely.

From the earliest times the regiment boasted a flourishing School of Arms, and no little of its distinction was due to Capt. Alfred Hutton, to whom reference has already been made. He attended the School regularly two nights a week for many years, and through his teaching Capt. Stenson Cooke and others gained their successes. A year or two before the war the School under Clr.-Sergt. F. H. Wallis became the centre of regimental life with 200 of the keenest men attending every night. It gave a couple of Assaults of Arms, which were better than anything similar to be seen elsewhere, and filled the tiers of seats round three sides of the Drill Hall for two nights each. At the same time other kinds of sports were taken up seriously and proved a great inducement to men of the right stamp to join the regiment, as they found they could get their exercise, amusement, and comradeship better and more cheaply therein than elsewhere. The success of a sports meeting at Stamford Bridge in the early summer of 1914 showed how much these various activities would have forwarded the interests of the regiment, if they had not been brought to a sudden close.

Easter was spent at Blackdown in Alma Barracks, which were occupied by the 2/60th, and the time employed in musketry on the Pirbright ranges.

On 2nd August the L.R.B. proceeded to Eastbourne for its annual training. The camp had been pitched at Whitebread Hole, just under Beachy Head, by the advance party, and the regiment arrived about 2.30 p.m. on the Sunday, but in consequence of the state of affairs on the Continent, it was obvious that great events might occur. At 5.30 p.m. on the same day the regiment marched back to the station and entrained for London, leading many of the men to think that they would be embodied on arrival, but they were all dismissed to their homes, and it was not until the following Wednesday that mobilisation began.

Thus ended the chapter of the L.R.B. as a Territorial regiment before the war. The regiment had been highly efficient from its earliest days, and an exceptional standard of discipline and of shooting had been invariably maintained. The discipline was incomprehensible to a critical outsider, and adjutants arriving fresh from their regular regiments were unable to understand how it was possible to carry on without the administration of military law. The intelligence of the men, and their determination to uphold the good name of their beloved regiment were the chief factors which solved this question. No sacrifice was too great if it in any way enhanced the regimental prestige, misconduct was practically unknown, and, if any small lapses occurred, the comrades of the man concerned could safely be left to deal with the matter. It may be wondered how it was possible for men of social equality, in short, gentlemen, to maintain discipline without familiarity. The fact remains that they did do so, and a long experience shows that it was quite possible for men seeing each other daily in civil life, business or friendship, to meet at headquarters in the positions of officer and private, and for the distinction to be fully maintained. No instance can be recalled of presumption when on military duty, and there can be no doubt that, by good sense and tact on both sides, a situation, in theory impossible, was actually maintained with most satisfactory results.

Officer and N.C.O. in Review Order, 1914

CADET CORPS

THE L.R.B. CADET CORPS was started in 1860 to train those who were too young to go into the ranks of the existing Volunteer Corps and who did not care to become buglers, in the hope that they would later join the battalion and prove useful recruits.

The Boys' Own Magazine of the period wrote : "The uniform is remarkable for its extreme neatness and general utility. It consists of a short tunic and trousers of black ribbed cloth with facings of black braid, a little forage cap which is worn on the side of the head, completely *à la militaire,* gaiters, black gloves, a broad belt of black patent leather with a frog for the bayonet and fastened by a black snake-hook." After that it is not surprising to learn that "it is readily adaptable for school or office wear."

After a flourishing start, with the numbers soon reaching 200, the strength gradually fell, but in 1885, began to rise again and continued to do so up to 1902, when there were 400 on the roll, as the effect of the South African War on volunteering. The turn of the tide was partly due to the battalion introducing the custom of taking the Corps out with it at Easter and this was continued until the training at that time of the year came to an end. Fresh interest was roused in 1895 when the Corps first took part in the Public Schools Camp, although its constitution was not quite the same as that of the other units there. On the formation of the O.T.C. in 1908 the schools from which the main supply of cadets came—The City of London, the Merchant Taylors', King's College, and University College—formed companies of that body, and the Cadet Corps died out.

Although undoubtedly smart and producing such noteworthy men for the L.R.B. as E. D. Johnson, E. G. Stenson Cooke, W. H. Whittow, and A. C. Feast, the corps never did what had been expected of it, through not having been handled in quite the right way. For many years the commander only held the rank of sergeant and consequently was not in his proper position, and when at last the popular and hard-working Sergt. Haig-Brown was promoted to Hon. Lieut, he was past the age for making the most of it. If steps had been taken at that time to secure a suitable younger man to learn his work in the Corps and ultimately to succeed to the command, better results would have been obtained, but the proper officering of these corps is always a difficult problem, and in any case the O.T.C. would have killed this one.

The commanders were: 1860 Sergt. Ladd, 1864 Sergt. Yewsbury, 1871 Sergt. Hooper, 1873 Sergt. Fletcher Bannister, 1881 Sergt. Elliott, and 1885 Sergt. Haig-Brown, who finally rose to be Hon. Captain in 1893, and retired as Hon. Major.

FIRST BATTALION

PART I.—AUG. 2, 1914—APRIL 22, 1915

Mobilisation—Moves to Bisley and Crowborough—Embarkation—Wisques—Plœgsteert—Essex Trench—The Wood—Steenwerck.

(The Maps referred to are A and No. 1 facing p. 86. References to A in roman: to No. 1 in italics. See p. xiii.)

ON Sunday, August 2nd, 1914, the regiment went down to Eastbourne for its annual fortnight's training, arriving about 2.30 p.m., but three hours later it was ordered back to London, where the men were dismissed with the feeling that they would soon be called together again: so the order to "mobilize" was received on August 5, with little surprise, and they reassembled at Bunhill Row conscious that they were wanted for much more serious work than any which they had previously undertaken. The mobilisation orders, it may be noted, had been framed some years earlier by Capt. J. A. W. Spencer, while he was adjutant, and were so complete that they had been adopted by Head-quarters for the whole Division. As the regiment was not at the time up to strength, Bunhill Row at once became a seething mass of men all clamouring to join, and the vacancies were immediately filled with men of the right type. Experience soon showed that there are drawbacks to regiments being composed of one class only, because the tailors and bootmakers required in a self-contained unit were not to be found, and very few of the men knew one end of a horse from another. However, men were fitted out, swords were sharpened, etc., and everything went so smoothly that by the fourth day all was ready, in accordance with schedule, except that the transport, which consisted of horses and waggons bought by the War Office from private owners, required time for its completion.

Drills took place in the Merchant Taylors' School Ground, and most impressive Church Parades were held there on

Sundays, at which the Bishop of London officiated. At first the men went home at night and travelled up to drill (free by train and omnibus as long as they were in khaki), but, after an alarm on the 10th August at 10 p.m. had only resulted in a small part of the battalion being collected, they were no longer allowed to go off, but had to sleep either at headquarters or the school. The failure, it is only fair to say, was not the fault of the men, but the result of all regiments trying to telephone to the police at the same time to knock their men up, which overloaded and blocked the lines.

On 15th August the battalion was asked if it would volunteer for foreign service, an idea which had been mooted before, but not so seriously. The Commanding Officer, Lord Cairns, addressed the L.R.B. and put the facts before them, saying amongst other things that the regiment had always claimed to be one of the foremost in the force, and that now was the time to prove it. The matter required consideration on the part of many, for they were in receipt of good salaries, and had heavy responsibilities to bear, but the predominant idea in the mind of all was that, if the regiment were to be kept together and go out as the L.R.B., they were prepared to make the necessary sacrifices, and Lord Cairns was in a position at once to say that 75%, the minimum number acceptable, would accept the foreign service obligation. The L.R.B. was the first battalion in the brigade to come to this decision, the others not doing so till a week or two later, but no one, or at least very few, had any conception at that time of what this would involve. The prevailing idea was, that all would be over by Christmas, and that the utmost use which would be made of Territorials would be to give them duties on lines of communication.

The original intention had been that the regiment should move to its war station at Harrow on August 11th, but the position there was required for other purposes and it was not until the 20th that the 2nd London Brigade consisting of the 5th (L.R.B.), 6th, 7th, and 8th (Post Office Rifles) Battalions left London by march route, and proceeded to Wimbledon via Clapham Road and Wandsworth Common. On the following day the L.R.B. was billeted at Hersham, near Walton-on-Thames, and on the 22nd the Brigade reached Bisley, where the L.R.B. camped on the ground usually occupied by the range officers. The march down had been a sort of triumphal procession with the people coming out of the houses cheering and offering refreshment, while the men were also in high spirits, but want of condition and hot weather combined made the casualties in the brigade very heavy, although they were not all due to exhaustion. The L.R.B. dropped only one man, and he had a fit. By the kindness of the National Rifle Association, as represented by Lieut.-Col. C. R. Crosse, the secretary, the officers were given the use of the permanent huts and the range officers' Mess.

The brigade was under the command of Brigadier-General the Earl of Cavan, who had been brigade major in 1899 when he was Lord Kilcoursie. No one who was present will readily forget the conferences held at short intervals by Lord Cavan, which were sources of inspiration instead of being formal and dull, because he possessed the power of implanting high ideals in the minds of all those under him. Training went on uninterruptedly on the old lines of company training, with a limited amount of digging as well, until 8th September, when the brigade left by march route for East Horsley and Effingham, where Lord Cavan received orders to proceed at once to France to take command of the 4th (Guards) Brigade. In his farewell order he said :—

"He wishes to thank all officers, N.C.O.'s and men for the loyal support they have given him during his short command, and he wishes to leave on record his convinced opinion that the 2nd London Brigade, as an active service unit, will prove themselves fit to take their place in the firing line alongside the Army that has already proved its worth. He wishes the brigade the best of luck, and an order to cross the seas as soon as ever they are trained for war, which he hopes will be at no very distant date."

The command of the brigade temporarily passed into the hands of Lieut.-Col. and Hon. Col. C. G. R. Matthey, of the L.R.B., by seniority, although in the regiment he was serving under Lieut.-Col. Lord Cairns.

On the following day the brigade marched to Reigate, and on 10th September reached East Grinstead, having had the honour of marching past H.M. King George on the way. After staying at East Grinstead till 16th, because water had not been laid on to their camp and the baggage had not arrived from Bisley, the brigade marched that day to Camp Hill, Crowborough, where it went under canvas. The arrangements which had been made by the authorities were very inadequate, as after a hot march the men were kept standing about in a cold wind before the tents arrived, and the feeding was bad. This was the case during the whole time there, and no great improvement at home took place until the subject was properly taken in hand, as it was later on, On 22nd September Brig.-Gen. W. McGrigor took over command of the brigade and the whole of the 1st London Territorial Division was then close together, with the exception of the 1st Brigade, which, after guarding the line of the London and South-Western Railway, left for Malta early in September under Brig.-Gen. the Earl of Lucan (formerly Lord Bingham), who had only recently given up the command of the L.R.B. The Bishop of London, Chaplain of the L.R.B., who had been with the regiment from almost the day of its mobilisation, as he joined at Bisley, came with it to Crowborough and remained under canvas until October, his influence and inspiration proving of great value. One of his early sermons had the effect of inducing a large number of men in other battalions of the brigade to volunteer for foreign service, and by his help and counsel, which were always at the disposal of officers and men alike whatever their regiments, he did much to prepare those who went to him for the times that were to come. He frequently visited the men in the lines, and was always welcome.

The training at Crowborough was much the same as before, although the men had some exercise in digging, especially with the small entrenching tool which each man carried, as very little information was received from the front about the requirements for the new style of fighting, and there was no one to show how they should be met. Everyone became wonderfully fit, but it would have been a great help if valises could have been issued earlier: they came only a few days prior to embarkation, and the men found them very heavy after carrying only a great-coat and mess tin. Leave was given very sparingly owing to fear of invasion, and most men only got a few hours at home before leaving for France. A number of practice "alarms" were given which were most useful but very tiresome to all concerned. New rifles were issued just before embarking, and every man fired a few rounds with them.

Towards the end of October complete new kits were served out and all ranks were inoculated twice against typhoid, signs that the L.R.B. had been selected for an early move, but nothing definite was known, though rumour gave France or India as its destination. The kit for officers was limited to 35 lb. including the valise, and it was reported that any kit overweight would be left at the base, so everyone discarded all but bare necessities. The C.O. then ordered all kits to be weighed, with the result that most of them turned the scale at something over 50 lb., and great were the searchings of heart before superfluous items were eliminated.

At midnight on 27th–28th October the adjutant was awakened to receive embarkation orders which were subsequently cancelled, and it was not until 3rd November that final orders were received to embark next day.

The officers and principal N.C.O.'s were as follows :—

Head-quarters

Lieut.-Col. W. D. Earl Cairns. Commanding.
Lieut.-Col. (Hon. Col.) C. G. R. Matthey. Second in Command
Capt. A. C. Oppenheim (60th Rifles). Adjutant.
Capt. A. L. Lintott. Machine Gun.
2nd Lieut. C. W. Trevelyan. Transport.
Lieut. P. A. Slessor. Intelligence.
Lieut. J. R. S. Petersen. Quartermaster.
Major A. D. Ducat. Medical Officer.
Regtl. Sergt.-Major A. G. Harrington (60th Rifles).
Regtl. Quartermaster Sergt. F. Bate.

"A" Company

Capt. R. H. Husey
Lieut. G. H. Morrison.
Lieut. G. H. Cholmeley.
Clr.-Sergt. A. Read.

"D" Company

Major N. C. King.
Lieut. J. G. Robinson.
Clr.-Sergt. W. G. Hamilton.

"E" Company

Capt. C. H. F. Thompson.
Lieut. H. B. Price.
2nd Lieut. H. G. Vincent.
Clr.-Sergt. P. O. Werdmuller.

"G" Company

Capt. and Hon. Major C. D. Burnell.
Lieut. E. L. Large.
Lieut. A. G. Kirby.
Clr.-Sergt. R. J. Adamson.

"H" Company

Capt. H. D. F. MacGeagh.
2nd Lieut. G. H. G. M. Cartwright.
2nd Lieut. K. Forbes.
Clr.-Sergt. G. H. Cotter.

"O" Company

Capt. M. H. Soames.
2nd Lieut. W. L. Willett.
2nd Lieut. G. C. Kitching.
Clr.-Sergt. F. H. Wallis.

"P" Company

Capt. J. R. Somers-Smith.
2nd Lieut. H. L. Johnston.
2nd Lieut. G. E. S. Fursdon
Clr.-Sergt. D. B. Sceats.

"Q" Company

Capt. A. S. Bates.
Lieut. R. E. Otter.
Clr.-Sergt. H. G. Marner.

The battalion had a great send-off from the other regiments of the brigade who were less fortunate, the band of the Post Office Rifles playing it to the station, and embarked on s.s. *Chyebassa* at Southampton on the evening of 4th November.

After a particularly calm crossing the L.R.B. disembarked at Havre next day (5th), and had a trying march, ending with a long hill, to No. 1 Rest Camp, which was found full of old soldiers, many of whom were "swinging the lead" and telling most sanguinary stories. This formed a very bad start for raw troops, and, to make things worse, owing to the shortage of tents a large number of the men had to spend the night, which was a frosty one, in the open. Iron rations had been issued on board, which, after considerable doubt as to their nature had been expressed, turned out to be the grocery portion only, and required, as was discovered later on, a tin of bully beef and six hard biscuits to be carried in addition.

While here the officers learnt that it was usual for them to be dressed like the men, so they gave up wearing the swords and Sam Browne belts with which they had come out, and drew equipments, which had not been issued to them previously, to take the place of the ruck-sacks that most of them had brought. The regiment entrained at the Gare des Marchandises in the evening of 6th November, and reached St. Omer via Abancourt, Aumale and Abbeville on the evening of 7th. The train consisted of 50 vehicles and carried 848 all ranks, with 22 vehicles, 2 machine guns and 68 horses. Only the one halt was made and the men were very uncomfortable in crowded trucks which many had seen in peace time marked "Hommes 40. Chevaux 8, en longue," but never expected to occupy. The arrival at St. Omer was apparently not expected by the authorities there, but, after a little delay, quarters were provided for the night in the cavalry barracks near the station, which were in a filthy state, and on the next day the regiment marched to the Benedictine Convent at Wisques about 3¼ miles W. by S. of the town, better known in 1915 as the G.H.Q. Machine Gun School. The building, which was both unfinished and unfurnished, was a large one and accommodated the whole battalion, but there was no water laid on, not a single fire-place, and no means of lighting it except by candles, which were most difficult to obtain. At first the men slept on the bare boards and showed a good deal of nervousness about candles and smoking, but it was not long before they drew straw and stuck lighted candles in it without any qualms. Of course all were very new to this sort of life and unable to make themselves as comfortable as they would have done later on, when they had gained more experience. For instance, at Wisques, thirty miles from the firing line, a guard of 25 men was mounted, whereas in Plœgsteert itself, only just behind the line, a guard of three was considered ample. The chief inconvenience came from the stringent regulations with regard to leaving the Convent, but those were necessary, as during the first battle of Ypres the L.R.B., one or two other Territorial battalions, and the North Somerset Yeomanry, were almost the only troops in reserve to the whole B.E.F., and they had to be ready to move at any time.

The following week was taken up with digging, practising the attack, and firing the new rifles which had been issued just before leaving England. For musketry a thirty yards' range was used in the fortifications round St. Omer, as well as one of twenty yards in a chalk pit. Rapid loading was practised in the Chapel of the Convent, but the rifles, which had been converted in order to take the new service ammunition, did not prove entirely satisfactory, and one or two rounds were fired unintentionally through the extractors failing to act. One day during the week Sir John French came over to see the regiment, but unfortunately was unable to do so, as it was out at work. The regiment also suffered its first casualty about the same time through a big transport horse, known as "The Pride of Hammersmith," ceasing to take any further interest in life. It was no easy job to bury him.

On 16th a move was made to Hazebrouck. As the work had been very hard and carried out to a large extent in the rain without any means of drying the wet things, a very tired and damp battalion paraded for the seventeen-mile march. However, although the road was principally uneven *pavé* and the men were not thoroughly accustomed to the weight of their packs, no one fell out: the exhaustion at the end was not entirely dissipated by the issue of a rum ration. On the following day Bailleul, eleven miles further, was reached, where the billets were behind the Church in a large school, which had formerly been used as a hospital, and after two nights there, an advance was made on 19th to Romarin, finishing in a snowstorm. There the regiment was attached to the 11th Brigade, under Brig.-Gen. A. Hunter Weston, of the 4th Division, under Major-General H. F. M. Wilson, of the IIIrd Corps under Lieut.-Gen. Sir W. P. Pulteney. The brigade consisted of the 1st Somerset L.I., 1st E. Lancs, 1st Hants and 1st Rifle Brigade, and the L.R.B. found great satisfaction in being with its own regiment. The following short account extracted from the diary of Capt. G. A. Prideaux, of the 1st Battalion Somerset L.I., explains the situation at Plœgsteert prior to the arrival of the L.R.B.

"On October 20th, 1914, the 11th Infantry Brigade marched to Ploegsteert (*U*. 25). At 5.30 a.m. the next morning the Germans attacked and drove the Inniskilling Fusiliers out of Le Gheer. At 9 a.m. two companies of the Somersets retook it and their battalion head-quarters were established between St. Yves (*U*. 15) and Le Gheer (*U*. 21). At 8 p.m. the same night the East Lancs made an attack on the left of the Somersets, but found the enemy had hurriedly withdrawn, and encountered no opposition. . . . On October 22nd, the Somersets appeared to be holding a line from the River Douve (*U*. 8) to Le Gheer village. . . . On November 1st owing to heavy artillery fire the forward line of British trenches was evacuated."

Capt. Prideaux also mentions as an item of interest that on Nov. 6th Very lights had that day been issued to them. It has often been stated that the Germans started the war with these as part of their regular equipment, but no good authority can be quoted. On November 7th the Germans gained a footing in the wood. The Inniskillings made a gallant effort to turn them out on the following day, but were unsuccessful and lost 5 officers and 150 men in the attempt.

So far as appears in the diary the situation remained unchanged from this time until the L.R.B. appeared on the scene and joined the 11th Infantry Brigade.

On 20th Nov., Brig.-Gen. Hunter Weston came to see the officers and made a speech welcoming the regiment, while later that day half companies were sent into the trenches to be attached to the regulars for instruction, when nothing could exceed the consideration which was shown them. Gratitude was expressed that the L.R.B. had come up to help the troops, who were tired out with their exertions during the first battle of Ypres which was just ending, and every possible help was given in teaching the duties required and how to make the best of the uncomfortable surroundings. After the remaining half companies had had a turn of instruction in the trenches, the companies went up as units.[1] During "D" company's preliminary tour in the trenches, Rfn. J. L. Dunnett, who was only 18 and very popular with his comrades, was killed by a shell while breakfasting. His loss, the first incurred by the regiment

[1] Regarding this Capt. G. A. Prideaux, says in some extracts in his Diary that were printed: "Nov. 20th, 1914. In the evening a platoon of the L.R.B. with two officers, Capt. Husey and Capt. Morrison, relieved some of our men in order to learn something of trench life. 21st. The L.R.B.'s are very keen and seem very efficient."

through the enemy, produced a deep impression. On 22nd the regiment moved up into Ploegsteert, just behind the line, and was billeted in the village, head-quarters at first being in a farm known as Report Centre (*U.* 19) on the Messines Road some 600 yards north of the village, and afterwards in some cottages nearer the billets on the east side of the road.

On 24th November the 4-company organisation, which had been laid down for the regular army about a year previously but not allowed up to this time for the Territorials, was adopted. "A" and "D" companies became No. 1 under Major King; "E" and "O" No. 2 under Capt. Soames; "G" and "P" No. 3 under Major Burnell; and "H" and "Q" No. 4 under Capt. Bates. The numbers were retained until after the second battle of Ypres, as it was thought that the use of the new letters at once might lead to confusion. From this date the battalion varied its turns in the trenches by finding working parties, mainly to convert "Bunhill Row" (*U.* 20), which was a ride about half a mile behind the front line, into a line of defence, and to construct two corduroy paths through the wood, which was almost impassable without them owing to the mud. The authorities made arrangements for baths as soon as they could, and the men went into Armentières where they bathed and were served out with clean underclothing, their coats and trousers being ironed, especially about the seams, to eradicate any little strangers who might have taken up their habitation there. Early in December, before the official arrangements came into being, use was made of a brewery, which had been disused since the tide of war rolled over it, and which stood on the east side of the road to Armentières, about 100 yards south of where the L.R.B. cemetery now lies. Thanks to the ingenuity of Alister Kirby the boilers were got to work, and the men tubbed in some of the brewing vessels. As this was the first bath since leaving England about a month before, it was particularly welcome, and the men had great fun and enjoyment out of it. The fact that they were under three-quarters of a mile from the front line disturbed them not one jot. The brewer raised objections to the place being used again: now it has been razed to the ground, so he might just as well have allowed the men to have comfort from it, but he didn't know the future. On 3rd December two platoons were sent to Nieppe, where they were passed in review by H.M. King George, who issued the following special Order of the day :—

"Officers, Non-commissioned Officers and men: I am very glad to have been able to see my Army in the Field. I much wished to do so in order to gain a slight experience of the life you are leading.

"I wish I could have spoken to you all to express my admiration of the splendid manner in which you have fought, and are still fighting against a powerful and relentless enemy. By your discipline, pluck, and endurance, inspired by the indomitable regimental spirit, you have not only upheld the tradition of the British Army, but added fresh lustre to its history. I was particularly impressed by your soldierly, healthy, cheerful appearance.

"I cannot share in your trials, dangers and successes, but I can assure you of the proud confidence and gratitude of myself and of your fellow-countrymen. We follow you in our daily thoughts on your certain road to Victory."

On 19th December an attack was made by the brigade with the object of rectifying its line, and keeping the enemy occupied. The L.R.B. was brigade reserve, and had two companies in Bunhill Row (which at that time was called Bunter Avenue), and two companies in support behind. The attack was not very successful owing to the mud, which entirely prevented men from getting forward, and the casualties were out of proportion to the success gained. Late that evening, in pitch darkness and torrents of rain, the L.R.B. was moved up to a line of breastworks in Hunter Avenue (*U*. 21) in case of a counter-attack, but fortunately this did not take place, as it would have been extremely difficult to deal with in the circumstances. At one time it was thought that the regiment would continue the attack next day, but the idea was abandoned, and the first experience of an offensive was not an encouraging one. The following Order by the Brigadier was issued :—

"The G.O.C., both 3rd Corps and 4th Division, have been personally to see the Brigadier and have asked him to convey to the officers and men of the 11th Infantry Brigade engaged in yesterday's attack, their sincere appreciation of the perseverance and gallantry under most trying circumstances. The Brigadier has already expressed his commendation of the conduct of the Brigade in the message he sent at the conclusion of the operations and in his personal visit to the battalions concerned in Ploegsteert Wood last night. The object of the operations was to tie the enemy to their ground by the fear of our attacks, and so to prevent him moving troops against the Russians. This object has been attained, and incidentally we have gained the edge of the wood and the houses which were troublesome to us as giving shelter to snipers. The 11th Infantry Brigade has always done well and has done well again."

In preparing for this attack various schemes were devised for getting over the German wire. One, for a small apron fence, which was tried with success and proved of some use, consisted of two lengths of wire-netting with straw in between which was carried, rolled up, by one man, who had to throw it over the wire, when the men could get over the obstacle by jumping upon it. This was not used in the actual attack.

When the regiment moved into Ploegsteert there was a good deal of frost, and many of the men suffered from it, particularly in their feet. Immediately afterwards rain set in and continued almost without a break during the winter, which was one of the wettest for some time. No small amount of pluck was required to step into trenches, which generally had two feet or more of icy cold water in them, on a dark night, knowing that boots and putties would be soaking wet for two, three, or four days, as the case might be. The soil was of clay, and the sides of the trenches fell in in lumps. Three men were required for filling a sandbag—one to hold it open, one to shovel, and one to scrape the mud off the shovel—and the bags when filled were of little use, for the mixture of clay and water could not be moulded into any proper shape: moreover no one had been taught the right way of revetting. The trenches were always getting filled with water from the field-drains, which had been cut through in digging, and, as some of them were in ground that was hardly any higher than the river Lys, baling was not much good because there was so little fall that the water trickled back through the sides of the trench instead of running off. Old buckets were used as braziers for the charcoal, which burned without smoke and was made behind the line at Steenwerck. Before the arrival of the L.R.B., the brigade had been frequently on the move and no one knew that it had settled down for the winter, so, while some battalions immediately set to work to put their trenches in order, others waited, thinking that they were only in the place for a time. The former were well repaid for their superior discipline and foresight.

On 23rd December each company was attached to one of the regular battalions, No. 1 to E. Lancs ; No. 2 to the Somersets ; No. 3 to the Hants, and No. 4 to the Rifle Brigade. The system was to have two companies in the line ; one in support just behind ; one resting in billets in Ploegsteert ; and one washing in Armentières. An attack by the enemy would not have been easy to meet, as very little provision was made against it and there was no proper second line of defence, but fortunately all was quiet, because the Germans were as worn-out as the British troops. In Armentières a troupe of "Follies," which was recruited from the Division, gave regular entertainments which were greatly appreciated, and enabled the men to forget for a time the hardships which they were undergoing ; the 4th Division troupe is believed to have been the first of its kind. The L.R.B. settled down extraordinarily quickly to their new life, so very different from anything that they had ever been accustomed to, one saving feature of which was that the food was excellent and abundant. The authorities provided goat-skin coats, worn with the hair outside, which were very warm but gave a most amusing appearance to the officers and the men. When going up to the trenches the men loaded themselves with all sorts of articles likely to minimise the discomforts in view, and a photograph of a company before setting out would have been an entertaining memento, but, as the start was usually made at dusk, there was no opportunity for taking one. The Christmas mail of the battalion was enormous, almost as large as that of all the rest of the division. People at home were most kind in sending out not only food, but comforters, socks and other things likely to be of use, to such a generous extent that large gifts, which were much appreciated, were able to be made to the regular regiments who were not so well looked after. The 2nd Battalion sent every man a wallet stamped "L.R.B. France 1914" containing writing paper; condensed milk and other useful articles of food were also sent, a kindness which was very greatly valued. Everyone received a card from their Majesties and an embossed tin box from Princess Mary containing a card, a pipe and tobacco or cigarettes, and many Christmas cards from the G.O.C. and others were circulated.

The Germans were also determined to keep the Christmas season if they could, and their trenches on 24th December were outlined with fairy lights, while Christmas-trees were in evidence as well. As the weather was very frosty just then, the British troops arranged a truce with the Saxons who were opposite this portion of the line, in order that burying parties might carry out their very necessary duties, and this led to meetings in No Man's Land and an exchange of courtesies, which ignorance at that time of German methods and intentions in the matter of poison-gas and other horrors made possible. In some cases visits were said to have been made to the enemy's trenches by adventurous spirits, and there were rumours of a proposed football match, but the authorities frowned upon ideas of this sort and stopped them, quite rightly, because it would have been most unwise to allow the Germans to know how weakly the British trenches were held. Anyhow the matter was essentially a question of paying proper respect to the dead, and not a shot was fired after Xmas Day until a message was received on New Year's Eve, that "The automatic pistol would recommence firing at midnight." It did, but the shots were purposely aimed high, and gossip said that the adjutant, who was going up through the wood, was very nearly hit.

About this time the first hand-grenades, which were of the stick variety, with two tails made of tape on the handle to steady the flight, appeared. A detonator was inserted before it was thrown, and the missile went off on impact, but it does not ever seem to have been much used. Rifle grenades of the same kind were also used, but were not much good, as the ground was too soft and muddy for the impact to explode them.

Later on the Mills grenade was largely used. This was an oval metal receptacle containing an explosive, in which a detonator was inserted, and was fired by means of a lever that was retained in its place by a pin. The pin was withdrawn before the grenade was thrown, and the lever sprang off, releasing a striker which exploded the charge five seconds later. This grenade was made more useful afterwards through having a threaded hole bored in the base into which a rod was screwed, so that the missile could be fired from the barrel of a rifle with the help of a special cup attachment. While in the wood an attempt was made to construct hand-grenades from old jam tins, which was partially successful, and, from data supplied by an Oxford Professor of Roman History, a catapult was constructed with which to propel them. Two saplings were chosen facing in the desired direction, and a sling was made of two or three strands of rope with a pocket in the centre. The "engine" was strained by a rope attached to the sling, but, as no satisfactory method of quick release was devised, it was never certain whether the bomb would be propelled in the direction of the enemy, or would drop gently to the ground; in the latter case the personnel had to make itself scarce with some speed. Sometimes, indeed, the bomb remained in the pocket, and the onlookers, who were all staring into the air to follow its flight, were liable to receive an unexpected shock. That the weapon was more dangerous to those who used it than to those at whom it was aimed soon became evident, and it was never employed against the enemy.

Some trench mortars also were sent up for experiment, crude affairs made after the pattern of an old-fashioned mortar with four legs, so that they somewhat resembled a frog squatting on the ground. They were fired by a fuse in the touch-hole, and were considered so dangerous that everyone left the fire-bay after the fuse had been lighted. On one occasion, and one only, was a direct hit made, and that seemed to cause confusion amongst the Huns, as they ceased sending over their grenades.

A good deal of new slang crept in from time to time, some of which may be worth noting as likely to be of interest in the future. One expression was, "To get the wind up," which was used in various forms, but meant to be nervous and fussy. Some say it arose from the sound of firing from miles away coming down the line. Amongst other words was "Blighty," derived from the Hindostanee "Belati," meaning "foreign." This was used by European soldiers in India to denote Europe or home. The word "Blighty" in France therefore originally denoted England, and was used as an adjective: "blighty one" applied to a wound meant a wound which took a man home to England: later the word was used very often as a substantive. "Camouflage" came from the French, and was used to denote disguise. "Strafe" came from the Germans, who frequently used the expression, "Gott strafe England," and its usual meaning was to inflict punishment or to give anyone a good talking to. "Scrounge" was a curious word, the origin of which is very obscure. Its meaning, to put it bluntly, was to steal, but not from an individual; thus anyone who could collect material for a dug-out from an R.E. dump without leave was said to "scrounge." Another phrase was "To swing the lead," which is probably an old one in the Navy though new to the Army, and meant that a man was escaping a duty by means of a false excuse. "Napoo" was a corruption of "il n'y en a plus" or "il n'y a plus," and meant that a thing was sold out or finished and done with. "Buckshee" was probably derived from "Backshish" and was used to denote anything that was over or was an unexpected gain; in returning stores, for instance, if more were brought back than were on charge, the surplus was said to be "buckshee."

On 27th December Lord Cairns went home on ten days' leave and Lieut.-Col. Matthey took over the command; this, the first leave granted, opened up great possibilities.

As the men were suffering from trench feet, owing to the frost and the water in the trenches, and scientific treatment of this complaint was then in its infancy, a good many of them went sick.

The total casualties for the month were—killed, Other Ranks, 11; wounded—Officers, 2; Other Ranks, 24. The officers were Lieut. A. G. Kirby and 2nd Lieut. W. L. Willet. Lieut. Kirby was hit in the head by a sniper and suffered from paralysis for some time, but eventually appeared to have recovered entirely. He did good work at home with an anti-aircraft battery for which he invented some most ingenious targets ; was an instructor at the Godstone School for Officers ; and also gave most valuable help to the 3rd Battalion. Later on he joined the staff of Brig.-Gen. Granet, commanding the artillery of 58th Division, and afterwards went to France on the staff of 63rd (Naval) Division, but he died in 1917 from the effects of his wound. 2nd Lieut. Willett, who was also wounded in the head while gallantly going to the help of a man who had fallen victim to a sniper, suffered, too, from paralysis, and was unable to take any further part in the war.

On 4th January, 1915, all the companies were recalled to billets at the south end of the village of Ploegsteert, preparatory to the battalion taking over a piece of the line for itself on the 7th. The sector was from the River Warnave (*U*. 28) to the Estaminet, but two days later the front was shortened to end at a point about 280 yards south of the Warnave with the E. Lancs on the left and the Monmouths (T.F.) on the right. The line, known as " Essex Trench," was held by one company, with the Support Company in a farm 300 yards south-east of the brewery having the greater part of one platoon in London Farm (*C*. 3), a ruined farmhouse, which had to be put into a state of defence, about 800 yards west of the front trench, a detachment in a farm known as Mountain Gun Farm (*U*. 27) (because there had been an emplacement for such a gun in a haystack on it), and another in the Red House (*U*. 27). The Reserve Company was billeted in the village and formed part of the Brigade Composite Reserve Battalion. The fourth company was in Armentières, resting and washing, with its billets in the Usine Electrique.

The " Essex Trench," which had been held previously by the Monmouth Territorials, was in shape rather like a lacrosse stick, lying with the handle to the south and the strings to the west. Almost all the northern curved portion was flooded, and went right up to the Warnave River, quite a small stream in reality, which flowed from east to west or *vice versa*, according to the direction of the wind, a peculiarity which caused it to be named on one of the official maps, " the Warnave or McKenna River," after a well-known politician. The main Le Gheer—Le Touquet road ran some 50 yards behind, and parallel to, the trench. Company Head-quarters were in a trench alongside the road, and for some weeks the O.C. Company could not enter the front trench by day owing to the communication trench being entirely flooded and unsafe. The German trenches were about 100 yards away at the south end and 400 at the north, while all reliefs had to be carried out by night, and a tour lasted three days.

On 8th January Lieut.-Col. Matthey went home sick, and Capt. Bates became Second in Command, Major King having also been invalided home. On one day during the month the War Diary records that "the shelling was severe," but the probability is that the enemy only fired a few more whiz-bangs than usual, because in the light of after-knowledge the battalion was never under anything which might really be called shelling while it was in the Ploegsteert neighbourhood. Much work was done in the trench without, however, making things entirely satisfactory, as Company Head-quarters were still not in touch with the front trench by day, nor could anyone from Battalion Head-quarters enter the trench at any time except under cover of darkness. During January 8 Other Ranks were killed, and 5 wounded.

On 1st February the first large draft arrived from home, consisting of 6 N.C.O.'s and 145 men; 2nd Lieuts. B. S. Harvey and J. E. Alcock had come in on 20th January with 2 N.C.O.'s and 15 men, and 2nd Lieut. B. E. Bland had arrived in late December. On 20th February 1 N.C.O. and 97 men came up from the base; all the above came from the 2nd Battalion. During this month the first commissions in the battalion were given, and F. H. Wallis, G. H. Cotter, R. E. H. Flindt and R. Russell were made 2nd Lieutenants, the last becoming Transport Officer vice Lieut. Trevelyan. On 26th February, which was very misty, Cpl. T. H. Jenkin went across to the German lines and captured a flag which had been stuck up just outside their trench. This was referred to in *Punch* as follows:—

"We are not surprised to hear that Cpl. Jenkin of the 1st Battalion London Rifle Brigade succeeded in capturing a German flag at the front. Cpl. Jenkin is an artist, and it was only natural that he should make for the colours."

The flag was repaired and is preserved at Bunhill Row.

When Brig.-Gen. Hunter Weston gave up command of the Brigade and went home to undertake other work, he was succeeded by Brig.-Gen. Julian Hasler, late of the Buffs, and the following letter was received by Lord Cairns :—

"MY DEAR CAIRNS,

"It is with real regret that I have to give up the command of the Brigade to which the L.R.B. belongs. You know how very close a bond binds me to the Officers, N.C.O.'s and men of the 11th Infantry Brigade, and I can give your officers and men no higher praise than that I consider you have proved yourselves worthy to form part of the Brigade.

"Your Battalion has done well all that it has been called upon to do, and I am confident that, when hard fighting comes, your men will stick it out both in attack and defence with the tenacity and courage that the original four Battalions of the old 'Stonewall Brigade' have displayed unfailingly in every phase of the war.

"Please ask your Company Commanders to tell this to your Officers, N.C.O.'s and men, and to give each and all God-speed and my best wishes. My close connection with you, my old schoolfellow, has been a great pleasure to me. You are a fine Battalion Commander, and both your Battalion and I have been fortunate in having you.

"The best of good luck to you,

"Yours ever,

"AYLMER HUNTER WESTON."

Gen. Hunter Weston had been most helpful to the battalion on its first arrival at the front, as he had devised a really good system for initiating it into its work, and all were sorry to lose him.

The following were the methods adopted by the L.R.B. to ensure continuity in the work which would otherwise have been difficult, as each company was only in for three days. Permanent parties to assist the O.C. Trench under direction from Battn. H.Q. were detailed as follows :—

(*a*) 1 corporal and 3 men for wiring under Cpl. H. Smith and, when he was wounded, Lce.-Cpl. J. H. Stransom.

(*b*) 1 corporal and 8 men for revetting, building, etc. A portion of them went up every night to superintend the pulling down and rebuilding of shelters in the trench. They lived in the village, and were under Lce.-Cpl. A. K. Dodds, who reported daily in person to the C.O. to discuss the next item of work to be tackled. The woodwork was prepared in the pioneer shop in the village. When Lce.-Cpl. Dodds received a commission, Cpl. D. W. Belcher took over his work. During this period, and until the battalion left the wood, this party did excellent work.

(*c*) 2 men for the purpose of using the pumps, and to advise as to redrainage, etc. Pte. G. D. Milward was put in charge of the pumps. The water difficulty was a great one. The country was very flat and the surface water showed no anxiety to flow in any direction. Pumps, of which any number were received, were a never-ceasing source of worry. The best one the battalion ever had in this sector was sent out by Lieut. A. G. Kirby, made to his design, and said to be "fool-proof." That this was not the case was proved by some ingenious person who endeavoured to get it to function when the intake pipe was connected to the delivery end of the pump.

On 1st March the battalion lost the services of its medical officer, Major Ducat, who was given another appointment. He had served in the regiment for many years, and everyone was sorry to lose him, though he was really much too senior to hold such a post as that of a Battalion M.O. He was succeeded by Lieut. E. F. Edmunds. On 16th March Lord Cairns was unfortunately invalided home. The regiment was very much indebted to him for his services, particularly after the outbreak of war, when the wisdom of the regimental rule that the Commanding Officer should always be an officer of professional experience was well proved. In spite of the good will and keenness shown by all ranks, a voluntary organisation in peace time could not have been turned into a battalion on war footing with anything like the same ease if a regular soldier had not been at the head. His knowledge of the right thing to do, and his sound judgment were invaluable; he possessed the confidence of all ranks; and his loss was undoubtedly a great one. He was succeeded in the command by Major A. S. Bates, who retained his position until he also was invalided in August, 1916.

After various contradictory orders had been received, on 21st March the battalion finally took over the trenches held by the Somersets, and the left trench of the R.B. The line was divided into three subsections, each allotted to one company, with the supports in Tourist Line (*U.* 21) and Hunter Avenue, the fourth company being in reserve billets in Plœgsteert, and changed every three days, so that each company held its subsection for nine days, and then went into reserve. All the drinking water was obtained from Essex Farm (*U.* 20). Lce.-Cpls. Belcher, E. F. Rice and Stransom, who were the heads of the building and wiring parties, were attached to Battalion Head-quarters, but the men of these parties were returned to their companies for duty. The new trenches were taken over on 21st March. On 23rd a further draft of 93 arrived from the base, who were all sent out from the 2nd Battalion.

A very large number of visitors came to the wood, probably because it was the only part of the British line in which visitors could get into a front line trench in daylight. Amongst others were Gen. Allenby, Admiral Sir Lewis Bayley, some Japanese officers, a Russian officer, Lieut.-Gen. R. Baden-Powell and Maj.-Gen. Sir R. Pole-Carew. On 27th March Lieut.-Gen. Sir Horace Smith-Dorrien, commanding the 2nd Army, visited Rifle House, which was Battalion H.Q. (*U.* 21), and expressed his regret to the Commanding Officer that he was unable to see the battalion as a whole. He added that he had always heard how well the battalion had done, and that he wished all ranks to realise how fully their good work was being appreciated. He hoped soon to be able to express his personal thanks to the battalion. At the end of the month three platoons of the 4th Lincolns (T.F.) were attached to the L.R.B. for instruction, and three more directly afterwards. The casualties for the month were, killed, 1 Officer and 10 Other Ranks ; wounded, 10 Other Ranks. The officer, Capt. G. H. Morrison, who was sniped, was a man whom the regiment could ill spare, as he was a fine leader of men, and beloved by his own men and by his brother officers.

At Easter the Bishop of London visited Ploegsteert, but to his great regret was forbidden by the Commander-in-Chief to enter the wood. He therefore had to content himself with sending his chaplain, Rev. G. Vernon Smith, who was also chaplain of the 2nd Battalion, in his place. The Bishop held a Celebration for the company in reserve billets and for a draft of 105 Other Ranks which had just arrived from the base. He also consecrated the L.R.B. cemetery in the village on Easter Sunday.

Some of the 5th Gloucesters (T.F.) came up about this time for initiation into trench warfare, and were followed shortly after by parties from the 4th Oxford and Bucks (T.F.). On 17th April the battalion was relieved by the 7th Worcesters (T.F.), of the South Midland Division, and marched to billets in the Steenwerck area, west of the "Grand Beaumar," on Le Veau-Steenwerck Road.

During the stay at Ploegsteert Sergt. A. W. Stapley and Pte. Slade had done some very good work in correcting a large scale map of the ground behind the division's trenches, which led to three men being asked for to start systematic work. Ptes. E. H. Slade, W. H. Pickard and T. W. May were sent before the battalion left, and on 11th July a letter was received from the G.S.O.3, in which the following paragraph appeared :—

"Your three topographers have been an unqualified success, and I do not know how we should have got on without them. The work they do now is perfectly extraordinary. I would like to give them a final testimonial in saying that they tossed up as to who was to go out with me at night, when I suppose the chances of being killed were considerably greater than if they had stayed at home. They are what Prowse would call stout fellows."

The battalion was continually being called upon to provide experts of all kinds for various jobs, and the men had the happy knack of always rising to an emergency.

The following translation of part of a letter written by a Mlle. Charlet to an officer in the 4th (Res.) Battalion Loyal North Lancs Regt., when Lieut.-Col. Bates was in command of it later in the war, gives a French view of the L.R.B. :—

" . . . You ask me about Mr. Bates. It is quite possible that I know him because the L.R.B. was at Ploegsteert in 1914–15. It was a superb regiment and the soldiers were held in great esteem by the inhabitants because they were such models of politeness, and were so amiable and grateful. I assure you that the whole village, even until 1918, regretted the absence of the L.R.B., and as for us, we never regretted any regiment so much because the officers who were with us always treated my family with such respect. Alas! when the L.R.B. left Ploegsteert everyone was heart-broken, seeing these noble and gallant Londoners, so appreciated in our country, leave for the bottomless pit, and the emotion was great when, about a month later, they heard that most of those brave boys had lost their lives in an attack on Ypres. Our good *curé* said Masses for these heroes, but we never saw that gallant regiment again. We often heard rumours of its return, but, unfortunately, they were never realised. In this regiment I knew Messrs. Somers-Smith, Large, Johnston, Price, Vincent, Alcock, Thompson, Burnell, Soames and many others whose names I have forgotten. How jealous you will be! However, your regiment, too, contained many brave and noble men. We lived at 20 Rue d'Armentières, in Ploegsteert. I am sure Mr. Bates must know our dear little house, where we were so happy because it was our country house. We had another at Lille, where we spent the greater part of the year. If you see the Colonel, please give him my best respects and congratulate him on belonging to a regiment so respected and esteemed in France. . . ."

The casualties for the month were: Killed, 1 Officer, 3 Other Ranks; wounded, 2 Other Ranks. The officer was 2nd Lieut. G. H. Cotter, who had gone out as a colour-sergeant and had been promoted in the field. He had done extremely well, and would have proved an uncommonly useful officer if he had lived.

The L.R.B. came out of the trenches for a rest on the night of 17th–18th April, and went into billets round Steenwerck. This was the first rest that the L.R.B. had enjoyed since its arrival in the firing line five months before, and the first time that the 11th Brigade had been out of the line for a rest since

August, 1914, so all ranks were in high spirits and looked forward to a long "easy." The billets were good, the weather was brilliant and sports were arranged for which the prizes had been bought, when the situation suddenly changed, and all the plans which had been made were upset.

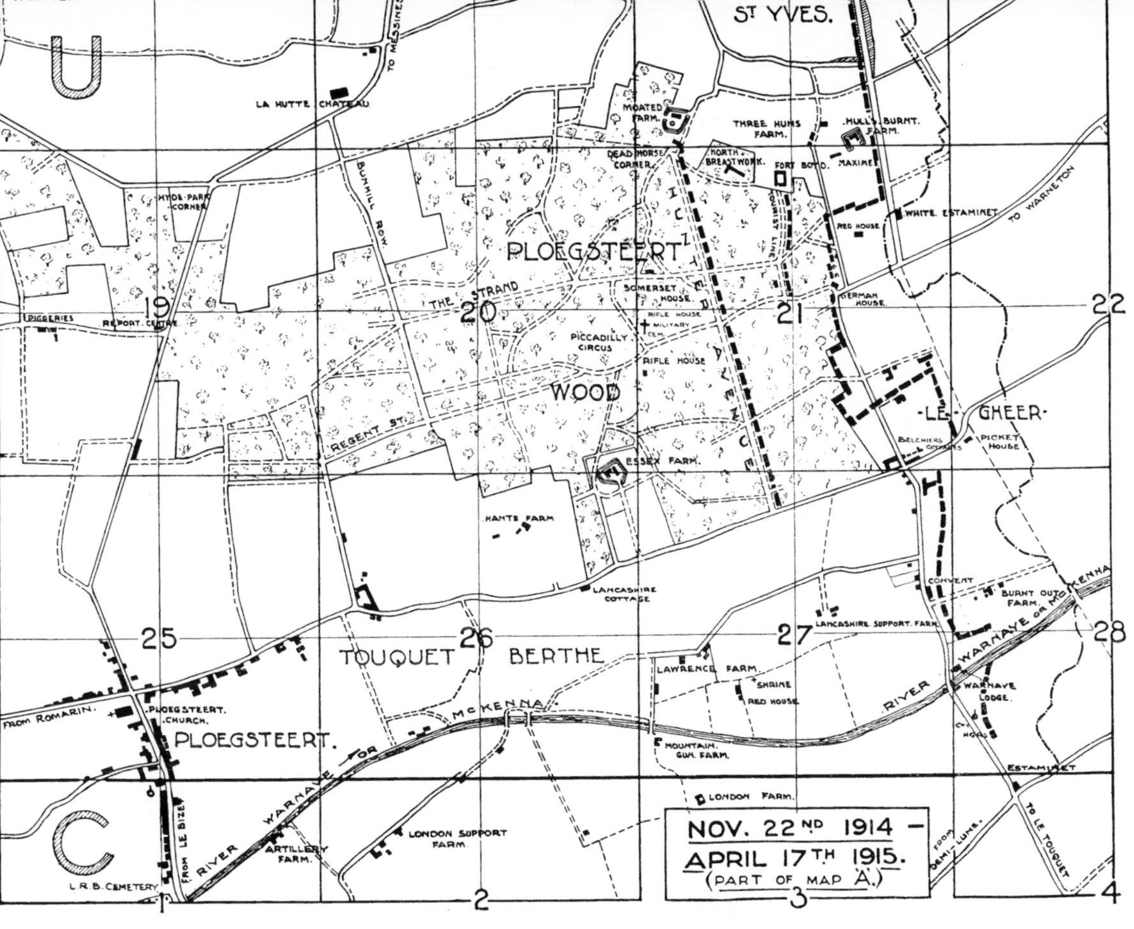

Sketch Map No. 1.

To face page 86

FIRST BATTALION

PART II.—APRIL 23—MAY 18, 1915

Second Battle of Ypres.

(The Maps referred to are A 7, 2 on p. 90, 3 on p. 96, and 4 on p. 102).

AN attack by the British on Neuve Chapelle in March, and attacks by the French in the Wœvre and Alsace, combined with the Russian descent of the Carpathians, were announced in *The Times* of 10th April as "the opening of the Allied offensive in the summer campaign of 1915." Neither the British nor the French attacks were productive of any real advantage to their side, and "the disaster which soon overtook the Russian plans had its effect upon the Allied designs in the West, and induced an attempt to menace the Germans in a quarter more likely to disturb their concentration on the East than a campaign against the St. Mihiel wedge or in the mountain frontiers of Alsace. The tender spot in the East was Lille, with its concentration of railways and importance as protecting the right flank of the German front along the Aisne and the left flank of their hold on the Belgian coast. The Germans learnt, divined or anticipated the design, and sought to parry or break the force of the projected blow by a defensive-offensive against Ypres. The attack was not their real offensive for 1915, but they developed the habit of distracting attention from their main objectives by decking out their subsidiary operations with some new devilry of ingenuity . . . and they treated the defenders of Ypres to their first experiments in poison gas. They had tried the effect on the humbler creation some time before, and had indicated their intentions by accusing their enemies of the practice they themselves had in mind, but it came as a ghastly surprise to the French Territorials and British and Canadian troops along the Yser on 22nd April. The attack had clearly been planned beforehand, because the preparation of the chlorine gas, arrangement of the gas tubes along the front, and delay for the requisite conditions of wind and weather required time; and the absence of any great concentration of troops merely showed that in view of their commitments in the East, the Germans only sought at Ypres a local and tactical success."[1] Ypres was bombarded on the 20th, and on the evening of the 22nd the gas attack developed.

The Officers' Mess has received a most interesting present from Major P. A. Slessor in the shape of framed facsimile copies of the original telegrams which passed between Sir J. French and the War Office on the occasion of the first use of gas by the Germans. Their text is as follows:—

From Sir John French

"O. a. 948, 23rd April. Germans used powerful asphyxiating gases very extensively in attack on French yesterday with serious effect. . . . Apparently these gases are either chlorine or bromine. . . . Will send further details later but meanwhile strongly urge that immediate steps be taken to supply similar means of most effective kind for use by our troops AAA. Also essential that our troops should be immediately provided with means of counteracting effects of enemy gases which should be suitable for use when on the move. . . . As a temporary measure am arranging for troops in trenches to be supplied with solution of bicarbonate of soda in which to soak handkerchiefs. . . . "Chief G.H.Q. 5.50 p.m."

Lord Kitchener's reply, dictated by him to the Adjutant-General, Sir Henry Sclater, *in whose handwriting it is*:—

"Your O. a. 948, 23rd April. The use of asphyxiating gases is, as you are aware, contrary to the Rules and Usages of war, before therefore we fall to the level of the degraded Germans I must submit the matter to the Government. In the meantime I should be glad if you could send me an example of diagnosis of the material used, and I am also having the matter fully gone into in our own Laboratories and by experts

[1] From *A Short History of the Great War*, by A. F. Pollard, published by Methuen.

in this country. These methods show to what depths of infamy our enemies will go, in order to supplement their want of courage in facing our troops."

Warning orders were received on 23rd April that the battalion was to be prepared to entrain at two hours' notice, and later in the day a further order was received detailing the brigade, less 1st East Lancs, to be prepared to move to Poperinghe (G. 2) by rail, and naming the entraining station for the L.R.B. as Steenwerck, but the transport was ordered to proceed by road. The battalion finally entrained on the following day, which was very wet, at 12.30 p.m., and, as nothing had leaked out in the ranks about the destination of the regiment, countless rumours were in circulation, which were assisted by the fact that the first part of the journey was away from the firing line. At Hazebrouck, however, the engine changed ends, and the train moved off on a line running north-east, passing on the way trains packed with refugees. It was the sight of these cattle trucks crammed tight with the civil population that finally convinced everyone that something very serious was happening and that, at last, the L.R.B. was really "for it." On arrival at Poperinghe at 4.30 p.m. the battalion marched out south-west to Busseboom (G. 16) and prepared to bivouac in the open, where the whole horizon was lit up by shell-flashes towards the east; but subsequently a few billets were found. The brigade was in Army Reserve, and late that night Operation Order No. 1 was received, ordering the brigade, less the E. Lancs, to march next day to Vlamertinghe (H. 2), starting at 6 a.m. in the following order: Somersets, Hants, R.B., L.R.B. It was added that the brigade would be under the orders of the Vth Corps, and was to be ready to move at short notice after reaching Vlamertinghe.

On 25th April the regiment started in weather which was as vile as that of the previous day, and arrived, after passing on the way several cavalry regiments in bivouac, at Vlamertinghe at 10 a.m., where they found numbers of ambulance and motor-buses, full of the less seriously wounded, continually rolling westwards. It was billeted on the west of the town, with three companies in a large hop warehouse, No. 2 Company in a separate building, and head-quarters in an

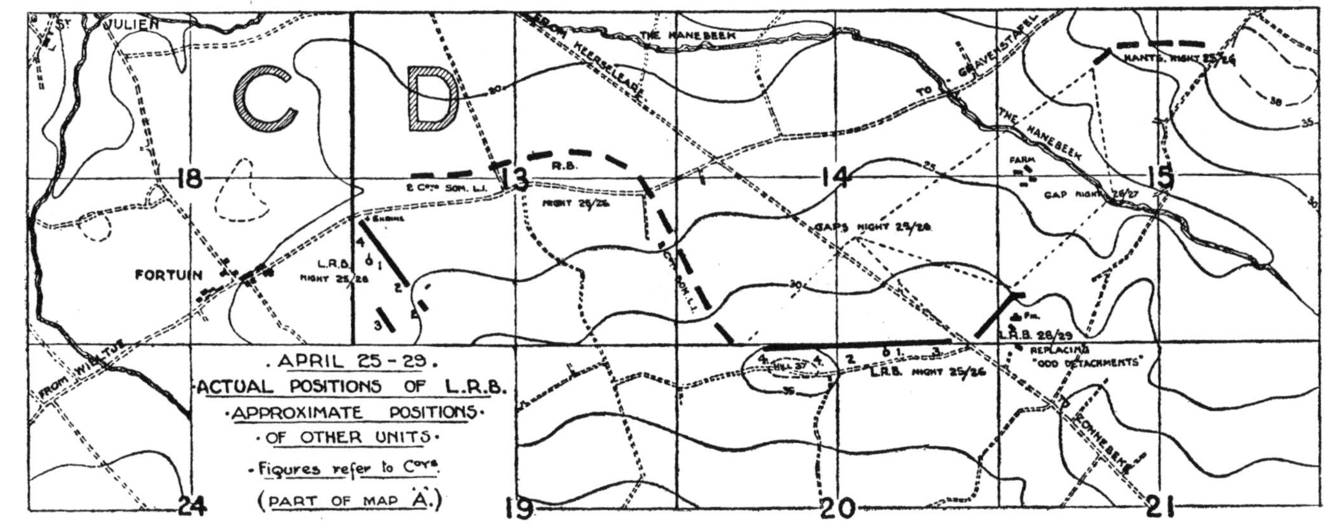

Sketch Map No. 2

estaminet close to the large billet ; but about midday orders were received that the brigade would move in the evening and must be ready to go at any time from 5.30 p.m. onwards.

The Brigadier, Brig.-Gen. J. Hasler, of the Buffs, held a meeting of C.O.'s at 4.30 p.m., at which he was not able to give much information as to the state of affairs, but instructed each C.O. to send two officers on bicycles, one towards Wieltje (C. 28) and the other towards Verlorenhoek (I. 6), to endeavour to discover the exact situation, and Capt. R. H. Husey, who was now Second in Command, and Lieut. H. L. Johnston were detailed from the L.R.B. for this. The brigade moved off at 6.15 p.m. on a march which proved a very trying one, as the battalion had, in common with the others, a considerable amount of transport and eight pack ponies. Ypres was skirted to the north, as it was being very heavily shelled and was on fire in many places. At times, in addition to the troops in fours, there were three columns of transport moving on a road which was by no means good and had suffered from continual shell-fire for many days. This made it quite impossible to keep the distances laid down, with the result that men in rear had to double, often in single file, in order to get through the press. Although the men were in fighting order, they carried full packs, and the strain on them was great ; but eventually St. Jean (C. 27) was reached, and the battalion closed up, to find that one tool limber had been ditched on the road, a misfortune which was to prove a great handicap in the subsequent operations. The two officers on bicycles rejoined the battalion with very little news, except that no one in front seemed to know much about the actual state of affairs. During the halt here tools were issued, and there was no doubt about the intensity of the struggle that was taking place. The indescribable destruction was made more terrible owing to the district having been very recently evacuated by the civil population. While there, the men experienced for the first time the effect of lachrymatory or tear shells, for which no antidote had so far been provided.

The battalion was subsequently ordered forward to Wieltje to act under the orders of Lieut.-Col. Compton of the Somersets, and arrived at 1.45 a.m. on the following morning (26th) at a position facing north-east about *D*.13.*c*. on the south side of the Wieltje-Fortuin Road. The order of companies was 4, 1, 2, from left to right, with No. 3 slightly in rear on the right. Nos. 4, 1 and 2 Companies managed to dig a shallow trench before daylight, but No. 3 Company, which was the last to line out and had taken up a position behind a hedge slightly in rear and to the right, was less fortunate. Not only had there been some delay in getting into position, but owing to the loss of a tool limber the supply of spades was wholly inadequate, in addition to which the roots from the hedge made it impossible to dig more than two feet deep. However, a morning mist made digging possible for an hour or two after daybreak, which was fortunate, as the ground was very wet and took time to work. Whether the line was front support, or reserve was uncertain, but it was finally ascertained that a platoon of the R.B. was in front, so sentries were posted as if the battalion was in support.

During the early morning intense fighting was witnessed to the left rear of the position. This was one of a long sequence of attacks made by the Lahore Division and the French to try to bring up the left flank and straighten the line to the north, and it was completely stopped by the enemy's barrage. At 10 a.m. two men from the Connaught Rangers, who formed part of the front line garrison, came through No. 1 Company and reported that a German machine-gun was causing great casualties by enfilade fire from the left. A F.O.O. (Forward Observation Officer R.A.), who was in the L.R.B. trench, set his battery on the cottage from which this gun was firing, and with their second round the gunners put it out of action by a direct hit. During the morning the enemy's shells fell clear of the trench, but the M.G. S.A.A. dump, which was in a small cottage to the rear of No. 3 Company, was destroyed by enemy shell-fire, and, in addition to the ammunition, all the spare parts of the machine-guns were lost. The enemy's gunners did not locate the whereabouts of the L.R.B. until about midday, but then considerable shelling started from the north and east, causing casualties to Nos. 1 and 3 Companies, owing to the position having been given away to an enemy aeroplane by men of other units, who came through and down the trench. Although, according to the newspapers, the

Allies had supremacy in the air, during the whole of the battle enemy planes came over with impunity, and met with no opposition whatever.

In the course of the afternoon two riflemen of No. 3 Company evacuated a stretcher-case in full view of the enemy, and in spite of both being hit by machine-gun fire brought it to the dressing station, an action which undoubtedly saved the life of the casualty by enabling amputation to be performed in time. About noon an order had been received to send one company to fill up a gap existing between the Hants and the Somersets. As the position of neither of those units had been given, Major Burnell was instructed to reconnoitre and took nearly three hours, during the whole of which he was under fire, to do so. He then reported that to take his company over the high ground would entail heavy casualties, so Lieut.-Col. Compton of the Somersets was asked by Major Bates, if the movement could be delayed till dark. The former communicated with the Brigade, which issued the following Order to the Somersets :—

"Yes, but it must be clearly understood that it must be done at the earliest moment. The whole L.R.B. must be put in so as to relieve the odd detachments. The safety of this part of the line is very important, as, if it is broken, the flanks and rear of the 28th Division are exposed."

This was despatched at 4.10 p.m. The "odd detachments" referred to a party, said to be about 250 strong, from five or six different units, which was entrenched holding an isolated farm and posts facing north-west at *D*.14.*d*.8·0, just north of the Kerselaere-Zoonebeke Road.

At dusk the whole battalion moved off in Indian file to endeavour to find the two flanks which it had to join up. Their positions had not been given even approximately, and it was only by sheer good luck that the Commanding Officer came across a battery whose commander was able to give him a certain amount of information, which was not, however, of a reassuring nature, as the enemy was reported to have penetrated the gap. The R.B. (also the Somersets) was found about *D*.14.*c*. in a line running south and the battalion proceeded to the cross roads *D*.14.*d*.8·0, where the Commanding

Officer with Capt. R. H. Husey, met an officer (Col. Bridgford or Bridgnorth) and found the "odd detachments" situated about *D*.14.*d*.91. Ultimately Col. Bridgford, who said that he had two and a half battalions (?), promised to join up from the right of the "odd detachments" to the left of the Hants, if the L.R.B. would join up from the left of the "odd detachments" to the right of the R.B. a distance of about 600 yards. At dusk the L.R.B. started to dig itself in on a line *D*.20.*a*.69—*D*.14.*d*.7·0. just north of the track with its right at the turning in *D*.14.*d*.80 and completed the work, which was carried out in bright moonlight and not without some casualties from shell-fire, by daybreak. The trench provided excellent cover for the battalion, being four feet six inches deep, heavily traversed, with a bullet-proof parapet thrown well forward, and some of the forward slope turfed. The position was on the crest of a hill, with a small house, from which water was drawn, immediately behind the centre, forming a most excellent ranging mark for the enemy's artillery. The two and a half battalions of which Col. Bridgford spoke never appeared, and the gap was not filled.

The battalion remained in this trench during 27th April, and at noon the following Order was received from Brigade :—

"As soon as possible this evening the R.B. will send out patrols to the cross roads and farm in *D*.14.*a*. On the information gained the O.C. R.B. will arrange to dig his battalion in about the line of the road east of the road, which will be held by R.B. If enemy is in occupation, he will be driven out, as the valley of the Hannebeek for 150 yards on both banks is swampy. This valley will be wired and controlled, protection being given by machine-gun cross fire. The Hants will supply the guns on the north bank of the Hannebeek. The 5th Yorks will be prepared to commence joining their trench north of the road in *D*.13.*d*. with the trench to be constructed by the R.B. as soon as possible. The Somerset L.I. will remain in their present trenches. L.R.B. will give the R.B. any assistance asked for, and will occupy the R.B. trenches on Hill 37 in addition to their own. L.R.B. will relieve with two platoons trenches now occupied by the mixed detachments, which will be sent to rejoin their own units." (11.25 a.m.)

In connection with this order the L.R.B. was asked to assist the R.B. by fetching its rations from Wieltje and provided a carrying party, though only by leaving No. 1 Company's lines with about one N.C.O. and one man in each platoon. After a three hours' wait at the ration dump, owing to the transport being delayed by the congested road and heavy shelling, the party did its work, but only finished by 5 a.m. on 28th and had to return after daybreak, so that it was seen by the enemy, who at once put down a barrage, which wounded several of the men. Owing to the serious opposition that was met with, the R.B. was not able to take all its objectives, and later in the day another L.R.B. party of about 100, which was bringing up wire, stakes and sandbags, came in for an exciting time, which ended in the loads being dumped on the road behind the position actually occupied by the R.B. instead of at the spot where that regiment should have been according to orders.

The battalion was shelled all day and in the morning a shell fell upon a house in the village of St. Jean, which blew down the side and killed R.S.M. A. G. Harrington, a typical rifleman and fine soldier, with three other men, who were sitting at breakfast, besides wounding the four other men of the party. Among these was the Medical Officer, Capt. Edmunds, who was so completely buried by the debris, that he was nearly overlooked, and was so badly crushed about the chest, that he was incapacitated for duty for a very long time. He was succeeded by Capt. J. M. Moyes. The casualties were not very heavy, as the trenches were good, but the rifles and packs, which were in those days generally laid upon the front and the back respectively, were considerably damaged, and the wounded were difficult to evacuate in the absence of any of the R.A.M.C. The different battalions in the brigade showed marked comradeship in the way that they helped one another, and after relieving the "odd detachments," which were sent to their proper brigades, the 11th set to work to consolidate its positions. During the day Brig.-Gen. Hasler was killed, a great loss to the brigade, in which he was very popular and on which his personality had made a deep impression, and Lieut.-Col. Compton took over until the evening, when Lieut.-Col. Hicks of the Hants assumed command pending the arrival of the late general's successor.

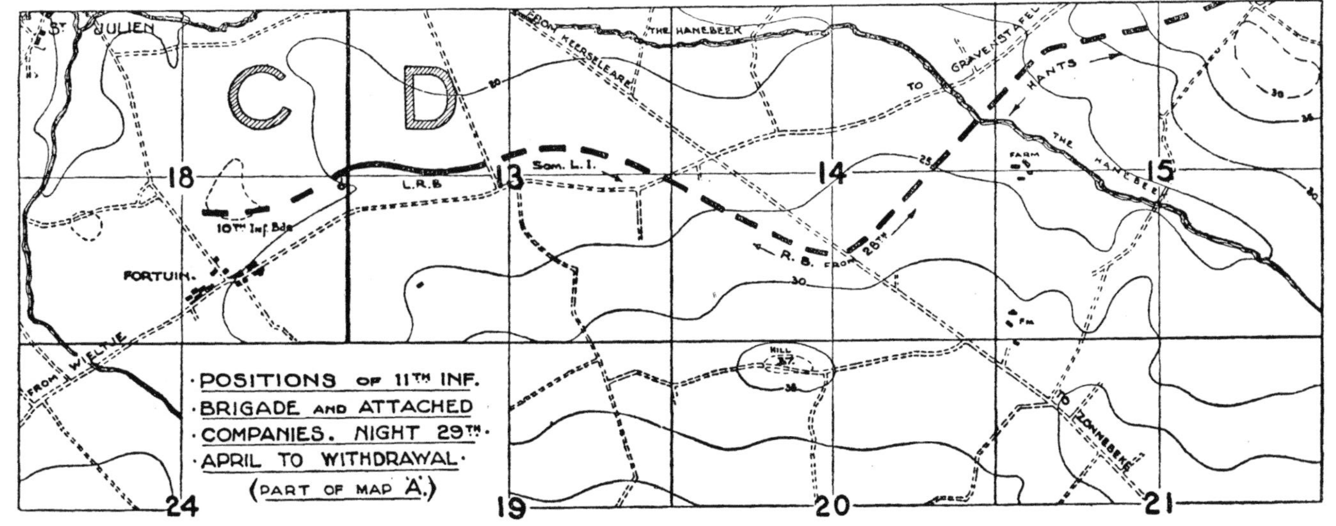

SKETCH MAP NO. 3

The 29th April was a beautiful day, and passed comparatively quietly. At 7.30 p.m. orders were received to relieve the 4th E. Yorks in the trenches north of the road *D*.13.*c*.39 to *D*.13 *central*, which not only proved to be very bad but did not provide sufficient accommodation for the battalion. There was a hitch in the relief owing to the orders reaching the E. Yorks after the L.R.B. had arrived, which resulted in the latter having to lie out behind the trench for half an hour, but, after they had taken over, several lengths of new trench were at once dug in rear. Two companies of the 4th Yorks, "Y" and "Z," were temporarily attached to the L.R.B. The dispositions on the 30th April, which was also a quiet day, were as follows: From right to left "Z" Company, 4th Yorks, Nos. 4, 3, 2 and 1 L.R.B., with battalion head-quarters in an unprotected wooden shelter at the end of a fence on the left of No. 1 Company. In support was "Y" Company 4th Yorks, in trenches about *D*.13.*c*.1·7. On the battalion's left were the Royal Irish, the junction being at about *C*.18.*b*.9·0: on its right, at about *D*.13 *central*, were the Somersets. On this date Brig.-Gen. C. B. Prowse, of the Somersets, took over command of the 11th Infantry Brigade.

On 1st May warning orders for the readjustment of the line were received, and the necessary instructions, which were to come into force on the receipt of further definite move orders, were issued at a conference of company commanders which was held in the open, so quiet were the enemy. During the day trench consolidation was carried on, small slip trenches being dug to provide more cover, and a number of British dead who were discovered in a field to the rear of the position were buried at dusk. At night a listening patrol in a cottage about a hundred yards in front of the left of the line reported that the enemy was apparently digging, so to the cottage a machine-gun party was sent, which opened rapid fire in the direction of the enemy who then withdrew.

On 2nd May the Germans started shelling this cottage at daybreak and succeeded in setting it on fire with their ninth round. During the morning a message was received stating that the French were making an attack on the left and that ten rounds were to be fired to attract the enemy's attention. This was done, and the enemy's artillery replied at once, but the French attack never developed. By midday the enemy's shell fire had increased, to a heavy bombardment, and, as salvos of H.E. were falling just forward of the line and shrapnel was bursting overhead and to the rear, all troops, with the exception of sentries, kept down in their trenches. Soon after 5 p.m. the "stand-to" was ordered, as large numbers of the enemy could be seen approaching from the high ground, but still a considerable distance off, about seven hundred to a thousand yards. At 5.20 p.m. the enemy released gas, and a heavy cloud appeared on the left, opposite the Royal Irish and in front of Nos. 3 and 4 Companies, while further over to the right, well clear of the battalion front, a very much larger one could be seen through the trees. Respirators (the first of their kind issued and of a very primitive description, as they consisted of mere strips of cloth, which, in the absence of chemicals, were recommended to be treated with urine) were at once put on, and the brigade was notified. The gas affected the front line for about ten minutes, causing much discomfort and a few casualties which were evacuated as walking cases at dusk. At 5.40 p.m. a telegram was sent to Brigade to the effect that the bombardment was still heavy, but that the gas had blown off. As soon as the gas had cleared, the enemy, who had previously been reinforced, began to advance, extending at the double directly they had left the cover of some small houses on the further side of the valley. The two companies of the L.R.B. on the left unfortunately had their field of fire screened by a hedge, but the right half of the battalion was able to bring a heavy fire on the enemy, as they advanced, with excellent results. A German machine-gun was set up near the gas cylinders and opened fire, causing some casualties, but the attack was held up in some dead ground from 100 to 300 yards off. By 6.30 p.m. active fighting had stopped, but sniping and machine-gun fire continued till dark and at 6.50 p.m. No. 4 Company, which had experienced very heavy casualties, was reinforced by two platoons of "Y" Company, 4th Yorks. An enemy aeroplane flew over low, presumably to see what effect the gas had had on the troops, and rifle fire was directed at it. By this time the men were thoroughly exhausted, for, not only had they been heavily shelled (our guns not having been able to give any reply in the form of counter-battery work), but they had been fighting all the afternoon, and were a good deal upset by the gas. Consequently the services of the E. Lancs were requisitioned for the ration and ammunition parties, and the last two platoons of "X" Company, 4th Yorks, were sent into the trench to assist No. 3 Company L.R.B. in every way, but particularly in the evacuation of the wounded. Owing to the shortage of stretchers great difficulty was experienced in getting the cases away, but eventually they were all removed, the last one, a wound through the thigh, at daybreak on a bicycle. At 8.25 p.m. the following report was sent to Brigade :—

"Situation quieter. Fear casualties very heavy, will report later. All supports now in trench. Improbable that we can hold length of trench without assistance. Men have had no sleep for seven nights. This, with the incessant shelling, has told on them. Germans are entrenching nearer to us, opposite to our centre. No. 3 Company, which is there, hopes that it did good execution on them. Can you send any Very lights ?"

At night an N.C.O. and three men went out from each company to put up wire. Cpl. G. G. Boston in charge of the party from No. 1 wired the whole company front, although within 50 yards of the enemy, and gained the D.C.M. for his gallantry.

The fatigue party of the E. Lancs, which had brought up the ammunition, was ordered to remain under the command of the O.C., L.R.B. About midnight two German prisoners were captured, the first taken by the L.R.B. in the war, but against this an L.R.B. listening patrol was lost that night, the first prisoners taken from the regiment.

Next morning (3rd May) at 2.45 a.m. Capt. Smith, who had sent up the fatigue party of the E. Lancs with ammunition, came up with the rest of his company. The ammunition party was withdrawn from the trench to the right of battalion head-quarters, two platoons were sent to relieve a platoon each of Nos. 1 and 4 Companies L.R.B., and the relieved platoons with the balance of Capt. Smith's company, all under his command, went into the support trenches. At daylight it was ascertained that the enemy had dug in all along the line about 200 to 300 yards off, with advanced trenches in some cases under 100 yards away, and that the cottage ruins in front of the left of the line were occupied. There was intermittent shelling all day, especially on the support trench. By 9 a.m. two of the battalion machine-guns had been knocked out. During the morning definite move orders were received, which stated that all wounded were to be evacuated, all dead to be buried, and all surplus kit, equipment, rifles and S.A.A. which could not be carried to be buried after dark. Consequently every unwounded officer, N.C.O. and man was hard at work from dusk up to the moment of withdrawal, when all the machine-guns, their spare parts and belt-boxes filled with S.A.A. were distributed among the companies and carried by hand the whole way back, no light work under the conditions. The 11th Brigade was ordered to retire through the new front line, which was already garrisoned, and move to woods in A.30 central.

The Brigade, which now consisted of the four regular battalions together with the L.R.B., the 4th Yorks and the 4th E. Yorks, was very fortunate in being able to carry out such a withdrawal with the Germans within at least 100 yards of the left of the line when it was evacuated, the L.R.B. which moved at 12.45 a.m. on 4th May being the last to leave. The road to be followed, which ran parallel to the trenches for some distance and less than 80 yards in rear, was blocked by at least three large trees, which had been blown down across it by shell-fire, but, in spite of these and the unavoidable noise made in trying to collect units, not a single shell was fired on the road during the whole night, not even at St. Jean, where another block occurred, although the cross-roads were a favourite spot for the enemy to shell every night. Elverdinghe Château was reached at 5 a.m., and, after spending the day in the grounds, the Brigade moved to a wood in A.30 central, where it bivouacked. In spite of their exhausted condition the men of the L.R.B. maintained their march-discipline admirably. At St. Jean the companies formed up and marched the rest of the way in column of route, overtaking the other battalions in the brigade. Those who took part in the march are undoubtedly justified in claiming, that on this occasion at any rate the Territorials held their own with the Regulars.

The following message was sent to all units in the brigade of that day :—

"The Brigadier wishes to congratulate the 11th Infantry Brigade on the gallant way they have held their positions during the past few days under most trying circumstances. He also congratulates them on the skilful way in which the most difficult and dangerous operations of withdrawal at night were carried out."

The casualties in the battle up to this time were : Killed—Lieut. H. B. Price, 2nd Lieut. R. Lintott (only gazetted on 29th April) and 77 Other Ranks ; wounded—H. C. Beard, C. D. Burnell, G. H. G. M. Cartwright, R. D. S. Charles, E. T. Edmunds (R.A.M.C.), R. E. H. Flindt, B. S. Harvey, E. L. Large (died 21.5.15), R. E. Otter, A. E. Sedgwick, A. B. White, L. E. Whitehead, A. S. Wimble and 246 Other Ranks ; missing—9 Other Ranks, and sick—2 Officers and 60 Other Ranks ; total, 408.

The accumulated mails of the battalion arrived that day and proved to be as large as those for all the other battalions in the brigade put together. The number of casualties in the L.R.B. resulted in such a surplus of good things that it was arranged that each company should invite a battalion in the brigade to share it with them, an act which still further cemented the good feeling already existing between the regiment and the rest of the brigade.

The battalion remained bivouacked in the wood until 8th May, upon which date it moved to virgin ground in the wood in A.16.a. During this time it was visited by Lieut.-Gen. Sir Herbert Plumer—commanding an augmented Vth Corps—who directed all ranks to be informed of his appreciation of their excellent conduct during the recent fighting, as well as by Major-Gen. Wilson, the Divisional Commander, who warmly congratulated it on its good work. The former asked Major Bates if he could do anything for him, and the C.O. replied that he would be grateful if his application for some N.C.O.'s to be given commissions could be hurried through. Whether as the result of this or not, three days afterwards a telegram came through granting commissions to S. M. Lines (killed two days later), E. C. Wills, F. D. Charles, G. G. Boston,

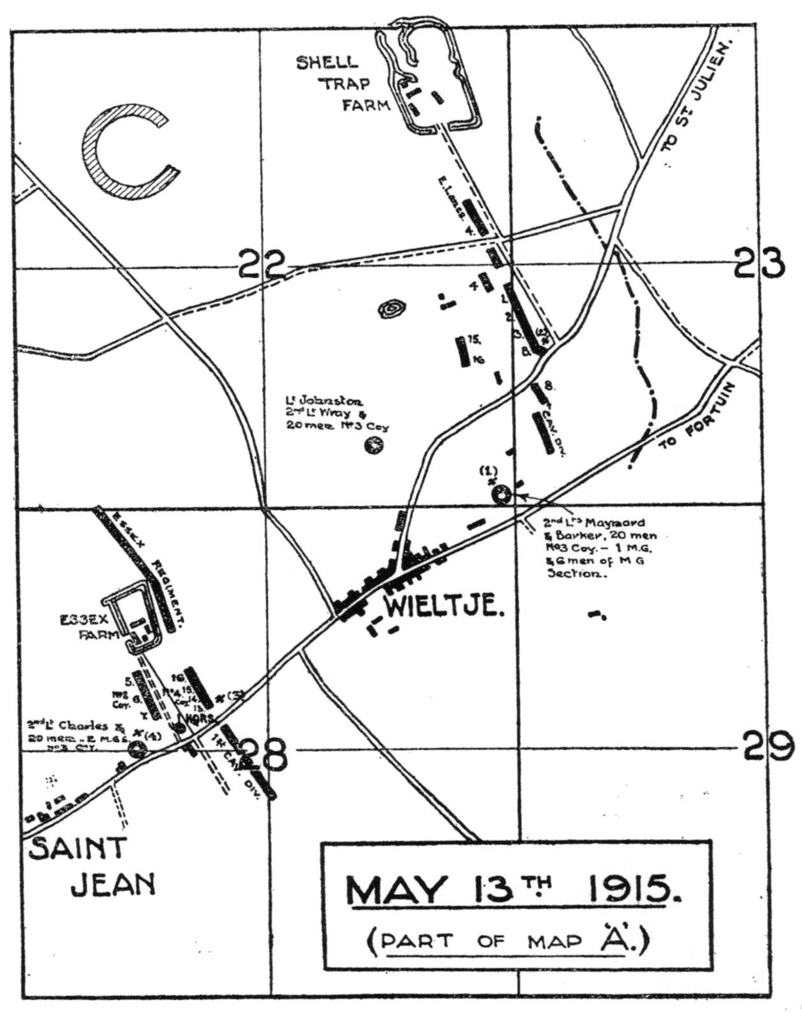

SKETCH MAP No. 4

M. Wray and A. C. Feast, with effect from 8th May. The battalion was promised three or four days' rest, so everyone proceeded to make himself as comfortable as possible, and the C.O. took off his boots for the first time since 23rd April, but at 11 p.m. a staff officer arrived with orders that the battalion was to be at Vlamertinghe Château (H.2.b.) by 6 a.m. next morning. The move was carried out, and the battalion bivouacked for the nights of the 9th and 10th in the ground of the Château, forming a working party on each night to dig trenches on the east of the Yser Canal, north of La Brique in C.26, a line which was at a later date and for many weeks the British front line.

On 11th May the battalion moved into French dug-outs on the bank of the stream, just west of the Yser Canal, north of Ypres in C.25.d.32—I.1.b.55, and there spent the night. On 12th May the L.R.B. was ordered to take over a bit of line held by the Dublins in *C.23.c.* with a minimum of 150 men, and also to occupy the three defended posts east of Wieltje village, with a garrison of 20 men in each. The remainder of the L.R.B. and its head-quarters were to be from the right of Essex Farm (*C.28.a.*), exclusive to St. Jean-Wieltje Road inclusive. Nos. 1 and 2 Companies took over the front line ; No. 3 occupied the defended posts ; and No. 4 Company was with head-quarters. One machine-gun was in the front line, and two in the defended posts round Wieltje. The companies were commanded—No. 1 by Lieut. C. W. Trevelyan ; No. 2 by Capt. J. R. Somers-Smith ; No. 3 by Lieut. H. L. Johnston ; and No. 4 by 2nd Lieut. F. H. Wallis. The M.G. officer was 2nd Lieut. H. R. W. Gooding.

The battalion was about 290 strong in the line when it took over from the Dublins on the night of 12th, a most difficult and dangerous relief, as, just in rear of the front line trench, there was the crest of a low ridge over which the relieving troops were obliged to pass. No. 1 Company and one platoon of No. 2 Company, who were all that the front line could accommodate, moved up the Wieltje-St. Jean Road to a point near the top of the rise, where, owing to machine-gun fire, it was necessary to continue in the ditch on the left of the road and then turn sharp to the left in the open dead ground in rear of the front line. The next move was to get into the front line without suffering heavy casualties from the enemy, who had, unfortunately, spotted the relief of some troops well over to the left, and were very active with their machine-guns, which continually swept the front line. All the conditions of the night assisted the enemy, because, not only was there a sky-line to cross, but every man, as he went over, was silhouetted by the glare of Ypres blazing in the background. However, the men lined out and doubled over, a section or half section at a time ; but when they reached the front line trench they found it in a very bad state, wide, shallow and partially blown in. The platoon on the extreme left was isolated, as about 30 feet of trench had been knocked completely flat, but on the extreme right, touching the road, the conditions were a little better. To add to the general discomfort rain started falling in torrents in the early hours of the morning, and continued to do so throughout the day.

At 4 a.m. on the 13th May a heavy bombardment, which was reported to Brigade at 4.20 a.m., was opened on the front and support lines, as well as on Wieltje. Half an hour later telegraph communications with the front line were severed, and all the rest of the day news had to go through by runners, who did magnificent work, crawling about the back of the front line fully exposed to the terrific fire of the enemy. During the morning a message came down from the left stating that it was possible for the wounded to get away by crawling down a hedge that ran back at right angles from Shelltrap Farm, which was the junction of the L.R.B. left and the right of the E. Lancs, so Capt. Somers-Smith gave orders that wounded men who were unable to use a rifle might try to get down this way, but several of those who acted on this permission were not heard of again, which was not to be wondered at considering that the bombardment was getting more intense every moment. At 6.43 a.m. a brigade message was received to the effect that the 11th Brigade line was to be held at all costs. At 7.35 a.m. three platoons of No. 2 Company and 20 men from No. 4 Company, under Capt. Somers-Smith, were ordered to reinforce the front line, but, before the men of No. 4 Company had got on the move, the remainder of that company was ordered to reinforce as well.

On reaching the line, which was in a horrible state, it was found impossible to accommodate all the reinforcements, and practically the whole of No. 4 Company had to remain out in shell holes, in the pouring rain and terrific shell-fire, for the greater part of the day. It is interesting to note that the L.R.B. reinforced by small parties in artillery formation suffered very few casualties from the very heavy shelling, but that a battalion of Regulars on the left, which reinforced at the same time in extended order with swords fixed, were caught very badly by the salvos of 5·9″ shells bursting in line at once. A runner squirmed his way up to this point in the line to enquire about the state of the garrison, and saw Capt. Somers-Smith, who told him to report that he could "hold on easily." The enemy was paying special attention to the defences on both sides of the road, which was broad and paved, with no obstacles of any kind on its face, and forming an excellent point for a break through. The machine-gun that covered the approach was knocked out during the morning, and the M.G. officer, 2nd Lieut. H. R. W. Gooding, who had only received his commission in the field about a week previously, and most of the crew, were killed. This left an undefended gap of about 30 yards between the right of the L.R.B. and a small piece of trench on the right of the Wieltje Road held by Sergt. Belcher and half a dozen men.

In the early afternoon the men defending the extreme right of the L.R.B. trench experienced a real thrill, for notwithstanding the intense fire there came scrambling into the trench a gun team, with machine-gun and box of ammunition, who had been sent up to take the place of the gun that had been knocked out. Loaded up as they were, it was little short of a miracle that had brought them over the high ground, in full view of the enemy, to the front line, which by this time was rapidly becoming a shambles, as the gap on the left had become much wider, and communication with the platoon on the extreme left been rendered almost impossible owing to German snipers and machine-guns. Early in the afternoon the enemy sent forward in front of the L.R.B. a line of skirmishers, who were shot down, but at a great cost to the garrison, which suffered many fatal casualties from the enemy's fire. This active resistance served to make the enemy realise that the line in that part was still strongly held notwithstanding the terrible punishment that it had received, and no further effort was made to come through on the L.R.B. front. On the left, Shelltrap Farm (*C.22.b.*), which formed the right of the E. Lancs position, changed hands several times during the course of the day, the enemy eventually being driven out at the point of the bayonet by the Essex.

It was difficult to see clearly what was taking place on the battalion's right owing to smoke and trees, but a message which came through battalion head-quarters from the 2nd Cavalry Brigade gives a good idea of the state of affairs there : "The left regiment of the 2nd Cavalry Brigade has been very much cut up by shell-fire, and its trenches practically destroyed. The remnants of the regiment retired. There is thus a gap of about 300 yards between my next regiment and your right. It is impossible to hold this gap thoroughly as we cannot dig trenches owing to machine-gun fire. Two squadrons are doing their best to occupy the gap by holding the shell holes. I have asked them to try and get touch with your right. Will you let me know how the right of your battalion is situated ?" This was received at midday and shows all too clearly how very serious the position was on the right of the battalion. The retirement of the remnants seems to have been due to a misunderstanding, and Capt. Husey, who saw what was going on from the head-quarter trench, was wounded while out in the open under very heavy fire trying to set matters right.

For 300 yards the line held by the 2nd Cavalry Brigade had broken, and left the 11th Infantry Brigade with its right in the air and nothing but Sergt. Belcher's post to protect its flank. So energetic, however, was the tiny garrison of nine men all told, of whom one was killed and three wounded, and so accurate their fire, that the attacking enemy was completely deceived as to the number holding that part of the line, and his effort to break through came to nothing. Sergt. Belcher was fully alive to the importance of the position he held, and continued to bluff the enemy till nightfall, when he and the remains of his small party were relieved. For organising this magnificent stand, which saved the right of the 4th Division, Sergt. Belcher was awarded the Victoria Cross, being the first Territorial in the ranks to receive this decoration. The following N.C.O.'s and riflemen were with Sergt. Belcher on this occasion: Lce.-Corpls. H. J. C. Rowe and J. H. Wheatley (wounded), Rfn. H. G. Buck (wounded), C. M. Evans, G. W. Freeman (killed), H. Parker, H. W. Rowe, R. S. Weeks (wounded). Lce.-Corpl. Rowe and Rfn. Buck were awarded Military Medals for their gallantry.

During the afternoon the enemy were observed, and caught by our rifle fire, massing behind a hedge in front of the battalion, but no attack developed. Though the bombardment continued with unabated fury, and what remained of the original front line was in a deplorable state, the garrison, in spite of being terribly handicapped by dead and wounded who could not be evacuated, continued to fire on the enemy till dusk, when the fighting eased up. The moment that it became sufficiently dark, Capt. Trevelyan ordered all the available men under his command to dig a new line to connect up with the isolated position on the extreme left, and the work was in progress when two companies of the King's Own came up to relieve the L.R.B. This regiment also provided the relief for No. 3 Company of the L.R.B., which had occupied the three defended posts in front of Wieltje about 250 yards behind the front line, and No. 4 Company with head-quarters, who were in a trench running from Essex Farm to the Wieltje–St. Jean Road. These support positions were extremely lucky throughout the whole of the 13th, suffering only one or two casualties, though one large shell fell in the middle of one of the defended posts, but fortunately without exploding.

The battalion, now reduced to 20 Officers and 218 Other Ranks, moved back at night to support trenches, one of which had been dug on the right of Essex Farm by No. 4 Company in about one hour at dawn under very heavy firing. The next day, the 14th May, passed quietly, there being only four casualties, all of which were caused by one shell; but the rain continued, and made the position thoroughly wretched. To add to their discomfort, the packs, which had been left under a hedge behind No. 4 Company before going into the line on the 13th, had all been rifled. After receiving the large mail mentioned earlier, most of the men had either food, tinned milk or chocolate, as well as their razors and washing things, stowed away in the packs, and practically the whole of these were missing. The men were utterly worn out, as the battalion had been on the go for over three weeks, and for the last twenty days the little sleep that was obtained had been in the open. In addition to Capt. Husey, who was Second in Command, Capt. Oppenheim, the Adjutant, had also been wounded on the 13th, and Capt. Somers-Smith and Lieut. H. L. Johnston took over their respective duties.

On the night of the 14th the battalion moved again, this time into Divisional second line. On the 15th orders came through that two companies of the 6th Northumberland Fusiliers, then on the canal bank, were to be attached to the L.R.B. These arrived after dark under the command of Major Headley, and went with the battalion when it moved up to take over a part of the 4th Division support line from the E. Lancs. There were only two casualties on this date, two men being wounded by spent bullets on the way up. On the night of the 16th–17th May the battalion moved back to the east bank of the canal and remained there until the 19th, when orders were received that it was being withdrawn from the 4th Division. While on the canal bank, the battalion and the two attached companies of the Northumberlands worked on the head-quarters' dug-outs for the Brigade on the west side of the canal. On the night of the 19th a move was made to Vlamertinghe, where the men were accommodated in some buildings in rear of the Château, and the battalion learnt that it was to proceed next day to Tatinghem and come under the orders of the G.O.C., G.H.Q. troops.

General Prowse, the Brigadier, came down to the canal bank to say good-bye to the regiment, and handed Major Bates the following farewell Order, in his own handwriting :—

"The Brigadier-General commanding the 11th Infantry Brigade has just learned that the L.R.B. is leaving his command to-night. He deeply regrets that he has therefore no opportunity of personally taking a farewell of all ranks of a battalion which has for the past six months made a reputation for itself which for courage, steadfastness and devotion to duty is second to none in the Expeditionary Force. He and all ranks of the brigade wish them a good time of rest and recuperation after their very trying experience in the late fighting, and hope before long that they may be back again among their old comrades of the 11th Infantry Brigade. Please communicate to all ranks."

In addition to the above message, Brig.-Gen. Prowse made a speech there in which he expressed a hope that he might shortly see the L.R.B. back again.

Before the battalion boarded the motor-buses for its journey, the Divisional Commander addressed all ranks behind his Divisional H.Q. His speech was congratulatory on the recent fighting, and it appeared that Major-General Wilson was really as sorry to lose the L.R.B. as the latter was to be leaving his command for the unknown one of G.H.Q. troops.

The ride to Tatinghem passed without incident, but it was an experience that no one who took part in it is likely to forget, owing to the intense contrast between the month's incessant fighting and the 32-mile joy ride on motor-buses in a westerly direction in glorious weather.

In connection with the foregoing operations, the following letter from the Divisional General was handed to the battalion by the G.O.C., H.Q. troops :—

"I have much pleasure in informing you that the G.O.C. 11th Infantry Brigade has referred in the following terms to the action of the L.R.B. during the operations east of Ypres from the 9th to 13th May : 'The behaviour of this battalion was most gallant and praiseworthy. It stuck to its trenches under heavy shell-fire, and was always dependable and ready for anything.' Signed, H. F. M. Wilson, Major-Gen. Comdg. 4th Divn."

Major W. W. Seymour, commanding the 1st R.B., wrote to Major Bates :—

"We are miserable at hearing that you are being taken away from us. I won't say more now, I cannot, but you will understand what we all feel at being bereft of the support of your braves. I will write as soon as I can find out what is happening to you all. In the meantime the very best of luck from all of the 1st R.B. to our old companions of the L.R.B."

And Lieut.-Col. C. W. Compton, commanding the 1st Somerset L.I., wrote :—

"We hope that we may some day find ourselves alongside the L.R.B. again."

In a subsequent letter Major Seymour wrote :—

"I don't think the very close ties binding the two battalions are likely to be loosed as long as the battalions exist."

It is much to be hoped that they will not. The L.R.B., which has always been intensely proud of its connection with the Rifle Brigade, was extremely pleased to find itself brigaded with one of its battalions, and asks nothing better than to be looked upon as a worthy comrade-in-arms, fit to fight by the side of the Brigade for which it has so much respect, admiration and affection.

During the whole of the battle, with the front line in a constant state of movement, there was not a single day on which the transport failed to get up the rations. This was largely owing to the energy and determination of Lieut. R. Russell, which were beyond praise.

The trench strength of the battalion on leaving Steenwerck on 24th April is not known, but the casualties from that date were : Killed, 4 Officers, 109 Other Ranks ; wounded, 17 Officers, 295 Other Ranks ; wounded, sick and missing, 2 Officers, 73 Other Ranks (of whom 60 were sick).

The battalion reached Tatinghem just after midday, its strength, including transport, then being 19 Officers and 344 Other Ranks, of whom 16 Officers and 196 Other Ranks, or 58 per cent, had come to France on 5th November, 1914, ten of the officers having been in the ranks at that time. While there the L.R.B. thought itself justified in following the custom of the Rifle Brigade, and substituting the term "Rifleman" for that of "Private," but the alteration of "Lance" rank to "Acting" rank was not made. The L.R.B., together with the 1/12th Londons (Rangers) and the 1/13th Londons (Kensingtons), formed a composite battalion, under command of Major H. J. Stafford of the Kensingtons, which was ordered to relieve the 6th Welsh in finding troops for the various railheads, and on 31st May the necessary details moved out. The L.R.B. kept 10 Officers and 113 Other Ranks with H.Q., the remainder being distributed over fourteen different points, and on 1st June the H.Q. details marched into St. Omer, the transport being disbanded. Lieut. Woolley, of The Queen Victoria Rifles (1/9th Londons), had won the V.C., and a telegram of congratulation was sent to them, to which the following reply was received :—

"The O.C. Queen Victoria Rifles, on behalf of the Officers, N.C.O.'s and Riflemen of the regiment, begs to thank the Officers, N.C.O.'s and Riflemen of the London Rifle Brigade for their wire conveying their congratulations on the occasion of Lieut. Woolley being awarded the V.C. The Q.V.R.'s send the best of wishes and good luck to the L.R.B., and hope to be able to send a similar wire to you soon."

A week or two later Sergt. Belcher was granted the V.C. for his gallant work on 13th May, and the following telegrams were exchanged :—

"To O.C., L.R.B. and Officers, N.C.O.'s and Riflemen, I beg to send on behalf of the 1st Battalion Queen Victoria Rifles serving at the front our most hearty congratulations to Lce.-Sergt. D. W. Belcher upon being awarded the V.C. and for the honour he has brought thereby to himself and the distinguished regiment that he belongs to. All Q.V.R.'s send our best wishes and good luck to all the L.R.B. Yours sincerely, V. W. F. Dickins, Lieut.-Col."

"To the Officer Commanding, Officers, N.C.O.'s, and Riflemen Q.V.R. On behalf of the Officers, N.C.O.'s and Riflemen of the London Rifle Brigade I wish to thank you for your letter of congratulation on Lce.-Sergt. Belcher being awarded the V.C. I am glad that the hopes expressed at the end of your letter in reply to our congratulations on Lieut. Woolley's V.C., have borne fruit so speedily. If the Press is correct in stating that Lce.-Sergt. Belcher used to be in your regiment, we do not grudge you the reflected glory. The best of luck to you all. Arthur S. Bates, Major, Commanding L.R.B."

A close intimacy had existed between the Q.V.R. and the L.R.B. since 1912, when after some manœuvres the latter put up the former in camp at Lulworth for a night, while in the following year the Q.V.R. entertained the officers and sergeants of the L.R.B. royally when in camp at Perham Down. The two battalions went to France on the same day, lay alongside each other in the rest camp at Havre, and later were both in the 169th Brigade, so that the friendship was firmly cemented.

FIRST BATTALION

Part III. May 19, 1915—June 30, 1916

St. Omer—Blendecques—Poperinghe—St. Eloi—Formation of 56th Division—Huppy—Magnicourt—Halloy—Hébuterne.

(*The Map referred to is A, and No.* 5 *facing p.* 398.)

ON moving to St. Omer on May 19th, the officers of the Composite Battalion were at first accommodated in billets, but subsequently went under canvas, and obtained permission to mess in the Salle d'Honneur of the 8th Regiment of French Infantry in the Caserne de la Barre. The colours of the regiment were captured at Waterloo, and a photograph of them was on the wall of the mess. When leaving G.H.Q. the officers of the L.R.B. presented a large and handsome inkpot with a silver lid on which the regimental crest was soldered and a suitable inscription engraved. The following acknowledgment of the gift was received :—

" My Colonel,

" I thank you and the officers of the London Rifle Brigade in the name of the officers of the 8th Regiment of Infantry for having sent us such a handsomely engraved inkpot. After the Victory, we will take it back with us to the Salle d'Honneur that you know at St. Omer where we shall always guard it as a souvenir of our glorious comradeship in arms. As Frenchmen we should dearly love to see you with us, and your presence in our barracks would surely be a token of respect to the glory that we have won, and a happy ending to the hopes that we have in common. With our kindest remembrances to all your officers and please accept my most cordial wishes towards yourself.

" *Vive l'entente cordiale,*

" Lieut.-Col. Roubert."

Early in June shoulder patches, with "L.R.B." in green on a black ground, were taken into use in place of the metal shoulder plates issued, a change which satisfied a wish of long standing. The patches were paid for by the men themselves for quite a long time, but, after special recruiting for the regiment was stopped, they were provided out of regimental funds. Leave was given almost at once to officers and men, and was very welcome. On 19th June a service was held in the Soldiers' Club, at the same time that a memorial service was held in London by the Bishop. On 30th June the Composite Battalion moved under canvas on the Champs des Manœuvres.

The duties on the lines of communication consisted in helping the railway transport officer, or other officer in charge, in every way possible, and the L.R.B. detachments carried this out so whole-heartedly and efficiently, that they won golden opinions from all under whom they worked. In addition to the ordinary duties, there were escorts to be found for British and German prisoners. After the battle of Loos every N.C.O. and rifleman was sent off post haste, and probably all the prisoners captured then were escorted by men of the Composite Battalion. The following officers joined from England: Lieuts. A. T. B. de Cologan, G. H. Cholmeley, G. E. S. Fursdon; 2nd Lieuts. C. G. Brodie, A. B. White, E. R. Appleton and P. J. Aste; and on the next day 2nd Lieuts. I. R. Pogose and E. W. Rose arrived, all sent out by the 2nd Battalion. On 27th June at 11.45 p.m. a hostile aeroplane dropped six bombs on the town, and did a good deal of material damage. The official report stated that they were dropped on the outskirts of St. Omer, but the nearest was only 200 yards from the house of the Commander-in-Chief. On 9th August, Lieut. B. S. Harvey rejoined from England, and 2nd Lieut. A. K. Dodds from Havre. On 11th August the Composite Battalion was resolved into its component units again. On 20th August, Capt. Trevelyan, Capt. A. L. Lintott, Lieut. de Cologan and Capt. R. E. Otter were placed in command of "A," "B," "C" and "D" Companies respectively, and Lieut. Harvey became machine-gun officer.

Early in September it became an open secret that a British offensive was shortly to be made and the use of gas on a large scale was said to be going to form a feature of the attack. Lieut.-Col. Foulkes, R.E., the Chief of the Gas School at Helfaut, quite close to St. Omer, came over and asked for the help of some L.R.B. officers. Lieut. Wallis and 2nd Lieuts. White and F. D. Charles, who were selected, went over, together with Capt. R. E. Otter, who was allowed to go at his own request, and within two days of their return on 28th September they wrote the reports, which will be found in Appendix A, while the events were fresh in their minds. In July 9 N.C.O.'s and riflemen were sent to the Cadet School at Blendecques for commissions in the field; in August 33 N.C.O.'s and men left for commissions, and 4 were sent to Blendecques; while in September 22 left for England for commissions, and 22 proceeded to Blendecques.

On 2nd October the L.R.B. was transferred from Line of Communications to G.H.Q. troops, when the following special Routine Order was issued by Col. A. Sprot, Commandant of No. 1 Section, Line of Communications :—

"The London Rifle Brigade is leaving this Section shortly. The battalion came from the front, where it had greatly distinguished itself, and it has since been employed on various and important duties on the Lines of Communications, often entailing much laborious work. These duties have always been performed with cheerfulness and zeal, and the conduct of all ranks has been exceptionally good. The Commandant heartily wishes all ranks of the battalion every success in the future."

Letters were also received from various others, under whom the battalion had served, all expressing high appreciation of the excellent work and conduct of the men. On the same day the battalion marched to Blendecques and went into billets there, the Artists very kindly lending their band, which went all the way and was much appreciated.

Intensive training and reorganisation were carried on until 25th October, when the battalion embussed for Ryveld. The strength by this time was 25 Officers and 806 Other Ranks, as large drafts had been received from the 3rd Battalion, which from this time forward supplied all reinforcements from the L.R.B. Unfortunately, for some unknown reason, the system of filling up the gaps from reserve battalions wherever possible was not adhered to, and things went so far in one case that men of one unit at the base were actually ordered to exchange badges with men of another, and the two parties were sent up in the same train to join their new battalions. Naturally the men, who had had the spirit and traditions of their own regiments instilled into them at home, were upset at finding themselves in an unexpected atmosphere, and the regiments to which they were sent had to start them all over again. To add insult to injury the Higher Authority, with a complete disregard of the paradox to which it was committing itself and with its customary lack of humour, was continuously thrusting the doctrine of the importance of *esprit de corps* down the throats of the infantry.

The L.R.B. was now attached in place of the H.A.C. to the 8th Brigade under Brig.-Gen. J. D. Maclachan, which consisted of 2nd Royal Scots, 4th Middlesex (which was subsequently replaced by the 8th Yorks), 13th King's Liverpool, 7th King's Own Shropshire L.I., and the L.R.B., and formed part of the 3rd Division, under Major-Gen. A. Haldane in the IInd Army. The billets in Ryveld were bad and very cramped and the weather was wet. Instructions were received to organise 68 Other Ranks as battalion bombers, and 14 as snipers; the latter were under Lieut. F. D. Charles, and the former under Lieut. G. G. Boston, and 2nd Lieut. R. L. Hill. On 28th information was received that the L.R.B. was to be trained as a Pioneer Battalion under R.E. instruction, which caused a good deal of dissatisfaction, but company as well as pioneer training was carried on until 14th November, when the latter ceased and the battalion was never used as a Pioneer unit. On 27th October a picked party of 20 Other Ranks, which included all N.C.O.'s and men whose names had been mentioned to "Higher Authority," under the Regimental Sergt.-Major J. Adams, formed part of a Composite Battalion which was inspected by H.M. the King. During the month 30 more men were sent away to take up commissions, 17 to England, and 13 to Blendecques. The officers serving with the battalion on 25th October were :—

Head-quarters

Lieut.-Col. A. S. Bates. Commanding.
Capt. R. H. Husey. Second in Command.
Capt. H. L. Johnston. Adjutant.
Lieut. J. R. S. Petersen. Quartermaster.
Lieut. R. Russell. Transport Officer.
Capt. B. S. Harvey. M.G. Officer.

"A" Company

Capt. C. W. Trevelyan.
Capt. G. H. Cholmeley.
Lieut. F. D. Charles.
2nd Lieut. P. J. Aste.
2nd Lieut. E. R. Appleton.

"B" Company

Capt. A. L. Lintott.
Capt. J. G. Robinson.
Lieut. E. C. Wills.
Lieut. G. G. Boston.
2nd Lieut. P. B. B. Oldfield.

"C" Company

Major C. H. F. Thompson.
Capt. A. T. B. de Cologan.
2nd Lieut. E. W. Rose.
2nd Lieut. H. C. Barker.
2nd Lieut. R. L. Hill.

"D" Company

Capt. R. E. Otter.
Lieut. F. H. Wallis.
Lieut. F. H. Crews.
2nd Lieut. R. Hogg.
2nd Lieut. I. R. Pogose.

Capt. Somers-Smith returned from England, where he had been kept back training the officers of the 3rd Battalion, on 1st November, and took over "A" Company, Capt. Cholmeley going to "D." On 8th November Capt. Otter went off for duty as Court-Martial Officer with the Ist Army, and Capt. Somers-Smith took over "D" Company, handing "A" to Capt. Trevelyan. On 20th Capt. Lintott proceeded to England to join the M.G. Corps at Grantham, and Capt. Somers-Smith took "B," handing over "D" to Capt. de Cologan. On 17th October the brigade, including the L.R.B., marched past Lieut.-Gen. Plumer, commanding the IInd Army, and on that night a barn in "B" Company's billet was destroyed by fire due to "spontaneous combustion," as ran the verdict of a court of enquiry, which contained two members who were lawyers. The usual training went on until 23rd November, when the brigade moved to Reninghelst (G.34) and Poperinghe. The L.R.B. marched to the latter place, 26 Officers and 751 Other Ranks, via Winnizeele and Watou, a distance of about ten and a half miles, over roads which were in a very bad and congested state, and billeted on arrival. The Rev. K. N. Crisford was attached to the L.R.B. on the same day. On 26th the C.O. and Company Commanders inspected the trenches at Voormezeele (I.31) and St. Eloi (O.2), and on 29th the battalion took over its allotted section, and head-quarters dug-outs. Orders had been issued for busses to take the battalion as far as Reninghelst, but these were cancelled at the last moment, and the men had to make a very long and tiring march. As the accommodation at Voormezeele was insufficient, one company was left behind under canvas at Reninghelst. The L.R.B. took over from the Liverpool Scottish, with the Royal Scots on its right and the K.S.L.I. on its left, the 76th Infantry Brigade being on the right of the 8th. The tour lasted till 5th December, and the attempt to get the trenches, which were very wet and in shocking condition, into something like shape involved a great deal of hard work. The rain was incessant, and the Boolaardbek stream, running by battalion head-quarters at Voormezeele, rose six or seven feet in one night, with the result that all the dug-outs near head-quarters, if not head-quarters themselves, were flooded. The battalion rested in Poperinghe till 12th, and the next tour lasted from 13th to 21st December, when, on coming out, a march was made to Vlamertinghe, where the battalion entrained in an armoured train and was taken to Poperinghe. During the tour there was an alarm on 19th, in consequence of a heavy bombardment to the north, where the Germans were attacking. Many lachrymatory shells were fired on the Ypres-Lille Road, some of which affected the head-quarter dug-outs, but otherwise the gas blew behind the line. The cloud-gas attack on this date was terrific, and its effects were felt beyond Poperinghe. The battalion was in the line again from 28th December to 4th January, 1916, and, on coming out, marched to Dickebusch (H.33). The casualties from 29th November to the end of the year were four killed and ten wounded. The next two tours were from 11th to 17th January and from 25th January to 1st February, and were uneventful. The casualties during the month of January were two killed and nine wounded. During the month Capt. Robinson and 2nd

Lieuts. Barker and Hogg returned to England, and the following officers came out: Lieut. P. Titley, 2nd Lieuts. B. Bromiley, H. M. Camden, G. E. Clode-Baker, F. E. Hewitt, B. L. E. Pocock, E. E. Pool, L. H. Pullen, C. H. Sell, H. Smith, F. M. Wheatley, and E. R. Williamson. With the exception of the first-named all these had been trained in the 3rd Battalion, and were the first to be sent out by it. 2nd Lieut. F. M. Wheatley was wounded during his first night at the Bluff (I.34) with a working party which had been sent to help the battalion on the left to consolidate after the Huns had blown up a large mine. Owing to the machine-guns (Maxims) being taken away from battalions in order to be brigaded as a separate force, the L.R.B. lost its four guns and personnel, including transport, and 2nd Lieuts. Pool and Pullen went with them. Lewis guns, which were issued in constantly increasing numbers, took their place in the battalion.

The whole winter was spent in the salient and was very wretched, but there were moments of brightness, as may be seen from the following correspondence, which explains itself and proves that even the Staff can unbend sometimes. Probably the owner of the pig obtained no compensation, but, as the battalion left the 8th Infantry Brigade after writing Minute 14, this cannot be said for certain. It is, of course, just possible that the dossier is still going wearily to and fro between the various departments of the Army.

The facts on which the correspondence was based were that a pig belonging to a farmer at Ryveld died on November 28th, 1915, from eating filth soaked in creosol, which had been spread broadcast in the billet by the troops owing to the disgusting condition of the farm. The owner wrote to the Claims Officer of the Corps and claimed 110 francs.

Min. 1.

D.A. & Q.M.G., Nth Corps. Q.V. 2108. 2/12/15.

To 3rd Division.

(Enclosing letter from farmer.)

For enquiry and adjustment please.

H. M. Montgomery, Lieut.-Col.
A.Q.M.G., Nth Corps.

2/12/15.

Min. 2.

A.A. & Q.M.G., 3rd Div. A/5993.

To 8th Inf. Bde.

Will you please enquire into this lamentable business ?

J. BUXTON, Major,
3/12/15. D.A. & Q.M.G., 3rd Divn.

To O.C., L.R.B. *Min.* 3.

For report as to attached letter.

J. N. MACREADY, Capt.,
3/12/15. Staff Capt., 8th Inf. Bde.

To 8th Inf. Bde. *Min.* 4.

Reference attached, all the billets at Ryveld were in an extremely insanitary condition and needed liberal sprinkling of creosol and other disinfectants.

The pigs at this billet were allowed to roam at will, and, although personally and forcibly warned on frequent occasions, they were always routing about in the latrines and rubbish pits.

R. H. HUSEY, Capt.,
7/12/15. For O.C., L.R.B.

Min. 5.

To H.-Qrs., 3rd Division.

Forwarded. Please see Minute 4.

J. D. McLACHLAN, Brig.-Gen.,
7/12/15. Commanding 8th Inf. Bde.

Min. 6.

D.A. & Q.M.G., Nth Corps. V.Q. 2108. 10/12/15.

To Nth Corps.

Please see Minute 4.

It appears that the pigs should have been kept under better control. Latrines are properly disinfected and are not fit places in which pigs should be allowed to feed.

It is not considered that this is a fair claim against the public.

R. H. COLLINS, Lieut.-Col.,
A.A. & Q.M.G. for G.O.C.
9/12/15. 3rd Division.

To 3rd Division. *Min.* 7.

Although, as you say, the pigs in question were not well under control, they were probably conforming to the customs of the country.

It seems clear that, but for the presence of British troops and creosol, the dead pig might still be alive ; in these circumstances the owner should receive compensation for the value of the pig. H. MONTGOMERY, Lieut.-Col.,

11/12/15. A.Q.M.G., Nth Corps.

Min. 8.

A.A. & Q.M.G., 3rd Div. A/5993.

To A.D.V.S., 3rd Division.

Passed.

Will you please express an opinion as to the demise of this unfortunate animal. In view of the habits and customs of this country, is it probable that swine fever is prevalent, and that, should the animal have had the seeds of the disease in him, his orgy of savoury feeding would only have been indirectly responsible for his untimely end ?

(for) J. BUXTON, Lieut.-Col.,

12/12/15. A.A. & Q.M.G. 3rd Divn.

Min. 9.

To A.A. & Q.M.G., 3rd Division.

I regret I am unable to give any opinion as to the cause of this miserable pig's death.

If you can arrange for the body to be brought to —— I will detail an officer to make a post-mortem examination.

G. CONDER, Major,

12/12/15. A.D.V.S., 3rd Divn.

Min. 10.

A.A. & Q.M.G., 3rd Divn. A/5993.

To Acting Claims Officer, 3rd Division.

As a considerable time has elapsed since the demise of the unfortunate animal the course suggested in Min. 9 would probably serve no useful purpose.

Will you, therefore, proceed with the adjustment of this claim. R. H. COLLINS, Lieut.-Col.,

16/1/16. A.A. & Q.M.G., 3rd Divn.

Min. 11.

To A.A. & Q.M.G., 3rd Division.

Could the officer who last saw this unfortunate animal alive give some particulars as to age, weight, etc., so as to enable me to arrive at a fair valuation ?

H. WARING, Major,
17/1/16. Claims Officer, 3rd Divn.

Min. 12.

A.A. & Q.M.G., 3rd Div. A/5993.

To 8th Inf. Bde.

Can the O.C., L.R.B., claim to be a judge of fat stock sufficient for him to express an opinion ?

J. BUXTON, Major,
18/1/16. D.A.Q.M.G., 3rd Divn.

To L.R.B. *Min.* 13.

Can anyone in your battalion who was acquainted with the deceased beast give an expert opinion as to its weight, age and condition when still in good health ?

A. DOWNS, Capt.,
for Staff Captain,
19/1/16. 8th Inf. Bde.

Min. 14.

To H.-Qrs., 8th Inf. Bde.

Reference, Min. 12—

(*a*) I regret that my experience is not sufficient to enable me to judge fat stock.

(*b*) The description given of the animal in the original claim is so sketchy that I fear no officer of my battalion can recognise the pig in question.

(*c*) In every sense of the word these animals were ubiquitous and they were extraordinarily similar to one another in form and habits. In fact, I consider the fact that only one died is proof of the extreme care taken by us in defending latrines and rubbish pits from pilferage (*vide* Min. 4).

(*d*) Under the circumstances I much fear that the owner

must set off the loss of this animal against the profit accruing from our visit. If he does this honestly, I am convinced that the balance will be in his favour and the pig's.

ARTHUR S. BATES, Lieut.-Col.,
Commanding L.R.B.

On 8th February the L.R.B. received orders to join the 169th Infantry Brigade which was then being formed, and on 9th it entrained at Godwaersvelde, detraining on 10th at Pont Remy and marching to Huppy in very fine cold weather. The strength was 29 Officers and 761 Other Ranks. The brigade formed part of the 56th Division under Major-Gen. C. P. A. Hull, which was in the VIth Corps commanded by Lieut.-Gen. Sir T. L. Keir, K.C.B.

The composition of the 56th Division was as follows :—

167th Infantry Brigade (Brig.-Gen. F. H. Burnell-Nugent, D.S.O., to 26/7/16, then Brig.-Gen. G. Freeth, C.M.G., D.S.O.):
- 1/7th Middlesex.
- 1/8th Middlesex.
- 1/1st Londons (Royal Fusiliers).
- 1/3rd Londons (Royal Fusiliers, broken up 30/1/18).
- 167th T.M. Battery.
- 167th M.G. Coy. (later 56th Bn. M.G. Corps).
- 512th Field Coy. R.E. (came out as 2/1 Lond. Field Coy. R.E.)

168th Infantry Brigade (Brig.-Gen. G. G. Loch, C.M.G., D.S.O.):
- 1/4th Londons (Royal Fusiliers).
- 1/12th Londons (Rangers, broken up 30/1/18).
- 1/13th Londons (Kensingtons).
- 1/14th Londons (London Scottish).
- 168th T.M. Battery.
- 168th M.G. Coy. (later 56th Bn. M.G. Corps).
- 513th Field Coy. R.E. (came out as 2/2 Lond. Field Coy. R.E.).

169th Infantry Brigade (Brig.-Gen. E. S. D'E. Coke, C.M.G., D.S.O.) :
- 1/2nd Londons (Royal Fusiliers).
- 1/5th Londons (L.R.B.).
- 1/9th Londons (Queen Victoria Rifles, broken up 30/1/18).
- 1/16th Londons (Queen's Westminsters).
- 169th T.M. Battery.
- 169th M.G. Coy. (later 56th Bn. M.G. Corps).
- 416th Field Coy. R.E. (Edinburgh).

1/3rd London Brigade, R.F.A.
No. 4 Coy. (216) Train.
2/3rd London Field Ambulance.

With the exception of the 1/7th and 1/8th Middlesex, the infantry of the division was composed of 1st line London Territorial battalions which had come out to France at an early date as separate units, and were now withdrawn from the various divisions in the B.E.F. to which they had been attached ; and the 1st, 2nd, 3rd, and 4th Londons, who had been sent to Malta as garrison in September, 1914, and afterwards to France. It remained without change until the end of the war except that certain units disappeared in 1918, when brigades were reduced from four battalions to three, and, as will be seen later, made no small name for itself by its gallant work. The brigade remained at Huppy training until February 27th, when it marched in a heavy snow-storm to Ergnies and went into billets for training. The casualties from 15th October, 1915, were: killed, 10 Other Ranks ; wounded, 1 Officer (Wheatley), 27 Other Ranks ; evacuated sick, 2 Officers (Aste and E. R. Williamson), 165 Other Ranks. Capt. Cholmeley went sick about January 7th and rejoined February 27th. On leaving the 3rd Division Major-Gen. A. Haldane wrote to the C.O. : " I wish to say how sorry I am that you and your fine battalion are leaving the 3rd Division after so brief a stay in it, and I wish you all good luck and God-speed for the rest of the war wherever you may be." While at Ergnies the Battalion Sports Meeting was held, at which " D " Company won the 4-mile Team Race, as well as a Guard Mounting competition under 2nd Lieut. I. R. Pogose on 3rd March. On March 11th an exciting Rugby match was played against the Q.V.R., and on the next day the L.R.B. had a tiring march to Gezaincourt, moving on 16th through Doullens to Sibiville, where it enjoyed six days' rest, in the course of which a demonstration of liquid fire was given with a flammenwerfer that had been captured at Hooge. On the same day (16th) " A " Company was sent to the head-quarters of the IIIrd Army at Beauquesnes, and, after moving with them to St. Pol, returned to the battalion on 24th April, but without Lieut. E. R. Williamson and 12 Other Ranks who were sent away to a Trench Mortar Battery.

On 22nd March the move was completed by a march to the village of Magnicourt sur Canche, where the inhabitants were found to be hostile and with strong objections to the military occupying their stables and barns. However, in spite of this the battalion, reinforced up to strength in officers and men, as well as playing, trained hard and in a very short time the standard was as high and *esprit de corps* as strong as ever. The men grew so keen about bomb throwing that it was looked upon as a pastime instead of a parade, and practised voluntarily in friendly rivalry. On 30th F.-M. Sir Douglas Haig passed through and caused a tremor when he told the Guard of Honour, which was "D" Company, L.R.B., to "slope" from the "present." Fortunately not a man moved until the command to "order" was given.

The battalion remained there during the whole of April, training in the morning and playing games in the afternoon. Besides route-marches to St. Pol, which were very popular on account of the open-air warm baths there, a Tactical Scheme was carried out on 6th, which will certainly live in the memory of the Transport Section, because of its acting as cavalry in an attack on Magnicourt made by the whole battalion with the exception of "B" Company, which was defending the village. Before very long a combined charge of Heavy Draughts, Mules, Riders, Pack-ponies and Julie (a mare brought out by Major King which became a battalion pet and served with it till the end of the war, when she was shot to prevent her sale to the Belgians) gained a great victory over the defending infantry, largely due to the argument of the Transport Officer, Capt. R. Russell who led the charge, that each horse represented a squadron and that only the imaginary animals had been killed. During the same month orders were received that steel helmets, of which a few had been issued previously as an experiment, were invariably to be worn on all parades and for all duties. At first they were rather jeered at, but the real value of them was soon recognised through their saving many lives, although they were heavy and hot to wear, owing to want of ventilation. Several internal changes took place. Capt. R. E. Otter was made staff-captain of the 168th Brigade; Capt. H. L. Johnston took over command of "C" Company; and Capt. F. H. Wallis became adjutant in his stead. Capt. Johnston was the first officer, not a Regular, to hold the appointment of adjutant in the 1st Battalion L.R.B., and, as he had great power of organisation and capacity for hard work which he brought to bear on all the routine work in the Orderly Room, he proved as conspicuous a success there as he had been in the trenches. Sergt. A. Gordon received a commission and took over the transport vice Capt. R. Russell, who had been invalided home; 2nd Lieuts. C. E. Ovington and W. G. Perrin, with 31 Other Ranks, left the battalion to form the 169th M.G. Company; Capt. Trevelyan handed over "A" Company to Capt. Cholmeley on being appointed A.P.M. at Boulogne. On 6th May Lieut. Petersen exchanged duties as Quartermaster with Lieut. W. Kelly from the 3rd Battalion.

On 7th May the brigade marched to Halloy and went into hutments there, joining the VIIth Corps. On 20th May it marched to St. Amand, and on 21st to Hébuterne (*K*.9), where the L.R.B. went into trenches in "Y" Sector, two companies being in the front line and two in support, with the 5th Notts and Derby on its left and the Kensingtons on its right, remaining there till 27th. In view of the offensive which it was common knowledge was about to take place, the division had been instructed to dig assembly trenches in advance of the existing front line, and, in order to secure this operation being carried out with as little interference from the enemy as possible, the L.R.B. was ordered to occupy the position known as "Z" hedge (*K*.10) for the two days before the work was actually done. This was a difficult task, because a small bank was the only cover in the hedge and no assistance except rifle fire could be given by day, so that the men had to lie absolutely quiet all through the hours of daylight, knowing that if they were seen by the enemy they must be wiped out. The following battalion order dated 24th May gives details of the operations:—

1. During the night of 24th/25th the Intelligence Officer will have "Z" hedge patrolled and ensure that it is clear and report to Lieut. Clode-Baker at 1.30 a.m. that it is clear of the enemy. Lieut. Clode-Baker will establish a post in the hedge of 15 men. This post will be maintained until relieved by covering troops of the 167th Infantry Brigade during the night of 26th/27th.

2. This post will drive off all hostile patrols and will act with utmost vigour. On night 25th/26th it is to forestall German

patrols and prevent interference with the pegging party. On evening of 26th it will act as covering party until relieved by troops of the 167th Infantry Brigade.

3. Lieut. Clode-Baker and 15 riflemen will form the day post on 25th. 2nd Lieut. Pogose and 30 O.R. will relieve Lieut. Clode-Baker at dusk on evening of 25th. Lieut. Bromiley and 15 riflemen will relieve 2nd Lieut. Pogose at 1.30 a.m. on the 26th and remain there until relieved by 167th Infantry Brigade troops that evening. Each party will carry 24 hours' rations and water with them.

4. Lieut. E. C. Wills and 20 O.R. will be in the trench ready to reinforce if necessary.

5. The O.C. above parties will ensure that no maps, papers or personal letters, etc., are carried by any man.

As an additional safeguard observers kept a close watch on the party, which could easily be seen from the British line all day. On the night of 25th/26th Capt. Somers-Smith, and about 110 Other Ranks from " A " and " B " Companies under their own officers, formed a covering screen about 4/500 yards in front of the British front line, while officers and R.E. from 167th Infantry Brigade marked out the new line with strings, and parties under " B " Company sergeants cut five lanes through the barbed wire for the following night's operations. The night was very dark, and rain fell heavily, which probably explains why the enemy never discovered that unusual work was in progress. On the night of 26th/27th the 3rd Londons and 7th Middlesex from the 167th Brigade came up, relieved Bromiley's party in the " Z " hedge on the way out, and dug the new line with communication trenches and wire, getting back to billets in Souastre by 3 a.m. Lieut.-Col. Bates was personally congratulated by Gen. Hull and the C.O.'s of the two digging battalions (3rd Londons and 7th Middlesex) on the excellent work done and the great help afforded by the L.R.B., while the scouts, under Lieut. Pogose, had also done very well. This line was garrisoned by strong posts of which the L.R.B. held five, with an officer, N.C.O., 10 men and a Lewis gun in each. The enemy tried to raid one of these posts which was held by " D " Company one night, but, after an exchange of bombs for some time, was driven off by Lewis gun fire. As daylight showed that he had left behind him a number of bombs, wire cutters, an automatic pistol, and equipment, some of which had been cut off wounded men, besides one dead man, the party must have been a fairly strong one. The doings on 27th can be best described by a quotation from a diary :—

" Guns were now being massed, and we had behind us artillery with an unlimited supply of ammunition. Never before had the battalion had such artillery support. Whenever we were bombarded by minenwerfers, four shells were immediately sent over for every one from the Germans. If the bombardment did not stop, the size of our shells was increased, 4–5″ Hows. taking over from the 18 pounders, 6″ joining in later, and finally the 9″ Hows. stopping all further argument as to who could last the longer. The R.F.C. gained complete mastery of the air, and German aeroplanes were only seen at rare intervals. At night, work was continued in the improvement of the new trenches. Communication trenches were duck-boarded, wire strengthened, etc., but this work was now carried out during frequent bombardments, heavy minenwerfers being the German's favourite weapon. On the night of 28th, this interesting and exciting trench tour ended by the Q.V.R. relieving us."

The casualties during the tour had been 2nd Lieut. Sawbridge, slightly wounded on 25th, and four Other Ranks killed, with 14 wounded. The L.R.B. then marched to Bayencourt and went into billets until 3rd June, finding large working parties each night. Although the enemy knew by this time exactly what was being done, and the shelling was heavier, the regiment had the good luck to have only two men wounded as its casualties. During the month the following Officers joined from the 3rd Battalion : Lieuts. W. Kelly and C. W. Long ; 2nd Lieuts. W. E. M. Gardiner, J. R. Carrier, G. St. J. Martin, B. F. Sawbridge, F. A. Balls, A. Warner, C. V. Balkwill, R. E. Petley ; Capt. B. S. Harvey rejoined, and Capt. L. Crombie was attached as M.O. All the 72 Officers sent out from home so far had reached the battalion, and 1408 out of the 1466 reinforcements despatched. The total strength at this time was 30 Officers and 936 Other Ranks, some of whom were at courses or temporarily absent.

On 3rd June the L.R.B. marched to Halloy and stayed there until 13th June, when it returned to Bayencourt. The time was spent in digging a copy of the hostile trench system, which was the objective, and practising the attack over it. On 9th June, the Lord Mayor of London[1] visited the battalion with the Divisional General and Brigadier, but, as he was very late in arriving and it was a Sunday afternoon, his remarks were listened to with some excusable impatience. The billets at Bayencourt were occupied until 16th, when a move was made to Hébuterne, and the Queen's Westminsters were relieved in "Y" sector, where the arrival of heavy batteries made more digging necessary. On 21st June the L.R.B. was relieved and marched to St. Amand, but moved again next day to Halloy, where work on the copy-trenches and practice of the attack took up the time up to 26th, when a full rehearsal took place with smoke, etc., before the Brigade, Divisional, Corps, and Army Commanders. The C.O. obtained leave for each man to take three bombs into action, but not without some difficulty, as the Higher Authorities fostered the idea that the attack would be a walk over. On 27th June the battalion marched to Souastre, and dumped surplus stores, kits, etc.

As the men had been having a hard time in one way and another, and the weather had been exceptionally bad, they found a rest, which was given them on 29th, very welcome. "Z" day was postponed for two days in consequence of the rain, but on 30th, a fine day, the L.R.B. moved up to "Y" sector, and took over from the 2nd Londons, in preparation for the attack next morning.

On this occasion orders were received for the first time that battalions were not to take more than 23 Officers into action and that Seconds in Command were to be left out, in order that regiments which were badly cut up might have a nucleus on which to build again: afterwards this became customary. As Major Husey protested strongly against being sent to the rear, duties were found for him which would allow him to be nearer the front.

[1] Sir Charles Wakefield.

FIRST BATTALION

Part IV. July 1—July 5, 1916

Battle of Gommecourt.

(*The map referred to is No.* 5 *facing p.* 398.)

THE object of the fighting on the Somme, which began on 1st July, was partly to relieve the French fighting at Verdun, and partly that the British might make an offensive after due preparation. The front was one of twenty-five miles, and extended from Gommecourt on the north to Fay, five miles above Chaulnes, on the south. The British and French lines met at Maricourt, and an advance side by side had many obvious advantages. If successful, the Germans would have been compelled to retire to what was afterwards known as the Hindenburg line—as, indeed, they did in the spring of 1917. The enemy had made vast preparations to meet the coming storm, of which, apart from other information, they were warned by the bombardment that began in the middle of June and increased in intensity as the month wore on. The Armies who began the attack were the Fourth British, under Sir Henry Rawlinson, and the Sixth French, under Fayolle, but before the fighting ceased there were few, if any, British troops which had not been drawn into the maëlstrom at one time or another.

The battle of Gommecourt took place on 1st July and the following special battalion order was issued by Lieut.-Col. Bates :—

" On the eve of what will probably be the biggest Action on the Western front, the results of which, if successful, will certainly shorten the war, the Commanding Officer realises that once the assault is launched nothing that he can do will materially affect the course of events.

"He is absolutely confident, however, that all ranks will do their duty and that the Battalion will fully accomplish its task and add 'Gommecourt' to 'Ypres' and its other battle honours.

"The reputation that the L.R.B. has won through sheer hard work is now second to no unit in the T.F. This must be maintained and should be enhanced.

"The C.O. wishes all ranks a clear course to their objective and a safe return when the Battalion is relieved.

"Those who fall will do so in the sure knowledge that they have done their duty. More is impossible."

The 56th Divisional Special Order ran as follows :—

"The General Officer Commanding desires to express to all ranks his appreciation of the good work they have done during the past weeks, often under very adverse conditions.

"All ranks of all arms have co-operated to establish a completely new system of trenches, with all the necessary gun positions, observation posts, dug-outs, stores, aid posts and signal communications ; and the heavy transport duties entailed in the provision of large quantities of material and stores have been most satisfactorily performed.

"The Division is now about to have an opportunity of proving itself, to which the General Officer Commanding looks forward with complete confidence."

The battle-orders issued by Lieut.-Col. Bates will be found in Appendix B, and deserve careful study.

The following appreciation of the situation and description of the day is taken from Capt. Wallis's diary :—

"To report the battle of Gommecourt fully and correctly would require many pages and much writing. Briefly, Gommecourt Park was the most westerly point of the German position, forming a very sharp salient. The park was a thick wood, and the village was behind the wood. The idea was for the 56th Division to attack on the south side of the wood, and the 46th on the north, joining up with the 56th in the village and establishing a line in the German trenches cutting off the German garrison in the park. The whole attack was a feint, keeping the Germans occupied, while the great attack on the Somme was launched. It would not materially affect the military situation if our attack were successful or not, and the 56th Division was sacrificed. [*Note.*—It was supposed that the artillery preparation would have obliterated the defences and defenders, but that this was not the case will be seen from the German account, which will be found in Appendix D.]

"The L.R.B. attacked on the left of the Division and the Q.V.R. on their right.

"Zero was at 7.30 a.m., and punctually at zero a terrific bombardment opened and clouds of smoke were discharged in a favourable wind. The attack was launched and, in spite of casualties, the objective—the German line—was reached with the same accuracy as had been done at the numerous practices at Halloy. Hundreds of Germans surrendered, but only a few were prisoners at the end of the day, as they could not be escorted back, and made their escape.

"The 46th Division's attack did not materialise, and shortly all the German guns were turned on to the 56th Division's front. A barrage was put down in old No Man's Land, making it impossible for even runners, who usually managed to go anywhere, to get across. Soon the S.O.S. was signalled by 'visual' accompanied by urgent requests for bombs. German prisoners could not be induced to cross to our line and were herded in their old dug-outs. Lieut. G. G. Boston kept a squad of Germans carrying German stick-bombs to him until he himself was badly wounded. The Germans counter-attacked in great strength, and our men had now thrown their last bomb. They were gradually driven back trench by trench, the prisoners escaped, and soon a small remnant only could be seen in the original German front line. The 1st July was a terrible day, as well as a glorious day, one that will always be remembered in English history. Capt. J. R. Somers-Smith and Capt. B. S. Harvey, two splendid officers, were killed, as well as Lieuts. A. Warner, C. B. Doust, A. L. Benns, C. V. Balkwill, G. E. Clode-Baker, and little Jerry Pogose. Curly Boston was severely wounded, Lieut. E. G. Thomas was shot in the head and blinded—he lay in No Man's Land for three days and was then found crawling about trying to find his way to our lines. Lieuts. P. B. B. Oldfield, B. L. E. Pocock, E. W. Rose, Horace Smith, Rex Petley, R. F. Lydall,

B. F. Sawbridge, and Capt. G. H. Cholmeley were all wounded, and over 500 N.C.O.'s and men were killed, wounded or missing."

A more detailed story of the course of the action can be gathered from the following report, which was sent in by the C.O. to his Brigadier :—

From O.C. 1/*London Rifle Brigade.*

To 169*th Infantry Brigade.*

I have the honour to submit diary of events and report as follows :—

Assembly (1) The battalion, 23 Officers and 803 O.R., was ready in its assembly trenches, as per Battalion Orders sent you, by 12.50 a.m. on July 1st.

In addition there were details of R.E., Cheshire Regiment and Trench Mortar Battery dispersed over the various waves.

Assault (2) The assault took place exactly according to the schedule.

The dispositions in brief were that the first 6 waves, i.e. 3 companies with the Lewis guns of the 4th, plus attached troops, should cross at about 80 yards' distance. The reserve company was to advance to the Boyau and wait my orders there. When it advanced it was to act as a carrying party for R.E., material, etc.

My own views were in direct disagreement with any delayed start of the 4th Company and a weaker strength in each wave, and I represented this to you as strongly as I felt I could from Bayencourt. I was of opinion, which events have in no way altered, that it would be easier and wiser to try and get every one across as soon as possible to be ready for any eventuality and then, if the widely expressed views that the enemy had no men or guns left to prevent us after the bombardment proved correct, the 4th Company could be used as "coolies" pure and simple. They would have to return for their first loads.

I do not consider that any troops who may have to fight should be asked to carry anything except what is vital for actual fighting.

7.30 a.m. (3) The reserve company ("B") moved over the open to Y.48.S. where the R.E. stores had been dumped instead of in the Boyau as arranged.

7.40 a.m. (4) The casualties up to this time from the assembly trenches who had passed Battalion H.Qrs. were 2 Officers and 52 Other Ranks wounded. The killed were unascertained.

7.50 a.m. (5) Enemy were putting up a heavy and accurate barrage on the "R" line.

7.58 a.m. (6) Reserve company reported in position in Y.48.S.

8.3 a.m. (7) Smoke cloud still as strong as ever.

8.7 a.m. (8) Capt. G. H. Cholmeley, O.C. my left company, who had been wounded in the shoulder on leaving our own trenches, but assaulted with his men and saw them into the Park, returned and reported to me that so far as his company was concerned everything had worked like clockwork.

He said the corner of the Park was quite unrecognisable owing to shell-fire.

8.18 a.m. (9) Smoke was clearing off and the enemy barrage was on our front and "R" line.

8.45 a.m. (10) Received report in writing from Capt. Somers-Smith, who had crossed with the 6th wave to superintend the operations in the German lines, timed 8.2 a.m., that "C" Company (in the centre) was apparently in position, that "D" (on the right) was in position, and that "A" (on the left) was having a stiff fight in the Park, which they reported as being full of Germans. He added that he had sent 1 section of the battalion bombers to assist them, and had ordered No. 5 platoon of the reserve company to go across from our lines to their support. The latter was unable to cross owing to the barrage, but I was ignorant of this till much later in the day.

9.0 a.m. (11) Capt. Somers-Smith reported in writing to me (received by me at 9.15 a.m.) that the left company had been unable to get its strong point and that he was sending for No. 6 platoon of the Reserve Company to go across and assist it. This platoon was unable to cross owing to the enemy barrage of artillery and M.G. fire. I had no reason, however, to think that it had not crossed. As a matter of fact both Nos. 5 and 6 platoons started, but suffered very heavy casualties and were unsuccessful.

9.3 a.m. (12) Although I had received no definite report that my 3 companies had all reached their final objectives I issued orders for what I believed to be the balance of my reserve company to go across with their loads as arranged. These orders never reached O.C. "B" Company owing to the two messengers being knocked out. I fear that I am to blame for not noticing, in due course, that I received no acknowledgment of these orders. It would, however, have made no difference, as continual efforts were made all the morning by small parties from this company to get across, but all in vain. (See para. 22.)

9.10 a.m. (13) I requested "Souart"[1] to barrage the Park as follows to assist my left company, K.4.c.57 —K.4.a.91. This was done at once.

9.15 a.m. (14) See para. 11 above.

9.38 a.m. (15) The barrage asked for in para. 13 was moved 50 yards more north-west.

9.45 a.m. (16) A very large party of 3rd Londons passed down Yiddish Street. I was unable to get

[1] The Field Artillery group covering the L.R.B. front.

hold of an officer to ask on what orders they were acting. I was told that they had been detailed to dig the continuation of the saps across to the German line, but had been ordered back as the fire was too heavy.

9.52 a.m. (17) I was getting very doubtful whether Capt. Somers-Smith would have enough men to carry out the task of clearing the Park and sent him a message asking this question. It was never delivered.

10.25 a.m. (18) Instructed "Souart" to stop the barrage (see paras. 13 and 15) at 10.30 in the hope that the clearing of the Park would start at that hour.

10.5 a.m. (19) Received aeroplane report from you that Fir, Maze and Eck were held in addition to other trenches.

10.45 a.m. (20) O.C. my right company reported from Eck (received through the Q.V.R.): "Platoon Q.V.R. adjoining my right reports unable to get into touch with the remainder own company on right owing to hostile bombing in Feud. Inform Dick.[1] As their platoon officer, Lieut. Fleetwood, is wounded I am taking command." I received this message at 12.35 p.m.

11.33 a.m. (21) Felon and Epte reported by you as being consolidated and Fellow and Fell as being held.

11.51 a.m. (22) Saw Sergt. Slade of my reserve company, who reported that the barrage of artillery and M.G. fire from F. 19 was so heavy that no one had been able to get across although they had been trying all the morning. He himself had been ordered back by Q.V.R. officer.

11.40 a.m. (23) Received R.F.C. report from you that Feud, Fellow and Fell were strongly held.

12.6 p.m. (24) Received R.F.C. report that the "Quadrilateral" was unoccupied.

[1] Code name for Q.V.R.

12.43 p.m. (25) A few smoke or gas shells were sent over, but fell short of the "R" line.

1.9 p.m. (26) Fen and Ferret were signalling with the Venetian shutter, "S.O.S. bombs." This was the first time any visual signalling had been observed from any of our men in the German lines. I now know that this message had been sent continually for some time, but as we were expecting to see signals from point 94 in the Park no one was paying a special attention to any other part of the line from the point of view of looking out for signals. No action in response to this message could be taken, as the hostile barrage was too heavy to allow any useful number of men to get across.

1.10 p.m. (27) Asked "Souart" to put on the blue barrage again north of the Maze and Eck. It was clear by this time that none of our troops were in these trenches. In this opinion I was not correct as is shown in attached accounts. I have, however, received no reports from any men who returned that our guns caused any losses in our own ranks.

1.21 p.m. (28) Could see men being driven back to Fen and Ferret. This is confirmed by the accounts attached from "C" and "D" Companies.

1.31 p.m. (29) Small parties were seen being driven across to our own lines. The reserve company made repeated efforts to reinforce, but any-one leaving the trench was at once knocked out by the barrage. This latter was as severe as ever. A hostile M.G. was firing from in front of Fig and was shooting very accurately.

3.5 p.m. (30) Fen and Ferret appeared to be manned by about 100 men lying down on this side of the parapet.

4.51 p.m. (31) The German front line appeared to be held by our men in greater numbers than at 3.5 p.m.

5.0 p.m. (32) In response to a request from you I counted the numbers of the battalion remaining in our own lines. There were 2 Officers and 87 O.R. unwounded. Although these were unwounded they were naturally somewhat shaken, having been exposed for some ten hours to hostile artillery fire of varying intensity.

6.0 p.m. (33) Reference para. 31 our numbers now appeared very much less.

8.20 p.m. (34) O.C. my reserve company reported from the front line that men were withdrawing from the German lines across the open.

. . . . .

Appendices (42) I attach four accounts written, and in no way edited, by the senior N.C.O.'s who came back from the enemy lines.

From these it appears that our objectives were reached by each company, that the centre and right ones met no serious opposition, but that the left one never really was able to get to work without interruption.

Casualties (43) The battalion lost, in killed, wounded (including shell shock) and missing, 83% of the Officers who went into the action and 70% of the N.C.O.'s and men. It is particularly regrettable that 2 Officers and no less than 279 Other Ranks are missing.

. . . . .

I have the honour to remain,

Sir,

Your obedient servant,

ARTHUR S. BATES, Lieut.-Col.,

Commanding 1st London Rifle Brigade.

8/7/16.

The personal accounts of the fighting referred to in Para. 42 follow :—

Sergt. W. M. Lilley of " A " Company writes :—

" The 1st wave found the wire in front of point 94 well cut by our artillery, but the wire used was very thick and owing to it being in long lengths was still an obstacle and had to be cut and trampled down. By the time this was completed the 2nd wave advanced from our trenches and came up to us without any trouble. It got through the German front line easily. On reaching there, 2nd Lieut. Doust was shot through the head by a German officer, whom we killed. Work was immediately started to clear the trench Firm—Fir and, with the 3rd and 4th waves arriving, we started to consolidate the position from point 94 through Fir and Eel to Feast. By this time Capt. Cholmeley and Lieut. Pocock were casualties and had proceeded back to our own lines. Throughout the day the enemy continually strove to force us out by means of bombers covered by snipers. Their forces steadily increased as time went on. We protected our left flank by means of a Lewis gun mounted at the point where Fen meets Fir. This gun traversed our left front and kept the enemy down. Our supply of grenades gave out and we had to search the trench for German grenade stores. ' During the afternoon we had to send all available grenades to ' D ' Company on our right, as they were being forced back on us traverse by traverse. Over 300 German grenades were used, and when the supply finally ran out the remainder of ' C ' and ' D ' Companies, also a few Q.V.R. and Q.W.R., were forced through to our position. About 7.45 p.m. the enemy finally bombed us from both flanks and from the front, upon which Capt. de Cologan ordered us to get away as best we could. A German M.G. was in position in the 4th line, also their snipers stopped any attack by us on their bombers. We sent back prisoners during the day to our lines without any escort.

" No equipment of any kind was worn by any Germans seen all day, grenades being carried in sandbags. We found the front line full of deep dug-outs supplied with bunks for sleeping in. There was a plentiful supply of food on the shelves. We had to leave behind us in a dug-out all the casualties which had taken place in the enemy lines who could not make their own way back. We also left a party of 16 prisoners in the next dug-out."

Sergt. H. Frost, also of "A" Company, wrote as follows :—

" Everything went well for the first few hours. We reached the enemy front line quickly and without many casualties, so far as I could see. Our formation was rather broken up owing to the difficulties *en route*, but the corner of the Park was distinguishable and we all got in somewhere near and spread along the trench allotted to the company. This trench was just inside the Park and hidden by a hedge still thick in parts, especially at the far end. The Germans remaining did not offer great opposition. A number of prisoners were taken and sent across by orders of Capt. Somers-Smith. About 40 more taken during the day were put into dug-outs and had to be abandoned in the final withdrawal. We never succeeded in gaining the whole of the 'strong point,' partly because our own artillery continued to play for some time on that section, and later on because of the stronger opposition offered by the enemy. Moreover, a few of our men from the far end of our position had to be bent back towards 'C' Company (in the centre) as there was a gap between ourselves and them at that point and Germans were still in sight there. The situation began to get critical about midday and we were attacked more and more by bombers and snipers, causing us a number of casualties. We managed to hold on to our bit of trench, however, and, in fact, it was the last piece of enemy trench to be evacuated. The credit for this is certainly due to Sergt. [W. M.] Lilley, who worked very hard and courageously throughout the day. I cannot say how much I admired his behaviour. Another who helped greatly was a youngster working the Lewis gun posted in our trench. He kept so cool and never hesitated to expose himself. I do not know his name, but McOwan would [Rfn. D. Reynolds]. During the afternoon a strong attack was made against the other end of the line, chiefly by bombers. I understand our own supply was exhausted and that our men were using German ones found in the trench. At 6 p.m. Sergt. Lilley went and reported to Capt. de Cologan that our position was serious. Nothing had been seen of Capt. Somers-Smith or Lieut. Clode-Baker for some time. From this moment we could see the other end of the line being gradually driven in towards our L.R.B. bit of trench. Twice we had seen parties leave the trenches and cut across the open. Finally at about 8 p.m. the remainder (possibly 100 of various regiments) came rushing along to 'A' Company trench followed by Germans who were showering bombs on them. There was no hope of holding on any longer and our party of 'A' Company joined in the rush for the open quitting at point 94. . . . What a pity we could not get up some supports. We could easily have cleared the Park then, I am sure. The result would have been so different. I was hit in right side of face when leaving the German trench and lost much blood. My body is badly bruised from concussion earlier in the day. [Sergt. H. W.] Munday was very good too, helping with the Lewis gun though badly wounded in the arm."

The account of Lce.-Cpl. J. H. Foaden of "C" Company ran :—

"On leaving our trenches with the 5th wave we encountered a barrage of shell fire and M.G.'s. The smoke was fairly dense, but after advancing 50 yards it was comparatively clear and the M.G. fire very heavy. The enemy was found in his dug-outs in Feast. I saw two taken prisoner and others shot or bombed. On reaching the Maze, which was little more than large shell holes, I bore to the left and took up a position in a large shell hole (K.4.d.28). I was rather uncertain whether my position was correct, but Capt. Harvey arrived and confirmed it as being so. There were about ten men at this point, which we held and commenced to consolidate at once. Snipers were very busy and killed one and wounded two during the first two minutes. We were filling sandbags whilst lying down, until there was sufficient cover to work our Lewis gun. We proceeded to consolidate the position as far as possible until 12.45 p.m., when we realised the futility of working further, owing to the continual landslides. At this period and also previously we heard rapid rifle fire, which seemed to be on our right and which we failed to understand at the time. About 1.30 p.m. the battalion withdrew to Fen, but of this fact I was ignorant. At 4 p.m. Sergt. [H. V.] Hember ordered us to withdraw also, but there being no communication trench I told him we could not do so until dusk, as we had our Lewis gun and heavy packs of S.A.A. He went back, as I presumed, to consult Capt. Harvey and ordered us later to wait till dusk. About 4 p.m. enemy bombers appeared in Fibre and threw bombs at us. I opened fire with the Lewis gun, whereupon the enemy threw up his hands, I took this to be a ruse and fired again. This occurred on three occasions. I then retired towards the Maze taking the gun with me. I saw the enemy again there and once more fired. I was now covering a large shell hole in which were Sergt. Hember and 14 men. Having but two grenades, we decided to try and reach the rest of the battalion, so I stripped the gun, rendering it useless to the enemy. The premature explosion of one of our own grenades wounded Sergt. Hember and five others. I then decided to retire with the remainder and get reinforcements. After several fruitless attempts to find Fen we managed to work round the outer edge of the Maze and reached Exe. On reaching Female we encountered more enemy bombers, at whom we fired and threw our last grenade. We had just previously passed four enemy dug-outs, in one of which was Rifleman W. G. Bates wounded and a prisoner. Near by were two wounded Germans. We eventually crawled down Exe and reached the remainder of the battalion at the junction of Fen and Exe. The enemy was kept at bay until the last grenade had been thrown. Bombing had been kept up for some time by means of grenades captured from the enemy. Our officers at this point were Capts. de Cologan and Harvey and 2nd Lieut. Petley, who got through to us at the last moment. The final withdrawal took place, when we were surrounded on three sides, about 7 p.m. or later and we were being bombed by the enemy, who were completely out of sight."

Cpl. R. F. Ebbetts of "D" Company made the following statement :—

"At 7.27 a.m. the 1st and 2nd waves advanced, the former went 150 yards and got down for a moment and then advanced again, cutting the German wire where necessary. In most places it was blown to pieces and the advance was straight forward. The enemy first line was reached without opposition and a party of company bombers, seven in all, under Lce.-Cpl. [H. G. F.] Dennis entered the German front line S.E. of Ems in Fern and bombed along Ferret to the base of Exe. This party encountered two hostile parties of about six each, all of whom were killed. All dug-outs were bombed. This party then proceeded along Exe and, finding no Germans in their second line, occupied Eck. By this time the 3rd, 4th, 5th and 6th waves had all reached the German lines and, finding no opposition, occupied Eck, which they proceeded to consolidate. Sentries were posted. Our wiring party put up 5 rolls of concertina and three strands of barbed wire. A German M.G. in the wood was put out of action, as were several snipers. By 7.50 a.m. all 'D' Company was in Eck as per schedule and were busy consolidating the position. The bombers had orders to bomb down Erin, if 'C' Company were not already doing so. As, however, the latter were doing so, ours stayed in Eck and worked. Our left was in touch with 'C' Company. One of our Lewis guns was in the left part of Eck and fired half left across the road in front. The second gun never reached the German trenches. From 8.0 to 11.30 a.m. the consolidation of Eck proceeded without interruption from the enemy with the exception of a sniper in the wood on the left and one on the right. Our right was in touch with the Q.V.R. until this time. Eck was in such a condition that the Company were in isolated groups in holes with heaps of earth between them. These heaps were very large, but communication was maintained between them by shouting and by men crawling over the top. The following officers reached Eck: Capt. de Cologan, 2nd Lieut. [H.] Smith and 2nd Lieut. Petley. By 11.30 a.m. the enemy were observed creeping to the edge of the trees in front and on the left, but only singly. From this time the snipers became more and more numerous, and began to fire along Eck. At 12.30 p.m. an enemy bombing party were seen advancing along Ems. A bombing party of ours and the Q.V.R. went down Exe and along Female. This party came up against the hostile bombers at the junction of Feed and Female and held it up. Another German bombing party was then seen coming down Emden. At 1 p.m. another enemy bombing party was seen in the Maze advancing towards Eck. Owing to lack of bombs our bombing party on the right was forced to withdraw along Female. About 1.30 p.m. an order was passed along from our left from Capt. Somers-Smith to Capt. de Cologan, 'Withdraw to German front line.' The garrison of Eck then proceeded down Exe into Fen and Ferret. Our bombers engaged the enemy in Ferret and along Exe. A party under 2nd Lieut. Petley was cut off in Eck, the message to withdraw not having reached them. They were ordered by 2nd Lieut. Petley to withdraw back to Fen and Ferret, but were almost surrounded by enemy bombers. These they held at bay and they finally succeeded in breaking through. There was a continuous demand for grenades, and all, both British and German, were passed along to the bombing parties on our right and left. All this time we were suffering very heavy losses from sniping on the left. About 8.30 p.m. the grenades were quite exhausted and an order was received from the right to close up. The men closed up and overflowing the trench started to crawl or run towards our own lines. Every man who was unwounded then left the German lines. The enemy were in force in the Park on the left before our men started and opened a very heavy fire on them as they crossed the open."

2nd Lieut. R. E. Petley, who was with "D" Company, wrote as follows from Hospital :—

"I will begin my narrative from the time of the assault. It was really magnificent the way every man, cool and collected, strolled out through quite a stiff barrage to the tape I had laid down 150 yards out during the night. The smoke lifted for a few seconds when we were out, and I noticed the men were inclined to bunch on the right. I shouted an order and they shook out as if they were on Wimbledon Common. We (the first wave) got straight to our objective, Eck, without very much trouble, and, before the whole of 'D' Company were up, I got into touch with the Q.V.R. on our right and with 'C' Company on our left.

"We got our wire out at once and started the work of consolidation immediately. Within a quarter of an hour of our arrival we were seriously troubled with snipers from the Park and Cemetery as well as a machine-gun from the rear. All apparently had gone well and Capt. de Cologan sent several messages to Capt. Somers-Smith to that effect. After we had been in our positions about an hour I worked my way along the whole of 'D' Company to see that the men were digging well, etc. I got a slight wound in my shoulder for my trouble, but still things seemed to be going well, and our casualties were comparatively slight. We were then hoping soon to hear that the Q.W.R. and South Staffs had reached their objectives.

"Then a Q.V.R. man came and reported that he had lost touch with his regiment and that only about a dozen of his men were on our right, also that they were being bombed. Smith (2nd Lieut. H., 'D' Company) went along to see what he could do and a message was sent back to head-quarters in Exe. I believe a party of battalion bombers tried to cut them off in the rear. However, it soon became evident to us that the Huns were bombing uncomfortably near us on the right, and Capt. de Cologan moved further down Eck towards Exe. I found myself in a sort of cul-de-sac, and managed to get into the main trench (if it can be so called) by making each man crawl singly over a big mound of earth, while we kept the Huns on our right down with bombs and sniping. As soon as we were all over, we turned this mound into a barricade and managed easily enough to hold the Germans back.

"I then went along to the left to find Capt. de Cologan, but could find no trace of the rest of 'D' Company nor 'C' Company. I at once sent a message back to advanced head-quarters asking for more bombs and men. I heard from Smith that this message did not arrive, and that as soon as de Cologan reached the front German trench, finding I was not there, he sent two different parties to try and reach us, but they were unable to get near. Apparently Capt. de Cologan had passed the order to withdraw down to me before he left Eck, but, as I did not receive it and as we were holding the Huns up on the right, I could see no reason for withdrawing without orders.

"I sent another message back for more bombs about 4 p.m.

"At 4 p.m. I sent the following to advanced head-quarters:

"'I sent a message to you about two hours ago to the effect that I am holding on to Eck with about 40 men, including a dozen Q.V.R. and one Q.W.R., and *that I wanted more bombs.* Quite out of touch to right and left. Have held off Germans on our right with barricade. It is quite absurd to lay here at night as we are.'

"At 4.30 p.m. Sergt. [F. S.] Robinson appeared. He explained what had happened and brought me verbal orders to withdraw. I gave him the following message for Capt. de Cologan and told him to lead the party out :—

"'Sergt. Robinson brings me verbal *orders* to withdraw which, of course, we reluctantly must obey. Sergt. Robinson is bringing all the men down to you, and Sergt. [H.] Austin and I are trying to get Sergt. [S. H.] Olorenshaw. Should like some hot dinner when we get back.'

"Sergt. Austin, Cpl. [F.] Thorpe and myself brought up the rear. Our idea was to try and bring one at least of the wounded back; as soon, however, as the party started we were bombed rather heavily from Female, and, of course, I had to order all wounded to be left alone. We managed to account for two or three of the Huns in Female and kept them down until the rear of our party had passed the top of Exe. We worked our way round to about the junction of Maze and Fibre, Austin and I bringing up the rear.

"We had no less than four different bombing parties to keep off, and the whole of my party got to the German second trench with only two or three casualties. It was in the independent rushes across the open, of course, that the casualties occurred, but even then, most of us, I believe, got to the German front trench, where apparently were the remnants of 'C' and 'D' Companies and a lot of Q.V.R.'s. Austin and I lay in a shell hole by the second line to cover as much as possible these final rushes. Our intention was to stay there until dark, but on a bomb bursting in our shell hole we cleared off before the smoke lifted. Austin muttered that he was hit, but we did not wait to argue. We ran in different directions and I have not seen him since. Although the bomb burst practically on us, I was unhurt except for a few tiny pieces in my legs.

"I worked my way to the German front trench and joined the others, Harvey, de Cologan, Smith, Cox of the Q.V.R., several other officers and about 60 or 70 men. They were being bombed from the right, and it was evident that we should have to clear.

"Most of the party, I am afraid, were hit in No Man's Land, and I fear Harvey and de Cologan [he was taken prisoner] were killed then. Smith and I with about a dozen others held the Huns off until the main crowd had cleared and then we rushed for the nearest shell holes. I was then hit in the knee and you can imagine the waiting till dark and crawling in, etc.

"There is an incident I should like to mention which shows that we had a decent lot of Huns opposite, and which would prove a source of consolation to the relatives of the missing. About 9.45 p.m. (early twilight) a German came out to us, and as I saw his red cross I prevented our men from firing. He came up, saw I had been roughly dressed, and went on nearer to our own lines to attend to one of his own men. Some of our men got up to go, and he shouted out and stopped one of their machine-guns. I think his action showed pluck and decency, and augurs well for our wounded whom we had to leave behind.

"I have already mentioned Sergt. Austin as being very useful in helping in our miniature rear-guard action. Cpl. S. A. Ebbetts, who was killed, also rendered me every assistance, and his brother was exceedingly useful in helping me and other wounded back.

"I trust by now the battalion is well back, and I hope to be out again before you return to the firing line."

One of the very few written messages from the front line assaulting troops was brought across by No. 647 Rfn. C. H. Hudson, as is shown in the following memo. received from the Commanding Officer of the Q.V.R. :—

"I herewith send a report from one of my officers, 2nd Lieut. Ord-Mackenzie, with reference to one of your brave fellows. I concur in what Ord-Mackenzie says. Rfn. Coventry of my battalion also gave me the same report at the time of delivering the message at my head-quarters on "Z" day, saying what a brave fellow Rfn. Hudson of your battalion was ; his only thought was his duty, although badly wounded. I hope the poor fellow is all right."

The report from 2nd Lieut. D. A. Ord-Mackenzie was as follows :—

"I have the honour to bring to your notice the gallant conduct of No. 647 Rfn. C. H. Hudson of the L.R.B. on the morning of July 1st in conveying and delivering messages from the advanced companies while severely wounded. The circumstances were as follows: At some time between 11 a.m. and noon I was in Y47 between Yankee Street and Yellow Street together with Rfn. Coventry examining the ground with a view to crossing to the German lines. I had stopped to adjust the bandages of a wounded man, when Rfn. Hudson came into the trench from the direction of the enemy's lines and collapsed, shouting that he had two messages and asking me to take the delivery of them. I read the messages and endorsed them, and upon examining his wound found him badly wounded in the stomach. I bandaged him to the best of my ability with a field dressing, whereupon he expressed himself able to reach head-quarters if helped. As the messages contained the answer to one carried by Rfn. Coventry I decided to send him back to assist Rfn. Hudson, and to deliver his message. Rfn. Coventry asserts that Rfn. Hudson displayed great courage and fortitude throughout, and I should like to call attention to the fact that his first thought, when he met me, was for his duty and not for himself. He stated that he was the third to make the attempt. I propose to allow Rfn. Coventry to read this report and affix his signature to signify that he is in agreement with the details thereof."

The above was signed by Rfn. Coventry and also endorsed by Lieut.-Col. V. W. F. Dickins, Commanding the Q.V.R.

Unfortunately this very brave Rifleman succumbed to the wounds he received, and, although the Commanding Officer urged his claims very strongly to Higher Authority, he was unable to obtain the award of any medal for him. His name will, however, live in the regiment as having performed one of the countless acts of gallantry and courage which, in so many cases, were unseen and therefore unrecorded.

The work of the L.R.B. was, of course, only a part of the battle, the larger aspects of which is dealt with in the Divisional Report, which will be found in Appendix C. Among some Divisional Notes and Conclusions, which have not been printed, the following pregnant sentences occurred :—

"As many grenades as possible must be carried forward by the assaulting troops." "I think we still have a tendency to overload our men, and that to get the best work out of bombers in particular they must be as lightly equipped as possible and free to use their arms." These form a complete justification for the opinions which Lieut.-Col. Bates evidently held from the first, and contended for so strongly in para. 2 of his report. A translation of the German report on the defence of Gommecourt will be found in full in Appendix D, and is reprinted by the courtesy of the Editor of the *Journal of the United Service Institution*, in which it appeared. It should be carefully read while the foregoing narrative is fresh in the mind, and the table of casualties compared with that of the British on p. 380. It shows the enemy's opinion of what the L.R.B. and the 56th Division accomplished.

The following were the officer casualties for the day :—

Killed or Died—		
Captains . .	2	Somers-Smith and Harvey.
Lieut. . .	1	Clode-Baker.
2nd Lieuts. . .	5	Balkwill, Benns, Doust, Pogose and Warner.
Wounded—		
Captain . .	1	Cholmeley.
Lieuts. . .	3	Boston, Oldfield and Pocock.
2nd Lieuts. . .	6	Lydall, Petley, Rose, Sawbridge, Smith and Thomas
Wounded and Missing—		
Captain . .	1	de Cologan. (Taken prisoner as is now known.)
	19	Total officer casualties.

The other officers in the action were Lieut.-Col. Bates, Capt. Wallis (Adjt.), Lieut. Long, 2nd Lieut. Ticehurst and the M.O., Capt. Crombie.

In addition to the officers left out at the Transport Lines (see O.O., No. 1, Part 1, para. 11), the following were either on leave or courses, etc., and were not present: Capt. E. C. Wills, Lieuts. Howe, Martin and Sell.

Capt. Cholmeley was the only officer who had gone over the top whom the C.O. saw again on this day. He was wounded prior to leaving the assembly trench, but gallantly insisted in leading his company to its objective and, after leaving it there safely established as he then thought, he called in at Battalion Head-quarters on his way back and reported the fact to the C.O.

The battalion's figures do not quite agree in detail with those in the official report and are as follows :—

	Officers	"A"	"B"	"C"	"D"	Total Other Ranks	Total All Ranks
Killed or Died of Wounds	7	14	13	21	17	65	72
Wounded	10	63	44	67	68	242	252
Wounded and Missing .	1	18	3	22	16	59	60
Missing	—	67	24	68	44	203	203
Missing, believed Killed .	1	—	—	—	—	—	1
	19	162	84	178	145	569	588
Of the above wounded there had returned to duty by 23/7/16 :—		10	7	11	13	41	

The following congratulatory messages were subsequently received :

From G.H.Q. to the G.O.C. Third Army.

"The Commander-in-Chief directs me to confirm in writing the verbal message already delivered by an A.D.C. to Gen. Snow, conveying his appreciation of the gallant efforts made at Gommecourt on the 1st and 2nd July by the 46th and 56th Divisions of the VIIth Corps.

"While deeply deploring the losses suffered by these Divisions, he is glad to be able to assure them that their vigorous and well-sustained attack has proved of material assistance to the success of the general plan of operations."

This was forwarded by the Third Army to the VIIth Corps, and by it to the 56th Division.

Prior to the receipt of the above the Corps had issued the following :—

"The Corps Commander wishes to congratulate all ranks of the 56th Division on the way they took the German trenches and held them by pure grit and pluck for so long in very adverse circumstances.

"Although Gommecourt has not fallen into our hands, the purpose of the attack, which was mainly to contain and kill Germans, was accomplished, thanks to a great extent to the tenacity of the 56th Division."

In forwarding this to the 169th Infantry Brigade the Division issued the following :—

"The General Officer Commanding the 56th Division wishes all ranks to know how proud he is of the splendid way in which they captured the German trenches, and of the way they held on to them until all their ammunition and grenades were exhausted. He is satisfied that the main task of the Division in containing and killing Germans was most thoroughly accomplished."

The Brigadier added the following :—

"In forwarding the foregoing congratulatory message, the Brigadier wishes to express to all ranks his praise and appreciation of the excellent work done during the preparations for the attack and of the gallantry displayed during the day's fighting."

It was on the march out of the line to St. Amand when passing Divisional Head-quarters that Major-Gen. Hull came out on to the road and saw the L.R.B.'s remnant march past. He then personally congratulated Lieut.-Col. Bates on the fine work of the battalion.

The *Times* of July 14th, as well as other papers, published what purported to be the text of a congratulatory message from Major-Gen. Hull to one of the battalions in the division. This was entirely imaginary, and Gen. Hull took the trouble to circulate a special memorandum to all three brigades disclaiming the "order" and closing with these words : "Where all have done so well, it would have been invidious to call attention to any special unit."

At 5 p.m. the officers who had been left out at the transport lines (see O.O. No. 1, Part 1, para. 11) were ordered to rejoin the battalion and help in reorganisation. Major Husey had been employed all day as Liaison Officer between the Division and those on its flanks, viz. 46th and 48th.

The night of the 1st/2nd was occupied with bringing in

wounded, and Capt. Wallis persuaded the Commanding Officer to allow him to search for Lieut. Pogose, who was known to be lying out wounded. He brought that officer back alive, though only alas ! to die next day, and also carried in unaided about a dozen other wounded men. For his gallantry he was awarded the M.C.

On July 2nd, about noon, the remnant of the battalion was ordered to withdraw to the "R" and "S" lines, and remain in the reserve trenches and orchards there. During the movement, the enemy put down an intense barrage on Hébuterne, which lasted about ten or fifteen minutes and inflicted several casualties on the L.R.B.

During the afternoon an unofficial armistice took place and the Divisional artillery stopped firing. All the stretcher bearers went out and brought in as many wounded as they could find.

The battalion was subsequently ordered to march to Bayencourt, where it was to have been billeted for the night, but owing to the enemy persistently shelling the village the companies moved into the open country and bivouacked.

The strength of the companies were as follows :—

"A." Lieut. F. D. Charles and 23 Other Ranks.
"B." 2nd Lieut. G. H. Howe (pending return of Capt. E. C. Wills from the Third Army School) and about 60.
"C." Lieut. C. W. Long and about 40.
"D." Capt. F. H. Crews and about 50.

On 3rd July the battalion marched to billets at St. Amand. The next two days were spent in bathing and cleaning up, and in recovering from the heavy strain of the Gommecourt fight.

Great determination, combined with good discipline, is necessarily required if the daily routine of a regiment is to be carried on after a long preparation and a heavy engagement, just when the inevitable reaction is being felt and the extent and nature of its losses realised. It was therefore a great blow, and one that was much felt at this trying time, for the regiment to receive a large draft, not from its own 3rd Battalion, but from the 2/7th Middlesex, which had been serving for eighteen months in Egypt, although the material was exceptionally fine and no complaint could be made about the fitness or training of the men. Undoubtedly in times of stress battalions must be filled up as quickly as possible without waiting for reinforcements from their own units, but a case in which this was unnecessary has already been mentioned, and, as time went on, it became evident that the Authorities were doing so of set purpose. For sentimental reasons alone, which are by no means negligible, this was bad, but it was still worse from the practical point of view, because there is no doubt whatever that men do better work and stand the hardships of a campaign more satisfactorily with their own unit than with strange ones. The officer responsible for this gratuitous mixing up may have the satisfaction of knowing that not only did he do much to make the lot of those who were fighting harder even than it necessarily was, but that their efficiency was at times distinctly lowered. There was at this time a large draft of the L.R.B. actually in France at the base, which made the matter all the worse, and it was no consolation to know that all regiments were treated alike, or that the Q.V.R. had representatives of no less than seventeen different units in its ranks. It is difficult to write temperately about the course of action pursued by those in authority, who paid no attention to the very strong protests put forward by all who were actually engaged in the fighting, not only Battalion Commanders, but officers of higher rank.

FIRST BATTALION

Part V. July 6—Oct. 9, 1916

Fonquevillers—Cauchy—Leuze Wood—Les Bœufs.

(The maps referred to are C and No. 6 *on p.* 159 *and No.* 7 *on p.* 168.)

On 6th July the L.R.B. marched to Fonquevillers, where it remained in reserve billets until the 8th, when " A " and " B " Companies relieved two companies of the 2nd London in " Z " Sector. The trenches were very deep, and in many places were flooded to a depth of three or four feet, because the front line trenches were on a lower level than the village, so that all the drainage from the village ran down there through the communication trenches. The men in the front line trench and the ration parties took off their trousers, and knotted their shirts between their legs, so as to keep themselves as dry as possible. At that time the following officers were serving with the battalion: Lieut.-Col. Bates, Major Husey, Capts. Wallis (Adjt.), Crews and E. C. Wills, Lieuts. Long and F. D. Charles, 2nd Lieuts. Bantoft, Howe, Gardiner, Ticehurst (attached from 2nd Londons, soon after transferred to the L.R.B.), Sell, Perowne, Martin, F. A. Balls and Crisp. 2nd Lieut. Gordon was Transport Officer, Lieut. Kelly was Q.M., and Capt. Crombie was M.O.

The only event of importance that occurred was in connection with some raids, which were made by all the battalions simultaneously on 13th July, in order to find out whether a rumour that a German relief had taken place on the divisional front was true, a matter of great importance. As the orders only came down late in the afternoon, there was no time to reconnoitre or opportunity to practise, and everyone of the raids failed, although the Q.W.R. bumped into an enemy listening patrol and captured an " elderly German gentleman," who was too much frightened to run away and unable to give any information of value, because it was his first visit to the trenches.

On 16th of July a move was made to rest billets at Bienvillers. The battalion by then had filled up more or less, and included 2/7th Middlesex, 494 Other Ranks; 6th Londons, 8; 7th Londons, 26; 8th Londons, 86; 20th Londons, 1; 2/2nd Londons, 1; all wearing their own regimental badges. On 18th 2nd Lieuts. C. R. Hughes, G. S. Sanderson, R. W. Unwin and J. W. Wilkins from 11th Londons arrived, and on 19th Sergts. P. T. Dyer, J. S. Lindsay, E. G. Moore, P. D. Radford, A. P. Sharman and E. H. Slade; Lce.-Cpl. R. D. Poland and Rfn. C. H. John (on 17th) were gazetted, with direct commissions as 2nd Lieutenants.

On the same day (19th) the battalion again went into the trenches in "Z" Sector at Hannescamps, and was relieved on 22nd. There was a heavy bombardment on the evening of 20th, when out of 188 shells of 4·2″ and 5·9″, 72 proved to be "duds." This, however, may have been done of set purpose, for gas shells were put over shortly after, which were hardly distinguishable from the "duds" and caused several casualties.

Unfortunately, on the very first night 2nd Lieut. W. E. M. Gardiner and Sergt. Bradford were both killed while on patrol. 2nd Lieut. Gardiner, a charming, gallant boy, had not been with the battalion long but had endeared himself to all both in the 1st and in the 3rd Battalions; Sergt. C. W. Bradford had served in France since 1914, and his name had been submitted for a direct commission in the battalion. During the same tour 2nd Lieut. G. S. Sanderson, who had only recently joined from the 11th Londons and had shown himself a brave officer, was killed in a patrol fight in No Man's Land.

From 23rd to 29th July the L.R.B. was at Bienvillers and Fonquevillers, but on 30th it went back to the same trenches as before, and remained there until 6th August. When publishing in Battalion Orders of 25/7/16 the list of N.C.O.'s and Riflemen receiving Divisional Cards, the following appeared: "The C.O. takes this opportunity of regretting that the gallant and heroic conduct of very many officers and other ranks in the Battalion must necessarily pass unnoticed owing to the nature of the action." On 4th a raid was attempted on the 5th Leicesters, who were immediately on the left of the L.R.B., accompanied by a very heavy bombardment which produced exceedingly small results. On 7th August the battalion marched to St. Amand, and on 10th Maj.-Gen. Hull presented medal ribbons on parade, followed by a march past of the 169th Brigade, the regimental march of each battalion being played by the Divisional band. The General took exception to the pace, 140 to the minute, at which the L.R.B. went by, but it was quite correct, the bandmaster being an old 60th man.

On 13th August Lieut.-Col. Bates, who had succeeded to the command when Lieut.-Col. Lord Cairns left the L.R.B. in February, 1915, and had commanded it during the second battle of Ypres and the battle of Gommecourt, left the battalion owing to ill-health. The first officer, for many years, not a regular who had commanded the 1st L.R.B., and, of course, the first to command it in war, he fully maintained the high reputation which Commanding Officers of the L.R.B. have always had, and is entitled to the greatest credit for having carried out his difficult task so well. Major R. H. Husey took over the command, and the regiment was fortunate in having such a capable officer ready and prepared to do so, and in not having an outsider foisted on to it.

On 15th the battalion returned to Hannescamps trenches for its last tour in that quiet part of the front, and relieved the 2nd Londons. The only incident of any importance occurring was that a patrol, consisting of 2nd Lieuts. Slade and Sharman and a Lewis gun, was attacked by a German one, of which three were killed. Three Staff officers from the Army Intelligence Department, who attempted to identify the bodies, found that according to their tunics two were Bavarians, from their trousers all were Saxons, while their shirts made them Prussians of Würtemburg, and when their boots were pulled off they were discovered not to be wearing any socks. They carried no discs or papers, and the solitary five pfennig-piece taken out of one of the pockets was claimed and kept by the M.O., a Scotchman of course, for "professional services rendered." On two occasions notice was received that poison gas was to be released on either side of the battalion, which meant considerable anxiety for those in command, until they knew that the men in the front line and listening posts, who had to be withdrawn to the second line, were all back in safety.

On 20th the following farewell order was received from the O.C. VIIth Corps :—

"The Lieut.-Gen. Commanding the VIIth Corps, in saying good-bye to the 56th Division on their leaving the Corps, desires to record his appreciation of the manner in which the Division has fought and worked while it has been in the VIIth Corps. The gallant manner in which the Division fought at Gommecourt will be appreciated in history, but the Corps Commander wishes the Division to know that the less spectacular but more irksome work that the Division has put into the line which they have been holding has not escaped notice. It is invidious to make distinction when all have worked so well, but he particularly congratulates those units who have so well repaired that part of the line knocked about in the fighting of 1st July. The Corps Commander wishes all ranks good luck, and feels sure that any task committed to the Division in the future will be completed in triumph."

On the same day the 8th South Staffords arrived from the Somme to take over the line for a "rest-cure," and the L.R.B. began a journey there which finished up in plenty of time to take part in the very heavy fighting that had been raging since 1st July. It moved to St. Amand that day, and, after one night in billets there, marched to Sus St. Leger, a little village eight miles away, and again billeted. On 22nd an early start was made and the 14 miles to Wavans covered by noon in stifling heat, which made things very trying. On 23rd after another early start, with breakfasts at 4.30 a.m., Cauchy, a very nice little place full of historical interest 15 miles off, was reached, the dinners being eaten on the way.

On 24th orders were received for intensive training to begin at once, and the 56th Division heard that, with the Guards Division, it had been selected to make an attack in conjunction with the tanks, which were to appear for the first time. From that time to 3rd September daily practices took place, occasionally with the tanks though generally with dummies, but the training and the orders were kept very secret, and special precautions were taken to prevent any information about the new engines of war leaking out to the enemy. In view of the large number of reinforcements which had not been initiated into the attack with liquid fire, introduced so successfully by the Germans at Hooge, a special demonstration of that form of warfare was given during this period. Col. R. B. Campbell, the bayonet fighting expert, also lectured to the battalion in his own wonderful way, inspiring every man with thrilling hopes of the use that he might be able to make of the weapon.

2nd Lieut. D. McOwan was appointed adjutant on 3rd Sept., and on the same day the battalion marched to St. Riquier, where it entrained for Corbie, near Amiens, arriving at 2 a.m. on 4th, with the belief that it would be there for a day or two, but shortly after noon orders were received to move "forthwith" to Happy Valley (F.27.c.), near Bray, which necessitated bully beef luncheons instead of thoughtfully chosen meals. A 14-mile march brought the battalion to the spot, which did not in the least live up to its name, as only 22 bell tents and 6 trench shelters were available on a rainy night for men who were already wet and cold, so many of them had to bivouac in the open, getting what cover they could from their ground sheets. The Lewis gun teams in charge of 2nd Lieut. Poland had a particularly hard task in dragging some unserviceable two-wheeled carts, better suited for perambulators than their intended purpose, across country through soft and wet fields. A good many of the carts did not survive this, and the remainder were soon scrapped, to every one's relief. The next day was much finer and the men were able to clean up, while the C.O. and some of the officers went round the trenches about Fricourt (F.3) and Mametz (F.5), and found on their return a communication which said that, owing to the great successes achieved by the French, the division was to hold itself ready to move at a moment's notice after 5 a.m. next day.

On 6th September the battalion "stood to" at 5 a.m., but did not get orders to move till 2 p.m., when it set off for the support trenches known as Chimpanzee Valley (A.5). The slow and trying march across country, which was in a terrible condition, and through Carnoy (A.14), where the mud on the roads was 12 inches deep, only finished at 8 p.m. and, as the S.O.S. went up from the front lines just as the battalion came in, the L.R.B. was treated to some terrific salvos from the British and French artillery, which were massed in the valley.

On 7th the battalion moved up the line at 3 p.m. and relieved the Kensingtons in trenches known as the Falfemont

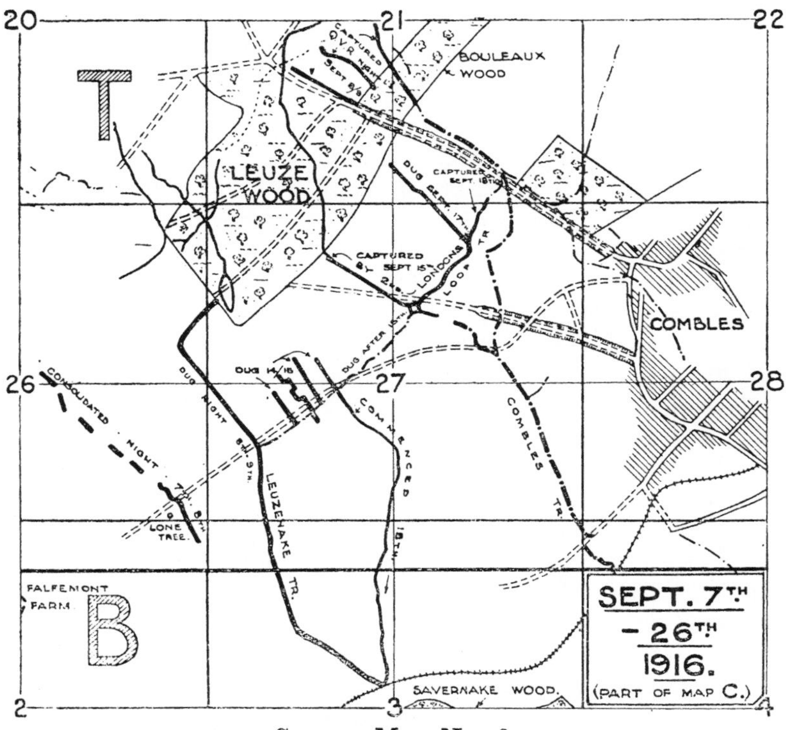

SKETCH MAP NO. 6.

Farm (*B*.2) line and a trench a little way in front, south-east of Leuze Wood (*T*.21). The march up was quite short, about three miles, but the going was very heavy, as it was through undulating country entirely devastated by shell fire. Farms and cottages had completely disappeared, and of the woods little remained except rugged stumps, while the slopes approaching Falfemont Farm trenches were strewn with British and French dead, killed in capturing the position on 5th.

The line itself, which had been a strongly held German

position, was typical of the whole Somme battlefield, but unrecognisable as a trench line; the whole position was blown down and the dead German defenders lay thick on all sides. The entrances to the dug-outs were still reeking from the effect of "P" bombs when the L.R.B. took over the line, and the unfortunate garrisons were found in some cases to have managed to get up the stairs into the open, only to die in a huddled heap around the entrance, horribly disfigured by the effects of the phosphorus. There was no time to bury the dead, as every one had to work tooth and nail at making cover of some sort, because, although the line was quiet at the time of taking over, heavy shelling was expected. One or two of the dug-outs which had escaped the phosphorus were fit to be occupied, and these were used as company head-quarters. The deep German dug-outs had been seen for the first time at Gommecourt, when our men, who penetrated to their lines, made use of them to shelter the wounded and to confine prisoners, but they were now met with again and proved of great service. They were invariably approached by two staircases, and averaged some twenty to thirty feet below the ground, some having as many as three chambers connected by galleries. The stairs were completely framed in wood, but the rooms, being cut out of the solid chalk, had not been lined or shored in any way. The Germans had been on this ground ever since the war became stationary, and an immense amount of time and labour must have been expended in fortifying it.

On the right the L.R.B. joined up with the French, and on the left it was in touch with the patrols of the Q.V.R., while battalion patrols were sent out to reconnoitre Combles trench (*T*. 27), as the position of the enemy was very obscure.

The night was fairly quiet, as things went in that locality,—at any rate no S.O.S. went up—and a lot of honest digging was done, which was the means of saving many lives from the incessant bombardment on the next day.

On 8th, the enemy's heavies shelled the valley round Brigade Head-quarters, and whiz-bangs fell on the L.R.B. trenches. At 11.30 p.m. the bombers of the L.R.B. and Q.V.R. carried out an attack, which resulted in the Q.V.R. occupying a trench (*T*.21.*d*.) that ran close alongside the north edge of the

Ginchy-Combles road, and the L.R.B. taking 200 yards of the Combles Trench south-east from Leuze Wood, although it was driven out at 5.15 a.m. next day by a strong counter-attack, which, however, failed to dislodge the Q.V.R.

Leuze Wood was on the left of the L.R.B. position, and was connected with Combles on the right by a sunken road, on the British side of which was German wire, and on the further side the enemy's trench. The road was occupied, and anyone approaching the wire was heavily bombed at once. The original orders were that the L.R.B. was to attack the sunken road and German Trench between Leuze Wood and the Loop (*T.27.b.*) Trench which ran round the north-west side of Combles. About 2 p.m., however, these orders were altered, and the L.R.B. was ordered to attack through the wood, and take the sunken road and trench in flank. The attack reached the edge of the wood with "B" Company on the right, "C" Company on the left and "A" Company in support, but after getting into the open was met by very heavy machine-gun fire combined with intense artillery co-operation, while the British barrage was practically non-existent, so the losses were very severe. Imperative orders had been given that the attack was to be pressed, and the men by valiant fighting carried the advance nearly up to the sunken road, but were finally held up, unable to get any further from want of men, after doing all that was humanly possible. Amongst the casualties was Capt. Nobbs, who was seen in a shell-hole shot through the eye and assumed to be dead until some three weeks later, when news was received that he was totally blinded and a prisoner; Lieuts. A. E. Sedgwick and E. S. Bantoft were mortally wounded and died next day. Lieut. Sedgwick, besides being a particularly gallant officer and one of the first promoted from the ranks, had in pre-war days been a prominent member of the School of Arms and its honorary secretary for three years. He was badly wounded at the second battle of Ypres, but, when he heard how many officers had been hit on 1st July, he insisted upon going to the front again, although he was still lame from his wound, because he found it impossible to remain at home while such strenuous work was going on. For some time he acted as assistant adjutant of the 3rd Battalion, where he did

M

most excellent work. Capt. H. L. L. Mathews (11th Londons) was also killed; Lieuts. E. G. Moore, Ticehurst, Sharman, Crisp, Radford and C. R. Hughes (11th Londons) were all wounded, and over 350 Other Ranks were either killed or wounded.

It used to be said in old days that a battalion which had been badly cut up was useless for some months at least. That this was not always so was proved by general experience several times during this astonishing war. For instance, on 1st July the casualties in the L.R.B. were about 70%, and yet some ten weeks later the battalion was twice able to sustain casualties of over 40% in attacks and to continue in the line without flinching.

The battalion continued to hold its section of the front line and was heavily shelled for the whole of 10th, when it was relieved at midnight, and went to the Citadel hutments, where it rested, was reinforced, and reorganised with a trench strength of 19 Officers and 395 Other Ranks. On 12th the battalion moved up to Billon Farm (F.30) and bivouacked in the open, which was hard on the reinforcements, who had only had some 12 weeks' training at home and no war experience. The L.R.B. was then in divisional reserve and on 13th moved to the trench system near German's Wood (A.10.a.), which was used as a resting-place for troops moving to and from the line. These trenches were shallow, with no head cover of any kind, and head-quarters occupied the only dug-out in the place.

At midnight on 14th/15th a move was made to Chimpanzee Trench, but the L.R.B. was obliged to halt in column of route for about half an hour in Death Valley, while the trenches that were to be occupied were being cleared by the troops about to make an attack. The British heavy artillery, which was putting down a heavy barrage, was all round, and the noise was simply terrific, but there was no counter battery work by the enemy, who were probably removing their heavy guns, and the only casualties were from some premature bursts of British shells. At 4 a.m. Chimpanzee Trench was reached, and at 6.20 a.m. the 2nd Londons, assisted by the few remaining L.R.B. bombers, practically all of whom became casualties, made a successful attack on the Loop Trench, which was partially occupied, the enemy still remaining in either end of it. The 2nd Londons had the assistance of one tank, which travelled successfully almost to its objective, but then broke down. This was the first time that tanks went into action, and the crew, after firing all their ammunition, set fire to it and then escaped. The L.R.B. moved in small parties during the day to Angle Wood (B.2.c.), a peculiarly unpleasant spot, as it was under perpetual artillery fire. That night a further draft of 102 men joined up.

On 16th the L.R.B. relieved the 2nd Londons in the captured trench in *T.27.a. and b.*, after having found heavy carrying fatigues all the previous night and morning through a continuous barrage. The trench was in a deplorable condition, and filled with German dead and British killed and wounded, the latter of whom were all evacuated, largely owing to the excellent work of the Divisional Field Ambulance which sent up bearers from the advanced post and continued carrying until daylight. A number of casualties was caused during the relief through one of the British heavy guns firing from the railway on the part of the trench occupied by our men, as our gunners did not know that we had captured it. One officer, who had to experience twelve hours of this, took the trouble to go to Brigade Head-quarters to express his feelings on the subject.

On 17th the weather was so bad that no active operations could be carried on, but assembly trenches (*T*.21.*d*.0.2—27.*b*. 4.8) for a frontal attack on the sunken road were dug by another unit, protected by a covering party found by the L.R.B. which was detected by the enemy and had a most trying time. Under the impression that this was the attack, the Boches put up a heavy barrage of hand grenades and opened fire, so that the men were withdrawn with the greatest difficulty.

On 18th the L.R.B. and Q.W.R. attacked to the north-west at 5.50 a.m. in a heavy drizzle, with very poor results. The L.R.B. captured, by means of a bombing attack, about 200 yards of trench towards the sunken road, which it managed to hold in spite of a determined counter-attack that night. The Q.W.R. had such a sweeping machine-gun fire brought to bear on their assaulting and supporting waves that their attempt failed completely, and they finally had to go back only 80 strong to Angle Wood to reorganise, while the L.R.B. took over the double front, i.e. the new Assembly Trench, as well as Loop Trench. The bad weather helped the enemy and crippled the British, as can be realised from the fact that a draft of 230, which left the transport lines at 8 p.m., did not reach Brigade Head-quarters till broad daylight on the next day, owing to the deep mud, and was unable to reinforce the battalion as intended. The next day the weather again put a stop to all action, but on 20th the enemy made some bombing attacks, which were all driven off, on the barricades before the Q.V.R. came up at dusk and relieved. The four days then spent in Angle Wood savoured of a busman's holiday, as the L.R.B. was hard at work every night and under ceaseless shelling all day in the wood, where 2nd Lieut. C. H. Sell was badly wounded through the simultaneous explosion of two 5·9″ shells, one on each side of him. On 24th the Q.V.R. made an attack on Combles, which failed owing to a German trench having been located wrongly, and the L.R.B. took over the Q.V.R. portion of the line in Loop and adjacent trenches at dusk. The next day, which was fine and warm, turned out to be one of the most successful ones in the Somme fighting. The 5th Division on the left captured Les Bœufs (T.4) and Morval (T.11), while the French on the right gained possession of the wooded slopes to the south and south-east of Combles, so that the enemy was overlooked from both flanks and in a precarious position. The 2nd Londons and the L.R.B. were patrolling all night, with German machine-guns and snipers firing persistently up to the early hours of the next day.

On 26th at 2.30 a.m. a patrol from "B" Company under 2nd Lieut. H. J. Simon pushed up the German (Loop) trench, climbed over the bombing block, and entered the sunken road leading to Combles. There it ran into and killed a party of five Germans, besides capturing a machine-gun, but was then stopped by a trench north-west of the village, strongly held by the enemy, which "A" Company was beginning to try to take by bombing the occupants out. By that time the French were reported to have obtained a footing in the south, and about 3.30 a.m. the resistance suddenly slackened and the bombing parties of the L.R.B. and the French met. This enabled the " B " Company patrol to enter the village and capture 200 prisoners, wounded and unwounded, who were handed over to the French, as no man could be spared for escort duties. By 9.30 a.m. the whole battalion, including headquarters, was in the village, still advancing, with two platoons holding the railway on the east, and by 4 p.m. the whole line had been carried 1100 yards east of the village up to a prepared position occupied by fresh German troops, which made any hurried advance impossible without the co-operation of artillery. This withdrawal by the enemy was evidently not prearranged, as the " B " patrol found breakfast ready in one house with hot coffee on the table. In addition to prisoners the following stores had been collected by the evening: 1800 rifles, 8500 bombs, 3 small minenwerfers, 3 flammenwerfers, of which one was a large one cemented into the floor of a house, and an enormous quantity of shells and S.A.A. At midnight the battalion was relieved by the 8th Middlesex and returned to Maltz Horn Farm (A.6.a) near Chimpanzee Trench, with as much of the captured material as it could carry.

On 27th, after sleeping through the morning, the battalion marched back to Meaulte (E.17), thinking that, as the whole Division had been relieved, it would have a week or ten days' holiday. It was rather a shock, therefore, to receive orders at 10 p.m. on 28th to be ready to move up again at short notice, in order to relieve the 6th and Guards' Divisions, as in the L.R.B. at the moment there were very few officers with any war experience and no battalion in the 169th Infantry Brigade had any bombers or more than a dozen Lewis gunners. To add to the general gaiety the rain came down in buckets, and on 29th the rest-cure ended with the L.R.B. occupying dugouts in the old German trenches at Talus Bois (A.9.c) in wretched weather. On 30th the battalion was in support at Guillemont (T.19), where the situation was very obscure. The trenches occupied by the 71st Infantry Brigade were only approximately known, the exact location of the French was a matter of speculation, no maps or aeroplane photographs were available, and one telephone wire had to satisfy the requirements of three battalions. Being in total ignorance of the enemy's position, the Q.V.R. pushed out patrols at once, who went over 500 yards forward without coming into contact with him.

On 1st October "A" Company was sent up to help in digging trenches for an attack which was going to be made on the main Le Transloy line. Its work was much hampered by the difficulties of the ground, the hostile artillery, and above all the lack of guides and accurate maps. The position was rendered a good deal clearer, although many points remained obscure.

Although the L.R.B. were not very deeply concerned in this episode, some extracts compiled from the report made by Capt. L. A. Newnham, Brigade Major 169th Infantry Brigade, about the operations throw a vivid light upon others which are merely mentioned or dismissed with a few phrases in these pages.

"1. At 6.15 p.m. the situation was very obscure, but as far as could be ascertained the Q.W.R. party had run up against the enemy in some strength in trenches and had mostly returned, leaving several missing. Q.V.R. left party had met with very heavy barrage and had not been able to go out from Foggy Trench. Q.V.R. right party had gone down the valley 400 yards and had not returned. Search parties were out several hours but could find no trace of the officer and several other ranks; a few were brought in wounded.

"2. Q.V.R. met with strong enemy barrage of H.E. for some considerable time before zero, shelling on front line had been heavy during the whole morning, and at 3.30 p.m. increased to intense. At 3.15 p.m. Foggy Trench was considerably damaged. Orders were very difficult to send owing to casualties to runners, touch between the various trenches was bad, no map showed the trenches accurately and the men were considerably shaken from the heavy bombardment.

"3. The intention for the night's work was to dig a trench southwards to connect with a small dug-in post. This was found impracticable as it was considered no starting point could be fixed to work from the north, especially as the northern end of Foggy Trench was an isolated post and exact position unknown. I therefore arranged to work in a northerly or north-easterly direction from advanced post, and arranged with

Q.V.R. for a covering party of three platoons to extend due north-east from the dug-in advanced post.

"2/2nd R.E. moved off at 9.10 p.m. to work on making Foggy Trench really tenable, to connect up the portions of trench, and join up with detached post on left flank.

"4. At about 10.5 p.m. party moved out to tape trenches and allot tasks. At the same time orders were issued to the three working companies to move down the main road and rendezvous. The country is extremely difficult to find one's way, few guides know the correct routes, and owing to trenches not being named it is very difficult to reach intended destinations.

"Tasks were allotted as follows: 2nd Londons and L.R.B. to dig a C.T. . . .

"At about 1 a.m. I led the Pioneer companies to their tasks and work progressed for 20 minutes. The enemy were sending up Very lights and one fell on the northern covering party. One or two men being new and untrained fired at the point from whence the Very light was fired; the enemy fired more lights into the covering party and opened rifle fire. Within 10 minutes a machine-gun also opened, and I could observe plainly that the covering party was under accurate and observed fire, as the bullets were dropping round them. The enemy then sent up red light signals and a heavy barrage, chiefly 4.2", was placed along the whole front. I ordered the northern covering party to withdraw man by man from the zone of Very lights and was also compelled to withdraw the platoons in the vicinity.

"5. The barrage lasted about half to three-quarters of an hour, causing considerable casualties.

"6. About 4 a.m. a small party moving from New Trench to Foggy Trench again attracted attention and, as working parties were withdrawing, at 4.15 a.m. a second barrage lasting an hour was placed over the whole area. Total estimated casualties: one Officer, 35 Other Ranks.

"7. The covering party of Q.V.R. remained particularly steadfast and all ranks, although mostly inexperienced, behaved well."

The Germans, who were located by this means and found to be in some shell-holes, trenches, and gun pits in front of Le

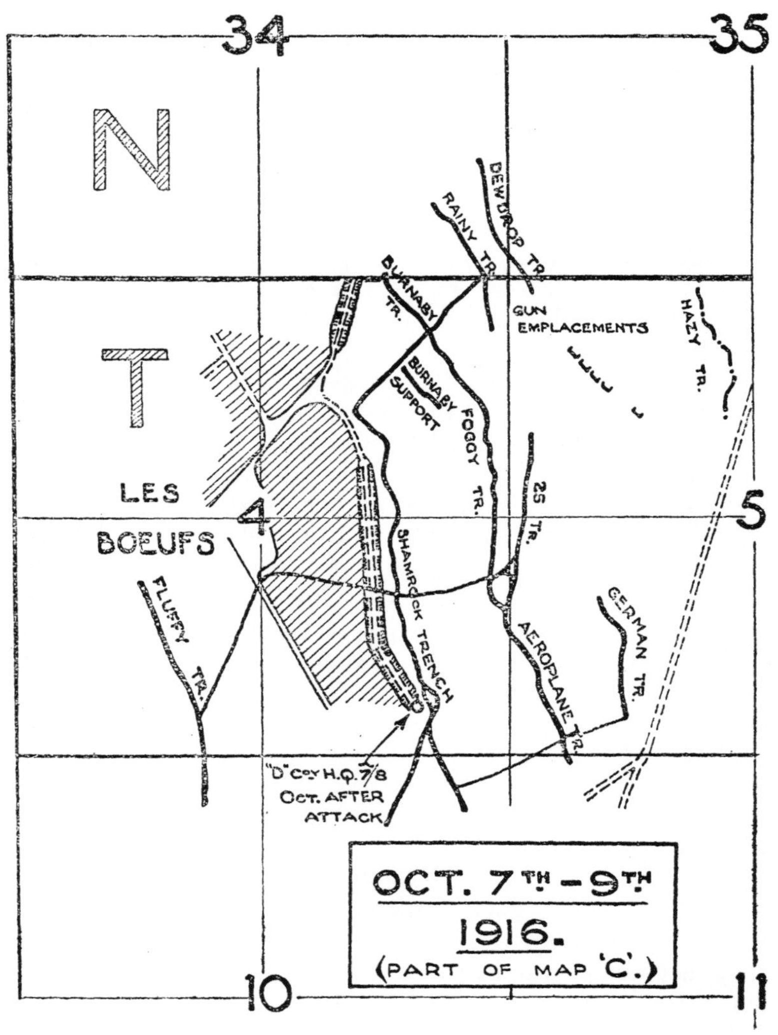

SKETCH MAP NO. 7

Transloy, and well supplied with machine guns, were extraordinarily clever in the way in which they managed, by means of their coloured light signals, to obtain such good co-operation from their artillery that they were able to hold their line easily.

On 2nd October the L.R.B. took over the line, which ran just in front of Les Bœufs, from the Q.W.R. and Q.V.R., but nothing of importance occurred until the evening of 3rd, when one Company spent the night in digging a communication trench with an unoccupied enemy trench that had been seized. The climatic conditions at that time made long tours of duty in the trenches impossible, and it was very difficult to carry out the necessary exchanges, as the muddy tracks and paths, combined with the innumerable shell-holes, made both travelling and fighting extremely hard. The London Scottish started that afternoon at 5 p.m. to relieve the L.R.B., but the latter did not reach its resting-place, some small dug-outs between Trones Wood and Bernafay Wood, three miles off, till 8.30 a.m. next day. The weather was so appallingly bad that the contemplated attack was put off, and the battalion spent two days in road-making, after receiving a special message sent by the Corps Commander, in which he expressed his great approval of the work done by the 56th Division with its tired troops. On 6th the Divisional Commander presented Distinguished Conduct Medal ribbons and divisional cards.

On 7th October the battalion was still at the same place, in Divisional Reserve, and not at all expecting to be called upon to do much more fighting, if any, in the Somme area. The 168th Infantry Brigade was known to be making an attack that day on Hazy Trench, a commanding position just in front of Le Transloy, which was to be used as a "jumping-off" spot for an advance on a large scale to be made by a division which had not been engaged in any serious fighting since 1st July, but, as no news came back about the result and several batches of prisoners went by, the battalion assumed that everything was going well and counted upon having a comfortable night's rest. However, this was not the case and at 11 p.m. orders were received to parade at 12, midnight, on the road facing Les Bœufs ready to relieve the London Scottish, who had failed to gain their objective and had been very much cut up in the attempt to do so.

Owing to the dark night, the congestion on the road which made it impassable for infantry, the muddy state of the ground by the side along which the men had to move, and the innumerable shell-holes which limited formations to single file, the march was very trying and slow. The result was, that it was daylight when the battalion reached the London Scottish Head-quarters, and the advance into the trenches, over a high ridge running between Les Bœufs and Morval and down the slope on the further side, had to be carried out in full view of the enemy. On reaching the position "D" Company, which was the last to come up, found that there was not sufficient room, through the L.R.B. being much stronger than the London Scottish, and was obliged to lie down on the back of what ought to have been its trench, until moved back to one which had been noticed on the way up, about 250 yards in rear, at the top of the hill. Finally things settled down with "A" Company in Aeroplane Trench, "B" and "C" in Shamrock Trench, less one platoon of "C" which was in Foggy Trench, and "D" in reserve in Fluffy Trench. The number of casualties during the operation was only nine, but this was entirely due to the calculated forbearance of the enemy, who realised that, if they could keep their dispositions concealed, they would later on have very much better opportunities for inflicting losses, as proved to be the case.

Within an hour warning orders were brought by runners that "A" Company on the right and "B" on the left were to attack Hazy Trench about 600 yards off, which was believed to be a line of consolidated shell-holes, with "C" in close support and "D" in reserve, and the tired men were at once ordered to get as much rest as they could. Very shortly afterwards every officer, N.C.O. and man in "D" Company was put to carrying tools, bombs and ammunition from Battalion Head-quarters to the front trenches, and heavy casualties occurred from shell-fire while doing this. About 1 p.m. final orders were received that zero was 3.30 p.m. and that the reserve company was to move forward to Shamrock Trench at the same time. It was known also that the Q.V.R. would attack simultaneously on the left, and that the French were on the right, but there was no information at all about what the latter intended doing.

As all the preparations had been made in broad daylight the attack had been well advertised, and, directly the first waves went over, the German red and green flares, which were sent up, brought on at once a terrific barrage. The smoke and the bursting shells made it impossible to distinguish the British creeping barrage which the lines had to follow, but " A " and " B " Companies pushed on through for about 500 yards, when they came under machine-gun fire from the direct front, and from some old disused German howitzer emplacements about 300 yards out on the left front, which had held up the London Scottish on the previous day, but had been, it was hoped, crushed on this occasion by the British artillery. The effect was disastrous as " A " and " B " Companies were wiped out, except for a few men who managed to reach the objective, where they may be presumed to have died fighting against overwhelming odds, but nothing more was heard of them, and the attack was completely held up.

At 4.30 p.m. " D " Company received orders to reinforce, and were subjected on appearing over the top to a barrage, which was, if possible, more severe than the previous one, but, as the men moved in artillery formation for 300 yards before extending, the advance was not very expensive and was continued until a line of shell-holes was reached in which some men of " C " Company were found. At this point the machine-gun fire was at its worst ; not a single officer of the first three companies was to be found, all of them having been passed lying dead or wounded on the way ; and further advance was impossible, as any movement brought on heavy fire at close range. The men were ordered to start digging and turn the shell-holes into a defensive line.

At dusk patrols were sent out to look for the French, as the consolidation was complete, while Capt. F. H. Crews of " D " Company, who handled his command extraordinarily well all through the day, reconnoitred the front with Lieut. J. H. Stransom, his only subaltern left unwounded, to look for men of " A " and " B " Companies. Later, Stransom went out by himself to try and find the French, and at a spot about 150 yards in advance of the British line found himself surrounded by half a dozen Germans who had risen from shell-holes behind him. On the principle that the offensive is the best defence, he called upon them to surrender (his revolver being choked with mud at the time), but only succeeded in frightening them away. Subsequent search with a rifle, which was not choked with mud, failed to reveal them. The first patrol that went out failed to return, and the second came back without any news of the first patrol or the French, but reported having seen numerous parties of the enemy. In consequence, a Lewis gun was placed on the right flank, which behaved so well in driving off the attacks made in that direction that Rfn. E. L. Kench, the commander of the team, was awarded the D.C.M. In the course of the evening 17 prisoners were captured and a machine-gun, which was found within 70 yards of the position and was no doubt the one that had caused so much trouble earlier in the day, was brought in. At 9.30 p.m. as it was clear that the L.R.B., which was not in touch with the French or the Q.V.R. who had been pinned all day to their trenches, must withdraw if it was to avoid being destroyed by the attack that was developing, the few survivors, 80 men or so, were reorganised into small parties which fell back one by one, carrying all the wounded that they could and covered by the Lewis guns under Rfn. Kench. By 10.30 p.m. they were all in their jumping-off trenches again.

The officer casualties for this one day were: Killed: Lieut. H. C. Beard, 2nd Lieuts. J. R. Carrier, C. H. Cole (11th Londons), H. Smith and G. O. Taylor; Missing: Lieut. M. J. Maynard and 2nd Lieut. J. E. Dewar; wounded and missing: 2nd Lieut. N. E. Baldwin; wounded: Capt. R. D. S. Charles, Capt. E. C. Wills, Lieut. A. Read, 2nd Lieuts. S. A. F. Alford, C. Hall, F. P. Machin, A. R. Thomson, J. S. Lindsay and W. C. Von Berg; invalided: 2nd Lieuts. P. T. Dyer, G. St. J. Martin and A. J. Newling (11th Londons).

During 9th October the stretcher-bearers showed much courage and determination, in spite of their being persistently shelled and very much hampered by the quagmire in which they had to work. Apart from this the day was quiet until about 5 p.m., when a terrific barrage opened, which led to preparations being made to meet an attack, but, as after 20 minutes the artillery stopped and machine-gun fire was put on the front line, it became evident that it was the enemy who was nervy about an assault. At 6.30 p.m. the R. Warwicks began their relief and, when this was completed, Capt. Crews with great difficulty obtained Lieut.-Col. Husey's leave to remain behind with the stretcher-bearers to search for his subaltern, Lieut. H. Smith, who was known to have been wounded, and any other man who might be saved. They worked all night and brought in many of the London Scottish, who had been lying out since the 7th, as well as their own men, but in the morning Crews, Lce.-Cpl. F. H. Stallman and one stretcher-bearer were the only survivors out of all the parties. The Warwicks also sent out a party which suffered very badly, as the officer and corporal were killed, and one man wounded, by a sniper at very close range.

Among the rescued was a sergeant, who was found crawling back bringing Lieut Smith's papers and personal effects and with a ghastly story to tell. The officer had been shot in both legs by a machine gun in trying to change his position, and had been put into splints made of his walking-stick and a rifle by his batman and the N.C.O., but was afterwards deliberately shot, though evidently still alive, by one of a party of three Germans who came up to the shell-hole in which he was lying. On the other hand, due credit must be given to one of the prisoners captured on the 8th, a stretcher-bearer, who, seeing that the L.R.B. were short-handed, bandaged at least 12 men and convoyed three serious cases safely back.

Meanwhile those of the L.R.B. who were left, only 2 Officers out of 21 (excluding the Head-quarter staff), and 108 Other Ranks out of 542 as compared with 1st October, marched back to their previous rest billets by Trones Wood, taking the whole night to do so. Owing to the congestion on the road and the appalling state of the ground the battalion soon got broken up into small parties, each in charge of an officer or N.C.O., and the principle tacitly adopted was that of "five minutes' march, ten minutes' sleep," as it was very difficult to keep awake, even while on the move, and any halt merely resulted in the men dropping in the road and falling asleep immediately.

This finished the fighting for the L.R.B. in the Somme district, and the work of 169th Infantry Brigade can be summarised as follows :—

8th Sept. Strong bombing attack by L.R.B. and Q.V.R.

9th Sept. Divisional attack on two-brigade front, L.R.B. and Q.V.R. 4.45 p.m. (Leuze Wood).

10th Sept. Q.W.R. 7 a.m. attacked Loop Trench; 3 p.m., with 2nd Londons, bombing attack.

15th Sept. 2nd Londons attacked Combles and Loop Trench 6.20 a.m.

15th and 16th Sept. (Night) three bombing attacks by 2nd Londons and L.R.B.

18th Sept. Q.W.R. attack Sunken Road Trench on two-companies front. L.R.B. bombing attack.

24th Sept. Q.V.R. bombing attack in conjunction with French.

26th Sept. Occupation of Combles—2nd Londons and L.R.B.

1st Oct. Strong patrols—Q.W.R. and Q.V.R.

8th Oct. Attack on two companies' fronts—L.R.B. capture of Hazy, Dewdrop, etc. (Les Bœufs).

The fighting was exceedingly bitter for the whole of this period and gave rise to many heroic actions. Sergt. W. A. Roulston accounted for 30 Germans in fighting his way down a trench to get touch with the Q.V.R. At Combles, Lce.-Cpl. C. Taylor killed two officers who were at tea, as well as two batmen who came in with fresh supplies. Rfn. A. E. Dunn, never resting or ever shirking under the heaviest fire, saved the lives of many, who will never forget him. "Little [F. A.] Crocker," the battalion runner, carried operation orders day and night, and on one occasion, in spite of being badly wounded, managed to deliver his message and bring the reply back, after which he fainted in battalion head-quarters. These instances, which are merely typical, show the spirit that animated the ranks, where everyone realised what the tradition of the L.R.B. was, and not a man failed.

FIRST BATTALION

Part VI. October 10, 1916—March 23, 1917

Picquigny—Richebourg—Lestrem—Laventie—Raid on Devil's Jump—Monchiet.

(*The map referred to is No.* 8, *p.* 178.)

ON 10th October the battalion went under canvas at Mansel Copse, bussing on 12th to Picquigny, where information was received that the division was going north, and after seven days' training it marched on 21st to Huppy. On 23rd it moved to Pont Remy, where it entrained for Berguette, and, arriving on 24th, marched from there to Paradis on that day. Two days were spent in training there, and on 27th a march was made to the Croix Barbee area, where the following order was received by the 56th Division from the G.O.C. Fourth Army (Lieut.-Gen. Sir H. Rawlinson), dated that day :—

"I desire to place on record my appreciation of the work that was carried out by the 56th Division during the battle of the Somme. The successful operations in the neighbourhood of Bouleaux Wood and Leuze Woods, together with the capture of Combles, between 9th and 27th September were feats of arms deserving the highest praise, and I congratulate the division on the gallantry, perseverance and endurance displayed by all ranks.

. . . . . .

"When after only two days' rest the division was again called upon to go into the line, they displayed a fine spirit of determination, which deserved success.

. . . . . .

"The enterprise and hard work which the division has shown in sapping forward and constructing trenches under fire has been a noticeable feature in the operations and I specially congratulate the infantry on the progress they made in this manner at Bouleaux Wood.

"It is a matter of regret to me that this fine division has now left the Fourth Army, but I trust that at some future date I may again find them under my command."

On 28th October the regiment relieved the 6th Worcesters in the trenches at Richebourg L'Avoue, near Neuve Chapelle, and remained in the line for the rest of the month. These trenches consisted entirely of breast works and were in a very poor, dilapidated condition, but fortunately the enemy was very quiet.

The casualties during the month were: Officers 20, of whom 8 were killed: Other Ranks 55 killed, 166 wounded and 97 missing. The officers joining up were: L.R.B.—2nd Lieuts. J. E. Dewar, S. H. Cross and S. Read; 11th London Regiment—2nd Lieuts. B. G. Ismay, D. W. Evans, C. J. Glover, H. J. Oakenfull and R. F. Bell.

During November spells of work in the trenches of a more or less light character occupied the greater part of the time, and the intervals were used for resting, cleaning up and training. On 3rd the battalion came out of trenches after being relieved by the 2nd Londons, and went back to Croix Barbee, where the second Chyebassa dinner was held on 5th in the sergeants' mess with Lieut.-Col. Husey in the chair. On 9th the battalion relieved the 2nd Londons, and during its second tour in the trenches made matters more lively for the enemy by means of trench mortar bombardments, until the 2nd Londons came in again on 15th, when the L.R.B. marched to Bout de Ville, as it was in divisional reserve. After six days' company and battalion training, the battalion on 21st took the place of the 2nd Londons for the second time, and developed its trench mortar work so much that a particularly severe effort on 23rd led to retaliation with heavy howitzer fire, after which matters were quiet on both sides until 27th, when the 1st Norfolks and 16th R. Warwicks came in relief, and the L.R.B. marched to Lestrem.

The casualties during the month were: Killed 5 Other Ranks and wounded 11. The officers joining were: Capt. A. B. White, Lieut. P. Titley, 2nd Lieuts. F. H. Ball, J. S. Calder,

F. S. Clark, F. G. Fass, L. H. Fotheringham, J. S. Godward, F. G. Hancocks, T. A. Prior, E. W. Rose, W. C. Von Berg (all L.R.B.), H. J. Simon (3rd Londons), H. N. Callcott (11th Londons), and Lieut. and Q.M. J. R. S. Petersen in exchange for Lieut. and Q.M. W. Kelly.

On 1st December, 1916, the battalion was at Lestrem, out of the line, and continued company training until the 8th. On 7th the Corps Commander, Lieut.-Gen. Sir R. Haking, who was accompanied by the divisional and brigade commanders, inspected the battalion and expressed his great approval of its steadiness and smart turn out. On 9th it relieved the 8th Middlesex in the line in the Neuve Chapelle sector (*M*.24.*d*.04 southwards), which was in an extremely bad state, with the wire very weak owing to the damage done by the enemy's "minnies," but the casualties were small. It came out on 15th, marching to Riez Bailleul, and returned to the line on 21st, taking up a position slightly to the left of the previous one.

In order to prevent any recurrence of the fraternising that went on at Christmas in 1914, which had not been forgotten by the authorities, the Corps Commander had prepared an elaborate programme of artillery and rifle fire, which began at 7 p.m. on 24th and continued with intense fire, steady fire, and a few quiet intervals until 7 p.m. on 27th. Not a Hun showed himself and the attempts at retaliation, which were very slight indeed, were silenced at once by the gunners, who co-operated whole-heartedly with the infantry. A prisoner had given full particulars of the Hun programme of Christmas festivities, which must have been sadly interfered with, as at 9.30 p.m. on 24th the British guns concentrated on a spot where a dinner was arranged to be held, and shelled it to pieces. On 27th an interesting tour came to an end by the 2nd Londons coming in and the L.R.B. going out to Riez Bailleul for six days, during which working parties were supplied to assist in repairing the much damaged front line.

The casualties for December were 7 Other Ranks wounded. The officers who joined were 2nd Lieut. B. Warner from England and 2nd Lieut. H. Taylor from direct commission.

If the honours of Christmas Day had belonged to the British, those of New Year's Day, 1917, were certainly in favour of

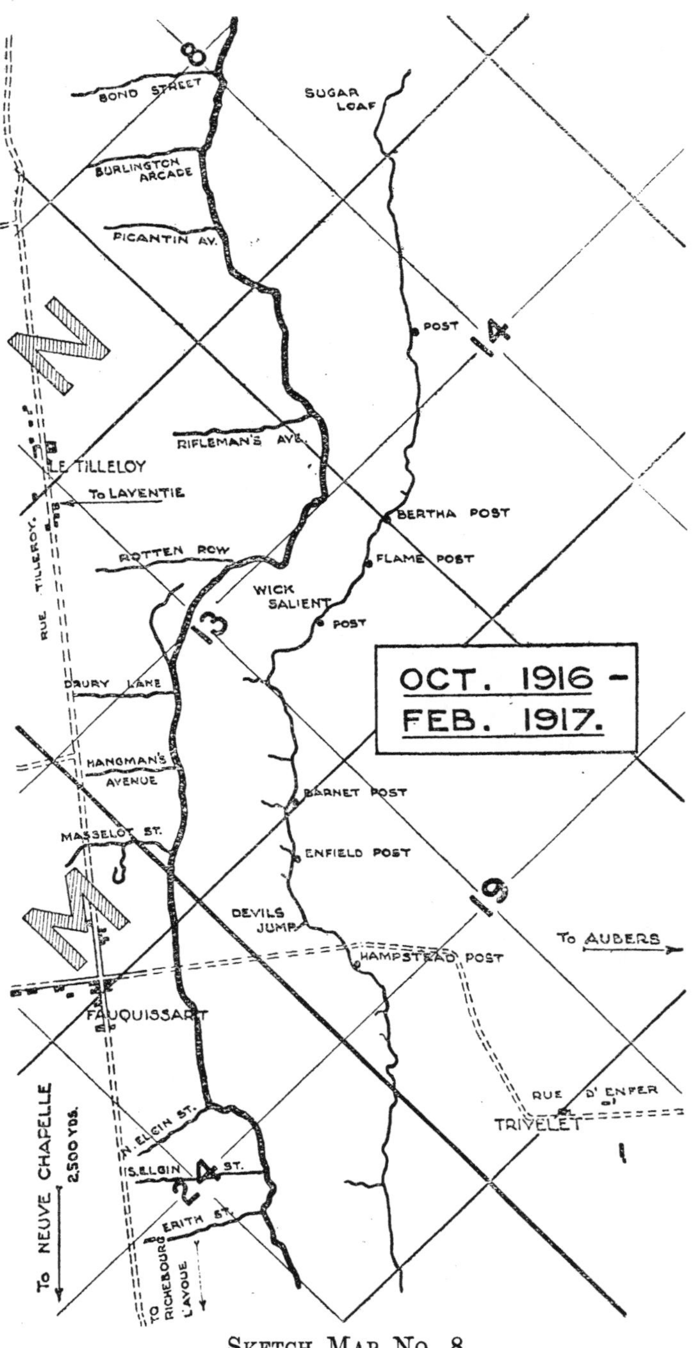

SKETCH MAP No. 8.

the Germans, who organized a shoot on a larger scale than had been seen in the neighbourhood for some time. Laventie, La Flinque, Pont du Hem, and other of the billeting places underwent severe shelling, which resulted in every house suffering from the lavish bombardment as well as, unfortunately, two field ambulances, but prompt steps were taken to retaliate.

On 2nd January the reply took place, in which much ammunition was expended, and the L.R.B. moved into divisional reserve at Grand Pacaut, a most popular place, for 12 days. Concerts and dinners were held there, besides regimental sports, in which "D" Company won the bayonet fighting and drill competitions, with the head-quarter personnel a good second in the latter, "C" Company won the bomb-throwing and tug-of-war, and "A" Company won the 4 mile team race, Capt. F. H. Crews being 1st, and 2nd Lieut. J. S. Godward 2nd. During this rest period the L.R.B. beat the Q.V.R. by 1 to 0 in a football match for the divisional cup, and an officers' mess dinner was held on 13th, at which 25 were present.

On 14th January the battalion went into support, with two companies in Laventie and two in Rue Bacquerot, and on 20th went into the line again, where it occupied Barnet (*N*.19.*a*) and Enfield, two posts which had been established in the German front line: the enemy had moved back to higher ground round Aubers in consequence of his old trenches being flooded. Digging and consolidation were almost impossible at that time, owing to the very severe frost. The ground in front of the trenches and posts was a sheet of ice, and the ditches and flooded communication trenches were frozen hard. On 24th January the Boches made a determined raid on the two posts, but were driven off on reinforcements arriving. On 26th the battalion was relieved, and on 29th these two posts, as well as three others which the brigade had established in the enemy's old front line, were abandoned. They had become increasingly difficult to hold owing to their being continuously shelled by the enemy, who knew their exact positions.

During January, 7 Other Ranks were killed or died of wounds and 20 were wounded. 2nd Lieut. H. N. Calcott was invalided to England, 2nd Lieut. D. W. Evans was transferred to the Machine Gun Corps, and 2nd Lieuts. W. E. Reed, T. E. Burroughs (both L.R.B.) and E. C. Warner (7th Londons) joined.

The following extract is taken from a communication received from XIth Corps relating to the operations by the 56th Division in the Fauquissart (*M*.24) section during January : "The Corps Commander considers that the enterprise and the fine fighting spirit shown in carrying out the operations is worthy of the greatest praise. . . . At 8.57 p.m. on 24th 30 Germans advanced along their old line to attack Barnet. They were able to obtain cover in their old trench owing to the hard ice. They then extended and attacked in a wave. This was held up by bombs and Lewis gun fire until the supporting platoon reinforced the post. After a fight lasting ten minutes they were driven off. Our Stokes' mortars put a barrage in front of the post immediately the alarm was given, and it is believed that casualties were thus inflicted upon the enemy. . . . The work done in connection with seizing and holding the Fauquissart posts, and the information gained by the persistent patrolling of the enemy's lines has been most valuable, and is a fine example of the policy of harassing the enemy by all means in our power, which it must always be our aim to carry out." The following letter from the Corps Commander, Major-Gen. Haking, to the Divisional Commander was circulated :—

"I shall be glad if you will convey to all troops of the Division under your command my appreciation of the operations they have carried out so successfully during the past month in establishing posts in the German front line and holding them, in spite of heavy bombardments and hostile infantry attacks. The effect of these operations is much greater than the troops that took part in them are probably aware of. They have shown the enemy the offensive and enterprising spirit displayed by our troops, and have encouraged other British formations to adopt similar tactics which will have a far-reaching effect. Brigadier-Generals Loch and Freeth, who conducted the operations at different periods when you were commanding the Corps, deserve credit for the determined manner in which they continued the pressure against the enemy in spite of serious opposition. The various counter-attacks by our troops, immediately delivered without waiting for any further orders and simply adhering to the plan laid down by you, show a fine military spirit on the part of the officers and men of the battalions engaged. I was particularly pleased . . . also with 'A' and 'B' companies of the L.R.B. under Lieut. Prior and 2nd Lieut. Rose, who held Enfield and Barnet posts in the enemy's line on the night January 24th/25th when these posts were shelled with lachrymatory shells and our men had to wear respirators. These posts were then heavily attacked and the supporting platoons quickly traversed No Man's Land before the hostile barrage was put down. I am also glad to hear that the artillery support on all occasions throughout these operations has been prompt and effective."

On 1st February the battalion relieved the Q.V.R. in the same trenches as before and stayed there till 7th in quiet, but in such intense cold that on 3rd 20 degrees of frost were registered. However, hard work was done in the only way possible, 817 coils of barbed wire being put out in addition to numerous "knife-rests," and, as the enemy was now able to occupy his front line again through the frost, it was decided to carry out a raid during the next tour in the line. On going back on 7th to billets in Laventie as Brigade Reserve, "D," the selected company, and the battalion bombers practised for the raid under Capt. Crews, 2nd Lieut. Perowne and 2nd Lieut. Godward.

On 13th the battalion was inspected and marched past the Commander-in-Chief, F.M. Sir Douglas Haig, and before going in again on 14th the Brigadier wrote to Lt.-Col. Husey: "Good luck; I hope you are choosing a pretty strong shelter for yourself for advanced battalion head-quarters. I want you to do so." He evidently knew how fearless Husey was and how careless of his own safety. The raid on Devil's Jump and Hampstead (*N*.19.*a*) took place on 17th/18th February, and the Brigadier's official report states "the night turned out very unfavourably, a thick ground mist combining with a clouded sky. The enemy trenches and their surroundings were much cut up by shell-holes, and it was entirely due to the excellent patrolling which the L.R.B. have been doing recently that there was not considerable confusion."

The report sent in by Major Wallis, who was in command that evening, owing to Lt.-Col. Husey having been slightly wounded while going round the front line to see that all arrangements were completed and sent down to the C.C.S., was as follows :—

"Owing to the severe frost causing the ditches and ground to become easily moved over, ample evidence was obtained from patrols, aeroplane photographs, etc., that the Germans were reoccupying their old front line. The L.R.B. received orders to raid some portion of the German line on their next tour in the trenches. It was decided to attack the German posts at *N*.19.*a*. 32 known as Hampstead and the Devil's Jump at *N*.19.*a*. 35.

"The raid was practised whilst the battalion was in reserve at Laventie. The success of the raid largely depended on the frost continuing, as the ground in front of the proposed objectives was not passable in ordinary winter weather.

"On 14th February the battalion relieved the Q.W.R. in the trenches. The same night reconnoitring patrols were sent out to report on Hampstead and the Devil's Jump, one patrol under an officer, 2nd Lieut. Godward, went out to reconnoitre Devil's Jump and our two old posts known as Barnet and Enfield. Barnet was found unoccupied, but considerable new work was found, including a new concrete dug-out containing German bombs and a telescope. Enfield was found to be held by the Germans and a bombing fight ensued, in which our entire patrol except one man became casualties. All, however, returned, except one N.C.O. killed, and brought back much valuable information. It was particularly unfortunate that the officer i/c the patrol, 2nd Lieut. Godward, was wounded, as he was the one detailed for the raid on the Devil's Jump, and knew the ground. The same day Capt. Crews, the officer i/c main raiding party, who had previously reconnoitred Hampstead on several occasions, was detailed to report at XIth Corps Head-quarters.

"A second patrol on the same night under Lieut. B. C. Perowne found Hampstead strongly garrisoned, and the enemy working hard in the post. A German fighting patrol of 25 men filed past our patrol within ten yards of them. A machine gun firing from Hampstead sprayed our parapet and No Man's Land. Fresh officers were detailed, and patrols again went out on the night 15/16th. A thaw had now set in and the ice broke in a few instances when the patrols were crossing ditches. The Germans were heard working, as on the previous night, and in several other places as well. Hostile machine-gun fire was active, firing from Hampstead. A German fighting patrol was also out, and approached our trenches ; they were fired on and dispersed.

" On the night of 16th/17th patrols were again out, but brought in no fresh information, except that the ground was very muddy and the ice very thin. During this day the wire in front of the right company was badly knocked about by hostile trench mortars and heavy artillery. At night a German patrol approached this company front and was fired on. It is known that at least one man was badly hit. Two German overcoats were recovered and numerous German bombs, all dated 17/1/17. One German rifle was also brought in.

" On the morning of February 17th the thaw set in in earnest and rain fell. It was decided that the raid should take place on this night. From 9.15 p.m. to 9.30 p.m. the 169th Machine Gun Company fired bursts of fire on No Man's Land. The artillery and trench mortars bombardment was carried out as prearranged.

" *Party 'A' objective Devil's Jump.* This party left our trench at 9.30 p.m. and, at zero, at once energetically pushed on to the objective, which it reached without opposition. The whole trench to the Rue d'Enfer (*N*.19.*a*) was thoroughly searched. The post was empty. No sign of any emplacement was discovered, and the trench itself was a mass of shell-holes. The patrol then took up a position in the German trench on Rue d'Enfer, and acted as left flank guard. It came into touch with the left flank of party 'B' which had lost direction.

" *Party 'B' objective Hampstead.* This party, under Lieut. T. A. Prior, *vice* Godward, left our trench at 9.40 p.m. and moved to assembly position. At zero the party advanced to the objective, which was reached without opposition. The left section lost direction and crossed the Rue d'Enfer, but quickly found its mistake and turned south to Hampstead. The trench from Rue d'Enfer to Hampstead was entirely obliterated and no dug-outs or emplacements were discovered. In Hampstead three Germans were found and killed ; the bodies were searched, but no papers or identity discs were found. A rifle was brought back. Owing to the thick mist and intense darkness it was extremely difficult to explore the position, but it was done as completely as possible in the circumstances. No machine-gun emplacement was found, or an emplacement of any kind. There is a semicircular very small sand-bag post in front of Hampstead, which was unoccupied.

"*Party* '*C*' left our trench at 9.30 p.m. to act as right flank guard. It suffered several casualties from one of our own shells during the intense bombardment, which severely wounded, amongst others, Lieut. Perowne, the officer i/c. At zero the remainder advanced and took up their prearranged positions. This party saw no signs of the enemy during the time of the raid.

"*Party* '*D*.' The supporting party under Capt. F. H. Crews was in position at 9.54 p.m. and telephonic communication was established with Advanced Battalion Head-quarters. The supports were not required to assist the raiders.

"At 10.20 p.m. the signal to withdraw was sounded and the parties gradually returned to our trenches.

"Casualties : 1 Other Ranks killed, and 1 Officer and 5 Other Ranks wounded. The German shelling of our line was accurate, several direct hits being obtained. His artillery stopped within a few minutes of ours ceasing to fire. No hostile barrage was put down in No Man's Land, and at no time during the night was there any enemy machine-gun fire opposite to our front.

"It is suggested that the Germans occupied their old front line in some strength during the time that the ditches were frozen over, with the object of preventing our patrols penetrating too far. The frost having now broken, the German trenches have become untenable, and the ditches are full of water. The night was very dark, which was made more intense by the mist. It was almost impossible to see our shells bursting when standing in our front trench."

It is interesting to note that the battalion buglers assisted in the raid by sounding the first part of the "officers' mess call" as the signal to withdraw.

On 20th February the L.R.B. was relieved by the Q.W.R. and went into brigade support, "A" and "B" companies being in billets in Laventie, and "C" and "D" in dug-outs in the Rue Bacquerot, and on 21st Lieut.-Col. Husey returned.

On 25th February the battalion was in the line again in the old trenches, but on 27th moved slightly to the right, and on 1st March finally came out. On 27th a medal ribbon presentation parade was held in the square at Merville, to which the L.R.B. sent 1 Officer (Capt. Crews) and 31 Other Ranks, Sergts. G. Hands and J. H. Wortley being among the recipients. The casualties during the month were, besides Lieut.-Col. Husey, 2nd Lieut. Godward, E. C. Wills, and Perowne wounded, Other Ranks 6 killed and 21 wounded. The following letter from the Corps Commander to the Divisional General was circulated :—

"On the departure of your division I am anxious to place on record my appreciation of the excellent work done by commanders, staff and all ranks throughout the division during the time it has been in the XIth Corps.

"In its higher leading and staff work the division is conspicuous for sound tactical judgment and forethought, and for its cheeriness and good fellowship in all its dealings both with those above and below.

"In the unit, brigade and divisional head-quarters I have always found that the basis of work is to help everyone else and not to make difficulties. A large number of regimental officers have been trained efficiently in staff work and have proved their value when they have been given definite appointments.

"The fighting spirit of all ranks is excellent, and this has been shown with the greatest success by the prosecution of raids into the enemy's lines, and by the operations carried out in bitter weather during January, when the front system of the German trenches was held by the division in a series of posts, and all attacks repelled with success until orders were received to withdraw.

"... I also wish to thank the chaplains of all denominations in the division for their devoted work to officers and men both in and out of the trenches.

"The football competitions got up by the divisional commander and the excellent entertainments provided by the 'Bow Bells' troupe have greatly assisted all of us to keep cheery and lively during the winter months.

"I have no hesitation in saying that this division is one of the best that has been in my corps, and there have been over 20 in it since it was first formed. I am convinced that wherever the division goes and whatever it is called upon to do, the officers, N.C.O.'s and men will always distinguish themselves.

"I wish the division an early victory to add to others it has already gained, and I part with it with the deepest regret, which is shared by all my staff."

On being relieved on 1st March the battalion marched to Vieille Chapelle and it continued to march daily until 8th, halting at St. Venant, Pernes, Fillievres, Le Boisle, Buire-au-Bois, Ivergny, and Fosseux, where it was billeted in Nissen huts. Lieut. D. McOwan, the adjutant, was invalided, and Lieut. Stransom took his place. A violent snowstorm took place on 8th, and the weather was bitterly cold. Soon after arrival the Commander of the VIIth Corps, Lieut.-Gen. T. D. Snow, visited the L.R.B. and expressed his pleasure at having the regiment, which had been under him at Gommecourt and until it left the Somme, again under his command. During the eight days' marching the L.R.B. covered 96 miles, a reference to which will be found on p. 58. The battalion rested until 14th March, when it marched to Dainville, and on 15th moved into Arras by sections after dark. During their few days in Arras the C.O., Lieut.-Col. Husey, and the Adjutant, Capt. Stransom, went up to the line held by the 2nd Londons (whom the L.R.B. were to relieve) to reconnoitre the trenches. These were in front of Beaurains, and the German line ran along the edge of the road skirting Beaurains, the No Man's Land being about 150 yards wide. The German trenches were protected by one of the thickest belts of wire yet seen, a good part of it being the thick "cactus wire." No sooner had these two officers arrived in the trench than a British plane, which had been observed to be flying very low and rather erratically over No Man's Land without being fired upon by the Boches, crashed between the British front and support lines. The 2nd Londons rushed out of their trenches to help the unfortunate occupants, but the fine target drew no fire from the enemy, which was explained by a message from the observer of the plane that there were no Boches in the front line, but plenty retreating down the valley behind Beaurains. Something of the sort had been suspected and the plane had apparently been watching for the move, the pilot being unluckily wounded in the thigh by one of the marksmen left behind in the line to help to prevent the fact of the retreat from being known for as long as possible. This was the L.R.B.'s first introduction to the voluntary retreat in the early months of 1917 which had begun sooner further south. The immediate result was the cancellation of the orders which had been issued by Brigade for an attack on Beaurains and beyond, and an immediate heightening of a *morale* already high. The enemy, of course, had his own reasons for retiring, but the good effect on the British *morale* undoubtedly played a large part in the attacks which took place on Easter Monday and after. On 18th brigade orders stated that Ficheux Mill was occupied by the 56th Division, the 89th Infantry Brigade being on its right. The 169th Brigade was on a two-battalion front, and on 19th the L.R.B. moved into Achicourt by platoons after dark. On 20th Lieut.-Col. Husey went into hospital, owing to his having neglected a nasty wound in the finger which he received on 17th February. His refusal to allow proper attention to be paid to the matter at the time threatened to lead to serious consequences, but fortunately all ended well. Capt. A. B. White was left in command.

On 24th the L.R.B. relieved the Q.W.R. in the left sector, several casualties being caused by shell-fire during the process. On 25th the posts were heavily shelled at night, and one was attacked, but the enemy was driven off by Lewis gun and rifle fire.

FIRST BATTALION

Part VII. Mar. 24—Aug. 11, 1917

Battle of Arras—Attack on Cojeul River—Sombrin—Bayenghem.

(*The Maps referred to are B and No.* 9 *on p.* 192, *and No.* 10 *on p.* 198.)

THE battle of Arras formed the spring offensive of the British in 1917; it was to some extent discounted by the German withdrawal to the Hindenburg Line, the strength of which enabled them to use their reserve in other threatened localities. Three lines of defences ran in front of the switch line from Queant to Drocourt and thence to Lens. This line was not finished at the beginning of April, and had the British attack been fully successful and had the attack by the French further south, which began just a week later, come up to expectation, the defences might have been broken and the Hindenburg lines turned. Up to a point the fighting was very successful, but the main object, to break the German lines, was not attained, and the success gained had to be exploited for more than it was worth in order to help the French, whose co-operation was almost a failure. Possibly unity of command might have produced better results, but this did not come for many months.

On March 26th Major Wallis, who had been on leave, assumed command of the battalion in Lieut.-Col. Husey's absence. The L.R.B. was holding the old German trenches in front of Beaurains, which had been evacuated by the enemy about three days before. Beaurains (M.11) was an important tactical feature from the enemy's point of view, on high ground, giving observation in Agny (M.9), Achicourt (G.33), Ronville, etc.

From patrol reports it was found that the Germans were holding a line across Telegraph Hill (N.7) and in front of

Neuville Vitasse (N.19). The L.R.B.'s front was held by "B" "C" and "D" companies, with "A" in support. Battalion head-quarters were in a German dug-out in Beaurains (probably in M.10.d.88, where they had been on 24th).

The front line ran along the Beaurains—Neuville Vitasse road.

"C" Company under 2nd Lieut. C. H. John, M.18.a.

"D" Company under 2nd Lieut. W. J. Grace (10th Londons) M.12.c.

"B" Company under Capt. P. Titley, M.11.d.

"A" Company under Capt. E. W. Rose in support south of Beaurains.

The right and centre companies each had three posts, and the left company one post. Each company had a platoon in support and one in reserve.

The trenches were in a very bad condition and there was only one dug-out, which was used by "C" and "D" companies for company head-quarters. "D" company's trenches were badly blown in and were not connected. In places they were only two feet deep. During the previous night and this day patrols were pushed out along the various communication trenches leading to the enemy lines. Posts were established in forward positions where possible.

On March 27th from 1 a.m. to 4 a.m. patrols were pushed out in the direction of Neuville Vitasse, and dispersed several enemy working parties, the Germans being feverishly engaged in putting out wire. British artillery fired on enemy carrying parties during the day. Hostile shelling increased considerably, especially on Beaurains, and rain made movement in the trenches very difficult. Otherwise the day passed off quietly.

Hostile artillery increased in severity on 28th in the battalion sector, but little damage was done. At 11 p.m. 2nd Lieut. Von Berg patrolled all along the enemy wire in front of Neuville Vitasse, and found the whole line strongly held with infantry posts every 10–15 yards. Heavy rain increased the discomfort at night, and continued during 29th.

At 3 a.m. on 30th our patrols reported that several of the old communication trenches leading to Telegraph Hill and Neuville Vitasse had been filled in by the enemy, and at 11 p.m. the battalion was relieved by the Q.W.R. and returned to billets in Achicourt. A few casualties were caused during the relief by hostile shelling.

The battalion spent 31st in cleaning up, bathing and resting.

On April 1st the battalion marched to Monchiet. The brigade was in divisional reserve. The route followed by the L.R.B. had been via the main Arras-Beaumetz-Doullens road, leaving Achicourt at 2 p.m. The roads were deep in mud.

The orders for the attack gave the information that the VIIth Corps would attack with the 30th Division on the right, the 56th in the centre and the 14th on the left.

The objective was approximately from east of Croisilles (T.23) 1000 yards east of Heninel (N.28)—500 yards S.E. of Guemappe (N.18). The attack would be launched at zero plus 3 hours by the centre and left divisions, while 3 hours and 40 minutes later all three divisions would advance together. The VIth Corps was to attack at zero so as to bring it up level with the VIIth. Of the 56th Division, the 167th Infantry Brigade was to attack on the right with the 168th on the left. The 169th was to be in Divisional reserve. Brigade head-quarters was to be situated at G.33.d.40. Sixteen tanks were allotted to the corps, of which the 56th Division got four.

After spending 2nd and 3rd in cleaning up, etc., the preliminary bombardment by the British artillery commenced in heavy snow and rain on 4th and the surplus personnel under Capt. A. B. White left for the divisional reinforcement camp on 5th.

April 6th, Good Friday, was known to be " X " day, and a voluntary church parade was held, at which practically the whole battalion was present. Heavy rain and snow fell all day, and news was received that " Z " day was postponed twenty-four hours.

At 7 p.m. on 7th the battalion moved to old British trenches south of Agny. Battalion head-quarters were at the junction of Girl Street and the Support Line (M.14.d.5.7). " Z " day was now known to be April 9th. The route up was through Dainville and Achicourt and the road seemed to be almost lined with artillery. The main Arras-Doullens road was very congested with traffic, and the fact that the enemy was paying particular attention to it did not tend to improve matters.

It was at the junction of this road with the one to Achicourt that a direct hit was obtained on " D " company's cooker, killing both horses and Rfn. C. Valentine and A. B. Tolhurst. The latter was the son of Alfred Tolhurst, late of " P " Company, one of the regiment's oldest friends and benefactors. Agny was reached at midnight. By this time the weather had cleared up and the moon enabled some shelters to be found. Altogether the conditions for the attack looked more hopeful.

On April 8th all packs were dumped in Achicourt and battle stores drawn. At 9 p.m. the battalion moved to trenches. The heavy bombardment continued without ceasing all day and night, but the enemy made very little reply. The weather continued fine.

On " Z " day, 9th, the attack was to be made by the First and Third Armies, zero hour for the former was 5.30 a.m. and for the latter 7.30 a.m. The attack on Neuville Vitasse and the Hindenburg Line by the 56th Division was successful, and by 3 p.m. British artillery was observed moving forward. At 4 p.m. the L.R.B. was placed under the orders of Brig.-Gen. Freeth, Commanding 167th Infantry Brigade, and moved to old trenches at Beaurains.

All officers reconnoitred the routes forward in case of any heavy counter-attack being made. Snow fell during the night. The position of the battalion at 12 noon on 10th was " A " Company in Manche Trench, " B " in Mince, " C " in Grundherr Stellung, and " D " in Maizieul Trench, battalion head-quarters being in Rechter Graben, in squares M.17d.18c. and 23b.

Divisional orders gave the information that the VIth Corps was in possession of the part of the Wancourt (N.23)-Feuchy (H.21) line, north of Feuchy Chapelle (N.4). The 56th and 14th Divisions were to assault the Wancourt-Feuchy line simultaneously with the 3rd Division at noon. The artillery of the 21st and 30th Divisions would assist. The 167th Infantry Brigade would attack on the frontage allotted to the division, and the Q.V.R. were placed at the disposal of the Brigadier-General Commanding 168th Infantry Brigade.

The attack was made in a snowstorm. The 167th Infantry Brigade was stopped at Nepaul Trench (*N*.21.*b*. and *d*.), which

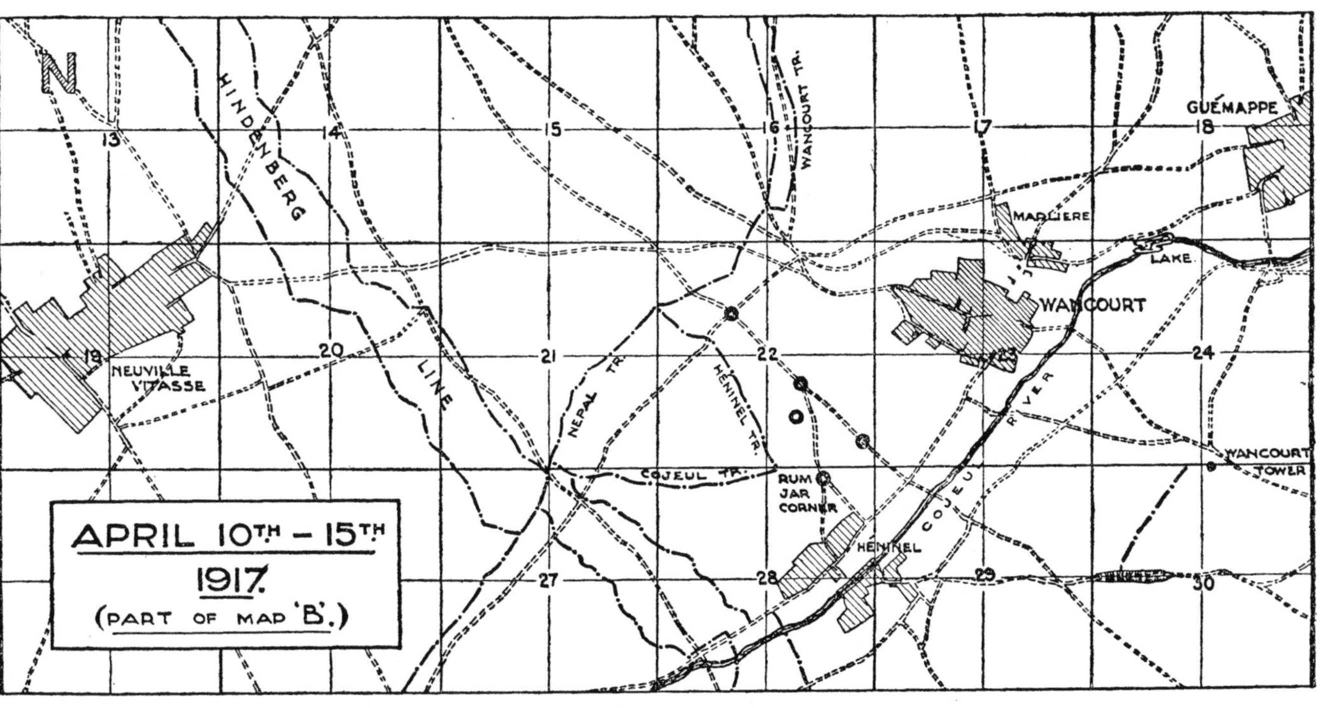

Sketch Map No. 9.

was the last German trench system, heavily wired with two belts of thick wire some 50 yards deep. This had been left untouched by the artillery. Our troops were reported as holding a line of shell-holes about 300 yards west of Nepaul Trench. The division on the left was similarly held up by the same trench.

The weather conditions were terrible on 11th April. The night had been bitterly cold and the men had had to stand in open derelict trenches through sleet, snow and freezing wind, which had been the normal conditions since leaving Agny. Two men died of exposure. The thick mud, too, caused intense discomfort.

At 11 a.m. Brig.-Gen. Freeth ordered the L.R.B. to relieve the 8th Middlesex as soon as possible. Their dispositions were obscure. Meanwhile the Q.V.R. on the right (lent to 168th Infantry Brigade) had penetrated Nepaul Trench (*N*.21.*d*.) and were successfully bombing southwards. It was arranged with the C.O. 8th Middlesex to send up a platoon immediately to enter Nepaul Trench and bomb northwards, and 2nd Lieut. Fotheringham was detailed for this work. The C.O. with 2nd Lieut. W. E. Reed then left to reconnoitre the front to be taken over, and, under cover of the thick snow, actually entered Nepaul Trench, which was said still to be held by the enemy. They traversed some 1000 yards of it northwards and found it untenanted. On their return they met Fotheringham's party, which encountered the enemy within 50 yards of where they had turned back. The battalion subsequently took over Nepaul Trench in advance of the 8th Middlesex. It was held by three companies with "D" in reserve at the old Middlesex company head-quarters. The L.R.B. arranged to bomb up Heninel Trench (*N*.22.*c*.) towards Rum Jar Corner (*N*.28.*b*.), to which point the 2nd Londons, who had relieved the Q.V.R., were also bombing up Cojeul Trench (*N*.28.*a*.). This relief of the Middlesex was complete by 7 p.m. and the battalion's frontage stretched from *N*.21.*d*.48 to *N*.22.*a*.45. 2nd Lieut. B. Warner was killed in the bombing operations up Heninel Trench, which resulted in the killing of 17 Germans and the capture of 2 wounded. Junction was made with the 2nd Londons, and posts were established at: (1) cross roads *N*.22.*a*. *central*. (2)

N.22.*d*.37. (3) *N*.22.*d*.9.2. (4) *N*.22.*d*.35 ; and (5) *N*.28.*b*.59. Warner made two unsuccessful efforts before his party finally cleared Heninel Trench, and was killed after he had gallantly succeeded in gaining his objective. He was the third and last of his family to be killed whilst fighting with the L.R.B. : one brother went out with the 1st Battalion and was killed at Ploegsteert, and another, Archie, was killed at Gommecourt. They were all fine soldiers.

On April 12th, at dawn, patrols were pushed out from the high ground and at 10 a.m. they reached the outskirts of Wancourt and passed through the village, which they were able to report as clear by that hour. Four prisoners were taken and handed over to the 14th Division. At *N*.22.*b*.56 a very large dug-out was found beautifully furnished with lounge chairs, beds with sheets on them, blankets, etc., and breakfast laid on a white cloth. Candles were still burning. It seemed in every way most suitable for battalion head-quarters, but the brigade thought it too large for a battalion and took it over later in the day. The battalion head-quarters then moved to a large dug-out, which had been an ammunition store at *N*.23.*a*.52. Capt. Titley led the first patrol into Wancourt and 2nd Lieut. W. E. Reed did excellent work in reconnoitring and searching that village, entering all the dug-outs with a single runner. His knowledge of the place was most useful subsequently. The above operations were described by a newspaper correspondent as follows : " After bitter fighting in the streets of Wancourt and Heninel the London troops pushed on, forded the Cojeul River and stormed the heights beyond." As a matter of fact no Germans were encountered in Wancourt, although two or three dug-outs still had candles burning in them on the arrival of our troops. The Cojeul River was not more than 18 inches wide where the L.R.B. stepped (" forded " sounds better) across it and the storming of the heights beyond was almost a bloodless battle, machine gun fire from Guemappe (N.18) and artillery fire causing all the casualties.

At 6 p.m. the battalion assembled on the rising ground east of Wancourt, with its left on Wancourt Tower (*N*.24.*d*.), for an attack on the following day on Cherisy (O.32) and the Sensee River. The situation was interesting as this was the first occasion on which orders were issued for open warfare. There were no trenches between the battalion and its objective, which was about two miles distant. The attack was subject to the 14th Division taking Guemappe, which was immediately behind and overlooked the battalion's assembly position. A few gas shells were sent over by the enemy during this time, causing some half-dozen casualties. The L.R.B. "stood to" all night and spent the time digging or improving assembly trenches.

The attack on Guemappe which took place on 13th failed, and, after remaining all the day expecting to receive notice of zero hour, the attack by the 56th Division was postponed.

At 9 p.m. orders were received that the battalion would be relieved by the Q.W.R. that night, and that the latter battalion would be ready to carry out the Cherisy attack if ordered to. The L.R.B. was ordered to move back to ground near Rum Jar Corner for rest. The large majority of officers and other ranks had had no rest since April 9th. Rum Jar Corner was reached next morning by 2.30 a.m.

This night of 13th/14th was noteworthy as being the first occasion on which the battalion's transport failed in getting rations up to the troops. Instructions had been sent to the transport that the battalion was east of Wancourt, followed by the news that it had been relieved. Capt. Gordon, the transport officer, dumped and moved the rations three times during the night and only gave up the search for the battalion at dawn, when, as it happened, the rations were dumped within a few hundred yards of where the L.R.B. actually was.

On April 14th, at 2 a.m., orders were received for the battalion to assemble behind the Q.W.R. ready for the attack that morning. Zero hour was 5.30 a.m. In order to complete the assembly by 5 a.m. it was necessary, owing to the exhausted state of the troops, to commence the move up to the area just vacated at 3.45 a.m.

The Q.W.R. were to attack on the left with the L.R.B. in support, the Q.V.R. attacking on the right with the 2nd Londons in support.

Further on the left the 151st Infantry Brigade was attacking. The idea apparently was to squeeze the enemy out of Guemappe.

From accounts given at the time by the C.O.'s of the 6th, 8th and 9th Battalions of the D.L.I., who were ordered to attack on the left of the L.R.B., it is surmised that their brigade was on a night march when orders were received that, instead of marching to billets, the brigade was to attack the next day on the left of the 56th Division. Wancourt Tower was given as an easy landmark for their flank, but by an unfortunate error it was given them as *their* left flank instead of the 56*th Division's* left. Later they were told to push on quickly as zero was at 5.30 a.m. and they were likely to be late. Their scheme was to move in artillery formation after passing Wancourt, and make a half-left wheel followed by a half-right wheel to get them on to their alignment under cover of the slope from the Cojeul. It would have been a sufficiently difficult manœuvre in peace time on even and open ground, but became an almost impossible one under the existing circumstances. To make matters worse Wancourt Tower had been blown up in the night, so their sole landmark was gone.

At zero the advance started and the attack looked for all the world like the crowd leaving the Crystal Palace after a cup final. The 169th Brigade with three battalions of the D.L.I. all mixed up on a frontage of about half a mile and a depth of 900 yards, moving up the hill with the Germans pouring machine gun fire from Guemappe into the mass. The attack failed from the outset and the advance was stopped dead. The Q.V.R. and Q.W.R. suffered heavily.

For the rest of the day the L.R.B. was under machine-gun fire from Guemappe, but the casualties were not so heavy as might have been expected. Battalion head-quarters was established at the cross-roads at *N*.29.*a*., as there was a deep dug-out there, but unfortunately it had only one entrance and the enemy paid special attention to it with 5·9's. Later in the day head-quarters were moved to the sunken road to an undercut at *N*.29.*b*.15.

From the high ground Germans were seen pushing towards Marliere (*N*.17.*d*.) in small parties from Guemappe. Machine-gun fire opened on the L.R.B. from the neighbourhood of the lake in *N*.18.*c*., but soon stopped.

Major Wallis was very anxious about the safety of brigade head-quarters and Wancourt, and consequently sent C.S.M.

A. J. R. Macveagh and his head-quarters' personnel to hold the sunken road from *N*.23 *central* to *N*.23.*a*.33. Luckily the enemy did not push through Wancourt. Had they done so Macveagh's party formed the only troops between them and brigade head-quarters at *N*.28.*b*.58.

This was the position when the L.R.B. was ordered to take over the front from the Tower to sunken road (*N*.30.*a*.). Arrangements were made gradually to occupy the trenches held by the D.L.I. and Q.W.R. with the understanding that, when the situation was straightened out, the battalion would be relieved by the London Scottish, if it could be done before daylight. The fact that the relief of the L.R.B. depended on the quick readjustment and reorganisation helped the movement materially, because by this time all ranks were almost dead beat.

The reorganisation was effected by 11 p.m., and the Scottish relieved the battalion by about 4 a.m. next morning. This relief was carried out without a hitch.

Capt. Stransom, who had won the D.C.M. at Ploegsteert while in charge of wiring parties during the winter 1914–15 and had been appointed acting-adjutant on 12th March when Lieut. McOwen had gone down sick, did admirably. He had been at work day and night since April 9th and had attended to every return, report, all reliefs and the nightly rations, etc., without any rest.

The medical officer, Capt. J. W. G. H. Riddel, worked untiringly. He attended to the wounded of all battalions at his aid post in a shell-hole on the Cojeul River under machine-gun fire and shell-fire in a most gallant manner.

From 15th to 20th April the battalion rested, the weather for the most part being bad with snow and rain, but on the latter day it moved to Faubourg d'Amiens, Arras, and from there bussed to Bienvillers. On 23rd a move was made to Souastre, on 24th to Wanquetin, and again on 26th to Berneville. At this time the strength of the battalion on paper was 972, but the fighting strength was only 488, with 14 officers, the remainder, except 104 with the transport, being distributed in various directions. Major C. D. Burnell arrived on 22nd and took over the command. On 28th April the battalion moved into the divisional support area west of

Wancourt, and the surplus personnel went into billets at Arras, including the following officers: Major F. H. Wallis, Capts. E. W. Rose, P. Titley, 2nd Lieuts. W. E. Reed and F. G. Fass, and Capt. F. H. Crews, who returned from the Third Army School on 29th. The following casualties occurred during April: 2nd Lieuts. H. E. Benstead (7th Londons) and B. Warner were killed; 2nd Lieut. E. G. C. Wadner (7th Londons) wounded, and 2nd Lieuts. C. H. John and W. E. Reed sent away on command; Other Ranks 17 killed,

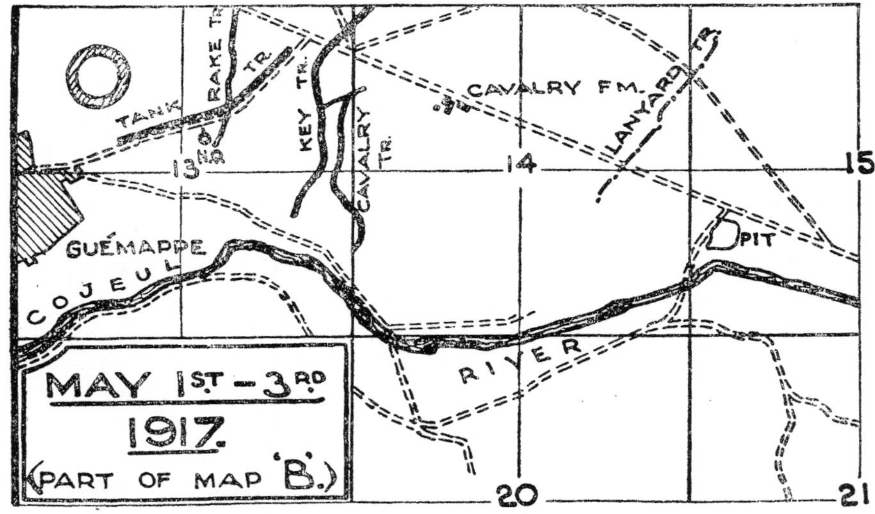

SKETCH MAP No. 10

62 wounded and 4 missing. Besides Major Burnell, 2nd Lieut. E. T. F. R. Chilman and 2nd Lieut. E. C. Hayes (Q.W.R.) joined the battalion.

On 1st May the L.R.B. relieved the Q.W.R., the line being Cavalry Trench (*O*.13), and spent the night in digging assembly trenches behind the front line, two companies being in the line and two in support, west of Guemappe. Brigade orders stated that the Fifth, Third and First Armies were attacking simultaneously, the main objective being a line Fontaine-Cherisy-St. Rohart Factory-Bois Du Vert-Plouvain Station (U.2–O.15–I.15). The attack by the 169th Infantry Brigade was to be carried out by the L.R.B. on the right, and the 2nd

Londons on the left, the Q.V.R. being in support, and the Q.W.R. in reserve. On capturing the objective the two attacking battalions were ordered to push forward patrols, duly supported, to gain ground, their first objective being the Cojeul River in O.16.a. and c. down to the Pont à Trois Gueules. The L.R.B. was ordered to attack in four waves, each of four platoons, and was disposed as follows: 1st and 2nd wave "D" Company, with one platoon of "B" Company, all under Capt. T. A. Prior; 3rd and 4th waves, "C" Company, and one platoon of "B" Company under Capt. A. B. White. The frontage of the battalion was 250 yards, with 100 yards between waves, and 15 yards between the two lines of each wave. A strong bombing party of 15 men of "A" Company, under 2nd Lieut. Grace (10th Londons), was ordered to cross to the south side of the Cojeul River and hug the southern bank, moving forward in line with the leading wave, to deal with any hostile machine guns which might be there. The attack was made on 3rd May, and the first two waves took and consolidated Lanyard Trench (*O*.14.*b*.) and occupied the shell-holes to the south of it, while the second two waves reached a line 25–30 yards from the Pit (*O*.15.*c*.), and occupied shell-holes, but no further advance was possible, owing to the failure of the attack by the battalions on the left. The brigade on the right was counter-attacked and driven back to its old line, and later in the day the Q.V.R. and Q.W.R. were ordered to hold the line as it was on 1st May, the L.R.B. having to withdraw and bivouac in rear of the Wancourt line, from which it moved on 4th to old German trenches south of Tilloy. From 5th to 17th May the L.R.B. was in the Harp N.1.a., and spent the time in salvage, cleaning up and reorganisation. On 19th a march was made to Duisans, where, on 20th, Lieut.-Col. Husey, who rejoined on that day, presented Divisional Cards to 18 men, and on the same date Major Burnell became Second in Command, Wallis again becoming Adjutant *vice* Capt. Stransom invalided. On 24th May a move was made to Agnez les Duisans, where the rest of the month was spent, and on 28th the Divisional General presented the D.C.M. ribbon to Sergt. E. G. Moore, at the same time congratulating the battalion on its good work in the recent fighting.

During a happy two weeks' respite it was possible to run an officers' mess, and the officers under Major Burnell beat the sergeants under R.S.M. Adams at football. Capt. Crews, who had done splendid work, went down to the base as instructor at the General Head-quarters Lewis Gun School by way of a rest.

The battalion remained in camp at Agnez Les Duisans until 9th June, when it moved forward, and on 10th went into support, the dispositions being as follows : Head-quarters in caves at Marliere (*N*.17.*d*.) ; " A " Company in Les Fosses Farm ; " B " Company in caves at N.12.c.26 ; " C " Company at *N*.17.*d*.87 ; and " D " Company, 3 platoons, immediately east of Marliere, with the remaining platoon at Wancourt. On 15th the L.R.B., which had been finding large working parties over this ground every night, relieved the 2nd Londons in the left sector, and at 2.30 a.m. on 16th the Huns attacked the battalion on its left, but without success. On 17th a further attack was made, in the course of which " A " Company suffered 18 casualties from shell-fire, owing to the main communication trench there being parallel to the road behind it, so that the shells that missed the latter hit the former, but as a set-off to this the company got some very useful moving-target practice at some slowly crawling Germans, who were considerably damaged. On 20th the L.R.B. was being relieved by the 2nd Londons, when a thunderstorm, which came on at the end of some very hot weather, caused so much delay that the platoons did not reach their billets in Beaurains until 6 a.m. next day. For the rest of the month the L.R.B. trained and carried out the usual routine. A German field-gun, which had been salved from the ground over which the battalion had attacked on 3rd May, came in during the month and was allotted to the L.R.B. as a trophy. The casualties for the month in regard to Officers were nil ; Other Ranks 13 killed, 45 wounded and 1 prisoner. The following officers joined during the month: Capt. W. G. D. Butcher, Lieut. B. L. E. Pocock, 2nd Lieuts. H. Cross, F. H. Ball, S. I. Wilson (23rd Londons), B. H. Sellon (11th Londons) and J. W. Brown (9th Londons). Those who left the battalion were Capt. F. H. Crews and W. E. Reed, on command ; 2nd Lieuts. L. H. Fotheringham, F. S. Clark and S. H. Cross, invalided ; and E. C. Hayes (16th Londons), who returned to his unit.

July was free from fighting and trench work, and the L.R.B., which had enjoyed little respite for a whole year, found the change very welcome. On 1st a memorial service was held for those who fell in the previous year at Gommecourt, and on 2nd and 3rd the battalion marched to Gouy-en-Artois and Sombrin respectively. The latter proved to be a pretty and clean little village, possessing a disused aerodrome with a large flat green plain just outside, which gave great possibilities for both training and sport. All billets were clean and good, and the population friendly and kind. One of the daily fatigues, to help the farmers on the land, was so popular that it was even volunteered for, but rumour said that feasts of strawberries and cream provided by the farmers were the real attraction.

H.M. the King was to have been present at a Church Parade on 8th, but the day was wet and the parade was abandoned.

On 14th a battalion sports meeting took place, which turned out a great success. Between this date and 17th the brigade held a two-day sports meeting in the grounds of the château in Grand Rullecourt which succeeded beyond anyone's hopes, as the enthusiasm was simply great and every winner had an immense reception. The Q.W.R. carried off most of the prizes, and the L.R.B.'s tug-of-war team was the battalion's only hope for one. The excitement was therefore intense when it was found that the Q.W.R. and the L.R.B. had to meet in the final pull, in which both teams pulled well, and the L.R.B. won by 2 to nil. 2nd Lieut. Poland was second in the high jump, Lce.-Cpl. Hornett second in the obstacle race, and the L.R.B. officers were second in the relay race.

In the mounted events Lieut.-Col. Husey was second in musical chairs, which Lynch (his horse) thoroughly enjoyed, and the transport section won first prize for Cooker and Team. Mule races afforded much amusement, and the day finished with "Retreat" played by the massed bands of the brigade. A point of interest in this performance was the ever-increasing rapidity of the step. All the four bands marched together, starting to the British Grenadiers by the fife band of the 2nd Londons at 100 to the minute, followed by the Q.W.R. at 110, quickened to 120 by the Q.V.R., and finishing with 140 for the L.R.B.

On 22nd Le Souich was reached by march route, and on 23rd the L.R.B. entrained at Bouquemaison for Wizernes, where it detrained and marched to St. Martin au Laert, moving on the next day to Bayenghem. The training-ground there was very large with splendid facilities for every sort of work, which were taken full advantage of for a fortnight.

During the month 2nd Lieut. G. E. Smith (Q.V.R.) was attached for duty, Capt. J. H. Stransom was invalided home, and 2nd Lieut. J. C. Slater, who joined the Depot Battalion on 20th June, but was sent to hospital from there on 2nd July, died on 6th without ever reaching the 1st Battalion.

On 4th August Major J. B. Whitmore (Q.W.R.) joined as Second in Command in place of Major Burnell, who had left to command the Divisional Reception Camp. On 6th the battalion went by rail to Abeele, where, after four days' intensive training, warning was received that it must be ready to move at an hour's notice, to take part in the battle of Ypres, which was then raging.

FIRST BATTALION

Part VIII. Aug. 12—Dec. 31, 1917

Attack on the Polygon—Lebucquiere—Battle of Cambrai.

(*The maps referred to are A and B ; No.* 11 *on p.* 204, *and No.* 12 *facing p.* 218).

THE object of the fighting in the Salient which took place in the late summer of 1917 was partly to endeavour to turn the Germans' flank, and partly to cut them off, if possible, from the Belgian coast, whence issued their submarines and other craft which were able to shelter at Bruges by means of using the canal between that and Zeebrugge. In June nineteen huge mines were exploded beneath the Messines-Wytschaete ridge and the Germans were forced to withdraw from all their positions in the Salient, but the advance was only a small one. For some reason the successes gained were not followed up, and it was not till July 31st that a further attack was launched. The weather was appalling ; rain fell in torrents and the ground became a morass. Small gains were made and the fighting continued till November, but the losses were terrible, and were accentuated because many wounded were smothered in the mud.

On 11th August the L.R.B. trained to Palace Camp, and on 12th a move was made in heavy rain along cross-country roads, which were deep in mud and exposed to shell-fire, to Halfway House (I.17.c.), a large dug-out, which served as Brigade, Artillery, R.E. and Battalion Head-quarters, as well as billets for two companies of the battalion, the remainder being billeted round it. On 13th the officers reconnoitred the route through Sanctuary Wood (I.24) to the front line, and on the following day Lieut.-Col. Husey was wounded while looking for a suitable shell-hole in which to write operation orders, after having attended a conference with the Brigadier,

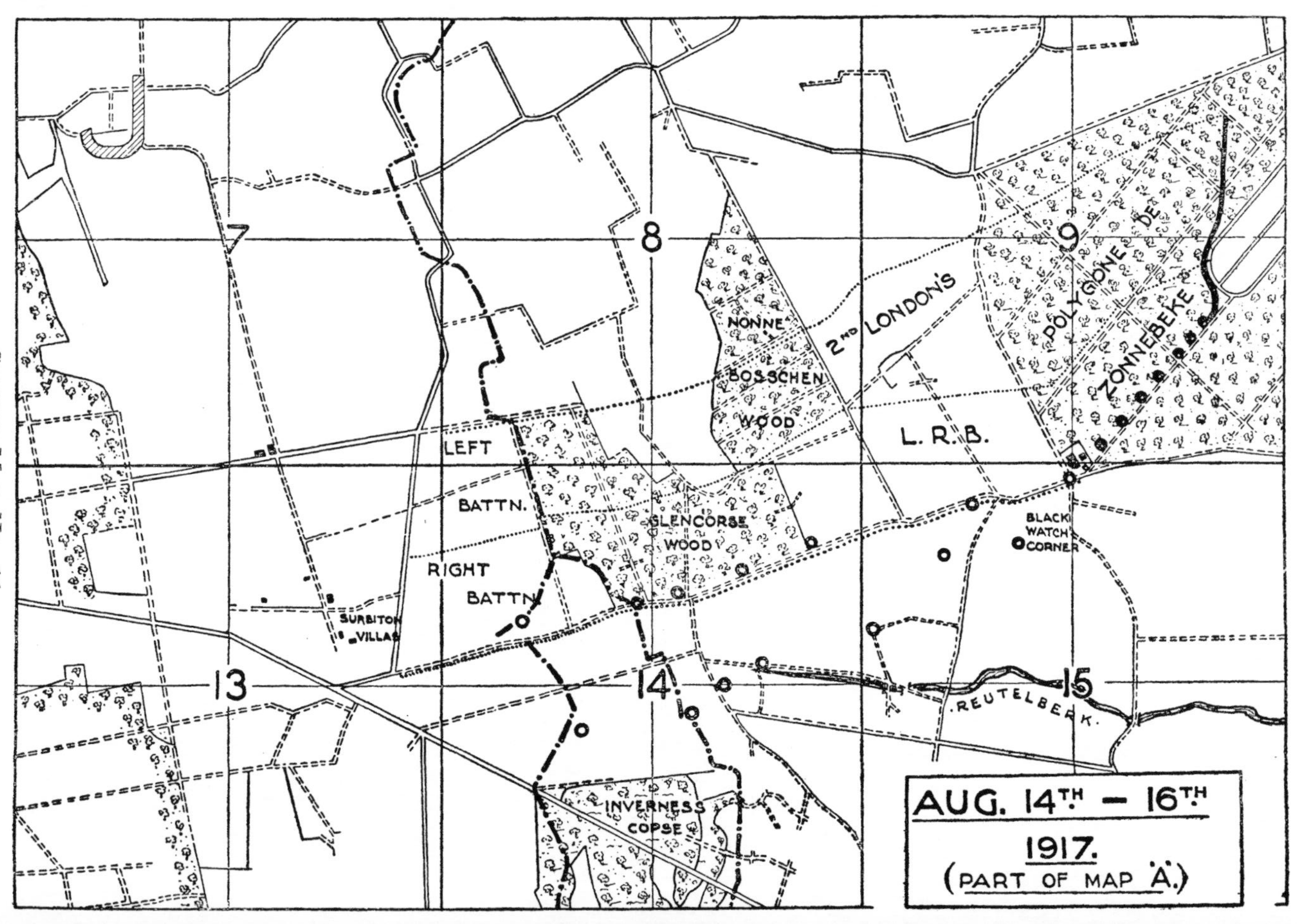

Sketch Map No. 11

The wound was severe and was the fourth he had received. Leave was obtained at Major Whitmore's request for Major Wallis to take over the command, and 2nd Lieut. Sellon (11th Londons) became Adjutant.

The Germans had held up the first stages of the battle by their good fighting at Inverness Copse (*J*.14), which was a nest of machine guns, and had successfully resisted all direct attack, so arrangements were made this time for the Fifth Army to attack to the north, leaving the copse in the enemy's hands, with the hope that he would evacuate it voluntarily when he saw troops pushing forward on his flank. The L.R.B. and 2nd Londons were to make the attack with the Q.V.R. and Q.W.R. in support respectively, the L.R.B. being on the right, with the Polygon de Zonnebeke (*J*.9) on the south-west edge of the race-course as its objective. The frontage was about 250 yards, but on reaching the objective the orders were that the battalion was to consolidate facing south, to reorganise in depth and hold the right flank of the Fifth Army for a distance of no less than 2000 yards, as shown on Map No. 11,

No one can deny troops the right to think, though criticism is not allowed, and rightly so when it is possible that the full reasons for particular decisions are not known. It is certain that the proposed plan of action was not viewed with much favour by anyone who was called upon to endeavour to carry it out, and it is whispered that Higher Authority stated that, if any such scheme had been set at Camberley, the officer responsible for it would have been asked to seek fresh pastures on which to graze. However that might be, it made no difference naturally to the attack, which was carried out with the gallantry for which the 56th Division was and ever will be famous.

Unfortunately no copies of Battalion Orders are available. The C.O.'s copy was in the possession of the Adjutant, 2nd Lieut. Sellon, who was mortally wounded as he was going forward with Battalion Head-quarters, and all his papers were lost at the advanced dressing station. His was a great loss to the battalion, as although he had not long been with it, he had become popular with everyone.

On 16th at 1.30 a.m. the battalion assembled in shell-holes in front of Surbiton Villas (*J*.13.*b*.) on a night which was so dark that only the good leadership of the Company Commanders, Capts. W. G. D. Butcher and A. B. White, and 2nd Lieuts. B. Sworder and P. Titley enabled the work to be carried out correctly. At 4.45 a.m. the British artillery put up the heaviest barrage that the L.R.B. had so far seen, the rate of advance being 100 yards per minute, and the attack developed satisfactorily, though the battalion suffered many casualties from the machine guns in Inverness Copse. "A" Company, which was leading, with the race-course for its objective lost Capt. Butcher, who was known to have been killed after passing Nonne Boschen Wood (*J*.8.*d*.), but beyond this nothing is certain, except that contact aeroplanes reported that "flares were lit on the south-west end of the race-course and our troops seen digging in," and that later in the day a pigeon brought in an untimed, unsigned message, "We are surrounded." All that can be said of this gallant band is that it went on with its work "according to plan," and upheld the regiment's fair fame, with no lime-light or applause to cheer it while engaged on its heroic yet doomed task. "B" Company was delayed through having to deal with Germans who came out of dug-outs after "A" Company had gone through, which it did very effectually, gallantly led by 2nd Lieut. H. Taylor, who took command early in the day when 2nd Lieut. Sworder was wounded. "C" Company lost Capt. A. B. White, probably on the outskirts of Nonne Boschen Wood; and by the time that Black Watch Corner (*J*.15.*a*.) was reached, which the battalion had been ordered to hold with 2 platoons, only 3 men—2 runners and Capt. White's batman—were available. After being held up for a time the battalion was compelled to fall back on to a line inside Glencorse Wood (*J*.14), and finally a German counter-attack, with organised troops, from Inverness Copse and the low ground of the Reutelbeek (*J*.15), was successful in driving the remnants back to their original trenches by 5 p.m.

Relieved that evening by the Q.V.R. the few men of the L.R.B. who had managed to get back marched to Halfway House by 2 a.m. on the next day, and from there to Café Belge (H.29.b.) on the Ypres-Dickebusch road, where motor-buses collected and took them to Abeele, 2nd Lieut. H. Taylor acting as Adjutant.

The casualties for the period 14–16 August were: Officers—11; Other Ranks—killed 24, wounded 172, missing 147, total 361. The officers in this list were: Capt. A. B. White, killed; 2nd Lieut. B. H. Sellon, died of wounds; Capt. W. G. D. Butcher and 2nd Lieut. J. W. Brown (Q.V.R.), missing; Lieut.-Col. R. H. Husey, Capt. F. H. Wallis, 2nd Lieuts. E. R. Boland, W. G. Percy, B. Sworder, P. Titley and S. I. Wilson (23rd Londons), wounded. The only officers not wounded were 2nd Lieuts. F. H. Ball, D. Hood and H. Taylor.

On 18th Capt. F. H. Wallis was appointed Lieut.-Col., and 2nd Lieut. W. C. Von Berg became Adjutant. Six days were spent in reorganising, though no reinforcements were received, and on 24th the battalion trained to Moulle, not far from St. Omer, where the news came that the division was to be moved to the Third Army area. On 30th the battalion marched to Wizernes, where it entrained for a ten-hour journey in cattle trucks via Arras to Miraumont, whence it marched via Achiet le Grand to an excellent camp at Bapaume, which was reached at 2 a.m. on 31st without a man falling out.

During August 2nd Lieut. H. Cross was invalided, and 2nd Lieuts. J. R. S. Ripley and R. C. Thompson joined. The only reinforcements were 35 Other Ranks.

The first three days of September were spent reconnoitring the front line and training, and on 4th the battalion took the place of the 7th K.S.L.I. at Lebucquiere, in the left battalion sub-sector of the Louverval sector, where it passed the happiest three months of its time in France. This was a well-organised, clean, comfortable rest camp with delightful country round. The Transport Officer pictured to himself a garden-city with special cottages for the mounted officers' horses, while the Quartermaster, with visions of an industrial town, at once began to build the famous Petersen railway line, which delivered rations to the stores and forage to the stables, as well as a branch line which ran out to the manure dump. The entrance to the lines was equal to that of the finest park and, with the buglers' gardens in working order as well as additional cottages completed, everyone was quite prepared to settle down for life.

The battalion sector of the front to be held, which was before Boursies and Louverval, and some 5 or 6 miles from Lebucquiere, was equally pleasing. The right of the line, which was over 1000 yards in length, with the enemy from 1000 to 2000 yards away, rested on the Bapaume–Cambrai road (*J*.6) on a high spur from which the clock-tower and the trains running into Cambrai could be seen. The left was on the Mœuvres road (*D*.29), also on a spur, while there was a third road in the centre, but the gully in each of the valleys between suggested trouble in the winter. The line was held by two companies, with two in support, in a number of posts all connected by a good series of spotlessly clean trenches, and battalion headquarters at Louverval, near the ruined château which had at one time been the head-quarters of the Crown Prince, was a well-built dug-out with garden, bedrooms, and a deep emergency dug-out in case of heavy shelling.

Every one took a lively interest in their quarters. The pioneers built a pretty stone house with a tiled floor and fire-place, and surrounded it with creepers and shrubs to prevent aerial observation. The mess had the regimental badge outside in black and white stone, made by Cpl. Edwards, R.A.M.C., who had been with the battalion since September, 1914. Units of the 3rd Division, the former occupants, had put up their regimental badges in coloured stone, and whether the R.F. badge of the 2nd Londons was superior or inferior to the L.R.B. crest is a question that has never been decided, but there is still a suspicion that the 2nd Londons were a little bit jealous!

On 5th September the battalion went into the line to relieve the 1st R.S. Fus., and, after eight days' quite without incident except for 12 shells fired by the Germans, were relieved by the 2nd Londons on 13th, Major W. D. Cheshire, 17th Lancs Fus., joining on the same day as Second in Command. On 17th the battalion was inspected by the 4th Corps Commander, Lieut.-Gen. Sir C. L. Woollcombe, K.C.B., who expressed his approval of the steadiness in the ranks, and especially of the turn-out of the transport and horses. Afterwards the Commanding Officer presented medal ribbons for the decorations won at Ypres on 16th August, and the battalion marched past the recipients. During the next tour in the trenches from 21st to 29th a British aeroplane was brought down in the enemy's advanced line on 24th, but a patrol which crawled out was unable to approach it or see any signs of the pilot or observer. On coming out the battalion moved into brigade support to the Q.V.R. and the 2nd Londons.

The following officers joined in September :—

Major W. D. Cheshire (17th Lancs Fus.) ; 2nd Lieuts. W. A. Thomson, R. F. L. Hewlett, H. L. Renwick, H. G. Higham, L. N. Thompson (all L.R.B.), and S. du Plessis (7th Londons), S. C. Gould (21st Londons), J. H. Bryant (20th Londons), A. R. Leslie (19th Londons), J. F. Maginn (18th Londons, transferred later to L.R.B.), E. Staples (17th Londons), and F. Adams (21st Londons).

From October 1st to October 23rd no incident occurred while the battalion was in reserve or in the line, which it occupied from 7th to 15th and entered again on 23rd, but on 24th the Lord Mayor of London (Sir William Dunn) paid a visit to the division and opened the Officers' Club at Fremicourt. Of course he did not see the L.R.B., but he inspected their transport lines and made a complimentary speech, besides sending a message to the battalion saying how sorry he was not to have met it.

At the very end of the month the R.E. Company of 62nd Division reported that the light railway was to be continued through Boursies (*J*.6) to the front line, and that the Cambrai road was to be widened at once. As this road, which ran in an absolutely straight line from Bapaume to Cambrai, was already broad and well paved, it was obvious that the additional width could only be required for bigger traffic, and the inference was that the existing peaceful life was coming to an end. This work proved to be the beginning of what was pro bably the best-organised offensive that had been made up to that time, and one which the presence of the British Divisions, which had to be sent to Italy in consequence of the German-Austrian attack there, would have made a complete success.

The attack at Cambrai was intended to break the Hindenburg lines and enable the remainder of them to be assaulted from the flank and rear. A further object was to divert the Germans from their Italian campaign. Tanks had been found to be useless in Flanders owing to the mud, and to the ground being cut up by the preliminary bombardment. In this case there was no warning of the attack ; the tanks broke through the wire; the Germans were completely surprised, and in the first day greater progress was made than in any one day before. But the arrangements were not perfect; the troops were too few to exploit the successes gained, and eventually, though our line was stabilised somewhat in advance of where it had been, a part of it was even further west than before owing to the large forces brought up to counter-attack.

On 31st October the battalion left for Lebucquiere, where every officer and man was set to work each night on the Cambrai road, and the Commanding Officer was officially informed that a surprise attack was to be launched in the near future.

During October, 2nd Lieuts. J. A. T. Derham (L.R.B.) and C. W. Woodward (18th Londons) joined, and Capt. A. Gordon returned. Lieut. and Q.M. J. R. S. Petersen, who had come out with the battalion in November, 1914, and done excellent work with it ever since, except for four or five months in the summer of 1916, went home on 16th for demobilisation, and was succeeded by Lieut. A. Denny, who had gone out in the ranks with the battalion in November, 1914.

On 5th November the Chyebassa dinner was held in the Cinema Hall and was attended by Col. Ducat, Lieut.-Col. Wallis, Major Burnell, Capts. Calder, Ovington, Slade, and Trevelyan, and 70 Other Ranks. On 11th, while the battalion was doing its last tour of peace in these trenches, it suffered its only casualties since 1st September—due to the collapse of a dug-out—and, when Louverval was quitted on 16th, the state of the preparations that had been made showed that the attack would take place at once.

The essence of the attack was surprise, and its success, which meant the capture of the whole of the defences running south from Arras known as the Hindenburg Line, depended on secrecy. Accordingly the whole of the work, even in the back areas, was done by night, and no movement of men, transport, or guns was allowed by day. Gradually batteries of artillery were massed and camouflaged; dumps that grew in the night were completely hidden by day; the Cambrai road was widened 12 feet without apparently showing any structural alteration, and the light railway ran up to the front line; and, finally, troops were massed in the existing camps without an extra shelter being put up in the area. The result was that the Germans were in complete ignorance of what was in store for them until the night before the attack.

The training, while these preparations were being made, consisted in teaching everyone how to deal with any contingency that might arise. No definite rôle was laid down for any battalion, but instructions and orders were drafted and issued for attack with artillery and after artillery preparation, for attack without artillery preparation or barrage, for attack in co-operation with tanks, for attack with a creeping barrage, and for dealing with a voluntary German retirement. Further instructions were issued to companies giving them the fullest information, and the steps to be taken with trench-stores, equipment, prisoners, delayed mines, etc. etc., while the Transport Officers instructed the Q.M. Sergts. in the supply of S.A.A. in open warfare. By orders from brigade, officers were detailed in advance as Town Majors of villages which it was anticipated would be captured. Company and battalion training was carried out, after sentries had been posted to watch for hostile aeroplanes, in all the above methods of advance, as well as in putting out a line of outposts, the duties of advanced guards, and open warfare.

The lie of the country and the preparations that the Germans had made must be realized before there is any attempt to describe the battle of Cambrai. Standing well back on a high hill and easily visible from Lebucquiere was Bourlon Wood, the key to Cambrai ; on the German right well in front, on a high piece of ground in front of Inchy (*E*.7), overlooking the Cambrai road for miles, was Tadpole Copse (*D*.24), the key to Bourlon Wood ; Mœuvres (*E*.14) was a little village, behind the Hindenburg Line, at the foot of the ground sloping down from Inchy and Bourlon. The line itself, which had been taken up when the Germans voluntarily withdrew in 1917 as the result of the Somme fighting, was considered impregnable. The trenches were admirably sited, and consisted of a front line, with a second line about 200 yards in rear and two similar trenches 250 yards behind the first pair, all joined together by good communication trenches which were fire-stepped and ready to be used as front line trenches in case an entry were made or footing obtained in any part of the line. In addition to these some miles of communication trenches were dug back to Inchy, Bourlon, etc., and emergency tunnel communication trenches also fed the front line in various places. The trenches themselves were deep, and wide enough in places for men to file along two deep ; they had dug-outs 50 feet deep, fitted up with electric light and the latest improvements, and well supplied with furniture from Mœuvres, Inchy, etc., while water was laid on in many of the larger ones. In front there were numerous belts of very thick wire.

On 17th November battle equipment was drawn in accordance with instructions ; on 18th the Commanding Officer conferred with the Company Commanders and gave them their final instructions ; and on 19th an attack behind dummy tanks was practised, and all packs and kits were dumped. Late that night it was announced that the attack would begin at 6.30 a.m. next day.

On 20th the attack was launched at the time laid down, covered by smoke discharges all along the line, but the 56th Division took no part in the advance. It had, however, put up during the night dummy tanks[1] in front of its lines which were heavily shelled up to noon, and figure targets were shown from the trenches, which drew a severe and destructive fire from artillery and machine guns as the smoke cleared.

By 9.15 p.m. the Q.W.R. had established posts 200 yards north of the Cambrai road and established touch with the 36th (Ulster) Division. On 21st the L.R.B. was in Divisional Reserve, but moved early on the morning of 22nd to the old front line in front of Doignies. At 3 a.m. orders were received that the Q.W.R. with the L.R.B. in support was to attack at 11 a.m. by bombing up the Hindenburg Line from *K*.3.*c*. and to capture Tadpole Copse, which was to be entered by the 36th Division, who would then advance against Mœuvres. The attack began in the face of a terrific bombardment, and the enemy's line proved such a maze of trenches that the L.R.B. was soon drawn into the fight, but by 7 p.m. Tadpole Copse was in British hands. The 12th R.I. Rifles after getting through Mœuvres were driven out by a German counter-attack. At the close of the day the two German front line trenches were in the hands of the Q.W.R. and L.R.B. from Tadpole Copse to the Mœuvres road (Houndsditch, *E*.19.*c*.), while the enemy occupied his old

[1]Motor-bicycle engines were set running in the trenches to complete the illusion.

support line. The front line was held by "A" Company (Capt. Calder) and "B" Company (2nd Lieut. Maginn), with "C" Company (2nd Lieut. du Plessis) and "D" Company (2nd Lieut. Hosking) supporting them respectively. Battalion head-quarters were established in a portion of the German outpost line, which was only two feet deep and contained a partly finished dug-out with only one entrance, and that directly facing a German battery. In the course of the day the L.R.B. took three German officers and over 100 men prisoners.

The night was spent in consolidating, making fire-steps, bombing blocks, etc., in addition to successfully meeting three counter-bombing attacks.

The battalion front was quiet on 23rd, but the London Scottish on the immediate left continued the attack and captured over 500 yards of trench, though some of this was lost to a counter-attack later on. On the next day a very determined German counter-attack drove the London Scottish back to Tadpole Copse, Lieut.-Col. Jackson, its Commanding Officer, having during the struggle to fight his way out of the battalion head-quarters, which were in the old German front line. The Scottish suffered heavy casualties, so one platoon of "D" Company under 2nd Lieut. Bryant was lent to them and remained in position with them till relieved on the following night by the 12th Londons. On 25th again no change took place on the L.R.B. front, and all was quiet at Mœuvres, but the Rangers and the 2nd Londons were fighting the Germans hard all day and finished by having a slightly improved position. The struggle led to the unusual sight of both sides sending up S.O.S. signals simultaneously. By 26th the whole Division was involved. The 169th Brigade was on the right, with its right flank not secure until Mœuvres had been captured; the 167th Brigade on the left, being constantly counter-attacked; and the 168th in the centre, holding 5500 yards of the British old front and also supplying a battalion every night for consolidation work. It must be borne in mind, too, that the L.R.B. had received no reinforcements to fill the gaps made at Ypres on August 16th, and had in addition lost many men in this action, as could also be said about most of the other battalions. After the Germans had again counter-attacked on the left and again been repulsed, the L.R.B. was relieved by the Q.W.R. at 9 p.m. and went back to Louverval to re-equip.

On 27th at 3.30 p.m. an intense bombardment of the front line and supports, which cut the telephone wires, sent the S.O.S. up all along the line, and was followed by a heavy counter-attack ; but at 5.30 p.m. a wireless message came through saying that the Kensingtons and Rangers had repulsed it. The battalion worked all night on digging communication trenches from the old British Trench to Houndsditch. On 28th the battalion head-quarters were shelled with 8″ shells, and all parts of the front were similarly treated, but for the first time no counter-attack was made, and the night and following day passed quietly.

On 30th at 3 a.m., owing to a 6″ battery having kindly taken up a position 50 yards from battalion head-quarters at Louverval, a concentrated gas bombardment began, which lasted for two hours and affected every officer and man there so seriously that by the following evening they were unable to keep their eyes open or talk out of a whisper. Indeed, so many of the staff were obliged to go to hospital that the personnel was reduced to Lieut.-Col. F. H. Wallis, 2nd Lieut. R. D. Poland, the M.O., Capt. J. W. G. H. Riddel, and about ten Other Ranks, all of whom were expecting to have to leave at any moment. The battalion had been at work all night in the trenches.

At 10 a.m. reports, which were subsequently confirmed, were received from the 2nd Division on the right, stating that the enemy were concentrating on their front and that one division was entering Mœuvres. At 10.45 a.m. the S.O.S. went up all along the line and the Germans counter-attacked with large bodies of men, after a heavy bombardment with guns of all calibres, as well as innumerable minnies which had been collected in their support line during the last two days.

A most extraordinary scene followed. Masses of Germans with mounted officers and horse artillery came advancing in the open down the sloping ground between Mœuvres and Bourlon, when, as if by signal, the British guns opened a fire to which no troops in the open had ever been subjected before. Horses, men and guns could all be seen being blown to pieces by the guns, which appeared to be using a new shell (said to have been employed for the first time on November 22nd) that exploded in a sheet of flame. The slaughter must have been terrific and the German advance was stopped dead.

The enemy had, however, also massed with more success by using Hobart Street (*E*.13.*b*), as he gained a footing in the British front line. From there he attempted to bomb his way down Short Street (*E*.19.*b*.), and, after forcing his way between the London Scottish and the 8th Middlesex, captured the latter's head-quarters dug-out, only to be pushed back again by their head-quarters staff. The 2nd Londons then attacked and regained touch with the 167th Brigade, and the Q.W.R. gradually got their trenches back.

As all the battalions engaged in this struggle had lost heavily, they were reinforced with companies from the battalions in the 167th Brigade and the 5th Cheshires (Pioneers). At 2 p.m. "B" and "C" Companies of the L.R.B. were sent up to occupy trenches that had been vacated by the Q.W.R., but at 3.20 they were ordered back. At 3.30 p.m. "D" Company, under 2nd Lieut. Hosking, went into the German outpost line, with secret orders to hold on at any cost and cover any retirement that might have to be made, and at 4 p.m. "A," "B," and "C" Companies assembled in the old British front line, ready to move at a moment's notice. At 8 p.m. two companies got forward to the Hindenburg Line in closer support, and at 9 p.m. the battalion relieved the Q.W.R., who had been very badly mauled. By midnight the relief was complete with the battalion all in the front line from *E*.19.*d*.9.7 to *E*.19 *central*, except one weak platoon of "D" Company, which was in the old front line German trench as reserve.

During the whole of December 1st a heavy artillery bombardment, which had been carried on during the night, was continued, and at 3.30 p.m. the S.O.S. was sent up, but the British artillery crushed the counter-attack and at 11 p.m. the shelling died down.

By this time the limit of endurance was being reached. The skeleton head-quarters staff could hardly see, in consequence of the previous day's gassing; the battalion was very weak through casualties; and the men, who had been fighting by day and digging or working on carrying parties by night, were worn out. It was therefore welcome news to hear that the gallant 51st (Highland) Division was coming in relief on the next day, and the C.O. visited every man in the front line, exhorting all to stick it out for one day more, kill as many Germans as possible, and be in a position to hand over the line intact.

That night Major Cheshire, Lieut. Burroughs and the whole head-quarters nucleus personnel rejoined late in the evening in the middle of an intense bombardment of the head-quarters dug-out. Burroughs, who took over the duties of Adjutant, saw as usual great humour in the situation and laughed till he cried, because of the splendid time which he was having. Following an anxious night, 2nd December proved a still more anxious day, filled up as it was with incessant shelling, although no counter-attack developed, but at 9.30 p.m. the 1/9th R. Scots arrived and the L.R.B. moved back to Lebucquiere.

The casualties for November were: 4 Other Ranks killed and 28 wounded. The following Officers joined: Capt. A. Gordon and Lieut. and Q.M. A. Denny, while 2nd Lieut. G. E. Smith (Q.V.R.) was boarded and struck off whilst on leave in England, and 2nd Lieut. N. A. Whitechurch went down to the Base; the reinforcements were 8 Other Ranks. The casualties from December 1st to 3rd were: Officers, 2nd Lieut. L. N. Thompson, killed, and 2nd Lieut. F. J. Maginn, wounded; 8 Other Ranks killed (or wounded and killed), wounded not ascertained.

The following message was sent to the Army Commander by Field-Marshal Sir Douglas Haig, dated December 1st, 1917:

"I congratulate you and the officers and men under your command upon the successful resistance maintained by the Third Army yesterday against the powerful attacks delivered by the enemy south and west of Cambrai.

"In particular I desire to convey to the General Officers Commanding the 2nd, 47th and 56th Divisions, and to all ranks serving under them, my warm appreciation of their magnificent defence of the important positions entrusted to them.

"Though exposed throughout the day to the repeated assaults of superior forces, they beat off all attacks with the heaviest losses to the enemy, and by their gallant and steady conduct contributed very largely to the security of the divisions engaged on the whole front of the attack."

The fighting gave opportunities for individual effort in which all did splendidly, but some especially so. Capt. Calder was responsible for repulsing the three counter-attacks of the night Nov. 22/23 ; 2nd Lieut. Maginn showed reckless bravery in patrolling ; 2nd Lieut. R. D. Poland went right up to the advanced bombing parties in his determination to keep brigade informed of developments ; and two South Africans, 2nd Lieuts. Hosking and du Plessis (7th Londons), proved themselves to be great leaders. The Medical Officer, Capt. J.W.G.H. Riddel, spent his time under perpetual bombardment at an aid-post, which was a hole dug in a small embankment, and a former corporal of "A" Company (Durrant), who was by this time an officer in the 14th Division, was awarded the D.S.O. in connection with Bourlon Wood.

The D.S.O. was awarded to 2nd Lieut. F. J. Maginn for his very gallant conduct during these operations : this decoration was only granted to junior officers in exceptional circumstances. 2nd Lieut. E. V. Briggs, of the 12th R.I. Rifles, was very severely wounded and unable to get away. 2nd Lieut. Maginn rushed forward with two stretcher-bearers, under very heavy M.G. fire and sniping, and by sniping the enemy single-handed for 15 minutes he made them keep their heads down, thus covering the stretcher-bearers, who were then able to bring the wounded officer back. When they had reached the British trenches, 2nd Lieut. Maginn returned by himself, unwounded.

The last paragraph of the *History of a Great Fight*, published by G.H.Q., runs as follows :

"At the end of this day of high courage and glorious achievement, except for a few advanced positions, some of which were afterwards regained, our line had been maintained intact. The men who had come triumphantly through this mighty contest felt, and rightly felt, that they had won a great victory in which the enemy had come against them in full strength and had been defeated with losses at which even the victors stood aghast."

On 3rd December, after reaching Lebucquiere early in the morning, the battalion entrained at Fremicourt at 11 a.m. for Berneville in very cold weather, which made it necessary to light fires as soon as the billets were reached. Curiously enough the Town Major reported several sign-posts as missing next day. The same day Lieut.-Col. Husey, who had managed to get himself passed as fit for duty again, rejoined, to everyone's intense delight. On 4th the battalion was paraded and complimented on its good fighting at Mœuvres by Brig.-Gen. E. S. Coke, and on 5th marched in the snow to Ecurie (A.27), as the 56th Division were taking over the Gavrelle Sector (C.25) from the 31st, which had been there for a very long time. The XIIIth Corps had an Officers' Club at Roclincourt (A.29), only half a mile away, and also churches, theatres, cinemas, canteens and baths, so that everyone was ready to remain there for the duration of the war. The L.R.B. was billeted at Ecurie Wood in Nissen Huts, which all had mattresses and stoves, while the transport lines were equal to those at Lebucquiere, but for the absence of the Petersen railway.

On 6th a reconnaisance of the front line produced a shock, as the back area had suggested the millennium, but the sight of the lines shattered all hopes of living in comfort and ease in them. A new system of defence was in force there, consisting of posts which were held in strength, with undefended gaps of about 1000 yards between them, many of the posts not being joined up. The trenches themselves were appalling, as they were shallow, only two or three feet deep in places, fast tumbling down, and not sufficiently wired to offer any serious obstacle to a determined raiding party. The enemy's trenches were very close and commanded, as might have been expected, those of the British.

On 7th the battalion relieved the 10th E. Yorks and spent its time in deepening the trenches by day and wiring by night, without much interference from the enemy, until 11th, when it gave way to the 2nd Londons and went into Brigade Support at Roundhay Camp (H.1.c.4.5). There it was hoped to have six days' rest, but on 14th the battalion took the place of the 2nd Londons at Mill Post, etc., at a time when things were somewhat " windy " with rumours of hostile tanks, guns of large calibre and a more deadly gas, but, although the enemy

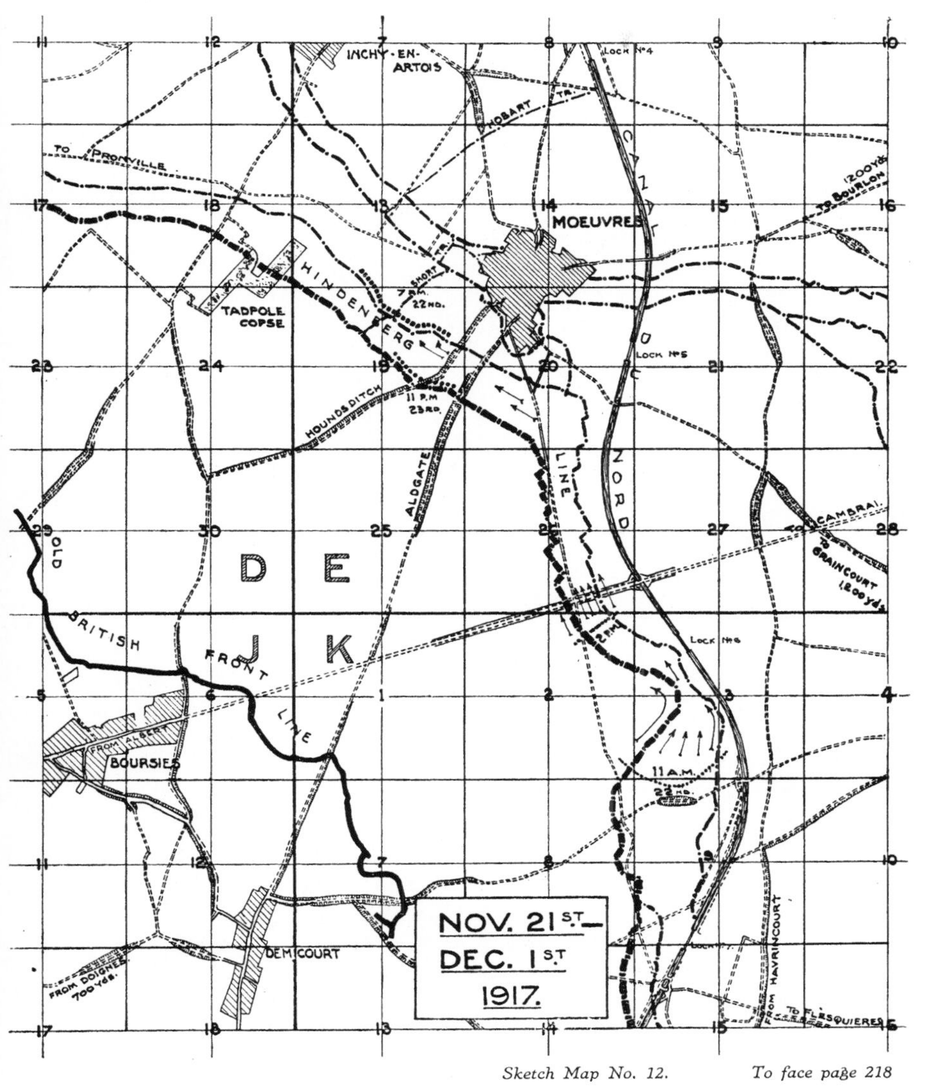

Sketch Map No. 12.

To face page 218

showed a marked increase in his offensive, nothing serious occurred. On 20th the battalion came out of the trenches expecting to have its Christmas dinner at Roclincourt, but warning orders came out that the Q.V.R. would have to be relieved on 24th, so the best was made of things, and the festivities took place on 23rd at Ecurie, the sergeants inviting the officers to their dinner. The relief was effected at 4 p.m. on Christmas Eve in rain and mud, and in the evening the Germans released some of their new gas, which was, however, carried off to the left by the wind. Christmas Day was spent in mild exchanges of fire, and on Boxing Day Lieut.-Col. Husey took over the command of the 169th Brigade for a month, an honour of which the L.R.B. felt very proud. On 28th the battalion, after being relieved by the Q.V.R., moved back to Roundhay Camp in real winter weather, and New Year's Eve was ushered in by the officers at the sergeants' dug-out.

The reinforcements for December were 3 Other Ranks, and the casualties 1 Other Ranks killed and 32 wounded.

FIRST BATTALION

PART IX. JANUARY 1—MARCH 31, 1918

St. Aubin—Raid on Crab Trench—German attack.

(*The maps referred to are B, and No.* 13 *on p.* 228.)

ON New Year's Day, 1918, the battalion took over the line from the Q.W.R., and, after two quiet days there, came out on being relieved by the Kensingtons to enjoy its much-longed-for rest. Next day the light railway, which was characteristically planned with a total disregard of the houses that it cut into on its way, took the L.R.B. to Marœuil, and, after one night's stay, the battalion trained to Savy, from whence it marched to Frevillers. The weather had changed by this time and ten happy days were spent there, the principal duty being to shovel the snow off the roads, eight miles of this being on record as one day's work. On 15th January rain came down, and on the next day the battalion marched in the wet to Tinques and trained to Marœuil, finally reaching Roclincourt on 16th by means of the light railway. For six days "A" and "B" Companies were employed in wiring the battle zone, and "C" and "D" worked with the Tunnelling Company R.E.; but on 24th the whole battalion, after training to Aubigny, marched to Caucourt and wound up the month with training. On 27th Lieut.-Col. Husey returned from commanding the brigade, and on 28th the Q.V.R., much to everyone's regret, left the division to join the 58th, in consequence of the order that all brigades were to be reduced to three battalions.

During January 2nd Lieuts. P. L. Grimwood, W. F. Harrington, K. W. Jones, W. R. B. Kettle and T. C. Kite-Powell joined, as well as the following from the 1st Rangers on being absorbed: Capt. R. W. Hunter, Lieuts. L. B. Burt, A. O.

Colvin, J. R. Monsell, S. R. Owen and S. R. Scott, and 2nd Lieuts. V. T. Farrant and C. S. Tresillian. The reinforcements were 292, of which 288 were 1/12th Londons. On 2nd January Lieut. Waters, of the U.S. Army, 2nd Lieut. Boyd, R.F.C., and 2nd Lieut. de Moyse Bucknall, 6th (Inniskilling) Dragoons, were attached for instruction in trench warfare.

February was occupied, when in the line, with improving the defences, principally by wiring, and every tour was fully taken up with hard work. While training during the first six days, time was found for the officers to play the sergeants at football and lose by 0–4. On 7th the battalion had a wet march to Marœuil and next day relieved the 2/7th Duke of Wellington's Regiment. The 2nd Londons came in four days later and the L.R.B. moved to St. Aubin, where it remained in Brigade Reserve until 17th, when it took over from the 2nd Londons in the Towey Post (*C.25.c.*) sector. Two days later the enemy put down a heavy barrage at 9.15 p.m., and at 4.45 a.m. on 20th a small L.R.B. patrol had its N.C.O. wounded, and one man wounded and captured, by a German patrol of from 10 to 12 men, which had penetrated an undefended bit of the line and laid in wait. On 21st the Q.W.R. came in, and the L.R.B. went to Brigade Reserve in Roundhay Park, where it drew 0–0 with the 2nd Londons in the Divisional Football Cup, before moving on 27th to St. Aubin, where the month was finished.

The casualties for February were : 2nd Lieut. E. T. F. R. Chilman, wounded ; Other Ranks, 2 wounded and 1 wounded and missing. The officers arriving were 2nd Lieut. F. S. Sills, 2nd Lieut. G. M. Newland (13th Londons) and Lieut. J. E. N. Pooley (4th Londons) ; those leaving were Lieut. A. O. Colvin to 4th Londons, 2nd Lieut. V. T. Farrant (4th S. Lancs, attached to 13th Londons), and 2nd Lieut. S. du Plessis (posted to 169th T.M.B.).

March opened with the battalion in Brigade Reserve at St. Aubin until it went into the line, which was arranged on a system that requires explanation in view of the German attack upon it at the end of the month.

The defence consisted in a series of "Defended Localities," which were strong posts containing garrisons varying from a platoon to a company, with gaps between them, in some cases of from 800 to 1000 yards, which were covered by artillery and machine-gun fire from the rear as well as that of Lewis guns from the posts themselves.

About 600 or 800 yards behind this line ran a continuous trench, known as Naval-Marine Line (Map 13), which contained battalion head-quarters, machine-gun and trench-mortar head-quarters, and a further 1000 yards in rear was the Red Line, strong and well sited, joining up another series of large posts. Behind this line again was the Point du Jour-Thelus Line, which lay on high ground, giving excellent observation all round especially over Gavrelle and Mill Post, ready to be occupied in an emergency. In addition to all this, anti-tank guns were sited so as to help to cover the Green Line, and all wire had been thickened and strengthened, particularly in front of the Red Line.

On 5th the battalion relieved the 2nd Londons in Gavrelle and Towy Post. The front was then in a state of much greater activity, the Guards' Brigade on the right was making a series of raids, minor offensive operations were continually taking place, and shoots of every variety were put down daily, but the L.R.B. had three quiet days on their own piece of the front. Then the Germans, who had also increased their efforts very largely, sent down on 9th a heavy gas bombardment, and battalion head-quarters in Naval Trench suffered from the accurate shooting from some 4·2's. For the next two days the gas attack was repeated, and the communication trenches became full of gas, which caused several casualties and interfered with the relief on 11th by the Q.W.R. During the next four days the battalion "stood to" every morning at 5 a.m., and the German assembly trenches were heavily bombarded every day from 3 a.m., but nothing materialized. The story was that, while the enemy were collecting for an attack on 13th of which information had been received from a prisoner, this fire had caught and scattered them.

From 12th to 16th, "C" Company, under Capt. J. S. Calder and 2nd Lieuts. T. C. Kite-Powell and S. P. de Moyse Bucknall, practised a proposed raid, while the rest of the battalion supplied carrying parties, besides being exercised in manning battle and strong-points in the Green Line. On the night of 15th 2nd Lieut. Kite-Powell laid a tape across No Man's Land to a gap in the first belt of German wire, and on the following night the raiding party made the attempt, of of which a full account follows.

RAID OF MARCH 16th, 1918

On 5th March the L.R.B. was selected to carry out a proposed raid on the trench known as Crab, from the junction of Crab Trench with Chaff Communication Trench (at *C*.25.*b*. 5.1) to a point 100 yards north of this junction, with the object of obtaining identification and killing any Germans who resisted capture.

Whilst in the line (5th–11th March), officers and N.C.O.'s patrolled No Man's Land nightly, and thoroughly learnt their way across to the German lines. A model of the German trenches to be raided was made near the Brigade Support camp, and practice on these trenches commenced the day after the battalion moved into Brigade Support on 11th March.

The raiding party was under the command of Captain J. S. Calder, who had with him 2nd Lieuts. T. C. Kite-Powell and S. F. de Moyse Bucknall, 9 N.C.O.'s and 57 Other Ranks and 4 stretcher-bearers. Total 73 all ranks.

The raiders were addressed by the Brigadier before marching off from Roundhay Camp at 6.30 p.m. A hot meal was served in Naval Trench at 8 p.m. and three-quarters of an hour later the party moved up to Willie Support Trench (*C*.25.*c*.), where rum was issued to those who wished it.

At 9.30 p.m. the raiding party commenced to file through the gap in our wire in front of Gavrelle Cemetery (*C*.25.*c*. 7.7) and formed up in assembly formation, as arranged, in front of our wire. Capt. Calder visited each party and found everything correct. The assembly was complete by 9.45 p.m.

At zero (10 p.m.) the artillery and Stokes' mortar barrage opened on the German front line, and the raiding party advanced in three waves at 30 yards distance. The first belt of wire was found cut to bits and formed no obstacle. The second and third belts were found to be serious obstacles, and the first wave became somewhat disorganised in its endeavour to cut a way through the wire.

At zero plus two minutes the barrage lifted to Crab Trench and the first wave had still not reached the third belt of wire. The other waves had halted in No Man's Land.

2nd Lieut. Kite-Powell cut and hacked his way through and reached the German front line. He found the enemy " standing to " and the trench closely packed. He emptied his revolver and claims to have killed three Germans. Meanwhile four other men struggled through the wire and joined him, but were at once wounded with bombs.

Capt. Calder with the third wave, after waiting four minutes, realised that the raiders would lose the barrage if the advance was not at once continued. He therefore rushed forward and ordered 2nd Lieut. de Moyse Bucknall to press on at all costs, whilst he himself cut his way through and joined 2nd Lieut. Kite-Powell.

2nd Lieut. de Moyse Bucknall was unable to get his men through the wire. They had scattered somewhat in order to force their way through and had become a little disorganised. At this moment the barrage lifted from Crab to Gavrelle Support, 400 yards further back. Only four other men had reached the German front line, the remainder of the raiders with 2nd Lieut. de Moyse Bucknall being still mixed up in the wire.

Capt. Calder realised that he could not possibly reach his objective by 10.30 p.m., at which hour it had been definitely ordered that the raiders were to be clear of Crab. He accordingly ordered the withdrawal. This was carried out in an orderly manner. Two flank parties were formed in No Man's Land with the L.G. section in the centre to deal with any German counter-offensive, which it was hoped would be made as had been done in a recent raid to the south. Two sections were extended across No Man's Land to search for any casualties, and the white tape which had been laid was rolled up and brought in. By 10.40 p.m. all the raiding party was safely back in the British line. . . .

Our casualties were 13 men wounded, none severely; 75% of these were in the first two parties and were caused by bombs thrown by the Germans over the heads of their men.

The following information was gained. The German wire was very thick and about 50 or 60 yards in depth. A dug-out existed about 50 yards north of Chaff. No Germans were wearing steel helmets, but several were armed with revolvers. The front line was strongly held. The front trench was very wide at the top and not deep. A space of eight to ten yards of clear ground existed between the German front trench and the first belt of wire.

The two subalterns had no difficulty in finding their direction owing to the frequent patrols they had done beforehand. Kite-Powell reached the enemy line at the head of Chaff. The small gap which he had cut for himself was much too small for the main party to get through, so it extended, and each man tried to cut his own way.

The artillery barrage was excellent and lifted punctually. The L.T.M.B. did specially good work, firing continually despite enemy retaliation. It is believed that one of their emplacements was blown in, and the mortar was at once taken to a shell-hole in front and went on firing. The Lewis guns of the Q.W.R. fired continually at the head of Chink (*C.25.d.*) and sprayed the German wire from dusk to shortly before zero. This firing was done from the open in front of our wire at Willie Trench (*C.25.c.d.*).

The raid was accepted at General Head-quarters and appeared in the communiqué as "we inflicted casualties in a successful raid carried out near Gavrelle." Capt. Calder was awarded a bar to his Military Cross, but was unfortunately killed on 28th March, two days before the award was made; he was a good officer and a brave soldier. He had served almost continuously since November, 1914, and his loss was a grievous one. 2nd Lieut. Kite-Powell received the Military Cross, and Lce.-Cpl. J. F. Morton, Cpl. J. A. E. Pembroke, Rfn. R. W. Story and Rfn. M. J. Bell were awarded the Military Medal for their action.

On 18th March the battalion moved to St. Aubin after ten very trying days, and everyone felt that the sooner the German attack was made the better, as all were hoping for "the day." On 21st the L.R.B. went into the line to take over from the 7th Middlesex at Mill Post (*C.19.c.*) and had a prolonged and difficult task in completing a relief, begun in a bombardment, which found the post itself partly blown in, sections of wire completely obliterated and the communication trenches impassable. The night was spent in digging trenches and trying to repair the wire, and after a quiet day the battalion stood to arms for practically the whole of the next night. The 23rd was a day of shelling, in which the defended localities were simply treated as bull's-eye targets, and Mill Post, as the highest point in the whole front, received specially accurate fire. After a particularly severe bombardment of the post at 4 p.m., and the explosion of a land mine in front of Gavrelle, the battalion "stood to," but nothing developed. The next day was quiet, but on 25th a prisoner was captured at 5.15 a.m. from a German patrol. That day the discovery was made that the entire garrison (1 officer and 6 men of the 2nd Londons) of Gavrelle (*C.25.a.*), an isolated post, was killed or missing, as the Germans had been able to reach it by crawling up a ditch in No Man's Land, while all the approaches to it from the British side were under direct fire. The same evening Lieut.-Col. Husey was full of pleasure, because the prisoner captured in the morning had given away the German plans. The enemy intended to attack with three divisions, whose objective was the Brigade Head-quarters, and, after securing this point, to turn their other divisions north and south to recapture Vimy Ridge as far as Lens and surround Arras. On 26th the Germans got into the L.R.B. trench at 5.45 a.m. under cover of a thick mist and a bombardment, but were immediately driven out. That night every battalion in the division attempted a raid on the enemy at 10.30 p.m., but not a single one scored a success, owing to the moon being full and the night clear.

On 27th Mill Post underwent a heavy bombardment, starting at 3 a.m., and, as the artillery had been treated to gas and the line to shelling from guns of very large calibre during the night, the attack was expected but did not develop. At 8 p.m. orders were received that the battalion was to take over a much larger front, in order (according to the War Diary) that troops might be withdrawn for a counter-offensive in the south. This resulted in every man having to be put into the front line, in quite new positions with the exception of Mill Post, and in many of the posts in the forward zone being left unoccupied. When by 4 a.m. next day the operation had been completed, " B " was in Mill Post under Capt. Grace, " C " in Bradford Post (*C*.19.*a*.) under Capt. Calder, " D " in Bird Post (*B*.18.*d*.) under Capt. T. A. Prior and " A " in Tyne Alley (*B*.23 *and* 24) under Capt. Slade.

The attack made by the Germans in March was their last throw to win the war. It began on 21st and was highly successful, being aimed at the junction of the French with Gough's Fifth Army about La Fêre. The main part of it did not fall upon Byng's Third Army, of which the 56th Division was part, but still the attacks to the south, where the L.R.B. was posted, were heavy, and in any case it was necessary to swing back the right of the Third Army to conform to the retirement of the Fifth. The 56th Division was about the pivot of the movement, and this accounts for the importance of its stand, of which an account follows. The Germans failed utterly, but, had the 56th given way, the results might have been disastrous to the British.

March 28th, 1918, was a day that can never be forgotten by anyone who took part in it. At 3 a.m., whilst the battalion was still engaged in taking over the new posts, the British artillery was drenched with mustard gas for an hour. At 4 a.m. Battalion Head-quarters (*B*.30.*a*.) in Naval Trench, which only, however, contained police, runners, etc., underwent a heavy bombardment from guns of various calibres and received several direct hits from 9″ shells. At 5 a.m. the batteries, and hundreds of minenwerfers as well, fired on to the posts with such effect that the one wounded man, who managed to get back from Mill Post while this was going on, reported that not a vestige of trench was left, the Lewis guns and trench mortars were destroyed, and the large dug-out, in which there were some men still, had had its entrance blown in. At 7 a.m. the guns lifted back to Naval Trench and the attack began. Masses of Germans appeared, advancing slowly with their loads of blankets, boots and seven days' rations and working in groups of 5 to 10, or coming on almost shoulder to shoulder in successive lines, and within a quarter of an hour Battalion Head-quarters and the fifty men in the trench found themselves repelling a frontal attack. In spite of heavy losses from " rapid fire," the enemy soon penetrated the undefended parts of the line and threatened to surround the L.R.B., Capt. Burroughs, indeed, being at one time alone on one side of a traverse and the Germans on the other, so Lieut.-Col. Husey ordered the remnants of his

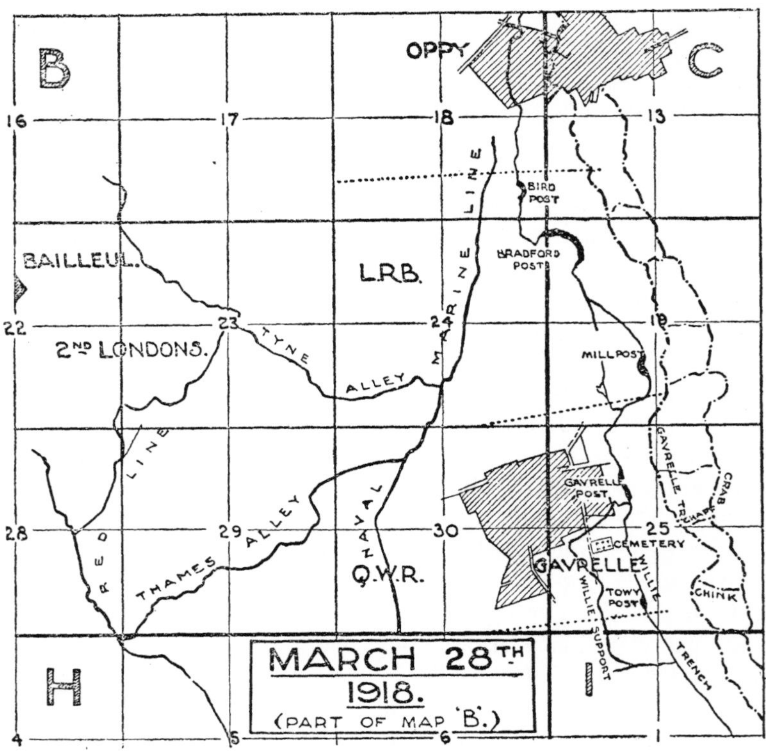

SKETCH MAP NO. 13

command to move to the head of Thames Alley (*B.30.a.*). After holding this point for a short time he began a retirement, man by man, with frequent halts for firing at the enemy, and finally was able by 10.30 a.m. to reorganise the battalion, reduced by then to 7 Officers and 64 Other Ranks, including a few survivors from Bradford and Bird Posts, in Red Line, and help the 2nd Londons, who were defending it in strength. In spite of bombardment and bringing their Horse Artillery up at the gallop to the outskirts of Gavrelle, only to be blown to pieces by the British guns, the Germans were able to make no further impression and their attack had failed. It had succeeded in capturing a series of isolated posts, but these were to have been given up on 30th, and the main line was intact. The fighting continued during the afternoon, but by 6 p.m. the enemy was spent, and by dusk patrols were out in front searching the ground to make sure that he was not assembling troops for a further attempt, although no attack was possible on the strongly held continuous line without a preliminary bombardment. When the 167th Brigade had come up the 169th began to feel free, and, after handing over to the 7th Middlesex, the L.R.B. started for Roundhay Park at 3.30 a.m. on 29th, feeling confident that the danger was over.

What that danger was Gen. Ludendorff revealed after the signing of the Armistice in the following November, when he said that the failure of this attack was the chief reason for the German downfall, and that, if the 4th and 56th Divisions had not held their ground, Vimy and Arras would have fallen, which would have been, in his opinion, the beginning of the end.

The day was crowded with incidents and acts of heroism. Lieut.-Col. Husey was always to be found where the fighting was hardest, but the part that he actually played will never be known, as it was so contrary to his nature to advertise himself that the War Diary, with stern self-suppression, gives no indication. However, he was personally congratulated by the Army Commander, and given a Bar to his D.S.O., facts which speak for themselves. Capt. Rose, who had been recalled from the boat at Boulogne on which he was going to England for a fortnight's leave, was hit and killed instantaneously while firing coolly at the Germans. Capt. Burroughs held three bombing blocks in succession and seemed to revel in it. The men for once were able to gratify a soldier's great ambition—to fire 15 rounds in a minute at an easy target at short range—to the full, and, whatever the battalion losses were, they were nothing to those of the Germans, who provided groups of men moving slowly at distances at which they could not be missed. A letter was received a month afterwards from a member of the Canadian Regiment, which took over the L.R.B. front, who wrote that he had always thought that his battalion killed Germans, but his patrols had reported that the ground was so littered with dead, that the battalion felt that it still had something to learn. One letter, written at Lieut.-Col. Husey's request, says, " The attack lasted all day and then died down, the Germans having wasted about two divisions on us and not reaching their objective. It was the finest day we have had, and afforded real pleasure in shooting Germans down at close ranges."

After reorganising into two platoons and a head-quarters platoon, and a day's rest, the battalion started on 30th March for Mont St. Eloi. While on the way, a halt was made at St. Aubin for dinners and a reinforcing draft of 400 men added to the ranks. This showed good staff work and proper attention to a matter of vital importance, and within the next two days the battalion was at full strength. A Canadian battalion, which had heard of the battle of Vimy and knew the losses which the L.R.B. had suffered, gave it a great reception there, and the Colonel gave a detailed account to his own men, finishing up by saying that the L.R.B. had fought to the last and it was now up to *them* to get the Naval Trench back. However, they had no chance of doing this, as that line was given up and the Red Line made the front lines.

On 31st, after reaching Mont St. Eloi, visits were paid by the Army, Corps, Division, Intelligence Departments and others, who talked about the wonderful fight that the battalion had put up. The Press correspondents turned up in full force, and, after interviewing Lieut.-Col. Husey, produced the accounts that will be found in Appendix E ; but these must be discounted by those who are unable to read between the lines, as he was the last man in the world to talk about himself or to sing the praises of his battalion in public.

The casualties for March were: Officers (L.R.B.), Capt. E. W. Rose, killed ; Capt. J. S. Calder, 2nd Lieuts. R. F. L. Hewlett, H. G. Higham, W. R. B. Kettle, T. C. Kite-Powell, F. S. Sills, R. C. Thompson, missing ; Capt. T. E. Burroughs, Lieut. S. R. Owen, 2nd Lieuts. W. F. Harrington, K. W. Jones, H. L. Renwick, wounded ; (21st Londons) 2nd Lieuts. F. Adams, S. C. Gould, missing ; (10th Londons) Capt. W. J. Grace, missing; (Q.V.R.) 2nd Lieut. G. M. Newland, missing; (7th Middlesex) 2nd Lieut. C. S. Tresilian, missing. Total Officers 1 killed, 5 wounded, and 13 missing. Other Ranks, 17 killed, 175 wounded, 437 missing; total, 629. The reinforcements were 495 Other Ranks.

FIRST BATTALION

PART X. APRIL 1, 1918—MAY 30, 1919

Beaurains—Lt.-Col. Husey promoted Brigadier-General—General advance—Armistice—Demobilisation—Return of Cadre.

(*The Maps referred to are B ; No.* 14 *on p.* 238, *and No.* 15 *facing p.* 250.)

THE first week in April was devoted to reorganising and getting ready to move to a new sector, and on 8th the battalion marched to Berneville, where it had to " stand to " during the night. From that date to 13th there were several alarms and on 11th a bombardment, but no attack was made. Perhaps the most quaint incident was that of a French farmer who started cursing a tank and thrashing it with his pitch-fork, because it had gone over his crops. On 14th a march was made to the old British trenches at Beaurains (M.11) to relieve the 8th Middlesex, and a week was spent there supplying working parties for the front line.

April was a quiet but busy month, as, although the battalion was always in reserve or support, there were plenty of working parties to be found by day or by night, and to " stand to " at 5 a.m. became almost a habit. On 14th a move was made to Beaurains to relieve the 7th Middlesex, and on 19th the battalion took the place of the Kensingtons, in support in Blangy and Ficheux Trenches. On 22nd Major F. H. Wallis went home to the Senior Officers' School, and on 25th Lieut.-Col. R. H. Husey was appointed temporarily Brigadier of the 167th Infantry Brigade, Major W. D. Cheshire taking command of the battalion. On 28th, after being relieved by the London Scottish, the battalion went to Dainville, where Capt. B. L. E. Pocock temporarily took over the duties of Second in Command, and Rev. F. L. Sheppard was relieved by the Rev. E. J. Passant.

The Officers joining during the month were :—

Lieut. C. H. John ; 2nd Lieuts. E. F. Byles (15th Londons), H. G. D. Coles, V. W. R. Crane, J. P. Gee, J. W. Grindey, L. R. Gyton, G. D. Hilder (15th Londons), W. A. Houghton, W. C. Lean, P. R. S. Spettigue, E. A. Thiede, H. B. Waters and M. W. Wright ; 359 Other Ranks also joined.

The casualties were : one Rifleman killed, nine Other Ranks wounded.

The 4th May was a red-letter day in the history of the regiment, as on that date Lieut.-Col. R. H. Husey, its most distinguished officer, was appointed to command the 25th Brigade in the 8th Division. With regard to this, Lieut.-Col. Husey wrote to a brother officer in England as follows :—

" 4/6/18. A very hasty line to let you know that I have been appointed Brigadier to the 25th Inf. Brig. ; who or what they are I know not. . . . These are giddy times to take over a new brigade, but it will be very interesting. I do hope that I shall be happy there—anyway I will let you know.—P.S. I've just heard that the 8th is a regular division—they *will* be pleased to get me ! "

On the same day the battalion relieved the 1st Londons in the front line, but nothing of importance occurred before 11th when Major C. D. Burnell assumed command, which he retained till the end of the war. The 1st Battalion was most fortunate in always being commanded by one of its own officers, and there is no doubt that this was one of the great factors in its efficiency. Burnell had served in the regiment from 1894–1912, when he retired, being senior captain. He rejoined on 4th August, 1914, coming back as a captain junior to many younger than himself. He went to France with the 1st Battalion, and was severely wounded at Ypres in May, 1915. On recovery, he did invaluable work in helping to train and fashion the 3rd Battalion, and in May, 1917, after passing through the Senior Officers School, he returned to France, and eventually brought home the cadre. On 15th, while digging a new forward trench which had been ordered, the enemy employed gas against the working parties, apparently from rifle grenades. It was the only occasion on which this method was experienced and the battalion was lucky to have had no casualties from it, as the troops on either side were caught rather badly. The work was continued in spite of hostility until 21st, when the 4th Londons came in and the battalion went back to Dainville, to move to Arras on 24th, returning to Dainville on 27th. During this period working parties were occupied in digging and wiring, but on 30th the front line was occupied again, Telegraph Hill being taken over from the 7th Middlesex, with head-quarters in N.1.a. On 27th the Germans made an attack on the Aisne, very skilfully concealed beforehand and covered by an exceptionally heavy bombardment, which opened without any previous preparation. It was after this action that Brig.-Gen. R. H. Husey was reported as missing, when the regiment suffered the irreparable loss of its most distinguished officer. This is not the place in which to enlarge upon his career, a full account of which will be found on p. 344.

The Officers joining during the month were : Capt. G. B. Vaile ; Lieuts. J. S. Godward, R. D. Poland, C. O. Tabberer (Q.V.R.), and 2nd Lieuts. N. Craig, E. Frey, R. N. Morley.

The casualties were : 2nd Lieuts. J. H. Bryant and J. A. T. Derham, wounded ; Other Ranks, 1 killed, 23 wounded and 2 missing.

In June the enemy's artillery was consistently active, but nothing of importance occurred until 10th, when a German sergt.-major was shot in our wire by one of our sentries. His body was brought in to our lines. On the 10th also the plans for a raid, which every battalion in the division was expected to make during its tour of duty, were discussed. The objective chosen did not allow effective observation to be made, so Capt. F. G. Hancocks, who provided the raiding party from "D" Company, sent out twice on night patrol every man selected for it, so as to become thoroughly familiar with the ground that he had to work over. The result was that when at 3 p.m. on 12th the raid advanced, covered by a barrage of shell and smoke, each unit found its way through some very poor wire to its respective objective without difficulty, and the enemy were, as was hoped, caught by surprise in their dug-outs. Only one German was seen above ground, who immediately ran to earth, and the others showed no desire to come out and fight, in spite of numerous P. bombs, except a few who fired from the fire-step, but were shot down. The dug-outs were then heavily bombed with Mills' grenades until at 3.10 p.m. the raiders got the signal to retire and withdrew, but without any prisoners. In addition to killing 24 Germans, as counted by the officers, three trench mortars were destroyed, and the barrage and bombing must have caused many casualties among those in the dug-outs. The enemy's position turned out to be some deep dug-outs, not connected with any trench system, and some small " bivvies " lying in a depression in the ground from which the British lines could only be observed to the north and north-west. The raiding party had three Other Ranks killed, 11 wounded and 1 missing. The Corps Commanding Officer sent the following message to the brigade : " My congratulations to the L.R.B. on success of Wednesday's raid, which does them much credit. Another time they must remember that live Boches are of value to us." This success was due to Capt. Hancocks' organisation, and particularly to the night patrol experience, as the only other information was that which could be obtained from aeroplane photographs.

After this things went on as before up to 17th, when the battalion was relieved by the London Scottish and went into divisional reserve at Berneville, where a distribution of awards was made ; on 26th it took the place of the 7th Middlesex in support at St. Sauveur (G.30), and remained there to the end of the month.

During the last week in June the effective strength of the battalion was very seriously affected by an outbreak of influenza, as many as 200 cases being evacuated to hospital at one time. The untiring energy and devotion to duty of the Medical Officer, Captain A. F. Horn, and his staff are worthy of special mention. They remained on duty the whole time although suffering severely from the complaint themselves.

The reinforcements during the month were : Officers 2 ; Other Ranks 16.

The casualties were : Other Ranks killed 13, wounded 23, missing 1.

Through the early part of July the enemy continued his activity, and the battalion was in the line at Tilloy from 2nd until relieved by the Canadians on 13th, a troublesome performance, as was the return one in the next month, owing to their still having four battalions in each brigade, which involved an entire redistribution of the line. The L.R.B. then had a series of moves, marching on 14th to Arras, travelling by train from Dainville to La Thieuloye on 15th, and marching on 18th to Beugin, where it trained until 30th, when it marched to Cambligneul, which village at this time seemed to be the objective of violent bombing attacks by night-flying enemy planes.

The reinforcements during the month were : Other Ranks 8 ; and the casualties : Other Ranks killed 2, wounded 4.

August was a month of marked variety, the first part quiet, the middle taken up with continual marches, which were very trying owing to the uncertainty of their object, and the end containing the four most strenuous days that the battalion was engaged in during the whole war.

On 1st a march to Mingoval and a journey by train to Dainville brought the battalion to Beaurains, where the Canadians were taken out of support by a troublesome relief. After wet weather up to 6th, when the padre, the Rev. J. M. Duncan, was wounded, the line at Telegraph Hill was occupied on 7th to relieve the Q.W.R. until 17th, when the battalion came out and went to Berneville, where it entrained and after a short run marched to Lignereuil. On 19th, with a view to deceiving the enemy about the movement of troops, his balloons were allowed to see the battalion embus before marching via Warlus and Dainville to Arras, which was left next day by another march via Dainville, Warlus and Wanquetin to billets in Hauteville. On 21st the battalion came to Saulty Labret via Fosseux and Barly Church. On 22nd warning orders were received to be ready to move at short notice to reinforce the 168th Infantry Brigade, which was attacking in the Boyelles sector, on the following morning. Nucleus and surplus personnel were withdrawn, and company commanders spent the day reconnoitring assembly and jumping-off positions. The battalion moved on 23rd to Bailleulval, where it bivouacked, knowing that an attack was on hand.

At 5 a.m. on 24th the battalion marched some six or seven miles to some gun-pits one mile east of Blairville, where battle equipment, etc., was issued ; at 6.30 p.m. it marched a further four miles to occupy Boyelles Trench, half a mile east of Boyelles (T.13), in support of the front line, which had been carried forward by that time to Summit Trench (*T*.10 *and* 16) along the top of the ridge three-quarters of a mile west of Croisilles (*T*.23) ; and it remained there to receive a bombardment of yellow cross gas during the night, as well as a heavy shelling in the morning and the afternoon of the next day.

At 6.15 p.m. on 26th the battalion left Boyelles Trench, and advanced by sections to Summit Trench to relieve the 7th Middlesex, prepared to attack ; at 9 p.m. it started against the trenches running north and south on the west side of Croisilles with the Q.W.R. on its right. "C" and "D" Companies, which were leading, with "B" in support and "A" in reserve, got 400 yards forward up to a sunken road (*T*.17.*a*.), when machine-gun fire from the front and both flanks held up the attack altogether, and ultimately the battalion withdrew to Summit Trench by order at 3.30 a.m. the next day in readiness for another attempt.

This was made on 27th at 9.30 a.m. with the same objectives, but with "A" Company and one platoon of "B" in front and the rest of the battalion in support, and again only 400 yards were covered before machine-gun fire from Croisilles and the trenches north of it produced so many casualties that no further progress could be made, and "A" Company could not get back while it was light. About 3.30 p.m. the battalion received orders to encircle Croisilles from the north by working down the Hindenburg Line from Fat Switch at *T*.5.*a*. This operation was carried out without any unusual incident until reaching the Sensee River, when, owing to the trench coming to an end 200 yards from the river (*T*.12.*d*.), the head of the battalion came under heavy machine-gun fire. However, by making a long detour the difficulty was surmounted, and eventually two trenches 500 yards east-north-east of Croisilles were occupied. Eventually the night was spent in Burg Support, about *U*.7. *central*.

On 28th "A" Company, which had, as already mentioned, been unable to withdraw after the first action on the previous day, rejoined at 11.30 a.m. and at 12.30 the attack was pushed further forward, but with the east side of Bullecourt as its

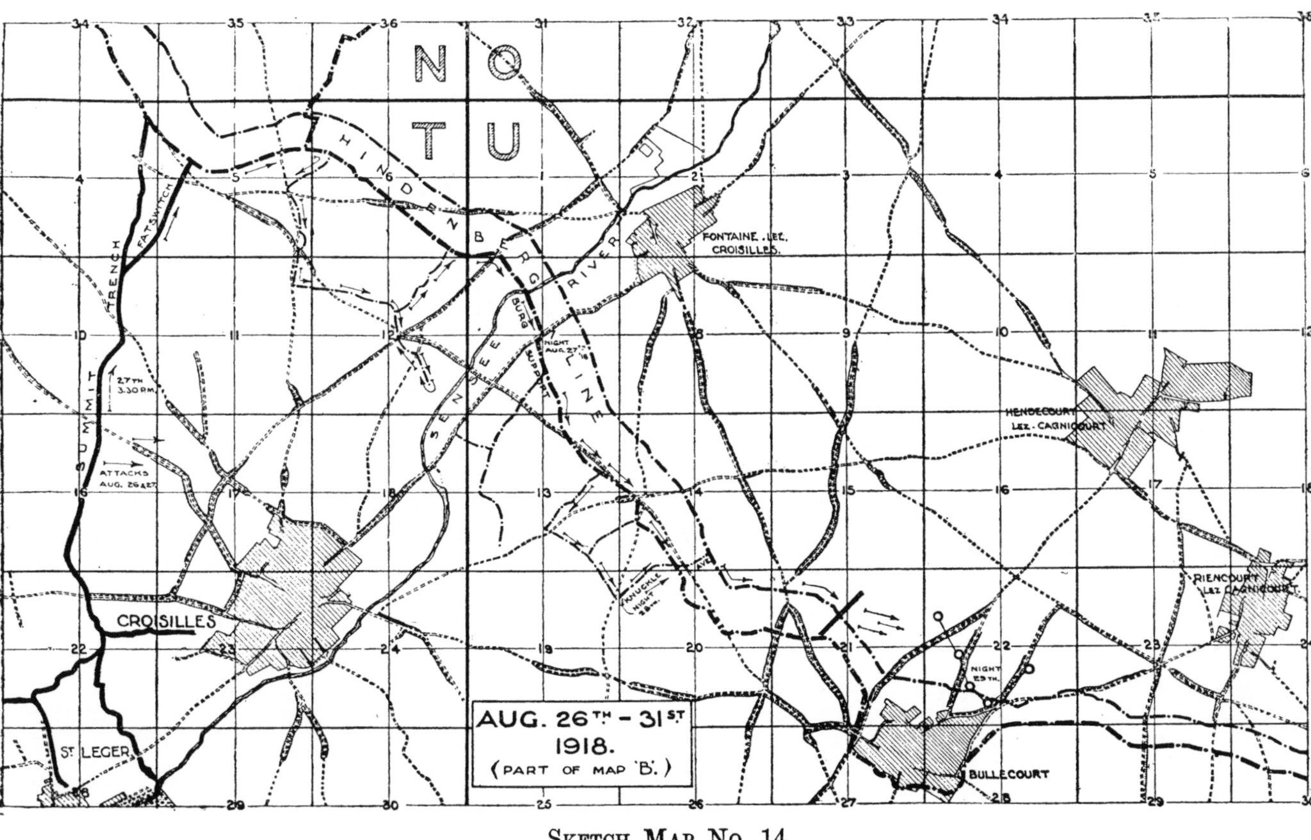

Sketch Map No. 14

objective, and the Q.W.R. in the front line with the L.R.B. in close support. Unfortunately " C " and " D," the left and centre companies of the L.R.B., lost direction, and bore off to the left, and were eventually compelled by machine-gun fire to hold up and consolidate north of Hendecourt (*U*.10.*d*.). The result of this mistake was that the head-quarters of the two battalions engaged found themselves unexpectedly fighting together as front line troops, almost surrounded by machine guns, a situation which was not cleared up till late in the afternoon. On the right (which was the open flank) the companies of the Q.W.R. were badly knocked about by a nest of machine guns about 200 yards off (*U*.13.*d*.) and by similar fire from Croisilles. " B " Company L.R.B. also suffered heavy losses and was pinned down, and an attack to outflank the nest from the south failed. In fact, the whole brigade was held up until 7.30 p.m., when Capt. Burroughs, with the help of two companies of the Kensingtons and two Stokes' mortars which had been sent for, organised a local operation which ended in the machine guns being rushed by " B " Company, L.R.B. Ten machine guns, 2 trench mortars and 10 prisoners were captured, and incidentally the head-quarters relieved from their embarrassing position. That night the battalion, which only consisted of " B " Company and a handful of " A," as " C " and " D " had not then come back, rested in Knuckle Trench and the Hindenburg Line (*U*.20.*a*.).

On 29th the battalion at 1 p.m. returned to the attack, its fifth in four days. The frontage that was given to it was 1500 yards and there were only about 100 men, " C " and " D " Companies not having yet got back, while the Q.W.R. in support had only 60 and the 2nd Londons about the same. However, the men went on with just the same dash as before, in spite of Capt. Burroughs having been badly wounded, capturing about 60 prisoners and eventually consolidating posts in *U*.22.*a*. *c*. *and d*., where they held on until relieved at dawn by the 7th Middlesex.

On 30th the relief had been completed by about 6.40 a.m., and the battalion was preparing to start off when the enemy counter-attacked on Bullecourt. Fortunately, however, the attempt fizzled out without the L.R.B. being called upon, and the move back to Burg Support (*U*.7. *central*) became possible.

An account of the doings of a single battalion in a battle of movement such as this can only be sketchy, and some extracts from a letter written by the Adjutant, Capt. W. C. Von Berg on 2/9/18, indicate one of the reasons for this.

"The battalion has covered itself with glory again, but not more so than at any other time in its history. All the 'Nobs' from the Corps Commander to the Brigadier are frightfully pleased with what we have done, and our tails are well up. . . . The good old division has made a record advance, further and more successfully than any other division has ever done in the time. . . . It was mighty stiff fighting at times and the lads stuck it well. . . . Our junior officers were just wonderful and did excellent work, but there is the same difficulty now that you experienced after Polygon Wood, viz., that there is no one left to tell us of any deeds of gallantry. We have managed to find a few however.

"Young Frey, whom you remember as a runner, was killed, also Capt. Welch, I fear, though he was last seen badly wounded. . . . Poor old Tom Burroughs got a nasty one through the body after doing magnificent work as O.C. 'B' Company. He was last seen in a C. C. S. and going well, so we are hoping he will recover. . . . If you can find him in England I hope that you will go and see him, and tell him how frightfully proud we are of him. . . . Cope was slightly wounded after doing good work as O.C. 'D' Company, but beyond that all other officer casualties are of new officers whom you would not know.

"All head-quarter officers came through all right, the C.O., John, Mills and yours truly feeling rather like chewed string, and I am up to my eyes in the usual work of reorganisation, etc. . . . The news is streaming in of further advances, and I think that the moral has never been better. . . . I do wish you were with us now, you would simply revel in this new kind of fighting. It is awfully exciting and I am quite looking forward to the next 'binge.'"

On 31st the brigade was relieved by the 155th Infantry Brigade and the L.R.B. moved into an old camp at Boisleaux-au-Mont.

The reinforcements during the month were: Capt. V. E. O. Welch, 2nd Lieut. S. F. J. Campbell (6th Londons), 2nd Lieut. W. E. Grant (7th Londons) and 8 Other Ranks.

The casualties were: Officers, Capt. V. E. O. Welch, 2nd Lieuts. S. F. J. Campbell (6th Londons) and E. Frey, killed; Capts. T. E. Burroughs, R. Cope, S. du Plessis and G. B. Vaile, Rev. J. M. Duncan, Lieut. H. A. Chodak, R.A.M.C., 2nd Lieuts. E. F. Byles (15th Londons), V. W. R. Crane, J. W. Grindey, W. A. Houghton, W. C. Lean, R. N. Morley and P. R. S. Spettigue, wounded. Other Ranks, killed 54, died of wounds 17, wounded 226, missing 2, total 299.

The first four days of September were devoted to reorganisation and training, and the battalion spent the fifth in marching out to a new area west of Bullecourt only to find that the orders had been cancelled and that it had to march back again. On the 6th the battalion was inspected and addressed by Lieut.-Gen. Fergusson, G.O.C. XVIIth Corps, on the occasion of the 56th Division leaving the Corps, and was highly complimented on the good work done in the recent fighting. On 7th it moved to Vis-en-Artois (O.22), where the 4th Londons were relieved, and on 8th it took over the sector of the front held by the 1st Black Watch. The next five days passed without any pronounced incident except persistent shelling, but on 12th a move was made into support at Dury (P.22), followed by a march on 18th to the area north of Guemappe. On 20th the battalion moved by road and across the old battlefield of 3rd May, 1917, to a position south of Vis-en-Artois, where it was accommodated in a vast cave called the Schmidt-Hohle. An idea of the size of these novel quarters may be gained by the fact that a battalion officers' mess was formed in one of the larger chambers.

Training, varied by bathing, filled up the time there until 24th, when a conference of battalion commanders discussed some impending operations in which the brigade's rôle was to mop up the Agache Valley including the villages of Cauchy-Lestree (Q.35) and Sauchy Cauchy (Q.34), if the main attack further east were successful. On the evening of 25th the battalion relieved the 21st Canadians in their positions, which were under direct observation so that no movement was allowed by day, and remained there in waiting for the attack.

In the operations which began on 27th August, the brigade was ordered to cross the Canal du Nord astride the Arras-Cambrai road, advancing through the 3rd Canadian Infantry

Brigade, who were to make the first assault, to attack the general line of the railway and clear the enemy from the ground between the canal and the river at Marquion. In order to carry this out the Q.W.R. had, after crossing the canal, to make one attack with the canal and the River Agache as its boundaries, and the 2nd Londons a separate one with the river on its left and some cross-roads as its limit on the right, while the L.R.B. co-operated with the two battalions.

"B" Company, L.R.B., was detailed to cover the passage of the Q.W.R. across the canal, clear its west bank, establish posts on the east side which were not to be withdrawn until the crossing was completed, and send out patrols to search for those of the enemy. This scheme did not work out as planned, owing to the Canadians getting hung up at Marquion and zero for the brigade being shifted in consequence from 14.20 to 15.25, and "B" Company was held up for some time by machine-gun fire before it was able to get forward. However, it eventually succeeded and covered the movement of the whole brigade, but not without having several casualties, including 2nd Lieut. H. Cross, who died the same day, and 2nd Lieut. G. J. Adams, who died the next. "D" Company under Capt. Hancocks had to connect the two attacking battalions, clear up any centres of resistance met with in the country between the two branches of the Agache and their junction, and assist in the capture of Cauchy-Lestree by firing on any of the enemy who might be seen at its western end and preventing any movement between that village and Sauchy Cauchy. This was carried out effectually, although the Company never passed through the Canadians as ordered because there were none to be seen, presumably through their having lost direction, but it also found hardly any Boches. "C" Company followed close up behind the right of the 2nd Londons, with "A" in support, in order to complete any mopping up that that battalion had not time for, and the four companies finished by collecting and reorganising in Cemetery Wood (Q.36.a.) preparatory to taking over the line which now ran from Palleul (Q.11) eastwards.

On 28th September the relief of the 2nd Londons which began at 7 p.m. was completed at midnight, and the next day was so quiet that all the posts were visited by daylight without shelling, although they were under observation. During 30th the battalion extended its front to the right, but otherwise nothing occurred. The front held now stretched from Palleul Lock to Canal in R.7 central.

The brigade gained great kudos for its share in this fighting, which from the battalion point of view was nothing like so strenuous as that near Croisilles or Bullecourt. Orders were issued well in advance, and everything was done to time, while the enemy hardly put up any fight at all, instead of hanging on with machine guns in every possible place.

The reinforcements during the month were : 2nd Lieuts. G. J. Adams, S. F. Belither, F. H. Brock, D. C. Cockerell, H. Cross, C. P. Darrington, S. F. Finch, L. Jessop, C. M. King (18th Londons), J. D. Keep, H. Ross (7th Londons), H. Stevens (18th Londons), J. W. Terry and 30 Other Ranks.

The casualties were : Officers, 2nd Lieut. G. J. Adams wounded and died next day ; 2nd Lieut. H. Cross, wounded and died same day ; Lieut. B. F. Sawbridge, 2nd Lieuts. W. A. Chrisp, N. Craig, J. P. Gee and G. D. Hilder (15th Londons) wounded ; Other Ranks, 8 killed, 3 died, 54 wounded.

On the morning of 1st October an enemy patrol surprised an L.R.B. post close to the Canal du Sensee, killing three of the garrison and wounding the fourth without, however, obtaining any identification. As the attempt was repeated the next night on the same post, which had been promptly re-established, it was evident that he felt very nervous about a bridge-head being made over the canal. On 3rd, after relief by the Q.W.R., the battalion went into support at Sauchy Cauchy, where the Germans had arranged excellent baths for officers and men, which were highly appreciated. On 5th the battalion was relieved by the 8th Middlesex and moved back to bivouac near Saudemont (P.24). On 9th a warning order was received to relieve the Kensingtons near Epinoy (R.34), but as they took Fressies, 4500 yards N.E. of Epinoy, on 11th the relief became complicated. However, this meant that there were no Germans south of the canal which made up for the difficulties, though unfortunately Capt. Hosking and Lieut. A. Macdonald (both 7th Londons) were badly wounded while taking over. On 13th the 2nd Londons crossed the canal on the L.R.B. left at Aubigny (R.10) and gained possession of the bridge-head, but were unable to retain the village itself. On 14th the 4th Canadians took over, and the next day the L.R.B. went by the Decauville railway from Marquion to Haute Avesnes in the Agnez Duisans area, a journey which seemed to cover half of France. There the battalion had a well-earned rest, the last during the war, and thoroughly enjoyed itself in the fine weather, officers, N.C.O.'s and companies all having most pleasant dinners in turn. During the stay fearful noises were heard one day in one of the huts, which investigation showed to be caused by the nucleus brass band practising. So much perseverance was displayed by the members and so much toleration of the discord by the rest, that a month later quite a first-class band was to be heard playing every day at the mounting of the Guard. On 17th Capt. F. H. Crews rejoined the battalion from the General Head-quarters' Lewis Gun School, and four days later Major F. H. Wallis rejoined from England for a month's attachment. On 31st the battalion embussed and moved via Arras to rest billets in Lieu St. Amand, a village which had seen very severe fighting but was able to produce about half a dozen inhabitants, the first that had been met so far. (See map facing p. 250.)

On 1st November orders were received for a move next day, when the battalion marched to Maing, where dinners were served and battle stores drawn, and afterwards went on to Caumont Farm, 12 miles in all. By 8 p.m. the 6th Duke of Wellington's had been relieved and the rest of the night passed quietly, but for a few shells, as the enemy was retiring. On 3rd information was received that the enemy was retreating all along the line and the L.R.B. moved forward in reserve at 2 p.m. to Moulin de Sameon, which was occupied by civilians, but later on went on to Saultain, also full of inhabitants, and passed the night there.

On 4th November at 6 a.m. the Q.W.R. attacked Sebourg with the L.R.B. in support and keeping touch with the brigade. By 9.30 touch had been lost, the Q.W.R. were having difficulties in the outskirts of the village, so the Commanding Officer decided to move up. The village was then easily captured and the Q.W.R. pushed forward across the bridge over the River Aunelle. The Germans had left a strong party of 25 men with 2 guns in a farmhouse on the far side near the bridge, and they kept in hiding until the patrols had gone by, but were satisfactorily dealt with when they showed themselves. The Q.W.R. pressed on until it was held up, and then had to meet a counter-attack, which was successfully driven off with the help of "B" Company L.R.B. under Capt. C. H. John and "C" Company under Capt. C. O. Tabberer. The day finished with all the ground that had been taken being in British hands, and there was no change during the night. In the course of the action about 30 prisoners were taken, in addition to a derelict disabled tank. The village was full of people, some of them refugees from Valenciennes, who were overjoyed to see the British and did all that they could for the troops. The Germans put down a heavy bombardment, beginning with a direct hit on the church, as well as gas shells, which between them considerably altered the appearance of the place and made things very uncomfortable.

On 5th November at 5.30 a.m. the battalion attacked Angreau to seize the village, push through and occupy a line on the east of the village along the railway line, besides establishing bridge-heads on the Angreau River, which was fairly deep but not wide. At first all went well, the guns put down a satisfactory barrage, a cluster of houses known as Nouveau Monde was easily cleared of Germans and the relieving party rewarded with coffee by the inhabitants, and Angreau itself soon reached and entered. The people received the troops with enthusiasm, and rumour, which the victim does not deny, states that the Mayor, unwashed and unshaven, insisted on saluting Major Wallis, who got no reward for his act of heroism, in the approved fashion on both cheeks. By 11 a.m the enemy's guns had been silenced and the battalion started to take up the ground east of the village, when the real trouble began. On the right lay Roisin, but for some reason or other no simultaneous attack had been arranged on it, and on the left, about one mile to the north, was Angre, which simply invited capture, but the London Scottish were so weak in strength that they could not go forward, and had to remain in their outpost line, the best part of a mile in rear. The result was that by noon "C" and "D" were forming a defensive flank on the north end of the village from the River Angreau, across a deep tramway cutting, to the left of the other two companies, which were holding the road on the east side running north and south. The enemy then began shelling the village and its approaches, besides paying special attention to the party on the north, who were also heavily attacked with machine guns that were brought down the cutting, and, although Roisin was taken during the afternoon and the Q.W.R. came up in close support, the situation did not appreciably alter during the day. At night "A" and "B" Companies were relieved by the 2nd Londons and moved in rear of "C" and "D," but Battalion Head-quarters instead of fetching Angreau found themselves in Roisin, so that it was fortunate that there had been a change of owners, though this was not the opinion of a Belgian there, who owned to being sorry that the Germans were not still present as one of them had borrowed his matchbox and gone off without returning it.

On 6th November the battalion attacked again, the final objective this time being Montignies, and started at 5.30 a.m. under cover of a creeping barrage, but the enemy replied at once with very heavy machine-gun fire from Angre and the banks of the River Honelle, which caused severe losses in the front line. As a matter of fact this attack was doomed to failure from the first as the men were not only wet and tired, but so few that they had to extend 20 or 30 paces, and even then the two leading companies appeared isolated and were certainly quite ignorant whether any advance had been made on their flanks or not. However, the River Honelle was forded and the attack up the slope begun, "C" Company first under Capt. Tabberer actually succeeding in reaching the objective, a sunken road, but the 2nd Londons got into great difficulty in the Bois du Beaufort. The enemy was not long in discovering how weak the attack was, and made a vigorous counter-attack with a battalion of reserves, which outnumbered the 169th Infantry Brigade completely. "B" and "C" Companies L.R.B. were isolated, and so nearly surrounded that they were called upon to surrender, but they refused, and with the help of the Lewis guns, which were admirably handled, gallantly fell back, fighting, to the river. At this point the 40 or 50 prisoners, whom the two companies had captured, showed a marked disinclination to getting their feet wet and required drastic treatment before they could be induced to cross. By 8.30 a.m. the battalion was back whence it had kicked off, exhausted, and none too cheerful, and for the next ten hours the Germans showered a concentrated hate upon the unfortunate village of Angreau. Eight-inch shells dropped round the church, and 5·9's and 4·2's were rained upon the village until not a house was left untouched; the whole place was in ruins, and the poor civilians had a terrible experience. At 9 p.m. the 7th Middlesex relieved the L.R.B., which went into rest billets at Sebourg.

This proved to be the last fighting in which the battalion was engaged. After a day's rest for cleaning up, it went across country on 8th November to Angreau, and two days later moved to Erquennes, where news was received on 11th that the Armistice had been signed, and in consequence the brass band played at Guard Mounting for the first time. On 13th orders, afterwards cancelled, were received that the battalion was to form part of the Army of Occupation in Germany, and on 15th 3 officers and 77 men represented it in a march past at Mons before Gen. Sir H. S. Horne, commanding 1st Army.

Road-mending, tree-felling and sports filled up the time until 26th, when the battalion marched to Harmignies with the band playing, via Rinchon la Folie, Blaregnies and Quevy le Petit. On 30th Lieut.-Col. Burnell proceeded home on leave, Major Cheshire taking over the command, and Capt. Tabberer, who had been appointed Education Officer, gave his first lecture.

The reinforcements during the month were: Capt. C. H. Marriott, Lieuts. H. J. F. Crisp and D. Hood, 2nd Lieuts. W. E. Anderson (51st R.B.), J. A. Bennett (3rd R.B.), J. M. Berkley (1st R.B.), V. W. R. Crane, A. Elliott (5th R.B.), W. J. Godwin (3rd R.B.), A. L. Milburn (5th R.B.), W. E. Page (15th Londons), C. Randall (8th R.B.), B. G. H. Stratton (2nd R.B.) and 109 Other Ranks.

The casualties were: Officers, 2nd Lieuts. E. Barnes (18th Londons) and D. C. Cockerell, killed; 2nd Lieut. C. M. King (18th Londons), wounded and missing; Lieut. C. P. Darrington, 2nd Lieuts. H. Stevens (18th Londons) and E. A. Thiede, wounded; Other Ranks, 22 killed, 8 died of wounds, 6 missing, 125 wounded; 161, total.

During December sports of every kind took place in the afternoons, many football matches were played and education was taken up seriously. On 3rd Rfn. W. Frampton was given a money prize by the division for the smartness of his transport turn-out, and on 8th Major F. H. Wallis ended his war service with the L.R.B., as he left to take command of the Kensingtons. He went to France as a colour-sergeant, was given a commission early in 1915, and for three and a half months in 1917 was Lieut.-Colonel commanding, in the absence of Lieut.-Col. Husey. With the exception of a month's leave in 1917 and the six months spent at home at the Senior Officers School and elsewhere in 1918, he had served with the 1st Battalion during the whole campaign, thanks to having been fortunate enough to escape a serious wound, to a strong constitution and a stout heart. He won a Military Cross with two bars, and was probably unlucky not to obtain a higher decoration. His determination and his power of persuading others to "stick it" undoubtedly did much to make the 1st Battalion what it was. Both in peace and war he rendered great and loyal service to the L.R.B., and his name is one which should not be forgotten in the regiment. On 20th the Brigadier came over and presented the medal ribbons won by members of the battalion, all attempts to arrange a divisional day for the purpose having failed. On Christmas Day the men were waited on by the officers and N.C.O.'s at their dinners, and in the evening a concert was held in the cement works, with free beer. On 31st the only reinforcements apparently for the month, 2nd Lieuts. L. B. Marrian and H. W. Snodgrass, joined.

January, 1919, was a blank month, by the end of which 6 Officers and 255 Other Ranks had been demobilised, and there was 1 Officer reinforcement, 2nd Lieut. C. Helm. During February 3 Officers and 187 Other Ranks were set free, and at the end of the month there were 31 Officers still serving, including Capt. H. L. Johnston and Lieut. J. E. N. Pooley, who joined during that period, and 180 Other Ranks. The last recorded incident in the war-history of the 1st Battalion L.R.B. is that on 26th February, 1919, "Jim.", the C.O.'s charger, won the XXIInd Corps $1\frac{1}{2}$ miles steeplechase (12 stone) at the Corps Race Meeting.

From this time forward all energies were devoted to preparations for returning to England. The 5 officers and 84 men due for the Army of Occupation were sent to the Q.W.R. and the regiment, after demobilising to cadre strength, marched on March 23rd to billets in Jemappes (Quaregnon), a mining village close to Mons, in order to be near a rail-head, as all animals had to be demobilised as well. The change from Harmignies was not at all appreciated, as no one was able to find anything to do in Jemappes.

The following letter from the Brigadier was received by the C.O.

"*20th April*, 1919.

"MY DEAR BURNELL,

"On leaving the Brigade after having commanded it over three years of such stirring times, I want to express to you my very high appreciation of your battalion. The gallantry of London Territorials is well known, and the units of the 169th Infantry Brigade have more than maintained the standard. But no less admirable have been the discipline and conduct. The absence of crime, the thoughtful consideration for the inhabitants, and the excellent spirit that has existed among all ranks have been most praiseworthy.

"I want also to thank you personally for the very soldierly and loyal way in which you have worked with me. Good luck to you all.

"Yours sincerely,

"E. S. D'EWES COKE.

After numerous orders and counter-orders, at last on May 17th the cadre entrained at Jemappes and moved to Antwerp, where 14 very pleasant days were spent in spite of a strike of tramway employees, the camp being well run and the city full of interest. Among other things a most successful dinner was held, at which everyone was present. On the night before leaving the Commanding Officer, Lt.-Col. C. D. Burnell, and Capt. H. L. Johnston were walking round the docks, when they recognised the s.s. *Chyebassa*, the boat in which the 1st Battalion had gone over to France, and on going on board they found two of the officers who had been with her on that occasion, but the captain was unfortunately on shore.

On May 25th the cadre reached Tilbury after crossing in perfect weather, and left at once for Newhaven to hand in stores. From there it went to London and ended its travels on May 31st, 1919, with a march past the Mansion House, which was most impressive, owing to the thousand and more members of the regiment who met their comrades at the station and fell in behind them. Of all those who went out on November 5th, 1914, only Lieut.-Col. C. D. Burnell, D.S.O., Capt. H. L. Johnston, M.C., and Lieut. and Q.Mr. A. Denny returned with the cadre to Bunhill Row.

ITINERARY OF FIRST BATTALION

Aug. 4, 1914—May 30, 1919 (*See Plan in pocket*)

1914.		
Aug.	4.	London.
	20.	Wimbledon.
	21.	Hersham.
	22.	Bisley.
Sept.	8.	East Horsley.
	9.	Reigate.
	10.	E. Grinstead.
	16.	Crowborough.
Nov.	5.	Le Havre.
	7.	St. Omer.
	8.	Wisques.
	16.	Hazebrouck.
	17.	Bailleul.
	19.	Romarin.
	22.	Ploegsteert.
1915.		
Jan.	7.	Ploegsteert (Essex Trench).
Mar.	21.	,, (Wood).
April	17.	Steenwerck.
	24.	Busseboom.
	25.	Second Battle of Ypres.
May	18.	(Second Battle of Ypres, Apr. 25–May 18)
	19.	Vlamertinghe.
May	20.	Tattinghem.
June	1.	St. Omer.
Oct.	2.	Blendecques.
	25.	Ryveld.
Nov.	23.	Poperinghe.
	29.	St. Eloi.
Dec.	5.	Poperinghe.
	13.	St. Eloi.
	21.	Poperinghe.
	28.	St. Eloi.
1916.		
Jan.	4.	Dickebusch.
	11.	St. Eloi.
	17.	Dickebusch.
	18.	Reninghelst.
	25.	St. Eloi.
Feb.	1.	Dickebusch.
	10.	Huppy.
	27.	Ergnies.
Mar.	12.	Gezaincourt.
	16.	Sibiville.
	22.	Magnicourt.
May	7.	Halloy.
	20.	St. Amand.
	21.	Hébuterne.

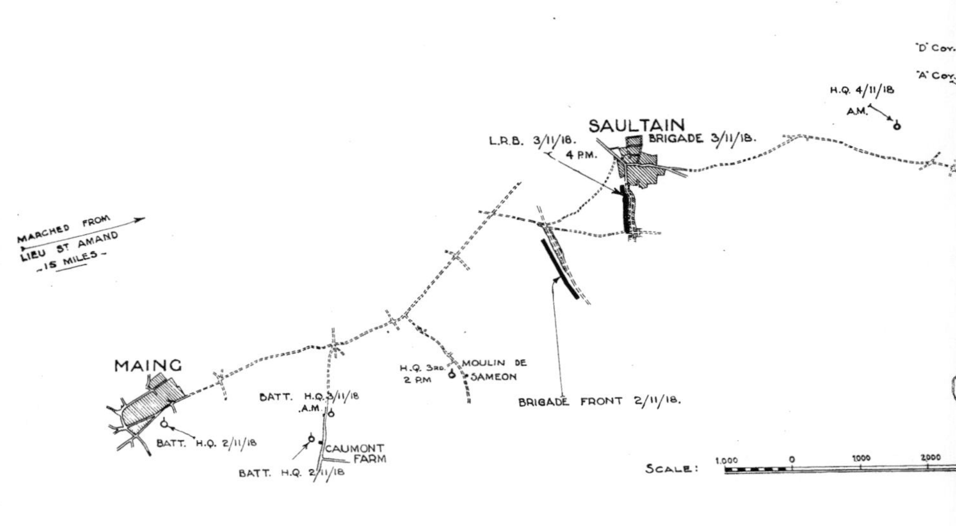

"D" COY.
"A" COY.
H.Q. 4/11/18
A.M.
SAULTAIN
BRIGADE 3/11/18.
L.R.B. 3/11/18.
4 P.M.
MARCHED FROM
LIEU ST AMAND
-15 MILES-
MAING
H.Q. 3RD. MOULIN DE
2 P.M SAMEON
BATT. H.Q. 3/11/18
A.M.
BRIGADE FRONT 2/11/18.
BATT. H.Q. 2/11/18
CAUMONT
FARM
BATT. H.Q. 2/11/18
SCALE:
1,000
0
1000
2000

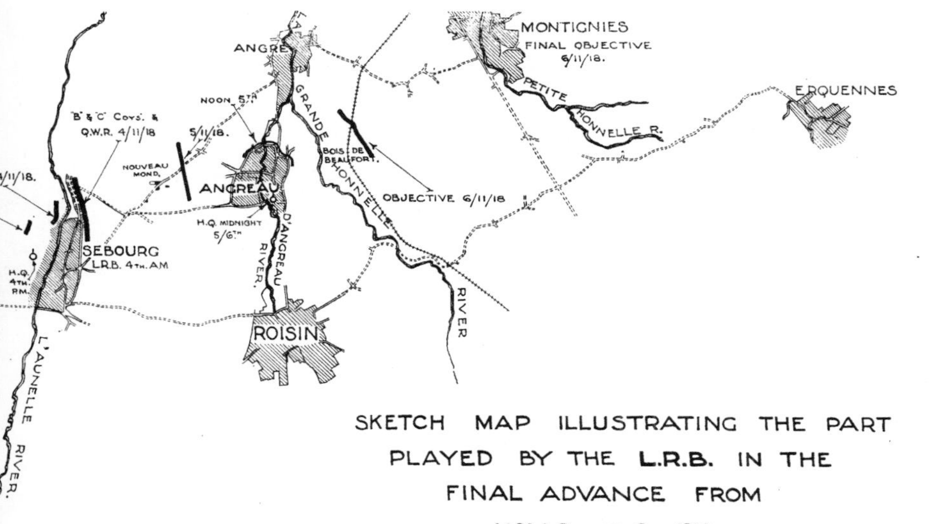

SKETCH MAP ILLUSTRATING THE PART PLAYED BY THE **L.R.B.** IN THE FINAL ADVANCE FROM NOV. 2ND. TO 6TH. 1918

ON NOV. 8TH THE BATTALION MOVED TO ANGREAU, REACHING ERQUENNES ON THE 10TH MARCHING TO HARMIGNIES 4 MILES S.E. OF MONS ON THE 26TH NOV. WHERE IT STAYED UNTIL IT MOVED TO JEMAPPES 4 MILES W. OF MONS ON MARCH 23RD 1919. WHENCE IT ENTRAINED FOR ANTWERP MAY 17TH AND SAILED FOR ENGLAND ON MAY 24TH 1919.

Sketch Map No. 15. *To face page 250*

May 28. Bayencourt.
June 3. Halloy.
13. Bayencourt.
16. Hébuterne.
21. St. Amand.
22. Halloy.
27. Souastre.
30. Hébuterne.
July 1. Battle of Gommecourt.
2. Bayencourt.
3. St. Amand.
6. Fonquevillers.
8. Hannescamps.
16. Bienvillers.
19. Hannescamps.
23. Bienvillers.
30. Hannescamps.
Aug. 7. St. Amand.
15. Hannescamps.
20. St. Amand.
21. Sus St. Leger.
22. Wavans.
23. Cauchy.
Sept. 3. Corbie.
4. Happy Valley.
6. Chimpanzee Valley
7. Falfemont Farm Line.
8. Leuze Wood Attack.
11. Citadel Hutments.
12. Billon Farm.
13. German Trenches.
15. Angle Wood.
16. Loop Trench.
18. Angle Wood.
24. Trench in front of Combles.
26. Combles.
Sept. 27. Meaulte.
29. Talus Bois.
30. Guillemont.
Oct. 2. In front Les Bœufs.
4. Between Trones and Bernafay Woods.
8. Attack on Les Bœufs.
9. Trones Wood.
10. Mansel Copse.
12. Picquigny.
21. Huppy.
23. Pont Remy.
24. Paradis.
27. Croix Barbée.
28. Richebourg L'Avoue.
Nov. 3. Croix Barbée.
9. Richebourg.
15. Bout de Ville.
21. Richebourg.
27. Lestrem.
Dec. 9. Neuve Chapelle Sector.
15. Riez Bailleul.
21. Neuve Chapelle Sector.
27. Riez Bailleul.

1917.
Jan. 2. Grand Pacaut.
14. Laventie.
20. Barnet and Enfield.
26. Relieved.
Feb. 1. Barnet and Enfield.
7. Laventie.

Feb. 14. Barnet and Enfield.
17. } 18. } Raid on Devil's Jump.
20. Laventie.
25. Barnet and Enfield.
Mar. 1. Vieille Chapelle.
2. St. Venant.
3. Pernes.
4. Willeman.
5. Le Boisle.
6. Buire-au-Bois.
7. Ivergny.
8. Fosseux.
14. Dainville.
15. Arras.
19. Achicourt.
24. Beaurains.
30. Achicourt.
April 1. Monchiet.
7. Agny.
9. } 15. } Battle of Arras.
20. Bienvillers.
23. Souastre.
26. Berneville.
28. Wancourt.
May 1. Harp Trenches.
3. Attack on Cojeul River.
4. Tilloy.
5. Harp Trenches.
19. Duisans.
24. Agnez les Duisans.
June 9. Beaurains.
10. Marliere.
15. Trenches.
20. Beaurains.
July 2. Gouy-en-Artois.
July 3. Sombrin.
22. Le Souich.
23. St. Martin au Laert.
24. Bayenghem.
Aug. 6. Abeele
12. Halfway House.
16. Attack on the Polygon
17. Abeele.
24. Moulle.
30. Wizernes.
31. Bapaume.
Sept. 4. Lebucquiere.
5. Louverval.
13. Lebucquiere.
21. Louverval.
29. Lebucquiere.
Oct. 7. Louverval.
15. Lebucquiere.
23. Louverval.
31. Lebucquiere.
Nov. 8. Louverval.
16. Lebucquiere.
20. Battle of Cambrai.
Dec. 3. Berneville.
5. Ecurie.
7. Gavrelle Trenches.
11. Roundhay Camp.
14. Mill Post.
20. Ecurie.
24. Mill Post.
28. Roundhay Camp.

1918.

Jan. 1. Mill Post.
4. Marœuil.
5. Frevillers.
16. Roclincourt.
24. Caucourt.

Feb. 7. Marœuil.
8. Gavrelle Trenches.
12. St. Aubin.
17. Towy Post.
21. Roundhay Park.
27. St. Aubin.
Mar. 5. Towy Post.
11. Roundhay Camp.
16. Raid on Crabb Trench.
18. St. Aubin.
21. Mill Post. German Attack.
29. Roundhay Camp.
30. Mount St. Eloi.
April 8. Berneville.
14. Beaurains.
19. Blangy Trenches.
28. Dainville.
May 4. Trenches.
21. Dainville.
24. Arras.
27. Dainville.
30. Telegraph Hill.
June 12. Raid.
17. Berneville.
26. St. Saveur.
July 2. Tilloy.
13. Relieved.
14. Arras.
15. Thieuloye.
18. Beugin.
30. Cambligneul.
Aug. 1. Beaurains.
7. Telegraph Hill.
16. Berneville.
17. Lignereuil.
19. Arras.
Aug. 20. Hauteville.
21. Saulty Labret.
23. Bailleulval.
24. Boyelles Trench.
26. Summit Trench.
27. Croisilles.
28. Knuckle Trench.
29.
30. Bullecourt.
31. Boisleaux-au-Mont
Sept. 7. Vis-en-Artois.
8. Recourt Wood.
12. Dury.
18. Guemappe.
20. Schmidt Hohle.
25. Trenches.
27. Canal du Nord.
28. Trenches.
Oct. 3. Sauchy Cauchy.
5. Saudemont.
9. Epinoy.
14. Haute Avesnes.
31. Lieu St. Amand.
Nov. 1. Caumont.
3. Saultain.
4. Sebourg.
5. Roisin.
6. Sebourg.
8. Angreau.
10. Erquennes.
26. Harmignies.

1919.
Mar. 23. Jemappes.
May 17. Antwerp.
25. Tilbury.
30. London.

SECOND BATTALION

Part I. September 4, 1914—January 23, 1917

Raising the Battalion—Haywards Heath—Norwich—Ipswich—Sutton Veny.

THE Second Battalion of the London Rifle Brigade was originally formed, as were most of those of other second line Territorial units, for home defence and to train recruits to fill the gaps in its first line unit. On 31st August, authority was given to the City of London Territorial Force Association for its battalions to re-commence recruiting for this purpose, and to enrol men for Home and Foreign Service in equal numbers. This was soon realised to have been a mistake, and was the cause of many troubles in the following year. Some say that the required number of men was found in two days, but whether this was so or not it was not till 4th September that the necessary work was got through and the establishment completed. There were enough candidates to fill two or three battalions, and many splendid men, finding their chances of joining the L.R.B. to be hopeless, joined other regiments.

The whole of the work at the beginning fell upon 2nd Lieut. C. Furze, the only officer of the 1st Battalion who was at Bunhill Row, but he threw himself into it with the energy and cheeriness which he showed in so many other duties later on, and endeared himself to all. Within a few days Capt. C. G. H. MacGill, M.V.O., and Capt. S. Bowers came back from the 1st Battalion, and Major J. Guppy, V.D., who had retired in 1913, rejoined and again took up the post of Quarter-master, which was no sinecure. Meanwhile negotiations had been going on to secure the appointment of Major G. R. Tod to the command, and on 6th September, the official date of the formation of the battalion, he took up the reins of office.

Major Tod was not only a regular officer, as the Regimental Rules required, but he had been one of the most popular and capable adjutants that the L.R.B. had ever had, so that he was quite familiar with the type of men with whom he had to deal. Major G. Harvest, another old 1st Battalion officer, also rejoined, as well as Lieut. Ambrose, who, when in the battalion before, had been an ardent member of the machine-gun detachment, but now came in as medical officer. Capt. MacGill was appointed adjutant.

By 21st the battalion had its eight companies, as the 4-company organisation had not then been authorised for Territorials, lettered after those of the 1st Battalion. "A" Company was under Capt. H. G. Nobbs, who had served in the ranks for some years and had been attached to the battalion in 1912, as an officer of a Canadian unit, for the training. "D" was under Capt. S. Bowers; "E" under Capt. H. B. Prior, a rejoined officer who had served in the regiment for a long time; "G" under Capt. C. R. Bland, another rejoined officer with long and valuable service; "H" under Capt. G. A. Redman. "O" Company was under 2nd Lieut. G. E. S. Fursdon until 2nd November, when Capt. J. M. Naylor was appointed; "P" under Lieut. C. Furze; and "Q" under Capt. C. E. Johnston, who had been an officer for a time in the early years of the century. Other officers had been posted to the battalion, and shortly afterwards further commissions were granted, chiefly to N.C.O.'s returned from the 1st Battalion.

Clr.-Sergt. H. Tyler, K.R.R.C., one of the permanent staff of the 1st Battalion, was made acting Sergeant-Major, and Lce.-Sergt. H. Cruse, another member with long service, was promoted Quartermaster-sergeant, but the selection of the other N.C.O.'s and the provision of instructors for the recruits presented great difficulties. Not many N.C.O.'s had come back from the 1st Battalion, and the retired N.C.O.'s who had rejoined were as a rule distinctly rusty, but, with the help of a few riflemen who were fit for a stripe, they set to work with a will at the task in front of them. Those who had had training in the Volunteers, Territorials, or O.T.C. were picked out and the promising ones promoted, which helped a great deal. "H" Company indeed, known as the "Schoolmasters' Company" because it contained so many of that profession, is reported to have solved the question of promotions by forming itself into a republic and making its own choices. This company produced in time a number of fine officers and N.C.O.'s, and its unique constitution broke up as military discipline developed and Army methods became better understood.

At first the grounds of The Merchant Taylors' School in Charterhouse Square, Cowper Street School, Middle Temple Gardens, the Archbishop's Park at Lambeth, and the City of London School were used for parades by the eager companies, but later on there were occasional marches by companies to Regent's Park and by half-battalions to Hanwell Park. The only form of shooting possible at that time was with miniature rifles, for which the Stock Exchange Rifle Club in Devonshire Square, and the National Reserve miniature rifle range near Blackfriars Bridge were available.

Up to the time that the battalion left London the men lived at home and drew ration, billeting and travelling allowances in addition to their pay. No uniforms were issued before October, and it was not until 19th November that plain clothes disappeared. There was no delay, however, about vaccination, and few who experienced it will ever forget the summary use of the hat-pin, with no time wasted in sterilization.

By October the battalion began to get into shape and early in the month a Signallers' Section got to work under Clr.-Sergt. Smith; the cooks began to train under Sergt. P. von Holtorp, and buglers were appointed. While in London the cooks had little professional work to do except before any big field day, when the joints were prepared over night at head-quarters to be ready for serving cold to the men. Eight of them were sent during November to a school of instruction at Windsor to be taught their duties thoroughly. Later on in the month the nucleus of the Transport Section was formed.

On 12th October a draft of 32 men was sent to the 1st Battalion at Crowborough to take the place of some who, to their bitter disappointment, had been rejected for foreign service on medical grounds. On 29th another draft of 26 men was despatched there under 2nd Lieut. B. E. Bland, who went down with a rear party to take over the camp and carry the good wishes of the daughter battalion to those who were about to embark on the s.s. *Chyebassa*, and 2nd Lieut. G. E. S. Fursdon was transferred to go out with them.

Up to November the battalion had had to be content with a few borrowed rifles, which had been passed from hand to hand and made the greatest possible use of, but during this month some E.Y. (Emergency) weapons were issued from the Tower. Their classification speaks for itself, and more than a year later the Musketry Officer was considered a very rash man when he demonstrated at Felixstowe that it was quite safe to fire them, but as a matter of fact all those that were tested proved quite accurate. About this time some N.C.O.'s were allowed to attend the Guards' School of Instruction in Drill at Chelsea, but it was not till the end of the month that vacancies were found for Lieut. Furze and a party of N.C.O.'s at the new Bisley School of Musketry.

On 9th the L.R.B., in accordance with custom, found the Guard of Honour for the Lord Mayor, being represented by "D" Company under Capt. Bowers, with the newly-formed bugle band under Bugle-Major Robinson. A short course of highly intensive training enabled the guard to maintain the regiment's reputation for smartness. On 11th the battalion carried out its one great operation while in London in the form of a route-march from the Merchant Taylors' School to Hampstead and back. The patriotic enthusiasm roused by the company marches through the streets of London, when the civilians used to walk with and cheer them, was nothing to that excited by this full parade with almost all the men in khaki. The keenness of the men was, however, considerably damped by the rain, which came down rather early, and the efforts of the newly organised cooks, who provided "skilly" among other things at the back of "The Spaniards," were not altogether appreciated. There was another expedition on similar lines to Catford about the same time.

It had already been known that the battalion would shortly move to some place in Sussex, and, in spite of their keen spirits, probably most of the men were at heart glad that they were going into billets and not into one of the hutment camps then being put up so hurriedly all over the country, which were no abodes of comfort in bad or wintry weather. As soon as

Haywards Heath was discovered to be the destination, Capt. C. R. Bland went down to pave the way and reassure the inhabitants, so, when the warning order was received on 16th November, the advance billeting party found things more or less made easy for them, and on 19th the battalion entrained, feeling sure that everything would be ready.

Haywards Heath

The Urban District Council with great generosity placed practically the whole of their offices at the disposal of the battalion, reserving only one small room for their staff. The Council Chamber made a fine mess room, though the difficulty of catering prevented the officers from dining together more than once a week, and the stiff formality of the furniture and the high tables reflected themselves in a certain lack of freedom in the mess. The experience at Haywards Heath, even under very favourable conditions, showed that the officers of a regiment can never get so well together if they are billeted as they can when living shoulder to shoulder in camp, and the same can be said about the men. One curious point connected with this, which would probably not occur to many people, was that a letter from the front stated that the "A" Company men in the January and February drafts of 1915, who had been billeted in "Kenwards" and "Red House," two uninhabited buildings, though no better in other respects, were harder and able to stand the severe life in the trenches more readily, when they first came out, than those who had been in the more comfortable billets.

The Divisional Head-quarters were at Crowborough, and those of the brigade (the 2/2nd London Infantry Brigade) at Borde Hill, about a mile and a half from Haywards Heath. Of the other regiments in the brigade the 2/6th and 2/7th Battalions were at Burgess Hill, and the 2/8th (Post Office) at Cuckfield, but the L.R.B. was not able to see much of the others before the Brigade Sports took place. Through the great kindness of the Bishop of London, his chaplain, the Rev. G. Vernon Smith, was allowed to leave his regular work to act as chaplain to the battalion. His splendid influence was responsible for the heartiness of the Church Parades, and for the fine moral tone which prevailed. On 21st November Major-Gen. W. Fry, commanding 2/1st London Territorial Division, held an inspection and expressed himself as having been very favourably impressed by what he had seen. Muster Green made an excellent battalion parade ground, with room for "A" and "D" Companies in the corners, and Victoria Park was the chief training ground for field work. Places further afield, such as North Common, Ditchling Common and Borde Hill Park proved better suited to more ambitious outdoor work, though much was done under cover in the Church Schools, Parish Room, Boys' Brigade Hall, and two unoccupied houses which were taken for billets, during the exceptionally bad weather of that winter.

The number of skilled instructors grew very slowly, and it was not until the battalion arrived at Ipswich that the supply began to increase at all rapidly, consequently the actual standard of training reached could not be said to be high; but the general condition of things was exceptionally sound, as, from the very first, the Commanding Officer, officers and N.C.O.'s took great pains to make the men realise the necessity for their acquiring the true soldierly spirit, encouraging them in every way to be proud of their regiment and show that they were so. The result was that the whole tone of the battalion was extraordinarily good, and this was to a great extent responsible for the praise which it obtained from the Higher Authorities in its early stages. A Finance Committee started by the Commanding Officer proved very helpful before, and continued to be of service even after, a Regimental Institute of the approved pattern was established.

The weakest point in the training for a long time, in fact right up to the middle of 1916, was the musketry, not through any fault of the instructors, but owing to the shortage of equipment. Charger-loading rifles were not issued at all until November, when 70 had to satisfy all requirements; ammunition was always hard, if not impossible, to obtain; and there were not sufficient ranges, even 30-yard ones. The men could only be stuffed with lectures and theory, with the inevitable result that they became fed up and began to hate the sight of a rifle.

In December the battalion was able to break new ground,

thanks to the generosity of the Medical Officer, Lieut. Ambrose, who presented it with 50 picks and the same number of shovels. In the course of the month, on the 15th, a draft of 15 Other Ranks was sent out to France. Gen. Ian Hamilton, who was then commanding the Central Force Home Defence, came down to inspect the brigade on North Common, and, in the remarks that he made afterwards, expressed himself as "particularly impressed by the fine appearance of the battalion and also by their steadiness on parade."

For some months after this a succession of drafts went overseas to the 1st Battalion: from Haywards Heath, 15 in January, 243 in February, and 207 in March; from Ipswich, 50 in July, 16 in August, and 75 in September. The number of men drafted across the water between 12th October, 1914, and 19th September, 1915—606—was far too great a drain for the battalion to stand, seeing that a large part of its strength consisted of men who had been unable to undertake the foreign service obligation and that recruits were not coming in sufficiently quickly to fill the gaps. The battalion, too, was at that time in the anomalous position of having to train as a unit for foreign service, although many of its members were not available for it. For the larger drafts Capt. Redman acted as Conducting Officer, and it was a great loss to the battalion when he was invalided out in the early spring after carrying on in considerable pain. The demands for officers were not so great, and after 2nd Lieuts. J. E. Alcock, B. E. Bland and B. S. Harvey went out in December very few were called for until July, 1915, when 15 went from Ipswich, some of whom had already been wounded, or invalided from the front.

The ranges were at Crowborough, and the men did the 17 or 18 miles by route-march in parties of 100 to 200, excellent training in itself. They had at first billets at Jarvis Brook, which were very indifferent except "The Bunches," which will be remembered by some of the officers. Later, huts were occupied near those in which the 1st Battalion had lived on Camp Hill, firing being done at Park Hill Range. Later on they used the Old Lodge Ranges, when the detachments were quartered in huts in the lines of the 2/10th Londons. The results were those which might be expected, considering that the weather was unfavourable and that the men could not possibly know their rifles.

On 11th January, 1915, the Double Company system was authorised for the Territorials and adopted by the battalion, but some time elapsed before everyone got accustomed to it and the mounted officers to their horses. When the new organisation was complete No. 1 Company, known later as "A," was made up of the old "A" and "D" and commanded by Capt. S. Bowers; No. 2 or "B" came from "E" and "O" under Capt. H. B. Prior; No. 3 or "C" from "G" and "H" under Capt. C. R. Bland; and No. 4 or "D" from "P" and "Q" under Capt. C. E. Johnston. This reconstitution was not allowed to interfere with the competition for the Inter-company Football Cup presented by Capt. Bland, for which each of the original eight companies had entered, in fact some of the best matches were played after it had been made. In the final, which took place in Victoria Park in March, "H" Company just managed to beat "D." The regimental team was a very good one, the difficulty being to pick the really best side out of the many candidates for places. On 21st subsistence allowance was discontinued and rations had to be drawn by all, much to the disgust of those who happened to be in comfortable billets.

In February the battalion got into touch with the recently formed 3rd Battalion. Capt. Johnston, with 100 men and the Bugle Band under Bugle Major Robinson, went up to London to help in a march, followed by a concert at Bunhill Row, organised with the object of stimulating recruiting, which was very slack at the time.

On 1st April the Regimental Sports were held on the Recreation Ground. Col. Cholmondeley, the Officer Commanding the 3rd Battalion, came down to look on and brought a bayonet-fighting team with him, which won its match against the 2nd. The great event for which everyone had trained hard was a marching competition from Brighton for company teams of 1 Officer, 1 Sergeant and 16 Other Ranks in full marching order. This was won by "B" under 2nd Lieut. Haggard and Sergt. Smiles, in a time which worked out at an average of $4\frac{3}{4}$ miles per hour. "D" won the Sports Cup presented by Col. E. Matthey.

On 10th April about half of the battalion went to Ore for field-firing, and it seemed a pity that more of this sort of practice could not be arranged. The routine training was varied by "periods of vigilance," which provided some of the most interesting work that was done. On such occasions one officer was detailed to march the unfit and the untrained back to comparative safety at Red Hill, while the battalion went south to meet the invaders on the Downs. By way of a change, parties consisting of an officer and 6 men were sent out on the Kaiser's birthday to picket the important roads in the neighbourhood. All this seemed very exciting at the time, but it was nothing compared with the feelings aroused when going out in the eastern counties because of an expected Zeppelin raid.

NORWICH

By this time rumours of a move were continually going round, and the men in the innocence of their hearts, whenever they heard that Commanding Officer, Medical Officer and Quartermaster had been to inspect a site, always believed that something would come of it, but nothing ever did beyond the news that some other regiment had filled the place. However, in course of time the 2/2nd London Infantry Brigade was moved and went up to Norfolk and Suffolk. On the night of 17th/18th May the L.R.B. entrained for Norwich in pouring rain, arriving there in a chilly state and not at all favourably disposed towards the city. First impressions were not changed by the nature of the billets, which were at the Catton end, but became considerably modified when a move was made to the Thorpe end, where arrangements were much more comfortable.

June turned out to be the hottest month of the year, when the training, and especially the route marches, proved very trying. "D" Company, which happened to have a trek sandwiched in between a brigade and a battalion march, was reported to have done 54 miles in 3 days, but was compensated in a measure by being quartered close to the river where the bathing was excellent. On Whit Monday the L.R.B., thanks to Ives, Markham, Morgan and others, took off nearly every prize at the Military Sports, open to the district, held on that day. The only real failure was in the tug-of-war, and that was perhaps a blessing in disguise.

On 19th June the men who had volunteered for foreign service moved to Ipswich. Those for home service or under age went down to Bawdsey and Hollesley Bay for coast defence, but a great number of them, especially the young ones, came back to the battalion later, to be transferred afterwards to the 3rd, if they were fit. By the irony of fate, many of these served in heavy fighting in France before those who had volunteered much earlier went out.

Ipswich

For the whole of the ten months' stay, which followed, the battalion was very popular with the townspeople, particularly those at the Norwich Road end, where most of the men lived, and there were no complaints about the billets from either side, the men being exceedingly well fed. In August central feeding was made compulsory, and the arrangements which were then made to carry out the scheme were for "A" Company to use the All Saints' Parish Hall in Blenheim Road, "B" an empty house nearly opposite head-quarters, and "C" to share a dairy in Brooke Hall Road with "D." This worked very well as long as the numbers were not large, but when recruits began to come in freely in February, 1916, the accommodation was found to be hardly sufficient. During this month the Division, hitherto known as 2/1st London Division, was renamed the 58th (London) Division, and the 2/2nd Brigade became the 174th Brigade.

For Battalion Head-quarters and the Mess, Wilbury, a large empty house about a mile from the centre of the town in the Norwich Road, was secured, and the quartermaster had his stores in the stables as well as in a greenhouse, which also afforded a chilly but serviceable guardroom. Many of the officers slept on the lawn in the summer, until some genius insisted on the tents being painted with a green distemper in order that they might not attract the attention of Zeppelins, the result of which was that their visibility was not in the least affected, but their power to resist rain was utterly destroyed and the occupants were flooded out. A convenient house for the Regimental Institute was found at Barrack Corner, about three-quarters of a mile from head-quarters, which also had a large lawn, besides bathrooms which were particularly appreciated in the winter.

The battalion always paid great attention to obtaining suitable ground on which to train its men, and made a great point of getting on good terms with the landowners, wherever it might be stationed, so that, as a rule, it was considerably better off in that respect than most of the others in the brigade. While at Ipswich, in addition to some brickfields and meadows near the Yarmouth Road, "A" and "D" Companies were provided with a digging ground beyond Claydon on the Norwich Road, though it meant a long march to get there; "C" secured the use of a piece of land beyond Whitton, and constructed experimental dug-outs out of the primitive materials that were available; and "B" obtained a much more accessible plot, close to the river, with a large field adjoining.

The disappointing thing was that the results did not in the least represent the trouble that had been taken, purely through lack of the necessary equipment. The machine-gun section (Maxim), which had been under Lieut. Whitaker, was disbanded and the men turned into Lewis gunners, but they had to start with only one gun, and it was a long time before there were more than two; company sections were formed minus guns; the platoon gunners were not trained and fitted out until just before leaving for France. No dealings with anti-gas measures were possible and very little field engineering could be carried out, but Lieut. G. F. Trenow was able to get on with his bombers without live grenades, and Lieut. G. L. Harvest did really well with his Intelligence Department. The transport section also steadily improved through the solid work of 2nd Lieut. A. J. Lintott, who instilled a fine *esprit de corps* which proved very valuable when the battalion went overseas.

About this time two important changes in the battalion staff occurred. Capt. MacGill, resigning the adjutancy, left to become brigade major to Lieut.-Col. Earl Cairns, who had by that time recovered from the effects of his experience with the 1st Battalion in France and been appointed brigadier of some third line units. Major Guppy, the invaluable quartermaster, finding that his age and health prevented him from going out to France, retired. Capt. F. Furze, a most capable and popular officer, was appointed adjutant, and held the position for two years. Lieut. N. Anderson became quartermaster, carrying out the duties very efficiently till January, 1916, when he was appointed court-martial officer (and afterwards D.A.A.G.) to 1st Army in France. He was succeeded by Lieuts. J. P. Dixon and W. E. Morgan in turn until Quartermaster-Sergt. H. J. Kent, a well-tried man, was promoted, and he remained until the battalion was broken up.

Training went on all the summer steadily and without any noteworthy incidents. In October the establishment had to be reduced, so eleven officers, of whom six came back in January, 1916, were sent to the 3rd Battalion. This would have afforded in the ordinary way a great opportunity for the officers of the two battalions to get to know one another intimately, but unfortunately the 3rd was for most of that time in billets at Sutton, so the acquaintanceship could not become as close as it would have been had the two sets been mixed in camp or barracks. In the same month Regimental Sergt.-Major Tyler was given a commission in another unit, and Company Sergt.-Major Maguire, K.R.R.C., took his place.

During the autumn considerable doubt was felt about the future of the battalion, which consisted of only 600 men, although 100 recruits had been received in June, another 100 some time later, and a few enlisted locally. However, the work went on and, among other things, a very good competition was arranged for company teams of 1 Officer and 30 Other Ranks, of whom ten were selected by the judges to shoot, in marching, digging and miniature shooting, which tested endurance as well as training. The first prize was won by Lieut. F. P. Barry with a squad from "B" Company, though he did not come out top in every subject, and a similar event on milder lines for recruits went to "D." In November a four-days' trek was made north-east as far as Halesworth, in the course of which the men were introduced to billets in barns and sheds, which they would have been delighted to get later on when they were in France. At times alarms occurred which meant entraining rapidly, but generally ended in a short quick journey out and home ; at other times positions had to be taken up for Zeppelin raids, but no one was asked to try to bring one down with an E.Y. rifle. In December, Mr. Roger Quilter, assisted by Messrs. Gervase Elwes and Thorpe Bates who gave their services, got up a concert for the L.R.B. Mutual Aid Fund, by which a considerable sum was realised. Practical musketry was impossible all this time as there was no ammunition except for recruits, who had to go through their firing at Felixstowe.

In January, 1916, the Inspector of Infantry came down and, after he had finished his investigations, said that the battalion was the best of the 69 2nd Line Territorial units which he had seen, but that in their anxiety to get ready for the front the members must not be too impatient and attach unwarranted importance to delays and deficiencies. At that time the average age of the men was 23½ and the average height nearly 5 ft. 10 in., so that they appeared more suitable for Guardsmen than Riflemen, and, though about 15 per cent were not of A1 category, their general physique was good. In February a draft of 240 recruits came, which gave rise to the hope that the division was going to be used for something more than the defence of the East Coast, but very few of the other units were reinforced so strongly and the 60th Division was known to have been sent to Salisbury Plain for final training, so the 58th had to be content to wait.

With the issue of 600 short rifles in March, musketry became a practical proposition for the first time and the battalion went over to Felixstowe, where five practices were fired. In April the division went under canvas, the camp of the 174th Brigade being at Foxhall Heath, about four miles from Ipswich, on ground which had not previously been used for that purpose, and proved very comfortable in the subsequent hot weather. Shortly afterwards a two and a half days' trek was made through Manningtree towards the East Coast; but the weather had changed and was wet and rough, making the bivouacs on the first night very uncomfortable. For the second night, billets were secured in a brewery and some schools near Mistley. On the return to camp, Gen. Sir William Robertson held an inspection.

Another long brigade march to Tunstall, begun in the rain,

was held in June. "B" and "D" spent the night on outpost, while the rest of the battalion bivouacked in comfort: but the return journey ended with only one man having fallen out. The Sports were held in the same month on the only available ground, a very rough field, but everybody was keen, and there were some very good performances. "C" Company won the cup presented by Col. Edward Matthey.

Sutton Veny

In July the 6th Londons had started on their musketry course at Felixstowe and the L.R.B. were expecting shortly to do the same, when the division received orders to take over the camp of the 60th Division near Warminster. The move to Sutton Veny was made on 13th, and on 17th the battalion began its musketry. At the end of 11 days the course had been completed with the exception of the recruits and field-firing, the average being the best in the brigade, and about level with that of the Q.V.R. in the division. The number of marksmen was naturally not very high, as there were not enough rifles for each man to have his own and know it, but that of the 3rd class shots was very low, a proof of sound instruction. The figures would have been still better if more practice could have been obtained in firing from behind cover on the miniature range, but this was probably the same for the other battalions.

The training now became more real and more strenuous, so the men gradually grew properly fit, a process still further encouraged by the granting of five days' leave by companies through the battalion. After a stiff march a night, which the Flanders veterans of 1915 declared to be more unpleasant than any they had ever experienced in the open, was passed in very rough and ready trenches near Yarnbury Castle, the highest and most exposed point on the plain, with a tempest raging. This spot was visited several times, and on the last occasion the battalion was able to see the divisional artillery using live shrapnel. The shooting was pronounced good by the experts, but the average rifleman was disappointed at the trench targets not being plastered with shot every time and would have preferred the sight of the more spectacular H.E.

In September the whole of the officers not on duty went over to dine with those of the 3rd Battalion, which was then at Fovant, and had a delightful evening. A group photograph of the officers of the two battalions was taken, and, Lieut.-Col. Bates, who had come home invalided, being present, the Commanding Officers of the three battalions were also able to be taken together. The intention was to have entertained the 3rd Battalion in return, but it was suddenly moved to Devonshire soon afterwards, so this could not be managed, nor were the N.C.O.'s able to meet.

By this time it was becoming evident that, in consequence of the losses incurred in the Somme campaign, the 2nd Line Divisions would be required in France in 1917, so the battalions were made up to strength, but with recruits instead of the, at least, partially trained men who would have been more helpful, as time was an element in the case. Although the battalion, after getting rid of all its men that were medically unfit, was short of but 70, it only just managed to bring these up to the proper standard of efficiency in January, 1917, by means of intensive training, owing to further weeding and delays in filling the gaps. Even then the musketry could not be said to be very good, owing to the bad weather prevalent at that time.

In November brigade competitions, which were not all finished when the move to France was made, were started in all branches of training as well as in athletics. The L.R.B. showed up well all round, but its strongest point was cross-country running, in which it was unbeaten in England and later on in France. The credit for this is primarily due to Capt. T. L. Forbes, a fine runner himself, who took charge of the team and made the most of the great interest in the sport shown by the men. All those in the slow pack were very keen to get promoted to the fast pack, which lived up to its name. The battalion also, after having been knocked out early in the 1915–16 football competition, determined to make no mistake this time, and won the final after a great match, which was played at Warminster a week before going overseas. The battalion team played several out matches as well, one at Swindon being particularly appreciated, and, besides the company matches for the Bland cup, which was won by "A" for the second time, even inter-platoon competitions took place. On the purely social side, the battalion orchestra played every week to the officers, N.C.O.'s and men, under B. M. King, who had succeeded B. M. Robinson, transferred as bandmaster to the 3rd Battalion early in the year; and that excellent concert party the "Transport Imps," which was directed by Sergt. Wood, was considered to be equal to "The Goods," the divisional party, which acquired a great reputation in France.

November was also noteworthy for a very unpleasant week under canvas at Imber, spent in digging trenches and positions for artillery demonstrations, an experience which was a good introduction to service conditions in winter. By great good luck the amount of work had been overestimated and when the 174th Brigade relieved the 175th, the L.R.B. had only two parties, or less than 200 men, to find: otherwise the time was fully occupied with completing the training. In spite of efforts no reserves could be trained for the Lewis guns; the remaining odd cooks, tailors, etc., who had to throw their three live bombs, were difficult to get hold of; musketry was confined to refreshers for 3rd class shots, night firing, and competitions; and up to the last field-engineering was cramped through the want of materials, though every man was a fairly efficient digger. At the end of the month five days' leave was granted all round and much appreciated.

During December the number of officers available for duty was very small, as vacancies for special courses, which had to be filled, were showered upon them, in striking contrast to the earlier days at Sutton Veny, when none were offered. On one Saturday a certain officer found that he was commander of his own platoon, commander of another company, brigade musketry officer, battalion musketry officer, intelligence officer, transport officer and orderly officer; so when, as luck would have it, the fire alarm was sounded for practice and the Brigadier came over to see how it was dealt with, he had great difficulty in deciding how he should report himself.

By Christmas the news came through that no embarkation leave would be given nor travelling by rail on short leave allowed. However, a privileged few, length of service being the principal qualification, were granted Christmas leave by road, and two motor-buses, one of which had an eventful journey back from London, were chartered, while some adventurous spirits got there and back in the 48 hours on cycles.

At the very last unexpected changes took place among the officers. Major C. R. Bland, to his intense disappointment, was found unfit for military service of any sort ; Capt. B. E. Bland, who had been successful in training of recruits, was pronounced unfit for a second tour overseas ; and Capt. C. E. Johnston was called upon to join the British Mission with the Portuguese Army, as he spoke that language. Capt. E. D. Johnson, a very old member of the battalion, who had been on Staff Musketry work since the early days of the war, re-joined and took command of " D " Company.

SECOND BATTALION

PART II. JANUARY 24—MAY 20, 1917

Embarkation—Souastre—German retirement—Bihucourt—Lt.-Col. Tod gives up command—Attack on Bullecourt.

(The maps referred to are B and C, and No. 16 on p. 285.)

DURING the early days of January, 1917, rumours, which had long been rife as to the battalion's immediate prospects, grew even more numerous and fantastic. Possible and impossible destinations were eagerly canvassed and discussed, while life became a burden to anyone who had the smallest claim to official confidence. The report that D.A.D.O.S. (Deputy Assistant Director of Ordnance Stores) had both European and Tropical kit in store, complete in every detail, for every officer and man in the division, did not help to elucidate the problem, but that the long-looked-for adventure was at hand was clear to all, despite previous disappointments. The quartermaster's stores were filled to overflowing with the final details of overseas equipment, box-respirators, steel helmets, and the like, whilst officers were called upon to discard everything beyond the absolute necessaries for a Spartan existence in the field. It was no easy matter to reduce kit to the official weight, whilst preserving a reasonable degree of decency and comfort ; but the Transport Officer, hardening his heart against supplication and excuse, was inexorable.

At last, on 24th January, the battalion entrained at Warminster for Southampton, *en route* for the war. The strength of the battalion was 903 N.C.O.'s and men, with 30 officers as follows :—

Head-quarters

Lieut.-Col. G. R. Tod. Commanding.
Major G. Harvest. Second in Command.
Capt. F. Furze. Adjutant.

Capt. F. L. Otter. Signaller.
Lieut. A. J. C. Lintott. Transport.
2nd Lieut. G. L. Harvest. Intelligence.
2nd Lieut. F. E. Pattisson. Lewis Gun.
Lieut. H. J. Kent. Quartermaster.
Capt. H. S. Palmer, R.A.M.C. Medical Officer.
Capt. Rev. G. Vernon Smith. Chaplain.
Regtl. Sergt.-Major J. E. Maguire.
Regtl. Quartermaster-Sergt. J. C. Turner.

"A" Company

Capt. C. Furze.
Lieut. C. Harrison Jones.
Lieut. A. S. Wimble.
2nd Lieut. E. G. Moore.
2nd Lieut. W. H. Mitchell.
C.S.M. Bottomley, C.
C.Q.M.S. Miller, R. W.

"B" Company

Capt. J. M. Naylor.
2nd Lieut. F. P. Barry.
2nd Lieut. E. W. Fuller.
2nd Lieut. V. A. Finlayson.
2nd Lieut. L. Forbes.
C.S.M. Smiles, A. O.
C.Q.M.S. Schonewald, C. S.

"C" Company

Capt. G. C. Kitching.
Lieut. G. Whitaker.
Lieut. H. G. Wilkinson.
2nd Lieut. C. F. Joyce.
C.S.M. Markham, P.
C.Q.M.S. Bonner, E. H.

"D" Company

Capt. E. D. Johnson.
Lieut. T. L. Forbes.
Lieut. V. E. O. Welch.
2nd Lieut. G. F. Trenow.
2nd Lieut. R. Cope.
2nd Lieut. J. F. Legg.
C.S.M. Timewell, A. W.
C.Q.M.S. Ide, C. W. N.

The 58th (2nd Line London Territorial) Division under the command of Major-General H. D. Fanshawe left England as a complete fighting unit and consisted of :—

173rd Infantry Brigade (Brig.-Gen. (—) Hunt).
1st, 2nd, 3rd and 4th City of London Regt. (Royal Fusiliers).

174th Infantry Brigade (Brig.-Gen. W. McGrigor), Brigade Major, Capt. R. M. Laverton, D.S.O., Staff Captain, Major D'A. Little.

5th (L.R.B.), 6th, 7th and 8th (Post Office Rifles) City of London Regt.

175th Infantry Brigade (Brig.-Gen. H. C. Jackson).
9th (Queen Victoria Rifles), 10th (Hackney), 11th (Finsbury Rifles), 12th (Rangers) County of London Regt.
Trench Mortar Batteries to each brigade, a Signalling Company, R.E., and the 503rd, 504th and 511th Field Companies, R.E., the 290th, 291st and 293rd Brigades Royal Field Artillery; a detachment of the Hampshire Yeomanry (Carabiniers), and complete administrative services, R.A.M.C., A.S.C., etc.

On arriving at Southampton, the Commanding Officer, with "A" and "B" Companies, embarked on the s.s. *Duchess of Argyll*, whilst "C" and "D" Companies, in charge of Major Harvest, went aboard the s.s. *Lydia*, with the Transport Section in the s.s. *North Western Miller*. A fair and still evening in the dock changed to rough weather ere Southampton Water was cleared, and, by the time that the ships reached the open channel, certain signs and portents were rapidly succeeded by the actual catastrophe which usually overtakes landsmen adventuring on the sea. Shortly after the escort was picked up, the *Duchess of Argyll* discovered discretion to be the better part of valour, and put back, so living to cross the next day, but the *Lydia* pursued her painful way. Be it noted that both vessels were of the West of Scotland type, forbidden in happier times to go beyond three miles from land.

Outside Havre there was a long wait while the pilot was signalled, and leisurely, very leisurely, proceeded to come aboard. The discomforts of this delay were in no wise diminished by the observation volunteered by the second officer of the *Lydia* that "it was about that particular spot that quite a number of ships had been torpedoed by the Huns."

All who served on the Western Front experienced the tedious, cold, disembarkation at Havre in the early hours of the morning, followed by the slow, fatiguing march around the docks, through the town, and up the seemingly endless hills to the camps of San Vic, above St. Adresse. In the greyness of dawn tea and tents were found and allotted, and, with four inches of snow outside and a porridge of melting snow and mud inside, all ranks were glad to forget their introduction to "La belle France" in uneasy slumber.

Little time was afforded for the exploration of Havre, for, on the morning of 27th January, the battalion was introduced to the luxurious rolling stock (" 40 hommes ou 8 chevaux en longue ") in which the exigencies of war compelled the soldier to travel. Such a journey, too ! The slow, meandering way of the train, via Rouen and Abbeville, being comparable only to the irritating tardiness of the leave train. Fifty-four consecutive hours in such a train *de luxe*, with 10 degrees of frost, make no joy ride, even though a thoughtful Y.M.C.A. provides a grateful and comforting hot drink at specified stopping places.

At length, during the night of 29th, billets at Rougefay, near Auxi-le-Château, were reached by a battalion wearied by the long march through the snow from railhead, stiff with cold, but welcoming the prospects of rest and shelter afforded by decayed barns and outhouses, regrettably redolent of their most recent animal occupants. Here two days were profitably spent in repairing the ravages of continental travel, and preparing for the line.

On 1st February the battalion, complete as it left England with the exception of a few sick, covered the last stage of the journey to the war in lorries via Doullens and Pas to Souastre, a village three miles behind the line which was reminiscent of the 1st Battalion's share in the opening of the Somme battles on 1st July, 1916. Deposited in the snow for a hasty cup of tea and rubbing of feet with whale oil, officers received final instructions, and the evening saw each platoon being guided up to Fonquevillers for initiation into the arts and crafts of real trench warfare. Head-quarters with " A " and " B " Companies were attached to the 6th Sherwood Foresters (46th Division), whilst the 8th Battalion of that famous regiment undertook the instruction of " C " and " D " Companies.

The strength of the platoons was a source of wonder and amazement to the hosts, as each was equal to at least one of their entire companies. This considerably complicated the question of accommodation, but, by midnight, all were settled down to listen, with becoming awe, to the hair-raising yarns with which the old soldier invariably regales the novice, ingeniously contrived to scare the latter whilst exalting the former to the sublimest heights of heroism.

Within 48 hours, through the courtesy and instruction extended by the Sherwood Foresters, the battalion was judged competent to hold the line by company sectors, interspersed with companies of their mentors. The morning of the 2nd brought the battalion's first casualty; Cpl. C. G. Adams, of "A" Company, famed on the running track, was mortally wounded by a shell splinter, and, as he had only just recovered from an operation for appendicitis, had not sufficient vitality to enable him to sustain the shock of a broken thigh. The same day a small Boche bombing party approached the lines, but was easily dispersed by rifle and Lewis gun fire, leaving two dead, whose bodies were recovered, and established the fact that a battalion of Guards Reserve was opposite. On the next night a heavy draught horse was killed by shrapnel whilst taking a company cooker from the line to Souastre.

These were the salient incidents connected with the battalion's introduction to war, and by the evening of 4th February it was considered that the battalion might be entrusted with the holding of the trenches in the Fonquevillers area, alone and unattended. At that time "C" Company was on the right, up Thorpe Street, by the "Mousetrap," and had the honour of being on the extreme right of the IIIrd Army. "B" Company was in the centre; "D" Company was on the left, with "A" Company in support of the battalion sector. The weather was bitterly cold but fine, with from 10 to 15 degrees of frost. At night a bright moon, lighting up all the snow-shrouded country, made patrolling in "No Man's Land" a task of considerable danger, and undoubtedly contributed to the first officer casualty. Early on the morning of 5th, Capt. Naylor was shot through the thigh by a sniper, whilst superintending a wiring party on his company front, whereupon Lieut. F. P. Barry took over the command of "B" Company.

A fact worthy of remark is that, despite the intense cold, the battalion had no cases of frostbite or trench feet; this was certainly due as much to good discipline, the energy of the Medical Officer, and an unfailing supply of whale oil, as to XVIIIth Corps Standing Orders which threatened dire penalties in the matter of suspension of leave to the unfortunate subaltern in whose platoon such cases should occur. For the following fortnight the battalion took alternate tours of duty in these trenches with the Sherwood Foresters, going into billets at Souastre for brief periods of rest when relieved from the line.

The earliest of the periods was notable as the occasion of the first bathing of the battalion in the war zone. This luxury, though properly appreciated, was far from a pleasant experience. Immersion in tubs of lukewarm water festooned with icicles, the while a piercing wind, heavily charged with snowflakes and in no wise frustrated by the broken sides of a crazy hut, made its determined effort to reach the quivering goose-flesh of the unhappy bather, was not a process calculated to inspire anyone with that affection for cleanliness which is commendable and infinitely desirable. The padre was heard to express a wish that the approach to Godliness might be made warmer.

On 22nd February the battalion trekked to Bailleulmont, reaching there at 5 a.m., and found it was a quiet village, practically undamaged, although only three miles from the line. Within two days trenches were occupied opposite Ransart, vastly inferior to those just vacated. The hard frost had broken, and the snow melted, filling the trenches with water and causing landslides everywhere. At some points of the front line the icy water and mud were waist deep, but that mixture was easy of negotiation compared with the firmer places where the mud was stickier. "Gum boots, thigh," were forthcoming in sufficient quantity to fit out everyone, but, whilst of great service, they caused much delay during reliefs. The store was situated on Ridge Road, close to Battalion Head-quarters, in full view of the Boche, and why he never strafed, when any number of men up to four or five hundred, with boots off, were clustered round Allouette, is one of the unrevealed mysteries of the war.

On 5th March the enemy carried out a raid against the troops immediately on the left of the battalion, which, though not actually concerned with it, had a very uncomfortable time during the bombardment. An interesting example of the value of the Amplifier was brought home about this time. In an orchard at Berles-au-Bois, which lay on the battalion's route to the trenches, was a battery of heavy howitzers which annoyed the Boche very considerably, with the result that he determined to put an end to its existence by concentrating all fire that could be brought to bear on the position at a given time. Fortunately his arrangements were overheard by our listeners just soon enough to evacuate all personnel from the neighbourhood, but all our guns were entirely destroyed. During a period of rest Lieut.-Col. Husey came over to see the battalion, the 1st Battalion being in billets only a few miles distant.

The next tour of duty, quite as muddy as the last, was memorable for two events. First, a visit in the line from Lieut.-Gen. Sir E. H. H. Allenby, K.C.B., who was then commanding the IIIrd Army. Secondly the Boche retirement, which had been anticipated. For several days and nights previous to 17th March somewhat indiscriminate shell-fire from guns of all calibres, which at times was exceedingly embarrassing, seemed to indicate that the enemy was using up his ammunition dumps in a reckless manner. Explosions had been heard, caused by the blowing up of dug-outs, dumps, etc., whilst the skyline had been lit up nightly by the red blaze caused by the organised burning of villages, châteaux and farms—the British Army's future rest-billets. After midnight 17th–18th March not a single Very light, rifle or machine-gun was fired from the German lines. Lieut. G. L. Harvest, attracted by this unwonted inactivity, took out a patrol to investigate the situation, penetrated to the enemy's support line, and came back to report that the Boche had vanished. Much to its disappointment, the battalion received orders to stand fast, whilst other troops were eventually sent in pursuit.

The peaceful atmosphere of the succeeding days, and the joy of the civilian population of the billeting areas about Bailleulval will never be forgotten. Young and old, with and without permission, hurried across the lines to Ransart and Monchy to see what remained of their erstwhile homes, but they soon came back when they discovered the havoc which the Hun had wrought. Cavalry patrols appeared and went forward; artillery and R.E. officers came up to arrange for the speedy advance of the guns; and an A.S.C. officer was seen in a car as far forward as what had been, twelve hours previously, the British Support Line. Many men went across to explore the enemy's trenches and dug-outs, and many were the souvenirs retrieved, despite the thorough manner in which the Boche had cleared up. It was not without consolation to find that the mud and water in his trenches were every whit as bad as in ours, and in places worse, but his wire was deep and immensely strong. Many traps for the unwary had been left, such as trip wires attached to bombs, explosives concealed in nicely laid fires, etc., but they were mostly so crude that no one was taken unawares. Several days were now spent in Pommier, and working parties were found to repair and construct roads across the old trench systems.

On 23rd March the battalion went forward as far as Boisleux St. Marc (Map B : S.11), marching right through the devastated area, the few available roads being thickly strewn with considerable mine craters, and congested with the heavy traffic of an advancing army. Everywhere was evidence of Teutonic thoroughness. Not a house or wall was left standing ; wells were filled in or else polluted ; trees, and even shrubs, had been cut down, including fruit bushes ; and vegetables and plants were uprooted. Churches were utterly wrecked, and, in some cases, tombs and vaults standing in graveyards were wantonly desecrated and destroyed. But it was instructive to note that the wayside shrines had been unharmed in nearly every case, the only items on the whole countryside that the Hun had respected. Passing Adinfer Wood, whence had come most of the shell-fire to the trenches just left, the enormously strong gun emplacements made of reinforced concrete six to nine feet thick were seen, looking like great caves, against which the heaviest ordnance was ineffective. For billets the heap of rubble that had once been the neat village of Boisleux au Mont (S.10) was allotted to the battalion ; but, with customary ingenuity, shelters were soon constructed from the wealth of material at hand, whilst house timber provided luxurious fires. That was before Town Majors installed themselves amid the ruins, labelling, numbering, and cataloguing each brick and stone, and forbidding unlicensed removal thereof under pain of condign punishment. The Transport Officer and the Quartermaster, both second to none in their uncanny ability for discovering super-billets, found welcome shelter in the large boiler of a wrecked sugar refinery.

Outposts in the neighbourhood of Boyelles (T.13), on the main Arras-Bapaume road, were taken up on 25th March, and the battalion had the (then) novel experience of digging its own front line trenches. It seemed a strangely peaceful war in those days, for, except one artillery strafe, the enemy were content to remain quiet. The skilful stalking by Lieut. G. L. Harvest and a few of his scouts of an officer of 99th R.I.R.[1] and his servant, which ended in the capture of the latter, was an interesting piece of work to those who were fortunate enough to witness it.

Relieved on the night of 27th/28th by the 12th Northumberland Fusiliers, the battalion commenced a long march back to Quoeux, near Auxi-le-Château, a distance of over 45 miles, staying at Pommier Grouches (which provided welcome change and refreshment at the shops and fleshpots of Doullens) and Bouret-sur-Canche, and reaching Quoeux amid a heavy snowstorm by midday on 2nd April. It was then announced authoritatively that the battalion would enjoy the benefits of at least three weeks' rest for refitting and reorganisation. In view of the date, there was warrantable suspicion that this was a cynical but belated endeavour of the practical joke department, for, hardly had the joys of good billets and plenty of local produce begun to be appreciated, when suddenly, on the morning of 4th, motor lorries arrived. Hastily the battalion embussed, leaving behind, amongst other surplus baggage, no less than 72 bags of mails which, owing to the exigencies of the preceding days of open warfare and continual trekking, had only just arrived, and three weeks passed before it was possible to get those mail bags to the battalion again. By evening billets were being improvised in Mailly Maillet (Map C : Q.7), amidst all the dirt and ruins of Hun devastation. During the following days the ill-health under which Major G. Harvest had been bearing up so stoutly, became too much for him, and then commenced the visits to hospital which ultimately resulted in his evacuation home at the end of April. A member of the regiment for many years, both in the ranks and as an officer, he had rejoined at the outbreak of war, when the idea was that the 2nd

[1] 99th German Reserve Infantry Regiment.

Battalion was for home defence and the furnishing of drafts, though he had been out of health for years and was more than fifty years old at the time. Always loyal to the L.R.B. and a thorough sportsman, he did much to instil the old spirit into the new battalion, and he went abroad with it after bluffing the medical authorities. The strain was altogether too much for him, and, not long after his return, he broke down completely, and died in the following year. He was extremely popular with all ranks, and their grief at losing him was sincere.

The march was resumed on 7th April, the route being through Beaumont Hamel (Q.11) and the valley of the Ancre. It was a sombre day of drizzling rain and grey sky as the column wound its way through that gloomy valley, where, instead of green woods and verdant water-meadows, the few gaunt, blackened trees that remained, with their shattered, tortured limbs standing in the shell-pitted ooze that had once been a pleasant river, bore mute witness to the fierceness of the battles of the previous November. Everywhere grove upon grove of small wooden crosses told dumbly of the awful price paid for that blood-soaked ground. Frequently a rifle stuck into the head of a pitiful mound was the only indication that there "in the corner of a foreign field was a spot that would be for ever England." [1] Complete and utter destruction, evidence of violent death everywhere, was the keynote of that terrible landscape, still littered with the melancholy debris of battle. Chilled were the spirits of all as they marched silently through the desolation of that dreadful valley.

By the afternoon the two Achiets had been passed, and a recently ploughed field close by Bihucourt reached, where, it was said, canvas would be delivered and a camp pitched. The exertions of "Q" department ultimately produced a quite insufficient number of bivouac sheets together with half a dozen bell tents, exhortations to further effort being met with a stony silence. "Q" was completely exhausted, and inclined to be flippant when it was suggested that one bivouac sheet formed an entirely inadequate shelter from the penetrating drizzle for eight cumbrously equipped soldiers. However, within a few days the camp was made reasonably comfortable,

[1] Rupert Brooke.

but only through the energy and enterprise of the men. The ground under each " bivvy " sheet was excavated, and the sheets raised on a framework of props, making quite a spacious shelter. Bell tents, at first distinctly scarce, gradually increased in number, principally at the expense of a recently evacuated cavalry camp near by, on which the guard was lamentably lax, especially at night. Improvised huts, built of material collected from the demolished farms and villages in the vicinity, soon housed the battalion stores, shops, canteen, etc ; and camp ovens were also constructed, delighting the heart of the quartermaster. A tarpaulin plunge bath, much appreciated during a subsequent spell of very hot weather, was due to the efforts of the Transport Officer. Soon, too, the Expeditionary Force Canteen opened a depot at Achiet le Grand, to the great content of all ranks. Beer, veritable British brewed beer, appeared in considerable, but never sufficient, quantity ; and many and questionable were the stratagems used to secure a case.

The battalion remained in this camp until 14th May, providing working parties for all and every purpose, day and night. At first it was attempted to put and maintain the Sapignies-Ervillers-Mory road into some sort of negotiable condition, but practically the only available material was rubble from the ruins of the villages, which proved a poor substitute for road metal, and soon turned to red, liquid mud under rain and the ceaseless heavy motor and artillery traffic. The road, especially forward from Mory towards Ecoust St. Mein, was frequently shelled, but fortunately the battalion suffered few casualties. A more popular job was assisting the Canadian Railway Construction Companies to lay a light line from Achiet via Mory to Ecoust, popular since the piece work system prevailed as against the soul-destroying time task set by our own R.E. But the most popular task of all, in so far as any work may be termed popular, was loading and unloading trains at railhead, since that was the situation of the aforementioned Expeditionary Force Canteen. Other work consisted in erecting sand-bag barricades for ammunition dumps, burying dead horses, improving the habitations of both Divisional and Corps Head-quarters, digging trenches for buried cable (very unsafe and unpopular), and filling in mine craters on the roads, of which more than one, operated by cunningly contrived, chemically actuated and delightfully simple delayed action mines, went up as long as six weeks after the treacherous Hun had departed.

A few high-velocity shells of large calibre occasionally came over, falling near, some almost into, the camp ; but, although there were some remarkably narrow escapes, no casualties resulted from that particular expression of enemy malevolence. Twice was the camp aroused in the middle of the night by gas alarms, but here again the evil intent of Hunnish hate was defeated by good discipline and box-respirators. When the Australians were surprised at Lagnicourt, the battalion, with the remainder of the division, received orders to stand by to counter-attack at an hour's notice, not an easy operation in view of the fact that the men were scattered all over the countryside on various working parties. In vivid contrast to the cool demeanour of the Commanding Officer, the Adjutant and orderlies suffered sudorific anxiety, not regaining their tranquillity until it was known that the situation had been restored by the gallant Anzacs themselves. Their characteristic reply to the division's telegram proffering assistance was sanguinarily brief and entirely unfit for publication. May 5th will be remembered for a terrific thunderstorm which washed out the camp, flooding tents and bivouacs completely. But it is an ill wind that blows no one any good, and most of the water drained into a very deep and broad German trench just below the camp, entirely filling it. Many men enjoyed a swim there, and even a race was organised.

During April many changes took place amongst the personnel of the division, brigade and battalion. Brig.-Gen. McGrigor relinquished command of the brigade, being succeeded by Brig.-Gen. C. G. Higgins, D.S.O. (Oxford and Bucks L.I.), whose forceful introductory address to the assembled officers of the brigade, a model of informative brevity and wit, will not readily be forgotten. Capt. R. Barrington Ward arrived as brigade major, whilst Major Little was succeeded by Major Bryant as staff captain. On 23rd April, to the infinite regret of every officer, N.C.O. and man in the battalion, who one and all suffered a feeling of personal loss, Lieut.-Col. G. R. Tod proceeded to England to take command of the 23rd (R)

Battalion of the Royal Welsh Fusiliers. His retirement was solely on account of age, a rule having recently been made that only comparatively young officers should serve in the field. Lieut.-Col. Tod had been adjutant of the regiment from 1898 to 1903, and the battalion had been very fortunate to secure him as its commander. He raised it, trained it, and brought it to a very remarkable state of efficiency, creating in all ranks a peculiar sense of devotion and duty. He was succeeded by Lieut.-Col. P. D. Stewart (3rd Dragoon Guards), who speedily won respect and admiration for his soldierly qualities and for the energy and driving power with which he inspired everyone. The departure of 2nd Lieut. E. W. Fuller to the Vth Corps School as Instructor was a loss to the battalion of a breezy personality and a capable officer. Capt. E. D. Johnson was admitted to hospital, passing thence to the base for permanent duty, and was followed in command of "D" Company by Lieut. T. L. Forbes.

The battalion now settled down to intensive training in earnest. Few will forget the subsequent days of battalion drill, field operations, etc., all the morning, tactical schemes for officers and specialist work for other ranks during the afternoon, with lectures for all on most evenings. Many looked back with real regret on the departed glories and comparative idleness of the days when eight hours' manual labour, with perhaps a nine-mile march added, was deemed sufficient to keep the long suffering soldier bright in body and mind. Brigade training followed, which culminated in a brigade attack on Loupart Wood, complete with creeping barrage and galloping umpires, ineffectually vociferous, under the eye of the Corps Commander. On one day there was a long march in the dust and broiling sun to a rendezvous where the whole division was to be gassed. There followed a long, long wait in the full blaze of the sun, head in mask, whilst perspiring specialist R.E.'s produced the wicked-looking cylinders. Then at last, when all was ready, the gas was released, hissing impotently into a light breeze which had sprung up suddenly, carrying the cloud right away from the massed and impatient division.

On 14th May, when the battalion moved forward to a camp near Mory, taking over from 2nd Royal Warwicks, it became evident that the division was to relieve the illustrious 7th Division in the maëlstrom of Bullecourt. Hardly had the battalion settled down for the night, when, amidst a roaring tumult of heavy guns, orders came to stand to and proceed to the high ground about L'Homme Mort, and to be ready to counter-attack. The grey, quivering dawn had given way to high noon ere the alarm died down. Then "A" Company went forward to the railway cutting south of Bullecourt (*U.27.d.*), which was then the British line, so far as the somewhat obscure situation permitted any particular spot definitely to be indicated as held. "B" Company, with Battalion Head-quarters, went up to Ecoust St. Mien, an exceedingly unhealthy locality. "C" and "D" Companies remained at L'Homme Mort.

At this time a footing had been obtained and held in the south-east corner of the ruins, but the remainder of the village was still in the hands of the enemy, who were in strongly fortified trenches, supported by numerous concrete "pill-boxes," the whole forming a large redoubt of the notorious Hindenburg Line. The 7th Division had captured the village once or twice, but had been driven out again; the 62nd (Yorkshire) Division had recently made a very costly but abortive attack from a south-west direction; so the final capture of the place was looked upon as a very tough proposition. About midday of 16th, without previous warning, orders were received that the half battalion would attack at 2 p.m., but fortunately these orders were modified and the attack postponed until 2 a.m. on 17th, which gave time for "C" and "D" Companies to be brought up and more precise plans to be made. Tapes were laid at dusk by the Intelligence Section under Lieut. G. L. Harvest, the shell-pitted ground in front of the railway cutting being the assembly and jumping-off place. Despite a pitch-dark night with torrents of rain, and the enemy's artillery and trench mortar fire combined with more than the usual number of unforeseen hindrances, "A" Company (Capt. C. Furze), two platoons of "B" Company under Capt. Barry, and one platoon of "C" Company lined up for the assault, whilst on their left 2nd Lieut. Trenow, with a party of bombers, got into position to storm Crucifix Corner (*U.27.b.*), a formidable strong point, possession of which would do much to secure the left flank of the operation. The objective of the main body was the road from the south-east corner of the village to Crucifix Corner, with supplementary orders to push patrols to the forward edge of the ruins. Zero was at 2 a.m. At zero minus two minutes a hurricane bombardment, directed against the enemy's assumed positions, seemed to cause unusual confusion, for the assaulting parties advanced, keeping touch and direction

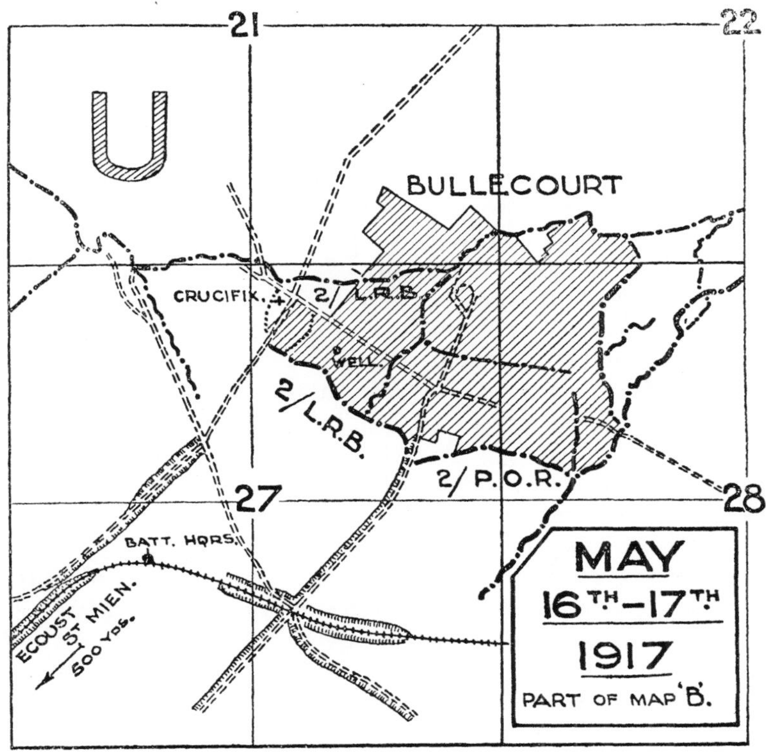

Sketch Map No. 16

in spite of difficult circumstances, amidst an unnatural silence, save for a few trench mortar shells and slight machine-gun fire. All objectives were gained, for the greater part with rather less opposition than had been expected, but on the left flank 2nd Lieut. Trenow and his men put in some pretty work with admirable effect. Casualties during the actual assault were slight, amounting to 1 Officer (2nd Lieut. A. H. Scholefield,

19th Londons) and 7 Other Ranks killed, and 21 wounded. Capt. Barry, though seriously wounded during the advance, carried on until his final objective was reached. Two other officers, Lieut. G. Shillito and 2nd Lieut. F. R. H. Newington (20th Londons), were wounded. Many Boches were killed and 23 prisoners taken, of whom 15 left the firing line at various times for Battalion Head-quarters, but, owing to a lamentable mistake, one party of 8 missed direction, and appeared in the dawn in rear of, and approaching the right flank of, the line. The men of " A " Company, taking no risks, opened fire with disastrous effect on two of them.

At daybreak it was possible to reconnoitre and connect up the flanks with adjacent units. The whole village was in our possession, but so many and wonderful were the stories spread by previously ejected conquerors, some of whom said that the enemy had a long tunnel through which he subsequently appeared in rear of their positions, that no chances were taken, all working with a will to make this the final and most successful operation in the village. " D " Company came up and assisted " A " Company in the consolidation of the forward edge of the ruins, whilst " B " and " C " Companies formed a support line. Daylight showed what an awful shambles the place had been, both British and German dead being piled in heaps everywhere, making an appalling stench, as the weather was hot for the time of the year. One dug-out afforded a gratifying example of the efficacy of British counter-measures in poison gas warfare, that product of *Kultur* peculiarly illustrative of German ideas of the chivalry of war, as it was full to the top of the stairs with dead Boches.

During the following night the battalion enlarged its front to the right by taking over a position held by the Post Office Rifles which was heavily shelled next day, with the result that there were several casualties. Whilst this arrangement was being completed, 2nd Lieut. V. A. Finlayson, who was leading his platoon, had the misfortune to fall down a well about 90 feet deep. Fortunately he was not seriously damaged by the fall, but as every one who came to the edge knocked bricks etc., down on to him, and his steel helmet had disappeared, he was in grave danger from this cause. An attempt to get him up was made by tying men's putties together, but, when he had been raised about half-way, they broke, and he fell back again, and a second attempt made with a piece of telegraph cable failed because it was not long enough. Eventually, after six hours' delay, some R.E. arrived with ropes and tackle by means of which he was at last rescued in a state of complete collapse. He was sent back to England, but rejoined before very long without showing any sign that his nerve had been in the least impaired by his terrible experience.

The surprise was that there were not more casualties of this nature, as the village was thickly sown with wells which were the only sources of water supply, and in the dark it was impossible to distinguish, amidst the litter of broken bricks that constituted the village, which was a house, garden or road, much less to see the mouth of a well. On the night of 18th–19th the battalion was relieved by the 2/6th Battalion, and, running the gauntlet of shell-swept Ecoust, returned to camp at Mory.

The total casualties sustained during these operations were 1 Officer and 11 Other Ranks killed, and 3 Officers and 33 Other Ranks wounded. Thus the battalion may be said to have been "blooded." Numerous congratulatory messages were received, amongst which were the following :—

From G.O.C. 7th Division to G.O.C. 58th Division.

"All ranks of the 7th Division offer their heartiest congratulations to you and your Division on your success in the final capture of Bullecourt. No one knows better than ourselves the difficult task your division had to undertake, and we are full of admiration for the gallantry and dash with which it was accomplished."

Reply from G.O.C. 58th Division to G.O.C. 7th Division :—

"All ranks much appreciate your kind telegram of congratulation. While the task of actually completing the capture of Bullecourt fell to this Division, we all realise that the success which attended our efforts has been due to the splendid offensive action on the part of the 7th Division, which broke the back of the enemy's resistance."

From G.O.C. 174th Infantry Brigade to O.C. 2nd London Rifle Brigade :—

"Please accept for yourself and convey to all ranks of your

splendid battalion my best thanks and congratulations for your magnificent success last night."

From O.C. 291st R.F.A. Brigade :—

" Heartiest congratulations."

Letters of congratulations were also received from officers, N.C.O.'s and men of the 1st H.A.C., 7th Division. The G.H.Q. intelligence did not depart from its customary laconic style :—

" After all night fighting, the village of Bullecourt was finally cleared of the enemy."

For gallant conduct the following decorations, the first earned by the battalion, were received :—

Military Cross : Capt. F. P. Barry ; Lieut. G. L. Harvest ; 2nd Lieut. G. F. Trenow.

Military Medal : Sergt. C. J. Potter, Sergt. J. A. Burton ; Cpl. F. J. Howells ; Lce.-Cpl. G. E. Foster ; Rfn. V. B. Ewins.

The Chaplain, Rev. G. Vernon Smith, with a few men volunteered the next night to go back to Bullecourt to place crosses on the graves of those fallen, some of whom had been buried practically in the front line. They arrived just as the battalion in the line was making a local attack to improve its position, and during the barrage and counter-barrage, which lasted for two and a half hours, this devoted party found what cover it could in shell craters on the outskirts of the village. All had incredibly narrow escapes, but fortunately no one was hit, and, having accomplished their self-imposed mission, they returned to Mory in safety.

SECOND BATTALION

Part III. May 20, 1917—Jan. 29, 1918

Longatte—Beaucamp—Poperinghe—Attack on Arbre, Von Tirpitz, and Stroppe Farms—Proven—Moreuil—Disbandment.

(The maps referred to are A and No. 17 *on p.* 297.)

AFTER this the battalion enjoyed eight days' rest, during which Capt. C. E. Johnston, who had been teaching our Portuguese Allies the art of war, rejoined after an absence of six months, and took over the duties of Second in Command. Capt. F. L. Otter, relinquishing his appointment as signalling officer, took command of "B" Company. R.S.M. Maguire returned to England, being succeeded by C.S.M. C. Bottomley.

Whit-Sunday was spent in support positions near Longatte, and that evening the battalion relieved the Post Office Rifles on the right of Bullecourt, "B," "C" and "D" Companies being in the front line, with "A" Company in support. During this tour both British and German Artillery fire was very heavy, whilst the firework displays put up by the Boches at night were as astonishing as they were appreciated. Evidently his casualties were considerable, since he was frequently seen evacuating his wounded by day under the Red Cross Flag instead of by night, as is usually the custom where there are no communication trenches. 2nd Lieuts. F. E. Pattisson and J. F. Legg (two most valuable Officers, of whom the latter had gone to France with the 1st Battalion in 1914), with 13 Other Ranks, were wounded on 2nd June. Before relief next evening by the 2/11th Battalion, great efforts were made to salve as much as possible of the enormous quantity of equipment, rifles, and other material which littered this gruesome area. During a subsequent period of rest at Mory working parties were sent up to the line every night, but, for the benefit of those luckier members remaining in camp, there were visits from the Divisional Band and Concert Party ("The Goods"). Games were organised as well, and the officers (captained by the Commanding Officer) played the sergeants a half soccer-half rugger match.

On the 14th June the battalion moved up to St. Leger and at 2 a.m. on 16th received orders to go forward at 6 a.m. to support part of the 173rd Infantry Brigade, who had made a partially successful attack east of Croisilles with the Hindenburg front and support lines as their objectives, and at 9 p.m. the same evening the battalion was ordered to relieve a portion of the line. "D" Company was detailed to move out in the formation of two strong fighting patrols to get into touch with some elements of the 173rd Brigade believed to be holding out —as the brigade front line—in the Hindenburg support line, whilst "A," "B" and "C" Companies relieved the Hindenburg front line. "D" Company's task was neither enviable nor simple, as the situation was more than usually obscure, even for this much fought over area; no time was available for personal reconnaissance, and, to add to their troubles, the guides from the 173rd Brigade failed to appear at the rendezvous. However, nothing daunted and determined to add to the laurels won by the battalion a month previously, the patrols set out. As one half of the company neared its objective, a heavy rifle, machine-gun, and rifle-grenade fire was opened on them, and rockets went up calling for artillery support, which made it very evident that the whole of the Hindenburg support line was in the hands of the enemy, and strongly held. The patrols therefore withdrew, and eventually took up positions in support of the remainder of the battalion.

This four days' tour was a sore trial from every point of view. Blazing sun alternated with torrents of rain, whilst abnormal artillery fire, combined with persistent sniping, took heavy toll. In his brave efforts to direct a Lewis gun which was keeping down enemy snipers whilst the wounded left behind by the 173rd Brigade were being evacuated, Lieut. G. L. Harvest, a gallant officer, was mortally wounded, and his loss was a severe one. He had gone out with the 1st Battalion in November, 1914, in the ranks, but had been given a commission in the 2nd some time before that battalion went overseas. Many wounded men of the 173rd Brigade, who had been hiding in shell-holes in No Man's Land since the assault on 16th, came into the British lines, some even from behind the enemy's front trenches, and great difficulty was found in evacuating them and the L.R.B. wounded. To assist in this merciful work the Chaplain, Rev. G. Vernon Smith, organised a party of volunteer stretcher bearers whose aid was invaluable, and for the courage and example shown by this fearless act he was rewarded with the Military Cross. But casualties were heavy ; 2nd Lieut. L. Forbes received a thigh wound of which he subsequently died ; Capt. T. L. Forbes, Lieut. Welch, and 2nd Lieuts. Brentford, H. C. Lintott and McKenzie-Smith (18th Londons) were all wounded ; 28 Other Ranks were killed, and 74 wounded. Every one was glad to see relief in the shape of 2/7th Battalion on the morning of 20th June, and to return to St. Leger, *en route* for a fortnight's rest at Courcelles Le Comte.

Reorganisation, refitting, and absorption of reinforcements was the first work. Capt. C. Furze's departure, owing to his having been accepted as an instructor at the base, left only " C " Company (Capt. G. C. Kitching) still under the command of the officer who came out with it from England. 2nd Lieut. E. G. Moore was appointed to " A " Company in command, and Lieut. H. G. Wilkinson to " D " Company. Soon the days grew busier and training more energetic, but every one worked with a will to earn commendation at the inspections which followed, first by the Brigadier, and then by the Divisional Commander. The indefatigable transport officer, Lieut. A. J. C. Lintott, organised successful Brigade Transport Sports, at which Brig.-Gen. Higgins won the bare-backed mule race in a canter amidst roars of applause. A privilege in those days, granted daily to a limited number of all ranks, was a trip to Amiens, an opportunity of spending a few hours in civilisation which was highly appreciated, and the extortions of " Josephines," the " Gobert," " Charley's American Bar," and other restaurants were suffered gladly after many weeks in the devastated area.

On 6th July the battalion set out by march route for Equancourt, via the ruins of Bapaume and Bancourt. On 8th trenches at Beaucamp, near Havrincourt Wood, were taken over from 2/5th and 2/8th Battalions of the Sherwood

Foresters. These trenches, which were conspicuous examples of the art of modern field defences, had been constructed by the Guards Division, and others. Another attraction, after the unpleasant times of May and June, was the fact that it was reported to be a quiet part of the line, and this, contrary to usual experience, proved to be true. In an eight days' tour the only incident meriting record was an ineffectual attempt at a raid at 3 a.m. on 10th July against the left of the battalion sector, and against the right of the trenches held by 2/7th Battalion, which was easily repulsed by "A" and "B" Companies. As soon as fire was opened, when the box-barrage had lifted, the Boches lost heart, dropped their bombs just outside the wire, and bolted back to dead ground, leaving seven killed and wounded, while the battalion had no casualties. Afterwards there were found some amateurish contrivances of three or four stick bombs tied together, operated by one fuse, and probably intended for our dug-outs. But of domestic incident there was full measure, pressed down and running over. Orders were received that all shelters, other than R.E. dug-outs, were to be destroyed, model fire-bays constructed, and that all men should eat, sleep, and live on their respective firesteps, things all excellent in principle, but, with human nature and the climate in France what they are, difficult to effect. On 16th, after relief by the 2/3rd Battalion, the L.R.B. went out to Ytres by light railway for a week's training. Major E. C. Hill Whitsun (Royal Scots) was posted to the battalion as second in command during the absence of Major C. E. Johnston at the Senior Officers' School, Aldershot.

By 23rd the battalion was in the line again at Le Trescault, forward of Havrincourt Wood, where an extremely quiet, but very busy, time was spent. Here No Man's Land was some six or seven hundred yards wide, wider than was advisable if the Boche was to be kept under proper surveillance, so every night was spent in digging an advanced outpost line three hundred yards nearer the enemy, and in erecting wire entanglements. Apparently the Germans were unaware of this work, or, if they knew of it, thought to leave well alone, for never was it checked or hindered in any way, and it was done so quietly, quickly, and efficiently, that the battalion earned much praise from Higher Authority. The South African

Brigade (9th Division) took over on 28th/29th July. After a few hours' rest at Ruyalcourt, the L.R.B. embussed for Bapaume, entraining there for Berneville via Arras. This was the first inhabited village that the battalion had lived in since March, so the estaminets and vendors of food quickly grew rich, and every one was pleased. A prominent feature of the village was a large canvas swimming bath, attractive both to hot, dusty soldiers, and to admiring civilians. Conscience, however, prompted the latter to represent to M. le Maire that the human form divine were better screened from the gaze of the local youth and beauty, so the delights of a cool plunge were denied to the troops until sufficient canvas for screening was extracted, by fair means or foul, from the stores of a stony-hearted and immodest C.R.E. Then battalion swimming sports were organised, duly eventuating on a very wet afternoon. Brigade athletic sports were also held when, as usual, the battalion did remarkably well. Both training and recreation were hindered by bad weather, much of the former having to be done in huts. Capt. F. Furze relinquished his appointment as adjutant about this time, taking command of " D " Company, and being succeeded by Lieut. R. Cope. He had carried out his difficult duties with conspicuous ability, and, while asserting his authority, had maintained his popularity with all ranks. An address from the Brigadier confirmed the rumour that the Division would shortly be going to Flanders to take its turn in the blood bath there.

On 24th August the L.R.B. proceeded by train from Arras to Godwaersvelde and Poperinghe (Map A: G.1), passing the 1st Battalion *en route*. The crowded streets of the latter town, boiling day and night with the ceaseless traffic of great battles, and its wonderfully resourceful restaurants, knew the battalion for four days ere battle surplus personnel departed westwards and the battalion eastwards to Reigersburg camp for a final spell of training. In many ways, besides the cramped accommodation, this camp was far from comfortable. It was frequently and accurately shelled, which meant continual movement, and also from this time onwards nightly bombing raids by enemy aircraft were disconcertingly regular. Meanwhile, two company commanders, with subaltern officers from each company, had been sent to XVIIIth Corps School for a week's complete immersion in the theory of battle as then being practised in Flanders. From all accounts they heard of nothing but battles by day, and were inspired to dream of them by night.

Ten days were passed at Reigersburg (H.6.b.), during which Major Hill Whitsun left to take command of 7th Argyll and Sutherland Highlanders, before the battalion went up into the line in front of Kitchener Wood (C.10.d.), north-west of St. Julien, for the privilege of surveying the kind of featureless morass which it later would have the honour of fighting in or on. The seemingly endless duck-board tracks, to stumble off which meant the risk of being swallowed up in the viscid mud, soon ceased to be a novelty. The slow tortuous and torturing journey from the Canal Bank to the Steenbeck across that desolate, shell-pitted, shell-swept waste, was in odious contrast to the safe communication trenches of the Havrincourt area. It was soon established that hostile fire exacted heavier toll from men when on the duck-boards than when in the front line.

After four days in "pill-boxes," and wet shell-holes, during which 2nd Lieuts. E. Higham and E. J. B. Miskin (19th Londons) were wounded, 7 Other Ranks killed and 16 wounded, relief was effected by the 2nd London Regt. (R.F.), 173rd Brigade, and the battalion came out via the Canal Bank dug-outs to Dambre Camp, near Vlamertinghe. But those four days gave opportunity for three more members to prove their courage and soldierly qualities. The Military Medal was awarded to Sergt. L. E. Cruwys, Lce.-Cpl. R. G. Bone and Rfn. F. H. M. Bolton, for devotion to duty in particularly trying circumstances.

The succeeding days were devoted to "dress-rehearsals" for the forthcoming battle over taped ground under the eye and personal direction of Gen. Sir H. Gough, K.C.B., commanding 5th Army, and Lieut.-Gen. Sir Ivor Maxse, K.C.B., commanding XVIIIth Corps, the latter especially paying keen and vocal attention to every detail. Certain remarks which he made at a meeting of officers of the brigade will not readily be forgotten. "Gentlemen, you lead your men creditably, but you are too polite. The spirit of the attack I have just witnessed savours more of the Sunday School than of the sanguinary battle. Far too gentle and kind. Your commands should be short and sharp : less ' if you please ' about them, more calculated to exact instant automatic obedience from the soldier's brain, half paralysed by noise and shock. Swear, gentlemen, swear : the men like it so long as you don't repeat yourselves. Cultivate a vocabulary." A vivid imagination is very necessary to stimulate much enthusiasm or language over a tree stump labelled " X Farm," representing a " pill-box " full of treacherous Boches, but the reality makes it comparatively easy and natural.

During the assembly of the brigade for one of these practice attacks, proceedings were enlivened and made realistic by the sudden arrival of a flight of enemy aeroplanes dropping bombs broadcast. Fortunately none fell in the area occupied by the battalion, although a large ammunition dump close by was fired, causing the extremely rapid and profane dispersion of a gorgeously gilded and glittering Staff, whose brains, though possibly half paralysed by noise and shock, were sufficiently active to exact instant, automatic obedience from their horses. But the utility of these practices was very evident when the time came for the stern reality, as every officer, N.C.O., and man knew his job exactly, and those who survived to reach their objectives carried out their orders to the letter, and not at all in the Sunday School spirit.

The brigade, with the 55th Division on its right and the famous 51st Division on its left, was to attack on a frontage of 450 yards, and to penetrate 1700 yards into the positions of the enemy, whose outpost line was parallel to and 200 yards east of the St. Julien-Poelcapelle Road. The Post Office Rifles were to lead the assault as far as Genoa-Hubner Farm (*D.*1.*c.*), where the L.R.B. would then pass through them with the line Road-Junction (*D.*7.*central*), Von Tirpitz Farm (*D.*7.*b.*) and Stroppe Farm (*D.*1.*d.*) as their objective, after which the 2/6th Battalion would pass through in their turn to capture Wurst Farm (*D.*7.*b.*). The 2/7th Battalion was in brigade reserve.

The order of battle for the battalion was " C " Company (Capt. Whitaker), " A " Company (2nd Lieut. Sharman), " D " Company (Capt. F. Furze)—right to left—with " B " Company (Capt. F. L. Otter) in support, their respective objectives being Arbre (D.7.a.), Von Tirpitz Farm and Stroppe Farm. The formation adopted in all the three assaulting companies was two lines of sections in single file at 25 yards' distance and 25 yards' interval for three platoons, with the remaining platoon, at 50 yards' distance, in one line of sections in file at 40 yards' interval, as the Company Commander's reserve. Sections were on an average some six men strong, including the leader. "B" Company was in one line of platoons in fours at 100 yards' distance and 100 yards' interval. The brigade assembly positions faced east, but the objectives were, generally speaking, in a south-east direction after the first 700 yards had been made good. On 18th September, "X" day, the battalion moved into a small camp close by the ruins of Reigersburg Château. During "Y" day it rested as much as possible, and flares, bombs, rifle grenades, message maps, rations, extra water and rum, sand-bags, and the hundred and one items which go to complete the modern infantry soldier's equipment for offence, were issued and overhauled.

At 10.45 p.m. Battalion Head-quarters and the companies moved out of camp for the long journey to the assembly positions by the Triangle, Keerselare (*C.6.c.*), via Canal Bank—Admiral's Road—Regina Cross, through the terrible din and noise of our gun positions, whence the massed artillery was belching forth death and destruction all night without ceasing. The ground quaked with the incessant shock of discharge, while the flash was so dazzling that to keep a sense of direction was nearly impossible in the darkness and rain. The route followed, being mostly across country and along obliterated roads, was difficult, slippery and exhausting. It had been previously reconnoitred and marked by the battalion scouts under 2nd Lieut. G. R. Reeve, who also laid the tapes to mark the assembly positions. The leading company was up by 3.30 a.m., and Battalion Head-quarters at the Moulin de Hibou was able to report the battalion present at 4.5 a.m. The men were very tired with the heavy loads and bad going, and in a few minutes were mostly asleep, despite the appalling uproar of artillery preparation and counter-preparation, and the immediate prospect of a battle. Casualties were unusually light, being only four on the way up to, and two whilst on, the tapes.

A party under the quartermaster, Lieut. Kent, drawn from the transport section, quartermaster's stores and the band, distributed the extra rations, water and rum which they had volunteered to bring up in order to lighten the weight carried by the fighting men. The party left Battalion Head-quarters only a few minutes before zero. Just before daybreak, though

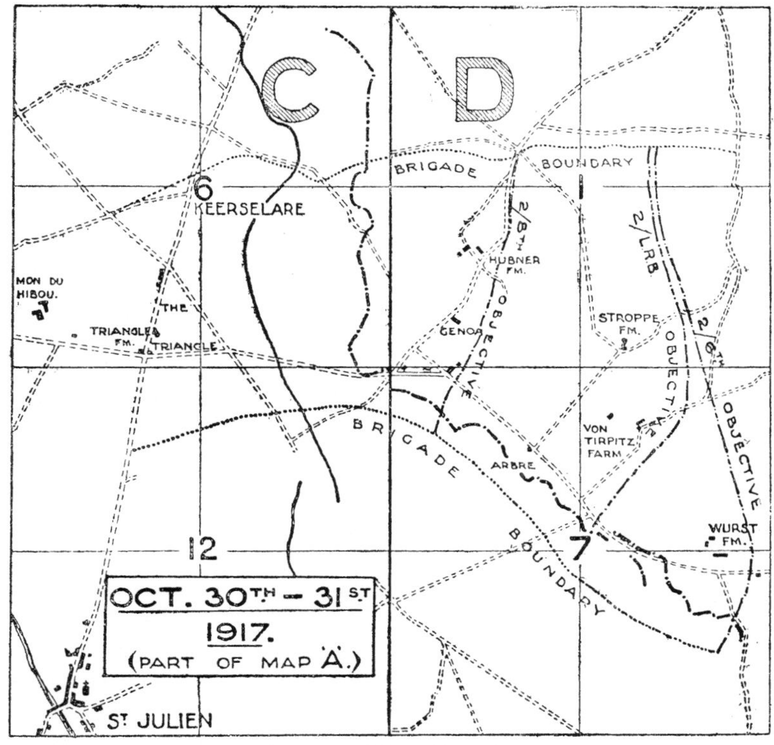

SKETCH MAP No. 17

the limit of noise seemed to have been reached already, the din was augmented by the barrage and searching fire of 16 machine-guns massed just in rear of the battalion.

On 20th September at zero (5.40 a.m.) the attack was launched, preceded by a creeping barrage. As an additional precaution against loss of direction both flanks of the battalion advanced on a compass bearing, but it was mainly owing to previous training and the fact that each section had maps that direction was maintained, since all company officers, save one, were casualties early in the advance. Within two minutes of zero coloured rockets went up from such of the enemy "pill-boxes" as had escaped destruction from the artillery preparation, showing the "S.O.S." call to their anxious gunners, and they were answered instantly by heavy curtain fire. This gradually thickened as the German gun teams took heart of grace and thought less of getting away than of assisting their perishing infantry, until at 6.45 a.m. it reached its greatest intensity, concentrating principally about Arbre and Hubner Farm. Hostile machine-gun fire was thick, accurate and actively maintained, and the ground was hardly won, but slowly, yard by yard, struggling and floundering through the morass of shell-holes, unsupported by the tanks which were to have aided them, the gallant men pressed on. The strong points fell according to plan, except that such fierce opposition was encountered at Hubner Farm that the Post Office Rifles needed the aid of the L.R.B. before this post was successfully carried. The enemy generally fought from his fortified shell-holes and concrete shelters until our men were upon him, but they seldom waited for the cold steel, and, when they did, it was "Kamarad," with the Boche ever clasping his too generous foe around the knees, as if to ensure safety by supplication and personal contact.

By 9.40 a.m. all the battalion's objectives had been successfully reached and were in course of consolidation, but the enemy's artillery fire was still strong, and the courageous runners who carried the glad tidings to an anxious battalion head-quarters had perilous journeys, oft-times only just struggling in, exhausted and wounded. The bag of prisoners was considerable. Von Tirpitz Farm, besides being a very strong point, was a medical aid post, and the Herr Doktor with his staff were all captured, but, before being sent down to Battalion Head-quarters, lent a hand in dressing our own wounded. Soon after midday the enemy tried to launch a counter-attack, but was seen assembling, with the result that it was crushed by artillery and machine-gun fire before getting within rifle shot. It is notable that this battle was the first in which machine-gun sections complete advanced with the leading waves of the assault. The experiment was amply justified by the result, for, besides helping with their fire to break up the immediate counter-attack, a machine-gun corps officer assisted very materially in the reorganisation of the left of the battalion front where no officers or senior N.C.O.'s survived.

The rest of that day, and also the following night, were quiet, but at dawn on 21st, after artillery preparation, the enemy made a determined attempt to attack, which was repeated again in the evening. No German, however, got within 100 yards of the line, woefully thin as it was, for the casualties had been very heavy, amounting to over 50% of the fighting personnel. Of the company officers engaged all were casualties, but Capt. F. L. Otter managed to carry on. Capt. F. Furze, for over two years the battalion's popular adjutant, capable and ever courteous, was killed. Wounded three times, twice severely, he refused to leave his men until he fell to the bullet of a sniper. His magnificent example of courage, endurance, and devotion to duty will ever remain a noble standard for the regiment. Capt. G. Whitaker, 2nd Lieuts. A. P. Sharman, G. H. Ticehurst, G. F. Trenow, W. H. L. Mitchell, D. T. Ward, L. S. Owen (12th Londons) and J. H. Hanna (19th Londons) also gave their lives in the great cause, and 2nd Lieuts. W. E. Green and H. G. Toseland (19th Londons) were wounded. Of the brave N.C.O.'s and men, 52 were killed, amongst whom was C.Q.M.S. C. S. Schonewald, a very old member of the regiment; 162 were wounded, and 25 were missing. On the night of 21st/22nd the 2/10th Battalion took over the outpost line, the remnants of the L.R.B. returning over the ground they had so hardly won, and via the light railway, to Reigersburg. The next night the chaplain, the Rev. E. M. Winter (the Rev. G. Vernon Smith had been invalided), took a party of volunteers back to the battlefield to search for and bury their fallen comrades, an act of no mean quality, for the area was still being heavily shelled.

For conspicuous gallantry in this battle, and for the splendid organisation which ensured such success, the following awards were made :—

D.S.O. : Lieut.-Col. P. D. Stewart ; M.C. : Capt. F. L. Otter ; D.C.M. : R.S.M. C. Bottomley, Sergts. F. H. Brock and T. W. Stapeley, Cpls. R. C. Hotz and T. A. Kingsbury, Lce.-Cpl. H. R. Porter ; M.M. : Sergts. E. H. Howard, H. B.

Hooson, G. M. Lee, L. Prike, W. H. Simmonds, Lce.-Sergts. H. Sears and W. S. Beauchamp, Cpls. P. Greenfield and W. N. Frentzel, Lce.-Cpls. F. T. Libby, G. R. Vaizey and A. Y. White, Rfn. A. E. Bazire, J. H. G. Box, D. Hernberg, E. A. Imber, D. Kibby, S. H. Timberlake.

Appended is an extract from Battalion Orders of 24th September :—

"The following messages have been received in connection with the recent operations :—

"From the Divisional Commander :—

"The Divisional Commander congratulates all ranks on their grand success, and the magnificent and whole-hearted way in which they have carried out the recent operations. All objectives have been taken, and the fine fighting spirit of the Division has been nobly upheld."

"From the Brigadier-General :—

"Please express to all ranks of your command my thanks and admiration for their great efforts on 20th and 21st, which ended in such unqualified success. The fighting spirit and discipline shown by the whole brigade, in capturing and holding this most important position against determined attacks, was beyond all praise."

"The Commanding Officer would like to add his appreciation and admiration of the gallantry and determination shown by all ranks under most trying conditions. The work of the last few weeks, which has often been irksome, has been well rewarded by the splendid successes gained, and the cheerful spirit and devotion to duty displayed on all occasions will ensure a fine fighting spirit being maintained in the battalion."

During the afternoon of 23rd, whilst on the road to Brake Camp, the Corps Commander (Lieut.-Gen. Sir Ivor Maxse) overtook the battalion, and leaned out of his car as it passed the column, shouting "Well done, boys. You did jolly well," but his further eulogisms, adorned with the choicest idioms of a peculiarly extensive vocabulary, were drowned in the noise of his motor.

Whilst at Brake Camp the massed drums and pipers of 51st

Division afforded diurnal inspiration, the martial magnificence of the drum-majors being only exceeded by the " joyful noise " of the pipes, which proved that the Psalmist was certainly not a Londoner. Battle surplus personnel having rejoined, the battalion entrained on 27th at Brielen (B.28) for Licques, a delightful area, " C " and " D " Companies being in the adjacent village of Herbinghem. Here, after rest, three weeks were passed in re-equipment and training, combined with football matches, concerts, and trips to Calais in lorries provided by a thoughtful Staff. Amongst other reinforcements came a large draft of Army Service Corps men, who, after training and some experience as infantry, took high places in the opinion of all for efficiency, cheerfulness and good comradeship in all circumstances. During this time Major-Gen. A. E. Cator, D.S.O. (Scots Guards), arrived to take command of the division, greeting the battalion during a morning's work, and Major C. E. Johnston rejoined from Aldershot.

By 29th October the battalion was back in the crater area, via Poperinghe, at Kempton Park, a hutted camp about 1½ miles west of the Steenbeck, and that night took up position as counter-attack battalion on the brigade front for the general operations of 30th October. The position occupied was a few hundred yards west of Poelcapelle, and was described on maps and in preliminary orders as Rose Trench, but it was not identifiable on the ground. Being a bitterly cold, wet day, the battalion's experience, scattered over the waste in brimming shell-holes and under considerable shell-fire for 16 hours, was far from enviable. The mud eclipsed its own evil records, and for that reason the attack, so far as the brigade front was concerned, did not make much progress. That evening the battalion took over the line just forward of the few unshattered " pill-boxes " that alone represented the once considerable village of Poelcapellè. The mud was beyond belief for its universality and adhesive quality, and no one who has not seen it, been stuck fast in it, or helped to unstick others, can possibly imagine what it is like. There is a record that, during this night, four strong stretcher-bearers of the L.R.B. worked hard for six hours to move a wounded rifleman of the 2/6th Battalion to a place of safety, but when day broke, and enemy sniping compelled the party to take cover, they had only succeeded in carrying him 50 yards. Patrolling to any extent was out of the question, for hours were passed in covering a few hundred yards. The activity and enterprise of runners was beyond praise, for there were no duck-boards nor any sort of landmarks discernible by night. Communication by day was kept up by signal lamps, as movement was impossible. To be lost hopelessly was the experience of all who had to move about at night. One officer, going round with his batman as runner, lost his way between his posts, and got into No Man's Land, where he heard groans, and after searching about found a man who, already wounded three times, had become hopelessly engulfed up to his waist in mud during the previous day's attack. Since to pull him out by ordinary means was impossible, and digging was impracticable owing to the liquid state of the mud, food and water were given him, with the assurance that a renewed effort would be made next night. This was done, and the wretched man, more dead than alive, was carried down to a forward dressing station. It will never be known how many British soldiers, officially reported "missing," perished, submerged in the blood-soaked mud of the plains of Flanders.

On the evening of 31st October, shortly before relief, "D" Company was ordered to attack a "pill-box" on their front which was believed to be occupied by only a few snipers, who were giving trouble. 2nd Lieut. L. H. Stokes, attached from the London Irish Rifles, gallantly led his platoon towards his objective, but progress owing to the mud was painfully slow, which gave the enemy sufficient warning and time to reinforce from occupied shell-holes close by. Before the party was within striking distance, fierce machine-gun and rifle fire was opened on them, and the officer fell mortally wounded within ten yards of his goal, and with him several of his men. One section, however, under the platoon sergeant (Sergt. J. Gration) got to close quarters and had the satisfaction of killing some of the enemy with their bayonets, but the party was too small to hold the position, and was compelled to withdraw in face of greater numbers. Whilst, strictly speaking, the attempt was not successful, it reflected greatly to the credit of the platoon. The expenditure of ammunition in an utterly useless barrage which the enemy put down, and maintained for over an hour, behind our support line immediately the attack became apparent, in the belief that general action was being resumed, must have cost many thousands of much needed marks. At this time the Germans were most lavish with their artillery ammunition in their efforts to bolster up and save their sorely tried and shaken infantry, especially in the vicinity of the Passchendaele Ridge. After only three days in this undesirable neighbourhood, the battalion suffered 75 casualties—1 Officer killed, and one wounded, 38 Other Ranks killed and 36 wounded—the great majority from shell-fire.

After relief by the 2/Queen Victoria Rifles, the L.R.B. proceeded to Siege Camp (B.20.d.) via Kempton Park, very gratefully completing the journey to camp from the latter place in motor lorries. There, thanks to the energy and persistent endeavour of the quartermaster, was awaiting every man a hot bath, with complete and much needed change of underclothing, and a square, hot meal. A week was spent in this camp, during which time a party of 200 men under Capt. Kitching was sent to assist the exhausted R.A.M.C. relay posts, which had had much hard work, and suffered many casualties carrying wounded on the duck-board tracks. On 4th November those officers then with the 2nd Battalion who had embarked for France in 1914 with 1st Battalion, viz. Capts. Kitching and E. G. Moore, and Lieut. Godward, celebrated the third anniversary of the sailing of the s.s. *Chyebassa* by a dinner at "Skindles" in Poperinghe.

By 10th November the battalion was again in the line, first in support in Pheasant Trench, and then forward in the old positions east of Poelcapelle. Circumstances were not quite so trying as during the previous tour, for the ground was firmer, a few duck-boards had been laid, and hostile shell-fire was less. Relieved by the 2/1st Londons on the 14th–15th November, the battalion passed through a very heavy gas shell bombardment on the way down. As the wearing of a gas mask on a dark and rainy night is no aid to the speedy negotiation of slippery, and oft-times broken, duck-board tracks every one was greatly relieved when, after interminable delays and exasperatingly frequent halts, the hard road was reached at last.

Siege Camp was occupied for 24 hours, after which it was

understood that the Division would proceed to a back area for three weeks' rest, but the "rest" was so broken up by continual moves that this euphemistic word more than usually belied its true meaning, and training was rendered very difficult. On 17th November the battalion proceeded by train to Hertzeele; on 25th it marched to Proven; on 26th trained to Wizerne, completing the day by a nine-mile march to Senninghem; and the next day it marched to Lottinghem, where a few days' training were arranged. These days will be remembered for two things. First, the great efforts that were made by platoons and companies on the parade ground in singing lessons in order to improve the singing whilst on the march; second, for the amazing energy expended by the transport section in order to turn out their horses, harness, carts and waggons the most lustrous of a glittering brigade.

On 4th December Capt. F. L. Otter, to the regret of all his old comrades, left the battalion to take up the duties of Camp Commandant and A.D.C. to the Divisional Commander. On 7th and 8th march route took the battalion back to Wizerne, via Colomby, and thence it trained to Elverdinghe (B.14). After three days at the correctly and descriptively named Dirty Bucket Camp, the battalion was moved forward to Huddlestone Camp, situated east of the canal, and about a mile south-west of Pilckem (C.2), amid the shattered remains of what had been the German front line at the opening of the Flanders offensive five months previously. For the following four weeks the whole brigade found working parties for the divisional sector. The work consisted chiefly in carrying R.E. material from dumps behind the reserve positions up to the front line, which entailed a nightly journey of over eight miles, principally along duck-board tracks that were frequently and accurately shelled. It was heavy, exhausting work, especially as the tracks and roads were covered with ice and melting snow for the first two weeks. In the minds of those concerned the names of Eagle Dump, Schreiboom, Olga Houses and Conde House will ever recall unpleasant memories, tempered by recollection of the good comradeship engendered amongst those who endure together hardship and danger.

It was at this time that the rumours of the coming great German offensive became concrete. New zones of defence were sited, dug, and wired, etc., not a little of the work in the Langemarck area being done by the battalion. A party from "C" Company, attached to a Tunnelling Company, laboured in the semi-liquid blue clay for over three weeks to disprove the fatuity that deep dug outs could be constructed in that sector of the Flanders marshes. Whilst at Huddlestone Camp Lieut. Eckle, of the 102nd U.S. Infantry, was attached to the battalion for a period of instruction, and was afforded ample opportunity of examining the battlefields in all their recent hideousness, as well as the systems of defence occupied and under construction. 2nd Lieut. A. G. Bower, attached from the 1st Royal Fusiliers, had the experience, novel but unpleasing, of being wounded whilst at tea in his company mess hut by a spent round fired from an aeroplane. Routine was unaltered on Christmas Day, but all ranks celebrated the festive season in the usual manner, thanks to the enterprise of the genial quartermaster in respect of turkey, and the far-sighted generosity of the Quartermaster-General in the matter of plum pudding. The Divisional Concert Party ("The Goods") having transformed the shell of the erstwhile brewery at Elverdinghe into an efficient theatre gave a splendid pantomime, with dresses, scenery and effects brought from London regardless of expense. At midnight on 31st December, 1917, the Boche treated the whole line to a magnificent display of fireworks, which speedily subsided into genuine "S.O.S." rockets when every British battery, of all calibres, fired a "crash" on selected nerve centres.

On 8th January, 1918, the battalion moved to Proven remaining there in a deplorably muddy hutment camp at Jans-Ter-Biezen for ten days. On 12th Lieut.-Gen. Sir W. Jacob, K.C.B., commanding IInd Corps, reviewed the battalion, and, after a congratulatory speech, presented ribbons of the M.C. to Lieuts. A. J. C. Lintott and Kent, the D.C.M. to three and the M.M. to 19 Other Ranks. During this period the Divisional Commander (Major-Gen. A. E. Cator, D.S.O.) summoned the officers of the division to an intensely interesting lecture in which he explained the influence that the Russian defection would have on the situation on the Western front, and expounded the principles and measures of defence that were being taken to combat the widely advertised offensive which the enemy would soon set in motion with probably superior numbers.

On 19th January the battalion left Proven by train for Villers Brettoneux, the head-quarters at that time of the Fifth Army. Every one was glad to say good-bye to the mud of Flanders, and, when Moreuil was reached, spirits were high at the prospect of a sojourn in a considerable town long innocent of troops, complete with delectable restaurants, shops and supplies, and affording the best billets that the battalion had known for many a long day. But a dreadful anxiety was hanging like a sword over the L.R.B. because it was known that the organisation of the Expeditionary Force was being radically changed, and that one battalion in every brigade would have to be disbanded. At any moment the fateful news might come and the sword fall, severing at a blow tried friends and trusted comrades, and dissolving the noble spirit of corporate pride so hardly materialised. The battalion was in no wise reassured when, at parade on the morning of 24th January, the Commanding Officer announced that he had been ordered to take over the 58th Divisional Machine-Gun Battalion, and that, deeply as he regretted the parting, he would have to leave the comrades of fair weather and foul whom he had had the honour of commanding for nine months. Three hearty cheers were given to Lieut.-Col. Stewart as the only means of expressing thanks for his gallant leadership, and the best wishes for his future. Although Lieut.-Col. Stewart left on this day, he officially gave up the command on December 27th, 1917, from which date Major C. E. Johnston, who got his acting rank on 11th January, 1918, took over. Rumour gave way to despair when it was known officially that the battalion would be broken up. Detailed orders for dispersal and destination quickly followed, and on the morning of 29th January the battalion, under Major C. E. Johnston, paraded for the last time as a unit in the square of Moreuil for a farewell address from Brig.-Gen. Higgins. After commending the battalion for its remarkable efficiency and fine fighting spirit, he said that he wished every officer and man to understand that the present course reflected no shadow of discredit of any kind on the L.R.B. Wherever any individual might find himself, and with whatever troops, they could have no finer standard of devotion to duty, to their King, their country and themselves, than that they had set up and always maintained. He wished them good luck and God-speed, with a fair share of the fight, until their unworthy and unchivalrous foe was finally crushed. Hardly had the cheers that concluded this short speech died away, when lorries appeared to carry "C" and "D" Companies to the 1/28th London Regt., the Artists' Rifles, then serving with the 63rd (Royal Naval) Division, in the 190th Infantry Brigade. The undermentioned Officers, with 450 Other Ranks, ultimately joined that battalion :—

Capts. C. Furze, G. C. Kitching, H. G. Wilkinson, E. G. Moore ; Lieuts. F. Williamson, J. F. Legg, R. E. Petley, 2nd Lieuts. H. C. Lintott, C. F. C. Brodie, H. W. Sampson ; L. G. Hummerstone, G. R. Reeve, A. C. Young, W. Gore (attached), J. T. Piggott (13th Londons), F. A. Newell, J. H. Morris, H. L. Higgs.

Later on the same morning the remainder of the battalion was addressed by the Divisional Commander (Major-General Cator) who congratulated the L.R.B. on its meritorious achievements, saying how sorry he was to lose it from his division, and wishing all ranks good luck. The next day "B" Company, with part of "A," 250 Other Ranks in all, embussed to join the 1/18th London Regt. (the London Irish Rifles), 47th Division, under the following officers :—

Capt. J. S. Godward ; Lieuts. C. Hall, R. F. Lydall, H. J. F. Crisp ; 2nd Lieuts. A. M. Pilcher (15th Londons), J. H. Wright, A. L. Jones, J. W. Carrington, R. Bronner, R. W. C. Hall (15th Londons).

On the 31st January the remainder of the battalion—150 Other Ranks—were absorbed into the 2/10th London Regt., 58th Division, with the following officers :—

Major S. Bowers ; Lieut. V. A. Finlayson ; 2nd Lieut. B. R. Power, L. Smetham.

Lieuts. C. Harrison Jones, A. J. C. Lintott and A. S. Wimble were retained on the staff of the 174th Infantry Brigade Head-quarters as Intelligence Officer, Transport Officer and Assistant Staff Captain respectively. After clearing up the administrative details of the battalion, head-quarters were disposed of as follows :—

Major C. E. Johnston was appointed to command the 8th London Regt., Post Office Rifles, taking with him the Chaplain, Rev. H. C. James. Capt. and Adjutant R. Cope became Adjutant of the IIIrd Corps Training Reinforcement Camp until joining the 1st Battalion L.R.B. The quartermaster, Lieut. H. J. Kent, proceeded to perform similar duties for the 47th Divisional Machine Gun Battalion. R.S.M. C. Bottomley was sent in the same capacity to the 1st L.R.B.

From 1st February, 1918, until the end of the war, the history of the 2nd L.R.B. becomes largely identified with the Artists' Rifles, and may be passed over briefly; but, as the two companies sent to them, together with some large drafts which had reached them from the 3rd L.R.B., brought it about that quite 75% of those in this battalion were really members of the L.R.B., its further proceedings merit record in the regimental history.

"C" and "D" Companies found the Artists out of the line, resting and training, at Beaulancourt, a few miles south of Bapaume. By the middle of February the battalion moved up into the line just west of Marcoing on to Welsh and Highland Ridges, where there had been fierce fighting when the enemy counter-attacked after the first battle of Cambrai. Tours in these fine trenches, with short rests in Havrincourt Wood, filled the apprehensive weeks up to the launching of the German onslaught in March.

The fine spirit of the two companies transferred was tried to the uttermost on 21st March and the succeeding days of the great German offensive. Following on a series of rear-guard actions, surrounded at Ytres on the night of 23rd/24th March, amid blazing ammunition dumps, with parts of other units of the Naval Division they fought their way out at daybreak to Barastre and Le Transloy, having to pass over open ground within 1000 yards of three enemy machine guns in enfilade. Capt. Kitching and Lieut. Petley were wounded and taken prisoner, whilst casualties amongst N.C.O.'s and men were heavy. The previous evening Lieut. F. Williamson and 2nd Lieut. A. C. Young were killed, practically the whole company with them being ambushed in the dark close to Ytres. 2nd

Lieut. H. C. Lintott had been mortally wounded on 21st: in civil life he was a portrait painter of no mean order, and war was very foreign to his nature and instincts, but he rose gallantly to the occasion and did his duty like a man. 2nd Lieuts. Piggott, F. A. Newell and Higgs were killed on 26th.

From Le Transloy (Map C : N.30), near which place touch with old comrades then in the London Irish was obtained, via Bazentin (S.8), Courcelette (R.30), Pozieres (X.4) and Thiepval (R.25), offering stubborn resistance in their endeavour to stem the overwhelming avalanche of constantly relieved and specially trained troops, often isolated, and generally outflanked, the remnant crossed the Ancre, and were at last relieved by the 12th Division on 26th March. The same evening, just when, owing to the exertions of Capt. C. Furze, the first square meal for five days was being enjoyed, the battalion was called out to form a defensive flank on the right of the 12th Division, as the line had given way. At dawn next day a counter-attack was made with the object of stopping the enemy from breaking out of Albert along the main Amiens road, which was the high-water mark of the German advance in this area.

The party which had gone to the London Irish Rifles had suffered equally badly as regards casualties, Lieuts. Hall, Lydall and Crisp being wounded, while 2nd Lieut. Carrington was wounded and taken prisoner. The members of the old battalion with the 58th Division had not been so heavily engaged, although that division had been on the extreme right of the Fifth Army front, and adjacent to our gallant French allies when the storm broke.

Little or no rest followed the staying of the enemy. After hasty reinforcement with representatives of no less than twelve different regiments, there followed a series of tours in the outpost line through Aveluy Wood (W.4). To the great grief of all who knew him, Capt. Claude Furze was mortally wounded during the evening of 5th April, and died next day. A gallant soldier and a cheery comrade, his loss made a large gap in the small band of those who had left England with the 2nd L.R.B. Lieut. Reeve was awarded the M.C. for bravery and fine example during a bombardment and raid on his company front. Towards the end of the month it became possible to relieve the tired divisions holding the line, and well-earned rest was enjoyed. Then came the opportunity to add lustre to the fame of the London Rifle Brigade. A competition to stimulate musketry, Lewis gun, and bayonet work, organised by the National Rifle Association throughout the British Expeditionary Force in France, with silver medals for the winning team in each division, was held, in which No. 13 Platoon of the old "D" Company, under Sergt. Canning, comfortably beat the other platoons of the 190th Infantry Brigade, and subsequently defeated all other competing platoons of the 63rd (Royal Naval) Division, with great credit to its members, and was handsomely congratulated by the Battalion, Brigade, Divisional and Corps Commanders concerned.

There followed a series of tours in the line in the area before Beaumont Hamel (Q 11). At the end of May, the Commanding Officer of the Artists' Rifles having been wounded, and the Second in Command following him into hospital, the command of the battalion passed to Capt. Wilkinson, with Lieut. Legg as Second in Command.

June and July passed, with marvellous recuperation of the British Armies, and in August the wonderful general advance over nearly the whole Western front began. In the early days of the month the Naval Division found itself in rear of the 58th Division just south of Albert, supporting the victorious advance along the banks of the Somme, and the battalion eagerly anticipated relieving old friends and carrying on the pursuit of the shaken enemy. But the Naval Division moved slightly north instead, and on 21st gave battle north of Bucquoy. Strangely enough the billets occupied on the night of 19th/20th August were at Souastre, and the route to the assembly position lay through Fonquevillers, over the old trenches where many of the officers, N.C.O.'s and men of the old 2nd L.R.B., now with the Artists, received their first tuition in the actual field of war.

This, the first of a final series of three major battles which the battalion saw before the enemy surrendered, resulted in an advance of over five miles during the first five hours, and in the capture of numerous guns, trench mortars and machine guns, with many prisoners, including some Austrian officers, and carried the line to a well-remembered spot, the railway at Achiet Le Grand, where in the preceding April much work had been done. This successful action, however, again reduced the ranks of the old 2nd L.R.B., as both Lieut.-Col. Wilkinson and Capt. E. G. Moore were wounded, besides numerous N.C.O.'s and men, but Major Legg took over the battalion, and commanded it for some weeks. Then followed further victorious actions, the first of which smashed the last hope of the enemy, the one remaining line of the famous Hindenburg system at Queant, while the second was a battle south of Cambrai, which gave the British Army final possession of the city.

On November 11th, 1918, the ever-to-be-remembered day on which the Armistice was signed, there remained with the Artists' Rifles only Major Legg, with some 80 N.C.O.'s and men, the survivors of the 18 Officers and 450 Other Ranks who had joined on 29th January that year from the 2nd Battalion of the London Rifle Brigade.

ITINERARY OF SECOND BATTALION

September 4, 1914—January 29, 1918

(*See Plan in pocket.*)

1914.		
Sept.	4.	London.
Nov.	19.	Haywards Heath.
1915.		
May	18.	Norwich.
June	19.	Ipswich.
1916.		
April	28.	Foxhall Heath.
July	13.	Sutton Veny.
1917.		
Jan.	25.	Le Havre.
	29.	Rougefay.
Feb.	1.	Fonquevillers.
	22.	Bailleulmont.
Feb.	24.	Allouette.
Mar.	18.	Bailleulval.
	23.	Boisleux St. Marc.
	25.	Boyelles.
	28.	Pommier-Grouches.
	29.	Bouret-sur-Canche.
April	2.	Quœux.
	4.	Mailly Maillet.
	7.	Bihucourt.
May	14.	Mory.
	15.	Ecoust St. Mein.
	17.	Attack on Bullecourt.
	19.	Mory.
	23.	Longatte.
	28.	Bullecourt.

June 3. Mory.
14. St. Leger.
16. Croisilles.
20. St. Leger.
21. Courcelles Le Comte.
July 6. Equancourt.
8. Beaucamp.
16. Ytres.
23. Le Trescaut.
29. Berneville.
Aug. 24. Poperinghe.
29. Reigersburg.
Sept. 7. Kitchener Wood.
11. Dambre Camp.
18. Reigersburg Chateau.
20. Moulin de Hibou. Attack on Arbre, Von Tirpitz Farm and Stroppe Farm.
Sept. 22. Reigersburg.
23. Brake Camp.
27. Licques.
Oct. 29. Kempton Park.
31. Poelcapelle.
Nov. 1. Siege Camp.
10. Poelcapelle.
15. Siege Camp.
17. Hertzeele.
25. Proven.
26. Senninghem.
27. Lottinghem.
Dec. 7. Colomby.
8. Elverdinghe.
11. Huddlestone Camp.

1918.

Jan. 8. Proven.
19. Villers Bretton-eux.
20. Moreuil.
29. Broken up.

THIRD BATTALION

NOVEMBER 26, 1914—APRIL, 1919

Raising the Battalion—Tadworth—Sutton—Fovant—Exeter—Dawlish—Blackdown—Shoreham—Disbandment.

THE 3rd Battalion of the London Rifle Brigade was established to find drafts for its other two battalions, and came into being on 26th November, 1914, the first recruits being enlisted on Monday, 1st December. As it did not, and was not intended to, go to the front its history, unlike the preceding ones, is perforce merely a plain record of steady efforts to turn raw material into a product worthy of the regiment.

The first Commanding Officer was Col. H. C. Cholmondeley, C.B., who commanded the mounted detachment of the C.I.V.'s in South Africa, a most fortunate appointment, as, being a regular officer, he complied with the regimental rule on this point, and as, having been Colonel of the London Rifle Brigade from 1890 to 1901, he was thoroughly familiar with the kind of men with whom he had to deal. The Second in Command was Major F. Cannon, who had served with the Royal Fusiliers Militia for some years. The first adjutant was Lieut. C. W. Long, but he was very shortly relieved by 2nd Lieut. J. F. C. Bennett, who, having served in the regiment since 1900, had been transferred to the 2nd Battalion because he found himself unable to undertake the foreign service obligation, and had been given a commission in it. Clr.-Sergt. C. Whittingham, who also had served in the L.R.B. for many years, was appointed Regimental Sergt.-Major and was the only one of the original staff remaining when the battalion was disbanded.

The Quartermaster, Lieut. W. Kelly, who had served with the Leinster Regt. in the same position, proved a treasure from the first, as he not only set about organising his own department and started training the cooks, tailors, etc., who were essential for the battalion and were available for the sister ones, but was also able and willing to help in teaching bayonet-fighting, Maxim-gun drill, etc.

Although the battalion, like the other Territorials then, was on a 4-company basis, only three—"A," "B" and "C"—were formed at this time, and 2nd Lieut. G. B. Vaile, lately a colour-sergt. in the 1st Battalion, 2nd Lieut. C. W. Long, an officer of the 1st who had been left behind to look after "details," and Capt. W. Paxman, who had served for many years in the Essex Volunteers, were the respective commanders.

1915

Training was not easy, as there were very few qualified instructors until ten N.C.O.'s who had been sent on January 10th, 1915, to the Chelsea School of Instruction returned, but there was a certain amount of squad-drill in the ground of the Merchant Taylors' School and at the City of London School; and many route marches were made, which were considerably enlivened by the music of the bands provided by the Lord Mayor's Fund, and certainly did much to shake the men together. In addition to this the Merchant Taylors very kindly lent some rifles which, with others borrowed from the Coopers' Company School, proved invaluable, as it was a long time before any were issued except a few for shooting, and altogether, with miniature rifle practice going on at Bunhill Row, training might be said to be moving the right way.

In February a concert was held at Bunhill Row in order to stimulate recruiting, which was by then very slack all over the kingdom, as the first rush was over. The principal speakers were Major-Gen. Sir Francis Lloyd, K.C.V.O., C.B., D.S.O., Commanding the London District, and the Bishop of London, the Chaplain to the Regiment, and a detachment of the 2nd Battalion with their bugles came up to lend a hand. If those who took up the parrot cry of "business as usual" had adopted the more practical one of "nothing as usual," this sort of stimulus would probably not have been required.

In March the battalion carried out a tactical exercise at Hampstead Heath, cooking the dinners in the field, and returning by route-march, but, though the experience was no doubt useful, the effort was distinctly ambitious at that stage of training. From the 12th of this month the battalion had to find two companies for trench-digging at Ongar in connection with the defence of London, all meals except breakfast being cooked on the ground, and also, after the first week, to mount a night-guard of 1 Officer and 8 Other Ranks, during which the officer was supposed to instruct the men in night work, but at this period it must have been rather a case of the blind leading the blind. In this month the battalion was fitted with equipment.

On 1st April the battalion seized an opportunity for making further acquaintance with the 2nd by sending a party down to their regimental sports at Haywards Heath and meeting it in a bayonet-fighting competition, the only one out of several suggestions which materialised. Lieut. Kelly took the team, who were all recruits, in hand, and trained each of them to avoid finesse and to go straight for his man with any sort of point that he could raise, with the result that the 3rd won by 6 to 4, a striking proof of the value of an old soldier's advice. In this month the battalion got in touch with the 1st for the first time, as it sent them out four officers, who had received, it is to be feared, a very sketchy military education.

Tadworth

On April 28th the battalion paraded at Wimbledon Station and marched to Tadworth, where in an excellent situation it lay in camps with other third-line units of the 1st and 2nd London T.F. Divisions, under Brig.-Gen. C. S. O. Monck. Here Lieut. Kelly again distinguished himself by laying out the regimental camp exceedingly well, and providing it with a particularly simple yet ingenious system of drainage which kept it dry and healthy. Sir Francis Lloyd, when he paid a visit of inspection at the end of the week, expressed himself as highly pleased with its state.

Up to this time the men had been living at home and coming up daily for drill, which meant loss of time and a necessarily patchy training, but now they were in a position to be taught a soldier's duties properly, and to acquire that true discipline, which the war had already proved to be essential, by living with and under it by day and night. The drill, however, was very conventional, with its areas allotted each week, extended order, attack and defence, outpost schemes by day and night, as had been customary for battalion training in peace time, instead of the subjects that were then occupying the regiments at the front.

On May 10th Col. Cholmondeley was given the command of the 173rd Infantry Brigade and went away shortly afterwards, leaving Major Cannon in charge. On June 4th Major N. C. King, who had gone out with the 1st Battalion to France and returned home invalided after only a short time there, came down and took over the command, which he retained until the end of the war. The strength at this date was about 800.

From his short experience at the front Major King had learnt enough to realise that training must be altered very much if men were to be sent out fit to go straight into the trenches, so he at once set to work to devise a scheme that would secure this with the limited number of instructors at his disposal.

His decision was to treat the battalion as one big school of instruction and to run it on Public School lines, using the instructors as masters, treating the platoons as Forms, and the companies as Houses. Accordingly the instructors were grouped by their specialities and put under specialist officers, who were held responsible for the proper teaching of their own subjects ; the men were rearranged and made up into platoons according to their state of efficiency ; and a programme was issued, corresponding to a school time-table, and made out each week as circumstances demanded. Each platoon had its own officer, who was responsible for his men in the usual way and marched them from the parade-ground to their class, where he fell in and was instructed with them, but was also called out by the instructor to put the men through what they had been taught, and so accustom himself to handling and looking after them. Each platoon also had an experienced N.C.O. allotted to it as drill sergeant. This system was a complete innovation at the time, but it was subsequently almost universally adopted, though often with modifications to suit requirements. Later on a syllabus was sent down from the War Office, and to this every one was expected to work as far as circumstances allowed. The specialist officers drew up a programme and kept a record of the lessons given to each platoon, so that the instruction was steadily progressive.

Training became much more practical through the starting of elementary bombing and the introduction of gas-masks, but the most useful step that was taken was to obtain the leave of a neighbouring public-spirited landlord to lay out a series of trenches in one of his adjacent fields. Here companies used to go out for a 48-hour tour, dig, do their own cooking, and live on the water that they took with them, besides being liable to night attacks. There was, however, still the same shortage of rifles, as only 100 were available for 800 men, and these were almost all required for musketry and firing on the range at Rainham, but thanks to schools like Epsom, Dulwich, Whitgift and Eton (who lent 400 captured Boer Mausers) enough were in hand during the summer holidays to teach the manual exercise and make the men learn to put up with the weight of the rifle on the march. No Lewis guns were yet issued, but only Maxims, and these had to be shared between battalions.

As by this time wounded men were coming back from overseas in considerable numbers, the missing company—" D "—was formed and reserved for them under Lieut. A. Read. The N.C.O.'s, if not all qualified as specialists, were invaluable in dealing with the other men, and the touch between the 1st and 3rd Battalions began to be real instead of theoretical.

A Y.M.C.A. hut, which was principally run by the local inhabitants, was a great comfort to the troops, especially when the summer began to wane. Having no chaplain of its own, like the 1st and 2nd Battalions, the 3rd was fortunate in having the Rev. Vernon Hanson attached to it. The Bishop of London came down and confirmed many men before they went out.

The Rifle Brigade custom of calling their men riflemen instead of privates was now adopted, since the 1st Battalion had done so after the first battle of Ypres, but that of calling lance ranks, acting ranks, was not. At the same time a long desired change was made and the metal shoulder plates were replaced by tabs with L.R.B. in green on a black ground, without any objection from higher authorities. These were not an issue and were paid for by the men, but towards the end of the war the regimental institute bore the expense.

In June and July Lieut. B. Ashton Warner, a pre-war officer who had been seconded for duty in Nigeria where he had charge of a district, came down and voluntarily spent a month of his leave in giving most valuable training to the officers, who profited enormously from his precepts and example. In July, Capt. R. H. Husey, on recovery from his first wound, put in an appearance, to every one's great pleasure, as did Capt. R. Somers-Smith shortly after, and these two also gave great assistance in the training, besides helping to drive home to all the real unity between the two battalions. Major M. H. Soames also joined and became Second in Command, Major Cannon having left early in July to take up recruiting duties.

On August 29th the first draft, 239 N.C.O.'s and men, was sent out, with considerable anxiety as to what would be thought of them, but the reports were altogether favourable and in some respects, e.g. bayonet fighting, they were ahead of the older soldiers, who had not up to then had a chance of learning the latest methods. From this time the co-operation between these two battalions was of the closest, reports and suggestions from the front being sent back regularly, with the confidence that they would be attended to and that the firing-line would receive the reinforcements it required.

During the late summer the Norfolk and the Suffolk Yeomanry were lying almost next door and advantage was taken of the opportunity to borrow horses and give some practice in riding to the younger officers. This was exceedingly popular as well as useful, and many of those who had never mounted a horse before showed great courage and determination to succeed.

In October Lieut. A. G. Kirby joined the staff and took over the training of the officers, which Capt. Somers-Smith had begun, as well as helping with the general training of the battalion, which up to this time had devolved entirely upon the Commanding Officer, owing to the adjutant being fully occupied with the very heavy routine and office work. From all accounts the officers trained regimentally by the 3rd Battalion and sent to the 1st were quite satisfactory, but, as some battalions were not able to organise a proper system and others, it is to be feared, did not trouble to do so, Young Officer Companies, and later Officer Cadet Battalions, were formed, which in many cases turned out men who, for all their book learning, had very little idea of how to use it to the best advantage, and did not in the least understand how to handle men. There can be little doubt that the training of officers in their own units was the best system, if properly carried out, as, when the demand for officers was very insistent and they only spent a week or two with their battalions after leaving the cadet units before they went to the front, the complaints from their C.O.'s of their lack of knowledge of the first duty of an officer, viz. to look after his men, were frequent. Quite as important as training was the selection of likely men for commissions, which was not difficult in the early days, because no one was recommended until he had been to the front, and reports as to actual conduct in the field were easily obtainable; but the demand for officers grew, and it was necessary to use men who had not been under fire, so from the early days of 1916 special classes were held for N.C.O.'s and candidates, under Lieut. H. C. Beard, Capt. H. L. Johnston, Lieut. C. Hall and Capt. E. C. Wills in succession, with Sergts. F. O. Harriss and T. Malone in charge. Each course lasted about three weeks, during which the members of the class, which was kept under close observation, were taught how to instruct in the ordinary elementary subjects as well as how to read maps, etc.; and at the end of the time a report on every member was made to the Commanding Officer, who interviewed each man himself. By judicious weeding out, the battalion was in the position to boast that not one man was sent back from a Cadet Battalion as incompetent or unlikely to make an efficient officer.

During the summer of 1915 the subjects to be taught were comparatively few; for instance, rifle grenades, Lewis guns and rapid wiring had not been introduced, so that there was time for two route marches a week, which not only made the men very fit, but introduced them to the lovely country surrounding the camp on all sides. On one occasion a long day was given to a march to the hills on the west side of Burford Bridge, when the men covered about twenty miles and were very much pleased with themselves in consequence. Musketry, which was a great feature of the training, was admirably taught under Capt. Vaile, and gradually a fine staff of instructors was built up with the help of Col.-Sergt. Instructor of Musketry

Price. Parties were sent away to Rainham, for about ten days each, to fire the course, and the figures steadily improved. All this time the battalion was left to itself, being very rarely inspected, and, though there was not a single Regular soldier connected with it, the training was never better or more thorough. No time limit was imposed on the training, and the average period was about six months, which enabled the men to be made really fit and to be taught the essentials of soldiering thoroughly. Amusements were not neglected; cricket was played on the fine ground at Tadworth Court and on that of a private school near the camp; and there were also sports for all the troops, at which the prizes were distributed by Mr. Lloyd George, then Minister of Munitions, whose house was near by. Concerts were given in the dining tents and in the Y.M.C.A. hut, and though at this time the battalion had not the fine musicians who joined it later, a fairly good show was made. Being so near London, a good many men were able to get to their homes during the week-end, a privilege which was rarely abused, though some battalions had very large numbers of men overstaying leave.

Sutton

On November 22nd the battalion moved to Sutton, where it was billeted for the most part in the residential district south of the railway. By great good luck the workhouse at Belmont was in the L.R.B. area, and, as the inmates were few, the courtyards and casual wards were made available for drill through the kindness of the Master. Recruiting was very brisk and the battalion was strong, so that a good place for drill with cover for wet days was invaluable.

Considering that the men were distributed in billets the training, while there, did not suffer as much as might have been expected, but the difficulties in the way of turning into soldiers men who were not quartered together in camp or barracks proved to be enormous. Discipline away from parades could not help becoming relaxed, corporate feeling could not easily be inculcated, and both officers and N.C.O.'s found their work very much increased without any adequate result. Fortunately, however, the stay was not a long one, and the place had the compensation of being so near London that nearly every one was able to spend Christmas at home.

Just before moving to Sutton the 2nd Battalion was ordered to send ten officers to the 3rd, which was most fortunate, because it enabled the two battalions to become better acquainted with one another, but it was a great drawback that facilities for meeting were not so good in billets as they would have been in a camp or barracks, and almost directly after the move to Fovant the majority of the officers returned to their own unit.

Fovant

On January 10th, 1916, the battalion was moved to Fovant, about twelve miles west of Salisbury on the road to Shaftesbury, and occupied a hutted camp at the bottom of a hill immediately below three other camps. As hardly any of the roads had been properly constructed and all the drainage from above ran down to the L.R.B. ground, it naturally was muddy, and the fact that all the huts had not got duck-boards did not make things more pleasant; but Lieut. A. K. Dodds was at once detailed to lay out and dig a system of drains, which was fortunate, because he had only just finished when a heavy snowstorm came down, which, when the snow melted, would have left the place in a terrible state if the work had not been done, and done so well as to stand this test.

Soon after reaching Fovant the battalion was granted leave to form a band, provided that all the members were fit for active service. Major Soames, who had made himself responsible for raising the money, was able to purchase a complete set of instruments, through the generosity of the Lord Mayor, Sir Charles Wakefield, who gave £200, and a grant of £50 from the *Daily Telegraph* Fund, and Mr. P. S. Robinson, who had been the bandmaster of the 1st Battalion before the war and acting as bugle-major of the 2nd Battalion, was transferred by the kindness of Lieut.-Col. Tod to the 3rd Battalion, and succeeded in enlisting a full band of professional, semi-professional and amateur musicians combined. The difficulties first of training the men and then in keeping them together were very great, but Mr. Robinson tackled them with characteristic energy and most satisfactory results, and the band undoubtedly proved a great asset to the battalion by filling up many an otherwise dull hour. A string band was also formed, which did excellent service within the battalion, and went out to play to wounded soldiers in hospital, besides giving performances for charities in Salisbury and elsewhere. During this year Bugle-Major Mould took the buglers in hand with such success that, having about 36 under him, it became possible to drop the drums, which had been presented by the 2nd Battalion and been of the greatest possible service, and to follow the practice of the Rifle Brigade in having bugles alone, and the bugles were plated.

This seems a suitable place at which to complete the general story of the brigade and its brigadiers. Shortly before going to Fovant the command of the brigade had been taken over by Col. S. H. Godman, D.S.O., of the Scots Guards, who had the whole of the third line of the 1st London Territorial Division under him at Fovant and at Hurdcott, which was adjoining. In the spring of this year (1916) the division was broken up into Group A, which contained the L.R.B., under Col. K. B. Williams, and Group B, under Col. Godman; in the summer, Col. Williams gave way to Col. A. C. Becher; and in the autumn the latter was replaced by Brig.-Gen. A. A. Howell, C.M.G., by which time various amalgamations had taken place (the L.R.B. was untouched), ending in the twelve battalions being reduced to eight under the name of the 1st London Reserve Brigade. Gen. Howell, who went out to Malta in the early days of the war in command of the 1/3rd Londons (Royal Fusiliers) and from there over to France, where he served until sent home for his new duty, was a man of marked individuality and pulled the brigade together, besides improving its training all round. On his death early in 1918, Brig.-Gen. R. Jelf, D.S.O., who came from the K.R.R.C., was appointed to fill the vacancy, much to the pleasure of the L.R.B., who were very glad to have a rifleman over them, as he understood riflemen's ways.

In the early spring the weather was very wet, and the parade ground, which was on a steep slope, was so slippery that men could hardly stand and scarcely any drill could be done out of doors. With a view to making the men fit and giving them practice in using pick and shovel, two tennis courts were made near the officers' mess, which proved the greatest boon to officers and sergeants during the summer. This led to a question in Parliament: "Is it a fact that 100 men are being employed at Fovant in making tennis courts for officers?" The answer was in the affirmative, but nothing more was heard of it. Lieut. A. K. Dodds was in charge of the work and rendered great help, not only by reason of his technical skill, but also by his wonderful acquisitive powers. As a picker up of unconsidered trifles he was unsurpassed, and on one occasion he collected a gate which really belonged to the R.E., and was subsequently traded back by him to the R.E. in exchange for some other article that he wanted.

In February Capt. Kirby left to take up staff duties and his place was taken by Lieut. A. E. Sedgwick, who acted unofficially as assistant adjutant, but after the 1st Battalion had been so much cut up at Gommecourt on July 1st he insisted on going to the front again although he was still lame from his first wound. The work he did was quite first rate, and he was one of the finest officers the regiment ever had. He was followed by 2nd Lieut. G. C. Chambers, who was eventually gazetted as adjutant in August, 1918.

Soon after reaching Fovant Major Soames was appointed A.P.M. of the division and was succeeded as Second in Command by Major C. D. Burnell, who was recovering from a severe wound received at the second battle of Ypres. He was a tower of strength, not only owing to his great ability as an instructor, but also on account of his personality and sound common sense.

At Easter, regimental sports were got up to which a large number of friends from the neighbourhood were invited, and they were followed in the evening by a revue arranged by Lieut. Stransom, assisted by Mr. Robinson and others, which was highly successful, though quite crude compared with those given later on. At this time also the Rifle Brigade custom of calling men to attention by the use of the word "Squad," "Company," "Party," etc., was adopted, and, soon after, that of doing all movements, except ceremonial, from the "stand at ease" position where possible.

During the severe fighting on the Somme the demands for drafts became heavier and the calls for officers were very difficult to meet. For a considerable period the time allowed for training men at home was reduced to nine weeks, including two anti-typhoid innoculations, which was too short for them to get properly fit, much less efficient, and the men had to complete their knowledge after they had landed in France; but from all accounts the training given at home was—at any rate, as far as the 1st London Reserve Brigade was concerned—by no means inferior to that obtained in France.

The shortage of rifles was gradually made up, first by the issue of what was called the "1914 pattern," which was made in America and was not a good weapon for rapid loading, besides being weak at the muzzle, and later by the issue of S.M.L.E. in adequate numbers. During the autumn orders were received that all bands were to be broken up, and, though this was subsequently modified so that they were allowed, provided they consisted of unfit men, it became very difficult to keep the numbers up. However, by good fortune and with Mr. Robinson's skilful training, the L.R.B. always managed to keep very useful bands, both brass and string, until demobilisation began. In the late summer Capt. H. L. Johnston joined on recovering from wounds, and he rendered invaluable help in all ways so long as he stayed with the battalion.

In May an order came down from the War Office which abolished the regimental subscription for the first time in the history of the regiment, but was an inevitable sequel to compulsory service. There was, however, no interference with the system of enlisting men of the type preferred, and, though a certain number of men of a different class were sent down, who were nicknamed the "Stratford O.T.C." and eventually made excellent soldiers, the general standard was on the whole maintained. It was not till 1918 that special recruiting was stopped and the regiment had to accept whatever men the recruiting officer sent them; but whatever men came in, they all soon became imbued with the spirit of the regiment and maintained its best traditions.

About this time also Army messing was taken in hand scientifically, for the first time, on a general plan. The L.R.B. had always been well fed, and the companies made responsible for looking after their men, so the system initiated by Lieut. Kelly, which had worked very well, was given up reluctantly, but the new one was an undoubted improvement. Capt. Paxman took charge, with a very capable helper in Staff-Sergt. Soman, and from the middle of 1916 onwards no unit could have been catered for better than the L.R.B.

During this year the category system of grading men came into force and originally had the following classes :—

A i. Men who were trained and fit to go abroad.

A ii. Men who were over 19, and were in training, but had not been overseas.

A iii. Men who had been overseas, who had come back wounded or sick, and who were hardening ready to go out again.

B i. Men who were fit for garrison duty abroad.

B ii. Men who were fit for duty in labour units, etc. abroad.

B iii. Men who were fit for light or sedentary duty at home or abroad.

C i. Men who were fit for garrison duty at home.

C ii. Men who were fit for light duty at home.

C iii. Men who were fit for sedentary duty at home.

D. Men who were temporarily sick

E. Men for discharge as unfit.

Later on category C was eliminated, as it was considered that any duty which the men could do in England they were capable of doing in France, and later still Class A iv was introduced, which contained A ii men who were under 19. All cases below A ii were frequently reviewed, and new cases seen by Travelling Medical Boards, which consisted of two medical officers and one combatant officer. In course of time men who were A iii or lower came to be called "category men," a terse if inaccurate description.

In order to give a rest to Lieut. and Quartermaster Petersen, who had been out with the 1st Battalion since the beginning, it was arranged that he should exchange duties with Lieut. Kelly for a time, and he came home from May till October, when these two again changed places. If transfers of this sort had been freely permitted, by arrangement between Battalion Commanders, it would have been most beneficial, for it would have given the war weary a rest, and draft-finding units the benefit of the latest experience from the Front.

The conditions for training at Fovant on the whole were good, as there was a good set of trenches, though facilities for digging were not numerous, and plenty of ground for manœuvre was available, so that Major Burnell was able to school the men in open order fighting until the time for training men was so very much shortened that this could not be fitted in.

Facilities for cricket were not great, though an attempt was made to make two concrete practice wickets. Brigade sports were held at which the L.R.B. maintained its reputation, and a match against the 3/Queen Victoria Rifles aroused much interest. One remarkably good runner, Rfn. Redhead, was unearthed, who was never beaten at three miles and over: with others he went down to the sports held by the 2nd Battalion at Ipswich, and it was hoped to find out how good he was by running him against Cpl. Ives, but unfortunately they did not meet in a race.

The concerts given during this summer and afterwards were of a very high class. A number of really fine musicians were now in the L.R.B., including as pianist Rfn. Gritton, as 'cellist Rfn. Tabb, and as singers Rfn. Ripley, Martin, Hayes, Williams, Lewis, Monument, Key, Church and C.S.M. Babbington.

In September the 2nd Battalion was moved to Sutton Veny, only some 15 miles from Fovant. Individual visits between the two battalions were freely exchanged, but unfortunately a scheme for each of them to march out half-way, so that they might all meet together, never matured owing to the exigencies of training. The 3rd Battalion officers had the great pleasure of entertaining their opposite numbers at dinner, and the evening will not readily be forgotten by those who were present.

Exeter

On November 17th, 1916, the battalion moved to Exeter, but only remained there for three weeks, which was fortunate as the billets were very much scattered, and places suitable for training purposes almost impossible to find. The battalion introduced an innovation here, to which some of the inhabitants of this cathedral city took exception, by giving a Sunday concert at the theatre in aid of the Mayoress's Fund for providing refreshments for soldiers passing through the station, but the building was packed and as many people were turned away as there were inside. The performance, which produced over £100 for the Fund, could hardly have been bettered out of London and would have been repeated if the battalion had remained longer. The string band was at its best and numbered some 30 members ; the singers were C.S.M. Babbington, Lce.-Cpl. Ripley and Rfn. Martin, while Rfn. Tabb played the 'cello and Rfn. Gritton the piano.

Dawlish

On December 8th, 1916, the battalion moved to Dawlish. On marching in its strength was weak, but, before leaving, it numbered over 1600 men and occupied every available space in the charming little town. This great increase in strength was due to leave having been granted at the beginning of the year (1917) to enrol boys of 18, of whom 700 were soon obtained. These boys were of an excellent type, and as, up to the date of the German push in 1918, it was possible to give many of them a year's training, because they were not sent out until they were 19 years old, they became really good soldiers. A large number of them proved suitable for commissions, and, besides providing officers for the regiment, furnished many to other regiments in the brigade. It may be noted here that all through the war men were being sent to the L.R.B. by other regiments to do their time in the ranks before applying for commissions. As material for making soldiers nothing could have been better, the standard of training reached was very high, the behaviour was excellent, and the reputation of the regiment was well maintained in all respects. Three new companies were added. A boxing competition took place at the Royal Hotel, in which no one proved very outstanding though the average was good.

The battalion was treated with the greatest kindness by everybody, and owes a great debt of gratitude to Mr. Peter Hoare, who allowed trench-digging to be practised in the grounds of Luscombe Castle, while a large field at Elm Grove provided a parade ground. The band played in the public gardens once a week, and on the front on Sunday mornings ;

concerts which raised a very useful sum of money were given every week in aid of the Regimental Prisoners of War Fund; the buglers played Retreat and Tattoo on the lawns once a week; and the battalion undoubtedly made a very good name for itself during its stay. At Easter sports were held, to which the whole of the neighbourhood was invited, as a small return for the many kindnesses received.

Early in 1917 an order was received that a large proportion of instructors were to be sent to France, which was reluctantly obeyed, and fresh instructors were put into training, who had only just finished their classes and begun to teach when the regiment was severely taken to task because the instruction was not good, and the C.O. censured for letting the instructors go. This was both unfair and disheartening, but the defects were soon remedied, and though the musketry returns, which are the only ones of training giving exact figures, fell off for a time, they soon recovered. The question of instructors was always made difficult because Higher Authority never seemed to realise that first-rate instructors are rare and require long training. It was quite right to insist that every one should take his turn at the fighting, but those who had been to France might well have been allowed to remain instructors so long as they retained their keenness. The problem of getting the best men was very difficult, and training was made much harder by the harassing orders received on this subject.

Blackdown

On April 23rd, 1917, the 1st London Reserve Brigade, including the L.R.B., was moved to Aisne Barracks, at Blackdown, where they found, as was to be expected, that the facilities for training were the best that had been met with. There was a range close at hand, plenty of trenches on Frith Hill, and unlimited ground for digging, assault courses, and bombing grounds, etc. Consequently the teaching could be more highly developed, and Lieut. J. S. Lindsay, a particularly good instructor, was able to do a great deal in the way of Field Engineering, as was Lieut. A. R. Thompson in rapid and other wiring. The musketry, too, which had been under Capt. A. C. Feast from early in 1916 and was now under Capt.

P. J. Aste, reached a very high standard and one worthy of the best traditions of the regiment. Except on a very few occasions, the L.R.B. headed the monthly Brigade Musketry Returns from now onwards. By this time Lewis guns were available and the subject was well taught under Lieut. P. T. Dyer, as were bombing and rifle grenades under Lieut. R. F. Lydall and afterwards Lieut. D. V. Lankester. The drill, which was successively under Lieut. Soman, Lieut. P. Titley, Lieut. D. McOwan, Lieut. H. J. F. Crisp, Capt. F. D. Charles and Capt. F. P. Barry, was always kept at a high level.

Organised games were soon started, and boys were allowed their choice of football, cricket, running, cycling, boxing, fencing, etc., in fact of any form of exercise, on two afternoons a week, besides amusing themselves on Saturdays and Sundays.

Major C. D. Burnell, who had attended the Senior Officers' School at Aldershot from January to March, was ordered out to France, and fortunately Major Soames returned to the battalion, becoming Second in Command, a position which he filled well until demobilisation. In May, Lieut. Kelly was ordered out to France and was succeeded as Q.M. by Lieut. Judge, late of the Queen Victoria Rifles.

During the stay at Aldershot, and particularly during 1917, there were numerous Command Competitions, and regiments who desired to do well had to take their men off proper systematic training in order to specialise, which was not good policy, and did not produce the result required, viz. a good standard of all-round training.

A new feature was introduced at the end of the summer in the form of platoon training. For this the men ready for draft were, for the last two weeks of the fourteen that were then allowed, struck off all duties and spent their time in learning open-order work and practising the use of the bullet and bayonet in the attack, which was at first carried out throughout the brigade on stereotyped lines that were liable to give a false impression, but afterwards on broader ones. During the second week of this course men were given the actual articles (or dummies made up in weight to represent them) that they would have to carry in fighting-order ; two nights were spent in the trenches ; and the training wound up with a field-firing practice. It was carried out under Capt. Feast, who latterly was assisted by Lieut. F. E. Pattisson and a special staff, and admirable work was done. The platoon was divided into four sections of riflemen (red), bombers (black), rifle bombers (yellow) and Lewis gunners (blue), each distinguished by a colour so that the men could easily be picked out for instructional purposes. The articles carried, with the weights, were as follows :—

PLATOON TRAINING

Dress and Equipment of a Rifleman

		Weight.
1.	Fighting Order. (Equipment : haversack on back, entrenching tool at side) . . .	$12\frac{1}{2}$ lbs.
2.	Small box respirator	$3\frac{1}{4}$,,
3.	Field dressing	—
4.	($7\frac{3}{4}$) pick or ($3\frac{1}{2}$) shovel	$3\frac{1}{2}$,,
5.	Ground sheet (Cardigan inside) . . .	$3\frac{1}{2}$,,
6.	Two grenades, with rods in side pockets . .	$3\frac{1}{2}$,,
7.	In haversack : Spare water-bottle, iron ration (sewn up), 2 days' rations, 1 pair socks, cap comforter, breech stick (2 per section) .	8 ,,
8.	Two sandbags	$\frac{3}{4}$,,
9.	120 rounds of ammunition (24 metal blocks) .	8 ,,
10.	Mess tin, with Tommy's Cooker inside . .	$1\frac{1}{2}$,,
11.	Extra flannelette in pocket	—
12.	Identity disc	—
13.	Steel helmet (red)	2 ,,
14.	Flare (improvised 5″, rod) in right breast pocket	$\frac{1}{4}$,,
15.	Wire-cutters and frog (2 per section) . . .	2 ,,
16.	Vigilant periscope in left breast pocket (2 per section)	$\frac{1}{4}$,,
17.	P. bomb (2 per section)	$1\frac{1}{4}$,,
	Total . .	$50\frac{3}{4}$ lbs.

Note.—No cleaning materials, no Rifle Grenade ammunition, and no pay-book or documents concerning operations. No knife, fork or spoon.

FIGHTING ORDER, 1918

Bomber

	Weight.
1 to 8 and 10 to 17, as above	$42\frac{1}{4}$ lbs.
13. Steel helmet (black). *Note*—weight included above	—
18. Bomb bucket with 5 bombs (No. 5) . .	8 ,,
9. 50 rounds of S.A.A.	$3\frac{1}{4}$,,
Total . .	$53\frac{1}{2}$ lbs.

Rifle Bomber

1 to 8, and 10 to 17, as above	$42\frac{1}{4}$ lbs.
13. Steel helmet (yellow). *Note*—weight included above	—
18. Bomb bucket with 5 bombs (23 S.), and rod and R.G. ammunition (25 rounds) . . .	$11\frac{1}{2}$,,
19. Cup attachment in side pocket . . .	$\frac{1}{2}$,,
9. 50 rounds of S.A.A.	$3\frac{1}{4}$,,
Total . .	$57\frac{1}{2}$ lbs.

Lewis Gunner

1 to 8, and 10 to 17, as above	$42\frac{1}{4}$ lbs.
13. Steel helmet (blue). *Note*—weight included above	—
9. 50 rounds S.A.A.	$3\frac{1}{4}$,,
20. Lewis gun equipment. (See L.G. Officer, or S.S. 143)	—
Total . .	$45\frac{1}{2}$ lbs.

The ample accommodation in the hutted barracks gave much more scope for arranging entertainments, and in the course of the time that the battalion was quartered here Capt. Stransom, who came back in the late summer of 1917, organised, with the help of Cpl. C. Hayes as author, and Rfn. E. Gritton as composer and accompanist, no less than three really high-class revues which were all witty, topical and tuneful. The last one was given for a week to big houses at the Garrison Theatre, and the Commander-in-Chief, Lieut.-Gen. Sir Archibald Murray, who was present one night, was so much amused by it that he stopped to the end, although he had intended to leave earlier as he had important business to attend to. The revues consisted for the first part of songs, etc., by the Pierrot Troupe, and for the second of small plays and interludes. An extremely clever caricature of a company orderly room, entirely sung to tunes of the day arranged to fit the words, was a very successful item, and the scenery made by Lieut. Lindsay and his assistants was a great factor in the success achieved.

The morning parade was a great feature and added much to smartness and efficiency. The whole battalion, which for a long time consisted of seven companies, fell in in line of companies in mass and was inspected and proved by the company officers. When the parade was complete it was handed over by the second in command to the Commanding Officer who, after proving it, gave the command to march off to the work of the day. Occasionally the men marched past in various formations on their way to work.

Ample funds were available for all purposes owing to the large rebate received from the canteen, and all the boys were supplied with white zephyrs and blue shorts for organised games. Inter-company competitions in running and walking were instituted, in which every man who finished in anything like reasonable time was able to gain a point for his company, and it was a fine sight to see nearly a thousand men all in clean white and blue stream across the parade ground.

War Savings Certificates were introduced early in 1917, and before the battalion was disbanded a sum of over £4000 was raised for the Government by this means. A photograph was sent to the battalion of an aeroplane, D.6949, which was purchased from this fund, and on it was "London Rifle Brigade, No. 1." A second plane was also provided.

For six months in 1918 the Rev. Guy Vernon Smith, M.C., the chaplain of the 2nd Battalion, was with the battalion, and the parade services, which were always good, were never better than when he was in charge of them. For the previous eighteen months the Chaplain had been the Rev. H. G. Walker, who did excellent work and was very popular with all ranks.

The battalion was visited at work by several distinguished visitors, including Field-Marshal Lord French and Lieut.-Gens. Sir William Robertson and Sir Ivor Maxse. On several occasions it put up demonstrations of various forms of training which won high praise. In 1918 it was honoured by a visit from H.M. King George, who spent some time in chatting with the C.O. The Guard at the Royal Pavilion on one night was found from the overseas company under Lieut. F. E. Pattisson, who had the honour of dining with their Majesties. The string band played for the Royal Party in both 1917 and 1918 and appeared to give great satisfaction.

In September, 1918, the battalion was sent with others to Newport to keep order during the railway strike. The inhabitants were delighted to have the protection of the soldiers, and, during a period of waiting in the streets, they provided tea and other refreshments, courtesies which had not been met with since the early days of the war. The bulk of the battalion was quartered in the Skating Rink, and the remainder in various schools. No rioting took place, and the four days change from the strenuous routine of training was very welcome. Wales was found to be a land of milk and honey ; there was no stint of butter and meat and, best of all, of the products of Messrs. Bass and Guinness, which had not been seen for many a long day.

The conclusion of the Armistice was celebrated by a bonfire in front of the Officers' Mess, when a hut of the coffee-stall nature, which had been used by the Physical Training Staff for storing gear, came to an untimely but glorious end. Rumours spread about the other camps that a hut had been burnt down, that £400 worth of damage had been done, that there had been a riot, and that the hose of the fire-engine had been cut when run out to extinguish the conflagration ; and there was almost disappointment, when it was found that the L.R.B. had not disgraced itself, but had merely had an uncommonly good evening's fun. On the next night the men were given a special hot dinner followed by a concert which went with a swing from start to finish.

There is no doubt that the 1st London Reserve Brigade

gained a good reputation. Major-Gen. Sir Francis Howard, an old rifleman, who must have been highly thought of by the authorities as he had to pass all divisions as trained for service before they went abroad, frequently inspected it, and said on his retirement in a letter to the Brigadier: "I cannot leave without thanking you and your brigade for the splendid way you have always played up to my strokes. You can hardly realise what an assistance it has been to me to feel that any suggestion I might make with regard to training would be taken up and thoroughly thrashed out on its merits by you and your lot, and I am very grateful to you for it."

During the war some 11,000 men were members of the London Rifle Brigade, and between seven and eight thousand of those passed through the 3rd Battalion. At first the men were young volunteers, more or less athletic; those who followed were older, and later the men were in many cases almost middle-aged; these, again, were followed by a large number of boys of eighteen and upwards, mostly from big secondary schools, and finally by boys of a less high social class and by transfers from other arms and units. Many of the men on joining had probably never left home before, and to be plunged into the publicity of a hut containing some thirty others, to perform ablutions in public and to have no privacy whatever was no doubt a severe trial. Even the everyday language was more or less strange. The discipline was strict, but in spite of this, and though many of the men were of a different class from those who generally joined the L.R.B., the amount of crime was negligible, and apparently, judging by the number of court-martial cases, far less than that in other units of the 1st London Reserve Brigade. Although every one was kept right up to the mark, the object was to help men to keep out of trouble, and not "to run them" when mistakes were due to inadvertence or inexperience. Rights in regard to leave were carefully respected, and the men had every ounce of food that belonged to them. The result was that the men played up to the best tradition of the regiment. An instance, not isolated, may be given. A detachment from another arm was posted to the 3rd Battalion. It arrived about 11.30 p.m. one night, and the men, after being taken to their huts, where they found their beds already laid down, were conducted to the dining-hall, where they had a square meal and were looked after by some of the sergeants, including the R.S.M. Next day they were reclothed, and generally tidied up, a very necessary process, and, before work started, the question of whether any leave was due to them was gone into. It was found that nearly all were due, and several were very much over due, for leave, and, although many of the men had distinctly bad conduct sheets, largely due to having overstayed leave previously, they were told that they started afresh with the L.R.B. and were sent away. They all came back to time, this party proved to be one of the best and smartest ever turned out, and crime was for the future entirely absent. All this was done without orders from the orderly room, and as a matter of course. To what is this very satisfactory result attributable ? Simply to the spirit of the L.R.B. No unit can ever possibly have had a better lot of commissioned and non-commissioned officers, and it is doubtful if any unit ever had as good. Their first thought was always for the men, to give them all that was their right and due, and to help them in every possible way. The result was that the men responded and the spirit of comradeship and good-fellowship that existed could not be surpassed. Many of the men did not realise what advantages they had had until they had lost them.

The battalion reached a very high state of efficiency in discipline, smartness, shooting and all that is required to make a good soldier. It was very frequently visited by officers and other ranks of the sister battalions when on leave from France, in itself a very healthy sign, and it is difficult to give too much praise to the staff which produced such good results. To have commanded men of such a kind is an honour which falls to the lot of few.

A *Record* edited by Capt. Pattisson, which gave briefly all the doings of the various battalions of the L.R.B., was issued from time to time in 1918 and proved most interesting, and it was a great pity that the idea was not thought of earlier. Many of the staff have been mentioned already. Capt. Bennett, the first Adjutant, carried out his duties, especially on the secretarial side, with great devotion, till he was succeeded in August, 1918, by Capt. Chambers, who had assisted the C.O. in all the training from July, 1916, and who deserves a special word of praise for his sturdy common sense, energy, coolness under a rain of orders from high authority, and clear-headedness in all matters of detail, which were very great factors in the good results attained. Regimental Sergt.-Major C. Whittingham did extremely useful work in regard to returns, which were always most admirably kept in spite of their complications, and also in the Sergeants' Mess, which owed its consistently high tone very largely to his influence. R.Q.M.S. Freeman and R.Q.M.S. Anderson, who succeeded him when he went off as Equipment Officer in the R.A.F., both performed their duties admirably, and Capt. Judge carried on the good work begun by Capt. Kelly, doing his best to assist every one. Lieut. Hall, who, as assistant adjutant, took over Capt. Bennett's secretarial work, was also very helpful, particularly in regard to unravelling the intricate details of demobilisation.

Two other names deserve special mention. One is that of Capt. H. S. Ferguson, who commanded the depot at Bunhill Row from the autumn of 1914 until the end of the war. The hard work that he did and his ready kindness and courtesy will not soon be forgotten by those who had the pleasure of working with him. The success of the Mutual Aid and Prisoners of War Funds were largely due to his efforts. The other is that of Sergt. T. Malone, who came to the L.R.B. as Sergt.-Major in 1897 and gave up the post in 1904 on the termination of his engagement. He then became assistant secretary and did valuable work in that capacity for ten years. On the outbreak of war, though no longer a young man, he rejoined the service and went to France with the 1st Battalion as a rifleman, with the acting rank of Officers' Mess Sergeant. There he remained until the summer of 1916, when in spite of his protests, he was sent home to help the training of recruits. Very shortly afterwards he was put in charge of the special N.C.O. class, and by precept and example, coupled with his good judgment of men, he was of the greatest help in that direction. He always refused further promotion, but served on until the Armistice. A fine soldier of the best possible type, absolutely selfless, and devoted to duty and the L.R.B., no record of the regiment would be complete without a special mention of his name, and he thoroughly deserved the

Meritorious Service Medal granted to him at the conclusion of hostilities.

In the early part of 1919 the battalion melted away very rapidly, as nearly every man was badly wanted for some post or other in civil life, but some stayed on loyally until all the men were disposed of. In the latter part of February the remains were moved to Shoreham, and a week or two later those who were not due for demobilisation were sent off to join the 5th Rifle Brigade at Rugeley, but it was not till the beginning of April that the head-quarters were moved to London for the final winding up. During the last two months Capt. Stransom, who had only stayed back in order to help, took over the duties of Adjutant, a thankless task at that time, and carried them out with his customary thoroughness and energy.

L.R.B. PRISONERS OF WAR FUND

THE Fund was originated in September, 1916, by a Committee consisting of Lieut.-Col. A. S. Bates, Mrs. Bates, Sergt. W. G. Payne, and Sergt. W. J. A. Tinkham, with Captain H. S. Ferguson as Hon. Secretary, the object being to provide for prisoners parcels of food and clothing which were transmitted through the Central Prisoners of War Committee.

At the close of the year 1917 there were 107 prisoners in Germany and 14 interned in Switzerland, entailing a cost of £268 13s. every four weeks. The necessary funds were provided from three sources: Total Adopters, Partial Adopters, and Subscriptions and Donations, aided by "The Ladies of the Regiment Fund," raised by Mrs. Arthur Bates. The number of prisoners rose rapidly during 1918 until it reached 484, and the cost of providing the individual parcels also increased, entailing an expenditure of £1345 10s. every four weeks. Towards this the regular income amounted to £649 only, and the funds in hand would have been exhausted in two months. At this juncture Lieut.-Col. King put the matter before Mr. Thomas Forbes and Mr. F. N. Large, who started a subscription list at Lloyds and raised for the Fund no less a sum than £3249 3s., thus relieving the Committee of pressing anxiety. The sending of parcels was stopped at the Armistice in November, 1918. On the return to England of the first man it was learned that many of the men taken in March, 1918, though they had been given camp numbers and addresses in Germany, had never been to these camps, but had been kept working behind the German lines in France and Flanders, and that, with few exceptions, the parcels and bread, addressed to them to the camps in Germany where they were supposed to be, had never reached them. The value of unacknowledged parcels from the regiment amounted to over £1000.

Of the total number of prisoners, 484, the number repatriated was 460, 18 died in Germany and 6 were unaccounted for. On returning to England the prisoners expressed their great gratitude for all that had been done for them, stating that, without the help rendered to them, they must have starved. Among the strong supporters of the Fund must be mentioned Mr. C. F. Wilbe, as Secretary, and the members of the American Market, Mr. F. L. Pattisson who organised the Stock Exchange Foreign Market Fund, the members of Lloyds, Mrs. Arthur Bates and the subscribers to the "Ladies of the Regiment Fund" (who subscribed in all £1611) and many other generous subscribers and adopters.

The total expenditure for parcels and supplies dispatched amounted to £6762 13s. 8d. and, upon the closing of the Fund, the unexpended balance of £3737 19s. 3d. was, with the generous consent of the donors, paid over to the Mutual Aid Fund.

In addition to this sum an unexpended balance of £374 7s. 4d., remaining in the hands of the "Ladies of the Regiment Fund," was by consent also paid over to the Mutual Aid Fund.

Among those who rendered invaluable help as members of the Committee or otherwise were Mrs. Arthur Bates, Mrs. G. R. Tod, Mrs. M. H. Soames, Sergt. Tinkham, Cpl. Yerbury, Sergt. Payne, and especially Capt. H. S. Ferguson, upon whom as Hon. Secretary very heavy work devolved.

L.R.B. MUTUAL AID FUND

FORMED in November, 1915, as a Fund "for the purpose of giving help to members of the regiment who may be in need of assistance owing to injuries or incapacity arising out of the war or to aid their dependents," the "Mutual Aid Fund" was the outcome of the "London Rifle Brigade Aid Society," formed and supported by the officers and members of the 2nd Battalion to provide comforts for the 1st Battalion in France. The objects of the Aid Society having ceased to be necessary, the larger scheme of a regimental "Mutual Aid Fund" was initiated by Major C. Riviere Bland and received the cordial approval of the officers commanding the three battalions and the officers and members generally. A scheme was prepared and submitted to Col. Earl Waldegrave, V.D., Lieut.-Col. Earl Cairns, C.M.G., and the Bishop of London, K.C.V.O., who consented to be named as Trustees.

The scheme provided that the Fund should be administered by a Committee of five, two of whom (to be old members of the regiment) were to be nominated by the Trustees, and one each by the officers commanding the three battalions (to be as far as practicable officers, N.C.O.'s or men actually serving). The original Committee consisted of Major C. W. Cornish, V.D., and Mr. W. J. M. Burton (nominated by the Trustees), Mr. Newton Dunn (for 1st Battalion), Major C. R. Bland (2nd Battalion), C.Q.M.S. Anderson (3rd Battalion), with Captain H. S. Ferguson as Hon. Secretary.

The formation of the Fund was notified in Orders, and from the first it received generous support from individual officers and members, canteen and mess funds, special entertainments and collections; old members and friends of the regiment were also liberal contributors. After the Armistice in November, 1918, and the closing of the Regimental

Prisoners of War Funds the unexpended moneys in hand of these Funds were, with the generous consent of the donors, transferred to the "Mutual Aid Fund," which thus benefited to the extent of £3760 5s. 4d. from the regimental "Prisoners of War Fund" and by a sum of £374 7s. 4d. from the "Ladies of the Regiment Prisoners of War Fund."

From the Annual Report at the 31st December, 1919, the Fund then amounted to £7110 4s.—the total of grants made out of the Fund prior to that date amounted to £709 5s. 8d.

The method of the Committee has been to get into, and to keep in, touch with the dependents in every case of men reported killed and with cases of serious injury, and to ascertain in what way, if any, help could be most effectively given. Some 228 cases in all have been dealt with. In many cases help was declined by dependents; in others temporary help was needed until pensions were fixed. Grants have been made to meet specific needs, such as for additional clothing, for the education of children, for keeping a home together, for expenses of sickness and convalescence, for assistance to obtain work or to earn a livelihood. Besides monetary grants, it has been possible to assist in finding work for men who were not reinstated by their old employers, and by obtaining nominations for children to the London Orphan School, Watford, the Orphan Working School, the Alexandra Orphanage and the Reedham Orphanage. (A generous donation to the London Orphan School by an old member entitles the regiment to five votes at each half-yearly election for thirty years.)

Many letters have been received expressing great gratitude for the help given. Providing assistance for the education of the children is likely for some years to come to constitute an important part of the work of the Committee.

For more than four years Capt. H. S. Ferguson as Hon. Secretary devoted himself unremittingly to tracing those in need of help, and giving kindly sympathetic consideration to their various needs. The Committee greatly regret the severe illness which, early in 1920, compelled him to relinquish his duties. He is succeeded as Hon. Secretary by Capt. A. Read.

A LAST WORD

THE preceding account of the L.R.B., in peace and in war, is offered as a tribute to all those who have laboured at any time for the welfare of the regiment in the truest loyalty and affection.

It is not feasible to render thanks or bestow appreciation individually, nor would it be the wish of members of the regiment of any period that this should be done. Just as they gave their services without thought of gain or personal advertisement, so would they now be content to rest assured that, if any recognition of their efforts were desirable, it would best take the form of the setting forth of the whole history of the L.R.B. and all for which it stood to them.

To those who gave their lives in the War no assurance of remembrance and gratitude could be more fitting than that we should think of them (as they always thought of themselves) in relation to the regiment to which they gave so much before they offered the greatest gift of all.

But this History is not dedicated to the past members of the regiment alone. It is offered also to the L.R.B. in its process of reconstruction and to all future members, in the hope that it may serve them not only as a record of a most gloriously worthy past, but also as an inspiration and encouragement in any and every enterprise upon which they may embark.

After the War, uncertainty as to the future hampered the life of the Old Members' Club. The questions of its relationship to the new regiment, and of what accommodation, if any, would be available at Head-quarters, combined to prevent its launching out on a definite line of its own. However, in November, 1919, one very definite step was taken towards holding all the members of the regiment together, when the *L.R.B. Record* was re-started as a monthly publication.

Containing as it does the latest Regimental information and previously unpublished statistics and records, as well as matter of a lighter nature, its appearance is now eagerly awaited by over a thousand subscribers.

The period of suspense, due to political considerations, in regard to the future of the whole Territorial Army came to an end in February, 1920, when the L.R.B. became an integral part of the scheme for the army of this country. From the point of view of the reconstitution of the regiment this interval was most deplorable, and its effect has been felt very considerably, as many old members had scattered or had formed new ties that left them less free than in the past.

The battalion is now, however, once more on its feet as a living and active body. Numbers are at the time of writing small, but the nucleus of past members who have re-enlisted (many after resigning their commissions in order to do so) is representative of those who took the lead in the many-sided activities of pre-war days. As the new generation comes along and more of the old members find themselves able to return, they will join a really live battalion. The inspiration of a tradition of past service and success is there, and behind them is a History, which will help to re-build the L.R.B. on the lines that proved so sound and valuable before.

One new and welcome asset there is. The story of the Territorials during the War has dealt a knock-out blow to the preconceived notions and prejudices of the Regular Army (and even of the general public) regarding the efficiency and value of a citizen army. The difficulty now lies in the contrary direction, owing to over-anxiety on the part of the authorities to help and offer facilities, but, contrasted with the past, this attitude can only be full of encouragement for the new Force. The fitting close, therefore, to this History is the hope that all success may attend the enterprises of the new battalion, and that it may quickly reach its full establishment, perpetuating the memory and carrying on the success of the London Rifle Brigade.

MEMOIR OF BRIG.-GEN. R. H. HUSEY, D.S.O., M.C.

RALPH HAMER HUSEY, the elder son of Charles Hubert Husey, was born on 25th November, 1881. After four years at Marlborough, followed by a year in Germany, he tried the Stock Exchange for a time, and then went into his father's office before finally deciding to accept an opening as a chartered accountant offered him by his uncle, Ernest Husey. With his customary energy he took up his old school subjects again for the preliminary examination, and, after passing that, went on with his professional studies, until he was on the point of qualifying when war broke out.

So far from looking upon Germany as his spiritual home, he came back from that country firmly convinced that the Germans, as a nation, were bent upon removing the British Empire from their path, and that, as war was inevitable, it was his duty to prepare himself to do his share when it came, and to induce others to do the same. Accordingly he joined the Hertfordshire Yeomanry as a trooper in 1901, and, after five years' service with them, accepted a commission in 1906 as 2nd Lieutenant in the London Rifle Brigade. He was posted to "A" Company and remained with it until he became a Field Officer, rising to Lieutenant in 1909 and Captain in 1912.

When the call came in August, 1914, he was one of the first to volunteer for active service, and so anxious was he to take part in the fighting, that the delays and uncertainties about the movements of his battalion led him to talk seriously at one time of exchanging, but he crossed with it in November to France. By January, 1915, he was commanding one of the double companies that were formed on the adoption of the new organisation by the Territorials, and on 17th April, after going untouched through the trench warfare at Ploegsteert, he was promoted Second in Command of his battalion.

During his first serious engagement, the second battle of Ypres, on 13th May, he went out into the open in characteristic fashion and endeavoured to restore the situation, which had become unsatisfactory owing to the retirement of some men of other regiments through misunderstanding an order. While engaged on this he was so severely wounded that he had to go back to England, where two shrapnel bullets were taken out of his knee, and it was not until 4th October that he was allowed, after a rest at Tadworth with the

Brigadier General R. H. Husey, D.S.O. and Bar, M.C.

3rd (Reserve) Battalion, L.R.B., to rejoin his own battalion which was then at Blendecques.

The following months were spent in harassing work in the line and in preparing for the attack on Gommecourt; but on the day itself, 1st July, 1916, he was not with the fighting line, as orders had just come out that Seconds in Command were in future to be sent back to the Transport lines. His protests, however, against being sent such a distance back were so vigorous and persistent that eventually a post was found for him as Liaison Officer at Divisional Head-quarters. A month later, while in the trenches on 3rd August, he received a slight wound on the head, which did not interfere with his duties, and on 15th he took over the command of his battalion in succession to Lieut.-Col. Bates, who was invalided home.

During the heavy fighting on the Somme from 5th September to 8th October he directed the operations of the battalion and then took it to Laventie, where he was wounded for the third time while going round the front line on 17th February, 1917, to see that all the arrangements for a raid, which was to be made that night, were complete. Although the top of his finger had been shot away, he insisted on having it merely dressed, and came away from hospital the next day, as his absence would have prevented Major Wallis, his second in command, from going on leave; but this unselfish neglect ended in his having to go back to hospital on 20th March, where his condition was found to be so serious that he was not allowed to leave until after the battle of Arras.

At the disastrous attack of 14th August on Polygon Wood he was wounded for the fourth time, very severely in the stomach, and again had to go back to England, but he rejoined on 3rd December, though only his iron determination and strong personality can account for any Medical Officer having been persuaded to sign him up as really fit for service by then. On 26th December he was appointed to the temporary command of the 169th Infantry Brigade, as much an honour to the man as a compliment to the regiment, and in January, 1918, his well-deserved D.S.O. was published in the Honours List.

He put the seal on his magnificent work by his conduct of the stubborn defence at Gavrelle against the great German attack on Vimy on 26th March, for which he was given a bar to his D.S.O. on the field, the official account being as follows:—

"During the enemy attack, when the enemy approached close to his Battalion Head-quarters, he held the forward end of a communication trench with the personnel of his head-quarters and a few other men, and largely assisted in breaking up the enemy's attack. He used a rifle himself at close range and inflicted many casualties on the enemy. He then conducted an obstinate withdrawal to the next line of defence, where the enemy were finally held up. He set a magnificent example of courage and determination."

Various accounts of what he was supposed to have said after the battle appeared in print, but those who knew him best were very sceptical about their accuracy, and those who were present state that his actual remarks were typically outspoken and very different from what they were represented to have been.

On 20th April he was appointed to the temporary command of the 167th Infantry Brigade, and on 4th May he was promoted Brigadier-General to command the 25th Infantry Brigade, which was stationed on the Aisne, but his gallant career was closed during the fighting there on 27th. The official statement was that in the early hours of that day the Germans attacked on the brigade front, and in a very short time reached the Brigade Head-quarters. When the enemy was only a few yards distant, Brig.-General Husey made his way to the river to organise a second line of defence. He also sent Lieut. Rice to organise the line, placing himself at the head of a bridge in order to make sure, before allowing it to be demolished, that all his troops had crossed. A few hours afterwards the enemy crossed the river and captured the village. It was a long time before anything more definite was heard.

The only facts known about his movements on the day come from Lieut.-Col. Henry C. Richardson of the 2nd R.B., who wrote :—

" I spoke to him on the telephone when the enemy was approaching my Battalion Head-quarters—very shortly after that I was hit, and when being helped back I passed Brigade Head-quarters outside which I saw your son and spoke to him, telling him what I knew of the situation ; it took me a long time to get back to the Aisne, but, when I got to the main bridge close to Germicourt, your son was standing there and I spoke to him again. He told me that he was shortly going to have the bridges blown up, and advised me to get back as quick as I could ; that was, I think, about 8 a.m. I never saw him again ; the shelling at the time, both gas and high explosive, all round the bridge was very heavy indeed. I was much distressed to see in the paper later when I was in hospital in London that your son was missing. Both he and I were new to the brigade, but I had already realised what a splendid man he was ; he knew several of my friends and I had tea with him only the evening before the attack ; we neither of us were expecting a big attack then, but I think he had already heard some rumours. He was absolutely calm when I saw him at the bridge and spoke to me as calmly as if nothing unusual was happening."

At last information was received that a German orderly had reported that he was brought into Le Thour unconscious from concussion, and that he died there. As he had always said that he would never be taken prisoner, and had always instilled into his men that their duty was to fight to the last, there can be little doubt that he was stunned with a rifle while living up to his words.

In addition to the honours already mentioned his name appeared four times in despatches—22nd July, 1915; 4th January, 1917;

24th December, 1917; and 29th December, 1918; and in March, 1917, he was awarded the 4th Class of the Montenegrin Order of Danilo.

Hard-working, cheery and self-sacrificing, *Ralph Husey* was welcome wherever he went, and a man whom anyone would be proud to call a friend. High ideals, shown by actions rather than words, guided his life, and they were accompanied by a modesty which was quite unaffected, and a directness of speech which never gave offence. A strong character, he exercised a healthy influence over all with whom he came in contact, and this was particularly marked in connection with the young officers who saw him during his stay at Tadworth. During his peace-time service with the L.R.B. he was always to the front when there was anything to be done, and could be depended upon to see it through. When the first party marched down to Brighton in 1911, he went down with it all the way for pure sport. In 1913 he led the battalion team to victory in record time over the twelve-mile course of the Territorial Marathon race, a trying run in marching order for a man who was quite unfit and had not intended to take part. In 1914 he was in command of the detachment which put up another record—over the Brighton march.

War proved, literally as by fire, of what steel his courage was wrought, and the heroic firmness of his spirit. A man of middle height, a well-built figure, well set up, always immaculate, in peace and in war, so far as circumstances would permit, no one could have set a higher standard in the matter of personal appearance. His eyes were his most arresting feature: nearly always the spirit of fun would show itself for those who could see, but on occasion a different fire shone out, and then it was well to beware. The war left its mark upon him, as is well shown by two photographs, both in almost the same position, one taken in the early days and the other reproduced here. In the former his light heart is evident: in the latter there is a sternness formerly unknown, but, if examined carefully for a little time, the underlying spirit is wonderfully apparent.

Absolutely fearless, never asking from others what he was not prepared to do himself, and able to say exactly what he meant without causing irritation, he had all the qualities required in a leader of men, and obtained their confidence so completely that they would follow him anywhere and respond loyally to any call that he made upon them. Though not professionally trained, he unmistakably possessed the faculty of gauging a military situation, as was shown by his letters while on the Aisne, and, though not good at finding his way by map, he had the gift of making the best use of ground. Despite the alleged want of appreciation displayed by the Higher Authority towards the Territorials, he had plenty of opportunities for going on the Staff, but refused them all, because he felt very strongly that, as long as his health remained comparatively unimpaired, his proper place was in the fighting line. He was genuinely diffident about his reception by the Brigade of Regulars which he was appointed to command, but a chance remark of one of the young officers in it revealed that he produced a fine impression while he was spared to carry out his duties with it. What his superior officers thought of him, can be gathered from their letters.

Maj.-Gen. W. Hastings Anderson, who served for a year with the 8th Division and is now Commandant at the Staff College, writes :—

" His career had been such a splendid one, and his gallantry and military knowledge had made him such a marked man that his death was regretted by a very great number in the army, both the older officers who had marked his career, and the others who had served with him and under him. . . . Regular soldiers started the war with every chance of advancement in their favour ; he made good by sheer force of character and soldierly qualities, which were bound to bring him to the front. I should like you to know the admiration I felt for him and the deep sense of loss which his very gallant death has brought."

Brig.-Gen. E. S. D'E. Coke, who commanded 169th Brigade, from its formation in January, 1917, until the Armistice, writes :—

" I regard Husey as the finest example of the ' Born Soldier ' I have ever met. Courageous and cool in emergencies, his men would follow him anywhere. One of his secrets of success was undoubtedly that he never asked more of any man than he was prepared to do himself. His great personal popularity naturally added to his influence, and I can recall no name in the whole 56th Division which stood higher than did Husey's."

Maj.-Gen. Sir C. P. A. Hull, K.C.B., who commanded the 56th Division during the greater part of its existence, writes :—

" Husey was one of those who always more than pulled his weight. A brilliant soldier and a good friend. I never saw him without a smile on his face, however vile the conditions of the moment might be. When we last met we were in hospital together in 1917 after he had been badly wounded ; he was still smiling and only anxious to be in harness again. I always thought he would go far, but it was not to be ; the army lost a great leader, and myself a great personal friend."

Maj.-Gen. W. Heneker, who was in command of the 8th Division, in which Gen. Husey commanded the 25th Infantry Brigade, writes :—

" . . . When his front line was broken Gen. Husey with his Brigade Major, Capt. Pascoe of the Rifle Brigade, collected the remnants of the brigade and made a stand outside the brigade dug-out and trench. Capt. Pascoe was, unfortunately, killed there leading a counter-attack. Gen. Husey, finding he was surrounded, decided to drop back to the Germicourt position on the Aisne itself. He reported that he was doing this to Divisional Head-quarters, and this was the last I ever heard of him. He was one of the best Brigadiers I had come across during the war—very gallant, full of energy, and resourceful. His men had the most perfect confidence in him, and would do anything for him. His loss was a grievous blow to me, and I missed his help very much when I came to reform the division after the Aisne retreat, and prepare it for the subsequent fighting which faced it."

This is not the place to say much about his home and private life, but he was a devoted son and brother, whose loss has left a blank that will never be filled, and to his friends he was a source of pure delight, the first man to be chosen when a party was to be formed. For some years he played for the Marlborough Nomads, but as he was one of the football unfortunates, who have more than their share of accidents, it was a relief when he gave the game up. A light weight with good seat and hands, he was a fine and daring horseman, who knew no greater pleasure than a day in the saddle.

Of the many names that will be for ever honoured by the London Rifle Brigade in connection with the war that of *Ralph Husey* will always stand first.

APPENDICES

APPENDIX A

Details of Work leading up to and the Attack with Asphyxiating Gas at Loos, September 25th, 1915

Capt. R. E. Otter, Lieuts. F. D. Charles, F. H. Wallis and A. B. White were attached to special companies of the R.E. on 3/9/15 and proceeded to Helfaut for instruction. On the following day a lecture was given by 2nd Lieut. Hill, R.E., on the mechanism of the gas cylinders, and these four officers were then put in charge of squads.

The cylinders were about 2′ 6″ high and weighed about 60 lb. each. They contained 60 lbs. each of gas in a liquid state, which took from 2 to 2½ minutes to discharge. Two pipes were used when discharging the gas, the parapet pipe, 10′ long (placed on the parapet when the attack took place), and a connecting pipe, preferably armoured and flexible, about 7′ long.

Squads were practised daily at connecting the pipes, and gas was occasionally turned on for exhibition purposes.

On September 13th the companies moved to Verquin and were billeted there until the day before the attack. Several visits were paid to the trenches from Verquin.

Each officer was given a section of 3 sergeants and 30 corporals. About 10 to 15 of each section were men, who had experienced trench warfare, specially transferred from regiments, and the balance were specially enlisted men with the rank of corporal who had knowledge of chemistry.

The 47th Division front, facing Loos, was served by 6 sections of No. 189 Company R.E. This company included the sections under Capt. Otter and Lieut. Wallis. The former also acted as second in command and superintended the left of the division line. Lieut. Charles's section occupied a front in the 15th Division's line (see below). Lieut. Wallis's section was on the extreme right of the line from which the attack was to be launched.

Plan of Attack

Each section had 12 to 14 batteries of gas, each battery consisting of 12 cylinders. On the right of the attacking line, from which no advance was made, three sections were detailed to discharge 6 minutes of gas and then smoke candles were to be burnt for 34 minutes.

It was known that the Germans were supplied with respirators, and that their machine gunners had oxygen helmets which protected them, if carefully used, for 30 minutes. Respirators only last for 15 minutes, and then require to be dipped again in hypo solution. It was hoped that, in the surprise caused by the gas, the Germans would use all their solution in the first instance. It was, therefore, originally proposed to discharge gas for 38 minutes followed by 2 minutes of thick smoke, thus ensuring that all the infantry and machine gunners would be accounted for. Our infantry was to advance under cover of the thick smoke. Unfortunately the supply of gas was cut down, and the final arrangement was 12 minutes of gas, 8 minutes of smoke, 12 minutes of gas and 8 minutes of smoke. At 38 minutes after zero an additional smoke candle was to be lighted, with a triple candle.

On the night of September 18th the cylinders arrived at railhead, and on the two following nights they were carried up to the dump by horse transport. All the wheels were muffled and, in many cases, the hoofs of the horses were put in partially filled sandbags. From the dump the cylinders were carried to the trenches by men of the 4th Battalion Welsh Regiment (T.F.).

The cylinders were dug in under the parapet and sandbagged. Capt. Otter superintended this work for the whole front of the 47th Division.

On September 24th the whole personnel moved into the trenches carrying pipes, spanners, etc. Each section was supplied with two Vermorel sprayers to clear the trench of gas in case of leaking pipes or broken cylinders. All the officers, N.C.O.'s and men connected with the gas wore special brassards on their arms.

In the 47th Division the front line was held by the Civil Service Rifles (15th Londons), but, with the exception of a few sentries, the actual front line was given up to the R.E. The 4th Welsh were detailed to supply two men to each battery as reserves and to light smoke candles. Orders had been given for all men to wear " smoke helmets," which were only to be pulled down to prevent asphyxiation by our own gas.

Bridges had been erected over the trenches to facilitate the advance of the infantry. Numerous scaling ladders were also supplied. During the whole night of the 24th the British artillery kept up a fairly heavy fire, to which the enemy made no reply. The Civil Service stated that no one could have lived in the German front trench that day.

The Attack by the 47th Division, 25/9/15

Between 4.30 and 5 a.m. word was sent that the gas attack was to commence at 5.50 a.m. and that the infantry would assault at

6.30 a.m. The wind was then blowing at about 3 m.p.h. from the south-west. Punctually at 5.50 a.m. the gas was discharged and was blown towards the enemy's trenches. Rockets were immediately sent up by the Germans, and their artillery commenced to shell our trenches with shrapnel and small H.E. In about a quarter of an hour two big howitzers got to work and paid particular attention to our C.T.'s behind Capt. Otter. Our own artillery plastered the German front line and support trenches during the gas and lifted when the attack took place.

The 1/6th and 1/7th Londons, who came into the assembly trenches 10 yards behind the front line, carried out the attack. The advance was exceedingly well done, the men being as steady as if at drill. They advanced under cover of the thick smoke, practically shoulder to shoulder. The enemy front line was entered and captured in a few minutes. Large bodies of Germans marched over from the right (in front of the three cylinder batteries) and surrendered. It was reported to the gas men that the front German trench was full of dead Germans. This was evidently correct, as practically no rifle or machine-gun fire hindered our infantry's advance. The Post Office Rifles and Civil Service were in support and reserve.

The Attack by the 15th Division, 25/9/15

The following is the account written by Lieut. F. D. Charles:

The R.E. section moved off from Mazingarbe at 5.30 p.m., 24/9/15, and the intervening two miles to our trenches in front of Loos were covered in about 3½ hours by my section, which got in first. The men were all carrying pipes and spanners, and a halt was called every hour. On arrival at the trenches our first job was to put everything in order in preparation for the attack, the exact hour of which was to be telegraphed later, and each man was instructed to put on his brassard, a red, white and green vertically striped affair, which, if clean, could not very well be mistaken for that of a staff officer. It served as our authority for giving orders, and also as a preventative against being ordered "over the top" with the assaulting infantry.

The time of the attack was telegraphed to me at 4.40 a.m. 25/9/15. The infantry, after being told the time of the attack by us, issued a rum ration to each man who wanted it, and then started getting their men together, instructing them slowly without hurry and very clearly, so that each man knew exactly what to do when the time came. It is a matter of interest that the time of the assault was taken from us.

At 5.50 a.m. we turned on the gas, which was slowly carried towards the enemy's lines. The wind was blowing at the time about south-west and very little over 1 m.p.h. The Germans, who had not fired a shot all night, immediately plastered our parapet with shrapnel, machine-gun and rifle fire. The shrapnel did a large amount of damage to our pipes, and, through this fact and the eagerness of the men to turn on the gas before tightening up the connections, our trench was very soon filled with gas. After about 20 minutes the rifle fire died away altogether to everyone's satisfaction, but then came our most difficult time. The infantry in the trenches, finding the heat inside their smoke helmets trying and experiencing some difficulty in breathing, were inclined to draw them up to get a couple of breaths of fresh air, with the result that quite a number of them were more or less seriously gassed. Directly these men found themselves coughing they wrenched their helmets off and staggered down the trench, making it very difficult for us to work or even to move at all. Also at this period the wind changed slightly and some of the smoke, which had been thickened, poured down the trench, but, fortunately, did not cause any confusion.

For some reason the assault did not go out exactly to the minute but waited for some 5 to 10 minutes. It may have been because, instead of each man climbing over the parapet opposite to himself, the attack was commenced in five columns which fanned out after passing through specially prepared gaps in our own wire. News from bombers, coming back for fresh supplies of bombs, reported that there was practically no opposition in the first German trenches, and within 20 minutes our infantry was practically through the 4th enemy line.

The Germans now commenced shelling our reserves with heavy H.E., but did not appear to have many guns and did no damage to us as all the supports and reserves came up C.T.'s.

At about 7.30 a.m. I started to get my section home, and, whilst being held up by troops coming up, crossing the head of a sap, I looked over the top out of curiosity and saw the guns galloping up over specially prepared bridges, the cavalry jumping their horses over trenches and the first batch of prisoners, roughly about 300, being brought in. Far away it was possible to see our infantry in a mass of confused figures, but, as I had no glasses, I could not distinguish exactly what they were doing.

September 26th.—My company was sent up at 10 a.m. to collect any unused cylinders, and all pipes and spanners. I got my section as far as the outskirts of Vermelles and then halted them to enable us to have a look round. On passing into the open in front of the houses I saw a most wonderful sight, just like the picture of a battle in a child's picture book before the war. There were batteries of guns practically wheel to wheel with their ammunition limbers some hundred yards in rear; the latter kept galloping up with fresh supplies. A little behind still were massed regimental transports, bridging trains, machine-gun limbers and even cookers with hot food or tea going.

The main Lens road was chock-a-block with G.S. wagons, limbers and fresh infantry going one way, whilst wounded men and relieved troops, mostly smothered in mud and with only their smoke helmets on their heads and nearly all with their swords still fixed, were going in the opposite direction. It was impossible for my men to work as two batteries of field guns were in action some 30 yards in rear of our old front line and the enemy was making excellent practice with heavy H.E.

The Attack of the 2nd Division, 25/9/15

The following is the account written by Lieut. A. B. White :

On 13/9/15 I joined the 186th Company R.E. at Busnes. Normally a company consists of 10 sections of 30 corporals with 2 sergeants and 1 officer. Actually, when I arrived, the company consisted of 17 sections, owing to the change of front allotted to it. Eventually it was divided into two halves and called 186th and 188th. I was given charge of a section, 2 sergeants, 30 corporals and a cook. These men had been drawn from three sources : (a) From battalions in the trenches, (b) from battalions at home, and (c) from special enlistment. The actual figures under these three heads in my section were as follows : (a) 11, (b) 10, (c) 11=32 N.C.O.'s. The cook was a Permanent Base man, but came up to the trenches with the section.

The front allotted to me was 350 yards long, measured as the crow flies. The position was astride the Bethune–La Bassee road, south-east of Guinchy. It was held alternately by the 1st Battalion King's Liverpools and the 1st Battalion Herts (T.F.) of the 6th Infantry Brigade.

On 17/9/15 we left Busnes on motor lorries and proceeded to our Brigade area, where we billeted. The next day I reported to the brigade and inspected the emplacements on our front. These had been planned by an officer of R.E. There were 14 in all on my front, but one, being a dangerous re-entrant, was not used. Each was intended to hold 15 cylinders. It was made by digging away the fire step and substituting a wooden platform supported by strong stakes, leaving ample room for the cylinders below it. All arrangements for carrying the cylinders into the trenches were in the hands of the Brigade. My men were solely responsible for placing them in the trenches. The cylinders were all in wooden boxes in a train. The latter was shunted into a siding at Gorre, where the arrangements were that a fatigue party of 1 sergeant and 10 corporals from each section should unscrew all the boxes, remove the cylinders and loosen all the dome covers. The cylinders were then to be replaced in their boxes and only one screw inserted. This system was carried out for a time until the arrival of a General Officer, who ordered all the cylinders to be put back into the train and no more to be opened there. This change of plan was not notified to Brigade or Section Officers. The result was that we found that many of the caps would not move at all when we got the cylinders into the trenches. It was, finally, necessary to obtain specially long spanners for the job, which could quite well have been done at the train. The cylinders arrived in lorries at a dumping point, where they were taken out of their boxes and slung on poles. These were carried by infantry carrying parties to the emplacements. Each cylinder was carried by two men and there was a relief for each. One N.C.O. was in charge of each group of four cylinders. A definite route in and out of the trenches was assigned to each party, and all C.T.'s were blocked by sentries to avoid congestion. The weight of a full cylinder varied from 120 to 160 lb. The arrangements worked very well, and, as the cylinders reached their emplacements, they were put into position and a sandbag wall was built up as protection. The cylinders arrived as follows : 4 per emplacement on the 18th, 4 more on the 19th, and 2 on the 20th.

September 21st.—I withdrew my men in the morning to the billets at Gorre in accordance with instructions, leaving six men in the trenches with two Vermorel sprayers. One more cylinder per emplacement arrived on the night of 21/22nd and a further one the next evening, making 12 per emplacement in all.

On the afternoon of the 23rd I left Gorre with my section and their pipes on two lorries, and unloaded them at the brigade dump. As soon as it was dark, the pipes were carried up into the trench and placed on pegs along the parapet. It was raining hard and the trenches were very muddy, rendering the task of carrying 10-foot pipes along narrow trenches and round the traverses exceedingly difficult. No arrangements had been made to accommodate my men in the trenches, so we returned to a supporting point, where the men slept in the cellars.

On *Friday, 24th*, the section returned to the front line and prepared everything for the attack. Each emplacement had two 10-foot iron pipes for throwing over the parapet and there was one spare one to every two emplacements. For connecting the cylinders with the jet pipes there were three different kinds of pipes, viz. iron, copper and flexible armoured tubes. As far as possible there was one flexible and one stiff tube per emplacement. In one or two difficult places two copper or flexible tubes were used. There were two spanners to each emplacement, one of them being adjustable. The men were told off as follows : two to each emplacement, one to each of the two sprayers, two spare men and one officer's orderly. Each sergeant was responsible for one-half of the front and he had at his disposal one spare man and one of the two abovementioned sprayers.

At 10 p.m. I reported to Brigade Head-quarters, about 900 yards from the front line, where I waited to ascertain zero hour. Here watches were set with Brigade, and I was made responsible for notifying the time of zero to the battalion on my front (1st Battalion King's Liverpool).

September 25th.—At 3.50 a.m. a message was received from the division that the hour of zero would be 5.50 a.m., I immediately proceeded to the front line, taking with me printed instructions for each emplacement as follows :

Zero to 0·12′ six cylinders gas.
0·12′ to 0·20′ four smoke candles.
0·20′ to 0·32′ six cylinders gas.
0·32′ to 0·38′ four smoke candles.
0·38′ to 40′ two triple smoke candles
0·40′ assault.

The instructions also provided for gas to be run concurrently with the smoke, if necessary, and that all cylinders should be turned off at 0·38′. My men had previously had the programme explained to them. By 5.30 a.m. I had everything ready to start at zero, and I went back a short distance to ascertain whether the wind was favourable. Finding it blowing very lightly from the S.S.W. and varying considerably in direction, I decided not to carry on and warned the men to do nothing without further orders. At 5.40 a.m. a mine was blown up in front of my line. The charge appeared to have been too weak as no debris was thrown up, only an immense cloud of smoke. From the direction in which the smoke drifted I was confirmed in my impression that it would not be safe to carry on. At 5.48 a.m. I got on to the Brigade on the telephone and informed the General that I was unable to carry on. He replied that he had already spoken to the 2nd Division about the wind being unsuitable, and that he had received a direct order to carry on.. In these circumstances he ordered me to let the gas off. I returned to the front line and ordered the gas to be turned on at about 5.58 a.m.

At first the gas drifted slowly towards the German lines (it was plainly visible owing to the rain), but at one or two bends of the trench the gas drifted into it. In these cases it was turned off at once. At about 6.20 a.m. the wind changed and quantities of the gas came back over our own parapet, so I ordered all gas to be turned off and only smoke candles to be used.

Punctually at 6.30 a.m. one company of the King's advanced to the attack, wearing smoke helmets. In some parts they advanced over the parapet from the front trench, and at others from sap heads. There was a certain amount of confusion in the front trench owing to the presence of large quantities of gas. Very little could be seen of the German lines owing to the fog of smoke and gas, but they appeared to have fires burning along their front line. Our infantry reached the enemy wire without a shot being fired, but were mown down there by machine-gun fire or overcome by the gas. One or two made their way back and reported that there were seven to ten rows of wire uncut, and that nobody had reached the front German trench. A report also came in that the enemy were not holding their front line, but were firing from their second line. During the 40 minutes in which the gas should have been let off, our artillery maintained a curtain of shrapnel over the German front line. When the attack started, the enemy shelled our front line and C.T.'s with shrapnel, but I did not see anything larger than field guns.

It is interesting to note that three out of the five machine-guns on my front were put out of action by the gas. Great difficulty was experienced in letting off the gas owing to faulty connections and broken copper pipes causing leaks. Nearly all my men suffered from the gas and four had to go to hospital. Two more were too bad to walk. After turning off the gas my men had orders to collect in deep dug-outs until the shelling was over. This they did, and by 2 p.m. I had all the emplacements sandbagged in and I was able to march back to Gorre, where we arrived wet through at 5 p.m.

On *Sunday, September 26th,* I was ordered to prepare for a fresh attack and returned to the trenches with my section and six men to replace my casualties. I took with me thirteen 10-foot rubber connecting pipes as one had been tried successfully in the first attack. After clearing out the empty cylinders, there was an average of eight full ones per emplacement. Late on Sunday night I received a message which made me feel certain that there would be an attack on Monday morning, so I withdrew my men to a shelter about 500 yards back. About 2 p.m. on Monday I received orders from the Brigade that I should probably have to co-operate with a large counter-attack, which was being organised in the south. I was given the probable hour as 5 p.m. I immediately ordered my men to stand by their emplacements and to be ready by 5 p.m., and informed the officers on my front. An hour or so later I received a message from the O.C. my company, who was at Divisional Head-quarters, giving the time of discharge as 25 minutes. Zero hour would be notified later. As I was responsible for giving zero hour to the two sections on my left I had two orderlies ready to take a message to them by two different routes. At 4.49 p.m. I was notified over the telephone that zero was 5 p.m., and immediately despatched the orderlies and informed my sergeants.

Punctually at 5 p.m. the gas was let off and continued for 25 minutes. There was some delay on the left, and the first 12 emplacements south of the canal did not start up at all, as, in the opinion of the section officer, it would have been dangerous to do so. The wind was N.W. and gusty and it was raining. The gas travelled well across the enemy's trenches, but, owing to the gap on the left and the direction of the wind, a large section of the German trenches south of the canal, including some of the brick-stacks, was untouched. Immediately the gas started the enemy threw out some kind of hand bomb, and within two minutes he had fires burning all along his front trenches. He also kept up a steady rifle and machine-gun fire. His artillery literally plastered our front trench with shrapnel and H.E. He also sent over all kinds of bombs and "minnies," blowing in our front trench in places.

The firing, however, did not become intense until the gas had ceased. In the case of both attacks the enemy was reported to have sent up coloured lights immediately the gas started, presumably for artillery assistance. Our infantry also reported that the enemy were standing up on their parapet waving to us, but did not explain why they were not shot down. On my front it was impossible to see anything more than the fires flickering through the cloud of smoke and gas. At the end of 25 minutes two smoke candles were lit at each emplacement and a patrol of three men went out from each battalion. These men were shot down at once, probably from the brick stacks, and any idea of attack was abandoned.

Once more there was considerable leakage in the trench and about 15 of the infantry were gassed, chiefly owing to the faulty use of gas helmets. Four of my men were slightly gassed and one wounded. After this I got my men back to the place where we had spent the previous night. It was raining very hard and it seemed quite impossible to get the pipes out and return to billets. About 9.30 p.m. I received two messages, the first one from my O.C. company, telling me to leave everything clear and return to billets with my pipes and spanners; and the second, which was apparently from Brigade, telling me to empty all my cylinders before I left. This appeared to me to be very unwise, and I went and explained my reasons to the B.G.C., who agreed and gave me permission to leave six men only in the trench as a guard.

Early on Tuesday morning I had all the available pipes collected and sent my section on with them and reported to Brigade. Here I was again ordered to empty all cylinders before leaving. After a considerable amount of telephoning, I finally got some men to replace my section, with a few pipes and spanners, also definite orders from Division to carry on independently as soon after 3 p.m. as possible. I was to give the Brigade three-quarters of an hour's notice to get the infantry under cover. Before leaving the Brigade I registered a final protest against carrying out this order, in view of the state of my equipment, fatigue of the men, and the uselessness of the whole proceeding. At 4.30 p.m. I was ready to carry on and telephoned the Brigade that I should start at 5.15 p.m. At 5 p.m. the wind had got round to S.S.W. and I passed the word not to let the gas off and telephoned the Brigade, which told me to stand by. Later on I received orders to leave things as they were. Once more I had my emplacements sandbagged in, pipes collected and men put under cover. As it was raining in torrents I decided to return to billets on the following morning. This was done, lorries meeting us at the brigade dump. The idea of another attack on the 30th was, fortunately, abandoned, although extra gas cylinders were brought up behind the line. It is interesting to note the behaviour of the different classes of men in my section. On the whole the specially enlisted men did excellent work and did not complain of hardship. Some of the trench men were inclined to get away at the earliest opportunity and with very little excuse. On the other hand they were very much better able to look after themselves in the trenches.

APPENDIX B

Operation Order No. 1 (Part 1)

By Lieut.-Col. A. S. Bates, D.S.O., Commanding 1st London Rifle Brigade

Reference, Hebuterne 1/10,000 and sketch maps issued.

Information. (1) The 46th Division will attack Gommecourt from the N.W. The 6th S. Staffordshire R. (137th Inf. Bde.) will be on its right, and therefore on the immediate north of this battalion.

Artillery. (2) The preliminary bombardment will have been carried out for five days. For an hour before zero the fire will be intense. The heavy artillery will continue to bombard Gommecourt and the park for three hours after zero (see para. 17).

Machine-Guns. (3) During the ten minutes before zero one section will fire heavy bursts on Maze, Eck and Cemetery. From zero to zero plus two minutes one clamped gun will fire on Firm towards Fibre. With this exception all firing after zero will be on K.6.a. only from these guns.

Move to Trenches. (4) "Bat" (L.R.B.) and "Dick" (Q.V.R.) will take over "Y" sector less Y.49 and Y.50 on afternoon of "Y" day. "Shou" (Q.W.R.) will move up into assembly trenches when the two former have assumed command of their battle areas.

Communication. (5) The brigade signal station will be established near junction of Yiddish Street and Y. 48.R. This method will only be used in case of failure of wire system. Each message so sent will be sent twice.

Task. (6) The battalion will assault and take Fir, Eel, Maze and Eck (excluding Ems and Cemetery). "Dick" is on our immediate right and "Shou" pass through the former. "Atten" (2nd Londons) is in Brigade Reserve.

Hour of Assault. (7) Zero time will be notified later. See para. 13 (e).

Watches. (8) The correct time will be sent round about midnight on night "Y/Z" to company commanders. Any company commander not having received it by 1 a.m. "Z" day will send a watch to Battalion Head-quarters to be synchronised.

Dress. (9) Fighting order with two bandoliers S.A.A., full

water bottles, mess tin, mackintosh sheet, iron ration, remainder of the day's ration and two smoke helmets. Officers will carry rifles and conform to the movements of their men.

(10) All N.C.O.'s and riflemen (excepting battalion scouts, signallers and stretcher-bearers) will carry two Mills grenades, one in each side pocket, and three sand-bags. Officers commanding companies will be responsible that the grenades are collected as soon as the situation permits. They will not be thrown by individuals except in grave emergency.

Officers and N.C.O.'s to be left Behind. (11) Third Army orders that not more than 23 officers are to go into action with the battalion. Capt. (Temp. Major) R. H. Husey, M.C., will remain at Sailly. The following will remain with the first line transport until ordered to rejoin by the Brigade, 2nd Lieut. (Temp. Capt.) F. H. Crews, 2nd Lieut. (Temp. Lieut.) F. D. Charles, 2nd Lieuts. Gardiner, Balls and Crisp. "A" and "D" Companies will take four officers each and "B" and "C" Companies five each into action. The Regimental Sergeant-Major and the following N.C.O.'s will remain with the first line transport until ordered to rejoin. Sergts. Sampson, Sharman, Burroughs, Reed, Lindsay, Baldwin, Sworder, Bradford, Radford and Todd.

(12) Capt. Somers-Smith will accompany the 6th wave and take up his position at junction of Fen and Ferret.

2nd Lieut. Pogose will accompany him and act under his orders. At zero plus two hours Capt. Somers-Smith will resume command of his company. See para. 17.

Assault. (13) Assault will be carried out by "A," "C" and "D" Companies.

(a) *Objectives.* "A" Company. Fir, point 94 of which is to be made into a strong point, Eel to be consolidated by small defended posts while the general consolidation is in progress.

"C" Company. Fen, Feast and Maze, which is to be made into a strong point.

"D" Company. Ferret, Exe, Female and Eck. The latter is to be treated as Eel.

(Separate orders *re* strong points have been issued to officers commanding companies concerned.)

(b) *Formation.* First four waves as practised, platoons being in depth. The first two waves will have to be strengthened to satisfy requirements of para. 4, Operation Order No. 1 (Part 2) of to-day. The special duty of the first wave is to clear any wire or obstacles which will hinder the succeeding waves. This is more important than making an immediate entry into the German front line.

Fifth wave one platoon "C" and one "D." See para. 18.

Sixth wave as for fifth wave.

(c) *Ladders.* These will be provided in, certainly, the front line and perhaps in others at a scale of one ladder for two men. Just prior to the time at which men are to leave the trench these will be placed in position and the two men will stand by. The man on the right going first.

(d) *Bridges.* These will be required to bridge over our front line, Boyau, Y.48.S. and Y.48.L for the rear waves. If special ones are not provided, floor boards will be taken up and put across each of these trenches. The senior officer in each trench is responsible that this is done and that the advance is not delayed.

Ladders and bridges to be prepared for the third and fourth waves. See para. 18.

The occupants of the Boyau will leave 10 ladders and 10 bridges on the parapet for the fourth wave to collect and carry forward. They will also leave 20 ladders and 20 bridges for the third wave to collect and carry forward.

(e) *Advance.* At three minutes before zero hour.

First wave will advance and lie down 150 yards in front of the front line.

Second wave will advance and lie down 70 yards in front of the front line.

At zero hour the first, second and third waves will advance simultaneously.

At zero plus ½ minute the fourth wave will advance.

At zero plus 1¼ minutes the fifth wave will advance.

At zero plus 2 minutes the sixth wave will advance.

ON NO ACCOUNT ARE THESE TIMES TO BE EXCEEDED.

If the trenches are wet sufficient allowance must be made to ensure no delay. Officers commanding companies are responsible for taking any steps they can to facilitate guiding their leading and succeeding waves across No Man's Land.

(f) *Compass bearings.* True bearings from the map are :

For left of " A " Company to point 94, 24 degrees 45′.

For right of " D " Company to point 63, 48 degrees 45′.

(g) *Silence.* Strict silence will be maintained during the advance through the smoke and no whistles will be blown.

ASSEMBLY TRENCHES. (14) First and second waves in new front line immediately south of Gommecourt Road.

Third wave in Boyau immediately behind it. (Both these lines extend to the south of Yellow Street.)

Fourth wave in Y.48.S. Fifth wave in Y.48.L (this was Y.48.R). Sixth wave in Y.48.L. These three last waves are all north of Yellow Street. Once in these trenches strict silence must be maintained and no smoking is on any account to be allowed.

DISTINGUISHING MARKS. (15) All ranks of " A," " C " and " D " Companies in the first six waves and all " B " Company, excluding 10 men detailed in para. 26 (c), will wear distinguishing marks as follows. " A " Company, blue ; " C," Yellow ; " D," red ; and " B," green tied on the left shoulder. In addition each N.C.O. or rifleman with wire cutters will wear a white bow on the right shoulder. This excludes battalion scouts and battalion bombers.

Reserve. (16) "B" Company will be in reserve (less 10 men detailed in para. 26, c), and will assemble in the "R" line north of Yiddish Street, moving up to the Boyau over the open through gaps in the wire, which will be marked, at zero plus five minutes. It will carry the dump (No. 7) of R.E. stores at head of Yellow Street (a list of these had been handed to officers commanding companies). These stores will be dumped about the base of Exe. Special parties are to be detailed for this fatigue and all the dump will be taken across. O.C. "B" Company will inspect the dump on the night Y/Z.

Clearing Gommecourt Park and Village. (17) This will take place at zero plus 3 hours and will be carried out by "B" Company as far as the park is concerned and by "Dick" for the village. Special instructions will be issued to O.C. "B" Company.

Tools, etc., to be Carried. (18) In addition to details in para. 9 the first wave will carry billhooks, wire cutters and wire breakers.

	Shovels.	Picks.	Bridges.	Ladders.
The second wave will carry—			(See para. 13, d).	
"A"	26	8		
"C" . . .	21	3		
"D"	13	3		
The third wave will carry—				
"A"	10	2	4	4
"C"	13	5	8	8
"D"	5	1	8	8
The fourth wave will carry—				
"A"	14	2	2	1 (and periscopes)
"C" . . .	16	2	4	4
"D"	22	6	4	5
	140	32	30	30
Extra to be carried as directed by O.C. "D" Coy. .	35			
	175			

In the fifth and sixth waves each platoon of "C" and "D" Companies will carry four boxes of S.A.A. from Y.48.L. They will be dumped as follows :

5 by "C" Company at point 94 for "A" Company.
5 by "C" Company at point 16 for their own use.
10 by "D" Company at the junction of Feast and Female.

The balance of men available in the last two waves will carry half man loads of R.E. stores, which will be in readiness behind Y.48.L. They will be dumped as follows :

(a) To point 94 for " A " Company } Details later.
(b) At north end of Feast }
(c) At junction of Exe and Eck.

The senior officer in Y.48.L. will be responsible that every man in these two waves has a definite load told off for him ; Section Commanders must ensure that unless their men are required as immediate reinforcements to their leading platoons their loads are carried across and dumped as directed. Periscopes for " C " and " D " Companies should be carried by these waves.

Trench Names. (18a) Boards will be carried as follows under Com. arrangements :

Fir Eel by " A " Company.
Fen, Feast and Maze by " C " Company.
Exe, Ferret, Female and Eck by " D " Company.

Battalion Bombers. (19) Will go across with the fifth and sixth wave and remain at point 16, base of Exe, point 63, for orders. Failing which, they will assist at any point which seems to be threatened.

Battalion Scouts. (20) Six will report to Capt. Somers-Smith, two to Lieut. Boston, two to Lieut. Oldfield and two each to officers commanding "A," " C," " D " Companies. The remainder will remain at Battalion Head-quarters. All will report on " Y " night.

Battalion Snipers. (21) Will be divided between " A," " C " and " D " Companies and be at the disposal of the officers commanding these companies.

Battalion Signallers. (22) Will man stations at Battalion Head-quarters and Report Centre in " Z " hedge. They will run a line in duplicate behind the sixth wave from the latter post to base of Exe via point 94. The call for this advanced report centre is " L."

Two thousand five hundred yards of wire will be provided. They will endeavour to establish a visual station from point 94. So long as the wires last the report centre need not be used, a clear line through to Battalion Head-quarters being left from advanced report centre.

Battalion Pioneers. (23) Will cross with the fifth wave and be at the disposal of officers commanding companies for skilled work.

Sanitary Men. (24) Will rejoin and accompany their companies.

Lewis Guns. (25) Will accompany third and fourth waves. Teams will carry two bandoliers each man. The guns will not fire unless definitely counter-attacked. " B " Company's guns will cross with Capt. Somers-Smith and act under his orders. (Teams carry 40 magazines per gun without assistance.) The L.G. Officer will superintend all L.G.'s. Twenty-two reserve buckets of L.G. magazines will be dumped under his arrangements at head of Young Street on night "Y/Z."

ATTACHED TROOPS. (26).

(a) *Cheshire R.* Two sections will report to O.C. "A" Company and advance with his last wave. They will assist in making his strong point at point 94. Two sections will advance with "C" Company in the sixth wave, remaining at the junction of Feast and Female for orders from O.C. "C" Company. They will assist in the Maze.

(b) *Royal Engineers.* One corporal and three sappers will report to O.C. "A" Company as in (a) above.

One sergeant and three sappers will advance with "C" Company as in (a) above.

(c) 169*th T.M.B.* A half section will cross with the sixth wave assembling in Y.48.L. A carrying party of ten riflemen from "B" Company will report to it and remain under its orders.

S.A.A. AND GRENADE DUMP. (27) Is at head of Young Street and during operations it can be drawn on. It contains 25 boxes of S.A.A. and 1000 Mills grenades. (The 20 boxes S.A.A. mentioned in para. 18 are on no account to be taken from here.)

REPORTS. (28) All messages to be sent to Advanced Report Centre at base of Exe, where they will be shown to any officer there and telegraphed or sent by runner to Report Centre in the "Z" hedge. If the message is urgent and is to be delivered by hand, Yiddish Street must be used. It must be remembered that negative reports are of value. If the opportunity offers frequent reports should be sent in. If these latter are to be telegraphed, brevity, provided it is perfectly clear, is essential.

FLARES. (29) Red flares will be carried by "A," C" and "D" Companies and lit when their objectives are reached.

(Signed) F. H. WALLIS, Capt. and Adjt.,
26th June, 1916. 1st Batt. London Rifle Brigade.

DISTRIBUTION.

No.	1. "A" Company.	No.	10. Capt. Price, Cheshire R.
,,	2. "B" Company.	,,	11. 2/1st Field Coy. R.E.
,,	3. "C" Company.	,,	12. 169th Inf. Bde.
,,	4. "D" Company.	,,	13. M.O.
,,	5. O. i/c Scouts.	,,	14. L.G. Officers.
,,	6. O. i/c Bombers.	,,	15. Head-quarters.
,,	7. N.C.O. i/c Signallers.	,,	16. War Diary.
,,	8. Capt. Somers-Smith.	,,	17. War Diary.
,,	9. Capt. Coote, 169 T.M.B.	,,	18. Adjutant.

Operation Order No. 1 (Part 2)

By Lieut.-Col. A. S. Bates, D.S.O., Commanding 1st London Rifle Brigade

The following are to be considered part of Operation Orders for "Z" day. They are issued in advance to avoid overcrowding of the actual attack orders, but are to be read in conjunction with them :

Battle Police. (2) O.C. "A" Company will detail battle police at point 94. O.C. "C" Company will detail battle police at about point 16, and O.C. "D" Company battle police at about junction of Fen and Ferret. Their special duties will be :

(a) To see that no one except linesmen use the new communication trenches across No Man's Land from the German side.

(b) To prevent any N.C.O. or rifleman leaving the German lines who is not wounded, or an orderly or other properly authorised person.

(c) To direct men who have lost their way, messengers or carrying parties, to the trench they want to find. It must be impressed on them that their duties are important and must be carried out implicitly.

Casualties. (3) Whenever reports or messages are being sent by hand an estimate of casualties should be added. In sending further reports it must be made clear whether the casualties reported in them are additional to any previously reported or are total. The latter is, probably, the best method as it avoids the mistakes that may occur if messages go astray.

Clearing Trenches. (4) Officers commanding assaulting companies will detail special parties to clear the German trenches which their waves have to pass over. All dug-outs will be thoroughly cleared. No dug-out will be left unentered. All wires of any description found in any German trench will be cut *at once*. When these parties have done their work they will remain in the trenches they have cleared and help to carry up R.E. stores as they arrive to their respective company objectives.

Communication Trenches. (5) Young Street and Yellow Street are only to be used towards the enemy. Their continuation across No Man's Land are to be used similarly. Yiddish Street is only to be used towards Hebuterne. It is of the utmost importance that no officer, N.C.O. or man (except linesmen) attempts to use a C.T. contrary to this order. Battle police have the strictest orders at once to turn anyone, whatever his rank, whether wounded or not, out of a trench in which he is endeavouring to walk in a wrong direction.

Flanks. (6) Particular attention must be paid to the flanks. No unit will leave its flanks exposed. Should the attack be held up on a flank, the unit which had been able to push on will, at once, form a defensive flank in a communication trench until the danger of being attacked on a flank is passed. Special care is to be taken to keep touch with " Dick " on our right.

Head-quarters. (7) Battalion Head-quarters will be in old Yiddish Street about 20 yards from the " R " line on the south side. They will be marked. An advanced head-quarters will be established by Capt. Somers-Smith at the base of Exe.

Looting. (8) All ranks are warned that the most extreme disciplinary action will be taken in the case of any officer, N.C.O. or rifleman detected looting, or found in possession of, or to have disposed of, any article from the dead.

Prisoners. (9) Prisoners will be sent to billet No. 141 in Hebuterne (entrance to Yankee Street) or to the western end of Yiddish Street. Units capturing them are responsible for sending them back. Escorts will be on the scale of 10 per cent. Officers will be kept separate from N.C.O.'s and men. They will be searched as soon as possible for concealed arms and documents. These latter will be sent to Battalion Head-quarters at once. The search should be carried out in the presence of an officer if possible. Escorts and guards are forbidden to talk to prisoners or to give them tobacco or extra food. Personal effects (except diaries, letters, etc.), badges, etc., will not be collected unless required by the G.S. Identity discs will not be taken from them.

Maps, Documents. (10) No copies of maps in which our present trenches are marked and no orders will be taken by assaulting troops. All private correspondence should be left behind.

Ration and Water Dump. (11) The food rations dumped at the head of Young Street are not to be touched without orders from the Brigade. The water may be drawn once the battalion is in the German line, but it may not be touched before the battalion leaves on any account. Officers commanding companies are responsible that this regulation is carried out. Whenever water is drawn empties *must* be returned. Tins are scarce and the battalion's future supply will depend on its having returned empty tins.

Regimental Aid Post. (12) Will be in old Yiddish Street. Evacuations from it will be made via Keep Street at K.9.d.37 to the Advanced Dressing Stations at K.9.c.23 and K.9.4.57. Directing sign-boards are placed at convenient points to guide stretcher-bearers and walking cases. Two stretcher-bearers per company will go forward as directed by officers commanding companies. They will be unarmed and without stretchers, but will carry additional field dressings.

Very Pistols and Ammunition. (13) Officers commanding companies in their objective line will send back specially for these during the afternoon of " Z " day. They will be drawn at Battalion Head-quarters.

War Standing Orders, 56th Division. (14) Special attention is called to the following:

No. 27. *Tending of Wounded.* All ranks are forbidden to divert their attention from the enemy in order to tend wounded officers or men. A wounded man who is unable to advance or to take any further active part in an action will hand over his ammunition to the nearest soldier.

No. 30. *White Flags.* The display or hoisting of a white flag by the enemy is not a sign of surrender, but merely implies that he has a communication to make. If a white flag be displayed during an action firing will *not* be discontinued on any account. The fact that a white flag has been displayed will be reported to Divisional Head-quarters.

Warning if Captured. (15) All ranks are warned that if captured by the enemy the only information they can be forced to give is as follows: Name, Rank, Regiment. On no account is any other information of any description to be given.

(Signed) F. H. Wallis,
Captain.
26/6/16. Adjutant, 1st London Rifle Brigade.

Distribution.

As for O.O. No. 1 (Part 1).

Operation Order No. 2

By Lieut.-Col. A. S. Bates, D.S.O., Commanding 1st London Rifle Brigade

Work in Trenches. (1) Immediately darkness permits, officers commanding "A," "C" and "D" Companies will detail special parties to—

(a) Remove the whole of the wire on the battle front.

(b) Remove portions of parapet and parados and insert floor boards securely as bridges. This will be done over every trench except C.T.'s forward of the "R" line (Ref. O.O. No. 1, Part 1, para. 13, d.)

(c) Distribute the half man loads and 20 boxes of S.A.A. for carrying forward.

(d) Erect ladders (Ref. O.O. No. 1, Part 1, para. 13, c). N.B.—All ladders are the same, and those to be carried forward will be drawn from those already in the trenches issued as sortie ladders. Officers commanding companies will report when their tasks have been completed.

Communication Trenches. (2) Must be kept clear after dark. Up to this time only Young Street may be used.

2 B

MOTOR M.G. (3) One section, No. 16 Battery, is available to assist in consolidation.

PATROL. (4) Officers commanding companies will arrange in conjunction with the Scout Officer (who will assist with his scouts) to patrol and report on the enemy wire in front of Fir, Fen and Feast. This must be done between 12 midnight and 1 a.m., during which time the artillery and machine-gun fire on front line trenches will cease. Reports from officers commanding companies must reach Battalion Head-quarters by 2 a.m. "Z" day.

SMOKE. (5) In event of a hand smoke thrower becoming a casualty during or preceding a smoke discharge, the infantry in the firebay must assist in carrying out the smoke programme.

46TH DIVISION. (6) Ref. O.O. No. 1, Part 1, para. 1, the 6th South Staffordshire R. will join hands with the Q.W.R. at junction of Indus and Fill. The 5th South Staffordshire R. will be employed in clearing Gommecourt Park and village. The 5th Leicestershire R. is the battalion which will be employed to reinforce either of these if required.

ASSAULT. (7) Special attention is drawn to line 1 of para. 13, e, of O.O. No. 1, Part 1, that our first two lines emerge from our front line at three minutes before zero, and that on no account is any wave to leave its assembly trench later than the times ordered in this paragraph.

SPECIAL BRIDGES. (8) Ref. O.O. No. 1, Part 1, para. 13, d, owing to the bad condition of the trenches the special bridges for carrying forward may have to be issued before entering the trenches. In this case officers commanding companies will earmark the men to carry them and they will be drawn as each section passes "K.Y.C."[1]

WATER. (9) *On no account will any water other than what is carried on the person or brought over from our trenches be drunk (whether boiled or not) in Gommecourt.* It is more than likely that all wells, etc., will be contaminated or even poisoned.

TIME. (10) All ranks are specially warned to wind their watches on "Y" evening.

BATTALION BOMBERS. (11) Ref. O.O. No. 1, Part 1, para. 17, the O. i/c battalion bombers will arrange to assist O.C. "B" Company in clearing Gommecourt Park.

(Signed) F. H. WALLIS, Capt. and Adj.,
28/6/16. London Rifle Brigade.

DISTRIBUTION. As for O.O. No. 1, Part 1.

Amendment No. 1 was, Lieut.-Col. Bates believes, sent out on a message form to company commanders, and consisted of only one paragraph.

[1] "K.Y.C." was the code signal for the old L.R.B. H.Q. in Hebuterne which were used during the battle by 169th Infantry Brigade H.Q.

Operation Order, Amendment No. 2
By Lieut.-Col. A. S. Bates, D.S.O., Commanding 1st London Rifle Brigade

(1) Ref. O.O. No. 1, Part 1, para. 29. The red flares issued will be used by all troops to indicate *final* objectives reached. Lights, long red, if issued, are to be used to indicate final objectives reached after smoke has cleared away. (N.B.—Blue lights are for the Q.W.R. only. Lights, long green, for the Q.V.R. only.)

(2) Ref. O.O. No. 2, para. 4. Patrols.

(a) The Brigade has altered the times between which these are to go out to between 11 p.m. and midnight to-night instead of between 12 midnight and 1 a.m.

(b) A detachment of R.E. with bangalore torpedoes will accompany these patrols and will report to Battalion Head-quarters at 10 p.m. to-night.

(c) Officers commanding "A," "C" and "D" Companies and Scout Officer will send the officers in charge of their patrols to Battalion Head-quarters at 10 p.m. to-night to consult with the R.E. and lead them to where the patrols start.

(d) A favourable method for using these detachments would appear to be as follows: An officer accompanied by the R.E. detachments with three patrols to advance about 300 yards, the three patrols to diverge dropping connecting files. The patrols on returning to report the exact state of wire and, if a large portion is uncut, the officer would then give the necessary instructions.

(e) The report called for in last line of O.O. No. 2, para. 4, must be rendered to Battalion Head-quarters by 1 a.m. and not 2 a.m. "Z" day.

(3) Ref. O.O. No. 1, Part 1, para. 7, an orderly from each company will report to Battalion Head-quarters at 11 p.m. to-night for the special task of conveying "zero hour" to officers commanding companies.

(4) Ref. O.O. No. 2, para. 1 (a). After removal, if possible, the wire is to be dumped on the Gommecourt road. Failing this the wire must be dumped in piles in front of the trench.

(Signed) F. H. Wallis,
Captain,
28th June, 1916. Adjutant, L.R.B.

Operation Orders. Additions and Amendments No. 3 By Lieut.-Col. A. S. Bates, D.S.O., Commanding 1st London Rifle Brigade

Soup. (1) An issue of soup will be made about two hours before zero. O.C. " B " Company will detail 24 men to carry the 47 two-gallon tins. They will report to billet No. 207 at three hours before zero. Instructions will be given how many are to be taken to each trench. Empty tins will be left in the trench but not damaged.

Work. (2) On arrival in their assembly trenches on evening "Y/Z" night O.C. " B " Company will detail 15 men to deepen a new piece of C.T. (commenced last night by 2nd London) between where Young Street joins Boyau immediately south of Gommecourt Road to half-way up eastern face of the " Z " hedge ; tools to be drawn from and returned to O.C. " A " Company.

Assembly Trenches. (3) Ref. O.O. No. 1, Part 1, para. 14. If the front line is too bad in places either from wet or hostile shelling, officers commanding companies will use their discretion as to putting their first two waves into the Boyau with their third waves. For the night "Y/Z" the line can be held with sentries and two L.G.'s in the front line. In no case, however, must the times at which the various waves leave be departed from. See O.O. No. 1, Part 1, para. 13 (e).

Bridges to Carry Forward. (4) Ref. O.O. No. 1, Part 1, para. 13 (d). The 30 bridges for this purpose will be issued at " K.Y.C." to companies as they pass. The special men detailed (see O.O. No. 2, para. 6) must draw them before entering the assembly trenches. These bridges are only to be used for carrying forward.

Bridges over Trenches. (5) If the front line is not occupied (para. 3 above) it must still be bridged on the scale of, at least four per platoon (see O.O. No. 1, Part 1, para. 13, d). This work must be done at night, but the parapet and parados must not be cut through so as to show definite gaps which would be noticeable to the enemy.

Ladders. (6) If sufficient sortie ladders are not obtainable steps must be cut to facilitate getting out of the assembly trenches. The senior officer in the Boyau will use every endeavour to assure the 10 required by the fourth wave (after the third wave has taken 20) being left on the parapet.

Advanced Parties. (7) It is probable that advanced parties from each wave may be able to go to Hebuterne before the battalion, and their duty will be to adjust the supply of ladders, etc., in the various trenches.

Reports. (8) Ref. O.O. No. 1, Part 1, para. 28. The first

report that each company has reached its objective will be sent by wire, if available, and by runner.

Bangalore Torpedoes. (9) Ref. O.O. Amendment No. 2, para. 2 (b, c and d). No torpedoes will be required and the carrying party from " B " Company will not be detailed. O.O. Amendment No. 2, para. 2 (c), need not be carried out.

Half Manloads. (10) Ref. O.O. No. 1, Part 1, para. 18. These are 60 in number and consist entirely of wiring material.

R.E. Dump. (11) Ref. O.O. No. 1, Part 1, para. 16. This may not exist either wholly or where laid down. O.C. " B " Company will endeavour to find what there is during the night "Y/Z," and any balance of men available will carry boxes of grenades from battalion dump at junction of Young Street and Y.48.S. behind the " Z " hedge. The R.E. loads have all been halved.

(Signed) F. H. Wallis,
Capt. and Adjt.,
1st London Rifle Brigade.

30th June, 1916.

Distribution.

As for O.O. No. 1, Part 1.

APPENDIX C

Report of Operations of the 56th (London) Division Culminating in the Attack on the S.W. Face of Gommecourt Salient on July 1st, 1916

Signed by the G.O.C. and issued by the Division S.G., 121/100, dated 18/7/16.

(1) On May 3rd and 4th the 56th Division moved from the VIth Corps reserve area east of Frevent and took over the front east of Hebuterne, from the Hebuterne-Puisieux road to a point opposite the western extremity of Gommecourt Park (K.3.d.36). The outline of the proposed attack was explained by the VIIth Corps, and reconnaissance and preparations began immediately.

(2) On the nights of 26/27th and 27/28th May, the line was advanced to include the road junction at K.10.b.07 and the "Z" hedge at K.10.a.79. The distance from the German front line was reduced from 600–800 yards to 250–400 yards.

(3) From May 28th to June 26th the new system of trenches was completed, 6250 yards of fire, support and assembly trenches, and 2,700 yards of communication trenches being dug. Battle Headquarters for one brigade and for eight battalions, stores for grenades, S.A.A. rations and water, emplacements for heavy, medium and light trench mortars and stores for their ammunition were constructed. Many new battery positions and observation posts were built; and a system of buried cables behind and in Hebuterne was completed. The work was very considerably delayed by wet weather, and, to some extent, also by the enemy's artillery and trench mortar fire. By June 24th (the first day of the bombardment) the preparations as far as they went were completed, but, had another month been available, our front line would have been pushed forward another 150 to 200 yards, and great improvements could have been carried out in the trenches themselves, in the trench mortar emplacements, stores and in extending the system of buried cables.

(4) A replica of the German front line system was dug in the neighbourhood of Halloy, and brigades and battalions selected for the assault rehearsed their attacks several times both with and without the assistance of smoke.

(5) On June 24th, the artillery bombardment commenced, wire cutting only being carried out on the first day. Five batteries of

18-pdr. guns remained directly under my orders for wire cutting. The remainder of the artillery was directly under the orders of the G.O.C. R.A., VIIth Corps, until zero hour on the day of the attack. During this period several intense bombardments with lifts were carried out both with and without smoke. The smoke discharges on each occasion drew a moderate barrage from the hostile artillery but very little rifle or machine-gun fire. The period of artillery bombardment was increased from five to seven days on 28th June, and July 1st was fixed for the day of the assault.

(6) During this period (June 24th to 30th) the 167th Infantry Brigade was holding the line, and completing the preparations. They suffered a fair number of casualties from hostile artillery fire, as did the artillery whose observation posts came in for a considerable amount of hostile shelling. On the whole, hostile retaliation was not very great, and very little counter-battery work was carried out by the enemy. The 168th and 169th Infantry Brigades during this period were practising for the attack.

(7) On the night of June 30th–July 1st the 168th and 169th Infantry Brigades moved into their positions of assembly without incident.

(8) On the morning of 1st July the units of the division were disposed as under :

168th Infantry Brigade. Head-quarters in Mardi Trench, K.10.d.27. Right assaulting battalion, 14th London Regt. (London Scottish). Left assaulting battalion, 12th London Regt. (Rangers). Right supporting battalion, 4th London Regt. (R.F.). Left supporting battalion, 13th London Regt. (Kensingtons), with the special task of digging fire trench from K.11.c.23 to German sap at K.11.c.64.

169th Infantry Brigade. Head-quarters in Hebuterne, K.9.d.48. Right assaulting battalion, 9th London Regt. (Q.V.R.). Left assaulting battalion, 5th London Regt. (L.R.B.). To go through Q.V.R. to Quadrilateral in K.5.a., 16th London Regt. (Q.W.R.) Brigade Reserve, 2nd London Regt. (R.F.).

167th Infantry Brigade. Head-quarters in Souastre with advance head-quarters in Hebuterne at K.15.b.29.

1st London Regt. in area "A," 600 men under C.R.E. to dig C.T.'s across No Man's Land.

3rd London Regt. in area "C," ditto, ditto.

7th Middlesex Regt. in the Keep, Hebuterne.

9th Middlesex Regt. at Souastre.

5th Cheshire Regiment. (Pioneers) had one company with each of the 168th and 169th Infantry Brigades. One company in Hebuterne under the C.R.E. and head-quarters and one company at Souastre (parties on roads, etc.).

Royal Engineers. One section 2/1st London Fd. Company with 169th Infantry Brigade. One section 2/2nd London Fd. Company, with 168th Infantry Brigade. The 1/1st Edinburgh Fd. Company was in Hebuterne. The 2/1st and 2/3rd London Fd. Companies, each less one section, were in Sailly in divisional reserve and to find reliefs for the sections with the 168th and 169th Infantry Brigades.

R.F.A. (after zero hour). Southern Group (4 18-pdr. batteries, 1 4·5″ How. battery) affiliated to the 168th Infantry Brigade. Northern Group of similar strength affiliated to the 169th Infantry Brigade. Counter-battery Group of 2 18 pdr. batteries, and 1 4·5 How. battery.

The C.R.A. had in his hands 2 18 pdr. batteries.

Trench Mortar Batteries. V.56 Battery 1 240 mm. mortar at K.10.d.21. 1 240 mm. mortar at K.9.b.43. X.56. (2″) Battery at K.3.d.32. Y.56. (2″) Battery at K.11.c.23 with 168th Infantry Brigade and Z.56. (2″) Battery in the "Z" hedge with 169th Infantry Brigade. The Stokes' batteries were with their respective Brigades except 167th Battery, which was divided between 168th and 169th Infantry Brigades.

Narrative of Operations by the 56th Division on July 1st, 1916

(9) The objective of the division was to capture and consolidate a line running approximately due north from strong point K.11.c. to junction of Fillet and Indus, joining hands with the 46th Division, who were to continue the line from this point to the "Little Z" and then clear Gommecourt village and park. The division attacked on a front of two brigades, which were given the following objectives :

168*th Infantry Brigade on the right,* which attacked on a front of two battalions, was to capture the strong point at K.11.c. Fame, Elbe between Fame and Felon, Felon junction of Felon and Epte. Strong points to be consolidated at K.11.c., Elbe and Et south-east of Nameless Farm, junction of Felon and Epte.

169*th Infantry Brigade on the left,* which attacked on a front of two battalions, was to capture Fell, Fellow, Feud, Cemetery, the Maze, Fir and junction of Fir and Firm. A third battalion was to push through up Ems and Etch, capture and consolidate the Quadrilateral in K.5.a., bomb up Fillet and establish a post to join 46th Division at junction of Fillet and Indus. Strong points to be established at junction of Fir–Firm, the Maze, Cemetery.

The attack was preceded by a bombardment lasting from 24th to 30th June, during which there were two discharges of smoke. On 1st July, the day decided on for the attack, an intense bombardment of guns of all calibres was opened on the enemy's lines at 6.25 a.m. At 7.20 a.m. (five minutes before scheduled time) smoke was discharged from the left of the line near the "Z" hedge. In five minutes the smoke was dense along the whole front. Shortly after this the infantry moved forward. At 7.30 a.m. the assault commenced, the artillery having lifted off the enemy's front line.

At about 7.35 a.m. our first lines reached the enemy's front trench, under cover of the smoke, with comparatively little loss. A hostile machine-gun in Gommecourt Park appeared to be firing high, and there was little fire from the Germans in the trenches. Shortly after this the enemy's artillery was reported to be shelling his own front line opposite our right.

At 7.50 a.m. the left battalion (L.R.B.) of 169th Infantry Brigade had gained all its objectives, and was beginning to consolidate. At 8.30 a.m. on the right the London Scottish held as far as Fame Farm and south-east corner of strong point K.11.c. The left battalion of the 169th Infantry Brigade (Rangers) held Felt, Fetter and Fate, but were held up at Felon, and its flank companies were reported to have been driven back. Two companies of the reserve battalion (4th Londons) were sent to carry this attack forward again. The right battalion of the 169th Infantry Brigade (Q.V.R.) held Feed, Feint and Fellow and was pushing forward. The left battalion (L.R.B.) was consolidating. The Q.W.R. had reached the line of the Nameless Farm road and were now mixed up with the Q.V.R.

9.30 a.m. By this time the hostile barrage on No Man's Land was very intense. Of the 168th Infantry Brigade the London Scottish holding strong point K.11.c. and Fall, Rangers in touch with Scottish on Nameless Farm road, and half a company of Kensingtons had reinforced the London Scottish in Farmyard, but lost heavily in crossing No Man's Land. Of the 169th Infantry Brigade the Q.V.R. after hard fighting were in possession of all their objectives. The Q.W.R. were still mixed up with the Q.V.R., but had succeeded in making some progress in Etch and Ems C.T.'s towards the Quadrilateral in K.5.a. It was shortly after this that the enemy in their turn commenced bombing down these trenches and were observed to be collecting behind the Cemetery, the company of the L.R.B. in the park *had been reinforced by two platoons and* was engaged in heavy grenade fighting. (Note by A.S.B.—The words in italics should be deleted, as they are incorrect. No reinforcement was able to be carried out.) Consolidation at all points was hindered by hostile rifle and machine-gun fire. Hostile artillery still very active.

11.15 a.m. Little change in the situation except that small parties of hostile bombers got between parts of the left company of Q.V.R. in Cemetery, and shortly afterwards others were seen moving through Gommecourt Park. No signs of any troops in the Quadrilateral. A small party of Rangers had been able to commence consolidation of the junction Felon–Epte.

12.0 noon. From this time onwards battalions of both brigades suffered from shortage of bombs, which could not be made good owing to impossibility of crossing No Man's Land. As an instance, two carrying parties of the London Scottish, 50 strong, started across between 9.30 a.m. and noon with grenades and ammunition. Of these no man got across and only three men got back. All along the captured line free use was made of the German grenades found in trenches and dug-outs. By 12.30 p.m. the enemy was launching determined counter-attacks down Epte, Ems and Etch, gradually forcing our troops out of his third line.

By 2 p.m. we were holding on the right a part of Fancy, west end of K.11.c. and Fall. On our left Ferret, Fibre and the corner of the park. Several parties from all posts of the German lines had returned to our trenches. (Note by A.S.B.—Mostly all wounded.)

3.30 p.m. At this hour we were still holding a part of K.11.c. occupied by the London Scottish on the right, and parts of Ferret, Fern, Fen and Fir on the left occupied by about 100 men of the L.R.B., Q.V.R. and Q.W.R. (Note by A.S.B.—It is clear that up to this hour the L.R.B. still held a portion of Ecke.)

4 p.m. The London Scottish having both flanks in the air and no munitions were forced to evacuate K.11.c. and withdrew to our trenches. Parties of the enemy massing in Fish, Firm and the vicinity of the Cemetery were dispersed by our artillery. Our hold on the left was gradually weakening (Note by A.S.B.—The L.R.B. had men actually fighting in the German third line up to 4.45 p.m.) and at 7.19 p.m. was reduced to about 70 men in Ferret. An hour and a half later all the survivors who were capable of movement had withdrawn and returned to our trenches.

At 5.45 p.m. I directed the 167th Infantry Brigade, less 3rd Londons, to relieve the 168th Infantry Brigade in the right sector, retaining the 7th Middlesex in divisional reserve. At the same time I ordered the 168th Infantry Brigade to concentrate and re-organise in the Divisional and Corps lines between Sailly and Hebuterne. I placed the 3rd Londons at the disposal of the B.G.C. 169th Infantry Brigade.

(10) On 2nd July the 167th Infantry Brigade relieved the 169th Infantry Brigade, which was withdrawn into the Divisional and Corps lines between Hebuterne and Sailly and later to Bayencourt, and the 168th Infantry Brigade moved to Souastre and St. Amand. On the nights 2/3rd and 3/4th the 168th Infantry Brigade relieved the 46th Division in the trenches east of Fonquevillers.

(11) The number of prisoners captured was 189 of the 170th Regiment and units of the 52nd Reserve Division and the 55th Reserve Regiment and units of the 2nd Guards Reserve Division. In addition some wounded prisoners were evacuated through our field ambulances. A considerable number of prisoners were killed by their own barrage while crossing No Man's Land. This number is estimated at 60 to 80 in front of the left brigade.

(12) A table showing casualties suffered on July 1st and for the period June 24th–July 3rd is attached.

(13) I wish to call attention particularly to the following:

(a) The energy and zeal displayed by all ranks of all arms in their efforts to complete the preparations against time, and under very adverse conditions of weather.

(b) The work done by my staff, especially by Lieut.-Col. J. E. S. Brind, D.S.O., and Lieut.-Col. H. W. Grubb. The success of the operations was in no small measure due to their grasp of detail and knowledge of what was required, combined with unceasing hard work.

(c) The careful and well-thought-out arrangements of Brig.-Gen. G. G. Loch, C.M.G., and the staff of the 168th Infantry Brigade. The good work performed by Lieut.-Col. A. F. Prechtel and the wire-cutting group consisting of the following batteries : A/282, B/282, C/282, C/283, A/280.

(d) The energy and determination displayed by all ranks of Y.56 and Z.56 Trench Mortar Batteries.

(e) The steady advance and determined resistance offered by the five assaulting battalions :

The L.R.B., Lieut.Col. A. S. Bates, D.S.O.
The Q.V.R., Lieut.-Col. V. W. F. Dickins, D.S.O., V.D.
The Rangers, Lieut.-Col. A. D. Bayliffe, C.M.G., T.D.
The London Scottish, Lieut.-Col. B. C. Green, C.M.G., T.D.
The Q.W.R., Lieut.-Col. R. Shoolbred, C.M.G., T.D.

With the small parties of the 2/1st and 2/2nd London Field Companies R.E. and of the 1/5th Cheshire Regt. (Pioneers) attached to them.

(f) The excellent arrangements made by Col. E. G. Brown, C.B., A.M.S., and the good work performed by the R.A.M.C. personnel of the division in the collection and evacuation of the wounded.

(g) The good work performed by the personnel of the 2nd Company 5th Battalion Special Brigade under Capt. Holland, R.E., and of the personnel of the 167th Infantry Brigade detailed for smoke duties under the Divisional Gas Officer, Capt. C. O. Lambert, 3rd London Regt. I wish also to acknowledge the assistance received from the 8th Squadron R.F.C. both before and during the operations.

Table showing Number of Casualties
From June 24th to July 3rd, 1916

	Officers.	Other ranks.	Totals.
Killed . . .	35	412	447
Wounded . .	107	2632	2739
Missing . .	40	1523	1563
Totals . .	182	4567	4749[1]

[1] Of this total, as will be seen from the next page, 4202 were sustained on July 1st.

56th DIVISION CASUALTIES ON JULY 1st, 1916.

Unit.	Officers. K.	W.	M.	Total.	Other ranks. K.	W.	M.	Total.	Total All ranks.
1st London Regt.	–	2	1	3	3	67	7	77	80
3rd London Regt.	1	3	1	5	19	124	4	147	152
7th Middlesex Regt.	–	3	–	3	2	36	–	38	41
8th Middlesex Regt.	–	1	–	1	–	29	–	29	30
4th London Regt.	2	8	3	13	28	178	56	262	275
Rangers	–	8	9	17	28	250	220	498	515
Kensingtons	3	11	3	17	34	184	82	300	317
London Scottish	3	8	3	14	47	234	263	544	558
168th Bde. M.G. Co.	–	–	–	–	1	4	–	5	5
2nd London Regt.	4	7	1	12	40	204	–	244	256
L.R.B.	7	10	2	19	56	210	299	565[1]	584
Q.V.R.	5	5	5	15	40	261	210	511	526
Q.W.R.	2	9	8	19	12	240	249	501	520
169th Bde. M.G. Co.	2	1	–	3	9	9	19	37	40
5th Cheshire Regt.	1	3	2	6	13	112	47	172	178
159th T.M. Battery	1	1	–	2	2	19	10	31	33
280th, 281st & 282nd Bdes. R.F.A.	–	2	–	2	–	6	–	6	8
Divisional Ammn. Col.	–	1	–	1	–	2	–	2	3
X56, Y56 & Z56 T.M.B.	–	1	–	1	4	1	3	8	9
Field Co.'s. R.E.	–	1	1	2	6	28	24	58	60
M.M.P.	–	–	–	–	–	1	–	1	1
2/1st & 2/2nd London F.A.	–	–	–	–	2	9	–	11	11
	31	85	39	155	346	2208	1493	4047	4202

An analysis of the above figures shows how the actual infantry battalions making up the three brigades fared :

KILLED, WOUNDED, AND MISSING

	Officers.	Other ranks.	Total.
167th Inf. Bde.	12	291	303
168th Inf. Bde.	61	1604	1665
169th Inf. Bde.	65	1821	1886
	138	3716	3854

[1] See p. 150.

APPENDIX D

REPORT ON THE DEFENCE OF GOMMECOURT ON JULY 1ST, 1916

(Translated from the German and reprinted from *The Journal of the Royal United Service Institution* by kind permission).

PART I

WAR DIARY OF THE 55TH RESERVE INFANTRY REGIMENT (2ND GUARD RESERVE DIVISION) FOR THE PERIOD JUNE 24TH TO JULY 1ST, 1916

(The Sector held by the 55th Reserve Infantry Regiment was from the Cemetery (*K.4.d.*) on the south up to and including the whole of Gommecourt Wood on the north. Sectors G.1, G.2, and G.3 referred to were on the left of the L.R.B.'s objective; G.4 ran from the E. of Gommecourt to the communication trench joining Fight and Firm; G.5 ran thence to the angle in Ferret. It was this last sector that the L.R.B. attacked. Kern Redoubt was a strong point about the figure 4 on sketch map.)

Saturday, June 24th, 1916. During the night the enemy dug a new trench about 250 metres in front of the right flank of the Regimental Sector north of the Gommecourt–Fonquevillers road. Wire not yet put up. Enemy's machine-gun and rifle fire unusually quiet.

6.30 a.m. Heavy continuous shrapnel fire on Sectors G.1 and G.2, which increased to an intense bombardment towards midday. Some medium shells on G.2.

A few enemy's aeroplanes about.

Weather : Dull and rainy. Casualties : 1 Other Rank wounded.

Sunday, June 25th, 1916. During the night continuous shrapnel fire on all approach roads and the area in rear. Heavy artillery fire on the whole sector, increasing in intensity.

8.45 a.m. The officer commanding G. Right Sector reports heavy fire on his trenches. Patrol reports cannot be forwarded owing to the danger of losing the runners. Sent later by telephone.

10 a.m. The bombardment less severe. Up to the present the casualties reported are :

1 man killed, 1 severely wounded, 1 slightly wounded.

11 a.m. Bucquoy and the Esarts road bombarded. Retaliation fire on Hebuterne is asked for.

12 noon. The field-cooker of the 12th Company has been destroyed by a shell.

Casualties : 1 horse of the 4th Company wounded and 1 man of the 12th Company.

12.30 p.m. G. Left reports continuous bombardment, especially on G.3–Kern Redoubt.

1 p.m. Permission from division for Regimental Command Post to remain in Bucquoy.

1–3 p.m. Heavy bombardment on Bucquoy and Essarts road, Many direct hits on the village.

10 p.m. Bombardment less severe.

11 p.m. Heavy shrapnel and machine-gun fire on the front line and communication trenches. Some trench mortar bombs on G.4. Great activity on the part of the enemy aeroplanes during the day.

Weather : Sunny, then clouded ; night very dark. Casualties : 1 Other Rank killed, 11 Other Ranks wounded.

Monday, June 26th, 1916. 8 a.m. Lively shrapnel fire on G. Right and Left.

10.35 a.m. Bombardment very heavy, almost continuous.

11.30 a.m. Gas was let off opposite G. Left. Our artillery opens heavy barrage fire. 91st Reserve Regiment [Ed. Note.—*This was on the right of the 55th*] reports that the enemy has prepared sortie steps between Monchy and X.2. 3rd Battalion 55th Reserve Regiment is ordered to stand to.

11.45 a.m. Report from front line that the gas cloud has passed high over trenches.

12 noon. Rain sets in.

12.20 p.m. Order for 3rd Battalion to stand to cancelled.

12.30 p.m. 170th Regiment reports gas attack towards the north. Gas cloud passes over our trenches at 12 and 1.30 p.m.

1.45 p.m. The enemy's fire lifts.

2 p.m. Draft of 165 men arrives from Field Recruit Depot.

2.15 p.m. A section of the Machine-Gun Company was sent forward to the 2nd Switch Line. G. Right reports things somewhat quieter since 1.45 p.m. G. Left also reports things quieter. One blind 9·2-inch penetrated a dug-out. The shell had no markings.

2.30 p.m. Bucquoy bombarded with heavy calibre shells.

Casualties : 4 Other Ranks wounded.

5.30 p.m. 517th Battery in Biez Wood received several direct hits.

9.20 p.m. Comparatively quiet in front line. Shrapnel fire concentrated on approach roads. In G.1 one dug-out badly damaged. Enemy's aeroplanes very active.

Weather : Dull. Casualties : 1 Other Rank killed, 10 Other Ranks wounded.

Tuesday, June 27th, 1916. 12.20 a.m. Comparatively quiet.

1.30 a.m. Bucquoy shelled with shrapnel.

2.30 a.m. Artillery fire increases.

3 a.m. The Brigade reports that an English attack will take place at 4 a.m.—unknown whether English or German time meant. 170th Regiment reports English prisoner's statement that an attack will take place at 4.55 a.m., German time. 3rd Battalion ordered to stand to.

5.50 a.m. G. Right reports wire south of the Gommecourt–Fonquevillers road still in good condition; also the English wire. North of the road fifty yards of the English wire has been removed Our wire in front of G.1 damaged. 170th Regiment reports a gas attack.

7.10 a.m. Shelling on Bucquoy grows heavier.

5.30 p.m. Brigade reports the enemy attacking south of the Ancre near Thiepval.

7.9 p.m. Bombardment exceptionally heavy—H.E. shells of all calibres.

8 p.m. Medium H.E. shells on left front. Almost continuous bombardment on Kern Redoubt.

9.30 p.m. Bombardment becomes less intense and finally ceases on the front line. Shrapnel fire on all the approach roads, increasing towards midnight. Front trench in G.1 badly damaged—one dug-out blown in. Support line in G.2 bombarded—one dug-out blown in. Several trenches badly destroyed. Enemy's aeroplanes active.

Weather: Dull. Casualties: 1 Other Rank killed, 4 Other Ranks wounded.

Wednesday, June 28th, 1916. 7.50 a.m. Artillery bombardment begins afresh—heavy and light calibres on the whole of the front line. Heavy and medium calibres on Kern Redoubt and the trenches in rear.

8.25 a.m. Right sector reports gas attacks in front of G.1–G.2.

8.50 a.m. G. Right reports that the shelling is much less violent.

No. 3 Company reports that white gas was released after a reddish flame had appeared. The gas cloud, however, remained in the hollow in front of our trench. No. 4 Company reports that gas was released but at once rose and dispersed in the air.

Major Bothmer reports Stössel Trench [Ed. Note.—*The main C.T. in G.*1] partly blocked. The Kern Redoubt partly blown in—repairs in progress. Second machine-gun in G.1 has been badly damaged by artillery fire. Telephonic communication with the trench mortars completely cut. The trench mortar emplacements were partly destroyed yesterday. Enemy appears to be using 15-inch shells (splinters).

9.15 a.m. Bucquoy shelled.

10.15 a.m. G. Right reports increase of artillery fire on the second line.

The telephonists again behave extremely well. In spite of the heavy bombardment, the linesmen succeeded in maintaining communication the whole time, except for the line to the battalion on the right, which will be repaired to-night. Hostile aeroplanes not so active.

Weather: Dull and rainy. Casualties: 3 Other Ranks wounded.

Thursday, June 29th, 1916. 9.15 a.m. Trenches badly knocked about, but still capable of defence. Wire not so badly damaged. Three trenches in G.1, rendered impassable, are being repaired. Heavy hostile trench mortar fire. One of our heavy trench mortars is moved back to a reserve emplacement—the other is buried by a shell. No change in the enemy's front trenches during the last four days. Gas and smoke bombs on G.2.

10.45 a.m. to 5.45 p.m. On the left sector, bombardment of the front line and Kern Redoubt by 6-inch shells. Comparatively quiet on the right. Some heavy shells on Gommecourt.

6 p.m. From the battalion dug-out one can see the enemy's line on the left—the trees have all been shot away. On the right it is somewhat better. Hostile aeroplanes active.

Weather: Dull. Casualties: 4 Other Ranks wounded.

Friday, June 30th, 1916. 7.50 a.m. Heavy artillery and trench mortar fire on G.1 and G.2. One dug-out blown in.

9.15 a.m. Comparatively quiet on both sectors—no signs of an attack.

9.45 a.m. Heavy bombardment of the sector on our left. Quiet on the front of the 91st Reserve Regiment. The impression of an attack on Gommecourt being imminent is not confirmed from the right sector.

10.30 a.m. Quiet.

2.30 p.m. An English prisoner makes the following statement: "No black troops present—no gas—nothing known about attack—rest billets at Sailly." Prisoner was leading a patrol of five men with the object of ascertaining effect of bombardment on our trenches.

5.45 p.m. Heavy shrapnel fire on G.1 and G.2, especially on the left of G.2. Opposite G.2, near the "Bare Pear Tree," several gaps have been made in the enemy's wire close together on a breadth of 15 metres.

6.55 p.m. Bombardment less intense.

Weather: Fine and warm. Casualties: 1 Other Rank killed, 11 Other Ranks wounded.

THE ATTACK. *Saturday, July 1st,* 1916. The intense bombardment shortly before the attack succeeded in rendering the front trenches in sectors G.1 and G.5 ripe for assault. The enemy attained this by concentrating a very great proportion of his artillery and trench mortars (up to the largest calibres) against these sectors. It was then evident that the main attack would be directed north and south of Gommecourt village (sectors G.1, G.5) in order to cut off the garrison of Gommecourt.

The operations of the regiment may thus be considered under the heading of these two sectors.

[NOTE.—*For the distribution of the 55th Reserve Infantry Regiment on July 1st, see Appendix I.*]

G.1 SECTOR. 7.30 a.m. An extremely violent bombardment began, overwhelming all the trenches and sweeping away the wire.

8.30 a.m. The enemy's fire lifted. The enemy's attack, which was made under cover of gas bombs, was perceived. In consequence of the sharp look-out kept by the commander of the 4th Company (Lieut. Graf von Matuschka) and by a platoon commander holding the most dangerous portion of the line, the shell-holes were occupied exactly at the right moment and the attackers were received with hand-grenades. The barrage fire which had been called for began at once.

8.40 a.m. Strong hostile skirmishing lines deployed from opposite G.1. They were at once met by heavy machine-gun and infantry fire. 2nd Lieut. Dobberke, of the 2nd Company, 55th Reserve Regiment, who was holding the third support line of G.1, recognised the superior strength of the enemy's attack which was being carried out against No. 4 Company. In spite of the intense bombardment, he decided to advance with his platoon over the open, and, crossing the second line, reached the front line of G.1 at the decisive moment to reinforce No. 4 Company.

The enemy built up his firing line and attempted to press forward with bombers and flame-projectors, but was repulsed everywhere. Landwehrman Siekmann and Pte. Tenbring of the 4th Company especially distinguished themselves. They sprang forward with a cheer and threw their grenades.

10.30 a.m. The fine spirit of the brave troops of the 2nd and 4th Companies succeeded by their stubborn resistance in annihilating the thick charging waves of the English. The ground was covered with numbers of dead, and in front of our trench lay quantities of English arms and equipment. Gradually the artillery fire recommenced on the front line trenches and rose to a pitch of extreme violence in the course of the afternoon. The fact that all attacks were completely repulsed without the enemy gaining a footing in the front line of G.1 at any point is due, next to the bravery of the troops, to the carefully thought-out arrangements of Major von Bothmer, to the care of the O.C. No. 4 Company (Lieut. Graf von Matuschka) and to the energy of platoon commanders, especially 2nd Lieut. Dobberke and Offizier-Stellvertreter Wortmann.

While the sectors G.2, G.3 and G.4 were kept under a heavy hostile bombardment, which was not followed by an infantry attack, an energetic assault was delivered against G.5.

G.5 SECTOR. 6.30 a.m. Intense bombardment of all calibres up to 15-inch commenced against G.5 with the result that most of the entrances to the dug-outs were blown in, the trenches were flattened out and the wire was destroyed. The front trench was enfiladed from the direction of Fonquevillers. Every round from the English guns pitched in the trench, thus rendering its occupation even by detached posts impossible.

7.30 a.m. Capt. von Schroetter of the 16th Battery, 20th Reserve F.A.R., observed as follows :

"The enemy has overrun sectors N.1. and N.2 (both S. of G.5) and has pushed forward between Süd Trench and Roth Trench beyond Gommecourt Cemetery as far as the beginning of the 1st Guard Line and the Kern Redoubt."

7.30 a.m. The enemy's bombardment lifted on to the Kern Redoubt and the first switch line. Directly afterwards, under the cover of smoke clouds, the enemy's assault began. On the left flank of G.4 (No. 6 Company) and the right flank of G.5 (No. 8 Company) the assault was completely repulsed, but in the meantime two platoons of this company were overrun by the attack, the garrison not having been able to leave the dug-outs in time owing to the entrances having been blown in. 2nd Lieut. Holländer, commanding the 8th Company, 55th Reserve Regiment, was only able to beat off the attacks of the succeeding lines which advanced from Patrol Wood, and to block a further advance, without being able to counter-attack the enemy who had already penetrated the front line. [Ed. Note.—*The Report included a sketch showing that British troops—all L.R.B.—had penetrated Fir, Fen, Ferret, Ems, Female, Exe and Feast, and were N. of the Maze.*]

The enemy forces which had penetrated into N.1 and N.2 were held up and driven back to Gommecourt Cemetery after a heavy bombing encounter with the men of the Infantry Pioneer Company of the 55th Reserve Regiment and of the 4th Company, 10th Pioneer Battalion, which were holding the Kern Redoubt. Elements of the entrenching company and of the 4th Company, 10th Pioneer Battalion, blocked the entrance to the Kern Redoubt. Continuous heavy rifle fire and bombing held up the enemy, who was at least two companies strong. In this struggle Cpl. Seiger, of the 3rd Company, 55th Reserve Infantry Regiment, and Cpl. Laufermann, of the 2nd Company, did well.

7.40 a.m. Capt. Minck, commander of G. Left, issued the following order :

"No. 7 Company (left of Kern Redoubt) will at once attack the enemy who has penetrated into G.5 and the sector of the 8th Company. The attack will be made through Süd Trench."

The 7th Company could not carry out this order at once, but prevented the enemy's further advance, which was held up about 100 yards south of the Kern Redoubt between Hauser Trench and Süd Trench on a front of 100 yards, where he had dug himself in and brought up two machine-guns. The enemy, who was amply supplied with machine-guns and every form of equipment for close fighting, offered a stubborn resistance. His exact strength could not be accurately ascertained, but he was known to be everywhere in far superior numbers. All telephonic communication had been destroyed by the bombardment, and even the cable, buried two metres deep, had been cut. The Regimental Head-quarters were thus without news of the progress of events.

7.50 a.m. Capt. Minck therefore issued the following order :

" No. 10 Company (in regimental reserve in the switch line) will leave small parties in the switch line and will occupy the left portion of the Kern Redoubt. No. 7 Company, 55th Reserve Regiment, will attack the enemy who has penetrated into G.5. Regiment informed."

The regiment received this information at 10.25 a.m.

8 a.m. Following order issued by Regimental Head-quarters :

" One platoon, 11th Company, 55th Reserve Regiment (Bucquoy), will advance and will occupy the 2nd switch line. The 10th Company (switch line) will leave the 2nd switch line clear. Acknowledge receipt to Regimental Head-quarters.

Following report received from 170th Infantry Regiment (*which was on the left of the 55th*—Ed.) :

" 8.35 a.m. Enemy attack developed Hebuterne–Gommecourt Rd. southwards."

9.5 a.m. Gas attack against the north sector.

9.15 a.m. Attack took place from S. of Hebuterne–Bucquoy Rd.

9.30 a.m. Enemy penetrated into G.5, threatening our right flank. We hold the third line trench.

9.30 a.m. Regimental order to the 3rd Battalion, 55th Reserve Regiment (battalion in rest billets at Bucquoy, under Major Tauscher) :

" The battalion, including its entrenching company, will advance by the 2nd Guard Trench and drive out the enemy who has penetrated into G.5. Report when ready to begin the operation. Machine-guns will be allotted."

9.40 a.m. The 8th Company, 77th Reserve Regiment, was placed at the disposal of the 55th Reserve Regiment, and billeted in Bucquoy.

11 a.m. Major Tauscher proceeded to Hill 147 and learnt that the enemy was still in N.1 and N.2. As the enemy who was pushing forward against the Guard Trench was already on the flank, the attack against G.5 was not possible. Major Tauscher, therefore, ordered the 11th Company (Lieut. Stolper) to advance to the attack through the Roth Trench and the 12th Company (Capt. Winkelmann) through the Lehmann Trench, while the 9th Company (Capt. Terberger) remained for the present in the 2nd switch line as reserve. The enemy had constructed several barricades in Roth Trench, Lehmann Trench and Becker Trench, and had occupied the intervening network of trenches.

3 to 4 p.m. The 11th and 12th Companies pushed forward after

extremely violent fighting at close quarters, with the result that the enemy suffered very heavy losses and took to flight, effectively pursued by rifle, machine-gun and artillery fire. In this fighting, in which portion of the 9th Company also took part, the company commanders are especially worthy of praise, and also Offizier-Stellvertreter Viedahl, who recaptured Roth Trench. 2nd Lieut. Weiland and Cpl. Wortmann should also be mentioned.

In the actual regimental sector the enemy had established himself at various points. In order to drive the enemy out, various local encounters ensued. Small parties of the 7th and 10th Companies resisted the superior enemy, who had already dug himself in. The enemy was held in check owing to their efforts, effectively supported by the surviving light trench mortar of the 6th Guard Minnewerfer Company.

No. 7 Company, under Capt. Brockmann, at the same time advanced through the second line from Hauser Trench. Parts of the 6th, 8th and 10th Companies, with bombing parties, attacked the third line trench of G.5 and the ground lying between it and the Kern Redoubt. Two English officers and seventy men were captured. 2nd Lieut. Kröger especially distinguished himself in these bombing operations.

Although we had not been successful in entirely clearing the superior forces of the enemy out of the line, by four o'clock portions of the front trench of G.5 sector had been won back by the 7th and 10th Companies. Parties of the enemy, who offered a stubborn resistance, maintained themselves in sectors of Süd Trench support line.

4.15 p.m. Major Tauscher could not carry out the order given him to advance and clear out G.5 with the 11th and 12th Companies, as the portions of N.1 and N.2 sectors which had been recaptured by these companies were only held with such weak parties of the 170th Regiment that an advance with the two companies of the 55th Reserve Regiment did not seem possible. At 5 p.m. the 170th Regiment recognised this and again placed the companies at the disposal of the 55th Reserve Regiment.

6.50 p.m. In the meantime it had been definitely ascertained at which points the enemy had established himself in our line. (See Sketch No. 3.)

7 p.m. to 10.45 p.m. Regimental Order : To Major Tauscher :

"The 11th and 12th Companies are again placed under your orders for further clearing out of G.5. The 2nd Battalion (Capt. Minck) is to be informed, as telephonic communication has not yet been established."

In the meantime, portions of the 11th Company had already pushed forward to G.5 on their own initiative and had recaptured the front line, almost up to Süd Trench. 2nd Lieuts. Steenbock, Meyenberg, Eilbracht, Sthamer and Cpl. Kauermann especially distinguished themselves. Major Tauscher sent forward another eighty men and the Infantry Pioneer Company through Roth Trench for further operations.

Owing to the skilful and energetic leadership of the O.C. 12th Company (Capt. Winkelmann) and of the O.C. 11th Company (2nd Lieut. Stolper), the counter-attack against the very superior enemy was successful, and after a hard struggle the enemy was cleared out of two company-sectors (N.1 and N.2) of the neighbouring regiment, as well as out of G.5, by 10.45 p.m.

12 midnight. Regimental order issued detailing the new distribution in the sector :

"The 1st Battalion will hold G.1 and G.2 and right of Kern Redoubt.

"The 2nd Battalion, including Infantry Pioneer Company and part of the 4th Company, 10th Pioneer Battalion, will hold G.3, G.4 and left of Kern Redoubt.

"The 3rd Battalion will hold G.5, 2nd Guard line, 1st switch line and left of 2nd switch line.

"The 8th Company, 77th Reserve Regiment, will hold the right portion of 2nd switch line."

Sunday, July 2nd, 1916. 12 midnight onwards. The new distribution was carried out. Units were reorganised, ammunition and supplies were brought up, working parties told off to put up wire and clear up the trenches. The enemy's artillery was quiet. Front line practically not shelled at all.

10 a.m. Thirty-eight shrapnel and twelve H.E. on the Kern Redoubt. Our artillery retaliated. Work done on reconstructing the trenches. Great aerial activity.

Weather : Fine and warm. Casualties : 8 Other Ranks wounded.

[Ed. Note.—*The Report included a sketch showing British troops in Fir, Fen, Ferret, Ems, Feast and N. of the Maze. Exe and Female are shown as clear of British troops.*]

PART II

Remarks by the 55th Reserve Infantry Regiment

(1) The sector held by the regiment was in an exceptionally unfavourable position. The trenches could be directly enfiladed the whole time from Hébuterne and Fonquevillers. Digging new traverses, therefore, afforded no protection. The English enfilading guns fired with such accuracy that every round fell actually into the trenches of G.5 sector, rendering the line untenable. The infantry assault was perceived only when the enfilade fire on the trench was lifted beyond the parados, and simultaneously the English bombers appeared on the parapet.

(2) A prisoner stated that it was intended to cut off Gommecourt

village. The greatest danger, therefore, lay in G.1 and G.5 sectors and on the left flank of the Kern Redoubt. When the position was taken over, the 2nd Guard line consisted of a fallen-in trench. Although its repair was pushed on by all available means, it was only possible to make the actual trench defensible ; dug-outs and shelters could not be provided.

(3) All telephonic communication had already been interrupted by the morning and could not be re-established again until the evening. Communication with Bucquoy remained intact throughout, and also with the second switch line and the regimental battle-post at Point 147. All messages for further forward had to be sent by runner. The wire which was run out by the linesmen during the day, under the heaviest bombardment, only remained intact for a very short time. All cables, which were buried two metres deep, were cut.

Even the tunnelled dug-outs, which were six metres deep, could not keep out the heavy 15-inch shells ; they were blown in. It was again proved that dug-outs should have at least two exits. This is the only way of preserving the occupants from being buried. Long dug-out periscopes are required ; they proved valuable.

(4) The wire was unable to withstand the systematic bombardment. Although all damage caused by the bombardment during the day was repaired during the night, after the bombardment of the morning of July 1st the wire in front of G.5, fifty metres wide, had completely disappeared.

(5) All the trenches bombarded on July 1st were completely flattened out. Only shell-holes remained.

(6) The English had excellent maps of our trenches. They were extremely well equipped with bridging ladders, equipment for close fighting, obstacles, machine-guns and rations, and were well acquainted with the use of our hand-grenades.

(7) Our own barrage fire opened promptly and was very effective. The enemy's barrage frequently failed.

(8) The maintenance of a supply of rations in dug-outs proved of value.

(9) The replenishment of ammunition and grenades was carried out without interruption. More grenade stores are, however, required in front line, and the reserve of belts of machine-gun ammunition must be still further increased.

Conclusion. In order to appreciate fully the efforts of the troops, a few words must be said about the enemy. Of the two attacking English divisions ten battalions have been identified by men captured and killed :

5th and 6th Notts and Derby.
5th and 6th North Staffords.
6th South Staffords.
5th, 9th, 12th, 14th and 16th London Regiment.
5th Cheshires (two companies), attached to the 56th Division.

It should also be mentioned that among the killed was a French artilleryman, apparently an observer.

It must be acknowledged that the equipment and preparation of the English attack were magnificent. The assaulting troops were amply provided with numerous machine-guns, Lewis guns, trench mortars and storming ladders. The officers were provided with excellent maps which showed every German trench systematically named and gave every detail of our positions. The sketches had been brought up to date with all our latest work, and the sectors of attack were shown on a very large scale. Special sketches showing the objectives of the different units, and also aeroplane photographs, were found among the captured documents. The list of the equipment captured gives an idea of the excellent preparations :

Prisoners :

16 officers.
251 men.

Arms and equipment :

39 machine-guns (including 29 Lewis guns).
95 drums of machine-gun ammunition.
5 machine-gun mountings.
2 reserve barrels for machine-guns.
2 shoulder-pieces for machine-guns.
6 trench mortars.
1 trench mortar bed.
915 rifles and carbines.
455 bayonets.
2 revolvers.
2 light-pistols.
65 steel helmets.
150 belts and frogs.
1 pack.
23 wire-cutters (including one for attachment to rifle).
10 knobkerries.
97 spades.
16 picks.
6 telephone instruments.
3 reels of wire.
1 signal apparatus.
42 anti-gas apparatus.
41 gas masks.
4 gas helmets.
4 sacks of English equipment.

Ammunition :

11 boxes of S.A. ammunition.
3880 loose cartridges.

44 boxes of machine-gun ammunition.
6000 belted rounds of machine-gun ammunition.
2 sacks of machine-gun ammunition.
214 rifle grenades.
381 hand grenades.
52 trench mortar bombs.

Our own losses :[1]

Our own losses on July 1st amounted to (not including the 2nd Reserve Ulanen Regiment or the 15th Reserve Infantry Regiment) :

Killed : 3 officers, 182 men.
Wounded : 10 officers, 372 men.
Missing : — officers, 24 men.
Total : 13 officers, 578 men.

Guns destroyed :

3 light field howitzers.
1 field gun (direct hit).
1 9-cm. gun (direct hit).

Though our losses are regrettable, they must be regarded as small when one considers the severity of the fighting. Many casualties were avoided by holding the front trenches, exposed to the most intense bombardment, with the minimum strength required for defence, and in nearly every case the garrison succeeded in leaving the dug-outs and manning the parapet at the right moment.

July 1st terminated in a complete victory for the 2nd Guard Reserve Division. Every man in the Division is proud of this result and of the success won. The most westerly point of the German line on the Western Front remains intact in our hands. Full of confidence, the brave troops maintain their watch with the same strength and endurance in order to annihilate every fresh attempt on the part of the enemy whenever it may come.

PART III

Lessons from the Fighting

(By Gen. Freiherr von Süsskind, Commanding 2nd Guard Reserve Division.)

(1) Effect of the Enemy's Bombardment on our Trenches. —(a) *The Obstacle.* Even an obstacle consisting of two belts of wire, each 30 metres wide, was unable to withstand the intense bombardment where not concealed from view. In spite of this, wire must be considered as an important factor in the defence of

[1] Apparently for the whole of the 2nd Guard Reserve Division, less the units mentioned.—Translator.

a position, as it protects the trench garrison from surprise attacks and minor enterprises up to the moment of the last preparatory artillery bombardment preceding the assault. It thus enables a considerable reduction to be made in trench garrisons, and preserves their defensive power.

When a new line is being dug or an old line is being repaired and the time is short in which work can be done undisturbed by the enemy's fire, it is recommended that the construction of the obstacle should be undertaken first of all. The construction of the actual trenches is easier to carry out than that of the obstacle when under hostile fire.

The principle must always be borne in mind that the obstacle should be concealed as much as possible from the enemy's view. With this object, and also to obtain the greatest possible enfilade effect, the trace of the obstacle should not be parallel to that of the fire trench. When time and labour are available, the wire must be artificially sunk below the ground level. The destruction of the wire by the enemy's artillery is rendered more difficult when the obstacle is at least 50 metres in front of the parapet. The destruction of the wire cannot then be carried out simultaneously with the bombardment of the trenches. It requires a separate expenditure of ammunition and time, the latter being all to the advantage of the defence. One condition is necessary, namely, that the whole of the obstacle, from its forward to its rear edge, is visible from the parapet. Another method of rendering the destruction of the wire more difficult is to construct it in two or three belts, with about 15 metres of intervening space between each.

In order that the wire may be repaired as far as possible during the pauses in the artillery preparation, it is necessary that materials for repair (e.g. rolls of barbed wire, *chevaux de frise*, loose wire for joining up broken ends and wire-cutters), should be distributed along the whole front in small trench dumps.

(b) *Traverses* must be 10 metres thick, in order to withstand the effect of heavy calibre shells and mortar bombs.

(c) *Sentry-posts* are of the very greatest importance. They should be of concrete and cannot be made sufficiently strong. When constructed in any other manner, they are simply swept away. Concrete recesses dug deep into the parapet, from which the sentry can observe with a periscope, are recommended. These, however, can seldom be made in the front trench under the enemy's fire. Splinter-proof sentry-posts can, however, be constructed in pioneer parks. These should also afford protection against splinters from the rear, and should have good broad observation slits. Sentry-posts of this description can be quickly dug in.

If the sentry-posts are destroyed by the intense bombardment, observation must be carried out from the dug-out entrances by means of long trench periscopes. A large reserve of spare mirrors for these periscopes is necessary.

(d) *Dug-outs.* The deep, tunnelled dug-outs, with 5 or 6 metres of earth covering, were only destroyed when they had been struck by several direct hits of the heaviest calibre. In many cases, both dug-out entrances were blown in. It is recommended that several dug-outs should be joined up by underground galleries. The heavy aerial torpedoes, which penetrate a long way before exploding, cause great damage to dug-outs. All mining frames must be strongly reinforced with props. In the trenches further back the dug-outs should be made 7 or 8 metres deep. The steps should be so constructed that there is at least 1·1 metres of earth above the first frame.

In the good dug-outs existing in the position the troops were able to endure the seven days' artillery bombardment without depreciation of their fighting power and to meet the infantry assault with vigour and energy. In chalk soil particular attention must be paid to the concealment of every shovelful of excavated chalk. Otherwise, aeroplanes flying low can at once mark down every dug-out. It is no use concealing them later on ; this, in fact, only shows the enemy that the excavation is complete and that the dug-outs are in use.

It is desirable that at least every Company Commander should have an aeroplane photograph of his own trenches in order to see for himself the weak points in their construction.

(e) The work done in *digging-in battery positions* has been of the greatest value. Especially good were the splinter-proof gun emplacements, as is proved by the small losses of the artillery in personnel and *matériel.* The use of timber frames, previously prepared in the pioneer park out of strong beams, made it possible to construct a gun emplacement in one night. This strong framework made possible subsequent reinforcement of the cover above and at the sides, according to the time and material available. The necessary lateral traverse for the guns was allowed for in every case.

(f) *Communication Trenches.* The communication trenches have proved suitable for the passage of runners as well as for the replenishment of ammunition and supplies, even when they were exposed to barrage fire. In constructing the communication trenches attention must be paid, as a first principle, to avoid straight lines exposed to enfilade fire ; otherwise, they must be provided with strong traverses. In order that they may be always passable, they must be provided with numerous deep sump-pits, which must be dug at the time of the original construction of the trench, and must be maintained by means of trench wardens permanently told off to them, who are responsible for keeping the sump-pits clear of mud. In general, there should be one man told off to look after between 4 and 6 kilometres of trench. Trenches should be at least 2 metres deep. A width of 1 metre floor and 1·8 metres surface measurement is preferable to smaller dimensions. Traffic is easier and the trench still remains passable even when knocked about by shell fire, and passing places are not so necessary. Numerous sortie-steps are necessary on both sides.

(2) LESSONS FROM THE ENEMY'S INFANTRY ASSAULT.—(a) According to prisoners' statements, our *artillery barrage* was extremely effective; but in spite of it the enemy appears to have been able to pass round the northern limits of the barrage, near X2. The lateral limits of the barrage must, therefore, not be too abrupt.

(b) *Machine-Guns.* All the prisoners were unanimous in recognising the moral and actual effect of our machine-guns. In order not to betray to the enemy their final emplacements, it is necessary to change their positions frequently. At ordinary times, fire should not be opened from the emplacements which are intended to repel an assault. An accumulation of machine-guns in the front line is to be avoided. Every opportunity should be seized for obtaining overhead and enfilade fire from positions further back, all positions suitable for this purpose are to be carefully reconnoitred beforehand and shown on a map, together with their principal arcs of fire and ranges.

(c) *Alarm Signals* of every kind have, in the main, proved useless in the din of battle. Men must be roused by special parties told off to run along the trench and give the alarm. Loud and shrill automatic syrens and large, easily handled bells are best suited for gas alarms.

(d) Rifles, knobkerries, ammunition, *hand-grenades* and entrenching tools must be ready to hand *in the dug-outs.* Ammunition and grenade stores must be provided in every company and sector dug-out in underground depots. On no account should an excessive number of grenades be stored in one place. Each regiment must have a reserve of 2000 grenades available in its pioneer park. A part of this reserve should also be kept in dumps in the intermediate position. The reserve of 8000 grenades laid down for every regimental sector is sufficient so long as the supply can be replenished from the divisional reserve during the battle when the grenade stores in the front line have been blown in.

(e) *The enemy's aeroplanes* had a most disturbing effect during the preparatory period as well as during the actual attack. In the attack each sector had an aeroplane told off to it. These airmen had already carried out preliminary reconnaissances. They gave the direction to the attacking troops, gave them warning against surprise, and in one case—in sector X—attacked with flechettes, the reserves coming up from the fourth line trench.

During the preparatory period the trench garrison must be afforded more protection against enemy aeroplanes. Light, mobile anti-aircraft guns must be provided, which can change position after every series, and can be used from the trenches without special previous arrangements. Anti-aircraft guns which are permanently dug in soon attract hostile artillery fire, are put out of action, and do more harm than good to the infantry. During the attack, this protection should be provided by battleplane squadrons.

(f) *Protection against Gas.* The experiences gained with regard to protection against gas are contained in a separate report. From a tactical point of view, the enemy appears to have made various gas and smoke attacks during the preparatory period, with the following objects :

(1) To tire out our watchfulness.

(2) To use up our anti-gas equipment.

(3) To draw our artillery fire in order to mark down the exact limits of our barrage ; and

(4) To cause us unnecessary ammunition expenditure.

During the assault, he endeavoured to form a screen with smoke bombs in front of our trench to cover his passage through the remains of our wire and penetrate into our trenches.

(g) *Reserves.* If the switch and intermediate lines cannot be permanently used for accommodating the sector reserves on account of insufficient dug-outs, it is recommended that reserves should be sent forward as soon as the imminence of an attack is recognised by the intense bombardment on the front trench. In this sector of the front, the reserves can reach the intermediate position without loss. They are then ready to reinforce any point where the hostile attack may have penetrated. The counter-stroke, however, must be made immediately, in order to allow no time to the enemy, tired out with the assault and unacquainted with our trench system, to reorganise, get his bearings, bring up his machine-guns, and consolidate the position gained.

(h) *Regimental Command Posts.* The regimental command post is best situated in or near the intermediate line into which all the communication trenches to the front debouch.

The regimental commander should be here close to his reserves. Even when telephonic communication from here to the battalion command posts further forward has been cut, rapid communication with the front by means of runners is still possible. The telephone lines from the intermediate position to the rear are only exposed to the danger of chance hits, and breaks here can be more easily mended. Alternative means of communication rearward must, however, also be arranged for by means of runners and cyclists. In the same way, the command post of higher formations must be prepared to send forward orderly officers in the event of the telephone lines being cut.

(3) Replenishment of Ammunition and Grenades. The replenishment of ammunition and grenades took place, even on July 1st, without interruption.

Artillery Ammunition. Taking advantage of the fact that during the morning the enemy's batteries paid little attention to the ground in rear, the replenishment of ammunition was begun as early as 10.30 a.m. ; and, in spite of being in full view, was carried out without casualties and in accordance with the pre-arranged plan. Not one of the batteries of all the different calibres ran the least danger of exhausting its ammunition supply. Artillery group commanders exercised their authority in the most exemplary manner in controlling the ammunition expenditure, so that the proper quantity of ammunition was used at the right times.

Infantry Ammunition. The quantity of small arms ammunition in the ammunition recesses in front line was in excess of the demand.

On the other hand, as regards machine-guns, the necessity was shown for the provision of a far larger supply of belted machine-gun ammunition than at present laid down (twenty belts for each machine-gun, and, in addition, a reserve of 200 belts with the machine-gun company).

Hand-grenades and "Priester" Grenades. These were brought up as far as Rettemoy Farm by motor lorry on several occasions.

(4) RATIONS. Rations were dumped in front line on the following system : Three ration dumps in each sector, each dump containing 2000 rations, besides ample supplies of chocolate and mineral water. This system proved of great value, as the troops in front line were thus assured good and sufficient food even when the rations could not be brought up from the rear. In consequence, their resolute and confident state of mind was maintained throughout.

(5) TELEPHONES. As far back as eight kilometres behind the front all lines must be buried to a depth of at least two metres, when possible.

When the cable trench is being dug, care must be taken that during and after its construction it is concealed at once from either direct or aeroplane observation by the enemy (concealed with turf, brushwood, etc.). This precaution is of particular importance in the neighbourhood of telephone exchanges. Points which are likely to be kept under heavy fire during an attack are to be avoided, e.g. gun-positions, cross-roads, etc.

Advantage must be taken of the ground to lay the line in dead ground and behind banks and to avoid the crests of ridges. The provision of lamp-signalling has again proved of value.

CONCLUSION. The most important preparation for successfully repelling an attack consists in fostering and constantly maintaining a healthy and active offensive spirit among the troops.

By careful instruction in all methods of close fighting, each individual man must be trained to feel and know himself superior to the enemy, in order that the penetration into our position of a hostile attack must involve its annihilation.

The united efforts and energies of the troops holding a defensive position in face of the enemy must be devoted to preparation for the final victory. No opportunity must be missed for causing the enemy casualties when at work, especially by wary, alert and boldly led patrols, and by artillery and machine-gun fire.

It is not a question of merely repelling the enemy's attack ; the object should be to annihilate him.

(Signed) FREIHERR VON SÜSSKIND.

APPENDIX I

Distribution of the 55th Res. Infantry Regiment on July 1st

	G. Left (2nd Batt.) *Sector Commander:* Captain Minck.			G. Right (1st Batt.) *Sector Commander:* Major V. Bothmer.	
	G. 5.	*G.* 4.	*G.* 3.	*G.* 2.	*G.* 1.
Front Line:	8*th Coy.* 170 Rifles. 3 M.G's.	6*th Coy.* 134 Rifles.	5*th Coy.* 171 Rifles. 1 M.G.	3*rd Coy.* 137 Rifles. 2 M.G's.	4*th Coy.* 126 Rifles. 2 M.G's.
Close Support:	8*th Coy.*	6*th Coy.* 26 Rifles.	5*th Coy.* 1 M.G.	3*rd Coy.* 12 Rifles.	4*th Coy.* 18 Rifles.
Kern Redoubt:	7*th Coy.* 158 Rifles. 2 M.G's.	*Inf. Pioneer Coy.* 150 Rifles.		1*st Coy.* 159 Rifles. 1 M.G.	2*nd Coy.* 90 Rifles.
1*st Switch Line:*	10*th Coy.* 62 Rifles.			2*nd Coy.* 62 Rifles.	
2*nd Switch Line:*			10*th Coy.* 100 Rifles.		
Intermediate Line:		M.G.			
Resting:	9*th and* 12*th Coys.* in Brigade Reserve. 11*th Coy.*, Regimental Reserve. In Bucquoy, 14 M.G's. and remainder of Inf. Pioneer Coy.				

Thus the front line was held with 738 rifles and 8 M.G's., with 56 rifles and 1 M.G. in close support.

The Kern Redoubt was held with 557 rifles and 3 M.G's.

APPENDIX II

Casualties of the 55th Res. Infantry Regiment for the period June 24th to July 2nd, 1916

Date.	Officers.			Other ranks.		
	Killed.	Wounded	Missing.	Killed.	Wounded.	Missing.
24th June, 1916	—	—	—	—	1	—
25th ,,	—	—	—	1	11	—
26th ,,	—	—	—	1	10	—
27th ,,	—	—	—	3	4	—
28th ,,	—	—	—	—	3	—
29th ,,	—	—	—	—	4	—
30th ,,	—	—	—	1	11	—
1st July, 1916	1	5	—	109	244	38
2nd ,,	—	—	—	—	8	—
Total	1	5		115	296	38
	6			449		

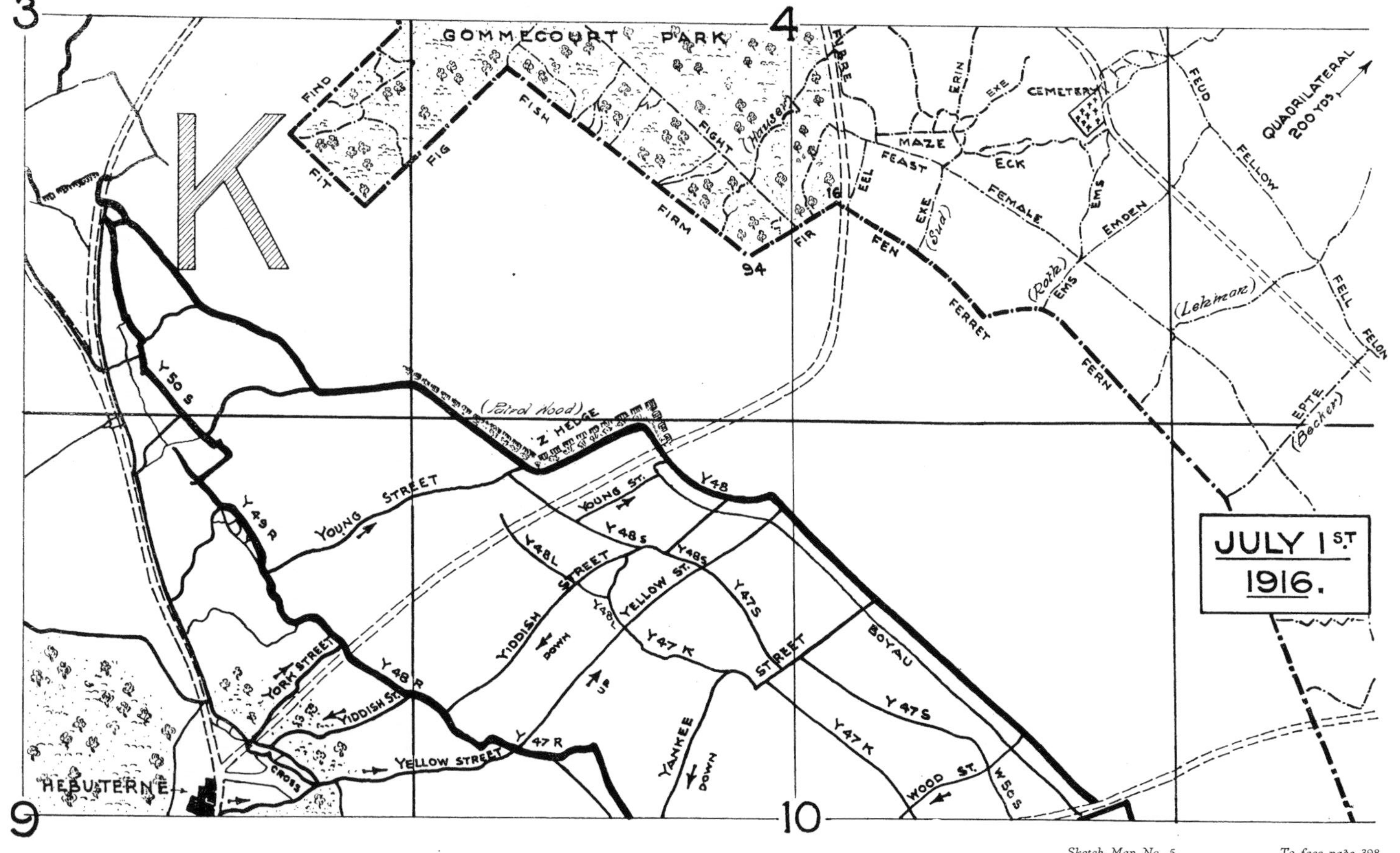

Sketch Map No. 5.

To face page 398

Missing (other ranks) :

7th Company	14
8th Company	22
11th Company	2
Total	38

APPENDIX III

AMMUNITION EXPENDITURE DURING THE PERIOD JUNE 24TH TO JULY 1ST, 1916, BY THE ARTILLERY OF THE 2ND GUARD RES. DIVISION

Date.	60 Field Guns and Hows.			20 Heavy Guns and Hows.				
	Field Guns 40.	Light Field Hows. 12.	9-cm. Guns 8.	10-cm. Guns '14 2.	15-cm. How. '96 4.	15-cm. How. '02/13 8.	Russian 15-cm. Guns 4.	21-cm. How. (old pattern) 2.
24th June . .	528	223	211	8	80	138	42	17
25th ,, . .	1,105	313	452	214	173	357	154	102
26th ,, . .	3,806	621	651	385	79	953	74	67
27th ,, . .	4,518	468	208	70	152	664	260	68
28th ,, . .	664	210	173	—	38	404	39	32
29th ,, . .	751	69	108	126	141	247	67	6
30th ,, . .	548	90	—	—	31	25	52	—
1st July . . .	11,683	4,429	2,070	609	481	2,821	258	252
Total . .	23,603	6,423	3,873	1,412	1,175	5,609	946	544

APPENDIX E

Arras, March, 1918

Special Correspondents' Notices

The *Daily Mail*, 2/4/18, Hamilton Fyfe.

". . . But these men—those I saw belonged to the London Rifle Brigade—did not want to play football. . . . Here was a man who had been buried in one of our outposts when the German push for Arras began with so terrific a bombardment. Only he escaped. Another post had the luck to be less heavily shelled. When the enemy came over the garrison strafed them with machine-guns until it was surrounded. Then it cut its way through them and, to the amazement of the Battalion Commander, rejoined the main body. . . . A man among men is the commander of this party. How he escaped alive no one can understand. He was in the thick of the fight. When the Germans were advancing he was firing into them with his rifle. He fired 300 rounds and he says 'you simply couldn't miss.' He was very much impressed by the way the advance was made. 'They came shoulder to shoulder. They wore huge packs. They carried six or seven days' rations, an extra pair of boots and two blankets. They evidently meant to go a long way. We stopped that all right.' It was stopped by the resolute courage of the men in the trenches and by the fierceness of our machine-gun fire."

The *Daily Telegraph*, 2/4/18, Philip Gibbs.

". . . Yesterday I saw some of the men who have been fighting in the battle of Arras, heroes of the heaviest blow the enemy has received since March 21st. There were some London Regiments among them, and their band was playing a tattoo as the evening sun set in and a great glory of gold flamed across the Western sky after a day of storm. The Colonel of their battalion, it was the London Rifle Brigade, came out after a sleep and a wash and a shave—all his kit had been lost in a dug-out, but he had borrowed a razor from his batman—and nobody would have guessed that this smiling man with perfectly bright eyes and easy manners had just come out of a battle where many of his comrades fell around him under frightful shelling, where he had been firing a rifle all day long at the crowds of Germans, and where he had seen dead bodies piled on dead as the enemy came up in waves against blasts of machine-gun bullets and the fire of our field artillery. He spoke just a word or two about the tragedy of losing many of his best and bravest and then put that thought aside and told of their heroic defence and the slaughter of the enemy. . . . This battalion was holding the foremost line by a system of posts in advance of the battle line, among them Mill Post, Bradford Post and Towie Post, and the enemy began the battle by a concentrating bombardment on these, while he gassed the support lines and the field artillery positions and brought his barrage backward and forwards over our main defences. . . . Most of these posts were blotted out utterly. . . . An officer of the L.R.B., who has been out since the beginning of the war, says he never saw such an intense bombardment, and when it lifted the enemy came over in close formation wave after wave. Behind them at some distance rode the Company Commanders on horses and behind them the field artillery. Each man carried a full pack and an extra pair of boots—one man had two extra pairs—as for a long march, and rations for six days."

The *Morning Post*, 2/4/18, Percival Phillips.

". . . The experience of some London Rifle Brigade lads will show what happened in our forward trenches. They were far quicker in action than their heavily laden foes. When the flood poured over the first parapet through broken wire draped with corpses, the Londoners gave them a bit of trench, blocked it off and fought them from the further side. As the flood extended so they fell back a yard at a time, throwing bombs and firing rifles point blank, sometimes so close that they nearly drove scorched cloth into the grey figures tightly wedged into the narrow alleys. The Germans who fell never got up again. Those carried down by the collapse of their comrades lay helpless, their cumbersome kit weighing them down, while others trampled over them to meet their death. The officers of the riflemen were as busy as the privates. The Commander and his Adjutant lay on the parapet beside two machine-guns that were pouring out an unruffled stream of bullets along the trench. They fired 600 cartridges between them in the first hour of the attack. 'You simply could not miss,' said one of them afterwards, repeating the phrase we have heard so often from troops at other parts of the front. Officers had more work with the rifle that day than since they first commanded men in the field. Still the Germans came on. The riflemen fell back slowly along a communication trench. They themselves lost heavily, but the regiment of which they were a part will record their deeds and those of their comrades who died so willingly as amongst the most glorious in its history."

The *Daily Graphic* gave Lieut.-Col. Husey's photograph headed "A Gallant Colonel" with the following letterpress:

"The heroic stand made by the London Territorials against the most determined attack delivered by the enemy during the past week has given unalloyed pleasure to Londoners. But the mention of any individual or unit might almost be invidious if it were not that the special achievement of Lieut.-Col. Husey, commanding the London Rifle Brigade, stands out as something unique and distinct. . . . Imperative orders that the line must be held at all costs reached Col. Husey, who rallied his men again and again when further resistance seemed all but hopeless. Realising that this was a soldier's battle, when every shot tells, the Colonel went himself into the ranks and fired over 300 rounds at the dull grey mass that threatened to overwhelm our force. . . ."

APPENDIX F

Honorary Colonels

1859–60, Col. J. Carter (Lord Mayor).
1860–1904, H.R.H. The Duke of Cambridge.

Commanding Officers

1859, Lieut.-Col. G. M. Hicks (late 41st, Welsh, Regt.).
1862, Col. George Warde (late 35th and 51st L.I.).
1876, Lieut.-Col. Sir A. D. Hayter, Bart. (late Grenadier Guards).
1881, Lieut.-Col W Haywood
1882, Col. Lord Edward Pelham Clinton (late R.B.).
1890, Col. H. C. Cholmondeley, C.B. (late R.B.).
1901, Col. Edward Matthey, C.B., T.D.
1901, Col. Lord Bingham (late R.B.).
1912, Lieut.-Col. Earl Cairns, C.M.G. (late R.B.).

1st Batt.

1915 (Feb.) to 1916 (Aug.), Lieut.-Col. A. S. Bates, D.S.O.
1916 (Aug.) to 1917 (Aug.), Lieut.-Col. R. H. Husey, D.S.O.
1917 (Aug.) to 1917 (Dec.), Lieut.-Col. F. H. Wallis, M.C.
1917 (Dec.) to 1918 (May), Lieut.-Col. R. H. Husey, D.S.O.
1918 (May) to 1919 (May), Lieut.-Col. C. D. Burnell, D.S.O.

2nd Batt.

1914 (Sept.) to 1917 (April), Col. G. R. Tod.
1917 (April) to 1917 (Dec.), Lieut.-Col. P. D. Stewart, D.S.O.
1917 (Dec.) to 1918 (Feb.), Lieut.-Col. C. E. Johnston, M.C.

3rd Batt.

1914 (Nov.) to 1915 (May), Col. H. C. Cholmondeley, C.B.
1915 (June) to 1919 (Aug.), Brevet Col. N. C. King, T.D.

Adjutants

1859, Capt. C. F. Mackenzie.
1860–1882, Lieut. A. T. Ewens (K.R.R.C.).
1860–1864, Capt. R. W. Smith (late 30th Foot).

1864–1865, Capt. R. C. Holmes (10th Hussars).
1865–1881, Capt. E. O'Callaghan (16th Foot, Bedfords).
1882–1888, Capt. C. Wortham (K.R.R.C.).
1888–1893, Capt. J. A. Skene Thomson (33rd Regt., Duke of Wellington's).
1893–1898, Capt. T. G. P. Glynn (8th Regt., King's Liverpool).
1898–1903, Capt. G. R. Tod (72nd Regt., Seaforth Highlanders).
1903–1906, Capt. B. H. H. Cooke (Rifle Brigade).
1906–1909, Capt. A. C. H. Kennard (Rifle Brigade).
1909–1912, Capt. J. A. W. Spencer (Rifle Brigade).
1912–1914, Capt. A. C. Oppenheim (K.R.R.C.).

1st Batt.

1914 (Aug. 4th) to 1915 (May 13th), Capt. A. C. Oppenheim, D.S.O.
1915 (May 13th) to 1916 (April 7th), Capt. H. L. Johnston, M.C.
1916 (April 7th) to 1916 (Sept. 12th), Capt. F. H. Wallis, M.C.
1916 (Sept. 3rd) to 1917 (March 19th), Lieut. D. McOwan.
1917 (March 19th) to 1917 (May 20th), Capt. J. H. Stransom, D.C.M.
1917 (May 20th) to 1917 (Aug. 14th), Capt. F. H. Wallis, M.C.
1917 (Aug. 14th) to 1917 (Aug. 15th), 2nd Lieut. B. H. Sellon (11th Lond.).
1917 (Aug. 15th) to 1919 (May 31st), Capt. W. C. Von Berg, M.C.

2nd Batt.

1914 (Sept. 6th) to 1915 (June 17th), Capt. C. G. H. Macgill, M.V.O.
1915 (June 17th) to 1917 (July 23rd), Capt. F. Furze.
1917 (July 23rd) to 1918 (Jan. 29th), Lieut. R. Cope.

3rd Batt.

1914 (Nov. 26th) to 1918 (Aug. 11th), Capt. J. F. C. Bennett.
1918 (Aug. 11) to 1919 (March 2nd), Capt. G. C. Chambers.
1919 (March 2nd) to 1919 (April), Capt. J. H. Stransom, D.C.M.

Sergeant-Majors

1859–1881, R. Southgate.
1861–1870, A. Talbot (2nd Batt.).
1870–1878, — O'Neill (2nd Batt.).
1881–1893, W. Gowling.
1893–1893, J. K. Williams.
1893–1897, J. H. Bedford.
1897–1904, T. Malone.
1904–1908, J. McLoughlin.
1908–1912, R. J. Kensdale.
1912–1915, A. G. Harrington.
1915–1919, J. Adams.

Permanent Staff

1868–1885, W. Grange.
1868–1871, — Smith.
1868–1884, D. Desmond.
1868–1876, — Membry.
1870–1874, — Brown.
1877–1881, W. Gowling (then S.M.).
1882–1889, G. Frier.
1885–1893, J. K. Williams (then S.M.).
1886– T. Donovan.
1892–1893, J. Bedford (then S.M.).
1894–1900, S. Brown.
1894–1900, J. O'Shaughnessy.
1900–1904, M. Moriarty.
1900–1904, J. McLoughlin (then S.M.).
1900–1906, J. F. Perrier.
1904–1907, C. J. Rush.
1906–1908, R. J. Kensdale (then S.M.).
1907–1908, H. J. Price.
1908–1909, H. E. Lydiart.
1908–1910, G. H. Thomas.
1909–1914, H. Tyler.
1910–1912, A. G. Harrington (then S.M.).
1910–1911, M. Turpin.
1911–1915, J. Adams (then R.S.M.).

Bandmasters

1859, J. R. Sutton.
1864, J. E. Stanton.
1876, H. Sibbold.
1882, H. Henton.
1903, S. Dodwell.
1909, P. S. Robinson.

Bugle-Majors

1860, Webb.
1864, J. E. Smith.
1865, Marston.
Pound.
1891, Bunce.
1894, J. Cavanagh.
T. Bryant.
1896, W. J. Raw.
1905, S. Dunbar.
1909, J. Berry.
1912, C. Vellenoweth.

1st Batt.
P. S. Robinson.
W. J. Mould.

2nd Batt.
P. S. Robinson.
A. S. King.

3rd Batt.
A. W. Wright.
W. J. Mould.

Secretaries

1859, — Richardson.
A. Clearson.
1868, Adjt. and Sergt.-Major (Capt. Ewens and Sergt.-Major R. Southgate).
1882, Lieut.-Col. Ewens.
1883, Lieut.-Col. Harvey (late Paymaster, R.B.).
1893, Lieut. E. Milliken (Honorary).
W. Gowling (Assistant).
1897, Capt. C. W. Cornish (Honorary).
1903, T. Malone (Assistant).
1908, Capt. E. D. Johnson (Honorary).
1913, Pte. C. A. Monson (Honorary Assistant).
1914, Major C. W. Cornish (Honorary).

Honorary Solicitors

1860, H. W. Vallance.
1870, Lieut. A. Rhodes.
1885, Clr.-Sergt. G. P. Rogers.
1888, Sergt. E. F. Debenham.
1895, Pte. H. Lattey.
1911, Sergt. J. F. C. Bennett.

Auditors

1861, Harding, Pullein and Co.
1872, — Ball (Harding, Whinney, Gibbons and Co.).
1885, (Honorary) Woodley Smith.
1893, „ C. F. Elles.

Honorary Surveyors

1860, H. G. Haywood.
1882, Capt. H. C. Boyes.
1902, R. B. Marsh.
1903–1912, *Nil.*
1913, H. C. Monson.

Strength

These figures cannot be taken as strictly accurate : they are so in some cases, but in others they are only approximate.

1860 (Jan.), 1116.
(July), 1516.
(Oct.), 1499.
1862, 1232.
1863, 998.
1867, 1209.
1868, 1046.
1871, 1006.
1873, 881.
1876, 720.
1877, 801.
1878, 754.
1882, 820.
1885, 787.
1886, 806.
1894, 805.
1895, 825.
1896, 807.
1897, 842.
1899, 691.

1900, 1159.	1907, 481.
1901, 1034.	1908 (Mar.), 465.
1902, 828.	(May), 241.
1903, 657.	(July), 333.
1904, 570.	1909 (Feb.), 371.
1905, 555.	(Mar.), 744.
1906 531.	1910, 898.

Annual Trainings

Easter, 1860, None.
,, 1861, None.
,, 1862, Brighton.
,, 1863, ,,
,, 1864, None.
,, 1865, Brighton.
,, 1866 ,,
,, 1867, Dover.
,, 1868, Portsmouth.
,, 1869, Dover.
,, 1870, Brighton.
,, 1871, ,,
,, 1872, ,,
,, 1873 to 1876, None.
,, 1877, Aylesbury.
,, 1878, Brighton.
,, 1879, Dover.
,, 1880, Lewes for Brighton.
,, 1881, Brighton.
,, 1882, Portsmouth, Fort Nelson.
,, 1883, ,, Fort Purbrook.
,, 1884, Dover, Fort Burgoyne.
,, 1885, ,, ,,
,, 1886, ,, Shaft Barracks.
,, 1887, None.
,, 1888, Walmer.
,, 1889, Eastney.
,, 1890, Winchester.
,, 1891, Shorncliffe.
,, 1892, Winchester.
,, 1893, Chatham.
,, 1894, Winchester.
,, 1895, Canterbury.
,, 1896, Windsor.
,, 1897 ,,
August, 1898, Aldershot, Bourley Bottom.
Easter, 1899, Brighton.
Whitsun, 1900, Salisbury Plain, Perham Down.

August,	1901,	Colchester, Middlewick.
,,	1902,	Aldershot, Cove Hill.
,,	1903	,, Farnborough Common.
,,	1904,	Newhaven.
,,	1905,	Seaford.
Easter,	1906,	Dover.
August,	1907,	Salisbury Plain, Perham Down.
,,	1908	,, Bustard.
,,	1909	,, Lark Hill.
,,	1910,	Bordon.
,,	1911,	Camberley.
,,	1912,	Lulworth.
,,	1913,	Salisbury Plain, Perham Down.
,,	1914,	Eastbourne. Cancelled owing to mobilisation.

APPENDIX G

The following N.C.O.'s and men served with the C.I.V. in South Africa:

Colour-Sergeants

Bate, F.
Beeton, G.

Sergeants

Goddard, T. E.
Gordon, S. C.
Hamilton, W. G.
Harding; H. P. E.
Henshaw, S. T. W.
Kingsford, D. P.
Potter, C. W.
Taylor, C. E.
Warcup, H. E.

Lance-Sergeants

Hyman, R.
Prentice, S.

Sergeant-Bugler

Dunbar, S.

Corporals

Britton, C. A.
Douet, H. E.
Evans, A.
Jenkinson, E.
Josephs, P. R. E.
Kettley, G.
Lloyd, E. A.
Paul, A. L.
Paul, C. H.
Waters, R. W.
Willcocks, M. F.

Privates

Abrahams, A. G.
Banks, F. L.
Barter, E. B.
Barton, G. C.
Beart, F. C. W.
Bulley, C. P.
Burrough, J.
Byshe, E. A.
Charge, J. A. W.
Clapham, C. A.
Clippingdale, C. H.
Conolly, L. M. S. N.
Davies, W. E.
Edwards, J. C.
Edwards, P. A.
Eustace, F.
Evitt, H. L.
Flowerdew, H. H.
Foster, A. H.
Freeman, H. E.
Fry, W. S.
Gate, W. P.

Gilliland, W. E.
Godwin, R. W. G.
Hampton, E. B.
Hampton, G. C.
Hampton, J. L.
Hart, B. A.
Hart, T. E.
Hawkins, A. K.
Holland, M. W.
Hooke, J. C.
Houghton, W. E.
Hunt, M. T.
Knight, W. C.
Lintott, A. J. C.
Long, E. J.
Miller, J. A.
Nicholls, C. E.
Œxle, W. H.
Paynter, J.
Petty, L. C.
Phillips, C. E.
Pocock, G. B.
Pollock, D. W.
Ruddle, C.
Semple, W. A.
Simpson, H. G.
Tipper, V. G.
Titley, P.
Webb, C. C. W.
Williams, G. M.
Wilson, G. F.

BUGLERS

Bransgrove, S.
Davies, C. J.

The following served in South Africa in units other than C.I.V. Abbreviations: I.Y.—Imperial Yeomanry. R.F.—Royal Fusiliers (service company). R.A.M.C.—Royal Army Medical Corps. A.S.C.—Army Service Corps.

From "A" Coy.:—
Adshead, Cpl. G. F., R.F.
Beckett, Pte. F. F., I.Y. (Paget's Horse).
Fry, Pte. J. H., I.Y. (Rough Riders).
Harris, Pte. E. R., I.Y. (Paget's Horse).
Lable, Pte. W., R.A.M.C.

From "D" Coy.:—
Bing, Pte. R. H., R.A.M.C.
Carson, Pte. J. O., R.F.
Dunn, Pte. T., I.Y. (Paget's Horse).
Hooper, Pte. R. E. P., I.Y. (Sharpshooters).
Lintott, Pte. A. L., I.Y.
Loup, Pte. H., 9th Gen. Hosp.
Marton, Pte. W. de G., I.Y.
McVeagh, Pte. A. J. R., I.Y.
Neil, Pte. A. J., I.Y. (Sharpshooters).

From "F" Coy.:—
Andrew, Pte. A. J., I.Y.
Campbell, Pte. E. J., I.Y.
Stevens, Pte. F. W., I.Y.
Winton, Pte. A. E., I.Y.

From "G" Coy.:—
Charge, Pte. H. W. W., I.Y.
Dickie, Pte. T., R.F.
Featherstonhaugh, Pte. W. R., I.Y.
Neal, Pte. E., R.F.
Neal, Pte. H. E., R.F.
Rice, Pte. W. J., R.F.

From "H" Coy.:—
Carter, E. J., R.F.
Dewsbury, H. B., R.F.
Foster, B. G., I.Y.
Hilhouse, C., R.A.M.C.
Leleu, F. H., R.A.M.C.
Saltmarsh, A. J., R.F.
Scoones, W., R.F.

From "K" Coy.:—
Ashby, F. R., A.S.C.
Jones, H. E., R.F.
Miller, R. W., I.Y.
Pledge, E. H., R.A.M.C.
Puzey, G. F., I.Y.

From "N" Coy.:—
Andrewes, G. S., R.F.
Curra, S. S., I.Y.
Edington, H. H., I.Y.
Matthew, J. H., I.Y.
Rowley, B. P., I.Y.
Sheaves, L. H., I.Y.

From "O" Coy.:—
Barnes, E. W., I.Y.
Barton, A. E., I.Y.
Soman, A. F., R.A.M.C.
Soman, H., R.F.

From "P" Coy.:—
Aucutt, F., I.Y.
Christie, H. A. R., I.Y.
Richards, W. R., I.Y.
Swan, R. J. G., I.Y.

From "Q" Coy.:—
Allen, F. J., R.F.
Cussans, J. S., R.F.
Prior, H., R.A.M.C.
Rowsell, E. S., I.Y.
Vallance, W., I.Y.
Wickes, L. J., R.F.
Cadet—
Taplin, F. J., I.Y.

The following took part in the Brighton March, 18th April, 1914. The party left the Duke of York's Column at 7.28 p.m., and were dismissed at 9.51 a.m. next day at Brighton:

"A" Company.—Capt. R. H. Husey, Cpls. E. S. Peddel and E. C. S. Phillips, Lce.-Cpls. F. D. Charles, E. A. Sedgwick, Ptes. F. H. Crews, A. C. Day, I. P. Cregoe, S. H. Halfpenny, L. F. Whittaker.

"D" Company.—Sergt. C. F. Joyce, Cpl. T. H. Jenkin, Ptes. A. W. Durrant, P. K. S. Ewen, E. Jones, F. C. Oakley, C. E. Ovington, J. W. Reading, A. C. Score, M. J. Maynard.

"E" Company.—Sergt. E. Warner.

"G" Company.—Lieut. E. L. Large, Cpls. A. P. Featherstonhaugh and A. W. Stapley, Lce.-Cpl. E. E. Haynes, Ptes. H. C. Godfrey, D. W. Leman, C. W. Martin, W. H. Peppiatt, P. H. Widgery.

"H" Company.—Sergt. G. H. Cotter, Cpls. L. E. Schultz and G. O. Taylor, Ptes. H. B. Balls, F. Eustace, W. Hurford, W. Staples, W. Waldheim, R. G. Wallis.

"O" Company.—Sergts. S. M. Lines and E. M. B. Gordon, Lce.-Cpls. T. A. Prior and J. J. Westmoreland, Ptes. G. J. Adams, D. Cue, H. L. Flindt, P. W. Belcher, R. J. Hewetson, F. A. Hovill, S. C. Legg, E. G. Moore, A. O. Smiles, M. Wray.

"P" Company.—Lce.-Cpl. F. Ward, Ptes. J. W. Aris, L. Furrell, — Klitz.

"Q" Company.—Cpl. G. H. Porter, Ptes. W. F. Swan, H. Turner.

NOTE.—Clr.-Sergt. Wallis did much work in raising and training the team, but was unable to actually march with it. However, he accompanied it in a car, and walked a good deal of the way. He was able to give a great deal of help and encouragement.

APPENDIX H

Regimental Plate with Inscriptions

The numbers correspond to those on the key to the photograph of the plate.

(1) The Walter McDougall Shield Challenge Trophy presented to the L.R.B. in memory of Pte. Walter McDougall, who died May 8th, 1899, by his brother Fred.

Won by—

1889, Cpl. F. Elkington.	1902, Lce.-Sergt. E. Dicker.
1890, Sergt. Z. V. Walker.	1903, Capt. E. D. Johnson.
1891, Pte. C. G. W. Lock.	1904, Pte. T. A. W. Andrew.
1892, Pte. J. E. Carew.	1905, Capt. E. D. Johnson.
1893, Sergt. Ashby.	1906, Capt. A. S. Bates.
1894, Cpl. F. Elkington.	1907, Sergt. E. Dicker.
1895, Pte. R. Griggs.	1908, Pte. A. B. White.
1896 ,,	1909, Capt. A. S. Bates.
1897, Pte. F. Elkington.	1910, Sergt. H. L. Botting.
1898	1911, Sergt. A. Wright.
1899, Clr.-Sergt. R. H. Tayton.	1912, Sergt. G. E. Puckle.
1900, Pte. R. Griggs.	1913, Capt. A. S. Bates.
1901, Pte. W. J. Burton.	

(2) 3rd Battn. Challenge Shield. Presented by Col. Edward Matthey, C.B., V.D., late Lieut.-Col. Commandant L.R.B. May, 1916.

Won by—

" D "	Company,	May, 1916.	" B "	Company,	Nov., 1917.
" G "	,,	June ,,	" G "	,,	Jan. 1918.
" A "	,,	July ,,	" A "	,,	Feb. ,,
" D "	,,	Aug. ,,	" A "	,,	April ,,
" G "	,,	Sept. ,,	" F "	,,	June ,,
" D "	,,	Oct. ,,	" A "	,,	July ,,
" E "	,,	April, 1917	" A "	,,	Aug. ,,
" A "	,,	Sept. ,,	" A "	,,	Sept. ,,

(3) Efficiency Shield presented to the L.R.B. by Lieut.-Col. Sir Alfred Kirby, Sheriff of London and Middlesex, 1886–7.

Won by—

1887, " G " Company, Capt. M. W. Marshall.
1888, " D " ,, Major Earl Waldegrave.

1889, "P" Company, Capt. C. T. Beresford-Hope.
1890, "G" ,, Major M. W. Marshall.
1891, "G" ,, ,,
1892, "P" ,, Capt. C. T. Beresford-Hope.
1893, "P" ,, Capt. G. Bicker-Caarten.
1894, "P" ,, ,,
1895, "N" ,, Capt. C. F. Pritchard.
1896, "N" ,, ,,
1897, "O" ,, Major G. J. Cuthbert.
1898, "P" ,, Capt. Bicker-Caarten.
1899, "P" ,, ,,
1900, "C" ,, Capt. F. H. Whittow.
1901, "B" ,, Capt. E. G. Stenson Cooke.
1902, "P" ,, Capt. G. Bicker-Caarten.
1903, "D" ,, Capt. P. L. H. Canning.
1904, "Q" ,, 2nd Lieut. M. H. Soames.
1905, "P" ,, Capt. C. D. Burnell.
1906, "P" ,, ,,
1907, "Q" ,, Capt. A. S. Bates.

(4) Silver Statuette presented to Col. Lord Edward Pelham Clinton on retiring from command of the regiment, having gained the esteem and affection of all ranks, 1881–90.

Presented to the Officers of the L.R.B. by Mrs. Farnham in memory of her uncle, Col. Lord Edward Pelham Clinton, who commanded the regiment for many years with the greatest pride and left it with the deepest regret. 1907.

(5) London Rifle Brigade Challenge Cup, 1900. Presented by Cpl. Newton Dunn, No. 3727, "K" Company, for competition between company teams for marching and shooting.

Winner.	*Capt.*	*Sec. Commander.*
1900, "K" Coy.	2nd Lieut. A. O. Devitt.	R. R. Steel.
1901, "D" ,,	Sergt. H. Frost.	Cpl. J. R. Collins.
1902, "O" ,,	Sergt. Shepherd.	Cpl. T. W. Motley.
1903, "A" ,,	Lieut. H. B. Prior.	Cpl. C. E. Willoughby.
1904, "O" ,,	Clr.-Sergt. T. Prior.	Cpl. L. G. Petty.
1905, "P" ,,	Clr.-Sergt. Walker.	Cpl. Petty.
1906, "K" ,,	Sergt. G. Kettley.	Cpl. C. Hilhouse.
1907, "P" ,,	Sergt. A. Wright.	Cpl. G. B. Vaile.
1908, "P" ,,	Lce.-Sergt. G. B. Vaile.	Lce.-Cpl. Sceats.
1909, "G" ,,	2nd Lieut. McGeagh.	Cpl. D. V. Frank.
1910, "O" ,,	2nd Lieut.F.W.Bewsher.	Cpl. J. A. Humphreys.
1911, "O" ,,	,,	Sergt.J.A.Humphreys.
1912, "O" ,,	2nd Lieut. R. J. Hunter.	,,
1913, "O" ,,	,,	Sergt. F. H. Wallis.

(6) The *Daily Telegraph* Cup, 1898. Presented by Sir Edward Lawson, Bart., on behalf of the proprietors for competition

combining marching and shooting between teams of the battalions of the Regular troops and Rifle Volunteer Corps in the Home District. Won by the L.R.B., May 7, 1898.

Capt. C. R. Bland, Clr.-Sergt. R. Tayton, "K" Company; Cpls. A. Evans, "K" Company, I. Maltby, "G" Company; Ptes. E. Stribling, "A" Company, F. L. Banks, "D" Company, H. J. Brett, "D" Company, J. L. Hampton, "D" Company, E. Collier, "H" Company, A. Little, "H" Company, J. Burroughs, "N" Company, W. R. Clark, "N" Company, W. P. Gate, "N" Company, H. Lattey, "O" Company, W. Bell, "P" Company, C. Webb, "P" Company.

(7) Cripplegate Ward Challenge Plate. To mark their appreciation of the patriotic and gallant spirit that has characterised the L.R.B. since its formation, and to encourage the practice of competitive rifle shooting. The inhabitants of the Ward of Cripplegate of the City of London have subscribed for and present this plate to the Council of the Brigade for competition annually amongst the members of the Corps. August, 1865.

Winners—

1865, Assist. Surgn. H. J. Stormount.
1866, Capt. Francis Goodliffe.
1867, Cpl. Thomas Fletcher.
1868, Sergt. William Walker.
1869, Pte. John Wyatt.
1870, ,,
1871, Pte. J. R. Saw.
1872, Pte B. Crosby.
1873, Cpl. G. E. Laverack.
1874, Pte. S. S. Young.
1875, Sergt. T. Mann.
1876, Capt. Earl Waldegrave.
1877, Cpl. H. Mardell.
1878, Pte. W. T. Russell.
1879, Pte. J. Runtz.
1880, Pte. C. F. Robinson.
1881, Pte. Nash.
1882, Pte. A. H. Ridgeway.
1883, Capt. Earl Waldegrave
1884, Sergt. R. H. Tayton.
1885, Cpl. J. J. Rothon.
1886 ,,
1887 ,,
1888, Pte. E. Siegert.
1889, Clr.-Sergt. R. H. Tayton.
1890, Sergt. J. J. Keliher.

1891, Pte. E. Siegert.
1892, Bd. Sergt. Preston.
1893, Lieut. E. Milliken.
1894, Pte. E. Skilton.
1895, Cpl. T. Elkington.
1896, Pte. H. Lattey.
1897, Pte. W. T. Bell.
1898, Pte. W. C. Luff.
1899, Clr.-Sergt. R. H. Tayton.
1900, Pte. E. Skilton.
1901, Pte. W. J. M. Burton.
1902, Pte. R. Salter.
1903, Sergt. B. T. Puckle.
1904, Pte. R. W. Brading.
1905, Capt. E. D. Johnson.
1906, Pte. S. F. Thol.
1907, Pte. T. W. Harvey.
1908, Capt. E. D. Johnson.
1909, Lce.-Cpl. W. H. Bassingham.
1910, Sergt. B. T. Puckle.
1911, Sergt. D. V. Frank.
1912, Lce.-Sergt. H. G. Burr.
1913, Sergt. S. M. Lines.

(8) *Daily Telegraph* Cup, 1897, presented by Sir Edward Lawson, Bart., on behalf of the proprietors for a competition combining marching and shooting between teams of the battalions of the Regular troops and Rifle Volunteer Corps in the Home District. Won by the L.R.B., 8th May, 1897.

Team.—Lieut. N. C. King, "F" Company; Cpl. A. E. Evans, "K" Company; Pte. J. Anthony, "A" Company; F. L. Banks, "D" Company; W. T. Bell, "P" Company; R. W. Brading, "N" Company; J. Burroughs, "N" Company; A. G. Clark, "P" Company; A. O. Clark, "P" Company; W. R. Clark, "N" Company; A. O. Devitt, "K" Company; H. Lattey, "O" Company; A. Little, "H" Company; W. C. Luff, "N" Company; I. Maltby, "G" Company; C. C. W. Webb, "P" Company; Clr.-Sergt. R. Tayton, "K" Company.

(9) Field Firing Challenge Cup, presented by Col. Lord Edward Pelham Clinton, late Commandant. To be held for one year by the best shot of the best Field Firing Section of the regiment.

Winners—

1895, Pte. W. C. Luff, "N" Company.
1896, Pte. J. Burroughs, "N" Company.

1897, Pte. W. R. Clarke, " N " Company.
1898, Sergt. Thomerson, " H " Company.
1899, Cpl. A. Evans, " K " Company.
1900, Sergt. P. Walker, " F " Company.
1901, Cpl. F. E. Tracey, " D " Company.
1902, Pte. W. E. Bowers, " D " Company.
1903, Sergt. F. Bate, " H " Company.
1904, Lce.-Sergt. Tyser, " H " Company.
1905 ,,
1906, Pte. D. V. Frank, " G " Company.
1907, Pte. G. L. Frank, " G " Company.
1908, Pte. E. F. Fossey, " D " Company.
1909, Lce.-Cpl. W. H. Bassingham, " O " Company.
1910, Lce.-Cpl. F. Frank, " G " Company.
1911, Cpl. A. B. White, " E " Company.
1912, Sergt. G. L. Frank, " G " Company.
1913, Lce.-Cpl. A. Daphne, " O " Company.

(10) Hanson and Ogg Cup (aggregate). Presented to their old comrades of the L.R.B. by Sir Reginald Hanson and Sir William A. Ogg, Sheriffs of London and Middlesex, 1881–2.

Won by—
1882, Cpl. F. J. Rothon.
1883, Pte. W. McDougall.
1884, Pte. F. Elkington.
1885 ,,
1886 ,,
1887 ,,
1888, Pte. R. Griggs.
1889, Pte. W. C. Luff.
1890, Cpl. F. Elkington.
1891, Sergt. J. J. Keliher.
1892, Pte. W. C. Luff.
1893 ,,
1894 ,,
1895, 2nd Lieut. P. W. Richardson.
1896, Pte. E. Skilton.
1897, Pte. F. Elkington.
1898, Pte. E. Skilton.
1899, Pte. F. W. Bond.
1900, Pte. E. Skilton.
1901, Pte. W. J. M. Burton.
1902, Pte. J. P. Hope.
1903, Capt. E. D. Johnson.
1904, Pte. T. A. W. Andrew.
1905, Pte. E. Skilton.
1906, Capt. A. S. Bates.
1907, Pte. E. Skilton.
1908 ,,
1909, Capt. A. S. Bates.
1910, Sergt. H. L. Botting.
1911, Sergt. G. L. Frank.
1912, Lce.-Cpl. H. D. Lidbury.
1913, Capt. A. S. Bates.

(11) Ambulance Challenge Cup. Presented by Surgn. Capt. A. Ducat, M.B. 1900.

Winners.—1900, " K " Company, Ptes. R. C. Bush, J. H. Pledge, G. E. Puckle, S. A. Hill.
1902, " P " Company, Sergt. P. L. Walker, Ptes. L. G. Paxon, C. P. Jones, A. H. Dodd.

(12) Edinburgh Cup. From Q.R.V.B. to L.R.B. 1888.

(13) Major Nicholson's Cup. Presented to the L.R.B. by Major J. M. S. Nicholson, V.D., on his retiring from the regiment after 35 years' service, 1863–98.

Won by—

1899, "D" Company.	1906, "O" Company.
1900, "N" ,,	1907, "O" ,,
1901, "P" ,,	1908, "O" ,,
1902, "D" ,,	1910, "H" ,,
1903, "P" ,,	1911, "A" ,,
1904, "P" ,,	1912, "A" ,,
1905, "O" ,,	1913, "O" ,,

(14) Signallers' Cup. Presented to the Signallers of the 4th London Volunteer Brigade by Capt. P. Slessor, L.R.B. 1902.

Won by—

1902, L.R.B. 1903, L.R.B. 1904, L.R.B.

(15) Inter-Company Regimental Challenge Shield. Presented by the Regiment, 1880. To be competed for annually for six years by all companies by teams of 8, distances 200, 500 and 600 yards. In the seventh year the winning companies will compete for final possession.

1880, Won by "H" Company, Capt. E. Matthey, 10th June. Score, 594 points. Team—Capt. Matthey, Sergt. Rix, Cpl. Adams, Ptes. Allison, Green, Howell, Shepherd, Siegert.

1881, Won by "N" Company, Capt. Miller, 28th June. Score, 543 points. Team—Lieut. Titford, Clr.-Sergt. Preston, Cpl. T. W. Jones, Ptes. Desmond, Gunyon, Anstee, Richford, Webb.

1882, Won by "F" Company, Capt. Boyes, 15th June. Score, 523 points. Team—Capt. Boyes, Lieut. Adams, Clr.-Sergt. Geen, Cpls. Adams, Mardell, Cocks, Ptes. Chapman, Pickard.

1883, Won by "N" Company, Capt. Miller, 1st September. Score, 600 points. Team—Clr.-Sergt. Preston, Cpl. Rankin, Ptes. Anstey, Desmond, Griggs, Partington, Richford, Webb.

1884, Won by "H" Company, Capt. Baggallay, 4th August. Score, 559 points. Team—Lieut. Holbrook, Clr.-Sergt. Rix, Sergt. Burton, Cpl. Rothon, Ptes. B. T. Cornish, H. M. Cornish, Heasman, Pullin.

1885, Won by "K" Company, Capt. Poulter, 7th November. Score, 657 points. Team—Lieut. Cave, Sergts. Tayton, Ellett, Cpls. Milliken, Fyffe, Ptes. Runtz, Siegert, Spon.

1887, Won by "N" Company, Capt. Porter, 26th July. Score, 641 points. Team—Clr.-Sergt. Preston, Sergts. Desmond, Rankin, Ptes. Anstee, Flemons, Griggs, Richford, Webb.

1888, Won by "K" Company, Major Porter. Score, 658 points. Team—Lieut. Cave, Sergt. Tayton, Cpls. Ashby, Milliken, Ptes. Mathews, Runtz, Siegert, Spon.

1889, Won by "N" Company, Major Porter, 1st October. Score, 637 points. Team—Arm. Sergt. Preston, Sergt. Desmond, Ptes. Griggs, Webb, Small, Flemon, Rankin, Luff.

1890, Won by "N" Company, Major W. W. Young. Score, 665 points. Team—Sergts. Preston, Desmond, Ptes. Griggs, Webb, Swale, Flemons, Anstee, Luff.

1892, Won by "N" Company, Major W. W. Young. Score, 407 points. Team—Band-Sergt. Preston, Sergt. Desmond, Ptes. Flemons, Griggs, Hawtrey, Luff, Skilton, Webb.

1893, Won by "N" Company, Major W. W. Young. Team—Arm. Sergt. Preston, Cpl. Winch, Ptes. Brading, Griggs, Hawtrey, Luff, Skilton, Webb.

1894, Won by "N" Company, Capt. C. F. Pritchard. Team—Arm. Sergt. Preston, Sergts. Desmond, Tarr, Cpl. Winch, Ptes. Brading, Griggs, Hawtrey, Luff.

1895, Won by "N" Company, Capt. C. F. Pritchard. Team—Arm. Sergt. Preston, Clr.-Sergt. Tarr, Sergt. Desmond, Lce.-Sergt. Harben, Cpl. Winch, Ptes. Brading, Griggs, Luff.

1896, Won by "F" Company, Capt. Milliken. Team—2nd Lieut. Chilver, Clr.-Sergt. Hemsley, Ptes. A. Cocks, C. J. Cocks, Dicker, Dove, Sherman.

1897, Won by "H" Company, Capt. C. W. Cornish. Team—Ptes. Andrews, Bond, Burton, Collier, Eley, Gould, Little, Wormell.

1898, No Competition.

1899, Won by "H" Company, Capt. C. W. Cornish. Team—2nd Lieuts. G. H. Foster, E. D. Johnson, Cpl. Tyser, Ptes. H. J. Andrews, F. W. Bond, W. J. Burton, E. Collier, R. A. Wormell.

1900, Won by "H" Company, Capt. C. W. Cornish. Team—Lieut. E. D. Johnson, 2nd Lieut. E. Collier, Lce.-Sergt. A. E. Tyser, Ptes. H. J. Andrews, F. W. Bond, W. J. M. Burton, J. Eley, A. Little, F. Thol.

1901, Won by "H" Company, Capt. C. W. Cornish. Team—2nd Lieut. E. Collier, Sergt. W. H. Noble, Lce.-Sergt. A. E. Tyser, Ptes. F. W. Bond, J. Eley, A. Little, S. F. Thol.

1902, Won by "H" Company, Capt. C. W. Cornish. Team—Lieut. Johnson, Lce.-Sergt. Tyser, Ptes. Bond, Burton, Eley, Little, Scarfe, Thol.

1903, Won by "H" Company, Capt. C. W. Cornish. Team—Lieut. Collier, Sergt. Noble, Lce.-Sergt. Tyser, Ptes. Bond, Burton, Eley, Hammond, Little.

1904, Won by "N" Company. Team—Ptes. Brading, Hooke, Hope, Luff, Richford, Simmons, Skilton, Winch.
1905, Won by "H" Company. Team—Lieuts. Collier, Peddie, Sergt. Noble, Lce.-Sergt. Tyser, Ptes. Bond, Burton, Collins, Eley.
1906, Won by "H" Company. Team—Lieuts. Collier, Peddie, Ptes. Botting, Burton, Eley, Platts, Schultz, Thol.
1907, Won by "H" Company. Score, 717 points.
1908, Won by "H" Company. Score, 730 points.
1909, Won by "D" Company. Score, 724 points.
1910, Won by "D" Company.
1911, Won by "O" Company.
1912, Won by "H" Company.
1913, Won by "H" Company.

(16) Officers' Challenge Cup. Presented to the Officers of the L.R.B. by a few of their old comrades, 1876.

Col. Close, Col. Rose, C. Allen, T. Blandford, James A. Carson, W. Clode, F. Cotton, W. S. Dean, T. D. Deighton, A. Dodd, J. G. Gilbert, Reginald Hanson, Charles Humphreys, John Jackson, W. A. Ogg, E. S. Palmer, John E. Pawson, Robert Pinckney, H. R. Poole, Anthony Sim, George Sims, F. Stretton, T. I. Thomas. Treasurer, James A. Carson. Hon. Secretary, Arthur Dodd.

Won by—

1879, Capt. H. Wadd.
1880, Lieut. A. Titford.
1881 ,,
1882, Lieut. M. W. Marshall.
1883 ,,
1884, Capt. Earl Waldegrave.
1885, Lieut. H. Parker.
1886, Lieut. C. C. Cave.
1887, Major Earl Waldegrave.
1888 ,,
1889 ,,
1890, Capt. M. W. Marshall.
1891, Lieut. E. Milliken.
1892, Capt. C. G. R. Matthey.
1893, Major Earl Waldegrave.
1894 ,,
1895, Lieut. P. W. Richardson.
1896, Capt. E. Milliken.
1897, Capt. F. N. Mellersh.
1898, 2nd Lieut. E. D. Johnson.
1899 ,,
1900, Lieut. W. J. S. Read.
1901, 2nd Lieut. E. Collier.
1902 ,,
1903, Capt. E. D. Johnson.
1904, Lieut. E. Collier.
1905, Capt. N. C. King.
1906, Capt. A. S. Bates.
1907, Capt. P. L. H. Canning.
1908, Capt. E. D. Johnson.
1909, Capt. C. G. H. MacGill.
1910, Capt. A. S. Bates.

(20) Cup presented to the L.R.B. by their comrades in arms from the Cape of Good Hope in remembrance of the happy days spent in their camp at Wimbledon, 1887.

Inter-Company Judging Distance Competition Challenge Bowl.

Won by—

1888, " N " Company, Major R. S. Porter.
1889, No competition.
1890, " D " Company, Major Earl Waldegrave.
1891, " P " Company, Capt. C. T. Beresford-Hope.
1892, " N " Company, Major W. W. Young.

(21) Aldershot Athletic Association Command Relay Race, Tournament, May, 1918. Winning team, 3rd L.R.B.

(23) Cup. The Officers of the L.R.B. from Col. Lord Edward Pelham Clinton, who commanded the regiment from 1881 to 1890.

(24) Sports Inter-Company Challenge Cup. Presented by Col. Edward Matthey, C.B., V.D., late Lieut.-Col. Commanding L.R.B., to 2nd Battalion L.R.B. April, 1915.

Won by—

" D " Company, Haywards Heath, April, 1915.
" C " Company, Foxhall Heath, June, 1916.

(25) The Samuel Cup. Presented to the L.R.B. by the Rt. Hon. Sir Marcus Samuel, Bart., Lord Mayor, 1903.

Winners—

1904. Pte. H. G. Lynn, " K " Company.
1905, Pte. W. C. Terry, " K " Company.
1906, Cpl. F. C. Beart, " K " Company.
1907, Pte. A. B. White, " E " Company.
1908, Pte. O. H. Gates, " E " Company.
1909, Lce.-Cpl. W. H. Bassingham.
1910, Pte. S. M. Lines, " O " Company.
1911, Pte. W. R. Scammell, " D " Company.
1912, Pte. C. Barr, " G " Company.
1913, Pte. W. F. Pothecary, " P " Company.

(26) L.R.B. Challenge Cup. Presented by the Lord Mayor and Sheriffs, 1892–3.

(27) Cup presented to the L.R.B. by the Grocers' Company, 1908, to replace a similar cup presented in 1877.

Won by—

1908, Sergt. A. M. Wright, " P " Company.
1909, Lce.-Cpl. J. F. Young, " F " Company.
1910, Cpl. E. C. Hawkey, " D " Company.
1911, Sergt. E. C. Hawkey, " D " Company.
1912, Sergt. G. L. Frank, " G " Company.
1913, Sergt. F. H. Oakley, " H " Company.

(28) Divisional League, 58th (London) Division, 1916–17. Presented by Major-Gen. H. D. Fanshawe, C.B.

(29) School of Arms Inter-Company Bayonet Competition.
1912–13, " G " Company. 1913–14, " G " Company.

(31) Boyes Cup.

(35) The Ewens' Memorial Plate, subscribed for and presented to the L.R.B. by past and present Officers and Members in memory of the late Lieut.-Col. A. T. Ewens, for twenty-two years Adjutant and, on his retirement from that post, Major in the regiment, 15th March, 1883.

Conditions.—This cup is to remain the property of the L.R.B. and to be shot for in the annual ranks' match to be held by the Commanding Officer for the time being.

Won by—

1882, Sergeants.	1892, Privates.
1883, Privates.	1893 ,,
1884, Sergeants.	1894 ,,
1885, Privates.	1895, Sergeants.
1886, Sergeants.	1896 to 1908, Privates.
1887, Privates.	1909, Corporals.
1888, Sergeants.	1910, Sergeants.
1889, Privates.	1911 ,,
1890 ,,	1912, Corporals.
1891, Sergeants.	1913, Sergeants.

(36) The Torrance Cup. Won by—

1904, Pte. W. T. Bell.	Score 49
1905, Sergt. A. Wright.	54
1906, Cpl. E. A. Adams.	49
1907, Pte. R. A. Oliver.	41
1908, Pte. E. H. Lloyd.	51
1909, Sergt. S. W. T. Henshaw.	39
1910, Sergt. G. B. Vaile.	70
1911, Lce.-Cpl. F. E. Smith.	
1912, Lce.-Cpl. E. A. Adams.	
1913, Clr.-Sergt. G. B. Vaile.	

(37) The Commander-in-Chief's Cup. Presented by Field-Marshal Earl Roberts (1903) to the National Rifle Association for the encouragement of rapid fire. Won by the L.R.B.

Team—Clr.-Sergt. R. H. Tayton, Ptes. T. A. W. Andrew, W. Bell, R. Brading, A. Cocks, A. Denny, F. Kensitt, C. Knights, G. E. Mead, R. J. Salter.

(39) 2nd Battn. Inter-Company Association Football Challenge Cup. Presented by Capt. Charles Bland.

(41) Jardinière. Presented to the Officers' Mess by Col. H. C. Cholmondeley, C.B., on retirement from the command of the regiment. 1901.

(42) Challenge Bowl. Presented July, 1883, to the L.R.B. by the Rt. Hon. Henry Edmund Knight, Lord Mayor, 1882–3. A member of the regiment, 1860–1.

Won by—

1883, "N" Company, Capt. Miller.
1884, "D" Company, Capt. Earl Waldegrave.
1885, "N" Company, Major Miller.
1886, "H" Company, Capt. Baggallay.
1887, "N" Company, Capt. R. L. Porter.
1888, "N" Company ,,
1889, "Q" Company, Major J. M. S. Nicholson.
1890, "N" Company, Major W. W. Young.
1891, "H" Company, Major W. R. Baggallay.
1892, "G" Company, Major M. W. Marshall.
1893, "F" Company, Major H. C. Boyes.
1894, "P" Company, Capt. Bicker-Caarten.
1895, "D" Company, Major Earl Waldegrave.
1896, "G" Company, Capt. E. S. Horner.
1897, "D" Company, Major Earl Waldegrave.
1898, "K" Company, Capt. F. N. Mellersh.
1899, "Q" Company, Capt. F. H. Green.
1900, "P" Company, Capt. Bicker-Caarten.
1901, "K" Company, Major F. N. Mellersh.
1902, "H" Company, Capt. C. W. Cornish.
1903, "H" Company ,,
1904, "D" Company, Capt. Hon. Sir S. K. McDonnell.
1905, "K" Company, Capt. A. F. Chilver.
1906, "H" Company, Capt. C. W. Cornish.
1907, "H" Company ,,
1908, "D" Company, Capt. P. L. H. Canning.
1909, "H" Company ,,
1910, "H" Company ,,
1911, "G" Company, Capt. C. G. H. MacGill.
1912, "G" Company ,,
1913, "G" Company ,,

(45) Commander-in-Chief's Cup. Presented by F.-M. Earl Roberts (1902) to the National Rifle Association for the encouragement of rapid firing. Won by the L.R.B.

Team—Clr.-Sergt. R. H. Tayton, Ptes. H. W. Andrews, W. Bell, R. Brading, A. Cocks, J. Eley, P. Kensitt, C. Knights, G. E. Mead, R. J. Salter.

The remainder of the plate, Nos. 11, 17, 18, 19, 22, 30, 32, 33, 34, 38, 40, 43, 44, is composed of specimens of cups belonging to different companies. These are so numerous that it was not possible to include them all.

Regimental Plate

2.
1.
3.
4.
5.
6.
7.
8.
9.
10.
11.
12.
13.
14.
15.
16.
17.
18.
19.
20.
21.
22.
23.
24.
25.
26.
27.
28.
29.
30.
31.
32.
33.
34.
35.
36.
37.
38.
39.
40.
41.
42.
43.
44.
45.

APPENDIX K

L.R.B. Gold Medallists

1861, Pte. T. Foster.
1862, Cpl. O. F. Giddy.
1863, Clr.-Sergt. R. T. Churchill.
1864, Pte. J. Wyatt.
1865, Clr.-Sergt. R. T. Churchill.
1866, Pte. J. Wyatt.
1867, Pte. J. M. Gardiner.
1868, Clr.-Sergt. R. T. Churchill.
1869, Pte. H. Frere.
1870 ,,
1871, Sergt. T. Fletcher.
1872, Pte. J. M. Gardiner.
1873, Pte. J. R. Saw.
1874, Pte. W. S. Smith.
1875, Cpl. H. Mardell.
1876, Pte. H. Smith.
1877, Sergt. W. Frazer.
1878, Pte. J. Runtz.
1879, Clr.-Sergt. J. C. Preston.
1880, Pte. G. J. Hood.
1881, Capt. Earl Waldegrave.
1882, Clr.-Sergt. J. C. Preston.
1883, Cpl. F. J. Rothon.
1884, Capt. Earl Waldegrave.
1885, Pte. F. Elkington.
1886, Pte. W. McDougall.
1887, Pte. F. Elkington.
1888, Pte. R. Griggs.
1889, Pte. W. C. Luff.
1890, Cpl. F. Elkington.
1891, Sergt. J. J. Keliher.
1892, Pte. W. C. Luff.
1893 ,,
1894 ,,
1895, Lieut. P. W. Richardson.
1896, Pte. E. Skilton.
1897, Pte. F. Elkington.
1898, Pte. E. Skilton.
1899, Pte. F. W. Bond.
1900, Pte. E. Skilton.
1901, Pte. W. J. M. Burton.
1902, Pte. J. P. Hope.
1903, Capt. E. D. Johnson.
1904, Pte. T. A. W. Andrew.
1905, Pte. A. Cocks.
1906, Capt. A. S. Bates.
1907, Pte. E. Skilton.
1908 ,,
1909, Capt. A. S. Bates.
1910, Sergt. H. L. Botting.
1911, Sergt. G. L. Frank.
1912, Lce.-Cpl. H. D. Lidbury.
1913, Capt. A. S. Bates.

The following First Prizes have been won by Teams and Members of the L.R.B. at the Wimbledon and Bisley Meetings of the National Rifle Association. The events are placed in alphabetical order.

Alexandra

1865, Sergt. Walker. 1909, Pte. E. Skilton.

Grand Aggregate

Pte. E. Skilton, 1906 and 1909.

Volunteer Aggregate
Pte. E. Skilton, 1906.

Association Cup
1874, Pte. Young. 1896, Pte. Dicker. 1906, Pte. E. Skilton.

Belgian Challenge Cup
L.R.B. Team, 1895 and 1910.

China Challenge Cup
City of London Team, 1892, 1901.
The whole team was from the L.R.B.

Commander-in-Chief's Prize
L.R.B. Team, 1902 and 1903.

"Daily Graphic"
1911, Pte. W. C. Luff.

"Daily Telegraph"
1908, Capt. A. S. Bates.

Donegal Challenge Cup (for Rifle Clubs)
1905, Lieut. A. S. Bates. 1906, Sergt. H. G. Burr.

Duke of Cambridge's Prize
1895, Pte. J. Wyatt. 1902, Pte. Hope.

Duke of Westminster's Challenge Cup
L.R.B. Team, 1892, 1893, and 1899.

"Graphic"
1888, Cpl. F. Elkington.

Handsworth
1902, Pte. S. F. Thol.

Queen's Prize and King's Prize
1st Stage : Bronze Medal
1907, Capt. A. S. Bates.
Final Stage : Gold Medal
1864, Pte. J. Wyatt. 1902, Lieut. E. D. Johnson.
1909, Cpl. H. G. Burr.

Mappin Challenge Cup
L.R.B. Team, 1891, 1894, 1895, 1896, 1897, 1900.

Martin's Challenge Cup
1907, Pte. A. Denny.

Mullens
L.R.B. Team, 1895.

Ranelagh Challenge Cup
L.R.B. Team, 1907 and 1910.

St. George's Challenge Vase
1903, Capt. E. D. Johnson.

Secretary of State for War
1878, Lieut. Piggott. 1897, Mr. J. Wyatt.

Stock Exchange
1904, Pte. W. Brooks. 1906, Pte. E. Skilton. 1908, Capt. A. S. Bates.

Wimbledon Cup
1869, Clr.-Sergt. Hayes. 1882, Capt. Earl Waldegrave.

Final Stages of Queen's and King's Prize

The following Members of the L.R.B. obtained places in the Final Stage of the Queen's Prize, 1860 to 1900, and in the King's Prize, 1901 to 1914. (Up to the year 1885 only 60 shot in the Final Stage; after that 100.)

1894, Pte. Ashby.
1909, W. H. Bassingham.
1913 ,,
1907, Capt. A. S. Bates.
1903, Pte. I. H. Beattie.
1908, H. L. Botting.
1913, C. J. Brooks.
1900, Sergt. H. G. Burr.
1901 ,,
1902 ,,
1905 ,,
1906 ,,
1907 ,,
1909 ,,
1910 ,,
1914 ,,
1870, Pte. Chapman.
1865, Pte. Churchill.
1867 ,,
1909, Pte. A. Cocks.
1910 ,,
1914 ,,
1903, Lieut. E. Collier.
1904 ,,
1904, Pte. C. J. Cruse.
1914 ,,
1914, Pte. J. Currie.
1870, Pte. Dean.
1913, Pte. A. Denny.
1886, Sergt. Desmond.
1868, Pte. Dunn.
1905, Pte. J. Eley.
1878, Pte. F. Elkington.
1890 ,,
1862, Pte. Foster.
1864, Pte. Frere.
1868, Pte. Gardner.
1861, Pte. F. Goodliffe.
1896, Pte. R. Griggs.
1900 ,,
1865, Pte. W. Hammerton.
1872 ,,
1907, Pte. F. W. Harris.
1909 ,,
1875, Pte. J. R. Hawkins.
1870, Pte. C. C. Hayes.
1872, Pte. T. W. Heath.
1886, Pte. J. P. Hope.

1890 Pte. J. P. Hope.
1893 ,,
1901 ,,
1907 ,,
1911 ,,
1872, Pte. Hutchinson
1902, Capt. E. D. Johnson.
1905 ,,
1906 ,,
1885, Pte. H. Lattey.
1891 ,,
1908 ,,
1909 ,,
1908, Pte. H. P. T. Lattey.
1894, Pte. W. C. Luff.
1877, Pte. W. McDougall.
1875, Pte. H. Mardell.
1879 ,,
1884 ,,
1888 ,,
1865, Pte. Marsh.
1889, Pte. Matthew.
1894, Lieut. E. Milliken.
1868, Pte. T. Munn.
1872 ,,
1904, Lieut. J. T. Peddie.
1906 ,,
1872, Pte. T. Phythian.
1907, Pte. D. J. Platts.
1913, Pte. W. F. Pothecary.
1911, Sergt. G. E. Puckle.
1867, Pte. Richards.
1886, Lieut. P. W. Richardson.
1887 ,,
1895 ,,
1896 ,,
1902 Lieut. P. W. Richardson.
1903 ,,
1907 ,,
1914 ,,
1887, Pte. F. J. Rothon.
1890 ,,
1898 ,,
1900 ,,
1901 ,,
1876, Pte. J. Runtz.
1886, Pte. J. R. Saw.
1880, Pte. E. Siegert.
1893, Pte. E. Skilton.
1896 ,,
1901 ,,
1905 ,,
1906 ,,
1908 ,,
1910 ,,
1913 ,,
1914 ,,
1864, Pte. Stormont.
1890, Clr.-Sergt. R. H. Tayton.
1891 ,,
1896 ,,
1885, Capt. Earl Waldegrave.
1868, Pte. Walker.
1906, Pte. L. G. Willcocks.
1869, Capt. Wortham.
1871 ,,
1873 ,,
1862, Pte. J. Wyatt.
1863 ,,
1864 ,,
1870 ,,

STATISTICS OF ENROLMENTS AND DRAFTS, 1914–1918

ENLISTMENTS

3rd Battalion

	1914.	1915.	1916.	1917.	1918.
January	—	163	81	156	19
February	—	116	123	621	131
March	—	203	276	232	76
April	—	197	233	72	262
May	—	141	263	75	38
June	—	124	18	52	41
July	—	139	145	60	13
August	—	105	288	101	43
September	—	74	304	46	142
October	—	110	77	57	5
November	72	715	34	77	11
December	116	339	23	20	—
Total	188	2426	1865	1569	781

Grand Total = 6829.

POSTINGS—					
From 101st Prov. Battn.	—	—	167	—	—
2/7th Lond.	—	—	23	—	—
2/7th Essex	—	—	73	—	—
2nd L.R.B.	—	—	—	43	—
30th Lond.	—	—	—	17	—
Command Depot	—	—	—	77	326
(?)	—	—	—	—	19
Labour Corps	—	—	—	—	7
53rd Y.S. Battn.	—	—	—	—	67
R.F.A.	—	—	—	—	12
25th R.B.	—	—	—	—	269
24th Recruiting Dist.	—	—	—	—	32
Total	188	2426	2128	1706	1513

Grand Total = 7961.

DRAFTS OVERSEAS.

	2nd Battalion	*3rd Battalion*			
	1915.	1915.	1916.	1917.	1918.
January	15	—	146	247	91
February	243	—	80	50	—
March	207	—	131	54	365
April	—	—	25	63	193
May	—	—	81	120	12
June	—	—	—	144	40
July	50	—	590	91	33
August	16	260	285	108	111
September	75	—	—	62	23
October	—	150	154	141	99
November	—	33	107	96	182
December	—	—	350	70	—
Total	606	443	1949	1246	1149

Grand Total of 3rd Battalion = 4787.

OTHER OUTGOINGS—					
To 2nd Battn.	—	427	378	3	—
101st Battn.	—	28	4	—	—
60th Divn.	—	—	200	—	—
2/13th Lond.	—	—	100	—	—
Heavy Art.	—	—	23	—	—
R.F.C.	—	—	5	—	—
M.G.C.	—	—	126	196	—
Labour Corps	—	—	—	214	—
2/4th Norfolk	—	—	—	26	—
2/7th Essex	—	—	—	13	—
29th Lond.	—	—	—	9	—
Batmen for U.S.A.	—	—	—	21	—
Command Depot	—	—	—	16	219
Various Units	—	—	—	—	709
T. Res. Bde.	—	—	—	—	68
Total	606	898	2785	1744	2145

Grand Total of 3rd Battn. = 7572.

STATISTICS OF CASUALTIES, 1914–1918

	OFFICERS, INCLUDING ATTACHED.												OTHER RANKS.													
	KILLED IN ACTION.[1]						WOUNDED, MISSING, ETC.						KILLED IN ACTION.[1]							WOUNDED, MISSING, ETC.						
	1st Battalion.					*2ndB.*	*1st Battalion.*					*2ndB.*	*1st Battalion.*					*2nd Battn.*		*1st Battalion.*					*2nd Battn.*	
	1914	1915	1916	1917	1918	1917	1914	1915	1916	1917	1918	1917	1914	1915	1916	1917	1918	1917	1918	1914	1915	1916	1917	1918	1917	1918
January . . .	—	—	—	—	—	—	—	—	1	—	—	—	—	8	4	7	—	—	1	—	5	14	20	—	—	3
February . . .	—	1	—	2	—	—	—	2	—	4	—	1	—	9	—	6	—	2	—	—	18	—	22	3	5	—
March . . .	—	1	—	1	7	—	—	—	—	—	16	—	—	10	—	7	17	4	—	—	10	—	43	612	5	—
April	—	1	—	1	2	—	—	5	—	1	—	—	—	} 112	—	17	1	—	—	—	} 323	—	67	9	1	—
May	—	6	—	1	3	1	—	10	1	1	1	3	—		4	28	1	14	—	—		16	166	25	55	—
June . . .	—	—	—	—	—	1	—	—	—	—	—	8	—	—	5	14	13	30	—	—	—	30	43	24	104	—
July	—	—	10	1	1	1	—	—	11	—	—	—	—	—	67	1	2	4	—	—	—	508	—	4	8	—
August . . .	—	—	—	3	8	—	—	—	1	9	13	1	—	—	1	46	71	—	—	—	—	2	322	228	—	—
September . .	—	—	4	—	7	9	—	—	14	—	5	4	—	—	82	1	11	101	—	—	—	365	5	54	222	—
October . . .	—	—	12	—	3	1	—	—	9	—	—	2	—	—	55	—	—	21	—	—	—	263	1	—	59	—
November . .	—	—	—	1	1	—	—	—	1	—	4	—	2	—	5	4	30	2	—	6	3	4	28	131	5	—
December . .	—	—	—	1	—	—	2	—	—	1	—	—	11	6	—	9	—	3	—	24	16	7	32	—	9	—
	—	9	26	11	32	13	2	17	38	16	39	19	13	145	223	140	146	181	1	30	375	1209	749	1090	473	3

Officers, Killed in Action: 78 (1st Battalion) + 13 (2ndB.) = 91 Killed (1)

Officers, Wounded, Missing, etc.: 112 (1st Battalion) + 19 (2ndB.) = 131 Wounded, etc.

Total Casualties: 222 Officers.

Other Ranks, Killed in Action: 667 (1st Battalion) + 182 (2nd Battn.) = 849 Killed (2)

Other Ranks, Wounded, Missing, etc.: 3453* (1st Battalion) + 476 (2nd Battn.) = 3929 Wounded, etc.

Total Casualties: 4778 other Ranks.

Total Casualties: 5000**

Records give our total killed all Ranks as	.	1671
Aggregate of (1) (2) and (3) equals only	.	1518
Leaving unaccounted for in this Table .	.	153[2]

*Included in this figure are missing and / or missing and wounded	.	1062
Number of prisoners known	. .	484
Balance, probably killed	. .	578 (3)

[1] Includes died of wounds and / or disease.

[2] This figure must belong to some month or months for which incomplete Records exist. It should be added to the figure 5000,** making the total casualties 5153.

NOMINAL ROLL OF OFFICERS

1859–1919

THE names in italics are those of officers who were attached to the regiment, but were never actually transferred to it. Those with an asterisk appeared under the name of the regiment in the Army List during the Great War, but were seconded, and never actually served with any of the L.R.B. battalions as officers.

Medals gained during the Great War are not included.

ADAMS, F. 21st Londons. Attached to 1st Batt. 27/9/17–28/3/18 (*missing.*)

ADAMS, G. J. 2nd Lieut. 25/6/18. Joined 1st Batt. 21/9/18–28/9/18 (killed in action).

ADAMS, JOHN BORGNIS. Served in the ranks. 2nd Lieut. 1876. Lieut. 1876. Capt. 1887. H./Major 1887. Posted to "F" Co. Comd. "K" Co. June 1887–Nov. 1888. Retired 17/11/88. Died 2/4/06.

ADDISON, V. *Ed.* Hilton College, Natal, South Africa. Served with the Natal Carabiniers, Zulu Rebellion, 1906. Medal and clasp. Served with Natal Carabiniers, 1914–15, German South-West Africa. Served with 2nd Batt. South African Infantry, France, July–October. Wounded 12th October, 1916, at Butte-de-Walencourt; nine months hospital. Commissioned to the L.R.B. 28/8/18. Served France, attached 1/28th London Regiment, Nov. 1918–March 1919.

AINGER, WILLIAM EDWARD. *Ed.* Epsom College. Joined L.R.B. in Dec. 1914 as a rifleman and went to the Front (Flanders) on 23rd Sept., 1915. Wounded at Hébuterne (Battle of Somme) 2nd July, 1916. 2nd Lieut. 28/11/17. Went to the Front for second time Feb. 1st, 1918. Attached 2/6th London. Gassed at Villers Bretonneux 20th April, 1918.

ALCOCK, JOHN EVELYN. *Ed.* Haileybury and B.N.C., Oxford. Haileybury College O.T.C. 1908–12. Oxford University O.T.C. 1912–14. 2nd Lieut. L.R.B. 1914. Lieut. 1915. Capt. 1916. France 20/12/14–18/2/15. (Wounded.) Staff-Capt. 192nd Infantry Brigade, July 1st, 1917–January 8th, 1919.

ALDERSON, R. L. 2nd Lieut. 1898. Retired 1899.

ALFORD, S. A. F. Joined as rifleman. 2nd Lieut. 13/1/16. Went to France 2/9/16 (severely wounded). Lieut. 1917.

ALLEN, CHARLES. Ensign 1860. Lieut. 1866. Retired 1871.

ALLEN, WILLIAM FERNELEY. Capt. 1859. First Captain of "B" Co. Retired 1862.

AMBROSE, ALEXANDER, R.A.M.C. (T.F.) Attd. Ed. *Felsted School, Dublin and Cambridge Universities. Private L.R.B.* 1900–3. *Lieut. R.A.M.C.* 1914. *Capt.* 1915. *With* 2*nd Batt. from formation to June* 1916, *then to hospital ships across Channel and Egyptian Exped. Force and to Italy in hosp. ship. O.C. hosp. ship "Jan Brydel" Feb.–Nov.* 1917. *M.O. Neurasthenic Hospital, Stannington,* 1918–*April* 1919.

ANDERSON, NEVILLE. *Ed.* Rugby and Oriel College, Oxford. Rugby O.T.C. Joined 2nd Batt. 2nd Lieut. 12/2/15. Lieut. 1/6/16. T./Capt. 19/4/16. T./Major 25/2/17. To France 24/1/16, as Court-Martial Adviser First Army. Appointed D.A.A.G. First Army 9th June, 1916, and so served to 19th March, 1919. *Honours.* O.B.E., M.B.E. Three mentions in despatches. *Games.* Oriel College Rugby XV 1900–1–2.

ANDERSON, ROBERT DUNCAN. In ranks 2/12*th Londons. Gazetted to* 11*th Londons and served with* 1*st Batt.* 24–30/9/16.

ANSON, THOMAS EDWARD (Viscount, afterwards Earl of Lichfield). *Ed.* Harrow and Trinity College, Cambridge. Joined 2nd Batt. 2nd Lieut. 1914. T./Lieut. 7/1/15. Capt. 1/6/16. In June 1915 was appointed A.D.C. to G.O. Commanding 58th Division and served in that capacity in France with the 58th Division from January 1917 till June 1918. Then returned on sick leave and so remained till end of war. *Honours.* Mentioned in despatches.

APPLETON, ERNEST ROBERT. *Ed.* Worcester and New College, Oxford. Commissioned in 2nd Batt. 2nd Lieut. 1915. Lieut. 1916. Served with 1st Batt. in France 18/7/15–20/12/15 (sick). Then employed recruiting duties. Attached Australian Staff 1/12/16. Invalided out 10/5/17 and became a master at R.N. College, Dartmouth

ARIS, JOHN WOODBRIDGE. Ed. *Whitgift. Enlisted in L.R.B.* 1913 *and went to France with* 1*st Batt. Nov.* 1914. *Commissioned in R.A.S.C. and remained in France till Nov.* 1917. *Posted to* 3*rd Batt.* 22/2/18 *and went to France again* 30/4/18. *Posted to* 2/10*th Londons* (*wounded* 8/8/18).

ASTE, PERCIVAL JOHN. *Ed.* Malvern College. Joined L.R.B. as a rifleman 9/9/14 and commissioned in 2nd Batt. 2nd Lieut. 11/2/15. Lieut. 1916. Capt. 1917. Served with 1st Batt. in France 18/7/15–4/2/16 (sick). On recovery served with 3rd Batt. to end of war. *Games.* Amateur Golf Champion of the Argentine 1909.

ATKINSON, ARTHUR EDWARD, R.A.M.C. Attached to 3rd Batt. 19/4/16–3/7/16.

ATKYNS, ALFRED, M.D. Asst.-Surgeon 1860. Surgeon 1862. Retired 1878. Died 1881.

BABINGTON, WILLIAM ALFRED. Joined L.R.B. March 1913, and went to France with 1st L.R.B. 5/11/14–9/11/17. 2nd Lieut. 27/3/18. Lieut. –/9/19. *Honours.* Mentioned in despatches.

BAGGALLAY, WILLIAM R. Sub-Lieut. 1874. Lieut. 1874. Capt. 1884. H./Major 17/11/88. Q.M. 1892. Retired 1895.

BAINBRIDGE, WALTER WILLIAM. Lieut. 1860. Capt. 1860. Retired 1865.

BAKER, ALFRED B. B. 2nd Lieut. 1881. Lieut. 1881. Retired 1882.

BAKER, ERNEST COUSINS. *Ed.* Lower School of John Lyon, Harrow-on-the-Hill. Joined as private L.R.B. Sept. 1909, and served continuously, going to France with 1st Batt. Nov. 1914. Severely wounded April 1915. 2nd Lieut. 6/1/16. Lieut. 1917. Subsequently joined 3rd Batt. and afterwards on Instructional Staff, Aldershot Command Sch. of Musketry, February–August 1918, and Western Command Sch. of Musketry, August 1918–May 1919.

BALDWIN, NORMAN EDWARD. *Ed.* Royal Masonic School, Bushey. Enlisted as a private in 1912 in L.R.B. and served continuously, going to France with 1st Batt. Nov. 1914. 2nd Lieut. 1916. Rejoined 1st Batt. 3/8/16, posted to "A" Coy. Wounded and missing 8/10/16 at Les Bœufs.

BALKWILL, CHARLES VINCE. *Ed.* St. Dunstan's College, Catford. Joined L.R.B. as private Aug. 1914, and went to France with 1st Batt. Nov. 1914. Promoted Sergeant Dec. 1914. Wounded 26/4/15 at Ypres. Commissioned in 3rd Batt. 2nd Lieut. 8/12/15. Rejoined 1st Batt. in France 27/5/16–1/7/16 (killed in action). *Games.* Played Rugby for Kent for six seasons.

BALL, FRANCIS HENRY. *Ed.* Trinity College, Toronto, Canada. University of Tennessee, U.S.A. Hillsdale College, Hillsdale, Mich., U.S.A. Enlisted in Canada Aug. 10th, 1915, joining the "Third University Company," reinforcements to Princess Patricia's Canadian Light Infantry. Arrived in England Sept. 12th, 1915. Went to France Oct. 22nd, 1915. Returned to England as Musketry Instructor Nov. 4th, 1915. Corporal Nov. 12th, 1915. Sergeant April 29th, 1916. Commissioned in 3rd Batt. 2nd Lieut. 5/9/16. Joined 1st Batt. 8/11/16–9/2/17. Rejoined 1st L.R.B. 23/6/17. Invalided 9/11/17. Batt. signalling officer, Dec., Jan., and Feb. 1916–17.

BALLS, FRANK AUBREY. *Ed.* Tonbridge School. Joined L.R.B. as private, Sept. 1909, and served continuously, going to France with 1st Batt. Nov. 1914–15. Commission in 3rd Batt. 2nd Lieut. 20/10/15. Lieut. 1/7/17. Rejoined 1st Batt. in France 27/5/16–11/7/16. Returned to England and subsequently seconded for service with Labour Corps.

BANNISTER, JOHN EDWARD. Ensign 1862. Retired 1865.

BANTOFT, EDWARD SPENCER. *Ed.* Queen Elizabeth's Grammar School, Ipswich. Inns-of-Court O.T.C. 1/10/14–2/4/15. Promoted to Corporal and Sergeant. Commissioned to 3rd Batt. 2nd Lieut. 2/4/15. Lieut. 1916. Went to 1st Batt. in France 5/7/16. Intelligence officer 20/7/16, and sniping officer 7/8/16 (approximately). Died of wounds 11/9/16.

BARKER, H. C. 2nd Lieut. 1893. Lieut. 1896. Retired 1896.

BARKER, HUGH CECIL. *Ed.* City of Oxford High School. Joined L.R.B. 29/4/09, "G" Co., and served continuously, going to France with 1st Batt. Nov. 1914. Commissioned at Ypres, 29/4/15. Took over command of M.G. sect. 12/5/15. Seconded to M.G.C. 16/10/16. Lieut. 3/12/16. Served with 186 Co. M.G.C. from 22/7/17–29/5/19 in Mesopotamia and N. Persia. *Shooting.* "St. George's" Prize list, 1914.

BARNES, ERIC. 18th Londons, att. 1st Batt. —/10/18. Killed in action at Angreau 6/10/18.

BARRETT, WILLIAM CLAUDE PERCY, R.A.M.C. Att. to 3rd Batt. 14/5/15–19/4/16.

BARRY, FRANCIS PATRICK. *Ed.* Repton. Joined as private Jan. 1914 and went to France with 1st Batt. 4/11/14–12/2/15 (wounded). Commissioned to 2nd Batt. 19/5/15. Lieut. 1/7/17. Went to France with it 26/1/17–4/8/17. Severely wounded. Afterwards served with 3rd Batt. *Honours.* M.C.

BARTLEET, HENRY BOOTH. *Ed.* Gresham's School, Holt, Norfolk. Joined 3rd Batt. as rifleman 1917 and commissioned in it 27/2/18. Went to France 2/8/18 and posted to 4th Londons (killed in action Sept. 10th, 1918).

BARTON, JOHN W. Ensign 1860. Retired 1870.

BATES, ARTHUR SYDNEY. *Ed.* Winchester. Private in 1st V.B. Hants 14/11/96–1/11/98. Joined L.R.B. as 2nd Lieut. 26/3/1900. Lieut. 13/11/01. Capt. 1905. Major 1915. T/Lieut.-Col. 16/4/15. Lieut.-Col. 4/6/17. Served continuously from date of commission and went to France with 1st Batt. 5/11/14–15/8/16. O.C. "N" Co. May, 1905; to Comd. "Q" May, 1906. Commanding "Q" and No. 4 Co. till 7/1/15. Second in Command L.R.B. 8/1/15–15/3/15. Commanded 1st Batt. 16/3/15–13/8/16. Invalided home 15/8/16. To command 3/5 Lanc. Fus. at Colchester 8/2/17, with them to

France 28/2/17. Home on duty 7/1/18. To command 4th (R.) Batt. L.N.L.R. 23/1/18. Disbanded Batt. 5/7/19. Offered temp. command of a Spec. Res. Batt. in Ireland by G.H.Q., but refused. *Honours, etc.* D.S.O., four mentions in despatches, French Croix de Guerre with palm, T.D. *Shooting.* Bisley 1902, won King's Bronze Medal and Badge ; 1905, "Donegall" Cup ; 1908, "Daily Telegraph" and "Stock Exchange." Hon. Sec. Eng. XX Club 1904–06. Shot for English XX, 1907. Mackinnon 1908 and 1909. Res. 1914. Res. United Services 1909. Adjutant British Olympic team 1908. Adjutant British Empire Team 1910 and 1913. Captain British Empire Team 1919. Won L.R.B. Gold Medal 1906, 1909 and 1913. Silver Jewel Eng. XX Club 1907. Was Organising Sec. for Rifle Clubs under the N.R.A. 1903–4.

BATTEN, JOHN. Ensign 1863. Retired 1865.

BEARD, HAROLD CLIFFORD. Joined 2nd Batt. as Private Aug. 1914. 2nd Lieut. 1915. Lieut. 1916. To France early in 1915 (wounded in April). Instructor to O.C.C. To France again 20/9/16 and killed at Les Bœufs Oct. 1916.

BEDDINGTON, HENRY E. Ensign 1871. Lieut. 1872. Retired 1873.

BELITHER, S. J. *Ed.* Cooper's Company School. Enlisted in 2nd Batt. Sept. 1914 and went to France with it Jan. 1917. 2nd Lieut. 31/7/18. To 1st Batt. in France 21/9/18 to end of war.

BELL, R. F. 11th Londons. Att. to 1st Batt. Oct. 1916.

BENNETT, JULIEN FREDERICK CHARLES. Joined as Private 1900. Sergeant 1908. 2nd Lieut. 14/10/14. Lieut. 1914. Capt. 11/1/15. Adjt. 3rd Batt. 1915–18, then served in the R.A.F. Hon. Solr. to L.R.B.

BENNS, ARTHUR LIONEL. *Ed.* Christ's Hospital. Joined L.R.B. as Private 1909 and served continuously. Went to France with 1st Batt. in Nov. 1914 as Lce.-Corporal. Wounded at Ypres March 1915. Commissioned in 3rd Batt. 28/9/15 and rejoined 1st Batt. in France 5/3/16. Posted "C" Co. (killed 1/7/16).

BENSTEAD, H. E. 7th Londons. Att. to 1st Batt. 11/3/17–14/4/17 (*killed in action*).

BERKLEY, JOHN MALCOLM. Served at home till commissioned in R.B. 20/2/18. *Att. to 1st Batt.* 13/11/18.

BERRIDGE, G. J. 2nd Lieut. 1896. Resigned 1899.

BETTS, A. W. THOMSON. Joined Grenadier Guards 1914. 2nd Lieut. L.R.B. 21/2/15. Lieut. 1917. Served twice in France and latterly employed in connection with W.O. Lands.

BEWSHER, FRED W. *Ed.* St. Paul's and University College, Oxford. 2nd Lieut. 1909. Lieut. 1913. Capt. 1915. Mobilized as A.D.C. to G.O.C. 1st London Div. Bde. Major 175th Inf. Bde. in 58th Div., Feb. 1915–May 1916. Att. to 5th Seaforths and H.Q. 152nd Inf. Bde., B.E.F., May 1916–June 1916. Bde. Major 152nd Inf. Bde. June 1916–July 1917. Commandant 5th Army Musketry Camp, July 1917–Jan. 1918. G.S.O. 2, 51st Div. Jan.–June 1918. G.S.O. 2, IV Corps, June 1918–March 1919. Sec. Status of Inf. Com. at W.O. March 1919. To Egypt as Bde. Major 1919. *Honours.* D.S.O., M.C., three mentions in despatches.

BICKER-CAARTEN, GERARD. Enlisted in L.R.B. Cadets 1870. Corporal 1872. Sergeant 1873. Enlisted in L.R.B., "Q" Co., 1875. Corporal 1879. Sergeant 1880. Lieut. 22/1/86. Capt. 1892, "P" Co. Major 9/12/02. H./Lieut.-Col. Aug. 1904. Retired 1912. *Honours.* V.D.

BINGHAM, GEORGE CHARLES, LORD (afterwards Earl of Lucan). *Ed.* Harrow. R.B. 1881–1896. Bechuanaland Exped. 1884–5. Joined L.R.B. as Major 1900. Lieut.-Col. Commandant 1901–12. Brig.-Gen. commanding 1st London T. Bde. 1912–16. European War 1914–16. *Honours.* K.B.E. (civil), C.B. (mil.), T.D., mention and home mention, 2nd Class Order of St. Stanislaus of Russia, 3rd Class Nile.

BIRT, ERNEST W. Served in the ranks. 2nd Lieut. 1896. Lieut. 1898. Retired 1902 and joined R. Garrison R. Subsequently joined Durham L.I. and became Major.

BIRT, L. H. Served in ranks. 2nd Lieut. 1900. Given S. African War com. in R. Berks Regt. Retired 1902.

BISCOE, VINCENT FREDERICK. *Ed.* Cheltenham College; Clare College, Cambridge. Cheltenham College Cadet Corps and Cambridge University R.V.C. 1905–8. Sergeant 1908. Joined L.R.B. as 2nd Lieut. 1909. Lieut. 18/5/12. Capt. 30/6/15. Seconded to the Political Service, Northern Nigeria, 1911. Assistant Resident 2/8/11.

BLAND, BRIDGMAN ELSEY. *Ed.* Felsted School. Served in the ranks of L.R.B. for about ten years before the War. Rejoined 2nd Batt. on the outbreak of war as 2nd Lieut. and went to 1st Batt. in France 23/12/14–9/3/15 (sick). After return from France served with 2nd Batt. and afterwards with Bucks Volunteers as Adjt. Died 1917.

BLAND, CHARLES RIVIERE. *Ed.* Felsted School. Served as 2nd Lieut. with 2nd V.B. Essex Regt. Joined L.R.B. as 2nd Lieut. 1892. Lieut. 1893. Capt. 1898. Commanded "G" Co. Retired 1904. Rejoined 2nd Batt. on outbreak of war as Capt. T./Major 1915. Transferred to Reserve 1916. *Sports.* Commanded L.R.B. *Daily Telegraph* Team (winner) 1908.

BLANDFORD, THOMAS. Ensign 1860. Lieut. 1862. Retired 1868.

BODDAM, HUNGERFORD T. Ensign 1873. Lieut. 1873. Retired 1877.

BOLAND, EDWARD ROWAN. *Ed.* Stonyhurst. Joined 3rd Batt. as rifleman May 1916 and commissioned in it 1/3/17. Joined 1st L.R.B. 20/5/17. Severely wounded 15/8/17, and gazetted out owing to wounds 1918.

BOSTON, GEOFFREY GREENWOOD. *Ed.* Weymouth College. Joined as Private 1912 and served continuously, going to France with 1st Batt. Nov. 1914. Commissioned in field 8/5/15. Bombing Officer 26/10/15. Lieut. 1917. A/Capt. 5/1/17. Severely wounded 1/7/16 and gazetted out 1918. *Honours.* D.C.M. *Athletics.* Winner of 169th Brigade 5 miles and ¼-mile May 1916.

BOURNE, W. K. 2nd Lieut. 1895. Retired 1895.

BOWER, ALFRED GEORGE. Commissioned in 1st Londons and att. 2nd L.R.B. 17/11/17. *till wounded* 22/12/17.

BOWERBANK, EDWARD W. Ensign 1872. Lieut. 1873. Retired 1875.

BOWERS, STANLEY. Joined as private 1899 and served continuously. 2nd Lieut. ("A" Co.) 12/3/06. Lieut. 1/8/08. Capt. 9/7/10 ("D" Co. 1910/14). Major 1/6/16. Transferred to 2nd Batt. Sept. 1914 and served with it for some time. Went to France 13/12/17 to 2nd Batt., and att. to 2/10 Londons Jan. 1918–Feb. 1919. *Honours.* T.D.

BOWYER, PERCY GEORGE. Joined 3rd Batt. as rifleman July 1915. In France with 1st Batt. Jan.–Sept. 1916. Then served with 3rd Batt. and commissioned in it 5/2/19.

BOYES, HENRY COWELL. Served in ranks for some years. Ensign 1873. Lieut. 1873. Capt. 1877. Hon. Major 1896. Hon. Lieut.-Col. 1899. Hon. Architect to Regt. Designed H.Q. in Bunhill Row. Architect and Surveyor to Grocers' Co. Died 1900. *Honours.* V.D.

BRADLEY, MAURICE, R.A.S.C. Posted to 3rd Batt. and att. to 1st Batt. 7/9/18.

BRAND, JOHN A. Ensign 1868 ("F" Co.). Lieut. 1870. Capt. 1874. Q.M. 1877. Retired 1880.

BRENTFORD, C. G. *Ed.* Haileybury. Joined from Manchester University O.T.C. as 2nd Lieut. 25/1/17. Lieut. 1918. Served in France 3/3/17– — (wounded), and 1/2/18.– — .

BROCK, FREDERICK HARROLD. *Ed.* Christ's Hospital. Enlisted 2nd L.R.B. 21/10/14, "P" Co., and went to France with it 24/1/17. Home for commission 23/12/17 as a Sergeant. 2nd Lieut. 21/7/18. Joined 1st L.R.B. 21/9/18. Posted "D" Co. To England sick 7/11/18. *Honours.* D.C.M.

BRODIE, C. F. C. Joined as rifleman 1916. 2nd Lieut. 19/12/16. Served in France 13/12/17. Lieut. 1918.

BRODIE, C. G. Commission in 3rd Batt. as 2nd Lieut. 28/1/15, and joined 1st Batt. in France 18/7/15–15/9/15. Joined R.A.F. 1916 (killed in action).

BROMILEY, BERTRAM. *Ed.* Coffe's Grammar School, Blackheath. Private Civil Service Rifles 30/8/14–15/1/15. 2nd Lieut. L.R.B. 16/1/15. Lieut. 1916. Capt. 1917. On commission joined 3rd Batt. To 1st Batt. in France 24/12/15–5/7/16, and 8/5/17–7/12/17. Asst. Adjt. 1st L.R.B. 5/5/16. 2nd i/c 1st L.R.B. 1/8/17–2/12/17. Commanding while Major Wallis was on leave in Sept. 1917. *Honours.* Mentioned in despatches.

BRONNER, R. Joined as rifleman. 2nd Lieut. 26/4/17. Served in France 17/6/17. Lieut. 1918.

BROOKS, ROBERT HANSON. 2nd Lieut. 1888. Posted to "G" Co. Retired 1890.

BROWN, J. W. 9th Londons. Att. to 1st Batt. 23/6/17–16/8/17 (*missing*).

BRYANT, J. H. 20th Londons. Att. to 1st Batt. 28/9/17 *till wounded* 15/5/18.

BURCHETT, W. J. One year with H.A.C. (Inf.). 2nd Lieut. 1917. To France Feb. 1918, and served with some other Regt. Lieut. 1919.

BURNELL, CHARLES DESBOROUGH. *Ed.* Eton; Magdalen College, Oxford. Eton College R.V.C. Private 1892. Col.-Sergeant 1893. 2nd Lieut. Oct. 1893. 1st Lieut. June 1894. 2nd Lieut. L.R.B. 1894. Lieut. 1898. Capt. ("P" Co.) 1902. Hon. Major 1910. Retired 1912. Rejoined as Capt. and Hon. Major 1914. Went to France with 1st Batt. 5/11/14–2/5/15 (severely wounded) and from 11/4/17–1919. Commanded 1st L.R.B. 23/4/17–19/5/17, and from 10/5/18. A/Lieut.-Col. 1918. Brought back cadre of the Batt. on 30/5/19. *Honours.* D.S.O. Twice mentioned in despatches. *Rowing.* Won Eton Junior Sculls 1892. 2nd Senior Sculls 1893 and 1894. Winning House Four 1893. Eton College VIII, Winner Ladies' Plate Henley 1894. Oxford University VIII, Winner 'Varsity Boat Race 1895, 1896, 1897, 1898. Magdalen College, Oxford—Head of the river 1895. Won Stewards' Cup Henley 1899. Won University Sculls 1898. Leander Club—Winner Grand Challenge Cup Henley 1898, 1899, 1900, 1901. Stewards' Cup Henley 1899, 1900. Cork International Regatta, Eight Oar Race 1902. Olympic Regatta, Eight Oar Race 1908.

BURROUGHS, THOMAS EDWARD. Enlisted in 2nd Batt. 31/8/14. Joined 1st Batt. in France 24/1/15–7/7/16, Sergeant. 2nd Lieut. 25/10/16 and rejoined 1st Batt. in France 5/1/17–

14/9/18. Bombing Officer 20/2/17–2/12/17. Adjt. 2/12/17–9/4/18. Lieut. 1918. *Honours.* M.C. and Bar. Died 1920.

BURT, L. B. 12th Londons. Att. to 1st Batt. 30/1/18.

BUTCHER, WILLIAM GUY DEANE. *Ed.* Eton and Trinity College, Cambridge. Cambridge O.T.C. Commissioned to 2nd Batt. 14/10/14. Lieut. 1915. Capt. 1916. Joined 1st Batt. L.R.B. 3/6/17. Commanded "A" Co. in attack 16/8/17, and was missing, since reported killed in action on that date.

BYLES, ERNEST FRANK. 15th Londons. Att. to 1st Batt. 25/4/18 *till* 29/8/18 (*wounded*).

BYRNE, LUCIUS WIDDRINGTON. *Ed.* Marlborough and Trinity College, Cambridge. Marlborough College R.V.C. 1890–94. Cambridge University R.V. 1894–97. 2nd Lieut. L.R.B. 1898. Lieut. 1900. Retired 1903. Joined R.N.V.R. Oct. 1914. Att. to Intelligence Div. of Naval War Staff as Special Service Officer Dec. 1914–Jan. 1917. Served in Ireland and various parts of Great Britain. Appointed to H.M.S. *President* for service under Director of Naval Intelligence Jan. 1917. Lent to Army Council for service under Director of Military Intelligence at War Office Jan. 1917–Jan. 1919. Demobilised with rank of Lieut.-Com. R.N.V.R. Jan. 1919.

CAIRNS, WILFRED DALLAS, EARL. *Ed.* Wellington and Sandhurst. Lieut. R.B. 1885. Capt. R.B. 1895. Retired 1895. Capt. 5th (Militia) Batt. R.B. 1895. Retired as Lieut.-Col. 1905. Joined L.R.B. as Lieut.-Col. Commandant 9/12/12, and took 1st Batt. to France 5/11/14–9/4/15 (sick). T/Col. 3/11/15. *Honours.* South African War (Queen's Medal, three clasps). Great War: C.M.G. Mentioned in despatches and home mention. Resigned commission on account of ill-health 23/3/16.

CALDER, JOHN STEWART. *Ed.* Hartley University College, Southampton, and also East London College, London University. Enlisted in 1st Batt. 5/9/14, and went to France with it in Nov. 1914 till Aug. 1916. Corporal 28/4/15. Sergeant 9/8/15. C.S.M. 3/2/16. Commissioned to 3rd Batt. as 2nd Lieut. 26/9/16. Lieut. 26/3/18. Rejoined 1st Batt. in France 8/11/16–28/3/18 (missing). *Honours.* M.C. and bar.

CALLCOTT, H. N. 11th Londons. Att. to 1st Batt. 2/11/16–30/12/16 (*invalided*).

CAMBRIDGE, H.R.H. G. W. F. C. DUKE OF, K.G., K.P., G.C.B., G.C.M.G. Hon. Col. of L.R.B. 1860 till death. Commander-in-Chief of Army *circa* 1860–1902. Died 1904.

CAMDEN, H. M. *Ed.* Whitgift. Commissioned to 3rd Batt. 1915 and went to France 9/1/16. Soon returned and resigned commission. Afterwards served in the ranks elsewhere.

CAMPBELL, S. J. F. 6th Londons. Att. to 1*st Batt.* 13/8/18–27/8/18 (*killed*).

CANNING, PHILIP LOVELL H. *Ed.* Winchester College. Served for some years in ranks. 2nd Lieut. 1898. Lieut. 1900. Capt. ("D" Co.) 1902. Retired 1910.

CANNON, FRANCIS. Royal Fusiliers (Militia) 1890. S. Africa, Queen's Medal, 4 clasps. Promoted Major and 2nd in command 1902. Granted rank Hon. Major in Army 27th July, 1902. Retired on retired pay with rank and uniform through illness contracted during Boer War 13th Aug., 1903. Joined 3rd Batt. as Major 16/1/15: found medically unfit. Subsequently Chief Recruiting Officer No. 10 District Eastern Command. Commanded 32nd Batt. (Service Batt.) Royal Fusiliers. T.F. Reserve 17/5/17. National Service as Asst. Sub-Commissioner for Trade Exemptions Jan. 1919. Ministry of Pensions.

CANTRELL, J. 2nd Lieut. 1/5/18. To France 2/8/18.

CARRIER, J. RUSSELL. *Ed.* St. Olave's School. Joined in ranks 1912 and went to France with 1st Batt. Nov. 1914. 2nd Lieut. 18/10/15, and rejoined 1st Batt. 14/5/16. Sick to Havre 25/6/16. Rejoined Sept. 1916 (killed 8/10/16).

CARRINGTON, J. W. Att. to 2nd Batt. and on its disbandment transferred to 18*th Londons.*

CARSON, JAMES ALEXANDER. Ensign 1860. Lieut. 1860. Capt. ("A" Co.) 1863. Retired 1867. Died 1909.

CARTER, JOHN WILLIAM. Lieut. 1859. Retired 1861.

CARTWRIGHT, GEORGE HAMILTON GRAHAME MONTAGU. *Ed.* Eton and New College, Oxford. 2nd Lieut. 19/2/14 and went to France with 1st Batt. Nov. 1914–May 13, 1915 (wounded). Lieut. 5/2/15. June 1915–June 1916 A.D.C. to G.O.C. Southern Army. June 1916 transferred to Coldstream Guards S.R. France 17/3/17–17/3/19 with Guards M.G. Regt. A/Capt. 18/3/18. A/Major 24/3/18. Co. Commander 24/3/18 to date. *Honours.* Mentioned in despatches.

CATLOW, NORMAN STAINES. *Ed.* Wyggeston School. Joined as rifleman 1917. 2nd Lieut. 27/3/18. Went to France 2/8/18, posted to 3rd Londons (wounded 1/9/18 at Bouchavesnes, France).

CAVE, CHARLES CAVE. *Ed.* Winchester and Trinity College, Cambridge. Lieut. Winchester College R.V.C. and Cambridge University R.V.C. Lieut. L.R.B. 25/3/85 ("K" Co.). Retired 1890. Served as private in Inns-of-Court V.R.C. 1915, 1916, 1917, 1918. *Sports.* Winchester College Shooting VIII Wimbledon 1871/72/73/74. Cambridge Shooting VIII 1875/6. Athletic Blue. Won 'Varsity Half-Mile 1875.

CHAMBERS, FRANK JOB. *Ed.* City of London School. Joined L.R.B. as private 1872. Lieut. 1882. Capt. 1892. Retired 1892. Special constable Aug. 1914, afterwards Anti-Aircraft Corps.

CHAMBERS, GEORGE COLIN. *Ed.* Christ's Hospital. Joined as private 1907 and served continuously. Went to France with 1st Batt. Nov. 1914 to May 6th, 1915. Severely wounded. 2nd Lieut. 19/5/15. Lieut. 1/7/17. Asst. Adjt. 3rd Batt. July 1916–Aug. 1918. Adjt. 11/8/18–2/3/19. *Honours.* Home mention in despatches.

CHAPMAN, WALTER G. *Ed.* Westminster School and University College, Oxford. 2nd Lieut. 1900. Lieut. 1902. Retired 1908. Major Commanding 3rd V.B. 13 Middx. Regt. in Great War.

CHARLES, FRANK DALLAS. *Ed.* St. Albans School. Joined ranks L.R.B. 1910 and served continuously. Went to France with 1st Batt. Nov. 1914 and served there till 16/9/16 (invalided). 2nd Lieut. 1915. Temp. att. 187th Co. R.E. for Loos gas attack 28/9/15. A/Capt. 1916. Lieut. 1917. Served with 3rd L.R.B. for fifteen months and then joined Indian Army temp. A/Adjt. and Adjt. 40th Pathans. Transferred to 1st D.L.I. 1/5/19 and served in Frontier War May–Oct. 1919. A/Adjt. D.L.I. and came home with it 12/2/20.

CHARLES, RICHARD DUDLEY STAFFORD. *Ed.* Harrow and Pembroke College, Cambridge. Enlisted in the H.A.C. Sept. 1914. Joined 2nd Batt. 2nd Lieut. 31/12/14. Joined 1st Batt. in France Feb. 1915–May 1915 (wounded). Sent to 3rd Batt. and rejoined 1st Batt. in France 20/9/16–16/10/16. Lieut. 1916. Capt. 1917 (substantive). Wounded at Les Bœufs. Rejoined 3rd Batt. Subsequently Adjt. 1/12th (Dulwich) Co. London V. Regt. May 1917–April 1918 and War Dep. Valuer, Directorate of Lands, War Office, April 1918–Feb. 1919. *Rowing.* Pembroke 1st Crew 2 years, Cambridge University Clinker Fours 1909. Wyfold Cup, Henley 1911.

CHATER, SIDNEY. Asst. Surgeon 1863. Surgeon 1865. Retired 1875. Died 1885.

CHESHIRE, WILLIAM DONALD. Enlisted Sept. 1914, 15*th R. Warwicks. 2nd Lieut. April* 1915 17*th Lancs Fus. Att. to* 1*st Batt. L.R.B. Sept,* 1917 *as Second in Command and so continued to end of war.* Honours. *M.C., Albert Medal. Mentioned in despatches.*

CHILMAN, EDWARD THOMAS FREDERICK REA. *Ed.* Godalming Grammar School. Leathersellers' College, London. Joined as rifleman May 1916. 2nd Lieut. 1/3/17. Joined 1st Batt. 18/4/17. Severely wounded 9/2/18 when in charge of " A " Co. Lieut. 1/9/18. Invalided out Nov. 7th, 1918.

CHILVER, ARTHUR FARQUHAR. *Ed.* Haileybury and Trinity College, Cambridge. Served 1 year in Haileybury R.V.C. and 5 years in Cambridge U.R.V.C. 2nd Lieut. 1889. Capt. 1890. Enlisted in L.R.B. 1892, Sergeant. 2nd Lieut. 1896. Lieut. 1898. Capt. 1902 ("K" and "G" Co.'s). Retired as Hon. Major 1908. *Honours.* V.D.

CHODAK, HENRY ALEXIS (now Gregory, H. A. C.), R.A.M.C. Att. to 1st Batt. (wounded —/8/18).

CHOLMELEY, GUY HARGREAVES. *Ed.* Eton. Magdalen College, Oxford. Eton College R.V.C. and Oxford University O.T.C. Joined L.R.B., 2nd Lieut. 1913. Lieut. 1914 and went to France with 1st Batt. Nov. 1914 to Feb. 20th, 1915 (invalided). Again to France 17/7/15–3/7/16 (severely wounded). Capt. 1916. Joined 3rd Batt. and subsequently was Instructor Officers Cadet Batt. 1917–18 and Adjt. Vols. 1918.

CHOLMONDELEY, HUGH CECIL. *Ed.* Rugby. Formerly Capt. R.B. Adjt. 4th Batt. Afghan War 1878–9. Adjt. 5th Batt. 1882–7. Afghan War Medal and clasp. Joined L.R.B. as Lieut.-Col. 1889. Lieut.-Col. Commandant 1890. Retired 1901. Commanded C.I.V.M.I. in S. African War. S. African War Medal and six clasps. Twice mentioned in despatches. Rejoined L.R.B. 1914 as Lieut.-Col. and commanded 3rd Batt. Promoted Brig.-Gen. Commanding 173rd Inf. Bde. May 1915. *Honours.* C.B., C.B.E. (Mil.).

CHRISP, W. A. Enlisted and went to France with 1st Batt. Nov. 1914–21/9/18. Promoted 2nd Lieut. 1918. Wounded Sept. 1918. *Honours.* Mentioned in despatches.

CHRISTIE, JAMES R. Ensign 1860. Lieut. 1863. Served in "C" and "H" Co.'s. Retired 1865.

CLARK, DAVID. Joined as private about 1894. 2nd Lieut. 1897. Lieut. 1900. Retired 1901.

CLARK, FRANK STUART. *Ed.* Dulwich College. Rifleman in 3rd Batt. March 1916. Drafted to France 9/7/16, joining 1st Batt. 20/11/16–18/5/17 (gassed). 2nd Lieut. 1917. Lieut. 1918. Served as Training Officer with 51st ("Grad.") Batt. the R.B. from March 1918–Dec. 1918. T/Capt. 1/1/19. The third generation in the L.R.B. of his family: the sixth member of it to join: total service 97 years. *Sports.* Dulwich XI; Surrey Rugby XV 1911–12.

CLARKE, REV. A. DAWSON. *Ed.* Christ's Hospital, Durham Grammar School, St. John's College, Cambridge. M.A. Served in Cambridge University R.V.C., Sergeant, and from April 1879–Dec. 1882 held a combatant commission in the 3rd Mx.V.R.C. A member of the Committee which originated the inter-'Varsity sports. Chaplain 1887. Retired 1908 and appointed Hon. Chaplain T.F. *Honours*. V.D.

CLEARSON, ALFRED. Lieut. Supny. 1862. Retired 1870.

CLIFFORD, WILLIAM GEORGE. Enlisted 7/9/14 *and served with* 1*st Batt. in France* 26/1/15–4/5/15 (*wounded*). *Commissioned as* 2*nd Lieut. in* 101*st Prov. Batt*. 14/12/15. *Bde. Bombing Officer* 213*th Inf. Bde. Feb*. 1917–*Feb*. 1918 ; *and to* 227*th* (*mixed*) *Bde. Feb.–Dec*. 1918.

CLODE, WILLIAM. Ensign 1860. Lieut. 1863. Capt. 1866 ("M" Co.). Retired 1873.

CLODE-BAKER, GEORGE EDMUND. *Ed*. Uppingham. Enlisted in L.R.B. in Sept. 1914. Transferred to Inns-of-Court O.T.C. in Dec. 1914. 2nd Lieut. L.R.B. 7/2/15. Joined 1st Batt. as T/Lieut. in France 24/12/15–1/7/16 (killed in action).

CLOSE, VERE HENRY. Late Capt. 90th Foot. Joined L.R.B. as Major 1860. Lieut.-Col. 1860. Retired 1862.

COCKERELL, DONALD CHESSUM. *Ed*. Dunstable Grammar School and on Continent. Rifleman Oct. 1914 in 2nd Batt. To France with it Jan. 1917. Returned as Sergt. for commission. 2nd Lieut. 31/7/18. Joined 1st L.R.B. 21/9/18 ("A" Co.) and killed in action 6/11/18.

COCKROFT, CHARLES. *Ed*. Eton. 2nd Lieut. 1901. Retired 1905.

COLE, CHARLES HENRY. 11*th Londons. Att. to* 1*st Batt*. 5/8/16–3/10/16 (*killed in action*).

COLES, E. R. Joined as rifleman 1917. 2nd Lieut. 27/3/18. Served in France 2/8/18.

COLES, HERBERT GORDON DECIMUS. *Ed*. St. Saviour's School, Eastbourne. Rifleman Jan. 1917. Commissioned 2nd Lieut. in 3rd Batt. 18/12/17. Joined 1st Batt. in France 25/4/18. Intelligence Officer 15/10/18–15/11/18. Lieut. 1919. Asst. Adjt. 2/8/18–2/3/19.

COLLIER, EDGAR. *Ed*. Eastbourne. Joined as private 1895. 2nd Lieut. 1900. Lieut. 1902. Capt. 1908. Retired 1910. Died 1911. *Shooting*. King's Badges, Bisley 1903, 1904.

COLLIER, OSWALD. *Ed*. Haileybury. Enlisted 1895. 2nd Lieut. 1910. Batt. Signalling Officer 1910–14. Retired 1914. Served with R.N.D. during the War. T.E. Medal.

COLLINS, A. J. Joined 3rd Batt. 2nd Lieut. 16/1/15. Trans. to Yeomanry 1917.

COLLIS, LESLIE WILFRID. *Ed*. Ipswich School. Two years in O.T.C. at Ipswich School. Despatch Rider R.E. in England Sept. 1914–April 1915. Joined 3rd Batt. as 2nd Lieut. 14/4/15. Lieut. 1916. Joined 1st Batt. in France 2/8/16–21/9/16. A/Capt. 1917. Invalided from the service with rank of Capt. 19/1/19.

COLMER, G. J. 2nd Lieut. 1908. Retired 1908.

COLTHURST, R. ST. J. J. Joined 2nd Batt. 2nd Lieut. 1914. Lieut. 1916. Capt. 1916. Did not serve abroad owing to ill-health.

COLVIN, A. O. 12th Londons. Att. to 1st Batt. 30/1/18–25/2/18.

CONDUITT, WALTER. Joined 1st Batt. as 2nd Lieut. and Transport Officer 5/8/14 and left Regt. in Oct. 1914. Subsequently in Remounts.

CONOLEY, NICHOLAS RICHARD. *Ed.* Coopers' Company's School, E., and London Hospital Medical College. University of London O.T.C. 3rd A.M. R.F.C. June 1917–March 1918. Posted to L.R.B. as 2nd Lieut. 27/2/18. Att. to R.A.F. 9/9/18–16/3/19.

COOKE, BERTRAM HEWETT HUNTER. *Ed.* Eton and Sandhurst. Joined 4th Batt. R.B. 1895. Adjt. Sept. 1899–March 1901. With 2nd R.B. Nile Exped. 1898 (Queen's Medal, Khedive Medal and clasp). S. Africa 1901–2 with M.I. (Queen's Medal, 5 clasps). Wounded 19/12/01. Served with L.R.B. as Capt. and Adjt. 1903–6. Passed Staff College 1910. France 12/8/14–28/2/18. Bde. Major 2nd Inf. Bde. Aug.–Sept. 1914. Battle of Mons. Battle of Marne (severely wounded, Courchamps 10/9/14). D.A.A.G. and A.A.G., G.H.Q. Oct. 1914–Dec. 1915. Present at 1st and 2nd Battles of Ypres, Neuve Chapelle, Festubert, Loos. D.A. and Q.M.G. XIV Corps Jan.–Dec. 1916. Operations Ypres Salient Jan.–July 1916. Battle of Somme July–Nov. 1916. D.A. and Q.M.G. IX Corps Dec. 1916–Feb. 1918. Battle of Messines June 1917. Passchendael July–Nov. 1917. Operations in South part of Ypres Salient Nov. 17th–Feb. 1918. *Honours.* D.S.O., C.M.G., C.B.E. (Mil.), Order of St. Stanislaus with swords, Belgian Croix de Guerre. Commander Order du Merit Agricole. Brevet Lieut.-Col. Five mentions in despatches.

COOKE, E. G. STENSON. Served in L.R.B. Cadets (Sergeant Instructor) and in ranks as private. 2nd Lieut. 1893. Lieut. 1896. Capt. 1900 ("B" Co.) Retired 1903. Joined 8th Cyclist Batt. Essex Regt. 21/9/14 with contingent of A.A. Motor Scouts, rank of Capt. Att. W.O. (A.G. 2, 8/1/15). Apptd. Staff Capt. Dec. 1915. Major June 1916. *Honours.* Two mentions in despatches. *Sports.* Fencing Bronze Medal Foils L.R.B. S. of A. 1891. A few firsts at Orion G.S., open Foils and Single-stick. *R.M.T.* 1896, 3rd Sabres. 1897 1st and Challenge Cup Sabres, 3rd Foils. 2nds and 3rds up to 1902 when 1st and Challenge Cup Foils. Olympic Team Foils, Stockholm 1912. 2nd Prize R.N. and A. M. T. Olympia. Foil Championship 1919.

COPE, R. Joined 2nd Batt. 2nd Lieut. 1915. Lieut. 1917 and went to France with it 29/1/17. Adjt. 23/7/17–29/1/18. Then Adjt. IIIrd Corps Training Reinforcement Camp. Later joined 1st Batt.

COOPER, JONES WORTH. Ensign 1860. Retired 1860.

CORNISH, CHARLES W. Private 1883. Sergeant 1889. 2nd Lieut. 1892. Lieut. 1893. Capt. 1898 ("H" Co.). Retired 1908 as Hon. Major. Hon. Sec. L.R.B. 1897–1908, 1914–19. *Honours*. V.D.

COTTER, G. H. Enlisted about 1900 and served continuously, going to France with 1st Batt. Nov. 1914 as Colour-Sergeant Promoted 2nd Lieut. 11/2/15 and killed at Ypres April 1915 *Sports*. Both Brighton March Teams.

COTTON, FRANCIS J. Ensign 1864. Lieut. 1865. Capt. 1870 ("P" Co.). Retired 1873.

COXWELL, HENRY. Ensign 1863. Retired 1865.

CRAIG, NORMAN. *Ed*. North-Eastern County School and Armstrong College. Served in North-Eastern County School O.T.C. 1912–16. Rifleman L.R.B. Nov. 1916. 2nd Lieut. 30/1/18. Joined 1st Batt. in France 8/5/18–29/9/18 (wounded).

CRANE, VICTOR WILLIAM RODEN. *Ed*. Hartlebury Grammar School. Rifleman April 1916. 2nd Lieut. 28/11/17 and joined 1st Batt. in France 25/4/18–28/8/18 (wounded). Rejoined 21/11/18–28/1/19. *Sports*. 2nd in Aldershot Command 3 mile flat race July 1917. 4th in 56th Div. Cross Country Race Aug. 1918.

CREIGHTON, MANDELL, D.D. (Rt. Hon. and Rt. Rev. Lord Bishop of London). Chaplain 1897. Died 1901.

CREWS, FREDERICK HOWARD. *Ed*. Eastbourne Municipal Secondary School. Enlisted 1910. Served continuously and went to France with 1st Batt. Nov. 1914–4/1/19. 2nd Lieut. 24/1/16. Lieut. 1916. Co. Commander July 2nd, 1916–June 2nd, 1917. Asst. Instructor "G.H.Q. Lewis Gun School"–3/6/17–16/10/18. Batt. L.G.O. 18/10/18–4/1/19. A/Adjt. 23/10/18–14/11/18. A/Second in Command 4/12/18–4/1/19. *Honours*. M.C. *Sports*. Member of L.R.B. Marathon Team 1913 and Brighton March 1914.

CRISFORD, REV. K. N. Att. to 1st Batt. 23/11/15–1/7/16 (wounded). Rejoined 20/11/16–15/1/18. *Honours*. M.C.

CRISP, HAROLD JOHN FRANCIS. *Ed*. Bournemouth School. Joined L.R.B. as private 7/7/11 and served continuously. Proceeded to France 5/11/14 as Batt. Runner; became Lce.-Corporal, Corporal, Sergeant. Returned home for commission 23/1/16. Landed as officer 27/5/16. Joined 1st Batt. 5/6/16. Asst. Int. Officer till 20/7/16. Wounded 10/9/16. Lieut. 1917. Relanded 29/12/17. Posted to 2nd L.R.B.

Trans. (att.) to 18th Londons 8/2/18–13/3/18 (sick). Relanded 15/11/18 and rejoined 1st L.R.B. 21/11/18–8/2/19. *Honours.* M.M.

CROMBIE, LAWRENCE, R.A.M.C. Att. to 1*st Batt.* 12/5/16– —/8/16.

CROOK, AUBREY HARRY. Posted to 2*nd Batt. in France* 17/11/17–11/1/18.

CROSS, H. 2nd Lieut. 28/3/17. To France 24/5/17. Rejoined 1st Batt. 11/9/18. Killed in action 27/8/18.

CROSS, STANLEY HERBERT. *Ed.* Dulwich College. Inns-of-Court O.T.C. 29/11/15–30/7/16. Rank of Lce.-Sergt. Joined 3rd Batt. as 2nd Lieut. 30/7/16. Served with 1st Batt. in France from 20/9/16– —/6/17 (invalided). Lieut. 1918. Subsequently served with Inland Waterways and Docks. *Honours.* M.C.

CROSSLEY, NEVILL MORGAN. Served with 1st City of London Artillery Volunteers 1895–1900. 2nd County of London Imperial Yeomanry (Westminster Dragoons) 1901–8. 1st V.B.Mx.R. Sept. 1914–June 1916. Commissioned to 3rd L.R.B. 25/10/16. Lieut 1918 East Coast April 1917–May 1919. Att. 14th Batt. S. Lancs. Signals Officer, Asst. Adjt. Adjt. Did not serve abroad owing to ill-health. Home mention in despatches.

CROSSLEY, THOMAS S. Ensign 1870. Lieut. 1872. Capt. 1873. Retired 1875.

CROUCH, W. G. 19*th Londons. Served with* 2*nd Batt.* 31/7/17–20/9/17.

CUTHBERT, GOYMOUR. Joined L.R.B. Cadets 1867. Private in L.R.B. 1870, " N " Co., rose to Col.-Sergeant. Lieut. 25/3/85. Capt. (" O " Co.) 12/4/92. Hon. Major —/11/97. Major 2/4/01. Hon. Lieut.-Col. 10/8/01. *Honours.* V.D. Died 26/2/02.

CUTHBERT, RANSOM M. Ensign 1862. Lieut. 1863. Retired 1865.

DALE, REV. CANON. Chaplain 14/2/62. Retired 1872.

DARRINGTON, CLARENCE PHILIP. *Ed.* Deal and Sandwich School. After serving in France with the London Scottish, was commissioned to the 4th London Regt. about July 1915. Joined that Regt. soon after in Malta and saw service at Gallipoli, from whence he was invalided home with enteric fever and frost-bite in the feet. Posted to 2nd Batt. L.R.B. at end of 1916. Transferred and went to France with it Jan.–May 1917. 2nd Lieut. 1916. Lieut. 1917. Served with 3rd Batt. and returned to 1st Batt 24/5/17 to —/7/17, and 21/9/18–8/11/18 when severely wounded, of which he died 27/11/18.

D'AVIGDOR, B. H. Ensign 1873. Lieut. 1873. Retired 1875.

DAVIS, STEPHEN JOHN. Enlisted in 2nd Batt. Sept. 1914 and went to France with it Jan. 1917–June 1918. Returned for commission. 2nd Lieut. 3/3/19.

DAWSON, VICTOR REGINALD. *Ed.* Christ's College, Finchley. Joined 2/7th Middlesex Sept. 1914. Arrived Gib. Feb. 1915. Arrived Egypt Aug. 1915. Took part in Senussi campaign on Libyan Desert. Arrived France May 1916. Joined 1st L.R.B. July 1916. Wounded Leuze Wood 9/9/16. Commissioned 26/4/17 and subsequently served with 3rd Batt.

DEAN, WILLIAM SENIOR. Ensign 1862. Lieut. 1865. Capt. 1868 ("F" Co.). Retired 1874.

DEBNEY, R. J. E. Lieut. 1882. Capt. 14/12/89 ("A" Co.). Retired 1892.

DE COLOGAN, ARTHUR THOMAS BERNARDO. *Ed.* Oratory School, Edgbaston, and Queen's College, Oxford. Oxford University O.T.C. Oct. 1909–Jan. 1911. Joined L.R.B. as 2nd Lieut. 2/4/13. Lieut. 1914. Asst. Dist. Com. Somaliland Protect. 3/7/14–30/5/15. Att. Somaliland Camel Corps as Co. Officer 5/4/15–12/5/15. Capt. 1916. To France, joined 1st Batt. 18/7/15–1/7/16. Taken prisoner 1/7/16.

DENNY, ADDISON. *Ed.* Taunton. In ranks 1896–1908. Rejoined Aug. 4th, 1914–Nov. 13th, 1917, when commissioned as Lieut. and Q.M. 1917. Went to France in the 1st Batt. 5/11/14–24/5/19, serving with it without break from the day it went out till the return of the cadre. *Honours.* Mentioned in despatches. *Shooting.* Won "Martin's" Rapid Firing Aggregate 1907 and King's Badge 1913 at Bisley. L.R.B. Silver Badge 1902.

DERHAM, J. A. T. 2nd Lieut. 27/6/17. Joined 1st Batt. 10/9/17 to —/5/18 (wounded).

DEVITT, ANDREW OLIPHANT. *Ed.* Marlborough. Served in Marlborough College Cadets four years. Private L.R.B. 1896. 2nd Lieut. 1900. Retired 1901.

DEWAR, JAMES EVAN. *Ed.* Haileybury College. Inns-of-Court O.T.C. 1/12/15. Commissioned to 3rd Batt. 8/7/16. To France and joined 1st Batt. 1/10/16–8/10/16 (killed). *Rowing.* Rowed and sculled for several years for the London R.C.

DEWEY, JOHN HERBERT JAMES. *Ed.* Mercers' School. Rifleman 1917. Commissioned to 3rd Batt. 27/3/18. Went to France 27/7/18 and posted to 2/2nd Londons (wounded at Maricourt 28/8/18 and wounded and prisoner at Epehy 10/9/18). *Honours.* Mentioned in despatches.

DIGHTON, THOMAS D. E. Ensign 1860. Lieut. 1862. Capt. 1864 ("A" Co.). Retired 1869.

DITTMER, A. R. *Ed.* Coopers' Company School, Durham University, and Salisbury Theological College. Joined Inns-of-Court O.T.C. May 1915. Gazetted to 3/8th Hants (Isle of Wight Rifles) Aug. 1915. Transf. L.R.B. Feb. 1916 as 2nd Lieut. 1916. Retired owing to ill-health July 1916 to resume studies. Subsequently ordained.

DIXON, JOSEPH PERCY. Commissioned to 2nd Batt. T/2nd Lieut. 1/4/15. 2nd Lieut. 15/10/15. A/Q.M. of 2nd Batt. 22/1/16–25/9/16. Lieut. 1/7/17. A/Capt. —/6/17. Appointment on Lands Branch W.O. as War Dept. Valuer 1/12/17. Did not serve abroad.

DODD, ARTHUR. *Ed.* City of London School. Joined L.R.B. as private No. 18 on first day of enrolments. Ensign 1860. Lieut. 1862. Retired 1866.

DODDRELL, REV. E. C. Att. to 3rd Batt. 12/10/16–9/1/17.

DODDS, ARCHIBALD KIRKWOOD. *Ed.* Mill Hill School. In ranks of Queen's Edinburgh R.V. Bde. (R.S.) 1903–06. L.R.B. 1908–11. Rejoined as private 1914 and went to France with 1st Batt. Nov. 1914. 2nd Lieut. 28/2/15. Sick 3/5/15–1/6/15. Gassed 2/10/15. Lieut. 1/6/16. Trans. R.E. (T.F.) 25/8/16. Italy 7/1/18–15/5/19. A/Capt. R.E. 18/1/18. *Honours.* M.C. Mentioned in despatches.

DOLLAND, GEORGE. Ensign 1859. Lieut. 1860. Capt. 1860. Retired 1866.

DOUST, CHARLES BOWDEN. *Ed.* Dulwich College. Enlisted 6/8/14, and went to France with 1st Batt. Nov. 1914. Wounded at Ypres April 1915. 2nd Lieut. 17/8/15 in 3rd Batt. Again to France and joined 1st L.R.B. 25/3/16 (killed in action 1/7/16).

DUCAT, ARTHUR DAVID, M.B. *Ed.* London University and St. Bartholomew's Hospital. London Scottish 1889–95, leaving with rank of Sergeant. Surgeon-Lieut. 1895. Surgeon-Capt. 1899. Major 1908 (trans. to R.A.M.C. when T.F. was formed). Served continuously and went to France with 1st Batt. Nov. 1914–March 1st, 1915. Trans. to No. 12 Stationary Hospital as Second in Command. July 1915 sent to Third Army to take charge of Medical Stores (No. 13 Advanced Depot Medical Stores). Jan. 1916 was sent to A.D.M.S. Office, 18th Div. After an accident was sent home for operation in Feb. 1916. On becoming convalescent was sent as Surgeon to Southwark Military Hospital, Dulwich, in July 1916. Sent again to France to take over command of 2/3rd London Field Ambulance, 56th Div. 2/4/17 to —/3/19. Lieut.-Col. 1918. *Honours.* D.S.O., T.D. Three mentions in despatches. Medaille d'Honneur avec Glaives "en vermeil."

DUNCAN, REV. J. M. Att. to 1st Batt. 6/8/18–7/8/18 (*wounded*).

DUNCAN, WILLIAM, F.R.C.S. Asst. Surgeon 7/3/85. Surgeon-Capt. 5/5/89. Retired 1891. Afterwards Lieut.-Col. commanding Mx. Yeo. Died 18/12/17.

DU PLESSIS, S. 7th Londons. Att. to 1st Batt. 11/9/17–24/1/18.

DUTTON, HUGH COLSTON. 18th Londons. Served with 2nd Batt. in France 24/6/17–25/8/17.

DYER, PERCY THOMAS. *Ed.* Central Foundation School and Goldsmiths' College. Enlisted in L.R.B. 5/9/14 and went to France with 1st Batt. Nov. 1914. 2nd Lieut. 19/7/16. Lieut. 19/1/18. Served only with 1st L.R.B. in France and 3rd L.R.B. in England. *Honours.* M,M.

EASTWICK, EDWARD BACKHOUSE. Late Lieut. Bengal Native Inf. Joined L.R.B. as Major 1860. Retired 1861.

EDMONDS, GEORGE H. Ensign 1866. Lieut. 1868. Retired 1874.

EDMUNDS, EDGAR FLETCHER. R.A.M.C. Att. to 1st Batt. 27/2/15–28/4/15 (*wounded*).

ELKINGTON, ARTHUR JOHN. *Ed.* St. Paul's School. Lieut. 1882. Resigned 1888.

ELLIOTT, A. 5th R.B. Att. to 1st Batt. Nov. 1918.

EMERSON, F. Joined 2nd Batt. as private Sept. 1914 and went to France with it Jan.–April 1917, when invalided home. 2nd Lieut. 1/5/18. Went to France and posted to 2/2nd Londons 14/8/18 and killed in action 26/8/18 at Maricourt.

EMMETT, A. H. Att. to 3rd Batt. 31/10/18.

EPPS, FREDERICK GEORGE. *Ed.* Southend High School. Joined 2nd Batt. Sept. 1914 and drafted 1st Batt. in France 25/3/15–20/5/17. 2nd Lieut. 31/10/17. To France and posted to 2/6th Batt. London Regt. 2/2/18–26/5/18 (twice wounded). Lieut. 1/5/19.

EVANS, D. W. 10th Londons. Att. to 1st Batt. 2/10/16–6/10/16 *and* 15/10/16–10/1/17.

EVANS, E. G. Served in ranks elsewhere and posted to L.R.B. on commission. 2nd Lieut. 1918.

EWENS, ALEXANDER THOMAS. Late Lieut. K.R.R.C. Lieut. and Adjt. L.R.B. 1860. Capt. 1860. Major 1882. For services to L.R.B. see Index. Retired and died 1883.

FARRANT, VICTOR THOMAS. 4th S. Lancs. Regt. Posted to 12th Londons. Att. to 1st Batt. 30/1/18–25/2/18.

FASS, FRANCIS GEORGE. *Ed.* Charterhouse. Served in ranks 1900–1903. Commissioned to 3rd Batt. 5/8/16 and went to 1st Batt. in France 7/11/16–15/3/18. Returned for six months' home service and subsequently served at Air Ministry. Lieut. 5/2/18.

FEAST, ARTHUR COOPER. *Ed.* Merchant Taylors' School. Served in Cadets 1895–99. Served in ranks 1899–1907 and 1910–15. Lce.-Corporal 1911. Corporal 1913. Sergeant 1914. Went to France with 1st Batt. 4/11/14–18/5/15 (invalided). Subsequently served with 3rd Batt. 2nd Lieut. 8/5/15. A/Capt. 11/3/17. Lieut. 1/7/17.

FERGUSON, HAROLD STUART. *Ed.* Eton College and R.M.A., Woolwich. Lieut. Royal Field Artillery 1871–4. Lieut. Reserve of Officers 1880–95. Commanded 2nd Batt. Nayar Bde. Travancore State Troops 1885–95. Joined L.R.B. as Capt. 2/12/14. R.M.A. XI two years, XV two years. Represented R.M.A. in sports in 1870 *v.* Sandhurst. Won long jump, 21 ft. 2½ in. Played for Scotland *v.* England at Association football. Coffee planting in Travancore 1875–9. In service of Travancore State, India, 1880–1905 in various capacities. J.P. and Special Magistrate. Director of the Museum and Public Gardens. Member of Legislative Council. Private Secretary to F.M. Lord Roberts 1905–14. Fellow of the Linnean Society. Fellow of the Zoological Society: on Council from 1918. *Honours.* M.B.E. (civil). Died 1921.

FINCH, FREDERICK GEORGE. Ensign 1859. Lieut. 1860. Capt. 1860 ("K" Co.). Retired 1870.

FINCH, STANLEY FREDERICK. Trooper in Essex Yeomanry. Lce.-Corporal in 2nd Essex Regt. France Dec. 1916–Oct. 1917 with 2nd Essex Regt. Posted to L.R.B. on commission. 2nd Lieut. 26/6/18. Joined 1st Batt. 15/9/18–Jan. 1919. *Appointments,* Assistant Transport Officer and Town Major of Blaugies and Noirchain after Armistice was signed.

FINLAYSON, VICTOR ALEXANDER. *Ed.* Tonbridge. 2nd Lieut. 4/9/15. Commissioned in 2nd Batt. and went to France with it 25/1/17–17/5/17 (sick). Lieut. 1/7/17–28/2/19. Rejoined 2nd Batt. 14/12/17–1/2/18. On disbandment transferred to 10th Londons 2/2/18–28/2/19. Intell. Officer Feb. 1918–May 1918 and Adjt. 15/9/18–27/2/19. A/Capt. 15/9/18–27/2/19. 29/2/19 to —/11/19 in Germany with 9th London Regt. Q.V.R. *Honours.* M.C.

FISH, ROBERT. Asst. Surgeon 1866. Retired 1869. Probably died about 1875.

FLINDT, RUPERT ERNEST HUNTLEY. *Ed.* Christ's Hospital. Christ's Hospital O.T.C. 1 year. Served in ranks from 1911 continuously and went to France with 1st Batt. Nov. 1914. Sergeant. 2nd Lieut. 11/2/15–6/5/15 (wounded and gassed). T/Lieut. 1/2/16. Lieut. 1/6/16. France 6/1/17–3/2/17. Attached New Zealand Division. Instructor Young Officer Co. and No. 4 Officer Cadet Batt. Oxford Dec. 1915–May 1917. T/Capt. 1/6/16–11/3/17 and 13/10/17–19/7/19. Qualified at

Staff Course Cambridge July, Aug. 1917. Staff-Captain Lowland Reserve Bde. 13/10/17–16/3/19 and No. 3 Section Forth Defences (new formation) 4/1/18–17/3/19. Capt. 19/7/19. *Honours.* Mention and home mention in despatches. *Sports.* L.R.B. Marathon team 1911, 1912, 1913. Winning Newton Dunn Team 1912, 1913. Winning inter-company 5 miles team race 1911, 1912.

FORBES, KENNETH. *Ed.* Winchester. Winchester College O.T.C. 2nd Lieut. 2/1/14 and went to France Nov. 1914 with 1st Batt. Killed at Ploegsteert 10/2/15. At Winchester was Head of his House and a Prefect, and was joint Editor of the *Wykehamist.*

FORBES, LAWRENCE. *Ed.* Marlborough. Artists' Rifles O.T.C. Commissioned to 2nd Batt. and went to France with it Jan.–June 1917 (died of wounds received at Bullecourt).

FORBES, THOMAS LAWRENCE. *Ed.* Winchester and University College, Oxford. Commissioned to 2nd Batt. 5/11/14. Lieut. 1916. Went to France with it Jan. 1917–17/6/17 (severely wounded). Capt. 1917. Worked under Air Ministry 1/4/18–9/1/19.

FOSTER, GERALD HARMAN (afterwards Betton-Foster). *Ed.* Haileybury and Magdalen College, Oxford. Haileybury College R.V.C. 1887–90. Shot for Cadets 1889. VIII 1890. Oxford University R.V.C. 1891–95. Shot for Oxford VIII and IV 1893–94–95. 2nd Lieut. L.R.B. 1897. Lieut. 1900. Retired 1900. Transferred to R.G.A. with University commission during S. African War 1900. *Rowing.* Rowed Head of River 1892–93–94–95. Trial Eights 1895.

FOTHERINGHAM, L. H. Served in German W. Africa. 2nd Lieut. L.R.B. 31/8/16 and went to 1st Batt. in France 8/11/16. Invalided and afterwards served at home. Lieut. 1918.

FOX, A. R. Enlisted 1915. To France 1916. Wounded at Arras 1917. Commissioned in 3rd Batt. 2nd Lieut. 27/3/18 and went to France 2/8/18 (wounded 26/8/18. Wounded and prisoner 10/9/18).

FOX, CHARLES D. Ensign 1861. Lieut. 1863. Retired 1865.

FOX, FRANCIS. Ensign 1869. Retired 1870.

FOX, HUGH WATSON. Capt. R.A.M.C. Attached to 3rd Batt. 1/6/18–8/2/19.

FRANKLIN, WILLIAM. Ensign 1873. Lieut. 1873. Capt. 1879. Retired 1881.

FRERE, GILBERT RAPER. *Ed.* Haileybury and B.N.C., Oxford. 2nd Lieut. 1909. Lieut. 1910. Retired 1913. Joined 10th R.B. Sept. 1914. Adjt. To France 21/7/15. Capt. 10/10/15 (killed in action 26/10/15). *Rowing.* Capt. of B.N.C. Boat Club and rowed at Henley in several events.

FREW, DAVID THOMAS CRICHTON. R.A.M.C. Att. to 1*st Batt.* 3/2/16–12/5/16. *Died.*

FREY, E. *Ed.* in Switzerland. Joined 3rd Batt. as rifleman 20/5/15 and drafted to 1st Batt. in France 15/10/15–31/5/17. Wounded 23/9/16. Rejoined 31/10/16. Gazetted 28/11/17 to the Rangers but was transferred back to L.R.B. and went to France 30/4/18, rejoining 1st Batt. 8/5/18–26/8/18 (killed in action).

FRODSHAM, CHARLES MILL. Ensign 1860. Lieut. 1860. Capt. 1863 (" F " Co.). Retired 1866.

FULLER, ERIC WILLIAM. *Ed.* Merchant Taylors' School. Rifleman 2nd Batt. 21/9/14–25/1/15. Drafted to 1st Batt. in France 1/2/15–29/8/15. 2nd Lieut. 30/8/15 and rejoined 2nd Batt. To France with it 25/1/17–3/5/17. Instructor Vth Corps Schools 3/5/17–30/12/18. Lieut. 1/7/17. Adjt. Vth Corps Concentration Camp 2/1/19–5/7/19.

FURRELL, B. Joined from Artists' Rifles. Gazetted to 3rd Batt. 19/12/16 and ordered off to a Lancashire T.F. Batt. 7/2/17 with which he went to France and did all his service.

FURSDON, GEORGE ELLSWORTH SYDENHAM. *Ed.* Westminster School and Trinity College, Cambridge. Westminster School O.T.C. Sergeant 1908–12. Cambridge University O.T.C. Sergeant 1912–14. 2nd Lieut. L.R.B. 20/9/14. Went to France with 1st Batt. 5/11/14–2/3/15 (wounded). Lieut. 31/3/15. Rejoined 17/7/15–9/9/15 (sick). Trans. to T.F. Reserve 23/5/16. Asst. Recruiting Officer Plymouth 11/11/15–5/6/16. Sub-area Commander Exeter 6/6/16–31/10/17. Recruiting Staff Officer to Director of Recruiting Bristol 1/11/17–31/12/18.

FURZE, CLAUDE. *Ed.* Repton and Jesus College, Cambridge. Repton and Cambridge University O.T.C. 2nd Lieut. L.R.B. 11/7/14. Lieut. 1914. Capt. 1916. Could not go out with 1st Batt. owing to ill-health. Posted to 2nd Batt. and went to France with it 25/1/17–6/4/18 (killed in action).

FURZE, FREDERIC. *Ed.* Charterhouse. Joined 1st Batt. as private Aug. 1914. Commissioned in 2nd Batt. 1914. Lieut. 1915. Capt. 1916. Adjt. 17/6/15–23/7/17 (killed at Menin Road 20/9/17). Senior Capt. and officer in action.

FYNES-CLIFTON, GEOFFREY. Ensign 1872. Retired 1873.

GARDINER, WILLIAM EDWARD MANSFIELD. *Ed.* Forest School. Forest School Cadet Corps. Inns-of-Court O.T.C. 6/5/15. Commissioned to 3rd Batt. 11/7/15. Went to France and joined 1st L.R.B. 11/5/16, " A " Co. (killed in action 19/7/16).

GARDNER, WILLIAM. Capt. 1859. Retired 1864.

GARDNER, WILLIAM (Junior). Capt. 1859. Retired 1861.

GARRARD, F. N. 2nd Lieut. 1888. Lieut. 1890. Retired 1896. Subsequently served in a Surrey Regt.

GAWITH, JAMES JACKSON. Asst. Surgeon 1879. Surgeon 1885. Retired 1887. Died 28/12/89.

GEE, JOHN PERCY. *Ed.* Grocers' Company's School. Inns-of-Court O.T.C. 2nd Lieut. L.R.B. 28/11/17. Lieut. 28/5/19. Posted to 3rd Batt. and joined 1st Batt. 25/4/18–12/9/18 (wounded). *Honours.* M.C.

GILBERT, JOHN G. E. Ensign 1860. Lieut. 1862. Retired 1862.

GILLBARD, GURDON. *Ed.* University College School. Enlisted in the Artists' Rifles 2/11/16. Gazetted 2nd Lieut. R.F.C. 5/7/17. Posted to 3rd Batt. 8/1/18. Lieut. 5/1/19. Labour and German prisoners of War Dec. 8th, 1918–April 26th, 1919. Att. to Gar. Batt. Suffolk Regt. in France July–Dec. 1918.

GILSON, G. 2nd Lieut. 30/1/18. To France 2/8/18.

GIVEN-WILSON, H. F. 2nd Lieut. 1900. Resigned 1901.

GLOVER, CYRIL JOHN, 10th Londons. Att. to 1st Batt. 4/10/16–8/10/16 (*killed in action*).

GLYNN, THOMAS G. P., 8th, King's Liverpool, Regt. Capt. and Adjt. L.R.B. 1893–1898. South African War. Transvaal, O.R.C., Cape Colony. Special service Feb. 1899–July 1899. Chief Staff Officer Volksrust District July 1899 to end of War. Great War Aug. 1914–1919, in France. Base Depot Commander, subsequently Officer Commanding Reinforcements, Calais. *Honours.* C.M.G. (S.A. War); O.B.E. Four mentions in despatches.

GODWARD, JOHN SYDNEY. *Ed.* Epsom College. Epsom College O.T.C. 1910–1913. Joined L.R.B. as private 6/8/14 and went to France with 1st Batt. 5/11/14. Rose to Sergeant. Returned for commission June 1916. 2nd Lieut. 5/9/16. Rejoined 1st Batt. in France 8/11/16–March 1917 (wounded), and France 14/7/17–Feb. 1918. Lieut. 5/3/18. Returned to England for 6 months instructor's course. To France May 1918 till demobilised in Feb. 1919. A/Capt. 28/6/18. Was Bombing Officer during the first period of commissioned service overseas. During later periods was Co. Commander.

GODWIN, W. J. 3rd R.B. Att. to 1st Batt. Nov. 1918.

GOODING, HERBERT ROBERT WILLIAM. *Ed.* St. Dunstan's College. Enlisted in L.R.B. in 1909. Served continuously and went to France with 1st Batt. 5/11/14. Commissioned in the Field 19/4/15. Appointed M.G. Officer 12/5/15 (killed in action 13/5/15).

GOODLIFFE, F. G. Lieut. 1863. Capt. 1865 (" P " Co.). Retired 6/11/69.

GOODMAN, SAMUEL. Ensign 1860. Retired 1860.

GOODSON, ALAN RICHARD LASSAM. *Ed.* Malvern. Commissioned to 3rd Batt. 7/2/15 and trans. to R.A.F. Went to France Sept. 1915 as Observer. Came back to England Feb. 1916 to take Pilot's certificate and returned to France May 1916. Lieut. 1916. Wounded and taken prisoner on a bombing raid at Hollebeke, June 3rd, 1916. Capt. 16/8/17. Repatriated Nov. 18th, 1918.

GORDON, ALBERT. *Ed.* Brompton H.G. School. Joined L.R.B. Oct. 1912 and served continuously, going to France with 1st Batt. Nov. 1914. 2nd Lieut. (Transport Officer) 9/4/16. A/Capt. 2/10/17. Lieut. 9/10/17. To England 17/10/17 for duty under Mil. Int. Directorate. Rejoined 7/11/17 as Q.M. and again to England (sick) 1/5/18. To France and posted to 1/17th Londons 15/11/18. Re-trans. to L.R.B. 16/12/18–14/4/19. Demobilised 17/4/19. *Honours.* D.C.M. Mentioned in despatches. *Sports.* Won Eastern O.C.D. Heavy-Weight Boxing Sept. 1918.

GORDON, H. E. 2nd Lieut. 1916. To France 5/1/17.

GORDON-LENNOX, NORMAN H. 2nd Lieut. 1909. Retired 1911.

GORE, WALTER. Regt. not known. Served with 2nd Batt. 2/10/17–*unknown.*

GOSNELL, R. C. 2nd Lieut. 1902. Lieut. 1906. Retired 1908.

GOULD, S. C., 21*st Londons. Att. to* 1*st Batt.* 27/9/17–28/3/18 (*prisoner of war*).

**GRACE, W. J.* 10*th Londons. Att. to* 1*st Batt.* 27/9/16–30/9/16 *and* 14/10/16–28/3/18 (*prisoner*).

GRANT, W. E. 7*th Londons. Att. to* 1*st Batt.* 12/8/18 *to* –/8/18 (*wounded*).

GRAY, ROBERT. *Ed.* Denmark Hill Grammar School. Sub.-Lieut. 7th Surrey R.V.C. 9/12/74. Retired as Capt. 30/11/85. Capt. " Reserve of Officers " 15/10/80–4/8/85. Private L.R.B. 30/11/85–28/4/86. 2nd Lieut. 1886. Lieut. 28/4/86. Resigned 1892. Rejoined 13/4/99–27/3/1900. 2nd Lieut. 27/3/1900. Lieut. 9/12/02. Resigned 1902 as Hon. Capt. Capt. Territorial Force Reserve. General List 9/11/15. Pte. for 11 months in 15th London Vols. Served in the Records Office, Alexandria, Egypt, from Nov. 1915–Aug. 1916. Retired on account of ill-health 19/11/16 with permission to retain rank. Master, Vintners' Co. 1913–14. *Honours.* V.D. 1903.

GREEN, C. E. Served in ranks 1907–12. With Fife and Forfar Yeomanry as private France Nov. 1916–March 1917. Gazetted to L.R.B. as 2nd Lieut. 1/5/18. Went to France 2/8/18 and posted to 2/2nd London Regt. (killed Aug. 1918).

GREEN, SIR FRANCIS HAYDN, BART. *Ed.* University College School. L.R.B. Cadets 1886–88. Private L.R.B. 1888–90. 2nd Lieut. Nov. 1890. Lieut. Jan. 1893. Capt. 1898 (" Q " Co.). Retired 1904 with Hon. rank of Major. Lieut. Reserve of Officers 1895–1905. Member of City of London T.F. Member of the Common Council of the City of London.

GREEN, WILLIAM EDWARD. *Ed.* Wellingborough School. Joined 3rd Batt. as rifleman April 1916. 2nd Lieut. 25/1/17. In France with 2nd Batt. from 28/2/17–26/9/17. Wounded on the Menin Road 20/9/17. Lieut. 25/7/18. From Sept. 1918 to Feb. 1919 att. to 52nd (Grad.) Batt. the R.B. (at Colchester) as Musketry Officer.

**GRIFFITHS, S. A.*

GRIMWOOD, P. L. Enlisted in 3rd London Oct. 1914 and served with it in Malta, Sudan, Dardanelles and France. On commission posted to L.R.B. as 2nd Lieut. —/10/17. Joined 1st Batt. in France 29/12/17 to —/3/19. *Honours.* M.C.

GRINDEY, JOHN WILLIAM. Enlisted 20/2/17. 2nd Lieut. 18/12/17. To 1st Batt. in France 19/4/18–28/8/18 (wounded). *Sports.* Aldershot Command, High Jump Championship 1917.

GROTE, ANDREW M. Late 87th Foot. Capt. Feb. 1866 ("D" Co.). Retired 1872.

GUINNESS, HON. ARTHUR ERNEST. *Ed.* Eton and Trinity College, Cambridge. Eton Cadets 1891–5. 2nd Lieut., L.R.B., March 1898. Lieut. May 1900. Retired 10/10/02.

GUINNESS, RUPERT EDWARD CECIL LEE (afterwards Viscount Elveden). *Ed.* Eton and Trinity College, Cambridge. Eton Volunteers. 2nd Lieut., L.R.B., Jan. 1894. Lieut. Dec. 1896. Capt. May 1900 (" O " Co.). South Africa—in charge of the Irish Hospital (Queen's Medal). Seconded from the L.R.B. 30/7/03 (gazetted out 21/3/05) to command the R.N.V.R., London Div. Lieut. R.N.V.R. 1903 Commander. A/Capt. 1915. Capt. 1919. In charge of Recruiting Naval Mission to Canada 1916–17. M.P. for S.E. Essex from 1912–18. For Southend-on-Sea since 1918. City representative of London School Board 1902 and at Asylums Board as a representative of the L.G.B. 1902. *Honours.* C.B., C.M.G. (for S.A.), R.N.V.R. A.D.C. to the King May 1916–July 1919. *Rowing.* Won Eton School Sculling 1892. Rowed in Eton winning crew for Ladies' Plate at Henley 1892. Won Diamond Sculls 1895. Diamonds and Wingfields 1896.

GULL, REV. C. G. *Ed.* Oxford. Chaplain 1900. Retired from Chaplaincy 1907. Commanded 4th Londons (Grocers' Co.'s School) during its existence. Master at Dulwich—Commanded Cadets 1876–81. Nov. 1905 to Malta as Chaplain of St. Paul's Collegiate Church.

GUPPY, JOHN. *Ed.* Cowper St. School and University College. Joined L.R.B. January 1883. Corporal 1884. Sergeant 1886. Clr.-Sergeant 1892. Q.M. Sergeant 1899. Hon. Lieut. and Q.M. July 1900. Hon. Capt. Sept. 1901. Hon. Major 1908. Resigned April 1914. Rejoined 2nd Batt. Aug. 1914. Att. to 101st Provisional Batt. on its formation June 1915, and was transferred to Territorial Force Reserve in Jan. 1917. *Honours.* T.D., Coronation Medal. Home mention in despatches.

GUTHRIE, STUART. *Ed.* Streatham High School and King's College School, Wimbledon. Private in L.R.B. Nov. 1914. Went to 1st Batt. in France —/8/15– —/12/15 (sick). 2nd Lieut. 28/11/17. Sent to France 1/2/18. Posted to 2/6th London Rifles. Acted as Liaison Officer between British and French Head-quarters (killed at Villers Bretonneux, Amiens, 4/4/18).

GWYNNE, H. A. 2nd Lieut. 1897. Retired 1898. Reuter's Special War Correspondent in several wars. Editor *Standard* from 1904–11. Editor *Morning Post* from 1911–19.

GYTON, LESLIE RONALD. Enlisted in the L.R.B. as a boy on the 22/1/14, age 16 years. Mobilised with the regiment in August 1914. Acting Bugler until 17 years of age. Transferred (being under age) to 2nd Batt. when 1st Batt. proceeded Overseas ; to 101st Provisional Batt. on 20/6/15 ; to 3rd Batt. on 17/9/16. 2nd Lieut. 28/11/17. Joined 1st Batt. in France 25/4/18–19/3/19. Lieut. 28/5/19.

HADFIELD, FRANK. *Ed.* Chesterfield Grammar School. Joined 3rd Batt. as rifleman 23/2/17. 2nd Lieut. 27/3/18. To France 1/8/18. Posted to 1/22nd Londons 22/8/18–2/9/18 (wounded).

HAGGARD, A. J. R. Served with 2nd Batt.

HAIG-BROWN, ARTHUR. Joined as Cadet 1860. Private L.R.B. 1863–68 "Q" Co., 1877–1903 "D" Co. as Sergeant. In 1885 as Sergeant took over charge of L.R.B. Cadet Corps to 1903, its strength increasing from 30 to 400. Hon. Lieut. 29/12/88. Hon. Capt. 1893. 2nd Lieut. 6/6/00. Capt. 1/7/00. Retired as Hon. Maj. 1903. Died. *Honours.* V.D.

HALL, CLEMENT. *Ed.* St. Paul's School. Three years St. Paul's School O.T.C. Resigned with rank of Sergeant. Four years University of London O.T.C. Resigned with rank of Clr.-Sergeant. Enlisted in L.R.B. April 1914 and went to France with 1st Batt. Nov. 1914–16/2/15 (wounded). 2nd

Lieut. 21/10/15. Again to France 3/9/16. Posted to No. 2 Entrenching Batt. Joined 1st Batt. 24/9/16–8/10/16 (wounded). Lieut. 1/7/17. Again to France 14/12/17 and joined 2nd Batt. 28/12/17. Att. 1/18th Batt. London Regt. 29/1/18–21/3/18 (wounded). Asst. Adjt. 3rd Batt. 11/8/18 to end of war.

HALL, G., 11th Londons. Att. to 1st Batt. 24–30/9/16 and 14/10/16–25/12/16. Transferred to R.A.F.

HALL, RICHARD WILLIAM COMPTON, 13th Londons. Att. to 2nd Batt. 25/9/17, and on its disbandment transferred to 18th Londons.

HAMMOND, EDWARD T. E. Ensign 1860. Lieut. 1862. Retired 1865.

HANCOCKS, FRANK GEORGE. *Ed.* Christ Church, Crewe. Served Feb.–Dec. 1913 Cheshire R.F.A. (T.F.) Corporal. Joined L.R.B. as private May 1914, and served continuously, going to France with 1st Batt. Nov. 1914 and remaining there till Jan. 1919. 2nd Lieut. 7/10/16. Lieut. 7/4/18. *Honours.* M.C.

HANNA, J. H., 19th Londons. Att. to 2nd Batt. 5/8/17–20/9/17 (killed in action).

HANSON, REV. E. VERNON. Att. to 3rd Batt. 13/6/15 to —/11/15.

HANSON, SIR REGINALD, BART. Ensign 1860. Lieut. 1860. Retired 1866. Alderman for Ward of Billingsgate 1880–1905. Sheriff 1881. Knighted 1881. Lord Mayor 1886–87. Baronet 1887. M.P. for City 1891–1900. Joined the regiment again as private after he was an alderman. Died 19/4/05 as Hon. Colonel of 6th Batt. Royal Fus.

HARBEN, KENNETH TUCKER. *Ed.* Christ's College, Finchley. Joined L.R.B. 13/2/17 as a rifleman. 2nd Lieut. 26/2/18. Posted to 12th Londons in France 19/6/18–9/8/18 (died of wounds).

HARE, SHERLOCK. Ensign 1872. Lieut. 1872. Retired 1874.

HARRINGTON, WILLIAM FREDERICK. *Ed.* Lawrence School, London. Joined City of London Yeomanry Rough Riders Aug. 1914. Egypt Mar. 1915. Gallipoli Aug. 1915–Oct. 1915. Motor cyclist despatch rider att. R.E. Signals. Senussi Campaign Dec. 1915–June 1916 and Palestine June 1916–April 1917. 2nd Lieut. 31/10/17. Posted to L.R.B. and joined 1st Batt. 29/12/17 to —/3/18 (severely wounded). Lieut. 1/4/19.

HARRISON, W. H. 2nd Lieut. 22/12/87. Lieut. 1888. Capt. 1896 ("G" Co.). Retired 1896.

HARVEST, GEORGE. *Ed.* Highgate School. Enlisted in L.R.B. some years before commission. 2nd Lieut. 1892. Lieut. 1894. Capt. 1898 ("N" Co.). Retired 1905. Rejoined as Major

18/9/14. Went to France with 2nd Batt. 29/1/17 to —/4/17 (invalided). Died at Brighton in Oct. 1918 of illness contracted on active service. *Honours.* V.D.

HARVEST, GORDON LINDSAY. *Ed.* Repton and Jesus College, Cambridge. Joined 1st L.R.B. as private Aug. 1914 and went to France with 1st Batt. Nov. 1914– —/4/15 (invalided). Commissioned to 2nd Batt. 1915. Lieut. 1916, and went to France with it 29/1/17–20/6/17 (killed in action). *Honours.* M.C.

HARVEY, BERNARD S. *Ed.* Malvern College and Trinity College, Oxford. Served in Oxford University O.T.C. Commission in 2nd Batt. 23/9/14. Lieut. 1915. Capt. 1915. Joined 1st Batt. in France —/12/14–1/7/16 (killed in action). *Rowing.* Trinity College Eight 1907–10 (Capt.).

HAY, SIR HECTOR MACLEAN. Served in 1st Middlesex R.V.C. (Victorias) for some years, retiring as Capt. and joining L.R.B. Ensign 1871. Lieut. 1872. Capt. 1872 "M" and "H" Co.'s. Major 1876. Retired 1877. Died.

HAYES, E. C. 16th Londons. Att. to 1st Batt. —/4/17 to —/6/17.

HAYTER, SIR ARTHUR DIVETT (afterwards 1st Baron Haversham). *Ed.* Eton and B.N.C., Oxford. Capt. Grenadier Guards. Joined L.R.B. as Capt. 1872. Lieut.-Col. Commandant 1876–1881. Resigned 1881. M.P. for Wells 1865–8, Bath 1873–85, Walsall 1893–5 and 1900–05. Jun. Lord of Treasury 1880–82. Financial Secretary to W.O. 1882–5.

HAYWOOD, WILLIAM. Joined as private. Lieut. 1860. Capt. 1860 ("P" and "O" Co's.). Major 1872. Lieut.-Col. 1876. Lieut.-Col. Commandant 1881. Retired 1882. Died.

HELM, C. Served in German W. Africa and elsewhere. Posted to L.R.B. as 2nd Lieut. 11/9/18 and joined 1st Batt. in France 15/11/18.

HENDLEY, PHILIP ARTHUR, Capt. R.A.M.C. Att. to 3rd Batt. 18/2/18–1/6/18.

HEWITT, FRANCIS EDGAR. Private in 6th Seaforth Highlanders T.F. 12th Sept. 1914 to 28th April, 1915. Joined 3rd Batt. on commission 29/4/15 and went to 1st Batt. in France 11/1/16–20/5/16 (sick). Gazetted out from ill-health 1916.

HEWITT, H. St. J. 2nd Lieut. 31/1/18. To France 29/4/18.

HEWLETT, R. F. L. 2nd Lieut. 30/5/17. To France 27/8/17.

HICKS, GEORGE MONTAGUE. Late Capt. 41st Foot. Joined L.R.B. as first Commanding Officer 1859–3/3/62. Retired. Governor White Cross Street Debtors' Prison. Died 25/12/05.

HICKS, RICHARD L. Joined as Capt. 25/5/70 ("B" Co.) from 12th Tower Hamlets on amalgamation of the latter with L.R.B. and commanded "A" Co. 1874–9. Retired 1879.

HIGGS, H. L. *Ed.* St. Peter's Collegiate School, Wolverhampton. Enlisted 4/9/14 and drafted to 1st Batt. in France —/2/15. Wounded 2/5/15 and 1/7/16. 2nd Lieut. 26/9/17. Left 3rd Batt. 13/12/17. Posted to 2nd Batt. in France and was missing 25/3/18 (afterwards reported killed).

HIGHAM, ERIC EDWARD. *Ed.* Eton and Oxford. Enlisted in Artists' Rifles 4/9/14–15/1/15. Commissioned to 3rd Batt. 16/1/15. To France 14/7/17–9/9/17 (severely wounded). Lieut. 21/3/18.

HIGHAM, HERBERT GOWAN. *Ed.* Owen's School, Islington. Joined 2/7th Middlesex on 16/9/14. Served with them in Gibraltar, Egypt and in Senussi Campaign Nov. 1915–March 1916. Sent to France April 1916 and transf. as rifleman to L.R.B. on 2/7/16– —/9/16 (wounded). 2nd Lieut. 1/8/17. Rejoined 1st Batt. 11/9/17–28/3/18 (prisoner of war). Lieut. 1/2/19.

HILDER, G. D. 15th Londons. Att. to 1st Batt. 25/4/18–26/9/18 (*wounded*).

HILL, R. L. *Ed.* Colf's Grammar School, Blackheath. Enlisted in L.R.B. Oct. 1909–Oct. 1913. Rejoined Sept. 1914 and went to France with 1st Batt. in Nov. 1914–April 20th, 1915. 2nd Lieut. 21/5/15 and served in France till 22/6/16. On 4/6/16 gazetted to permanent Regular Commission in Middlesex Regt. (att. M.G.C. 20/11/16). March 1917–Feb. 1918 Mesopotamia, att. 132nd M.G.Co. Feb. 1918–May 1919 India, att. M.G. Depot Mhow, C.I. May 1919–Sept. 1919 Afghanistan, att. 263rd M.G. Co. 12th Sept. 1919 and onwards India, att. 263rd M.G. Co.

HILL-WHITSON, E. C. Maj. Royal Scots. Att. to 2nd Batt. as Second in Command 20/7/17–5/9/17.

HILLHOUSE, J. R. Ensign 1872. Lieut. 1872. Resigned 1877.

HOGG, S. R. Joined 3rd Batt. 2nd Lieut. 7/2/15. Served with 1st Batt. in France April 1915–Jan. 1916. Transf. to R. Fus. *Honours.* D.S.O., M.C. and Bar.

HOLBROOK, EDWARD. Enlisted Nov. 1871. Lieut. —/4/83. Capt. 1892 ("H" Co.). Retired 1898 as Hon. Major. Died 5/11/03. *Honours.* V.D.

HOLLAND, GEORGE EDMUND. Private Victoria Rifles (1st Middlesex) 1863. Capt. 4th Middlesex (West London) Rifles 1866. Major 1872. Sub.-Lieut., L.R.B., 1874. Lieut. 1874. Capt. 1879 ("H" Co.). Retired 14/12/89. *Honours.* V.D.

HOLLIDAY, ALFRED ROWLAND. *Ed.* Stationers' and Southgate County School. Joined 3rd Batt. as rifleman March 1915. 2nd Lieut. 25/10/16. To France and posted to the R.B. 5/1/17–20/11/17 (killed in action).

HOLMES, ROBERT CHARLES. Late Capt. 10th Dragoons. Adjt. 1863. Retired 1865.

HOOD, DOUGLAS. *Ed.* St. Paul's School. Joined the R.N. Div. Sept. 1914. Transf. to Army for commission July 1916. Commissioned in Q.W.R. and transf. to L.R.B. 2nd Lieut. 19/12/16. Lieut. 19/6/18. Served with 1st Batt. Jan. 1917–18. Six months with 3rd Batt. and rejoined 1st Batt. 24/11/18. *Honours.* M.C.

HOPE, ADRIAN ELIAS. Major 1874. Lieut.-Col. 1882. Retired 1889. *Honours.* V.D.

HOPE, CHARLES T. BERESFORD. 2nd Lieut. 1872. Lieut. 1880. Capt. 1887. Retired 1892. Died 1906.

HOPKINSON, CHRISTOPHER. Ensign 1860. Lieut. 1860. Capt. 1861. Retired 1864.

HOPKINSON, WILLIAM. Ensign 1859. Lieut. 1860. Capt. 1860. Retired 1866.

HORE, C. W. C. *Ed.* Harrow and Cambridge. 2nd Lieut. 1909. Lieut. 1910. Retired 1912.

HORN, ANDREW FERGUSON. R.A.M.C. Att. to 1st Batt. 9/5/18.

HORNER, ERNEST SIMMS. Served some years in the ranks. 2nd Lieut. 1890. Lieut. 1892. Capt. 1896 ("G" Co.). Retired 1898. Died.

HOSKING, S. T. 7th Londons. Att. to 1st Batt. 1/9/17– —.

HOUGHTON, WILFRED ARTHUR. *Ed.* Merchant Taylors' School. Enlisted as private Nov. 1912. Served with 1st Batt. in France 29/1/16–1/7/16 (wounded). 2nd Lieut. 18/12/17 and rejoined 1st Batt. 25/4/18–29/8/18 (wounded). Lieut. 18/6/19. *Shooting.* N.R.A. Silver and Bronze (Recruits) and King's 200, 1914.

HOWARD, H. S. 2nd Lieut. 1892. Lieut. 1896. Capt. 1900. Retired 1902.

HOWAT, JOHN B. Ensign 25/3/67. Lieut. 1870. Retired 1872.

HOWE, GEORGE HUBERT. *Ed.* Merchant Taylors' School and Guy's Hospital. Private, Artists' Rifles, 1911–15. Served in France with them Oct. 1914–April 1915. 2nd Lieut. L.R.B. 11/4/15 and served with 1st Batt. in France 27/5/16–19/8/16.

HOWELL, EDGAR H. Ensign 1866. Lieut. 28/4/68. Retired 1873. Died.

HOWELLS, FRANK JAMES. *Ed.* Bridgend. Enlisted in 2nd Batt. Sept. 1914, and went to France with it 23/1/17–1/10/17. 2nd Lieut. 1/5/18 and served in France 2/8/18–25/6/19. *Honours.* M.M.

HUBBARD, ARTHUR JOHN. Asst.-Surgeon 1886. Retired 1888.

HUGHES, C. R., 11th Londons. Att. to 1st Batt. 18/7/16–17/9/16 (wounded).

HUGHES, EDGAR ALFRED, F.R.C.S. Surgeon-Lieut. 1891. Surgeon-Capt. 1892. Retired 1899.

HUGHES, EDWARD BLYTHE HURST. Capt. R.A.M.C. Att. to 3rd Batt. 29/4/17–13/12/17.

HULSE, JAMES HOLT. *Ed.* Wallasey Grammar School. Joined 3rd Batt. in ranks March 1917–Dec. 1917. 2nd Lieut. 18/12/17. To France, posted to 1/19th Londons, 19/4/18–5/9/18 (wounded). *Honours.* M.C.

HUMMERSTONE, L. G. *Ed.* Christ's Hospital. Joined 3rd Batt. as rifleman Aug. 1916. 2nd Lieut. 26/4/17 and served in France 7/6/17–March 1918. Lieut. 5/7/18. Came to England and was att. to R.A.F. for training. Returned to France as Observer, R.A.F., June 1918 (killed in action 21/8/18).

HUMPHREYS, OCTAVIUS. Ensign 1860. Retired 1863.

HUNTER, SIR CHARLES RODERICK, BART. Late Capt. R.B. Retired 1890. Joined L.R.B. as Major 1890. Retired 1895. South Africa 1900 with Imperial Yeomanry. Inspector of Musketry Imperial Yeomanry 1900. Divisional Musketry Officer 1914–15. M.P. for Bath 1910–19. A.D.C. to General Lord Alexander Russell commanding in Canada 1884–8.

HUNTER, JAMES CECIL. 2nd Lieut. 18/12/17. Posted 1/19th Londons in France (died of wounds 2/9/18).

HUNTER, RICHARD JOCELYN. *Ed.* Winchester, Harvard University, U.S.A., and B.N.C., Oxford. 2nd Lieut. 1910. Lieut. 1912. Resigned March 1914 and rejoined 2nd Batt. as Capt. 16/1/15. Went to France 27/4/17 and, after being att. to a Brigade Staff for a few months, was att. to 1/21st London Regt. as Capt., where he remained until 25/8/18 when wounded and died the following day. *Games.* Winchester College XI (12th man) 1905–1906. Played cricket and football and rowed for Brasenose College, Oxford.

HUNTER, R. W. 12th Londons. Att. to 1st Batt. 30/1/18.

HUSEY, RALPH HAMER. *Ed.* Marlborough and in Germany. In the ranks of the Hertfordshire Yeomanry from 1901–6. 2nd Lieut., L.R.B., 12/3/06. Lieut. 1908. Capt. 26/11/12 (" A " Co.). Served continuously and went to France with 1st Batt. Nov. 1914. 2nd i/c 1st Batt. 18/4/15 till wounded 13/5/15. Rejoined 1st Batt. as 2nd i/c 4/10/15. Major 1/6/16. Wounded at duty 3/8/16. Commanded 1st L.R.B. 13/8/16 till wounded 14/8/17. T/Lieut.-Col. 13/9/16. Rejoined 2/12/17. Commanded 169th Inf. Bde. while Brigadier on leave 26/12/17–27/1/18. Commanded 1st Batt. till 20/4/18. In temp. command of 167th Inf. Bde. 21/4/18–3/5/18. Assumed command 25th Inf. Bde. 4/5/18. Brig.-

Gen. 8/5/18. Wounded and taken prisoner 27/5/18. Died in enemy hands 29/5/18. *Honours.* D.S.O. and Bar, M.C., Montenegrin Order of Danilo (4th Class). Four mentions in despatches. *Games.* Three times led the Regimental Marathon team, finally winning in record time in 1913. Established a record with the Regimental Team in the March to Brighton.

HYSLOP, HAROLD. *Ed.* Winchester. 2nd Lieut. 1900. Lieut. 1901. Retired 1902.

ISMAY, B. G. 10th Londons. Att. to 1st Batt. Oct. 1916.

IVENS, REV. A. L. Att. to 3rd Batt. 26/2/16–14/8/16.

JACKSON, JOHN. Ensign 1865. Lieut. 25/3/67. Retired 1871.

JACOB, W. S. C. Served in ranks and rose to Clr.-Sergeant. Ensign 28/4/68. Retired 1871.

JAMES, REV. H. C. Att. to 2nd Batt. circa *Jan.* 1918.

JARVIS, M. J. 2nd Lieut. 1897. Retired 1898.

**JENKIN, M. W.*

JENKIN, WILFRED DUDLEY. *Ed.* Dulwich College. Joined as private Feb. 1911 and served continuously, going to France with 1st Batt. Nov. 1914–April 1915 (wounded). 2nd Lieut. 26/4/17. Served in France with 2nd Batt. 7/6/17 to Sept. 1917. Then rejoined 3rd Batt. Lieut. 26/10/18. *Games.* L.R.B. Marathon Team 1912 and 1913.

JESSOP, LANCELOT. *Ed.* Haileybury College. Joined as private Aug. 1914 and went to France with 1st Batt. Nov. 1914. Transf. to Bde. M.G. Sect. March 1916. Rejoined L.R.B. June 1916. Wounded 1/7/16. 2nd Lieut. 31/7/18 and rejoined 1st Batt. 26/9/18.

JOHN, C. H. *Ed.* Churcher's College, Petersfield. Joined as a private Aug. 1914 and went to France with the 1st Batt. in Nov. 1914–Dec. 1918, all of the time with L.R.B. except seven months with 3rd Corps School. 2nd Lieut. 17/7/16. Lieut. 17/1/18. A/Capt. 14/9/18. *Honours.* M.C.

JOHNSON, ERNEST DARLEY. *Ed.* King's College School, London, and Aldenham School. L.R.B. Cadets 1890. Sergeant Instructor 1893–97. Private L.R.B. 1896. 2nd Lieut. Dec. 1897. Lieut. Jan. 1900. Capt. Dec. 1902 ("B" and "O" Co.'s). Retired 1908. Served in S. Africa from April 1900–July 1901 with 20th Batt. Imp. Yeomanry and Imp. Light Horse. S. African Medal, Queen's Medal and 4 clasps. Mentioned in despatches. Rejoined 1914 and served as Musketry Staff Officer (graded as Brigade Major) to 15th, 30th and 41st Div. in succession Aug. 1914–Feb. 1916. Musk. S.O. and G.S.O. 3 at Scottish Command Feb. 1916–Oct. 1916.

Posted to 3rd Batt. as Capt. 13/10/16. Posted to 2nd Batt. and went to France with it Jan. 1917–21st April 1917. Invalided to Base 21/4/17. Prisoner of War Co. May and June 1917. Chief Instructor Third Army Musketry Camp 4/7/17. Invalided home 5/10/17. *Shooting.* Won King's Prize 1902. "St. George's" 1903. King's Badges 1902, 1905 and 1906. Shot for English XX. "Volunteers" in United Services and "Mother Country" in Kolapore Cup and for "England" in Mackinnon Cup. Championship N.L.R.C. 1899. Championship English XX Club 1905. Won L.R.B. Gold Medal 1903.

JOHNSTON, CHARLES EVELYN. *Ed.* Eton and New College, Oxford. Eton College R.V. 1893–96 Sergeant. 2nd Lieut. L.R.B. 19/9/1900. Lieut. 29/1/06. Resigned 1906. Rejoined 2nd Batt. as Capt. 20/9/14. Att. British Mission, Portuguese E.F., Dec. 1916–May 1917, France. A/Major 20/5/17. Second in Comd. 2nd L.R.B. 20/5/17–27/12/17. Commanding 2nd L.R.B. 27/12/17–21/2/18. A/Lieut.-Col. 11/1/18. Commanding 8th London Regt. (P.O.R.) 20/4/18–31/7/18. T/Lieut.-Col. 31/7/18. Commanding 7th London Regt. 31/7/18–10/4/19. *Honours.* D.S.O., M.C. Mentioned in despatches. *Rowing.* Oxford University VIII 1899–1900.

JOHNSTON, HUGH LIDDON. *Ed.* Radley and Magdalen College, Oxford. Five years Oxford University O.T.C. 2nd Lieut., L.R.B., 26/8/14. Went to France with 1st Batt. Nov. 1914 till wounded 16/6/16. Adjt. 14/5/15–6/4/16. Lieut. 30/6/15. T/Capt. 29/4/15. Capt. 1/6/16. To France and posted to 6th London 24/6/18–8/2/19. A/Major 26/10/18–9/7/19. Rejoined 1st Batt. 8/2/19. *Honours.* M.C.

JONES, A. L. 2nd Lieut. 28/3/17. To France 7/6/17.

JONES, CHARLES HARRISON. *Ed.* Reading School and St. John's College, Oxford. Reading School Cadet Corps. 2nd Lieut. 1901–2. Oxford University R.V.C. 1902–6 (Lce.-Sergeant). Ceylon Planters' Rifle Corps 1908–14 (rifleman, Lce.-Corporal and Corporal). 2nd Lieut., L.R.B., 29/1/15. Lieut. 1/6/16. Joined 2nd Batt. and went to France with it Jan. 1917–March 26th, 1918. Brigade Intelligence Officer, 174th Inf. Bde., Sept. 24th, 1917–March 1918. *Rowing.* Oxford University Trial VIII's 1904 and 1905.

JONES, KENNETH WILLIAM. *Ed.* Owens School. Joined 3rd Batt. as rifleman in Feb. 1917. 2nd Lieut. 31/10/17 and served in France 29/12/17–11/3/18 (wounded).

JOPSON, REGINALD KEITH. *Ed.* Owens School, Islington, and London University. Enlisted in 3rd Batt. 17/10/16. 2nd Lieut. 18/12/17. Went to France and posted to 1/19th Londons 20/4/18–1/9/18 (wounded).

JOURDAIN, ALBERT. Ensign 1860. Lieut. 1862. Retired 1868.

JOYCE, CYRIL FRANCIS. *Ed.* Elstow School, Bedford. Joined as private Feb. 1909 and served continuously, going to France in the 1st Batt. Nov. 1914, holding ranks of Sergeant, C.Q.M.S. and C.S.M. Commissioned in 2nd Batt. 20/9/15, Lieut. 1/7/17, and went to France with it Jan. 1917–July 1917. Then att. 174th Bde. L.T.M. Battery Aug. 1917–March 1919.

JUDGE, FRED. Served 36 *years in Q.V.R. of which* 15 *were as R.Q.M.S., ending* 30/9/14. *Served with C.I.V. in S. African War. Mention. Q.M.* 2*nd Q.V.R.* 1914 *and went to France with it Jan.–Mar.* 1917 (*invalided*). *Posted to* 3*rd L.R.B.* 28/6/17 *and there continued till end of war.* Honours. *T.D.*

KEDDIE, G. D. F. 2nd Lieut. 16/1/15. Served in France with 1st Batt. 1915. Joined R.A.F. 1915. Lieut. 1916. Capt. 1917.

*KEELING, JOHN HENRY. *Lieut.* 15*th W. Yorks* 27/12/14. *Transf. to to L.R.B.* 26/2/16. *Capt.* 1/7/16. *Seconded for duty with R.E. Adjt. stores section I.W.D. Richborough* 4/10/17–10/5/19.

KEEP, J. D. 2nd Lieut. 1918. Joined 1st Batt. Sept. 1918.

KELLY, WILLIAM. Joined Army 9/1/92. Promoted 1st class W.O. Feb. 1907, and was commissioned Oct. 1909. Retired Aug. 1914 and joined the 3rd Batt. as Hon. Lieut. and Q.M. 8/1/15. Served with 1st Batt. 1/5/16–4/11/16. Rejoined 3rd Batt. To France, posted to 10th Londons, 5/7/17–Dec. 1917. Capt. 1/7/17. Then served at home with R.B. Home mention in despatches.

KENNARD, AUBERON CLAUD HEGAN. *Ed.* Eton and New College, Oxford. 2nd Lieut. L.R.B. 1893. Retired 1894 on obtaining commission in R.B. S. Africa 1902 (Queen's Medal, 4 clasps, and King's Medal). Rejoined L.R.B. as Capt. and Adjt. 1906–9. Retired from the Army 1911. Elected to London County Council 1913. Went to France as Major 19th Londons. Lieut.-Col. commanding 2/1st London Regt., Egypt and France. Major and A/Lieut.-Col. 1/1st London Regt. at Battle of Somme. Afterwards served as a Labour Group Commander till end of war; retiring as substantive Lieut.-Col. Mentioned in despatches.

KENNARD, EDWARD. Ensign 1860. Retired 1861.

KENT, HERBERT JOHN. *Ed.* Norwich. Joined 2nd Batt. as private Sept. 1914. Served in all ranks up to R.Q.M.S. until 10/1/17. Lieut. and Q.M. 11/1/17. Served with 2nd Batt. L.R.B. in France from 20/1/17–20/2/18. Transf. on disbandment of 2nd Batt. to 47th Machine Gun Batt. and served with this Batt. in France from 21/2/18–10/6/19. *Honours.* M.C. Mentioned in despatches.

KETTLE, WILLIAM RAYMOND BURLING. Joined 7th Londons in the ranks on 30/11/14. Served in France with 1/7th Londons from 18/3/15–28/3/17. Posted to L.R.B. on commission. 2nd Lieut. 31/10/17. Joined 1st Batt. in France 6/1/18–28/3/18 (prisoner of war). Lieut. 1/5/19. Mentioned in despatches.

KING, C. M. 18th Londons. Att. to 1st Batt. 21/9/18–4/11/18 (*wounded and missing*).

KING, NORMAN CAREW. *Ed.* Haileybury. Haileybury College R.V.C. 1887–9 (Sergeant). Victoria Rifles (1st Mx. R.V.C.) 1890–92 (Sergeant). 2nd Lieut. L.R.B. —/11/92. Lieut. 26/5/94. Capt. 1900 ("A" Co.). Major 22/7/12. Served continuously and went to France with 1st Batt. Nov. 1914–Jan. 1915, when invalided. Commanded 3rd L.R.B. 4/6/15 to demobilisation 1919. Lieut.-Col. 23/3/16. *Honours.* T.D., Brevet Col. 1/1/19. Home mention in despatches. *Sports.* Haileybury 2nd XI 1889. Mddx Hockey XI 1896–98. Commanded L.R.B. *Daily Telegraph* Team (winners) 1897.

KINGSFORD, THOMAS H. Ensign 1866. Retired 1867.

KIRBY, ALISTER G. *Ed.* Eton and Magdalen College, Oxon. Took a leading part in founding Oxford University O.T.C., in which he served as Lieut. Joined L.R.B. as Lieut. 1908–12. Retired. Rejoined as Lieut. 4/8/14 and went to France with 1st Batt. Nov. 1914 till wounded in Dec. Then served with Anti-Aircraft Force, Young Officers' School and 3rd Batt. Subsequently on staff of 2/2nd London Divn. Artillery and R.N. Divn. Died, as result of wound in 1914, March, 1917. *Rowing.* Eton VIII 1904–5. Oxford University VIII 1906–7–8–9. President 1908–9. Capt. of Leander 1912, and won Olympic Regatta VIII's at Stockholm that year.

KITCHING, GEOFFREY CHARLES. *Ed.* Oundle School and Jesus College, Cambridge. 2nd Lieut. L.R.B. 15/10/14. Joined 1st Batt. and went to France with them Nov. 1914–17th Feb. 1915. Lieut. 7/9/15. Capt. 1/7/16. Posted to 2nd Batt. and went to France with it 23/1/17–24/3/18 (prisoner of war).

KITE-POWELL, T. C. Served in ranks four years before war and went to France with 1st Batt. 4/11/14–16/2/16 (wounded). 2nd Lieut. 25/1/17. Again to 1st Batt. in France 29/1/17–28/3/18 (taken prisoner). Lieut. 25/7/18. *Honours.* M.C.

LANKESTER, DOUGLAS VERNON. Enlisted in 3rd Batt. May 1915, and drafted to 1st Batt. —/10/15 to —/2/17. 2nd Lieut. 14/9/16. Invalided 12/2/17. Lieut. 14/3/18. Thence served with 3rd Batt.

LARCOMBE, R. F. City of London Yeomanry. Att. to 3rd Batt. and went to France 2/8/18. *Missing, presumed dead,* 10/9/18.

LARGE, E. LYNTON. *Ed.* Charterhouse and New College, Oxford. Served in Charterhouse Cadets. 2nd Lieut. L.R.B. 1913. Lieut. 1914. Went to France with 1st Batt. Nov. 1914. Capt. 1915. Died of wounds May 1915. *Sports.* Second in Command Brighton March Team.

LEAN, W. C. Joined as rifleman. 2nd Lieut. 28/11/17. Joined 1st Batt. April 1918.

LEE, GERALD MOORE. *Ed.* Malvern. Joined 2nd Batt. as private and went to France with it in Jan. 1917 till sent home for commission 7/3/18. 2nd Lieut 30/10/18. *Honours.* M.M.

LEGG, JOHN FRANCIS. *Ed.* King's College School. Joined as private 1903 and served continuously, going to France with 1st Batt. Nov. 1914. Company Sergeant-Major May 1915. Commissioned in 2nd Batt. 7/10/15 and went to France with it in Jan. 1917. Lieut. 1/7/17. Home, and to 2nd Batt. again 13/12/17–21/2/18, and, on disbandment, transferred to "Artists." Capt. 8/4/18. Second in Command "Artists," and commanded them 23/8/18–22/9/18.

LESLIE, A. R. 19th Londons. Att. to 1st Batt. 28/9/17–21/3/18.

LETHBRIDGE, CHRISTOPHER. Ensign 1863. Lieut. 1865. Retired 1868. Died 1910.

LEWTHWAITE, ROBERT PIERSON. Att. to 2nd Batt. 25/9/17–30/10/17 (*wounded*).

LICHFIELD, EARL OF. *See* ANSON.

LIDDON, REV. CANON HENRY PARRY, D.D. Chaplain 12/5/88. Died 1890. Wrote the Regimental prayer.

LINDSAY, JOHN SEYMOUR. Joined 2nd Batt. as private Sept. 1914. Drafted to 1st Batt. Jan. 1915–July 1916. 2nd Lieut. 19/7/16. Wounded Sept. 1916 and then served with 3rd Batt. Lieut. 19/1/18. *Honours.* D.C.M.

LINDSAY-HOLT, GEORGE. *Ed.* Merchant Taylors' School. Served in Inns-of-Court. Joined 3rd Batt. L.R.B. as rifleman May 1916. 2nd Lieut. 25/10/16. Did not serve abroad. Invalided out 1917.

LINES, SIDNEY MARTIN. *Ed.* St. John's College, Finsbury Park. Joined K.R.R.C. Cadets when about 16 years of age and rose to rank of Sergeant, during which time he was Musketry Instructor. Transferred to L.R.B. as a rifleman and went to France with 1st Batt. Nov. 1914. 2nd Lieut. 8/5/15 (killed 13/5/15).

LINSTEAD, E. G. 2nd Lieut. 1908. Lieut. 1909. Retired 1909.

LINTOTT, ALFRED LORD. *Ed.* Mercers' School and King's College, London. Enlisted Oct. 1899. Commission in I.Y. April 1900 and served in S. African War 1901–2. Queen's

Medal and 5 clasps. 2nd Lieut. L.R.B. 1902. Lieut. 1906. Capt. 1909 ("H" Co.). Transferred to Reserve June 1914. Mobilised 4/8/14, going to France with 1st Batt. Nov. 1914–Dec. 1916. 2nd i/c April–Nov. 1915. Dec. 1915–Dec. 1916 commanded 52nd Bde. M.G. Co. Major April 1916. W.O. General Staff Jan.–Oct. 1917. Army of Black Sea Dec. 1917–1920 with 26th and 28th Divns., and on Staff of C.-in-C. Mediterranean Fleet. Served in Macedonia, Bulgaria, Roumania, Novorossik, S. Russia, Turkey-in-Europe, Greece, Asia Minor. *Honours*. D.S.O. Two mentions in despatches.

LINTOTT, ARCHIBALD JOHN CHILD. *Ed.* Lancing College. Served in the ranks of the L.R.B. 1899–1903. C.I.V. M.I. South Africa 1900. Queen's Medal, 3 bars. Ceylon Mounted Rifles 1907–14. Joined 2nd Batt. as 2nd Lieut. 12/2/15 (Transport Officer). Lieut. 1/6/16, and went to France with it Jan. 1917. Until Jan. 1919 in France and Flanders with 58th London Division. Att. 6th Batt. London Regt. (Capt. (addtl.) April 1918.) Feb. 1918–Sept. 1918. Brigade Transport Officer 174th Infantry Brigade Sept. 1918–Jan, 1919. *Honours*. M.C. *Games*. Lancing Football XI 1905–7. All Ceylon 1907. Colombo Rugby 1907–9. Lancing 2nd Cricket XI.

LINTOTT, H. C. Joined from Artists. 2nd Lieut. 19/12/16. Went to France 28/2/17 (wounded). Went out again 15/12/17 to 2nd Batt. (died of wounds 22/3/18).

LINTOTT, RICHARD. *Ed.* St. John's College, Hurstpierpoint. Served in ranks and went to France with 1st Batt. Nov. 1914. Commissioned 2nd Lieut. 29/4/15 (killed in action 3/5/15).

LLOYD, CHARLES FREDERICK. *Ed.* Eton and Trinity College, Cambridge. Eton College R.V.C. 1881–5 (Clr.-Sergeant). 2nd Lieut. L.R.B. 1889. Lieut. 1891. Retired 1894. During the war served in the 2nd Batt. County of London Volunteer Regt., Company Sergeant-Major and Musketry Instructor.

LONG, CHARLES W. *Ed.* Cambridge. Served in Cambridge O.T.C. (Colr.-Sergeant). Joined L.R.B. as 2nd Lieut. 1914 and remained behind as Depot Officer when 1st Batt. went to France. Lieut. 1915. Subsequently served with 3rd Batt. and went to France 26/5/16. Soon invalided and left the regiment 1916. Subsequently Capt. and Adjt. 2nd V.B. London Regt. Aug. 1917–Jan. 1920.

LORD, WALTER. Late Capt. Indian Army. Joined L.R.B. as Capt. 1860 ("Q" Co.). Retired 1865.

LUCAN, EARL OF. *See* BINGHAM.

LUCAS, EVELYN P. *Ed.* Eton. 2nd Lieut. 1900. Retired 1901. Served in R. Berks Regt. in Great War and won M.C.

2 H

LUCAS, REGINALD J. *Ed.* Eton. 2nd Lieut. 1900. Lieut. 1901. Retired 1903. Joined Hants Militia. M.P. for Portsmouth. Died. *Games.* Eton XI (Capt.).

LYDALL, ROBERT FRANCIS. *Ed.* Borough Polytechnic and South London College, Dulwich. Joined as private Jan. 1914 and went to France with 1st Batt. in Nov. 1914–Jan. 1916. 2nd Lieut. 24/1/16. Rejoined 1st Batt. 9/6/16–7/7/16 (wounded). Lieut. 24/7/17. Joined 2nd Batt. 29/12/17–24/3/18. Then served with 3rd Batt., and as Bde. Bombing Officer with 1st London Reserve Brigade.

McCARTHY, GEORGE. *Ed.* Wilson's Grammar School. University of London O.T.C. Mar. 1917–Dec. 1917. 2nd Lieut. L.R.B. 30/10/18.

McCAUL, SAMUEL. Ensign 1860. Lieut. 1862. Retired 1864.

MACDONALD, A. 7th Londons. Att. to 1st Batt. —-11/10/18 (wounded).

McDONNELL, HON. SIR SCHOMBERG KERR, G.C.V.O., K.C.B. *Ed.* Eton and Oxford. 2nd Lieut. 27/5/93. Lieut. 13/5/96. Capt. 4/4/00 ("D" Co.). Served in South Africa with C.I.V. Queen's Medal. Retired 1904. Served at home on Intelligence Sept. 1914 till summer 1915, and then joined 5th Cameron Highlanders (killed in action 1915). Private Secretary to Lord Salisbury, Prime Minister 1888–92, 1895–9 and 1900–02. Secretary to Office of Works 1902–12.

MACGEAGH, HENRY DAVIES FOSTER. *Ed.* St. Paul's and Magdalen College, Oxford. 2nd Lieut. 12/3/09. Lieut. 1910. Capt. 18/9/13 "(H" Co.). Went to France with 1st Batt. Nov. 1914–20/1/15 (invalided). Att. to H.Q. Second Army to initiate duties of Court Martial Officer 31/8/15–4/12/15 (invalided). Military Asst. to Judge Advocate-General 1916–19. D.A.A.G. War Office 23/2/17. A.A.G. 6/4/18. *Honours.* C.B.E., Brevet Majority. Home mention in despatches.

MACGILL, CAMPBELL GERALD HERTSLET, M.V.O. Served as private in 1st Wiltshire V.R.C. 1/2/97–2/12/98. 2nd Lieut. 3/12/98–20/12/00. Lieut. 21/3/00–15/2/03. Joined L.R.B. 2nd Lieut. 16/2/03. Lieut. 29/1/06. Capt. 8/12/08 ("G" Co.). Adjt. 2nd Batt. 6/9/14–17/6/15. Staff Capt. 3/1st London Divn. 24/7/15–2/5/16. Bde. Major "B" Group 1st London Divn. 3/5/16–31/8/16. Major 1/6/16. Officer attached for Staff duties 1st London (R.) Brigade 1/9/16–6/4/18. *Honours.* T.D.

MACHIN, FRANK PERCY. *Ed.* Friern Barnet Grammar School. Joined as private May 1914 and proceeded to France with 1st Batt. in Nov. 1914. 2nd Lieut. 14/9/16. Lieut. 14/3/18. Served until 13/10/16 with L.R.B. and from 2/3/17–12/5/19 with G.H.Q. 3rd Echelon. Mentioned in despatches.

MACKENZIE-SMITH, M. C. K., *18th Londons. Att. to 2nd Batt.* 15/6/17–25/6/17 (*wounded*).

McLACHLAN, WILLIAM. Ensign 1859. Lieut. 1860. Capt. 1860 (" N " Co.). Retired 1867.

McOWAN, DOUGLAS. Joined as private 1909 and served continuously, going to France with 1st Batt. Nov. 1914–1/4/15 (wounded). 2nd Lieut. 28/9/15. Rejoined 1st Batt. 14/7/16. Adjt. 3/9/16–19/3/17 (invalided). Lieut. 1/7/17. Invalided from the Army on account of ill-health on 26th June 1919. *Honours.* Mentioned in despatches.

MAGINN, J. F. Served in London Irish, and subsequently transf. to L.R.B. as 2nd Lieut. 1917. *Honours.* D.S.O. Mentioned in despatches.

MARRIAN, LIONEL BERNARD. *Ed.* University College School. Enlisted in Queen's Westminster Rifles Feb. 1908 and served with them in France Dec. 1916–Dec. 1917. Posted to L.R.B. on commission as 2nd Lieut. 25/9/18. Joined 1st Batt. 31/12/18.

MARRIOTT, ARTHUR WILLIAM. Ensign 1862. Retired 1866.

MARRIOTT, CECIL HENRY. *Ed.* St. Paul's School. Enlisted in L.R.B. 1908–12. Inns-of-Court O.T.C. 1/11/14–6/2/15. 2nd Lieut. L.R.B. 7/2/15. Lieut. 1/6/16. Capt. 1/7/17. Joined 3rd Batt. and served at home as Batt. Signalling Officer, and from 17/5/17–2/11/18 Asst. Bde. Sig. Officer 1st London Res. Bde. (Adjt. Bde. Sch. of Signalling). Joined 1st Batt. in France 8/11/18–8/4/19. From 6/2/19–8/4/19 Demobilisation Officer 56th Division.

MARSH, H. C. 11th Londons. Att. 1st Batt. 24–30/9/16 and 14/10/16–16/2/17 (invalided).

MARSHALL, MATTHEW WILBERFORCE. Served in ranks 1872–77. 2nd Lieut. 4/7/77. Lieut. 1879. Capt. 17/8/86 (" G " Co.). Capt. L.R.B. Shooting Team 1881–1900. App. Q.M. 25/12/95. Retired 1900 as Hon. Major. *Honours.* V.D.

MARTIN, CECIL WILLIAM. *Ed.* Ardingly College. Joined L.R.B. 1912 as private and went to France with 1st Batt. 4/11/14–27/1/15 (invalided). Afterwards served with 3rd Batt. as Sergeant until commissioned as 2nd Lieut. 5/2/19. *Sports.* Brighton March Team 1914.

MARTIN, G. ST. J. Joined 2nd Batt. 2nd Lieut. 1915. Transf. to 3rd Batt. and went to France 6/5/16. Lieut. 1917. Subsequently went to Indian Army in 1917.

MATTHEW, WILFRID JOHN. *Ed.* St. Paul's School. Private in the London Scottish 1901–2 and Bombay Light Horse 1902–7. Joined 3rd Batt. in ranks 1917. 2nd Lieut. 30/1/18. Went to France 29/4/18 (killed in action 19/5/18).

MATTHEWS, H. L. L. *11th Londons. Att. to 1st Batt.* 5/8/16–9/9/16 (*killed in action*).

MATTHEY, CYRIL GEORGE RIGBY. *Ed.* Charterhouse, Royal School of Mines and in Germany. Served four years in Charterhouse R.V.C. Enlisted in L.R.B. 1880–5. Lieut. 6/8/85. Capt. 5/10/92. Served in S. African War with C.I.V. ("C" Co.). Queen's Medal. Hon. Capt. Army 1/12/00. Major 28/5/01. Lieut.-Col. 16/4/02. Hon. Col. 17/4/07. Served continuously with L.R.B. and went to France with 1st Batt. Nov. 1914–12/1/15 (invalided). Posted to T.F.R. 18/6/15, and commanded 105th, 107th Provisional Batts., and 31st London Regt. on E. coast. Att. Fifth Army H.Q. 1917 and subsequently was Area Commandant in France. Invalided from service Dec. 1918. *Honours.* V.D.

MATTHEY, EDWARD. *Ed.* Forest School, Epping, and Royal School of Mines, London. Served in ranks of Victoria Rifles 1859–72. Enlisted in L.R.B. 21/1/73. Gazetted Ensign 1/6/73. Lieut. 1/6/73. Capt. 15/6/78 ("H" Co.). Major 16/4/84. Lieut.-Col. 2/8/90. Commandant 27/2/01. Retired 1901 as Hon. Col. Hon. Col. 4th London V.R.C. from 1900–04. *Honours.* C.B., V.D. Died 22/10/18.

MAY, WILLIAM COSTALE. Surgeon 1859. Retired 1864. Died 2/1/96.

MAYNARD, M. J. *Ed.* Tottenham County School. Joined as private Jan. 1914, and went with the 1st Batt. Nov. 1914 to France. 2nd Lieut. 8/5/15. Lieut. 7/6/15. Became Railway Transport Officer 1915 and transf. to R.T. Establishment 7/10/15. Rejoined 1st Batt. 4/8/16. Capt. 13/9/16 (missing, presumed killed 8/10/16). *Sports.* Brighton March 1914.

MELLERSH, FREDERIC N. 2nd Lieut. 1888. Lieut. 1890. Capt. 1896 ("N" Co.). Major 1902. Resigned 1904.

MEREDITH, WALTER WELLS. *Ed.* Clapton College. Joined 3rd Batt. in ranks May 1915 and served in France with 1st Batt. Oct. 1915–July 1916. 2nd Lieut. 28/11/17. Served with 3rd Batt. till commissioned and then had an operation.

METCALF, JOHN HENRY. *Ed.* Clark's College, Forest Gate, and Cambridge. Joined 2nd Batt. in ranks Sept. 1914 and went to France with it Jan.–Oct. 1917. 2nd Lieut. 29/5/18. Returned to France 2/8/18 and att. 2/17th London Regt. until demobilised.

MILBURN, A. L. *5th R.B. Att. to 1st Batt. Nov.* 1918.

MILLER, CHARLES J. 2nd Lieut. 1879. Lieut. 1881. Retired 1886.

MILLER, CLAUDIUS MONTAGUE. Asst. Surgeon 1870. Surgeon 1877. Retired 1878. Died 19/11/93.

MILLER, JAMES. Ensign 1863. Lieut. 1865. Capt. 1868 ("N" Co.). Resigned 22/1/86 as Hon. Major.

MILLIKEN, ERNEST. Joined as private Feb. 1878. 2nd Lieut. Jan. 1889. Lieut. March 1890. Capt. 18/4/96 ("F" Co.). Hon. Major Aug. 1901. I. of M. and Capt. Regt. shooting team 1891–6. Was Hon. Sec. of the Regt. Died 19/6/03.

MILLS, LESLIE THOMAS, 7th Londons. Att. to 1st Batt. 11/9/17 *to end of war.*

MISKIN, ERNEST JAMES BICKFORD. 19th Londons. Att. to 2nd Batt. 31/7/17–8/9/17 (*wounded*).

MITCHELL, HENRY. *Ed.* Technical Schools, Southend. Served in ranks Feb. 1909–Feb. 1914. Rejoined in ranks Aug. 1914. 2nd Lieut. 25/10/16. Lieut. 25/4/18. To France 5/1/17–17/2/17 (wounded), and then with 3rd Batt.

MITCHELL, HUBERT JAMES. *Ed.* Christ Church, Barnet. Enlisted in L.R.B. Sept. 1915. Joined 1st Batt. in France Feb.–1/7/16 (wounded). Transf. to 2/17th London Aug., and continued in France until Dec. 1916. Landed Salonica Dec. 1916. Returned to England July 1917. Rejoined L.R.B. as 2nd Lieut. 17/12/17. To France 29/4/18. Att. 1/20th Londons to end of war.

MITCHELL, WALTER. Lieut. 1870. Retired 1872.

MITCHELL, WILLIAM HENRY LISTER. *Ed.* Coopers' Company's School. Served in the ranks. Went to France with 1st Batt. Nov. 1914 (wounded). 2nd Lieut. 25/10/16. Returned to France Jan. 1917 (killed in action with 2nd Batt. 20th Sept. 1917).

MIVART, F. ST. J. Asst. Surgeon 1883. Resigned 1884.

MOGER, H. J. *Ed.* Crossleigh School. 2nd Lieut. 9/1/93. Lieut. 15/7/96. Retired 1898.

MONSELL, J. R. 12th Londons. Att. to 1st Batt. 30/1/18.

MOORE, CUTHBERT FRANCIS. *Ed.* St. Bernardine's College, Buckingham. Enlisted in 3rd Batt. 19/7/15 and joined 1st Batt. in France Feb. 1916. Wounded June 1916 and Arras May 1917. Sergeant May 1917. 2nd Lieut. 1/5/18. Returned to France 2/8/18. Posted to 6th Londons till end of war.

MOORE, ERNEST GEORGE. *Ed.* Christ's Hospital. Joined in ranks Oct. 1913 and went to France with 1st Batt. Nov. 1914–22nd Dec. (wounded). Returned to France Sept. 1915–Sept. 1916 (wounded). 2nd Lieut. 19/7/16. Returned to France with 2nd Batt. 25/1/17–24/8/18 (wounded). Lieut. 19/1/18. *Honours.* Mentioned in despatches. *Sports.* L.R.B. Brighton March Team 1914.

MORGAN, HUGH BROOMING TAYLOR. *Ed.* Christ's College, Brecon, and Edinburgh University. Private Vol. Med. Staff

Corps Edinburgh University. Surgeon-Lieut. L.R.B. 1899. Surgeon-Capt. 1903. Retired 1906. Mobilised first day of war. Capt. R.A.M.C. (T.) 5th S. General Hospital, Portsmouth. Sailed for Salonika June 1916 with 29th Station Hospital. Remained two years, then sailed with Hospital for Italy, where remained till demobilised May 18th, 1919. O.C. 29th Station Hospital, Italy, and O.C. Detention Hospital, Cremona, Italy.

MORGAN, W. E. Somerset L.I. Posted to 2nd Batt. and was Q.M. 25/9/16–11/1/17.

MORLEY, ROBERT NISBET. *Ed.* St. Dunstan's College, Catford. Enlisted in 3rd Batt. Feb. 1917. 2nd Lieut. 30/1/18. Went to France and joined 1st Batt. 29/4/18–28/8/18 (wounded).

MORRIS, JOHN HAROLD. *Ed.* Christ Church School and Teddington Schools, Teddington, and at Clark's College, Surbiton. Enlisted in 3rd Batt. April 1916. 2nd Lieut. 29/8/17. Joined the 2nd Batt. in France 19/10/17; 1st Batt. Artists' Rifles Jan.–27/9/18 (severely wounded).

MORRIS, WILLIAM. 2nd Lieut. 1880. Lieut. 1881. Retired 1884.

MORRISON, GERARD HUMPHREY. *Ed.* Harrow and Magdalen College, Oxford. Oxford University O.T.C. 1908–11. Joined L.R.B. as 2nd Lieut. 1911. Lieut. 18/9/13. Capt. 25/3/15. Went to France with 1st Batt. Nov. 1914 and was shot by a sniper in Ploegsteert Wood 31/3/15. *Sports.* Harrow Football XI.

MOYES, JOHN MURRAY. Capt. R.A.M.C. Att. to 1st Batt. 28/4/15.

MUXWORTHY, T. Att. to 3rd Batt. 13/11/18.

NAYLOR, JOHN MURRAY. *Ed.* Eton and Cambridge. 2nd Lieut. Montgomeryshire Yeomanry 1910–13. Joined 2nd Batt. as Capt. Nov. 1914, went to France with it 24/1/17–4/3/17 (wounded). Invalided out Feb. 1918. *Sports.* Eton XI 1906–1907.

NEWELL, FRANCIS ALLISTER. Enlisted and went to France as rifleman July–Oct. 1916 (wounded). 2nd Lieut. 29/8/17. To France 9/10/17–24/3/18 (killed in action).

NEWINGTON, FRANK REGINALD HAYES. 20th Londons. Att. to 2nd Batt. — –17/5/17 (*wounded*).

NEWLAND, GEORGE MICHAEL. 13th Londons. Att. to 1st Batt. 27/2/18–28/3/18 (*killed*).

NEWLING, ALFRED JOHN. 11th Londons. Att. to 1st Batt. 5/8/16–7/10/16 (*invalided*).

NICHOLSON, JOHN M. S. Served some years in ranks. Sub.-Lieut. 1874. Lieut. 1874. Capt. 1885 ("Q" Co.). Hon. Major 30/7/87. Retired 1898 as Hon. Major. Died 1911. *Honours.* V.D.

NOBBS, H. GILBERT. Served in ranks for some years. Went to Canada and obtained commission. Resigned. Rejoined L.R.B. as Capt. 1914 in 2nd Batt. Transferred to 3rd Batt. and went to France 2/8/16. Blinded and taken prisoner on Somme Sept. 1916. Repatriated and invalided out 1917.

NORTON, DANIEL. Ensign 1868. Lieut. 1871. Capt. 1874. Retired 1878.

OAKENFULL, H. J. 11th Londons. Att. to 1st Batt. Oct. 1916.

O'CALLAGHAN, EDWARD. Late Capt. 18th Foot. Capt. and Adjt. 1867. Retired 1873.

OGG, WILLIAM A. Capt. 1863. Retired 1873. Sheriff of London 1881.

OLDFIELD, PERCY BERTRAM BOYD. *Ed.* Radley. 2nd Lieut. 7/2/15. Went to 1st Batt. in France 1/5/15–1/7/16 (severely wounded). Lieut. 1/6/16. Subsequently Instructor No. 16 O.C.B. 29/1/17–11/2/19. Capt. 16/8/17.

OPPENHEIM, AUGUSTUS CHARLES. *Ed.* Eton and R.M.C., Camberley. Commissioned in K.R.R.C. 22/10/02. Capt. and Adjt. L.R.B. 1/1/13 and went to France with 1st Batt. Nov. 1914–13/5/15 (wounded). Returned to France 1/12/15 to 2nd Batt. K.R.R.C. Second in Command Jan.–June 1916. Bde. Major 48th Bde. June–July 1916. (Sick). Returned home for operation. Returned to France 27/12/16 to 2nd Batt. K.R.R.C. Second in Command 24/3/17 (wounded). Then Instructor at R.M.C., Sandhurst. *Honours.* D.S.O. Twice mentioned in despatches.

ORTON, WILLIAM HUNT. R.A.M.C. Att. to 2nd Batt. 21/7/17–

—

OTTER, FRANCIS LEWIS. *Ed.* Harrow and University College, Oxford. Enlisted —/9/14. Commissioned in 2nd Batt. 2nd Lieut. 14/10/14. T/Lieut. 7/1/15. T/Capt. 14/8/15. Capt. 1/7/16. T/Lieut. (R.E.) 19/10/17. A/Capt. 28/9/18. To France Jan. 1917–Jan. 1918 with 2nd Batt. Then H.Q. (58th) Div. and Signal Service Training Centre, Bedford, April 1918–April 1919. *Honours.* M.C.

OTTER, ROBERT EDWARD. *Ed.* Harrow and University College, Oxford. Two years Harrow School Cadet Corps. Joined L.R.B. as 2nd Lieut. 1908. Lieut. 1910. Served continuously and went to France with 1st Batt. Nov. 1914–5/4/16. Capt. 1915. Staff-Capt. 168th Inf. Bde. 5/4/16–29/4/17. D.A.Q.M.G. 66th Div. 29/4/17–12/5/19. D.A.Q.M.G. 2nd Corps Cologne, but did not take up appointment. *Honours.* M.C. Twice mentioned in despatches. French Croix de Guerre with palm. Brevet Majority.

OVINGTON, CHARLES EDWARD. *Ed.* Tottenham County School. Enlisted L.R.B. Oct. 1913 and went to France with 1st Batt. Nov. 1914–29/4/15 (wounded). 2nd Lieut. 5/8/15. Rejoined 1st Batt. in France 12/3/16 and seconded to 169th Bde. M.G. Co. in April. Appointed Second in Command 167th M.G. Co. 1/12/16. Lieut. 1/7/17. A/Capt. 1917. Addl. Capt. 193rd M.G. Co. Sept. 1917. O.C. 167th M.G. Co. Dec. 1917. Second in Command 56th Batt. M.G.C. Jan. 1919. A/Major 1/3/18. Served 3 years and 5 months in France and participated in every engagement in which 56th Div. took part. *Honours.* M.C. *Sports.* Brighton March 1914.

OWEN, L. S. Embarked to join 2nd Batt. 14/7/17–20/9/17 (killed in action).

OWEN, S. R. 12th Londons. Att. to 1st Batt. 30/1/18–11/3/18 (*wounded*).

PAGE, W. E. 15th Londons. Att. to 1st Batt. Nov. 1918.

PALMER, EDMUND S. Ensign 1870. Lieut. 1872. Retired 1873.

PALMER, HUGH SALISBURY. R.A.M.C. Att. to 2nd Batt. 8/7/16 *and went to France with it.*

PARKER, H. Lieut. 1883. Retired 1/4/1887. Died July 1905.

PARKER, R. M. A.S.C. Att. to 3rd Batt. about Jan. 1918 *and went to France* 29/4/18.

PASSANT, REV. E. J. Att. to 1st. Batt –/4/18– —.

PATSTON, HENRY RICHARD. *Ed.* Hugh Middleton School, London. Enlisted in 8th London Regt. and served with them in France from 17/3/15–20/11/17. On commission posted to L.R.B. as 2nd Lieut. 25/9/18. To France 15/11/18. *Honours.* M.M.

PATTERSON, W. 2nd Lieut. 1893. Retired 1895.

PATTISSON, FREDERICK EDWARD. *Ed.* Rugby. Enlisted 10th R. Fus. Aug. 1914. Commissioned in 2nd Batt. 2nd Lieut. 29/5/15. Lieut. 1/7/17. Went to France with it Jan. 1917–2/6/17 (severely wounded). Served with 3rd Batt. to end of war.

PAWSON, JOHN ELLERTON. Lieut. 1860. Capt. 1860. Major 1864. Retired 1865 and rejoined as Major in 1868, retiring again 1872.

PAXMAN, WILLIAM. *Ed.* Privately and University College, of London. Gazetted Lieut. 2nd V.B. Essex Regt. 18/7/85. Capt. 9/1/91. Resigned 30/11/01 as Hon. Major. Joined 3rd Batt. as Capt. 16/1/15 and served with it as Co. Commander.

P.R.I. and Messing Officer. *Honours.* O.B.E., T.D. Home mention in despatches.

PAYNE, HENRY. Ensign 1872. Lieut. 1873. Retired 1876.

PEARSE, LOUIS O. Served in the ranks, rising to Clr.-Sergeant. Ensign 1872. Lieut. 1873. Capt. 1877 (" G " Co.). Retired 29/6/86 as Hon. Major.

PEDDIE, J. TAYLOR. 2nd Lieut. 1904. Lieut. 1908. Retired 1909. *Shooting.* King's Badges 1904, 1906. Ontario and Mx. Gold Medals, and Final "St. George's" four times. Member of several International Teams.

PELHAM-CLINTON, LORD EDWARD W. P. *Ed.* Eton. Joined R.B. and served with them in the Crimea, retiring as Lieut.-Col. Joined L.R.B. as Lieut.-Col. 1881, and commanded 1882–90. M.P. for N. Notts 1865–8. Master of Household to Queen Victoria 1894. Groom-in-Waiting to King Edward 1903. *Honours.* G.C.V.O., K.C.B. Died 1907.

PELLIER, CHARLES DE CHAUVAL. R.A.M.C. Att. to 3rd Batt. 3/7/16–29/11/16.

PENBERTHY, E. H. Joined from Inns-of-Court. 2nd Lieut. 1916. Went to France Aug. 1916. Subsequently transf. elsewhere. Lieut. 1917.

PERCY, WILLIAM GEORGE. *Ed.* St. Olave's Grammar School. Enlisted in 3rd Batt. April 1916. 2nd Lieut. 1/3/17. Served with 1st Batt. in France 13/5/17–16/8/17 (severely wounded). Lieut. 1/9/18. Invalided out April 1919.

PEROWNE, BERNARD CUBITT. *Ed.* Bishop's Stortford G.S. Served ten years in the Norfolk Yeomanry. Commissioned in 3rd Batt. 2nd Lieut. 28/9/15. Served with 1st Batt. 5/7/16–17/2/17 (severely wounded). Lieut. 1/7/17.

PERRIN, WILLIAM GORDON. Enlisted in Dec. 1909 and served continuously, going to France with 1st Batt. Nov. 1914. Invalided home and granted a commission. 2nd Lieut. 28/9/15. Rejoined 1st Batt. 16/3/16, left 17/4/16 to 169th M.G.Co. With M.G.Co. until Oct. 1916. Invalided home. Proceeded Overseas March 1917 to G.H.Q. 3rd Echelon as Officer i/c Records. Lieut. 1/7/17. Invalided home in Sept. 1917 and relinquished commission on account of ill-health 19/4/18.

PERUGINI, EDMUND CHARLES. Ensign 1865. Lieut. 1867. Retired 1870.

PETERS, T. G. Posted to L.R.B. as 2nd Lieut. 1918 after serving in France with some other unit and passing through an Officers' Cadet Batt.

PETERSEN, JOHN RICHARD SYDNEY. *Ed.* Dulwich. Enlisted Jan. 1896. R.Q.M.S. at date of commission. H/Lieut. and Q.M. 29/4/14. Served continuously and went to France with 1st Batt. Nov. 1914–4/5/16. Came home on exchange for rest and rejoined 1st Batt. 8/11/16–16/10/17 when demobilised. Capt. and Q.M. 1/7/17.

PETLEY, REGINALD EDMUND. *Ed.* St. Anne's School. Enlisted 1911 and served continuously, going to France with 1st Batt. Nov. 1914–22/1/16. Came home for commission. 2nd Lieut. 24/1/16. Rejoined 1st Batt. 6/5/16–1/7/16 (severely wounded). Lieut. 24/7/17. Served with 3rd Batt. and joined 2nd Batt. in France Dec. 1917–Jan. 1918. On its disbandment posted to "Artists'" 27/2/17–24/3/18, when severely wounded and taken prisoner. *Honours.* M.C.

**PHILLIPS, E. S.*

PIGGOTT, FRANCIS T. Lieut. 1878. Retired 1882.

PIGGOTT, JOHN T. 13th Londons. Att. to 2nd Batt. 25/9/17, *and transferred on its disbandment to "Artists'."*

PILCHER, ALFRED MARK. 15th Londons. Att. to 2nd Batt. 18/3/17–29/1/18. *Then transferred on disbandment to 18th Londons.*

PINKNEY, ROBERT. Ensign 1860. Lieut. 1860. Capt. 1861 ("C" Co.). Retired 1874.

POCOCK, B. E. *Ed.* Mill Hill School. Joined L.R.B. as rifleman in Aug. 1914 at the age of 18 and went to France with 1st Batt. Nov. 1914. Commissioned on field 29/4/15–13/5/15 (killed in action).

POCOCK, BERNARD LANGDON ELLIOTT. *Ed.* Emanuel School and Bancroft's School, Woodford Green, Essex. Served in ranks of C.S.R. 26/2/14–24/3/15. Given commission in 3rd Batt. as 2nd Lieut. 24/3/15. Joined 1st Batt. in France 23/12/15–3/7/16. Lieut. 1/6/16. From 24/5/17–27/2/19 France with L.R.B. and on Staff Learners' Course. Appointed A/Staff Capt. 167th Inf. Bde. 6/2/19. *Honours.* Mentioned in despatches.

POGOSE, IVOR REGINALD. *Ed.* Arlington Park College, Chiswick. Enlisted in the 10th Batt. K.R.R.C. on 5/9/14. Joined 1st Batt. as 2nd Lieut. 26/7/15–2/7/16 (died of wounds).

POLAND, R. D. *Ed.* King's College. Enlisted in L.R.B. and went to 1st Batt. in France —/9/15 to —/7/16. 2nd Lieut. 19/7/16. Lieut. 19/1/18. Served with 1st Batt. till July 1918 when joined R.A.F.

POOL, ERNEST EDWARD. *Ed.* Northampton and North Sydney (Australia) Grammar School. Enlisted in 2nd Batt. Sept. 1914. Commission in 3rd Batt. 2nd Lieut. 28/5/15. Joined 1st Batt. 9/1/16. Transferred with L.R.B., M.G. Sect., to 8th Bde. M.G.Co. 28/1/16. Invalided home May 1916. Lieut. 1/7/17. Joined 47th Div. M.G.Batt. in France Nov. 1918.

POOLE, HENRY R. Late Anglesea Militia. Capt. 1859. Retired 1867.

POOLEY, J. E. N. 4th (or 9th) Londons. Att. to 1st Batt. 28/2/18.

PORTER, FREDERICK. *Ed.* King's College School, London. Enlisted 1874. 2nd Lieut. 1878. Lieut. 1881. Retired 1882.

PORTER, ROBERT S. *Ed.* King's College School, Strand, London. Joined L.R.B. as private in 1865. Sub.-Lieut. 1875. Lieut. 1875. Capt. 1886 ("N" Co.). Retired 1889. Joined 1st V.B. Cheshire Regt. as Capt. 1893. Major 1897. Retired 1898 as H/Lieut.-Col. *Honours.* V.D. Member of W. Lancs T.F.A.

PORTER, WILLIAM McN. Ensign 1866. Lieut. 1870. Capt. 1872 ("G" Co.). Retired 1874.

POULTER, THOMAS J. Ensign 1870. Lieut. 1873. Capt. 1877 ("K" Co.). Retired 1/4/87. Died 1911.

POWER, BASIL ROY. *Ed.* Wilson's Grammar School, Camberwell. Joined 2nd Batt. H.A.C. 29/11/15. Cadet 2nd Batt. Artists' Sept. 1916. Gazetted 2nd Lieut. L.R.B. 19/12/16. Served with 2nd Batt. in France from March 1917–Feb. 1918 when att. 2/10th Londons. Lieut. 19/6/18. Appointed Divl. Gas Officer 18th Div. July 1918 with rank of A/Capt. Capt. 20/9/18.

PRESCOTT, H. W. Ensign 1868. Retired 1872.

PRICE, CHARLES CAMERON. Ensign 1863. Retired 1865.

PRICE, H. B. 2nd Lieut. 1914. Joined 1st Batt. and went to France with it Nov. 1914 (killed in action 3/5/15).

PRIOR, HENRY BURRELL. Enlisted 1895. 2nd Lieut. 28/2/00. Lieut. —/4/02. Capt. 29/5/05 (E. Co.). Retired 1912. Rejoined as Capt. 19/9/14. Was not passed for foreign service owing to loss of an eye. Served with 2nd Batt. till middle of 1916, then on garrison duty on East Coast till end of war.

PRIOR, THOMAS ASHLEY. Enlisted 1909. Served continuously and went to France with 1st Batt. Nov. 1914–May 1915 (wounded). 2nd Lieut. 28/9/15. Served in France again with 1st Batt. March–June 1916 and Nov. 1916–June 1918. Lieut. 1917. *Sports.* Member of Brighton March and Marathon Teams. Died 1921.

PRITCHARD, C. F. Lieut. 27/4/86. Capt. 1893 ("N" Co.). Retired 1898.

PRITCHARD, H. G. 2nd Lieut. 1894. Lieut. 1898. Retired 1898.

PROPERT, JOHN LUMSDEN. Asst. Surgeon 1859. Surgeon 1863. Retired 1865. Died 7/3/02.

**PUCKLE, GERALD EUSTACE. Joined as private Feb.* 1900 *and served continuously to Nov.* 1914, *when transferred to 2nd Batt. being then C.S.M. 2nd Lieut.* 12/1/16 *and seconded for duty at Div. Musketry Schools, etc.*

PULLEN, LESLIE HOWSON. *Ed.* Merchant Taylors' School. Commissioned in 3rd Batt. as 2nd Lieut. 4/5/15 and went to 1st Batt. in France Dec. 1915–Jan. 1916. Transferred to M.G.C. and served with it in France Jan. 1916–Dec. 1918. Lieut. 10/5/17. Acting D.M.G.O. 3rd Div. Dec. 1918–Jan. 1919. *Honours.* M.C.

QUILTER, PERCY CUTHBERT. *Ed.* Eton. 2nd Lieut. 1900. Lieut. 1901. Retired 1904.

RADFORD, PERCY DENMAN. Enlisted March 1913 and went to France with 1st Batt. Nov. 1914–2/5/15 (wounded). 2nd Lieut. 19/7/16. Wounded 29/9/16. Subsequently served at War Office. Lieut. 19/1/18. *Honours.* Home mention in despatches.

RANDALL, C. 8th R.B. Att. to 1st Batt. Nov. 1918.

RATCLIFFE, N. T. Att. to 3rd Batt. —/10/18.

READ, ARTHUR. *Ed.* City of London School. Enlisted Jan. 1900 and served continuously, going to France with 1st Batt. Nov. 1914–May 1915. Came home for commission 3rd Batt. 2nd Lieut. 7/5/15. Went to France again 20th Sept. 1916 till 8/10/16 (wounded). Then served with 3rd Batt. Lieut. 30/5/17.

READ, SYDNEY. Joined from Inns-of-Court as 2nd Lieut. 1916. Went to France 20/9/16 and soon transferred elsewhere. Lieut. 1918. *Honours.* M.C., 3rd Class St. Stanislas.

READ, W. J. STONE. 2nd Lieut. 1899. Lieut. 1900. Retired 1902.

REDMAN, GEORGE ALFRED. *Ed.* Rossall School and Trinity Hall, Cambridge. Rossall School Cadets. Cambridge University V.R.C. (Capt.). Joined 2nd Batt. as Capt. 1914 and was Draft Conducting Officer Feb. and March 1915. Invalided out 1915.

REED, WILLIAM EDMUND. *Ed.* Monkton Combe School. Enlisted in L.R.B. October 1910 and went to France with 1st Batt. Nov. 1914–July 1916. 2nd Lieut. 25/10/16. France 5/1/17– —/6/17 with 1st Batt. Lieut. 25/4/18. Subsequently served with 29th London Regt., 193rd Bde. Signal School and 52nd Mddx.

REEVE, GEORGE ROBEY. *Ed.* Carpenter's School. Enlisted in 3rd Batt. July 1916. 2nd Lieut. 26/4/17. Joined 2nd Batt. in France June 1917–Feb. 1918. Intelligence Officer and Asst. Adjt. July 1917–January 1918. On its disbandment attached to Artists' Rifles till 6/4/18 (wounded). Lieut. 26/10/18. Joined 1st Batt. in France Nov. 1918 till end of war. *Honours.* M.C.

REEVE, WILLIAM A. A. Ensign 1870. Lieut. 1871. Retired 1874. Rejoined 2nd Lieut. 1877. Retired 1878.

REID, DAVID WILLIAM. Capt. R.A.M.C. Att. to 3rd Batt. 29/11/16–22/4/17.

RENWICK, HENRY LANGDON. *Ed.* Ilford County High School and St. George's College. Enlisted in 3rd Batt. April 1915. 2nd Lieut. 27/6/17. Joined 1st Batt. in France 27/8/17–28/3/18 (wounded). Lieut. 27/12/18.

RHODES, ABRAHAM. Ensign 1864. Lieut. 1865. Capt. 1871. Resigned 14/2/85 as Hon. Major.

RICE, EDWARD FELIX. *Ed.* Emanuel School, Wandsworth Common. Served in School O.T.C. Enlisted in L.R.B. 7/8/14 and went to France with 1st Batt. Nov. 1914–May 1915 (wounded). 2nd Lieut. 5/8/16 and rejoined 1st Batt. 30/9/16. Att. T.M.B. 11/11/16 (killed 18/2/17).

RICHARDSON, PHILIP WIGHAM. *Ed.* Rugby and King's College, Cambridge. Served in ranks of 2nd Warwicks 1880–83 and 2nd Cambridge 1883–86. Lieut. 5th Durham R.V. 1887–91. Capt. 2nd V.B. Northumberland Fus. 1891–95. Joined L.R.B. as 2nd Lieut. 1895. Resigned 1897. Served in 2nd, then 5th Northumberland Fus. 1897–1908. Major 1908. Commandant N.R.A. School of Musketry 1914 to end 1918. Att. 2nd Army France Feb. and March 1916. Lieut.-Col. November 1916. *Honours.* O.B.E. Brevet Lieut.-Col. Home mention in despatches. V.D. *Sports.* Capt. British team to Australia 1907 and Olympic team, Stockholm 1912. Won L.R.B. gold medal 1895. King's badges in 1886, 1887, 1895, 1896, 1902, 1903, 1907, 1914. Shot English XX 1887, 1889, 1893, 1896, 1899, 1901, 1902, 1914; capt. 1903, 1905, 1906, 1907, 1908. Shot Mackinnon 1905, 1906, 1912, 1913, 1914; capt. 1903, 1913, 1914, 1919. Shot Elcho 1902, 1906, 1912, 1913, 1914. Shot Kolapore 1902; capt. 1904, 1906, 1908. Shot United Services match 1887, 1906; capt. 1903, 1904, 1907, 1909. At Bisley won M.R. Assoc. cup, Duke of Cambridge, etc. English XX gold and silver jewels. English VIII gold and bronze jewels. Vice-President N.R.A. and Vice-Chairman of Council. Vice-President English XX Club.

RICHES, JOHN FREDERICK. Served in City of London School O.T.C. Enlisted in 2nd Batt. Dec. 1914 and went to France with it in Jan. 1917. Returned for commission May 1918. Gazetted after end of war.

RICHMOND, ARTHUR. Ensign 1861. Lieut. 1863. Retired 1865.

RICKARDS, ARTHUR GEORGE, K.C. *Ed.* Eton and B.N.C., Oxford. Served in the Inns-of-Court R.V. 1873–78 (Sergeant). Joined L.R.B. as 2nd Lieut. 1878. Lieut. 1880. Capt. 1888

("K" Co.). Retired 1896 as Hon. Major. Organising Officer of the Kensington National Reserve 1914–19. A member of Gloucestershire and London Military Appeal Tribunals 1916–18. *Honours.* V.D.

RIDDEL, JAMES WILFRED GEORGE HEWAT. R.A.M.C. Att. to 1st Batt. circa *April* 1917.

RIMINTON, HENRY. Ensign 1866. Lieut. 1868. Retired 1872.

RIORDAN, JOHN LEONARD. Enlisted in 8th London Regt. Served in France, and posted to L.R.B. on commission. 2nd Lieut. 29/5/18. Att. again to P.O.R. in France 2/8/18, and killed in action 8/9/18.

RIPLEY, J. RICHARD S. *Ed.* Manchester Grammar School. Joined in ranks June 1916. 2nd Lieut. 28/3/17. Joined 1st Batt. in France 19/8/17. Invalided home Nov. 1917 and invalided out 1/6/18.

ROBERTSON, REV. O. H. Att. to 3rd Batt. 12/1/17–1/2/17. *Subsequently enlisted in 16th Londons.*

ROBINSON, JOHN GRAHAM. *Ed.* Uppingham and Trinity College, Cambridge. Uppingham School R.V.C. 2 years. Joined L.R.B. as 2nd Lieut. —/1/10. Lieut. 26/11/12. Went out to France with the 1st Batt. Nov. 1914. Capt. 30/6/15. Served Central Training Staff, Rouen. Instructor in Trench warfare, drill, etc. Subsequently Instructor to R.A.F. Cadets.

ROGERS, JAMES. Ensign 1863. Lieut. 1865. Capt. 1868. Retired 1868.

ROGERS, REV. WILLIAM. Act. Chaplain 1873. Retired 1896. (Known as "Hang Theology Rogers.") *Honours.* V.D.

ROSE, ERIC WOLLASTON. *Ed.* St. Edward's School, Oxford. Enlisted in Sussex Yeomanry Oct. 1914 and joined 2nd Batt. as 2nd Lieut. 3/4/15. To France and joined 1st Batt. 22/7/15–1/7/16 (wounded). Lieut. 1/6/16. To France, rejoined 1st Batt. 8/11/16–28/3/18 (killed in action). *Honours.* Mentioned in despatches.

ROSE, OSWALD HARMAN. *Ed.* King's College School and Archbishop Tenison's School, London. Enlisted 1908–1912. Commission in 2nd Batt. 2nd Lieut. 17/11/15. Went to France 27/5/16 to 1st Batt. Invalided 12/6/16, and soon after left the service.

ROSE, WILLIAM ANDERSON. Capt. 1859. Major 1860. Retired 1870.

ROSS, HUNT. 7th Londons. Att. to 1st Batt. 19/9/18.

ROSS, PATRICK WILLIAM S. Lieut.-Col. 1866. Retired 1867.

ROWSELL, EDMUND P. Enlisted in 1859. Ensign 1860. Lieut. 1862. Capt. 1865 ("Q" and "G" Co.'s). Retired 1877.

ROWSELL, SAM JOHN. Enlisted 1860, rose to Clr.-Sergeant. Ensign 1868. Lieut. 1871. Capt. 1874 ("Q" Co.). Retired 1878.

RUNTZ, J. Joined as Capt. on absorption of 12th Tower Hamlets in 1870. Retired 1872.

RUSH, HENRY C. Ensign 1865. Retired 1868.

RUSSELL, REGINALD. *Ed.* Dulwich College and Germany. In ranks King Edward's Horse 1904–11. Enlisted in L.R.B. Aug. 1914 and went to France with 1st Batt. Nov. 1914. 2nd Lieut. 11/2/15. Transport Officer from commission till 20/4/16, when sick to England. Lieut. 1/6/16. Subsequently served with 3rd Batt. *Honours.* M.C. Mentioned in despatches.

SAMPSON, H. W. 2nd Lieut. 25/1/17. To France 3/3/17 (killed in action May 1918).

**SAMUEL, T. A.*

SANDERSON, G. S. 11th Londons. Att. to 1st Batt. 18/7/16–22/7/16 (*killed in action*).

SAWBRIDGE, BARTLE FRERE. *Ed.* Winchester and University College, Oxon, 1902–6. Inns-of-Court O.T.C. May 6th, 1915. Joined 3rd Batt. 2nd Lieut. L.R.B. 11/7/15 and went to France to 1st Batt. 6/5/16–25/5/16 (slightly wounded) and 5/6/16–1/7/16 (wounded). Lieut. 1/7/17. Commandant No. 6 Area Gas Sch., Southern Command, with rank of Capt. 18/12/16–22/6/18. Rejoined 1st Batt. in France 2/8/18–12/9/18 (wounded).

SCHOLEFIELD, ARTHUR HOYLE. 19th Londons. Att. to 2nd Batt. 17/3/17–18/5/17 (*killed in action*).

SCOTT, S. R. 12th Londons. Att. to 1st Batt. 30/1/18– —.

SCOTT, R. F. G. 2nd Lieut. 1900. Retired 1901.

SCOUGALL, DOUGLAS MUIR. 4th Londons. Att. to 1st Batt. 11/3/17–4/5/17 (*killed in action*).

SEDGWICK, ARTHUR EDWARD. *Ed.* Bedford Modern School. Enlisted 1912 and went to France with 1st Batt. Nov. 1914. Commission in the field as 2nd Lieut. 26/2/15–2/5/15 (severely wounded). Served as A/Adjt. with 3rd Batt. and rejoined 1st Batt. in France 21/7/16–10/9/16 (killed in action). Lieut. 1916. *Sports.* Brighton Marching Team 1914.

SELL, CHARLES HENRY. Enlisted 1907 and served continuously, going to France with 1st Batt. Nov. 1914–27/4/15 (wounded). Commissioned in 3rd Batt. 2nd Lieut. 28/9/15. Rejoined 1st Batt. 17/1/16–22/9/16 (severely wounded.) Subsequently served with 3rd Batt. Lieut. 1/7/17.

SELLON, BRUCE HECKFORD. 11th Londons. Att. to 1st Batt. 23/6/17–16/8/17 (*died of wounds whilst A/Adjt.*).

SEWELL, THOMAS DAVIES. Lieut. 1859. Capt. 1860 ("G" Co.). Regimental No. 1. Retired 1870. Died 1916.

SHARMAN, A. P. *Ed.* Caversham House School, Caversham. Served through the Boer War as a trooper in the S. African Constabulary. Served also as a private and N.C.O. in the Artists' Rifles and L.R.B. from the latter part of 1914. Joined 1st L.R.B. as 2nd Lieut. 19/7/16–9/9/16 (wounded). Rejoined 1st Batt. 14/7/17 (killed in action 9/9/16).

SHEPPARD, REV. F. L. Att. to 1st Batt —/—/— -28/4/18.

SHILLITO, GEORGE. Att. to 2nd Batt. 25/3/17–17/5/17 (*wounded*).

SILLS, FREDERICK S. Sergeant Instructor 3/6th R. Sussex Regt. April 1915–Aug. 1916. In France Aug. 1916–May 1917 with 8th R. West Kent. Posted to L.R.B. on commission. 2nd Lieut. 31/10/17. Served with 1st Batt. 4/2/18–March 1918 when taken prisoner.

SIM, ANTONY. Ensign 1866. Retired 1867.

SIMMS, GEORGE. Lieut. 1859. Capt. 1860. Retired 1864.

SIMON, H. T. 3rd Londons. Att. to 1st Batt. —/11/16–4/3/17.

SLADE, EDWARD H. *Ed.* St. Dunstan's, Catford. Enlisted May 1912 and went to France with 1st Batt. Nov. 1914. Employed on 4th Div. H.Q. for Field Sketching and Map Work from March 1915–Dec. 1915. Rejoined 1st Batt. 1/1/16. 2nd Lieut. 19/7/16. Employed on 169 Bde. H.Q. as Intelligence Officer Nov. 1916–Feb. 1918. Lieut. 19/1/18. Rejoined 1st Batt. till 15/6/18 (sick). Subsequently served with 3rd Batt. *Honours.* M.C., M.M.

SLATER, JOHN CYRUS. *Ed.* St. Paul's School. Enlisted in 3rd Batt. May 1916. 2nd Lieut. 25/10/16. Joined 56th Div. Depot Batt. in France 20/6/17. To hospital 2/7/17. Died 6/7/17 (never actually joined 1st Batt.).

SLESSOR, PAUL A. *Ed.* University College School, London. L.R.B. Cadet 1885–88. Enlisted 1890–95. 2nd Lieut. 1/7/98. Lieut. 1900. Retired 1903. Rejoined as Lieut. 4/8/14. Went to France with 1st Batt. Nov.–22/12/14 (invalided). Subsequently Staff Capt. South-Eastern Mounted Bde. (Yeomanry T.F.) 1/4/15–31/12/15. General Staff Officer 3rd Gde. H.Q. Eastern Command 1/1/16–2/4/16. General Staff 3rd Grade H.Q. Southern Command 3/4/16–10/9/19. Capt. 1/6/16. Brevet Major 1/1/19. Liaison Officer Inter-Allied Mission of Control in Germany 10/9/19. *Honours.* Brevet Majority. Home mention in despatches.

SMETHAM, L. Joined in ranks. 2nd Lieut. 27/4/17. To France 7/6/17. Lieut. 1918.

SMITH, G. E. 9th Londons. Att. to 1st Batt. 4/7/17–10/11/17.

SMITH, REV. GUY VERNON. *Ed.* Winchester and New College, Oxford. Joined 2nd Batt. as Chaplain Nov. 1914 and went to France with it Jan. 1917. Eventually invalided and served with 3rd Batt. March–Aug. 1918. *Honours.* M.C. Redeemer, Officers' Class (Greece).

SMITH, HORACE. *Ed.* Manchester and Eton College Choir School. Enlisted in 2nd Batt. 2nd Lieut. 28/5/15 in 3rd Batt. Went to 1st Batt. in France 19/1/16–1/7/16 (wounded). Rejoined 1st Batt. 21/9/16–8/10/16 (killed in action).

SMITH, ROBERT W. Late Capt. 30th Foot. Capt. and Adjt. 1860. Retired 1863.

SMITH, SIR WILLIAM ROBERT. Asst. Surgeon 26th Kent R.V. (afterwards 3rd V.B. R. West Kent Regt.) att. to L.R.B. for appointment as Bde. Surg.-Col. to the 4th London V. Bde. 1898–1908. *Subsequently Sanitary Officer of 2nd London T.F. Div. On Dec.* 1914 *appointed Specialist Sanitary Officer* 67*th Div.* 2*nd Army, demobilised Nov.* 1917. Honours. *V.D. Home mention in despatches. Sheriff of London* 1918–19. *Holds various foreign decorations.*

SNODGRASS, H. W. Served elsewhere in ranks and posted to L.R.B. on commission as 2nd Lieut. 10/8/18. To France 15/11/18.

SOAMES, MERVYN H. *Ed.* Eton and Trinity College, Cambridge. Served in Inns-of-Court. Joined L.R.B. as 2nd Lieut. 1901. Lieut. 1906. Capt. 1908 ("O" Co.). Served continuously and went to France with 1st Batt. Nov. 1914. Invalided June 1915 and subsequently served as A.P.M. 1st London R.B. and Second in Command 3rd Batt. Major 1916.

SOMAN, HERBERT D. *Ed.* Cowper St. School. In ranks April 1897–July 1910. Served in S. African War. Rejoined as 2nd Lieut. 1/12/14. Lieut. 1/7/17. Served with 3rd Batt. and 38th and 40th R.F.

SOMERS-SMITH, JOHN ROBERT. *Ed.* Eton and Magdalen College, Oxford. 2nd Lieut. 1908. Lieut. 1913. Capt. 9/6/14. Served continuously and went to France with 1st Batt. Nov. 1914. Invalided and served with 3rd Batt. June–Oct. 1915. Rejoined 1st Batt. in France Oct. 1915–1/7/16 (killed in action). *Honours.* M.C. Mentioned in despatches. *Rowing.* Capt. of Boats at Eton 1906. Spare man to Oxford University Eight and stroked Magdalen College, Oxford, four, winning Visitors and Wyfold's 1907, and Olympic and Stewards' (record) 1908.

SOTHERS, EDWARD DUDLEY. *Ed.* Highgate Grammar School, Windermere Grammar School, and St. John's College, Cambridge. Enlisted Sept. 9th, 1914. 2nd Lieut. 3/10/15. Resigned owing to ill-health 22/11/16.

SPENCER, JOHN ALMERIC WALTER. *Ed.* Harrow and R.M.C. R.B. 2nd Lieut. 11/8/1900. Lieut. 6/1/02. Joined L.R.B. as Capt. and Adjt. 22/10/09. Staff Capt. Base Aug. 9th, 1914–Nov. 1914. Co. Commander 3rd Batt. R.B. Nov.–Dec. 1914. G.S.O. 3, 27th Div. Jan. 1915–Aug. 1915. Bde. Major 3rd Canadian Brigade Aug. 1915–Jan. 1916. Major 1/9/15. G.S.O. 2, Staff School, Cambridge, June 1916–Dec. 1916; Egypt Jan. 1917–June 1917. G.S.O. 1, 75th Div. June 1917–Dec. 1917. G.H.Q. Dec. 1917–Nov. 1918. B.G.G.S. G.H.Q. E.E.F. Nov. 1918–March 1919. Bt. Lieut.-Col. 1/1/19. *Honours* C.M.G., D.S.O. Mentioned in despatches four times.

SPETTIGUE, PHILIP ROY SPENCER. *Ed.* Holloway County School and Imperial College of Science, S. Kensington. Enlisted in 3rd Batt. 1/3/17. 2nd Lieut. 18/12/17. Joined 1st Batt. in France 25/4/18–31/8/18 (wounded). Rejoined 16/10/18 to be demobilised. *Honours.* M.C.

STANFIELD, P. H. 2nd Lieut. 27/2/18. To France 19/6/18.

STAPLES, E. 17th Londons. Att. to 1st Batt. 28/9/17– —/6/18. *Transf. to 44th Bde. and later died of wounds.*

STEIN, CECIL. 2nd Lieut. 11/11/87. Retired 1890.

STEVENS, H. 18th Londons. Att. to 1st Batt 26/9/18–5/11/18 (*wounded*).

STEVENSON, RALPH TAPLEY. *Ed.* Alleyne School, Dulwich. Twelve months in R.A.F. as Cadet, then as 2nd Lieut. Posted to L.R.B. as 2nd Lieut. 27/2/18. Served in France June–31/8/18 (killed in action).

STEWART, PATRICK DOUGLAS. Ed. *Eton. Capt. 3rd D.G. Commanded 2nd Batt.* 23/4/17–8/2/18. Honours: *D.S.O. Mentioned in despatches.*

STICKLAND, A. G. R.A.S.C. Att. to 3rd Batt. 6/5/18 *and went to France* 19/6/18.

STOKES, HENRY FRASER. Asst. Surgeon 1881. Surgeon Capt. 1887. Surgeon Major 1897. Resigned 1898.

STOKES, LEICESTER HENRY. 18th Londons. Served with 2nd Batt. 15/10/17–31/10/17 (*wounded and missing*).

STORMOUNT, HENRY J. Asst. Surgeon 1864. Retired 1867. Died 9/1/90.

STRANSOM, JOHN HOWELL. *Ed.* Framlingham College. Enlisted 7/8/14 and went to France with 1st Batt. Nov. 1914–28/4/15 (wounded). 2nd Lieut. 29/4/15. Lieut. 1/7/16. Served with 3rd Batt. Rejoined 1st Batt. 20/9/16–7/7/17. Adjt. 19/3/17–20/5/17 (invalided). Subsequently served with 3rd Batt. Adjt. Mar.–April 1919. *Honours.* D.C.M.

STRATTON, B. G. H. 2nd R.B. Att. to 1st Batt. Nov. 1918.

STRETTON, F. WELLINGTON. Ensign 1860. Lieut. 1860. Retired 1863.

SUTHERLAND, ROBERT KERR SOUTAR. Capt. R.A.M.C. Att. to 3rd Batt. 3/6/18–20/7/18.

SWORDER, B. *Ed.* Bancroft's School, Woodford. Served in ranks 1899–1904. Rejoined Dec. 1914 in ranks. Drafted to 1st Batt. in France 23/3/15–7/7/16. 2nd Lieut. 25/10/16. Served again in France 18/4/17–16/8/17 (severely wounded). Lieut. 25/4/18.

TABBERER, CECIL OSMOND. Q.V.R. Att. to 1st Batt. 1918 *and served there till end of war.* Honours. *M.C.*

TATCHELL, EDWARD ROBERT. Ensign 1868. Retired 1871.

TATLOW, ERIC MARK. *Ed.* Wolverhampton School. Enlisted L.R.B. 5/2/17. 2nd Lieut. 2/5/18. To France and posted to 2/2nd London 2/8/18–25/8/18 (wounded).

TAYLOR, A. T. Served in ranks, came to 3rd Batt. and afterwards joined Aldershot Gymnastic Staff, remaining with the Batt. Gazetted 2nd Lieut. 3/3/19.

TAYLOR, CHARLES REGINALD. *Ed.* Clifton College and B.N.C., Oxford. Joined R.A.M.C. Mounted Field Ambulance Aug 1914 Commission in 3rd Batt. as 2nd Lieut. 11/2/15. Lieut. 1/6/16. Recruiting Sub-Area, Stoke Newington, 1916–17. In charge of Leave Office at Havre 2/5/17–20/2/18.

TAYLOR, FREDERICK GEORGE. *Ed.* St. Dunstan's College, Catford. Served in ranks March 1908–March 1914. Rejoined Aug. 1914 and went to France with 1st Batt. Nov. 1914–May 1915. 2nd Lieut. 20/1/16. Lieut. 20/7/17. Batt. Bombing Officer 30th Batt. London Regt. 1918.

TAYLOR, GEORGE OSSORY. *Ed.* Cowper Street School. Enlisted about 1907 and served continuously, going to France with 1st Batt. Nov. 1914–March 1915. Commissioned in 3rd Batt. 2nd Lieut. 28/9/15. Rejoined 1st Batt. 21/9/16–8/10/16 (killed in action).

TAYLOR, H. 2nd Lieut. 13/12/16.

TAYLOR, J. M. Went to France with 2nd Batt. 24/1/17.

TERRY, JOHN WHITAKER. *Ed.* Whitgift Middle School. Joined 2nd Batt. Sept. 1914 and went to France with it Jan. 1917–12/9/17 (wounded). 2nd Lieut. 31/7/18 and served with 1st Batt. 18/9/18 to end of war. *Honours.* M.C.

THIEDE. EDGAR ALAN. *Ed.* Princeton University, U.S.A. Enlisted in 3rd Batt. —/10/15. 2nd Lieut. 28/11/17. Joined 1st Batt. in France 25/4/18–5/11/18 (wounded). Lieut. 28/5/19.

THOMAS, EDWARD GEORGE. Enlisted in 2nd Batt. Sept. 1914 and commissioned therein as 2nd Lieut. 4/9/15. Transf. to 3rd Batt. and went to 1st Batt. in France 27/5/16–1/7/16 (severely wounded). Lieut. 2/7/16. Invalided out totally blind 1917.

THOMAS, J. THOMAS. Ensign 1864. Lieut. 1866. Retired 1872.

THOMPSON, CECIL HENRY FARRER. *Ed.* Harrow and Trinity College, Cambridge. Harrow School R.V.C. 1897–1901. 2nd Lieut. 12/3/09. Lieut. 1910. Capt. 1913. Went to France with 1st Batt. Nov. 1914–26/4/15 and 31/7/15–10/6/16. D.A.Q.M.G. Fourth Army B.E.F. 3/2/17–25/3/19. Major 30/5/17. Subsequently served in N. Russia. *Honours.* D.S.O., O.B.E. Four mentions in despatches. Fr. Croix de Guerre with star.

THOMPSON, LESLIE NORTHCOTE. Enlisted in 3rd Batt. June 1916. 2nd Lieut. 1/8/17. Joined 1st Batt. in France 27/9/17–2/12/17 (killed in action at Cambrai).

THOMPSON, RODERICK CHARLES. *Ed.* Haberdashers' Company's Schools. Enlisted in Artists' Rifles 11/12/15. 2nd Lieut. 3/8/17. Served in France 19/13/16–28/3/18 (prisoner of war). Lieut. 3/2/19.

THOMSON, ALEXANDER ROSS. *Ed.* Whitgift Middle School, Croydon. Enlisted in London Scottish Aug. 1914 and served with it in France March–May 1915. Commissioned in 2nd Batt. 2nd Lieut. 20/10/15. Transf. to 3rd. Joined 1st Batt. France 3/9/16–8/10/16 (wounded), and afterwards served with 3rd Batt. Lieut. 1/7/17.

THOMSON, J. A. SKENE. Capt. 2nd Batt. West Riding Regt. Capt. and Adjt. L.R.B. 1888–93.

THOMSON, WALTER ALAN. *Ed.* Whitgift Middle School, Croydon. Enlisted Aug. 29th, 1914 in the Res. Batt. London Scottish. Commissioned in 3rd Batt. L.R.B. 2nd Lieut. 30/5/17. Served in France 28/8/17 to end of war. Lieut. 30/11/18. *Honours.* M.C.

THOMSON, W. Y. *Ed.* St. Edward's School, Oxford. Enlisted in London Scottish Aug. 29th, 1914. Commissioned in 2nd Batt. 2nd Lieut. 25/10/15. Went to France with it Jan. 1917 and att. to 174th L.T.M. Battery to end of war. Lieut. 1/7/17. A/Capt. commanding 174th L.T.M.B. 20/9/17. *Honours.* Mentioned in despatches.

THORNTON, FREDERICK DU PRÉ. Ensign 1863. Retired 1865.

TICEHURST, GORDON HARRY. *Ed.* Battersea Polytechnic Secondary School. Served in London University O.T.C. Gazetted to 2/2nd London R. 14/7/15. Served with it in Ga lipoli Oct –Dec. 1915 and Egypt Feb.–April 1916. Posted to 1st Batt. in France 4/6/16 and subsequently transf. to L.R.B. Lieut. 2/7/16. Wounded 9/9/16 (at Leuze Wood). Referred to in " Englishman Kamerad ! " as " Chislehurst." Returned to France, att. to 2nd L.R.B. March–20/9/17 (killed in action).

TITFORD, ARTHUR. Joined L.R.B. as a private in Feb. 1860 and promoted to Corporal and Clr.-Sergeant. 2nd Lieut. 1874. Lieut. 1874. Capt. 14/2/85 ("P" Co.). Retired 1887 as Hon. Major. *Honours.* V.D.

TITLEY, PETER. *Ed.* St. John's School, Leatherhead. Enlisted in ranks in 1900. Served continuously and went to France with 1st Batt. Nov. 1914–March 1915 (wounded). 2nd Lieut. 17/6/15. Rejoined 1st Batt. 17/1/16-—/6/16 (wounded) and 8/11/16–Aug. 1917 (severely wounded). Lieut. 1/7/17. A/Capt Nov. 1916. *Sports.* Brighton March Team 1911.

TOD, GEORGE RUSSELL. *Ed.* Wellington College. 2nd Lieut. 23/10/80. Joined Seaforth Highlanders (72nd) 1880. Lieut. 1/7/81. Egypt 1882 (Medal and clasp, Khedive's Star). Adjt. 1887–91. Capt. 25/10/89. Capt. and Adjt. L.R.B. 1898–03. Major 19/7/99. Rejoined L.R.B. as Lieut.-Col. to command 2nd Batt. 6/9/14 and took it to France 24/1/17–24/4/17 (invalided). Subsequently commanded 23rd Batt. Royal Welsh Fus. 4/6/17–4/6/19. *Honours.* Mention in despatches. Home mention. Brevet Col. 3/6/18. Subs. Col. 26/3/20.

TOD, WILLIAM NORMAN. *Ed.* Eton. Two years in Eton R.V.C. Commissioned in 2nd Batt. 2nd Lieut. 18/11/14. After going to a Home Service unit was transferred to 3rd Batt. and went to France. Joined 1st Batt. 7/9/16–9/9/16. Served in W.O. as attached Officer Dec. 1916–Nov 1918 Lieut. 1/7/17. Then served as G.S.O. 2, at War Office, until June 1919. Gazetted out of Army on account of ill-health with rank of Major Nov. 1918. *Honours.* O.B.E. Home mention in despatches.

TOSELAND, H. G. 19*th Londons.* *Att. to* 2*nd Batt.* 9/8/17–20/9/17 (*wounded*).

TOWERS, EDWARD. Ensign 1866. Lieut. 1868. Retired 1873.

TOWSE, CHARLES. 2nd Lieut. 1878. Lieut. 1880. Retired 1885.

TOWSE, WILLIAM WRENCH. Ensign 1860. Lieut. 1860. Capt. 1863. Resigned 1865.

TRENOW, GEOFFREY FOVEAUX. *Ed.* Sutton Valence School, Kent. Private in 2nd Batt. H.A.C. Aug. 1914. Commissioned in 2nd Batt. 22/7/15 and went to France with it Jan. 1917–20/9/17 (killed in action). *Honours.* M.C.

TRESILLIAN, C. S. 12*th Londons.* *Att. to* 1*st Batt.* 30/1/18–28/3/18 (*missing*).

TREVELYAN, CHARLES WILLIAM. *Ed.* Wellington and Magdalen College, Oxford. Wellington College R.V.C. N.C.O. 1902–06. Oxford University O.T.C. (Cavalry Squadron). N.C.O. 1907–10. Joined L.R.B. as 2nd Lieut. 29/9/14. Went to France with 1st Batt. Nov. 1914–28/4/16. Lieut. 28/3/15. Capt. 3/5/15. Subsequently served with Provost Marshal's Branch in France and Belgium. *Honours.* M.C. Three mentions in despatches.

UNWIN, REGINALD WILLIAM. 11th *Londons. Att. to* 1*st Batt.* 18/7/16–30/9/16 (*killed in action* 8/10/16).

VAILE, GEORGE BERKELEY. *Ed.* University College School. Enlisted 26/10/99. Sergeant 22/3/09. Clr.-Sergeant 10/4/11. Commissioned in 2nd Batt. as 2nd Lieut. 24/10/14. Transferred to 3rd Batt. Lieut. 1/7/16. Capt. 16/10/16. Subsequently served on Bde., Divl. and Southern Command Musketry Staff. Served in France with 1st Batt 5/5/18–2/9/18 (wounded).

VALLANCE, HENRY FLETCHER. Ensign 1860. Lieut. 1860. Retired 1870.

VEZEY FITZGERALD, JOHN V., K.C. *Ed.* Rugby and Balliol College, Oxford. Capt. 1st Oxford R.V.C. Joined L.R.B. as Ensign 1873. Lieut. 1873. Capt. 1879 ("Q" Co.). Retired 1886 as Hon. Major.

VINCENT, HAROLD GRAHAM. *Ed.* Haileybury and Jesus College, Cambridge. Served in Haileybury O.T.C. 2nd Lieut. L.R.B. 14/9/14. Went to France with 1st Batt. Nov. 1914–May 1915 (invalided). Lieut. —/3/15. Then served some time as Instructor at Signalling Schools. Capt. 1/7/16. To France Aug. 1917–Dec. 1917. Seconded to Army Signal Service from 1917 onwards. *Cricket.* Cambridge XI 1914.

VON BERG, WILFRED CLEMENT. *Ed.* Whitgift Grammar School. Enlisted in 3rd Batt. March 1915 and went to 1st Batt. in France 1st Sept. 1915–April 1916. Came home for commission, 2nd Lieut. 5/8/16, and rejoined 1st Batt. 21/9/16–6/12/17 and 1/4/18–20/5/19. Lieut. 5/2/18. Adjt. 1st Batt. 16/8/17–31/5/19. *Honours.* M.C.

WADD, HENRY C. Ensign 1866. Lieut. 20/4/68. Capt. 1872 ("O" Co.). Retired as Hon. Maj. 1894. Died 1913.

WADDELL, JAMES. Sub.-Lieut. 1874. Lieut. 1874. Retired 1881.

WADNER, E. G. C. 7th Londons. Att. to 1*st Batt.* 27/1/17–12/4/17 (wounded).

WALDEGRAVE, RT. HON. WILLIAM FREDERICK, EARL, P.C. *Ed.* Eton and Trinity College, Cambridge. Eton College R.V.C. 1864–69. Cambridge University Rifle Volunteer C. 1869–72 (Capt.). Joined L.R.B. as Ensign 1873. Lieut. 1873. Capt. 1874 ("D" Co.). Major 1901. Retired 1901 as Hon. Lieut.-Col. *Honours.* Queen Victoria's Jubilee Medal and bar. King Edward's Coronation Medal. V.D. *Shooting.* Eton winning team in Ashburton Shield 1860. Cambridge winning team against Oxford 1872. King's Badge 1885. Won Snider Wimbledon Cup 1882. Won L.R.B. Gold Medal 1881 and 1884. In Kolapore team 1882. Capt. English Elcho team 1895 to date. Capt. English XX. Shot English XX 1877, 1878, 1885. Capt. of the Yeomen of the Guard 1896–06. Lord-in-Waiting to Queen Victoria 1886–92, 1895–96.

WALE, CHARLES WILLIAM. *Ed.* Stationers' Company's School. Enlisted in 3rd Batt. 22/3/16 and drafted to 1st Batt. in France 14/7/16–6/9/17. 2nd Lieut. 18/12/17. To France. Posted to 1/19th Londons 20/4/18 and transf. M.G.C. Grantham 22/7/18.

WALKER, REV. H. G. Att. to 3rd Batt. 1/2/17–16/4/18.

WALKER, J. B. Hon. Qmr. 1865. Retired 1867. Died 1867.

WALKER, ROBERT. Transf. as Lieut. 1870 from 12th Tower Hamlets on absorption. Capt. 1873 ("A" Co.). Retired 1879.

WALLIS, FERDINAND HOWSHIP. *Ed.* Doncaster and Priscas Grammar School. In ranks of L.R.B. 6/1/99–26/1/07 and from 8/3/09 served continuously and went to France with 1st Batt. Nov. 1914. 2nd Lieut. 11/2/15. Lieut. 1/6/16. Capt. 3/2/18. Served continuously with 1st Batt. to 25/3/18, being Adjt. 7/4/16–12/9/16 and 20/5/17–14/8/17. At various times was in command and was Lieut.-Col. commanding 15/8/17–2/12/17. Came home to attend Senior Officers' School, and on return commanded 1/13th Londons for a time after the Armistice. Slightly wounded 14/8/17. *Honours.* M.C. and two bars. *Sports.* Hon. Sec. L.R.B. School of Arms 1903–7 and 1911–14.

WARD, D. T. 2nd Lieut. 25/1/17. *To France* 3/3/17–20/9/17 (*killed in action*).

WARDE, GEORGE. Late Capt. 51st Foot. Lieut.-Col. Commandant 1862. Retired 1876.

WARDE, H. F. 2nd Lieut. 1887. Lieut. 1888. Retired 1893.

WARE, M. 2nd Lieut. 29/5/18. To France 7/9/18.

WARNER, ARCHIBALD. *Ed.* Whitgift and Queens' College, Cambridge. Enlisted in the Artists' Rifles June–Oct. 1915. Commissioned in 3rd Batt. 2nd Lieut. 29/10/15, and went to 1st Batt. in France 27/5/16–1/7/16 (killed in action).

WARNER, BERTRAM. *Ed.* Reading School. Joined the 1/8th Batt. Worcesters 8/8/14 and went to France with it 31/3/15 as Corporal and was promoted Sergeant. Returned for commission. 2nd Lieut. L.R.B. 26/9/16. Went to France and joined 1st Batt. 6/12/16–12/4/17 (killed in action).

WARNER, BRODRICK ASHTON. *Ed.* Winchester College. Served in Winchester College Rifle V.C. (Corporal). 2nd Lieut. L.R.B. 1909. Lieut. 9/7/12. Capt. 1915. Uganda Civil Service 1912 to date. Two mentions in despatches on German E. Africa campaign.

WATERS, BERNARD STANLEY. 4th Londons. Att. to 1st Batt. 11/3/17–3/5/17 (*killed in action*).

WATERS, HARDY BEDWELL. *Ed.* Hove College. Served in 6th (Cyclist) Batt. Royal Sussex Regt., and 1st Batt. East Surrey Regt. in France July–Oct. 1916 (wounded). Posted to L.R.B. on commission as 2nd Lieut. 31/10/17 and served with 1st Batt. April 1918 to end of war.

WATKINS, C. D. Posted to L.R.B. as 2nd Lieut. 1917.

WEBB, GEORGE. Ensign 1860. Lieut. 1863. Capt. 1865 ("B" Co.). Retired 1868.

WEBB, GEORGE HENRY. Served at home and in France as Cyclist Despatch Rider. Posted on commission to L.R.B. as 2nd Lieut. 26/6/18, and transf. to R.A.F. Aug. 1918.

WELCH, VERE EDWARD OSBALDESTON. *Ed.* Harrow. Harrow School O.T.C. 1910–14 (N.C.O.). Commissioned in 2nd Batt. as 2nd Lieut. 31/12/14. Lieut. 1/6/16. Went to France with 2nd Batt. 25/1/17–17/6/17 (wounded). Capt. 22/2/17. Instructor Aldershot Command School of Instruction for N.C.O.'s 9/9/17–3/6/18. Returned to France to join 1st Batt. 2/8/18–30/8/18 (killed in action).

WEST, HORACE C. G. 2nd Lieut. 1880. Lieut. 1881. Retired 1882.

WEST, LESLIE GOWER. Enlisted in L.R.B. 1917. 2nd Lieut. 27/2/18. Went to France 2/8/18 and posted to 2/2nd Londons (killed in action Oct. 24th, 1918).

WETHAM, ARTHUR. 2nd Lieut. 1877. Lieut. 1879. Retired 1887.

WHEATLEY, FLETCHER MORTIMER. *Ed.* Harrow. Enlisted in Artists' Rifles Sept. 1914. Commissioned in 3rd Batt. 2nd Lieut. 4/5/15 and joined 1st Batt. in France 9/1/16. Severely wounded almost at once and subsequently served with 3rd Batt. and as A/Adjt. London Command Depot. Lieut. 6/12/16.

WHITAKER, GEORGE. *Ed.* Whitgift Grammar School. Enlisted in Rifle Brigade 14/9/14. Commissioned in 2nd Batt.

L.R.B. 2nd Lieut. 17/1/15. Lieut. 9/9/15. Went to France with it 29/1/17–20/9/17 (killed in action). Capt. 30/5/17.

WHITE, ARTHUR BRYAN. *Ed.* St. Paul's School and Geneva. Enlisted in L.R.B. some years before the War. Served continuously and went to France with 1st Batt. Nov. 1914–29/11/14 (wounded). 2nd Lieut. 8/2/15. Rejoined 1st Batt. 22/2/15–2/5/15 (wounded). Rejoined 1st Batt. 25/7/15–23/10/15 (sick). Lieut. 1916. Rejoined 1st Batt. 12/11/16–16/8/17 (killed in action). Capt. 19/10/17. *Honours.* Mentioned in despatches.

WHITECHURCH, NOEL ARTHUR. *Ed.* Arundel House School, Surbiton. Enlisted in 3rd Batt. March 1916. 2nd Lieut. 1/3/17. Joined 1st Batt. L.R.B. overseas 30/4/17–1/11/17 (invalided). Att. to R.A.F. as pilot 24/5/18–27/2/19. Lieut. 1/9/18.

WHITEHOUSE, REV. CANON F. E. Att. to 3rd Batt. 2/10/18–—/1/19.

WHITMORE, JOHN BEACH. Q.W.R. Att. to 1st Batt. 3/8/17–28/9/17.

WHITTINGTON, REV. RICHARD. Chaplain 1891. Retired 1897.

**WHITTOW, A.*

WHITTOW, FRANK HERBERT. *Ed.* University College School. L.R.B. Cadet Corps 1886–92. Enlisted in L.R.B. 1892. 2nd Lieut. 1894. Lieut. 1898. Capt. 1900. Retired 1903.

WILCOX, HENRY. Asst. Surgeon 1879. Retired 1881.

WILKIN, WALTER REGINALD. *Ed.* Harrow and Trinity College, Cambridge. Enlisted in 2nd Batt. H.A.C. 29/11/15. Commissioned in 3rd Batt. L.R.B. as 2nd Lieut. 19/12/16. Att. 2/7th Lanc. Fus. from 5/2/17–21/8/17, and att. 66th Div. Reinforcement Wing 21/8/17–23/3/18 (wounded). Lieut. 19/6/18. Again to France and posted to 22nd London 20/8/18–30/8/18 (wounded).

WILKINS, J. W. 11th Londons. Att. to 1st Batt. 18/7/16–12/10/16.

WILKINS, R. C. 11th Londons. Att. to 1st Batt. 20/7/16– —/9/16.

WILKINSON, HERBERT GORDON. *Ed.* Radley. Enlisted 2nd Batt. L.R.B. 5th Sept. 1914. 2nd Lieut. 4/2/15. Lieut. 1/6/16. Went to France with it Jan. 1917–Jan. 1918. Capt. 11/7/17. On disbandment posted to Artists' Rifles and served with them to 23/8/18 (wounded), being in command from 31/5/18. *Rowing.* Henley 1901–2–3. Ladies' Plate. Wyfolds, Thames, Cup, etc.

WILLETT, WILFRID LESLIE. *Ed.* St. Paul's School and Trinity College, Cambridge. Lieut. Cambridge University

O.T.C. Joined L.R.B. as 2nd Lieut. 10/8/14 and went to France with it Nov. 1914–13/12/14 (severely wounded). *Honours.* Mentioned in despatches. *Shooting.* School Shooting VIII 1906–09. Cambridge University Snap Shooting 1910–11. Cambridge County X 1911. Territorial VIII United Services 1911. London Hospital IV 1914.

**WILLIAMS, R. B.*

WILLIAMSON, EDGAR ROWE. *Ed.* Repton. Joined 2nd Batt. in the ranks 15/9/14 and drafted to 1st Batt. in France 24/1/15–30/3/15. 2nd Lieut. 9/2/15. Rejoined 1st Batt. 7/1/16. Lieut. 18/1/16. Posted to 169th L.T.M.B. 6/4/16 (killed in action 10/9/16). *Honours.* M.C.

WILLIAMSON, FRANK. *Ed.* Churcher's College, Petersfield. Enlisted 1902 and served continuously, going to France as Sergeant in 1st Batt. in Nov. 1914. Invalided home early in 1915. Commissioned in 3rd Batt. 2nd Lieut. 4/6/15. Demobilised for a time for munitions. To France again to 2nd Batt. 24/5/17. Lieut. 1/7/17. On disbandment posted to Artists' Rifles 24/3/18 (killed in action).

WILLOUGHBY, EDWARD F. Asst. Surgeon 1868. Surgeon 1877. Retired 1878. Died 29/7/06.

WILLS, E. C. *Ed.* City of London School. In ranks of L.R.B. from Mar. 1909. Served continuously and went to France with 1st Batt. Nov. 1914. 2nd Lieut. 8/5/15. Lieut. 8/16/15. Severely wounded 8/10/16. Relinquished commission on account of wounds received in action and retired with Hon. rank of Captain 10/9/18.

WILLS, WILLIAM ANTHONY. *Ed.* City of London School. Enlisted in Artists' Rifles 9/10/15–20/6/16. Joined L.R.B. as 2nd Lieut. 21/6/16. Joined 1st Batt. in France 19/9/16–3/5/17 (severely wounded).

WILSON, F. M. Served in ranks and went to France. Severely wounded and commission received after return home. 2nd Lieut. 17/5/17. Lieut. 1918. Served with 3rd Batt. till demobilised.

WILSON, SIDNEY IRVIN. 23rd Londons. Att. to 1st Batt. 1/6/17–16/8/17 (wounded).

WIMBLE, ARTHUR STANLEY. *Ed.* Tonbridge School. Enlisted L.R.B. 8/8/14. Lce.-Corporal Sept. 1914. Went to France with 1st Batt. Nov. 1914–2/5/15 (wounded). Corporal Dec. 1914, Sergeant March 1915. Commissioned 2nd Lieut. 29/4/15, Lieut. 1/7/16, and ordered to 2nd Batt. Went to France with it in Jan. 1917. Appointed Staff Capt. 24th Inf. Bde 17/4/18–27/5/18 (prisoner of war). *Honours.* Mentioned in despatches.

WINNINGTON-INGRAM, ARTHUR FOLEY, D.D., LL.D., LORD BISHOP OF LONDON. *Ed.* Marlborough College and Keble College, Oxford. Joined L.R.B. as Chaplain 1901. Visited French Front April 1915; Grand Fleet July 1916; Harwich Fleet July 1917 and 1918; Salonica Front Oct. and Nov. 1918. *Honours.* K.C.V.O. Mention in despatches. Grand Cross of the Redeemer (Greece). Order of St. Sava (Serbia), 1st Class.

WINTER, REV. E. M. Att. to 2nd Batt. 27/7/17.

WOLFE, REV. P. R.C.C.F. Att. to 3rd Batt. 19/7/16– —/11/16.

WOOD, TREVOR LEY CODNER. *Ed.* Trinity College, Cambridge. Enlisted in Artists' Rifles. Commissioned in 3rd Batt. as 2nd Lieut. 16/1/15. Owing to ill-health employed at W.O. and subsequently with Labour units. Lieut. July 1917. A/Capt. Nov. 1918.

WOOD, WILLIAM EDWARD RAMSDEN. *Ed.* Harrow and Cambridge. Served in Harrow School Vol. (Sergeant) and Cambridge University Vol. 1870–2 (Capt.). Lieut. L.R.B. 1873–8. Asst. Surgeon L.R.B. 1878. Surgeon 1889. Retired 1890. Surgeon 3rd Cheshire Vol. 1894–5. *Shooting.* Shot for Harrow at Wimbledon 1867 and for Cambridge 1871–2.

WOOD, WILLIAM E. R. Ensign 1873. Lieut. 1873. Retired 1878.

WOODWARD, CHARLES WILLIAM. 18th London. Att. to 1st Batt. 19/10/17.

WORTHAM, C. Late Capt. K.R.R.C. Capt. and Adjt. 1882. Major 1884. Retired 1888.

WRAY, MAURICE. *Ed.* Dulwich College. Served in Dulwich College O.T.C. 1908–09 (Corpl.). Enlisted L.R.B. June 1911 and served continuously, going to France with 1st Batt. Nov. 1914–June 1915. 2nd Lieut. 8/5/15. Seconded with R.B. 15/3/16. Lieut. 1/7/17. Subsequently served in Egypt and Salonica. *Honours.* Mentioned in despatches. *Sports.* Brighton March Team 1914.

WRIGHT, C. L. Served in ranks of H.A.C., and went to France. Posted to L.R.B. on commission. 2nd Lieut. 25/9/18. To France 15/11/18.

WRIGHT, J. H. Att. to 2nd Batt., and on disbandment transferred to 18th Londons.

WRIGHT, MARTIN WISBEY. *Ed.* Isleworth County School. Enlisted in 2nd Batt. Sept. 1914 and went to France with it Jan. 1917. Promoted Sergeant 1917. Came home for commission. 2nd Lieut. 31/10/17. Joined 1st Batt. 25/4/18 till end of war. Lieut. 1/5/19 *Honours.* Mentioned in despatches.

WRIGHT, REGINALD GEORGE STUART, *18th Londons. Att. to 2nd Batt.* 15/10/17.

YALDEN, JAMES. Ensign 1872. Lieut. 1873. Retired 1877.

YOUNG, ALAN CATCHPOOL. 2nd Lieut. 30/5/17. Served with 2nd Batt. in France. Transferred, on its disbandment, to Artists 29/1/18.

YOUNG, WALTER WILLIAM. Joined 19th Middlesex R.V. Oct. 1859. Resigned as Sergeant 12/3/64. Joined 1st Middlesex Engineers Vol. 28/1/64. Sergeant Jan. 1867. Resigned 2/11/74. Enlisted in L.R.B. in 1874. 2nd Lieut. 1878. Lieut. 1881. Capt. ("N" Co.) 1889. Retired 1893 as Hon. Major. Died 1919.

ALPHABETICAL ROLL OF HONOURS, BRITISH AND FOREIGN, AND MENTIONS

WON BY

PRESENT AND PAST MEMBERS OF THE L.R.B. OF ALL RANKS IN THE GREAT WAR, 1914–19

HONOURS, AWARDS AND MENTIONS

THE following list gives the details of the Honours, etc., won by 473 past and present members of the regiment :—

V.C.	1	D.F.C.	2
K.C.V.O.	1	D.C.M.	36
K.B.E. (Civil)	1	M.M.	174
C.B. (Military)	2	Bar to M.M.	2
C.M.G.	3	M.B.E. (Military)	4
C.B.E. (Military)	5	,, (Civil)	1
D.S.O.	20	M.S.M.	22
Bar to D.S.O.	1	M.V.O. (6th Class)	1
O.B.E. (Military)	9	Brevets Colonel	2
,, (Civil)	2	,, Lieut.-Colonel	3
M.C.	136	,, Major	4
1st Bar to M.C.	10	Mentions in the Field	143
2nd Bar to M.C.	1	,, at Home	28

FOREIGN—

French Legion of Honour	4	Italian Bronze Medal for Valour	1
,, Croix de Guerre	9	Greek Redeemer	2
,, Medaille d'Honneur	1	,, George 1st	1
,, Merit Agricole	1	Servian St. Sava	1
Belgian Croix de Guerre	6	Egyptian Nile	1
,, Decoration Militaire	1	Montenegrin Danilo	1
Russian St. Stanislaus	3	Chinese Excellent Crop	1
,, St. Anne	1		
			648

In addition, 72 N.C.O.'s and Riflemen, none of whom figure in the above list, received "Divisional Cards" for gallantry in the Field.

Name and Rank	Regiment	Honours
Adams, Sig. Sergt. E.A.	L.R.B.	D.C.M.
Adams, R.S.M. J.	K.R.R.C. att. L.R.B.	D.C.M., M.M.
Alesbury, Rfn. R. E.	L.R.B.	M.M.
Allison, Rfn. R.	L.R.B.	M.M.
Anderson, R.Q.M.S. F. H.	L.R.B.	Home Mention
Anderson, Major N.	L.R.B.	O.B.E. (Mil.), M.B.E. (Mil.), Mention (3)
Andrews, Rfn. L. W.	L.R.B.	M.M.
Atkinson, Rfn. W. L.	L.R.B.	M.M.
Axten, Capt. C.	R.F.A.	M.C.
Babington, Cpl. W. A.	L.R.B.	Mention
Bailey, Rfn. S. E.	L.R.B.	M.M.
Baker, Rfn. G. G.	L.R.B.	M.M.
Baker, 2nd Lieut. H. B.	1st London	M.C.
Baker, Sergt. H. G.	L.R.B.	D.C.M.
Baldock, Rfn. W. T.	L.R.B.	M.M.
Banks, Rfn. W.	L.R.B.	M.M.
Barker, Rfn. H.	L.R.B.	D.C.M.
Barker, Lce.-Cpl. H.	L.R.B.	M.M.
Barrell, C.S.M. A.H.	L.R.B.	D.C.M.
Barrett, Sergt. A.	L.R.B.	M.M.
Barry, Capt. F. P.	L.R.B.	M.C.
Barter, 2nd Lieut. H. B.	1st London	M.C.
Bates, Lieut.-Col. A.S., T. D.	L.R.B.	D.S.O., Mention (4), Fr. Croix de Guerre (with Palm)
Bazire, Rfn. A. E.	L.R.B.	M.M.
Beauchamp, L/Sgt. W. S.	L.R.B.	M.M.
Belcher, L/Sgt. D. W.	L.R.B.	V.C.
Bell, Lieut. D. H.	1st Camerons	M.C.
Bell, Rfn. M. J.	L.R.B.	M.M.
Bennett, Lieut. H. B.	5th K.O.R.L.R.	M.C.
Bennett, Capt. H. S.	K.R.R.C.	M.C.
Berry, Rfn. W. H.	L.R.B.	M.M.
Best, Capt. B. G.	12th London	M.C.
Bewsher, Capt. F. W.	L.R.B.	D.S.O., M.C., Mention (2)
Billington, L/Cpl. L. W.	L.R.B.	M.M.
Bird, Lieut. E. T.	21st London	M.C.
Birt, Lieut.-Col. A. W.	4th W. Yorks	O.B.E. (Mil.)
Birt, Capt. L. H.	1st R. Berks	D.S.O., Mention (2)
Bishop, Rfn. W. S.	L.R.B.	M.M.
Blofeld, 2nd Lieut. D.	22nd London	M.C.
Blofeld, Capt. R. M.	22nd London	M.C. and Bar
Blumson, L/Cpl. W. J.	L.R.B.	M.M.

Name and Rank	Regiment	Honours
Bolton, Rfn. F. H. M.	L.R.B.	M.M.
Bone, L/Cpl. R. G.	L.R.B.	M.M.
Boorman, Capt. D. S.	4th London	M.C.
Booth, Capt. S. P. B.	7th North. Fus.	M.C., Mention
Boston, Cpl. G. G.	L.R.B.	D.C.M.
Bottomley, R.S.M. C.	L.R.B.	D.C.M.
Boutall, 2nd Lieut. W. J.	4th London	M.C.
Bouverie, Sergt. C.	L.R.B.	M.M.
Bowmer, Flight-Sergt. W .R.	R.A.F.	Home Mention
Box, Rfn. J. H. G.	L.R.B.	M.M.
Bradford, Rfn. C. W.	L.R.B.	M.M.
Bradford, Sir J. R., K.C.M.G.	Ex-L.R.B. Cadet	C.B. (Mil.), C.B.E. (Mil.), Mention (5)
Branch, L/Cpl. S. O.	L.R.B.	M.M.
Brandle, 2nd Lieut. S.	Tank Corps	M.C. and Bar
Bridges, L/Cpl. E. L.	L.R.B.	M.M.
Britton, Lieut. A. F.	R.A.F.	M.C., Fr. Croix de Guerre
Brock, Sergt. F. H.	L.R.B.	D.C.M.
Bromiley, Capt. B.	L.R.B.	Mention
Brown, Pay Lieut.-Com. W. W.	R.N.R.	Chevalier, Legion of Honour
Bryer, L/Cpl. A. E.	L.R.B.	Mention
Buck, Rfn. H. G.	L.R.B.	M.M.
Bully, Capt. C. P.	4th Hants	M.C.
Bunyan, Lieut. R. M.	3rd London	M.C.
Burnell, Lieut.-Col. C. D.	L.R.B.	D.S.O., Mention (2)
Burningham, Rfn. C.	L.R.B.	M.M.
Burroughs, Capt. T. E.	L.R.B.	M.C. and Bar
Burton, Sergt. J. A.	L.R.B.	M.M.
Bush, Sergt. F. T.	L.R.B.	Mention
Bushell, Rfn. W.	L.R.B.	D.C.M.
Butler, Lieut. L. G.	11th Essex	M.C.
Buxton, Rfn. P.	L.R.B.	M.M.
Byham, Capt. G. R. G.	8th Middlesex	M.C., Mention
Cairns, Lieut.-Col. W. D. Earl	L.R.B.	C.M.G., Mention, Home Mention
Calder, Capt. J. S.	L.R.B.	M.C. and Bar
Cambray, Lieut. W. C.	2nd London	M.C.
Carle, L/Cpl. G.	L.R.B.	M.M.
Carpenter, L/Cpl. C.	L.R.B.	M.M.
Cartwright, Lieut. G. H. G. M.	Coldstream Guards	Mention
Chambers, Capt. G. C.	L.R.B.	Home Mention
Chapman, L/Cpl. E. J.	L.R.B.	Mention

Name and Rank	Regiment	Honours
Charles, L/Cpl. P. D.	L.R.B.	D.C.M., M.M.
Chart, Rfn. H. B.	L.R.B.	M.M.
Chater, Lieut. S. W.	M.G.C.	M.C.
Chodak, Lieut. H. A.	R.A.M.C. att.	M.C.
Cholmondeley, Hon. Brig.-Gen. H.C., C.B.	Late L.R.B.	C.B.E. (Mil.), Home Mention
Chrisp, Cpl. W. A.	L.R.B.	Mention
Clark, Lieut. A. H. B.	5th Worcesters	M.C.
Clark, Rfn. R. S.	L.R.B.	D.C.M.
Clarke, Rfn. H. G.	L.R.B.	M.M.
Clarke, Lieut. J. W. D.	6th Oxford and Bucks L.I.	M.C.
Collins, Sergt. C. A. V.	L.R.B.	M.M.
Cooke, Major E. G. Stenson	8th Essex	Home Mention (2)
Cooke, Lt.-Col. B. H. H.	R.B. (late Adjt. of L.R.B.)	C.M.G., C.B.E. (Mil.), D.S.O., Brevet Lt.-Col., Mention (5), St. Stanislaus 3rd Class with swords, Belgian Croix de Guerre, Com. Ordre du Merit Agricole
Cooke, Capt. D. G.	R.A.F.	M.C.
Cope, Capt. R.	L.R.B.	Mention (2), Fr. Croix de Guerre
Cowley, Rfn. J.	L.R.B.	M.M.
Cowley, Sergt. W. J.	L.R.B.	M.M.
Crews, Capt. F. H.	L.R.B.	M.C.
Crisford, Rev. K. N.	C.F. att.	M.C.
Crisp, L/Cpl. H. J. F.	L.R.B.	M.M.
Crocker, Rfn. F. A.	L.R.B.	M.M.
Crockford, Sergt. A. H. J.	L.R.B.	M.M.
Croll, Lieut. A. G.	4th London	M.C.
Cross, 2nd Lieut. S. H.	L.R.B.	M.C.
Crossley, Lieut. N. M.	L.R.B.	Home Mention
Cruwys, Sergt. L. E.	L.R.B.	M.M.
Cutting, L/Cpl. H.	L.R.B.	D.C.M.
Daniel, Capt. H. W.	13th R. Fus.	M.C. & Bar., Mention
Dare, Sergt. E. C.	L.R.B. att. 8th London	D.C.M.
Daubeny, Col. R.	A.P.D.	C.B.E. (Mil.), Bt. Lieut.-Col., Home Mention
Davies, Rfn. T.	L.R.B.	M.M.
Davis, Capt. I. H.	?	M.C.
Deacon, L/Cpl. W.	L.R.B.	M.M.
Deacon, 2nd Lieut. W. W.	5th K.O.R.L.R.	M.C.

NAME AND RANK	REGIMENT	HONOURS
Dearing, Cpl. C.	L.R.B.	M.M.
Denny, Lieut. & Q.M. A.	L.R.B.	Mention
Denny, Capt. A. C.	Middlesex R. att. M.G.C.	M.C.
Dewey, 2nd Lieut. J. H. J.	L.R.B.	Mention
Dickson, Sergt. J. H.	L.R.B.	M.M.
Dippie, Capt. H.	11th R.W.S.R.	M.C., Mention (2)
Dobinson, Lieut. H. H.	Tank Corps	M.C.
Dodds, 2nd Lieut. A. K.	L.R.B. att. R.E.	M.C., Mention
Doughty, Cpl. C.	L.R.B.	M.M.
Dowley, 2nd Lieut. A. E.	5th E. Surrey	M.C.
Ducat, Lieut.-Col. A. D., T.D., M.B.	R.A.M.C. (T.F.) att. L.R.B.	D.S.O., Mention (3), Medaille d'Honneur avec Glaives "en vermeil"
Ducker, Rfn. R. F.	L.R.B.	M.M.
Dunk, Rfn. H. W.	L.R.B.	M.M.
Dunnett, Rfn. W. E.	L.R.B.	M.M.
Dunnett, 2nd Lieut. W.E.	R.F.A.	M.C.
Du Plessis, Capt. S.	7th London att. L.R.B.	Mention
Durant, Rfn. A.	L.R.B.	M.M.
Durrant, Capt. A. W.	23rd London	D.S.O., Mention
Dyer, Sergt. P. T.	L.R.B.	M.M.
Dyer, 2nd Lieut. W.	2nd London	M.C.
Ebbetts, Cpl. R. F.	L.R.B.	M.M.
Edington, Rfn. A. F. H.	L.R.B.	M.M.
Ellen, Rfn. H. F.	L.R.B., transf. R.E.	M.M., Belgian Croix de Guerre and Decoration Militaire
Elleray, Rfn. E. D.	L.R.B.	M.M.
Ellis, 2nd Lieut. A. C.	R.F.A.	M.C., Mention (2)
Evanson, A/R.Q.M.S. E.	L.R.B.	M.M.
Ewing, 2nd Lieut. G. C.	4th London	M.C.
Ewins, Rfn. V. B.	L.R.B.	M.M.
Farrant, Capt. V. F.	4th S. Lancs, attd. L.R.B.	Mention
Feather, Rfn. E.	L.R.B.	M.M.
Feeley, L/Cpl. P. F.	L.R.B.	M.M.
Ferguson, Capt. H. S.	L.R.B	M.B.E. (Civ.)
Finlayson, Capt. V. A.	10th London	M.C.
Fish, Lieut. F. J.	12th R.B.	M.C.
Fletcher, Capt. H. E.	R.A.F.	D.F.C.
Flindt, Capt. R. E. H.	L.R.B.	Home Mention (2)

Name and Rank	Regiment	Honours
Flint, Capt. N. S.	Bucks Battn. O. & B.L.I.	M.C., Ital. Bronze Medal for Valour
Foaden, L/Cpl. J. H.	L.R.B.	M.M.
Ford, Lieut. J.	23rd London	M.C.
Foster, L/Cpl. G. E.	L.R.B.	M.M.
Fowle, L/Cpl. V. L. A.	L.R.B.	M.M.
Foxall, Cpl. A. T.	L.R.B.	M.M.
Francis, Lieut. W. A.	2nd London	M.C. and Bar
Freemont, Rfn. L. T.	L.R.B.	M.M.
Frentzel, Cpl. W. N.	L.R.B.	M.M.
Frost, C.Q.M.S. A. A.	L.R.B.	M.S.M.
Fry, Capt. W. M.	R.A.F.	M.C.
Fuller, Sergt. A.	L.R.B., attd. R. Fus.	M.M.
Gale, Capt. F. R.	R.A.O.C.	M.B.E. (Mil.)
Gant, Rfn. F. A.	L.R.B.	M.M.
Gates, Rfn. W. R.	L.R.B.	M.M.
Gee, 2nd Lieut. J. P.	L.R.B.	M.C.
Gibson, Lieut. C. L.	17th London	M.C.
Gibson, L/Cpl. C. G.	L.R.B.	Belg. Croix de Guerre
Glynn, Lieut.-Col. T. G. P., C.M.G.	Late Adjt. L.R.B.	O.B.E. (Mil.), Mention (4)
Godsmark, Cpl. P.	L.R.B.	M.M.
Golton, Rfn. L. G.	L.R.B.	M.M.
Goodall, Rfn. A.	L.R.B.	M.M.
Gordon, Tr./Sergt. A.	L.R.B.	D.C.M.
Gordon, 2nd Lieut. A.	L.R.B.	Mention
Gordon, Rfn. G.	L.R.B.	M.M.
Gordon, Sergt. S.	L.R.B.	M.M.
Gould, Capt. F.	23rd London	M.C., Mention
Grain, Sergt. C. (?G.)	L.R.B.	M.M.
Grainger, Rfn. P. T.	L.R.B.	M.M.
Gratian, Sergt. J.	L.R.B.	D.C.M.
Gray, Rfn. A.	L.R.B.	M.M.
Greene, Rfn. F. N.	L.R.B.	M.M.
Greenfield, Cpl. P.	L.R.B.	M.M.
Grimwood, 2nd Lieut. P. L.	L.R.B.	M.C.
Guppy, Major J., T.D.	L.R.B.	Home Mention
Hall, Lieut. G.	L.R.B. att. R.F.C.	Mention
Hall, Lieut. R. M.	9th Cheshire	Mention
Hamilton, R.Q.M.S. W. G.	L.R.B.	M.S.M.
Hammond, Sergt. S. A.	L.R.B.	M.M.
Hancocks, Capt. F. G.	L.R.B.	M.C.
Hands, Major A. S.	18th Middx.	M.C.

Name and Rank	Regiment	Honours
Hands, Sergt. G.	L.R.B.	D.C.M.
Harding, J. R., Esq.	B.R.C.	O.B.E. (Civ.)
Harvest, Lieut. G. L.	L.R.B.	M.C.
Hastings, Lieut. W. J.	Notts & Derby	M.C.
Hawthorne, Rfn. W.	L.R.B.	M.M.
Hayes, L/Cpl. J.	L.R.V.	M.M.
Haylock, L/Cpl. J O.	L.R.B.	M.M.
Haynes, Sergt. G. E.	L.R.B.	Mention
Helsham, Rfn. G. D.	L.R.B.	M.M.
Hernberg, L/Cpl. D.	L.R.B.	M.M.
Hettler, Capt. B. H. C.	K.O.Y.L.I.	M.C.
Hilay, E. J.	L.R.B.	M.M.
Hill, Lieut. T. I.	4th Essex	M.C.
Hilling, L/Cpl. J. A.	L.R.B.	M.M.
Hoadley, Cpl. V. S.	L.R.B.	M.M.
Hodges, Sergt. H. W.	L.R.B.	M.M.
Hodgkinson, Rfn. E. W. G.	L.R.B.	M.M.
Hogg, Lieut. S. R.	R. Fus.	D.S.O., M.C. and Bar, Mention
Holland, Rfn. E.	L.R.B.	M.M.
Holtorp, Sergt. P. von	L.R.B.	M.M.
Hood, 2nd Lieut. D.	L.R.B.	M.C.
Hooson, Sergt. H. B.	L.R.B.	M.M.
Hosking, Capt. S. T.	7th London att.	Mention
Hotz, Cpl. R. C.	L.R.B.	D.C.M.
Houghton, Rfn. H. R.	L.R.B.	M.M.
Houston, Cpl. J.	L.R.B.	M.M.
Howard, Sergt. E. H.	L.R.B.	M.M.
Howells, Sergt. F. J.	L.R.B.	M.M.
Hughes, Sergt. E.	L.R.B.	M.M.
Hulse, Lieut. J. H.	L.R.B.	M.C.
Humphrey, Cpl. G. L.	L.R.B.	Mention
Hunter, Rfn. T. W.	L.R.B.	M.S.M.
Hurndall, Lieut. M. J.	52nd Notts and Derby	M.C.
Husey, Brig.-Gen. R. H.	L.R.B.	D.S.O. and Bar, M.C., Mention (4), Danilo, 4th Class
Imber, Rfn. E. A.	L.R.B.	M.M.
Ingle, Rfn. F.	L.R.B.	M.M.
Jackson, Major R. N.	A.P. & S.S.	D.S.O., Mention (2), Chevalier Legion of Honour, Fr. Croix de Guerre with three gold stars

Name and Rank	Regiment	Honours
James, Rfn. A. E.	L.R.B.	M.M.
James, Rfn. F. A.	L.R.B.	M.M.
Jarvis, A/Cpl. O. V.	L.R.B.	M.M.
Jenkin, Cpl. T. H.	L.R.B.	Mention
John, Capt. C. H.	L.R.B.	M.C.
Johnson, Lieut. R. S.	5th D.L.I.	M.C.
Johnston, Lieut.-Col. C. E.	L.R.B.	D.S.O., M.C., Mention
Johnston, Capt. H. L.	L.R.B.	M.C.
Johnstone, Lieut. J. I.	5th K.O.S.B.	M.C.
Keele, Sergt. F. C.	L.R.B.	M.M.
Keeping, 2nd Lieut. J. T.	12th K.R.R.C.	M.C.
Kelly, Capt. and Q.M. W.	L.R.B.	Home Mention
Kench, Rfn. E. L.	L.R.B.	D.C.M.
Kench, Sergt. W.	L.R.B.	M.M.
Kennard, Lieut.-Col. A. C. H.	1st London	Mention
Kent, Lieut. and Q.M. H. J.	Gen. List att. L.R.B.	M.C.
Kibby, Rfn. D.	L.R.B.	M.M.
Kiddle-Monroe, 2nd Lieut. C. S.	4/10th Middx.	Fr. Croix de Guerre (with Palm)
Kidson, Lieut. N. S.	6th London	M.C.
Kimber, 2nd Lieut. A. E.	2nd London	M.C.
King, Lieut.-Col. N. C., T.D.	L.R.B.	Bt. Col., Home Mention
Kingsbury, Cpl. T. A.	L.R.B.	D.C.M.
Knight, Capt. W. C.	Linc.	O.B.E. (Mil.), Mention
Latham, Rfn. E. B.	L.R.B.	M.M.
Latham, Capt. R.	R.A.S.C.	M.C.
Lea, Lieut.-Col. E. I.	5th Warwicks	M.C., Mention (3), Chev. Legion d'Hon.
Leapman, 2nd Lieut. L. C.	6th London	M.C.
Lee, Sergt. G. M.	L.R.B.	M.M.
Leech, Rfn. R.	L.R.B.	D.C.M.
Le Good, Lieut. E. C.	R.G.A.	M.C.
Leon, Major J.	R.A.S.C.	O.B.E. (Mil.), Mention
Levy, Capt. R. P.	8th Middx.	M.C.
Lewis, Sergt. S. H.	L.R.B.	M.M.
Lewis, Capt. W.	23rd London	M.C.
Libby, L/Cpl. F. T.	L.R.B.	M.M.
Lichfield, Capt. The Earl of	L.R.B.	Mention
Lilley, Sergt. W. M.	L.R.B.	D.C.M., Fr. Croix de Guerre (with Palm)
Lindsay, Rfn. J. S.	L.R.B.	D.C.M.

Name and Rank	Regiment	Honours
Lintott, Major A. L.	L.R.B. att. M.G.C.	D.S.O., Mention
Lintott, Lieut. A. J. C.	L.R.B.	M.C.
Linzell, Lieut. H. H.	Border	M.C.
Lockhart, Rfn. W. E.	L.R.B.	M.M.
London, Bishop of	C.F. att. L.R.B.	K.C.V.O., Mention, Grand Cross of Redeemer, 1st Class St. Sava
Lovett, Sergt. G.	L.R.B.	M.M.
Lowe, L/Cpl. H. S.	L.R.B.	M.M. and Bar
Lucan, Hon. Brig.-Gen. G. C., Earl of	Late L.R.B.	K.B.E. (Civ.), C.B. (Mil.), Mention, Home Mention (2), Nile (3rd Cl.)
Lucas, Lieut. E. P.	4th R. Berks	M.C.
Macadie, Rfn. S. C.	L.R.B. att. K.R.R.C.	D.C.M., M.M.
MacGeagh, T/Lieut.-Col. H. D. F.	L.R.B.	C.B.E.(Mil.), Bt. Major, Home Mention
Machin, 2nd Lieut. F. P.	L.R.B.	Mention
Mackay, Sergt. D.	L.R.B.	M.S.M.
McLoughlin, Rfn. M. N.	L.R.B.	M.M.
McOwan, 2nd Lieut. D.	L.R.B.	Mention
Macveagh, C.S.M. A. J. R.	L.R.B.	Mention, Belg. Croix de Guerre
Maginn, 2nd Lieut. F. J.	L.R.B.	D.S.O., Mention
Maitland, Lieut. V. K.	Tank Corps	M.C.
Malone, Sergt. T.	L.R.B.	M.S.M.
Manbey, C.S.M. B. K.	L.R.B.	Mention
Manbey, 2nd Lieut. B. K.	R.F.A.	M.C.
Mann, Lieut. J. C.	2nd R.W.Fus.	M.C., Mention
Martin, L/Cpl. A. G.	L.R.B.	M.M.
Martin, Sergt. A. J.	L.R.B.	M.M.
Martin, Lieut. E.	1st London	M.C.
Martinnant, Capt. L. W.	2nd R.B.	M.C.
Maskell, C.S.M. L. S.	L.R.B.	D.C.M.
Mason, Sergt. W. G. T.	L.R.B.	M.M.
Maude, L/Cpl. B.	L .R.B. att. K.R.R.C.	D.C.M.
Meldrum, Capt. H.	14th Gloucester	M.C.
Mellor, 2nd Lieut. H. E.	R.F.A.	M.C.
Mieville, Capt. W. S.	28th London	M.C., Mention
Milcovich, Sergt. M.	L.R.B.	M.M.
Miller, Rfn. F. W. M.	L.R.B.	M.M.
Millward, Lieut. G. D.	1st Herts	Mention

Name and Rank	Regiment	Honours
Milne, Lieut. D. W.	11th R.W.S.R.	M.C.
Moore, Capt. E. G.	L.R.B.	Mention
Moore, Sergt. G. G.	L.R.B.	D.C.M.
Moore, Rfn. N. C.	L.R.B.	M.M.
Mortimer, 2nd Lieut. F. S.	8th London	M.C.
Mortimore, Sergt. P. J.	L.R.B.	M.S.M.
Morton, L/Cpl. J. F.	L.R.B.	M.M.
Munday, Sergt. H. W.	L.R.B.	M.S.M.
Murrell, Sergt. S. A.	L.R.B.	M.M.
Newell, Rfn. W. H. O.	L.R.B.	M.M.
Newing, Rfn. A. B.	L.R.B. att. K.R.R.C.	M.M.
Newman, Rfn. C.	L.R.B.	M.M.
Newman, 2nd Lieut. H. R.	4thW. Riding	M.C.
North, L/Cpl. F.	L.R.B.	M.M.
Odhams, Lieut. D. W.	R.A.S.C.	M.C.
Oexle, A/R.S.M. W. H.	L.R.B., attd. 30th Lond.	M.S.M.
Oppenheim, Capt. A. C.	K.R.R.C. att.	D.S.O., Mention
Otter, Capt. F. L.	L.R.B.	M.C.
Otter, Capt. R. E.	L.R.B.	M.C., Bt. Major, Mention (2), Fr. Croix de Guerre (with Palm)
Over, Sergt. E.	L.R.B.	M.S.M.
Ovington, Major C. E.	L.R.B. att. M.G.C.	M.C.
Page, Cpl. W. E.	L.R.B.	M.V.O. (6th Class)
Palmer, Capt. H. S.	R.A.M.C. att.	Mention
Parker, Sergt. G. S.	L.R.B.	Mention
Parslow, Sergt. R. E.	L.R.B.	M.M.
Parsons, Rfn. A. R.	L.R.B.	M.M.
Paxman, Major W.	L.R.B.	O.B.E. (Mil.), Home Mention
Payne, Rfn. H.	L.R.B.	M.M.
Pearson, Rfn. R. S.	L.R.B.	M.M.
Peck, Rfn. R. E.	L.R.B.	Mention
Pembroke, Cpl. J. A. E.	L.R.B.	M.M.
Penney, A/Sergt. G. C.	L.R.B.	M.S.M.
Perkins, Capt. L. A.	T.F. Res.	M.B.E. (Mil.)
Petley, 2nd Lieut. R. E.	L.R.B.	M.C.
Phillips, Lieut. E. S.	L.R.B. att. 30th London	Home Mention
Pilley, Rfn. F.	L.R.B.	M.M.
Pocock, Lieut. B. L. E.	L.R.B.	Mention

Name and Rank	Regiment	Honours
Porter, Lieut. C. C.	M.G.C.	Medal St. Anne, Order St. Stanislaus
Porter, L/Cpl. H. R.	L.R.B.	D.C.M.
Pothecary, Sergt. W. F.	L.R.B.	D.C.M.
Pothecary, A/Major W. F.	Hants	Bt. Major on promotion to Capt.
Potter, Sergt. C. G.	L.R.B.	M.M.
Powell, Sergt. H. H.	L.R.B.	Home Mention
Powell, 2nd Lieut. T. C. K.	L.R.B.	M.C.
Powell, L/Cpl. W. F. D.	L.R.B.	M.S.M.
Pratt, A/Sergt. A. D.	R.A.S.C.	M.S.M., Home Mention
Pratley, Sergt. L. A.	L.R.B.	M.M.
Preece, 2nd Lieut. F. G.	R. Fus.	M.C.
Prike, L/Sergt. L.	L.R.B.	M.M.
Prince, 2nd Lieut. V. C.	2/4th London	M.C.
Pringle, Sergt. E.	L.R.B.	M.S.M.
Pullen, Sergt. C.	L.R.B.	D.C.M.
Pullen, Lieut. L. H.	L.R.B. att. M.G.C.	M.C.
Pumphrey, Capt. A.	D.L.I.	D.S.O., Mention
Radford, Lieut. P. D.	L.R.B.	Home Mention
Raines, Rfn. C.	L.R.B.	M.M.
Rayment, Lieut. C. L.	R.A.F.	D.F.C.
Rayner, Rfn. A. H.	L.R.B.	Mention
Read, Lieut. S.	L.R.B.	M.C., St. Stanislaus (3rd Class)
Reeve, 2nd Lieut. G. R.	L.R.B.	M.C.
Rice, Capt. C. E.	Mx. R. attd. Tank Corps	M.C., Mention
Richards, L/Cpl. K. D.	L.R.B. att. 2/10th London	Mention
Richardson, Major P. W., V. D.	Gen. List	O. B. E. (Mil.), Bt. Lieut.-Col., Home Mention
Richmond, Sergt. W. J.	L.R.B.	M.M.
Riddell, Capt. J. W. G. H.	R.A.M.C. att.	M.C.
Rippengall, Cpl. C. G.	L.R.B.	M.M.
Robinson, Sergt. F. S.	L.R.B.	M.M., Mention
Robinson, Rfn. T. J.	L.R.B.	M.B.E. (Mil.)
Roche, Lieut. & Q.M. G. D.	6th London	Mention
Rogers, Cpl. R.	L.R.B.	M.S.M.
Rolph, By.S.M. H. A.	L.R.B. att. L.T.M.B.	Mention
Rose, Capt. E. W.	L.R.B.	Mention
Ross, 2nd Lieut. R. S.	11th London	M.C.
Ross, Rfn. R.	L.R.B.	M.M.

Name and Rank	Regiment	Honours
Roulston, Sergt. W. A.	L.R.B.	D.C.M.
Rowe, Capt. G. F.	D.L.I.	M.C.
Rowe, Lieut. H. W. W.	10th Cheshire	M.C.
Rowe, L/Cpl. H. J. C.	L.R.B.	M.M.
Rowe, Rfn. W. T.	L.R.B.	M.M.
Rowland, A/Lieut.-Col. R. H.	8th R.W.S.R.	D.S.O., Mention
Russell, Capt. R.	L.R.B.	M.C., Mention
Sayers, Lieut. R. H.	6th W. Riding	M.C.
Sceats, C.Q.M.S. D. B.	L.R.B.	M.S.M., Mention
Schultz, 2nd Lieut. L. E.	Wilts	Mention
Sears, L/Sergt. H.	L.R.B.	M.M.
Sells, C. de G.	Late L.R.B.	O.B.E. (iv)
Shepard, 2nd Lieut. C. W.	K.O.Y.L.I.	Mention
Simmonds, Sergt. W. H.	L.R.B.	M.M., Mention
Slade, Sergt. E. H.	L.R.B.	M.M.
Slade, 2nd Lieut. E. H.	L.R.B.	M.C.
Slade, L/Cpl. J. H.	L.R.B.	M.M.
Slessor, Capt. P.	L.R.B.	Bt. Major, Home Mention
Small, L/Cpl. A. E.	L.R.B.	M.M.
Smith, Rfn. A. M.	L.R.B.	M.M. and Bar
Smith, L/Cpl. F. A.	L.R.B.	M.M.
Smith, 2nd Lieut. A. E. S.	6th London	M.C.
Smith, Rev. G. Vernon	C.F. att. L.R.B.	M.C., Redeemer (Officer's class)
Smith, Sir W. R.	R.A.M.C (late att. L.R.B.)	Home Mention, Com. Order of George I., Excellent Crop, 2nd Class with Grand Cordon
Somers-Smith, Capt. J. R.	L.R.B.	M.C., Mention
Spencer, Lieut.-Col. J. A. W. C.	R.B. (late Adjt. L.R.B.)	C.M.G., D.S.O., Mention (4), Legion d'Hon.
Spettigue, 2nd Lieut. P. R. S.	L.R.B.	M.C.
Stapeley, Sergt. T. W.	L.R.B.	D.C.M.
Stephens, Rfn. E. F.	L.R.B.	Mention
Stewart, Lieut.-Col. P. D.	D. Gds. att. L.R.B.	D.S.O., Mention
Stillwell, Lieut. C. D.	R.A.S.C.	Mention
Stock, Rfn. C.	L.R.B.	M.M.
Stockdale, Rfn. H.	L.R.B.	D.C.M.
Stone, Capt. F. R.	23rd London	M.C.
Stonnill, L/Cpl. R. H.	L.R.B.	M.M.

NAME AND RANK	REGIMENT	HONOURS
Story, Rfn. R. W.	L.R.B.	M.M.
Stow, L/Cpl. H.	L.R.B.	M.M.
Straker, C.Q.M.S. S. E.	L.R.B.	M.S.M., Mention
Stransom, L/Cpl. J. H.	L.R.B.	D.C.M.
Sullivan, S/Sergt. L. J.	L.R.B.	M.S.M.
Swan, Sergt. W. F.	L.R.B.	Mention, Belg. Croix de Guerre
Tabberer, Capt. C. O.	Q.V.R. att. L.R.B.	M.C.
Tatterton, Rfn. W.	L.R.B.	M.M.
Taylor, Lieut. A. C.	Middlesex	D.S.O., Mention
Taylor, L/Cpl. C.	L.R.B.	D.C.M.
Taylor, 2nd Lieut. H.	L.R.B.	M.C.
Teakle, Capt. W. A.	7th Essex att. 8th R.B.	M.C.
Terry, 2nd Lieut. J. W.	L.R.B.	M.C.
Thomas, Rfn. A. C.	L.R.B.	M.M.
Thomas, Rfn. A. J.	L.R.B.	M.M.
Thomson, Capt. W. Y.	L.R.B.	Mention
Thompson, Major C. H. F.	L.R.B.	D.S.O., O.B.E. (Mil.), Mention (4), Fr. Croix de Guerre with Star
Thompson, Rfn. L.	L.R.B.	M.M.
Thompson, 2nd Lieut. W. A.	L.R.B.	M.C.
Thurnell, L/Cpl. C. G.	L.R.B.	M.M.
Timberlake, L/Cpl. S. H.	L.R.B.	M.M.
Tod, Lieut.-Col. G. R.	L.R.B. att 23rd R. Fus.	Bt. Colonel, Mention, Home Mention
Tod, Capt. W. N.	L.R.B.	O.B.E., Home Mention
Todd, Sergt. R. V.	L.R.B.	D.C.M.
Treherne, C.S.M. F. M.	L.R.B.	M.M.
Trenow, 2nd Lieut. G. F.	L.R.B.	M.C.
Trevelyan, Capt. C. W.	L.R.B.	M.C., Mention (3)
Turner, Lieut. R. W.	R.W.K. att. 24th London	M.C.
Turner, L/Cpl. H.	L.R.B.	M.M.
Turner, R.Q.M.S. J. C.	L.R.B.	M.S.M.
Turner, L/Sergt. T.	L.R.B.	M.M.
Tytler, Sergt. A. B.	L.R.B.	M.M.
Vaizey, L/Cpl. G. R.	L.R.B.	M.M.
Virgo, Col.-Sergt. S. R.	L.R.B.	M.S.M.
Von Berg, Capt. W. C.	L.R.B.	M.C.
Wade, Rfn. A. W.	L.R.B.	M.M.

Name and Rank	Regiment	Honours
Wade, Rfn. G.	L.R.B.	M.M.
Walkinshaw, Lieut. I. C.	3rd London	M.C.
Wallis, Cpl. E. S.	L.R.B.	M.M.
Wallis, Lieut.-Col. F. H.	L.R.B.	M.C. and two Bars
Ward, Rfn. A. R.	L.R.B.	M.M.
Ward, Cpl. E. J.	L.R.B. att. 8th London and 174 L.T.M.B.	Mention
Ward, Lieut. F.	Scots Guards	M.C., Mention, Fr. Croix de Guerre
Warner, Capt. B. A.	L.R.B.	Mention (2)
Waterer, Capt. J. W.	Middlesex R.	Belgian Croix de Guerre
Waugh, Q.M.S. E. A.	L.R.B.	M.S.M.
Webb, Rfn. H. J.	L.R.B.	Mention
Welton, Major C. W.	R.G.A.	M.C.
Weston, L/Cpl. C. J.	L.R.B.	M.M.
White, Capt. A. B.	L.R.B.	Mention
White, L/Cpl. A. Y.	L.R.B.	M.M.
White, Capt. H. J.	13th R. Sussex	M.C. and Bar
Whittingham, R.S.M. C.	L.R.B.	Home Mention
Willett, 2nd Lieut. W. L.	L.R.B.	Mention
Williams, Lieut. Sedley G.	Devon and R.A.F.	M.C. and Bar
Williams, Rfn. W. W.	L.R.B.	M.M.
Williamson, 2nd Lieut. E. R.	L.R.B. att. L.T.M.B.	M.C.
Wilson, Sergt. P.	L.R.B.	M.M.
Wimble, Lieut. A. S.	L.R.B.	Mention
Winkley, 2nd Lieut. C. W.	M.G.C.	M.C.
Woodward, C.Q.M.S. S. J.	L.R.B.	M.S.M.
Wortley, Sergt. J. H.	L.R.B.	D.C.M.
Wray, Capt. M.	L.R.B. att. 20th R.B.	Mention
Wright, 2nd Lieut. M. W.	L.R.B.	Mention
Wright, Rfn. T. F.	L.R.B.	M.M.
Wynne-Williams, Rfn. T. H.	L.R.B.	M.M.

COMMISSIONS FROM THE RANKS

Although no battalion of the L.R.B. was ever treated as an O.T.C., 1350 members of the regiment obtained commissions.

INDEX

Ed. Note.—The original intention was to give a few words of description of each entry, but the references are so numerous that the plan had to be dropped. Incidents and matters of interest are inserted, but names of places in the story of the Great War are omitted. Nearly all of them can be found in the itinerary, and the date there gives the clue to the page. Individuals are given, but, in the case of members of the Regiment in the War, mostly without rank as this varied up and down so frequently.